203
B68
D53

Bouyer, Louis, of the Oratory
AUTHOR

TITLE
Dictionary of Theology

DATE DUE | BORROWER'S NAME

c.c.

230

203
B68
D53

DICTIONARY OF
THEOLOGY

DICTIONARY OF
THEOLOGY

by

Louis Bouyer, of the Oratory

translated by
Rev. Charles Underhill Quinn

Originally published in French under the title:
Dictionnaire théologique (© 1963 by Desclée & Co., Tournai, Belgium)

The publishers wish to express their appreciation for the permission to quote from the Revised Standard Version of the Bible, © 1946 and 1952 by the Division of Christian Education of the National Council of the Churches of Christ in the United States of America.

IMPRIMATUR

✝ Terence J. Cooke, V.G.
November 24, 1965
New York,

The nihil obstat and imprimatur are official declarations that a book or pamphlet is free of doctrinal or moral error. No implication is contained therein that those who have granted the nihil obstat and imprimatur agree with the contents, opinions or statements expressed.

English translation © 1965 by Desclee Co., Inc.

Library of Congress Catalog Card Number: 66–13370
Manufactured in the U.S.A.

LIST OF BIBLICAL ABBREVIATIONS

The abbreviations used are those of the Douay and Confraternity texts. Where book titles of the RSV differ, they are given in italics.

The Old Testament

Abdias	Abdias, *Obadiah*
Aggeus	Aggeus, *Haggai*
Amos	Amos
Bar.	Baruch
Cant.	Canticle of Canticles, *Song of Solomon*
Dan.	Daniel
Deut.	Deuteronomy
Eccles.	Ecclesiastes
1 Esdras	1 Esdras, *Ezra*
2 Esdras	2 Esdras, *Nehemiah*
Esther	Esther
Ex.	Exodus
Ezech.	Ezechiel, *Ezekiel*
Gen.	Genesis
Hab.	Habacuc, *Habakkuk*
Isa.	Isaias, *Isaiah*
Jer.	Jeremias, *Jeremiah*
Job	Job
Judges	Judges
Joel	Joel
Jon.	Jonas, *Jonah*
Josue	Josue, *Joshua*
Judith	Judith
1 Kings	1 Kings, 1 *Samuel*

2 Kings	2 Kings, 2 *Samuel*
3 Kings	3 Kings, 1 *Kings*
4 Kings	4 Kings, 2 *Kings*
Lam.	Lamentations
Lev.	Leviticus
Mal.	Malachias, *Malachi*
1 Mach.	1 Machabees
2 Mach.	2 Machabees
Mich.	Micheas, *Micah*
Nah.	Nahum
Num.	Numbers
Osee	Osee, *Hosea*
1 Par.	1 Paralipomenon, 1 *Chronicles*
2 Par.	2 Paralipomenon, 2 *Chronicles*
Prov.	Proverbs
Ps.	Psalms
Ruth	Ruth
Ecclus.	Ecclesiasticus
Soph.	Sophonias, *Zephaniah*
Tob.	Tobias
Wis.	Wisdom
Zach.	Zacharias, *Zechariah*

The New Testament

Acts	Acts of the Apostles
Apoc.	Apocalypse, *Revelation*
Col.	Colossians
1 Cor.	1 Corinthians
2 Cor.	2 Corinthians
Eph.	Ephesians
Gal.	Galatians
Heb.	Hebrews
James	St. James
John	St. John

vi

1 John	1 St. John
2 John	2 St. John
3 John	3 St. John
Jude	St. Jude
Luke	St. Luke
Mark	St. Mark
Matt.	St. Matthew
Phil.	Philippians
Philem.	Philemon
1 Pet.	1 St. Peter
2 Pet.	2 St. Peter
Rom.	Romans
1 Thess.	1 Thessalonians
2 Thess.	2 Thessalonians
Titus	Titus
1 Tim.	1 Timothy
2 Tim.	2 Timothy

*"Gentlemen, believe me! If we put into books
only what relates to the subject, first of all we
would be writing fewer of them, and then they
would be very tiny."*

E. Osty, P.S.S.

FOREWORD

This book does not presume to compete with a work of the magnitude of
the *Dictionnaire de théologie catholique*, edited by Vacant, Mangenot
and Amann, which consists of a series of monographs, many of them the
equivalent of full-length books. Our aim was considerably more mod-
est. We have sought to give precise definitions of theological terms, and
at the same time provide a concise synthesis of Catholic doctrine in terms
equally understandable to the layman and the specialist. In this way, we hope
to render a service to preachers and catechists by giving them a very brief
account of each major question, covering the essentials required for an
understanding and correct explanation of Catholic doctrine; and, to divinity
students as a general introduction to their formal studies. This simplified
approach may also be helpful to writers and journalists (even Catholic
ones!), by providing them with a ready reference to the meaning of the
various theological terms they may have occasion to use.

As brief as the articles are, we have always endeavored to give the biblical
texts essential to them, together with a minimum of necessary comment, and
the chief texts of the Church *magisterium*. Otherwise, we have limited our
references to St. Thomas Aquinas, the "Doctor Angelicus" *par excellence*,
and have been content to mention only the most important points of his
thoughts, as given in the *Summa Theologica*. Other scholars' work has been
included only when a particular doctrine has been developed apart from
the work of St. Thomas. We have limited ourselves as far as possible to the
basic author or text in question. Of course, for complete bibliographies, the
major dictionaries and theological manuals should be consulted. Let us add
that we have not dealt with details of Christian morality in this volume, but
have restricted our comments to the basic principles of theology in the strictest sense, i.e., dogmatic theology. The same is true with regard to historical
background, where we have only discussed what is essential to an understanding of the evolution of a problem or the meaning of a Church definition.

We began this undertaking with the hope of having the help of several
colleagues. We wish to thank Father Michel Birolet, of the Oratory, to
whom we are indebted for several philosophical articles, which will be recog-

nized by his initials. We must also express our thanks to our other colleagues of the Strasbourg Oratory, who, short of active participation, were never sparing with their friendship and encouragement. If we were to enumerate here all those to whom we are indebted, we should have to write another, even larger, book. May we, however, take this opportunity to once again express our gratitude to our revered teacher, Guy de Broglie, S.J. As we wrote these articles, we were more than ever aware of the soundness of his teaching, and if we have been successful in using St. Thomas as a beacon and not merely a landmark, it is due to Father de Broglie's influence. Lastly, we should never have been able to bring such a work to completion had we not been frequently consoled along the way by the meditation of a golden phrase of another of our most cherished teachers, E. Osty, who is one of the most affable, though not the least learned of the wise men of St. Sulpice. No other phrase could offer such a fitting preamble to the apparent rashness of our undertaking.

L. B.

TRANSLATOR'S NOTE

Because of its clarity, accuracy and completeness, the American Revised Standard Version has been used in general for the biblical quotations, as well as the traditional spellings of biblical names, which have become more or less standard in our language.

In those instances where etymological references in the French text are irrelevant, they have either been omitted, or an English equivalent has been substituted (such as in the article on the Church), for which the translator takes sole responsibility.

The titles of the articles are alphabetized according to the first letter of the phrase, and not under the principal word. Thus, Divine Attributes, for example, will be found under "D" and not under "A."

Considering the proverbial difficulties of reproducing the exact meaning of a philosophical or theological concept from one idiom to another, the translator assumes responsibility for any inaccuracies or lack of clarity.

C. U. Q.

A

ABBESS   The superiors of women's monastic communities were given (or took for themselves) a number of the privileges acquired by *abbots* (q.v.). Among these were not only the use of pontifical insignia (crozier, ring, pectoral cross, candlestick, etc.), but even, in some cases, the appointment of parish priests in the territory dependent upon their abbeys.

ABBOT   A term derived from the Semitic languages (from the Syriac *abba*, meaning "father"), which was used quite early in monastic literature to denote an experienced monk who, by his teaching, could fulfill the role of spiritual father. Later, in cenobitical monasticism (monasteries organized on the basis of community living) it came to refer more specifically, and finally exclusively, to the superior of the community. This was notably the case in the West, particularly through the influence of St. Benedict's Rule. It was during the Middle Ages that the abbotship came to be conferred only on priest-monks, and the privilege of exemption from the bishop's authority was extended to them, as well as an increasing use of pontifical insignia. This, and the fact that the ceremony of the blessing of an abbot was similar to the consecration of a bishop, ultimately led to a closer identification of the two offices. In fact, some abbots who were designated abbots *nullius dioecesis* came to exercise quasi-episcopal jurisdiction over their abbey dependencies.

Abbots are generally allowed to confer minor orders on their subjects. Some Cistercian abbots in the past even seem to have received from the popes the power of conferring major orders, including priesthood.

ABDICATION   Voluntary and free surrender by the possessor of ordinary authority of both the exercise and possession of that authority. Since abdication is generally recognized as valid only when a higher authority gives consent to it, theologians and canonists have doubted that the abdication of a pope would be valid, e.g., the case of St. Celestine V (1294). A decree of Pope Boniface VIII which was received into the *Corpus Juris Canonici* put an end to this doubt.

ABJURATION   The public and solemn disavowal before the Church authority of a heresy, schism or pagan worship professed prior to accepting or returning to the Catholic faith and communion. The Holy Office recently authorized a simple and positive profession of faith to take the place, on occasion, of abjuration in the case of those whose good faith in their prior attachment to error appears to have been beyond question. The liturgy of baptism, nevertheless, still includes a brief but explicit formula of abjuration for all adult candidates coming from any religious group outside the Church.

ABLUTION   A washing rite used particularly with reference to the *purification* (q.v.) of the chalice and the fingers of the celebrant after Mass or the distribution of Communion. Its purpose is to avoid any possible profanation of the remains of the sacramental species. Although it is difficult to give a precise date for its introduction into the eucharistic liturgy, the rite is to be found both in the liturgies of the East and that of Rome. It is thought to have been inspired by the analogous rites set down in Leviticus for the Temple worship, or by those rites which the Jews introduced into synagogue worship (e.g., after touching the sacred scrolls of the Law). In the present-day Roman rite, there are two ablutions in the Mass, one for the chalice with wine alone, and one for both the fingers and the chalice with a small quantity of wine and a greater quantity of water. The celebrant drinks the product of these ablutions. The ablution of the fingers after the distribution of Communion outside of Mass is made simply with water, which is then poured out into the *piscina* (sink for ritual remains).

ABROGATION OF LAWS   The repeal of a law by the lawmaker. Although abrogation can therefore be considered in the context of positive law, a problem is posed in an instance where a positive divine law would seem to abrogate a natural law, as in the case of divorce, allowed and regulated by the Law of Moses; or in the case of the Pauline privilege, even though the indissolubility of marriage is a consequence of the natural law. It is true that in such cases it is not, properly speaking, a question of the abrogation of a law, but rather of its tolerated suspension, which is justified in a particular case or series of particular cases by a higher objective. On the other hand, it must be noted that although abrogation is necessarily the act of the lawmaker himself, his intervention may be made *per conniventiam*, as in the case of a *contra legem* custom, which gains the force of law through the lawmaker's tacit consent.

The New Testament clearly abrogated the Law of Moses. But this is understood not with reference to the precepts of that law which merely specify obligations arising out of the natural law, but only to its positive and temporary provisions, as, for example, the ceremonial prescriptions of Leviticus. Yet, St. Paul speaks as though the Gospel abrogated every prior law (cf. Rom. 6,14; 7,4; 8,2; Gal. 5,18; Eph. 2,15). Paul's statements have to be understood in the sense that the revelation of grace, which is the fundamental principle of the New Testament, transcends all law. It is not then so much a matter of abrogation in the juridical sense, but rather of going beyond the purely juridical plane in our relationship with God. It is through charity, as St. Paul, echoing our Lord, expressly indicates, that the law, far from being repealed, is "fulfilled" in a manner that is above all law (cf. Gal. 5,14 with Matt. 5,17).

ABSOLUTE   The term *absolute* can be considered in two senses: (1) that which is independent of any other being (in this sense it is contrasted with *relative*), although the dependence of one or several other beings upon itself is recognized; and (2) that which is independent of every other being, to the exclusion of any relation whatsoever. In both senses it can be used in a number of different frames of reference, e.g., substance is an absolute in relation to accidents; there is absolute temperature in physics; and absolute value in mathematics.

The only frame of reference that will concern us here is that in which the term absolute is used to signify the final object of philosophical reflection, the idea of divinity. This use of the word is relatively recent, since its first appearance is found in the works of Nicholas of Cusa (*De docta ignorantia*, 1440). In France its introduction into philosophical vocabulary can be traced to Victor Cousin. However, philosophical interest in the subject goes back to earliest antiquity, and the conflict between the two senses of the word constitutes one of philosophy's most important problems.

Considering the different shades of meaning that the various philosophical systems have accorded the term, we can arrive at the following: Is reality, considered as a whole, merely an indivisible unity, or may an idea be formulated that allows for a certain type of determinable relation between its source and its elements, and if so, are these relations absolutely necessary, or do contingent relations also exist?

From the many forms of pantheism in which God is believed to be, in one way or another, merged with the total universe, to agnosticism in which the Absolute is inaccessible, and only phenomena are knowable, the various philosophical systems can be arranged on one or the other side of these extremes. We shall show, by following an historical sequence, what is essential in order to arrive at the Christian concept of the Absolute, and ultimately at an explanation of its deviations.

The well-known sophisms of Zeno of Elea (e.g., it cannot be demonstrated that an arrow is actually moving in the air, nor that Achilles will ever quite catch the tortoise) have popularized the teaching of Parmenides, who has the honor of being the first to have advanced the doctrine of the "oneness" of Being: Being is unique and indivisible, consisting of one homogeneous whole, enclosed within the limits of its own sphericity. It is not surprising to realize that the teaching of Parmenides, intact and unrevised, has been a heavy weight on the whole compass of Greek thought and on many aspects of modern thought as well, and as a result has been at the root of many theological weaknesses. How could such an idea of God actually ever admit the existence of anything other than God himself?

Through an intuition that was perhaps more religious than philosophical, Plato was able to avoid the stumbling block of a similar monolithic position. He is among those who were able to define relations between the eternal source of all things and those very things themselves with enough flexibility to maintain for this source its absolute character; and he attributed to the soul enough initiative for it to be something other than a mere subdivision. The Absolute is then certainly the One, identical with Being, and with the Good. The world of men, on the contrary, is the world of becoming and of multiplicity, the world of the Other. However, between Plato's Absolute and man, relations do exist. First of all, the world was unquestionably not created but modeled in an eternally existing matter by the demiurge which is its soul and the most beautiful of non-divine beings. In the second place, the soul of man is immortal, sharing in the divinity of eternal Ideas, and the fact that it found itself enmeshed from the very beginning in multiplicity makes contemplation of the sunshine of the Good impossible for it. But through memory of its previous life the soul recognizes the eternal beauty in things, and through love is thereby capable of going progressively back over the degrees of knowledge until it arrives at the perfect intuition of the absolute Good. The influence of this lofty teaching on Western thought in general and Christian thought in particular has never ceased to be a living one, even though Aristotle gave it the worst reproach possible to a philosophical system, by saying that it was unreal.

Aristotle brought Plato down from heaven to earth, according to his celebrated formula. Aristotle asserted, contrary to Plato, that Ideas are general, and that the general cannot have an existence of its own, heavenly or not. Ideas are of the earth insofar as they are the common note in each category of being that they define. Thus there could be no question of relying on them by attempting through intellectual processes to reach the fundamental source of things. This gives Aristotle's Absolute a completely different character from Plato's. Certainly, Aristotle affirmed, like Plato, and unquestionably more so, the existence and the unity of God. But while all Platonic thought was an effort to reach God, interest in this aspiration is totally excluded from Aristotle's concern. He held that the fundamental element of the world is motion, i.e., the passage from one state to another, from one form to another form of eternal matter; the passage from potency to act, i.e., from a lesser to a greater degree of intelligibility. But motion can only exist if it is moved and finalized by something (one could not say some*one* here) which itself is entirely intelligible, entirely realized. That something is Pure Act. Aristotle's Absolute is the Prime Mover, the source of motion, itself unmoving, but without which motion would be unintelligible. It remains that this Absolute, complete in its own sealed perfection, is perfectly ignorant of the world it is leading along, and that the relation which unites the mobile world to itself is irreversible. In Aristotle's world, there is no hope of ever arriving at or participating in the Absolute. Nevertheless, Aristotle's influence on Christian thought since the 13th century has been immeasurable, and has contributed to giving a realism and a strength to it which Platonic thought had not been able to impart. A genius and a saint, however, was still necessary.

It is to the Stoics that we owe the idea of Providence. Here the Absolute has a name, Zeus. Not the creator, but the organizer of the best of all possible worlds where everything was made for man. But this term Providence in the thought of the Stoics is something quite different from the idea we have of it today, for if the godhead entangles itself in the world from such a close vantage point, it is because it is actually indistinguishable from it. The Logos or fire of Zeus is involved in all parts of the world which for that very reason is itself understandable. Popular piety as well as philosophical reason are therefore founded on the possibility of direct relations with the Absolute. But if everything is understandable, it is because everything is determined. The world is fated to die, and to begin all over again in the same manner. There is nothing left for human freedom but to accept its lot. Therefore, as with Aristotle, the Absolute is completely man's condition: it imposes fatality, but allows no hope.

No other system except Christianity, about which we will speak further, has brought anything new to the concept of the absolute. But since Christianity introduced the idea of the infinite, a new understanding of the concept of the absolute became necessary. This new concept was judged by Kant to be impossible. Man's understanding can grasp only the finite, the phenomena, and not the infinite, the *noumenon*, which remains unknowable. Kant ushered in the era of the agnostic.

It is from this dichotomy between the insufficient finite and the inaccessible infinite, that Hegel's philosophy was born. The infinite of Hegel is an Idea. It is in no way contained in the consciousness of a person, but really exists of itself and even constitutes the total reality. At first unaware of itself, it progressively arrives at awareness over the course of history. It reaches the point of awareness by a dialectical movement where each stage of development of the Idea (thesis) is contradicted by an antithesis, a contradiction that will be resolved in a temporary synthesis. For the first time the absolute itself has become a *becoming*, a synthesis of Parmenides' Being with the Non-being that is its opposite. The world of physical and organic nature represents the first stages in the realization of the Idea, which continues in the awareness of the individual and that of society. History is not a train of contingent events, but a rigorously determined dialectical linking of events, where facts contain their own justification wholly within themselves. But the Idea, at first, only reaches a full awareness of itself in Art, where idea and the perception of the senses are united; then in religion, especially Christianity, where "the universal substance is realized in the awareness of the individual"; but more especially in philosophy where the absolute Mind, beyond representation, becomes entirely aware of itself in the thought of the philosopher. Is this absolute Mind a God in whom all thinking awarenesses participate, or a pure immanence totally within the confines of human thought? It is difficult to say. Whatever it may be, this concept of the Absolute has radically transformed the terms of the problem and has had a definite influence on all forms of subsequent thought.

The consequences of Hegelianism have made themselves felt on Catholic theology since the first half of the 19th century. Understanding from the outset the dimensions of such a system, as well as the dangers to the faith that might result from it, Günther, in keeping with his age's shelving of scholasticism, attempted a new theological synthesis on Hegelian lines. His intention was to link faith and reason in such a rigorously logical way that the result would impose itself with incontestable evidence on whatever mind came in contact with it. The implication was that reason could be raised to a level where it would be able to comprehend mystery, in much the same way that it grasps those truths which are normally considered to be its object. He modified the Hegelian idea of contradiction, calling it contraposition, and thus avoided in his demonstration the pitfall of having everything arise necessarily as an emanation of the Idea of God. But he was nevertheless impelled to show that, once revelation had been given to man, everything was thereafter necessarily linked together. He even affirmed that revelation, which he called "second" to distinguish it from Creation, would have been of no use if the mind had not been engulfed in idolatry. God, therefore, who is not pure act as he is for Aristotle, is actuated in his Son, who is his awareness of himself. The Holy Spirit is the unity of the contemplating Father and the object of that contemplation, the Son. To the Trinity, formed of three distinct substances, there is opposed a non-divine world, a world which God in the love that he has for himself creates by a necessary act of the will. Creation itself is an act of the non-divine spirit, of non-spiritual nature, in which this mind and nature are synthesized without being confused. We may say of this teaching that it erred in making the Trinity a threefold substance, in distorting the unity of the Word made flesh with man, and in turning the philosopher into the arbiter of theology and dogma. It was condemned in the First Vatican Council (D.B. 1655–58).

The divine Absolute is not an idea subjected to necessity, even to an internal necessity. The Christian working out of the concept of the Absolute finds the identification of the True, the Beautiful and the Good, in Plato, whereas in Aristotle's philosophy it is a thought, First Cause of all things and Prime Mover of all motion. Stoicism helped to conceive of the absolute as Providence, and finally Hegelian philosophy recalled expediently that there is no doubt that the Absolute makes itself known in time, and through history accomplishes its ultimate triumph. But more than all of this, Holy Scripture teaches something which modifies completely all of these theories. It is that the Absolute is personal, and spoke of himself in that way to Moses: "I am who am" (Ex. 3,14). Nor is it surprising that the term absolute is never used in traditional theology to designate the divine Being. The word absolute is nothing more than an adjective used to qualify one or another of God's attributes. The ultimate object of philosophical reflection is seen as life itself, not merely as the utmost proposition of knowledge. (For a further explanation of this teaching, see GOD.) We are concerned here only with the concept of the divine Absolute as found in the theories we have already discussed insofar as this may be considered the ultimate object of their thought.

God is absolute Being, in and through himself, not dependent upon any other being, knowing everything in himself, and nothing except in himself. He is absolute Truth and absolute Thought, and, as such, implies the term, the Word, the unique idea that God has of himself. In short, in the measure that he knows the Word, and the Word knows him, there is a total compenetration, absolute relation, absolute Love. Since he knows everything in himself, he has a singular idea of every-thing. This is the principle of Creation. Now, as absolute Will, God makes singular objects arrive at being in an absolute manner, that is, from nothingness, and in a free manner since their existence adds nothing to his perfection. As the Will that desires nothing but the Good, he is their Providence. Creation is itself *perfect* only in its knowledge of the divine Absolute. However, Creation does not reach this knowledge by intuition, but in the space-time conditions of its existence. It arrives first at a knowledge of the Absolute from itself, as its Being and its Crea-tor, and then supernaturally, through the revelation which the Absolute gives of itself as Love and Life. A relation with the Absolute is thus al-lowed not on a merely intellectual scale, but more deeply in a person to person relationship, made possible by the Word's bursting into time. This Word, precisely because he is the divine Absolute, is the human absolute. "Before Abraham was, I am" (John 8,58).

M.B.

ABSOLUTION This name is given to the act of the priest in the sacrament of penance, whereby he exercises the power of Christ, entrusted by Him to his apostles in the Church, and for the good of the Church, to forgive sins: "Whose sins you shall forgive, they are forgiven them . . ." (John 20,23; cf. Matt. 16,19 and 18,18). In the Latin liturgy of today this statement is in the indicative: *Ego te absolvo*. In the past, however, as well as in the Eastern rites today, the Church has admitted the validity of deprecative or subjunctive forms, as for example: *Deus te absolvat*. The Council of Trent, as an answer to the teaching of the Reformers, decreed that absolution was not merely a simple declaration similar to the general preaching of forgiveness, but rather a juridical act (Sess. XIV, chap. 6, can. 9; D.B. 902 and 919). It is clear then that the absolution given by the priest is not merely a statement of forgiveness. It also effectively grants that forgiveness in the sacrament to those who, of course, fulfill the necessary conditions. (Cf. articles on ATTRITION, and PENANCE; also, St. Thomas Aquinas, *In IV Sent.*, bk.IV, dist. 17–19; *Sum. Theol.*, IIIa, qq.84–90.) From the 15th century on, the question whether or not absolution may be given conditionally has been posed. It is generally admitted that in some cases absolution may be granted conditionally as long as that condition does not have the effect of annulling the sacrament, as would be the case with a future condition. The condition may be tacit. However, its use is lawful only if either the spiritual welfare of the penitent would be gravely jeopardized if absolution were withheld, or if unconditional absolution might expose the sacrament to the danger of profanation.

The term general absolution is given to two different rites that deserve noting. The first is the apostolic blessing *in articulo mortis*. The second is the general absolution given on certain days to members of certain religious orders (or third orders). Both of these rites constitute means of granting a *plenary indulgence* (q.v.) in the name of the Sovereign Pontiff. In its form the latter rite is related to a more widespread practice that lasted for many years on Holy Thursday in cathedrals and some other churches, and which was a survival of the public absolution once given to penitents at the end of Lent (*see* PENANCE). This survival may be looked upon as a sacramental, prompting one to contrition.

ABSTINENCE Refraining from the use of certain good things for a spiritual good, either as a response to a simple counsel, or in obedience to a positive law. It refers particularly to abstaining from certain foods, or from sexual relations. Mosaic Law had numerous prescriptions of this type. For example, it forbade the eating of the flesh of certain animals that were considered unclean, the use of leavened bread during Passover, or the eating of blood, and therefore the eating of any strangled animal. This latter prescription was followed for a time by the Christians themselves (Acts 15,20 and 29). Further, just as the Old Covenant required one to refrain from sexual relations at certain times, the canons prescribed this same type of abstinence before Communion. Both clerical celibacy and fasting (including the eucharistic fast) are, in the broader sense of the word, forms of abstinence. In a more restricted sense, abstinence in the West today is understood as refraining from eating meat on Fridays, and on those other days which are indicated by general or particular laws. In the East, as was once the case in the West, abstinence, particularly during Lent, may be extended to include other foods such as eggs or cheese. The purpose of these prescriptions is to exhort the faithful to the practice of self-denial, so necessary for anyone seriously desiring to lead a Christian life. These imposed prescriptions are actually the minimum that each Christian should selflessly impose upon himself in order to attain the greatest height in his spiritual progress. On the other hand, various circumstances may allow for a dispensation from definite canonical obligation (age, health difficulties, and others). But nothing can dispense a Christian from the general endeavor to abstain, which is the *sine qua non* of every effectual struggle against the selfish and sensual inclinations of our fallen natures. The definition we have given of Christian abstinence precludes any condemnation, either temporary or permanent, of those things from which we abstain. It is rather that our use of some particular good should not deprive us of a greater good. (Cf. St. Thomas Aquinas, *Sum. Theol.*, IIa-IIae, q.146 ff.)

ACCIDENT The word *accident* is used to distinguish that which may or may not be proper to a being, from that which constitutes its essence. Learning, therefore, since it may or may not be possessed by man, is called an accident in relation to man's nature. This is a logical accident. In a particular being, a physical accident is also a concrete reality distinct from the substance of that being. In the theological explanation of transubstantiation a distinction is therefore made between the physical accidents of bread (whiteness, characteristic taste, etc.) that remain unchanged after the consecration, and its substance, which is mysteriously replaced by the substance of Christ's body. Similarly, sanctifying grace is said to be an accidental quality infused into human nature by the supernatural action of God. We must further note that an accident (in contradistinction to a substance) cannot exist in itself, but exists, rather, in a substance. In consideration of this, the question is often raised as to how the eucharistic accidents can subsist, once their substance is no longer there. St. Thomas answers that the first of all accidents of a body is its extended quantity and all the other accidents of the bread arise from it; from then on it assumes the role with regard to accidents that ordinarily is held by the substance (*Sum. Theol.*, IIIa, q.77, a.5).

ACOLYTE   A minister in minor orders (the fourth in rank in the Latin rite), with the special function of carrying the candles and presenting the wine and water at the offertory during the eucharistic celebration. Formerly, acolytes also had the duty of carrying the Eucharist as follows: (1) they held the *sancta* (the sacred particles reserved from previous Masses) which were mingled in the chalice to denote the continuity of all the eucharistic celebrations in the same locality; (2) they carried the *fermentum* which united the celebration of priests of second rank with the principal celebration (i.e. of the bishop), and (3) they carried the sacred species destined for the Communion of the faithful outside of Mass. This ancient function still survives in certain local rites, notably in Bayeux where the chief acolyte still holds the paten today (which in a previous age contained the *sancta*) in Solemn Mass, as the subdeacon does in the Roman rite.

ACT   According to Thomistic theology, following the lead of Aristotelian philosophy, act is correlated to potency: first, in a being's motion, in that act changes a being's prior state (potentiality) into its proper form (actuality); and then, more generally, in any actualization of what a thing is, in contradistinction to its latent possibilities. In this regard, the fact of a given substance being simply what it is, is considered as its *first act*. Any subsequent operation is merely *second act*. On the other hand, only God is *Pure Act*, for he alone has nothing of potency in him. In all of his relations he is perpetually in act; his existence is not distinct from his essence. However, in the teaching of St. Thomas, the angels, even though they are pure spirits, do have an existence distinct from their essence, an operation distinct from their operative potency. For this twofold reason, they are not pure acts, nor, for even stronger reasons, are beings such as men, who are composed of both matter and spirit. At the other end of the scale of being, prime matter is considered to be pure potency. (Cf. St. Thomas Aquinas, *In Metaph.*, IX; *In IV Sent.*, I, dist. 19, q.2, a.1.)

In moral theology on the other hand, a *human act* is one over which man is the master by his reason and his will, in opposition to those acts of man that do not proceed from his resolute will (St. Thomas Aquinas, *Sum. Theol.*, Ia-IIae, q.1, a.1, and 3). The act that issues immediately from the will, namely, the choice of end or means, is called an "elicited act" (*actus elicitus*), while a "commanded act" (*actus imperatus*) is the submission of an inferior to a superior power. To love God is an educed or elicited act, but to meditate on his mysteries or to give alms out of love for him is a commanded act. The latter then may be an interior as well as an exterior act. (Cf. St. Thomas Aquinas, *Sum. Theol.*, Ia-IIae, q.9, a.3; also *In IV Sent.*, III, dist. 27, qq.2 and 3.)

ADAM   In the early chapters of the book of Genesis, Adam appears as the father of the human race, the first man. Because of Adam's failure to prove his faithfulness to the call of the divine Word, mankind in its infancy was dragged down with him into the contumacy of those spirit-powers that had rebelled against their Creator. Here Adam's fall, involving as it does the whole race, results in man's succumbing to the intuitive allurements of a self-centered sensuality, thus choking off God's call to faithfulness.

Such is the fact that Catholic faith obliges us to recognize in the imagery of this account. Although an historical fact, it is at the same time deeply mysterious both in the events described, and in its further import. In affirming the historicity of the account, there is no question of conflict with scientific knowledge of the material conditions surrounding mankind's appearance on the earth, which in itself is still obscure. The biblical account states explicitly that man was formed "out of the dust of the earth," and at the same time possesses a soul which relates him to God. This is not in opposition to the possibility of an evolutionary development of the human body from animal forms, provided that the Providence which presided over this evolution is not denied, and that God's special intervention in the creation of the human soul is not overlooked. But even more delicate is the problem posed by the hypothesis that certain modern scientists advance under the name of polygenism. If this hypothesis implies that the passage made from the animal to the human state took place in different stages and in different places on the globe, the biblical assertion of the unity of the human race as destined would run the risk of being in danger. With this in mind, various pontifical documents have warned Christian thinkers against too facile an approval of this supposition, which, at the moment, has little to compel its acceptance.

As for the longstanding description theology has endeavored to give of man's state before the fall, it has always been recognized for the most part as conjectural. Instead of presenting a complete picture of the conditions of the first man's life, it rather represents an attempt at encompassing the possibilities for development that would have been present had man been faithful from the first to the grace given him, and had he not lost that grace by his original act of faithlessness. All the Church had defined in this area is that Adam, by his sin, fell from the state of holiness and righteousness in which he had been created, and thus lost for himself and for us both of these qualities, and was, as a result, impaired in body and soul (Council of Trent, Sess.V, cans.1 and 2; D.B. 788 and 789; cf. St. Thomas Aquinas, *Sum. Theol.*, Ia, qq.90–102). St. Paul erects a parallel of deep theological importance between Adam and Christ. In the Epistle to the Romans he shows how, just as sin and its consequent result, death, came into the world through one man, so also through the obedience of one man we have regained righteousness and life (5,12 ff.). And, in his first letter to the Corinthians, he extends the parallel further. Keeping in mind that Adam means "man" in Hebrew, he calls the risen Christ the "second man," the "heavenly man," the "last Adam," who has become the "lifegiving spirit," in opposition to the "earthly man," who was created from the dust of the earth. And just as we have borne the likeness of earthly man, we are now called upon to bear the likeness of heavenly man (1 Cor. 15,45 ff.).

This parallelism seems to underlie other Pauline texts, especially the hymn of Phil. (2,6) where the declaration that Jesus did not seek to carry off his equality with God as a prize, can only be explained as a contrast with what Adam, tempted by the devil, had striven to do (cf. Gen. 3,4). Inversely, Christ's humble obedience achieved precisely that exaltation which is opposed to the disgrace merited by the arrogant lust of the first man. It is probable that the same parallelism is at least in the background of other Pauline contrasts between the old man which we must put off, and the new man we must put on (Col. 3,9 and Eph. 4,22; cf. Rom. 6,6) or between the exterior man who is decaying, and the interior man who is being renewed (2 Cor. 4,16; Eph. 3,16; cf. Rom. 7,22).

AD EXTRA, AD INTRA These Latin expressions designate the divine operations according to whether their effect is interior, or exterior, to the Godhead itself. Only *ad intra* operations can be proper to one of the three divine Persons to the exclusion of the other two, while *ad extra* operations are common to all three. To deny this would have the disastrous result of dividing one's allegiance by maintaining the existence of three Gods. It is only by *appropriation* (q.v.) that one can attribute to one Person rather than to another a particular action with respect to creatures (D.B. 284 and 703). However, this must not be misunderstood. Although *ad extra* operations are necessarily common to all three Persons by *efficiency*, they can still establish relations with creatures which are properly exclusive to one divine Person. This is principally the case of the Incarnation, whose only subject is the Son. In the same way, by the grace which the three divine Persons in common produce in us, we are conformed to the Son, adopted by the Father, and made the living temples of the Spirit, who is given to us by the Father and the Son. (Cf. St. Thomas Aquinas, *Sum. Theol.*, Ia, q.43 and Q.45, a.6 and 7.)

ADONAI   This special Hebrew form meaning "my Lord" (*adoni* is the common form) is applied exclusively to God in Hebrew liturgical usage. It was substituted in very ancient times (prior to the Septuagint Greek translation which presupposes it) for the divine name YHWH as a circumlocution to avoid any possible profanation, so that we no longer even know how the name was actually pronounced. The introduction into the Masoretic text of the vowels in this word, placed beneath the consonants of the divine name, is the origin of the solecism, Jehovah, which is the result of the misreading of the word Yahweh. Yahweh was always read aloud as Adonai.

ADOPTIONISM   The heresy which sees Christ not as God made man, but as a man especially adopted by God. Not only is this concept opposed to the great texts of St. Paul (Phil. 2; Heb. 1), and the first letter of St. John (1), which assert the preexistence of the Son of God before his relationship to his humanity, but it is already implicitly excluded by Jesus's own assertions about himself in the Synoptic Gospels, which regard his divine sonship as a constitutive reality of his person, which is to be taken in a transcendent sense in relation to the sonship of grace which is given to us. (Cf. Mark 13,32, and the great discourses of Matt. 11,27 and Luke 10,22.) It appears that the first adoptionists were Ebionite Christians, i.e., Judaizers who saw in Christ only the greatest of the prophets. They rejected the Gospel accounts of the infancy and held that the sonship of Christ was the result of the descent of the Holy Spirit on the occasion of his baptism. *Nestorianism* (q.v.) which sees the Saviour's manhood only as the temple of his divinity, tends toward a similar position. In the 8th century, adoptionism was again championed by Archbishop Elipandus of Toledo, who was opposed by Alcuin, and subsequently condemned by Pope Adrian I and by the Council of Frankfurt (D.B. 309 ff.). Abelard took up the error again in the 12th century, provoking a new condemnation by Pope Alexander III (D.B. 393), which was aimed directly at an old formula found in Peter Lombard. Protestant rationalists and liberal theologians teach adoptionist theories.

ADORATION   The Latin word *adoratio* (like its Greek equivalent, *proskynesis*) originally referred to a simple reverence made to a being who was considered divine, or to the likeness of that being. In this sense we still speak of the adoration of the cross on Good Friday. The stricter sense in which the word is presently considered designates the homage that can only be rendered to God, and to no one else. We adore the manhood of Christ, but only because the person whom we worship is divine. The same is true with regard to the Blessed Sacrament, since the sacramental species, deprived as they are of their proper substance, no more than signify the presence of Christ's humanity which cannot be separated from his divinity. This worship of adoration, exclusively reserved for God, is given the name *latria* in theology to distinguish it from the worship of *dulia* (homage excluding adoration) given to saints, their relics and images. A misunderstanding regarding this developed between the East and the West because the word *proskynesis* retained its original meaning of undefined homage among the Greeks, while the Latin *adoratio* had come to be used only in the sense of *latria*. The declaration of the Second Council of Nicaea (787) resolved the misunderstanding by making a precise distinction between *proskynesis* (ritual homage) and *latria* (reserved for God alone) (D.B. 302). The Protestants in turn, through a similar misunderstanding, saw idolatry in the worship given to saints, relics and images. However in this later controversy, the misunderstanding is often aggravated among those who attack the traditional practices by the Nestorian or adoptionist tendencies of their own theologies, which tend to deprive the Incarnation of its real meaning. Catholics, on the other hand, must exercise the greatest care in their demeanor and in the expressions of their piety to avoid ambiguous practices and formulas which could in fact lead, particularly among some of the less enlightened faithful, to idolatry, a thing totally repugnant to Catholic faith.

AGAPE   A Greek word meaning the love of charity. It is distinguished from *eros*, the physical aspect of love. *Agape* was the name given by the first Christians to their fraternal banquets, during which the primitive Eucharist was originally celebrated. Once the Eucharist became separated from these meals, the agape had only a very short independent existence before it was revived to some extent in the monastic meals, which the monks developed into a liturgy. In our own day, one might cite the use of blessed bread in certain areas as another survival of the agape.

AGNOSTICISM   A term coined by T. H. Huxley in 1869, and now accepted in current vocabulary. It serves to denote the whole school of

thought which, although admitting the existence of a reality beyond the
perception of the senses, denies that the human mind has the ability to
know anything about this reality.

Agnosticism, then, is a midway point between absolute skepticism and
absolute dogmatism. As such, its most important theological consequence is that it destroys any possibility of a natural theology (theodicy),
in that it denies that the intelligence can ever grasp the ultimate substance of things, even through a process of reasoning.

Throughout the history of human thought, there have been many
forms of agnosticism. From the Sophists, in the time of Socrates, to
Montaigne, and those thinkers who have been undeservedly called the
Neo-Academicians, there have always been men who refused to consider
any idea as being solidly founded, insisting that our senses deceive us,
and our reason falters. We shall not waste time considering these
patterns of thinking, because they only reveal the absence of serious
thought, and do no more than bear witness to the intellectual weakness
of those who propound them. The advent of modern science and its
unquestionable success has demonstrated that conclusions of incontestable certitude can arise from the alternate play of the senses and reason.
But at the same time these demonstrations have allowed agnosticism to
find strict critical bases, which we must now examine. By arriving at
scientific certitude in mathematics and physics, the human mind, if we
are to believe the agnostics, seems to have reached the limits of its
knowledge. One argument maintains that it is useless to go outside these
limits, to aspire to truths about things that are beyond nature, i.e.,
metaphysical certainty.

How did this conclusion come about? The greater part of the work of
Kant is devoted to its formulation, but essentially it consists of a few
relatively simple propositions: Knowledge is generally considered to be
built around two types of judgments, analytical and synthetic. Synthetic
judgments are more than a simple analysis of what the subject reveals
about itself, and are called *a posteriori* judgments because their assertion
presupposes experience. Such judgments are both enriching and informa-
tive, but are unsafe because they are contingent judgments. On the other
hand, analytical judgments are those in which the truth of the attribute
arises directly from a simple analysis of the subject. Such judgments are
called necessary, or *a priori*, and do not depend upon an experience; but,
because they do not teach us anything they are sterile. Thought then
finds itself caught between the following alternatives: it must either be
content with a sum total of tautologies, or move forward on the ever
shifting ground of a knowledge without security.

But Kant believed there are judgments (those on which science is
based) that possess a double quality of being, i.e., both *a priori* and

synthetic. He explains this in the following manner: The human mind is constituted in such a way that it possesses within itself a need for a unification of the sensations and perceptions it experiences in its surrounding environment. The senses cannot perceive anything except within the confines of time and space, and the understanding cannot grasp anything except within the context of the categories that are its own. Thus knowledge involves both experimental conclusions of a synthetic type, and *a priori* conjunctions made by the forms of human reason.

But with regard to what may exist beyond phenomena, whether of the exterior or interior world, Kant insisted that man can know nothing with certainty, since he is incapable of passing from that knowledge whereby he perceives everything through the forms of his senses and categories of his understanding, to a knowledge of an object that goes beyond the scope of these forms and categories. Therefore, the noumenon is unknowable.

Without submitting these critical bases to question, positivism relies upon, and reinforces the positions of Kantian agnosticism to the effect that scientific knowledge is considered without question the only valid form of knowledge. The knowledge of the Ages of Theology and Metaphysics is rejected. All that remains is the knowledge of the Age of Positivism. But even this age is nothing more than a passing moment. Certainly positivism is aware of the value of its own methods, and has disciplined itself not to make use of other methods to arrive at another object of inquiry that it knows from the start to be fruitless. These methods, however, become outdated one after the other, because the results they produce are related only to the precise moment at which they are used. Scientific knowledge follows a route that is asymptotic to the line of truth. It will never reach it. Furthermore, to Auguste Comte, who is even more emphatic on this point than Kant, the undertaking of a metaphysical quest is useless from the start. It would mean aiming at an objective that is out of possible range. Add to this what Spencer says about the thinking process itself: That every idea is symbolic, and the more we become concerned with abstraction, the less meaningful these symbols become, until they gradually blur, and finally cease to represent anything at all. On the level of metaphysics, all we do is juggle words, nothing more. We become lost in the maze of nominalism. So, since we no longer have any real certitude, as regards those things which are beyond phenomena, that we ourselves say has meaning, let us remain silent about the unknowable!

Since the time these theories were first proposed, philosophical reflection has retreated somewhat from its definitive claims. A more acute awareness of the problem posed by the unstable character of the axioms of mathematics and the principles of science has led it back over paths where it has again come face to face with the question of the nature of the mind. It is not enough to verify the mind's harmony with phenomena and the benefits derived from them, and therefore maintain that everything has been said and that nothing further has any meaning. Without a doubt we can be grateful to the positivists for having thoroughly taken the heart out of the scientific method. The intelligence, certainly, has everything to gain by avoiding nebulous speculation. This bears out the old scholastic adage that things must not be multiplied unnecessarily. But it does not necessarily follow from this that, except for the objective premise and its mathematical explanation, words have no meaning. A prejudice of method need not become a doctrinal prejudice. This is fundamentally the positivists' error.

Although the majority of scientific thought no longer holds to the conclusions of positivism, this does not mean that the Kantian critique of knowledge has become a dead issue. Rather, it is still one of the most lasting attainments of philosophy, and as it is only concerned with the mechanics of the mind in constructing scientific certitudes, the Kantian theory cannot be considered useless, even though it may have been superseded on certain points that are justifiably connected with the progress of science. What path, then, remains for the mind to take in its attempt to reach those realities that are beyond the phenomenal order?

A path does open up once one realizes that all reality is not contained in those intelligible relations that we perceive from it. The individual cannot be reduced to a universal, and scientific experimentation derives infinitely less from the object presented to it by the senses, than that which the object gives to the concrete universal experience. What is essential certainly remains essential. However, the existence of an individual being is not resolved in the mere fact of its existence, that is, a distinction exists between essence and existence. Scientific knowledge teaches us nothing about the mystery of this existence, and its judgment goes awry when it pretends to remove this mystery. The fact of an object's "being there" cannot be denied, but it is this presence itself that must be explained.

To get a clear idea of the way in which existing objects are present, we look to a causal explanation. Only one being exists whose essence gives a clear and integral idea of its existence, and that is God. This premise lays the groundwork for the ontological argument in a way which the Kantian critique cannot grasp, since it does not consider existence apprehended by the intuition as something that involves the whole man and not merely his thought. At the same time this premise also lays the foundation for the validity of analogical reasoning, which by tracing the causes of existing objects back to an uncaused cause, does not begin a procedure of infinite regression. Rather it seeks to find, in the idea of a being that exists by itself, the reason for being of the objects that analysis shows to be incapable of sustaining themselves in existence by their own power. Merely stating the structure of intelligible relations by which the elements of the world are linked together and interact does not sufficiently explain their presence.

Actually what was most lacking in Kant was that he was not a poet. A flower, the forest, the sky, reveal to me splendors of a quite different nature than those experienced by the naturalist and astronomer. Kant's deficiency becomes even clearer when one passes from the plane of *things* to that of *persons*. The sociologist or psychologist, not really knowing a friend of mine, can easily transform him into a mere motion in a series of collective motions, or the final balanced result of the pulsings and tensions found in every man. They will not plumb the whole mystery of his presence. I know very well, through our conversations, that my friend is in a state of constant development. Neither the sociologist nor the psychologist will ever be able to track down the source of the inventiveness that is precisely the act whereby my friend has an unquestionable existence. In other words, if one cannot expect scientific certitudes to shed light on the mystery of presence, one cannot merely dismiss that mystery. Let us be grateful to systematic agnosticism for having pointed out that these problems are distinct, and for helping to ascertain more accurately what should be expected from the order of knowledge.

But the endowments of my friend and his invitation to love him, have another possible answer than pure and simple objectivity. "No one knows the Son except the Father, and no one knows the Father except the Son, and anyone to whom the Son chooses to reveal Him," the Gospel tells us (Matt. 11,27), and again St. Paul: "Ever since the creation of the world His invisible nature is clearly perceived through created things" (Rom. 1,20). In addition, when the First Vatican Council decreed: "Our Holy Mother the Church affirms and teaches that God, the beginning and end of all things, can be known with certitude from creation by the rational light of human reason" (D.B. 1885), it made no claim that the proper function of scientific study was to attain to the knowledge of God. Rather it happily charges us to believe that human reason is not to be restricted to the possibility of establishing intelligible relations between the objects of the world. The scientist is required, once he has shed light upon the mysteries of the world, to turn without discouragement and devote himself to an elucidation of the mystery of the world itself.

M.B.

ALLEGORY   A distinction must be made between the general use of the word, and its traditional and special application in Christian theology. Generally, allegory is the use of a text in a sense other than the literal one immediately arising from its context. This practice was abused by the ancient writers, both Jewish (like Philo) and Greek (the Neo-Pythagoreans) in the Hellenistic period. The Fathers of the Church in turn employed allegory in their biblical exegesis, following St. Paul both in practice and even in the use of the term (Gal. 4,24).

However, it is necessary to distinguish between a literary process common to a whole period that was at times merely reduced to a rhetorical device, and that which actually constituted a genuine theological system. A primitive form of this system is found not only in the *Haggadah* (edifying commentary) of the rabbis, but also in the Old Testament itself. The New Testament draws upon the symbolic inferences of the Old Testament, and it remained for the Fathers, and subsequently for the scholars of the Middle Ages, to clarify these inferences. Since the time of the great prophetic writers, it is evident that biblical revelation is not a simple process of logical deduction from previous events, nor the mere addition of radically new truths, but rather a deepening of these first revelations and a consecutive transposition of the expressions given them. In this way the prophets (Osee, Ezechiel, the second part of Isaiah) interpret the Babylonian captivity and the return of the refugees as a second exodus. Following the example of Jesus, who transfigured the meaning of the titles Messiah, Son of Man and Servant of the Lord, and applied them to himself, the New Testament writers express the revelation of the Gospel in terms borrowed from the ancient Scriptures, but with new import. There is nothing artificial in principle here, since it is the meditation of the Old Testament in the light of Christ's actions and teachings that enabled the first disciples to understand Christ, while the Saviour himself enlightened their reading of the Bible with the light of a new day to come.

In the same sense medieval writers, following Origen and the Alexandrians, although not exclusively, came to distinguish in the biblical text a triple allegorical sense which they called *mystical* (hidden from view) or *spiritual* (revealed by the Spirit of Christ). The first and dominant allegorical sense (later called *typical*, according to the usage of the Antiochenes like Theodore of Mopsuestia) transposes and applies to Christ and the Church what is said about the People of God (as St. Paul does in Gal. 4,24), and the *providential* personalities of the Old Testament. The second sense is called *tropological* or moral in that it is applied to the Christian himself, considered in the Church, and made as one with Christ. Finally there is the third sense, called *anagogical* or, more specifically, mystical, which is the ultimate application of what is said about the People of God respective of their progress toward life everlasting, as the consummation of existence. It is allegory understood in this sense that is at the root of the liturgy's use of Holy Scripture and of its enlightening marriage of the Old and New Testaments. Here the sacraments are explained by allegorizing the acts of salvation in relation to us. And in turn, traditional mysticism finds its strength in symbolizing the sacramental experience with regard to everlasting life.

Quite different, however, is that allegory, frequently called *accommo-dative*, which is little more than a purely literary process that takes the words or images of Scripture in a figurative sense. Although this may be quite ingenious, it is nonetheless a groundless veneer. The main difficulty presented in the patristic and medieval writers is that they constantly confounded the two senses. This explains why frequently only the second of these senses was seen in their exegesis, and why all of it therefore seemed merely a gratuitous artifice (a proof, one might add, for not slavishly copying them, on the pretext of creating a spiritual exegesis).

ALTAR The Epistle to the Hebrews states that we have an altar from which those who are engaged in the service of the tabernacle may not eat (13,10). No serious question is posed here about its allusion to the Eucharist. However, if this statement is examined in the light of the whole Epistle, it appears that the term altar is referring to the mercy seat of heaven, rather than simply to the eucharistic table itself. While the Church Fathers and all Christians of antiquity did indeed maintain that the Eucharist was the Christians' sacrifice, they generally emphasized that this sacrifice is completely different from any other, in the sense that it does not involve material immolation of a victim, but rather an unbloody *re*-presentation of the Crucifixion. Consequently, even when they speak of the altar in reference to the Eucharist, as does St. Ignatius of Antioch (Magn. IV,7; Philad. 4), it seems that the text does not refer directly to the divine table, but rather to the Church assembly itself, which is considered as both temple and altar. Progressively, from the patristic period, once pagan sacrifices had vanished into the background, a more direct application of sacrificial *formulae*, particularly the term altar, was actually applied to the matter of the Christian rites themselves.

Interestingly, today in the East, the word is not applied to the table itself, but to the whole sanctuary surrounding it. Originally this table was of wood and had no particular consecration other than its use in the eucharistic celebration. Eventually the custom of celebrating martyrs' anniversaries over their tombs was extended to all celebrations. Relics were introduced beneath the altars which possibly contributed to spreading the custom of having fixed altars of stone. Subsequently, ablutions and anointings were added to this rite, a usage still common today to both Byzantine and Roman liturgies. In the West, however, a distinction was made between those fixed altars that were not portable and were consecrated in their entirety, and movable altars, i.e., simple stone reliquaries that were consecrated according to what had by this time become the ritual of anointings and ablutions. To the latter, the East has preferred the use of the *antimension*, a piece of consecrated cloth into which relics are sewn, and which makes the celebration possible on any table whatsoever. Let us note, however, that the principle of having but one altar in each church (and one daily celebration) has been better preserved in the East than in the West. It well suits that strong sense of unity which the Eucharist ought to produce among all the faithful, and which we find expressed in all the Christian writings of antiquity. In a Christian church the eucharistic table may be called an "altar" only by virtue of the presence of Christ in that celebration for which it is destined, and which the divine table permanently recalls. Therefore it is supremely fitting that the Sacred Elements always be placed in close proximity to this table.

ANALOGY   This term has two theological uses which must be distinguished. When we speak of the analogy of being (*analogia entis*), we mean that the being of God and the being of creatures are neither univocal nor equivocal, i.e., the word *being* in both cases does not stand for the same reality, nor does it signify two entirely different realities. Creatures proceed from God, and from God alone. Nevertheless, they proceed from him in such a way that they are not similar to him, nor do they add anything to him. Everything they are proceeds from him, but they are not simply as he is. Consequently we can transfer to God concepts that we have derived from creatures (otherwise we should be completely unable to speak about Him), but only in accordance with an analogy of proportionality. For example, although God is completely different from man, and his acts are entirely different from ours, when we say that God is good, we mean that there is between God and what proceeds from him an analogous relation with what characterizes a good man and what he does. Understood in this way, the analogy of being allows us to speak of God, and to be assured that what we say has a meaning, although we realize that we can never dispel the mystery that envelops him by analogy. Actually we only reach Him by an analogy in the second degree, i.e., between the relations that are applicable to divine realities and those applicable to human realities (cf. St. Thomas Aquinas, *De Veritate*, q.2 a.1, q.23, a.7 ad 9). This is why the *via affirmationis*, by which we assert qualities about God which we find in creatures, must always be completed by the *via negationis*, by which we then deny them, at least such as they are found in creatures themselves, to arrive at the *via supereminentiae*. This latter reasserts them, but goes beyond the negation itself by acknowledging that our ignorance appears all the greater as we advance in the analogical knowledge of the divine mystery.

When we speak of the analogy of faith (*analogia fidei*) we mean something that is strictly connected with the preceding, but which goes much further. The analogy of being, in permitting us to speak of God, with his creatures as point of departure, makes revelation possible. It is through revelation that he communicates himself to us more intimately, and to do so he borrows expressions taken from this world. Nevertheless, if revelation allows us to penetrate further into God's mystery than our created reason could, the validity of the expressions used would be affected by a new limitation. It is only in the total context of revelation and in relation to it as a whole that the expressions used are applicable to God. Therefore, we can in no way deduce from the fact that God has a Son, that this Son, like the children of men, should be subsequent to the Father, inferior to him, capable of having other sons, etc. The analogy of faith forbids us to do this because revelation which calls him Son, also calls him Logos, i.e., Thought and Word which are inseparable from the existence itself of the eternal Father. Conversely, the fact that the Logos is called Son, does not permit us to conceive of him as a simple accident of the Father's substance, but impels us to see in him a personal subject distinct from the Father. Thus, mutual corrections and completions are given to the terms used by revelation, and when we explore it in the light of the analogy of faith, it guides us toward the point where the analogy of being is applicable only to those expressions whose use surpasses our reason. (Cf. Vat. Council I, Const. *Dei Filius*, chap. 4; D.B. 1795 ff.)

ANATHEMA   In its original use in secular Greek, the word *anathema* referred to any object consecrated to a divinity. From its use in the Greek Septuagint version to translate the Hebrew *herem*, which designated an object (or a person) that was destined for destruction by God, it came to mean to the Hebrews and later to the Christians anything that was the object of a curse, and ultimately the curse itself. In the language of the Councils, anathema is specifically the condemnation of a proposition that is judged heretical or scandalous (i.e., *male sonans*).

ANGELS   The word comes from the Greek *angelos*, meaning "messenger" and was used in the Septuagint to translate the Hebrew *mal'ak*. This meaning underlines the fact that the Bible speaks to us of angels only insofar as they intervene in man's salvation, that is, principally in order to transmit God's Word to men, and thus become instruments of that Word among them. We cannot find sufficient data in revelation to construct any complete scientific knowledge of the angelic world. The angelic world immeasurably surpasses ours, and becomes knowable for us only to the degree that its history encounters ours. The doubts that many modern Christians harbor about the world of angels are too often provoked by the intemperance of some preachers and theologians who, while pretending to furnish a complete view of such mysterious realities, only produce a grossly mythological caricature. The same is true of too many iconographic representations where traditional symbolism has given way to puerile imagination, degraded to the most tasteless sentimentality. In itself, however, the idea of angelic beings in no way appears contemptible or unbelievable to the best modern minds, even those foreign to Christian tradition, such as the poet Rilke and the philosopher Souriau.

However, we must still dispel historical prejudice against biblical angelology. It has been claimed that belief in the existence of angels was introduced in Israel under Persian influence. Underlying this belief there is some confusion. The Persians' belief in the influence of individualized spirits who intervene in the course of human affairs, found an echo in Israel. The Zoroastrians, like the Jews, combined the most decided monotheistic belief with an assurance of the existence of other created spirits besides men. But this belief, which was found in Israel from the earliest times, with genuine characteristics, naturally evolved to a definition out of opposition to beliefs that Israel encountered over the course of its history. It seems that even if Hebrew monotheism did not arise from some sort of tribal henotheism (*see* POLYTHEISM), as was thought in the last century, the belief in the uniqueness and sovereignty of God is still accompanied in Hebrew monotheism by an acknowledgement of sacred "powers" that are immanent in the world, without, however, being considered divine (cf. Gen. 1,26 and 3,22.).

These *elohim*, as they were first called, are indeed like a primary refraction of divine glory for our world, since they are God's court or council. But the *elohim* are themselves no more than the first of his servants, and the error of idolatry is to put them in his place by giving them worship due only to God. It is certain that idolatry for Israel is not simply an empty form of worship, but one that has been perverted. When false gods are declared powerless, or even called nullities by the prophets, it is false to interpret this as a rationalistic denial of their existence. It is rather a question of vehement dispute about the divinity attributed to them. This is manifested to the fullest in the visions of the great prophets (Isa. 6, or Ezech. 1, ff.), in which the angels are described with characteristics attributed by Israel's neighbors to the elementary powers of the cosmos, while at the same time they are considered subject to the invisible God, and are his primary worshippers and natural representatives among men. This is specified in these assertions: the spirits faithful to the Creator fulfill the function of manifesting him to man, while idolatry (and therefore every sin) is the repercussion in mankind of the perverseness of spirits who wished to break away from the Creator and make other creatures their slaves. The first assertion implies the very ancient idea of the "Angel of the Lord," in whom the Lord manifests himself, but who remains nevertheless distinct from Him (cf. Ex. 12,21 and 14,19; also Judges 2,1 ff., and 13,9 ff.). The second assertion introduces the idea that the angelic fall is prior to the fall of man, and that man's fall hinges upon it (cf. Gen. 3). In the later books of the Old Testament, apocalyptic literature, beginning with the book of Daniel, arrives explicitly at the idea that the present reality of the visible world, although completely created by God, and remaining in his hands, reflects the spiritual conflict between the "powers" that remained faithful to the Creator and those that were in revolt. In Judaism this is translated by the idea of two spirits, one good, the other evil, between whom man is endlessly torn. It is in the world to come (*venturum saeculum*) that God will reassume his rule over the world, a rule which today is still partially usurped by the rebel powers.

In the New Testament (particularly the Gospels of Mark and John), the work of Christ is represented as that reassumption. This is why the account of the Saviour's temptation by Satan is put into such bold relief at the beginning of His earthly career (Mark 1,12–13 and parallels). It is evident in this text that Jesus, as a man, repairs the initial fault of Adam, and as the Son of God, reestablishes the Creator's rule over the world. This is emphasized by the place given in the Gospels to the casting out of devils in the work of the apostles and of their Master as well, and by the teaching of Jesus who explained this work in the parable of the strong man and the stronger man (cf. Mark 1,23 and 3,15–22 ff., with their parallels). On the other hand, the infancy accounts and the two Resurrection narratives attest to the indwelling of the divinity in Christ's manhood, through the ministry of the faithful angels. In the view of St. Paul, Christ is the second Adam, precisely because he rejects the suggestion of the devil, and thus ends the reign of sin and death which had become one with the reign of Satan and those powers that had revolted with him (Rom. 5,12 ff; cf. 2 Col. 2,9–15). This latter text shows with particular clarity that it is evident to St. Paul that the Crucifixion of Christ has put an end to the momentary and apparent reign of the faithless angels and at the same time frees men from their enslavement. (Cf. 1 Cor. 2,6–9, where the powers he mentions are both the visible powers who rule over the world, and behind them the infernal powers conceived of as their inspirers.) In these views St. Paul subscribes to an opinion about the law, as given to man by the angels, that was common among the Jews themselves; therefore he does not hesitate to place it on an equal plane with the idolatry of cosmic powers, since both things belong to the domination of the angels, good or bad, over the world. However, the economy inaugurated by Christ and his work establishes an immediate Kingdom of God, where man himself is seen as partaking of the divine triumph and Kingdom (Gal. 3,19 thru 4,7; cf. Acts 7,53 and Heb. 2,2). In a similar passage the Apocalypse, in describing the future of redeemed mankind, relates the arrival of the immolated but glorious Lamb into the heavenly assembly where the angels see God and glorify Him face to face (7,9 ff.).

The early Church especially retains from these biblical concepts the idea that the Eucharist associates us with the glorification of God by the faithful angels, while at the same time, like the cross, it dispels the effort of the rebel powers to enslave us in their usurped domination over the cosmos. It is with this in mind, that the Pseudo-Dionysius in his *Heavenly Hierarchy*, to which is appended the liturgical mysticism of his *Churchly Hierarchy*, described the spiritual world as a gradual awakening that approaches nearer and nearer the divine illumination, bringing about a unanimous ascent in praise, with the earthly Church as a prolongation and imitation of this heavenly worship. We must put ourselves in the same frame of mind in order to understand the original meaning of belief in guardian angels, and the angels who assist at the judgment (Matt. 18,10 and 13,39).

It is remarkable to ascertain even among those Fathers of the Church who were most opposed to the views of the Gnostic heretics, the very firm and practically unanimous belief that the Christian view of the universe is distinct from both the popular pagan view and that of Greek rationalism. It is a vision of a universe that is above all a society. Everything in this world is the interplay, not of abstract principles or sovereign powers in conflict, but rather of created persons who, however eminent they may be, are nonetheless all bound together, all equally dependent upon one sole Creator, all ultimately destined to the same glory or the same condemnation, depending upon whether or not they cooperate in the redemptive work of the Creator. It is quite wrong to assume in the Fathers' speculations on the invisible world simply a result of their real or supposed Platonism. Even when they express their thoughts on this subject, like St. Augustine or St. Gregory of Nyssa, in terms borrowed from Platonism or Neo-Platonism, speaking for example of the intelligible world, the substratum of their vision of the world remains essentially biblical. For that entire universe of Platonism that is divine when viewed from its spiritual point of view, or fallen in its material aspect, their vision substitutes an entire universe that is created, and in which the spiritual has a personal rather than an ideal existence, and gives life to matter.

In this speculation concerning the angels there is a problem that assumes a prominent place, which it kept throughout the Middle Ages, particularly in the Pseudo-Dionysian speculations. The problem concerns the hierarchy both in the angelic world, and between the angelic world and the human world. Here more than ever it appears at first glance that Christian theology has been content to reproduce a Neo-Platonist schema, such as one finds in Proclus, namely, that of a strictly ordered (i.e., compartmentalized) universe, progressively graded from pure spirit to matter. Once again, it is a question of misleading appearances. Faced with this Greek concept and the speculations of the Gnostics that further crystallized its dualism, Origen represented the extreme of Christian reaction by admitting at the beginning of things only a universe of created and strictly equal spirits, among whom further differences would be the only result of the determinations of their individual freedoms. After Origen, Christian thought through St. Thomas Aquinas inclusively, has more and more consciously assumed a less simple attitude in distinguishing between different degrees of being that result from the original will of the Creator, but which, far from excluding another gradation of free beings, furnish a basis of departure for the exercise of their freedoms. Thus, in the view of St. Thomas, a hierarchy of holiness is placed above a metaphysical hierarchy, and it is in accord with this hierarchy of holiness that the spirits of lowliest origin (i.e., men), by their faithfulness to grace, are capable of filling the ranks left vacant by defectors even in the most eminent of angelic cohorts, and, (as in the case of the Virgin Mary) of rising above these ranks. Still more profoundly, not only in St. Thomas but previously in Pseudo-Dionysius, it is very plain that the hierarchical concept does not imply any partitioning that would forever separate lesser beings from divinity. On the contrary, it is precisely the central characteristic of hierarchy according to the Pseudo-Dionysius that, according to their individual possibilities and response, causes the lowliest beings to share in the very gifts which are given to the highest, so through mutual assistance they all arrive together at an immediate contact with God. In this way, the hierarchy of creation is the occasion given for the generosity essential to charity, to the *agape*, which God communicates to his creatures: the most eminent cannot remain in their ranks without becoming involved with the lowliest, who in turn, in proportion to their faithfulness to the graces received, can become equal to those who were more endowed from the beginning.

Another problem, which has come more and more to the fore in the reflections about the angels, is that of their spirituality. The Thomist school is opposed to the Franciscan school in that it admits the pure spirituality of all spirits which are understood to be completely incorporeal (St. Thomas Aquinas, *Sum. Theol.*, Ia, q.50, a.1 and 2). The

Franciscans on the other hand, following St. Bonaventure (*In II Sent.*, 3,1,1,1, fund. 4um), purely and simply identify matter with potency insofar as it is opposed to *act* (q.v.), and see in all created spirits a composition of matter and spirit. Since both schools admit, on the one hand, that there is only one pure act, God, and on the other, that angels in any case remain associated with the material world (not only as guardians of men, but as managers of the visible universe), the difference is less than it might seem.

However, it remains true that the Thomistic synthesis on this subject is primarily a dialectic of the pure but created spirit. In this way we are led to see in each angel an individual whose species is completely unique in itself. But, however interesting it may be to think about this aspect, we must not disregard the fact that to St. Thomas, faithful to the lines of biblical revelation, the world of angels is principally the world itself, seen in its primordial aspect of spiritual reality created in persons. These persons remain associated with the human world in its fall, as in its reconstitution, although its principal salvation remains the work of Christ, and of Christ alone as God made man.

A final problem with regard to angels, that must be mentioned, is their eternal destiny. In spite of the fact that they are called in grace to share in God's own life, it does not appear that they are, like men, subject to salvation. In the view of Catholic tradition, which has become progressively freed from any possible hesitancy, they must be conceived as settled in faithfulness or unfaithfulness from the beginning of cosmic history. This is because their spirituality is higher than man's, and, because of a more perfect unity of their being, implies an immediate lucidity, confirming them from the very first in good, or locking them irremediably in evil. The uncertainties on this point that can be found in some ancient writers such as Origen, based on biblical texts in which the angelic world appears to be somewhat divided, can be explained by the erroneous application to individual spirits of the conflict between faithful angels and the fallen ones.

In conclusion, the exact definition of the nine choirs of angels which St. Thomas took verbatim from Pseudo-Dionysius, because he attributed a quasi-apostolic authority to him, is only a figurative expression of certain principles which can be helpful in forming a concept of the levels of created spiritual existences. (*See* St. Thomas Aquinas, *Sum Theol.*, Ia, qq.50 to 64 and 106 to 114; *Contra Gentiles*, III, chaps. 91–101.)

ANGLICANISM   The form of religion that characterized the Anglican Church after the schism consummated by King Henry VIII. Torn at first between a relative faithfulness to medieval Catholic tradition and a Protestantism of a Zwinglian (with Archbishop Cranmer) or Calvinist tendency, Anglicanism assumed the aspect of a compromise during the reign of Elizabeth I, when the profession of faith in the Thirty-Nine Articles was added to the liturgy composed by Cranmer. This combined a conservative humanism with a Zwinglian concept of the sacraments, especially of the Eucharist. The result was a hierarchical structure dominated by royal authority, a liturgical framework that retained many Catholic elements, and a moderately Protestant doctrine. The influence of the great theologian Richard Hooker, and after him, the Caroline theologians Andrewes, Laud, Cosin, etc., tended to put greater emphasis on the Catholic elements in developing the idea of a restoration of the Church of the Fathers (opposed explicitly both to post-Tridentine Catholicism and continental Protestantism). Despite the reinstatement of this school after the ultra-Protestant interlude of Cromwell's Commonwealth, the toppling of the Stuart restoration left few followers except those in the milieux that were influenced by the Non-Jurors (i.e., those who refused to take the oath of fealty to King William). After the pietistic revival (see PIETISM), started by Wesley, and the schism in the 18th century called Methodism, which was its result, a second renewal in the 19th century, the Oxford Movement, gave new life to the Anglo-Catholic tendencies (also called "High Church") in Anglicanism with Keble, Newman and Pusey. But as the movement came closer and closer to Rome, it resulted in numerous defections to the Roman Church (Newman's among them) and, often in a very external imitation of modern Catholicism.

Today the "Erastian" tendency to consider the Church only as the religious aspect of the State (prevalent since the downfall of the Non-Jurors) is without a doubt weaker in the Church of England than it has ever been, and practically nonexistent in its numerous extensions in other countries (Scotland, Wales, the United States, etc.). Anglicanism remains divided among various tendencies, "High Church," "Low Church" (influenced by an evangelical revivalism of Wesleyan origin) and "Broad Church" (or modernist, in the rationalistic or scientistic sense), which evolve from a common ground of syncretism between a taste for tradition (especially liturgical tradition), a sympathy for Protestantism, and an attraction toward critical liberalism. Although this syncretism often remains in a state of simple compromise, it is sometimes surpassed among more enlightened Anglican theologians (such as the incumbent Archbishop of Canterbury, Dr. Michael Ramsey) in ecumenical endeavors, such as genuine efforts to synthesize faithfulness to the tradition of the ancient Church, with understanding toward what is most positive in Protestant yearnings, and care for critical thought. It may be recalled that the Holy See, in the letter *Apostolicae Curae* of Leo XIII declared Anglican orders invalid from the Catholic Church's point of view (D.B. 1963–1966). Anglicanism in the U.S.A. has been styled for two centuries "The Protestant Episcopal Church," or, in common language, "The Episcopalian Church."

ANNUNCIATION   The ancient feast of the 25th of March that bears this name commemorates the announcement made by the angel Gabriel to Mary (Luke 1,26 ff.) that she was destined to become the mother of the Saviour. The Byzantine liturgy in particular emphasizes Mary's appearance in the Gospel account as the new Eve in relation to the second Adam. In her conversation with the angel prior to the Incarnation of the Saviour of fallen mankind, she appears as the living image of faith in God's Word through her sacrificial obedience, which consecrates Mary in her virginity to the divine motherhood, as the disobedience of the unbelieving Eve, beguiled by desire for the forbidden fruit, delivered mankind over to the power of the devil. (Cf. St. Thomas Aquinas, *Sum. Theol.* IIIa, qq.27–30.)

ANOINTING   A rite consisting of an applying of oil. The liturgy distinguishes in this regard the oil mixed with balm, called *chrism* (q.v.), and the other oils consecrated for the anointing of catechumens, and of the sick. These different ritual anointings always emphasize the communication of spiritual strength. *See also* MESSIAH.

ANOINTING OF THE SICK   Commonly called extreme unction, prior to the Second Vatican Council, the sacrament of the sick consists of an anointing with oil ritually blessed for this purpose, performed by the priest and accompanied by a formula approved by the Church that varies according to local rituals. In the West, until the Carolingian renascence, it does not appear that any practice was known other than the custom of having the sick anointed with an oil blessed by the bishop (according to formulas, the most ancient of which we have is found in the *Apostolic Tradition* attributed to St. Hippolytus, 3rd century) that could be administered to the sick by anyone at all. Under Eastern influence the practice of anointing came to be reserved to priests alone.

Recognized by the West and the East, as well, in the Council of Lyons of 1274 (D.B. 465), the full sacramentality of the anointing of the sick was justified from a reference to the text of the Epistle of St. James (5,13–16), which mentions the *presbyteroi*, the anointing along with the "prayer of faith," the salvation (or "health," referring to physical and spiritual health) of the sick person, and the remission of his sins (cf. Mark 6,13). Scholasticism tended to retain scarcely anything more of the sacrament than the aspect of remission of sins, which it generally specified as the remission of the temporal punishment still due for sins forgiven. Thus, it neglected the first aspect of helping to cure the sickness itself, and did much to reduce this anointing to a sacrament of the dying. If it appears to be reserved for grave illnesses, it is certainly not limited to those cases where there is immediate danger of death, and if it does not effect an automatic healing, then it is of a nature to prepare us for the definitive healing of the resurrection, by helping us bear our illness in union with the Lord's cross. (See St. Thomas Aquinas, *Sum. Theol.*, III, *Suppl.*, qq.29-33.) The Council of Trent defended the sacramentality and the true import of this rite against the Protestants (Sess. 14; D.B. 907-929). It must be noted that the oil of the sick, blessed in the West on Maundy Thursday by every bishop before the conclusion of the Canon of the Mass of Chrism, is, in the East, generally blessed by the priest himself before each administration of the sacrament.

ANTHROPOMORPHISM A manner of ascribing human attributes to either God himself or his actions. Anthropomorphic expressions abound in the Old Testament, with references to the "hand of God," his face, his mouth, etc., and attributing to him feelings of anger and compunction, and even describing the prophets' vision of him with human features, albeit surrounded by an incomparable glory (cf. Ezech. 1,26). The Hebrews, to whom these expressions were familiar, always considered them metaphors, finding a particular justification for them in the biblical belief that man was created in the image and likeness of God (Gen. 1,26).

Everything that characterizes man can therefore be considered especially suitable in representing God to us. Nevertheless, religious reflection puts us on guard against the extreme literalistic tendency which could come very close to idolatry, and, since Judaism, has come to specify not only that God is not corporeal, but that he is not subject to time, nor to any of the limitations of a created being. Properly speaking, he could not be moved by feelings that would imply a passivity regarding other beings, or show any change. Yet, we must realize that the expression of divine life through abstractions that are necessarily taken from our experiences is no less profoundly anthropomorphic than the rudest images. Consequently, this intellectual expression is no more adequate for describing the divine essence than such manifestly imperfect imagery. But, because of its relative spirituality, it runs the greater risk of deluding us with regard to the possibilities open for describing this essence. On the contrary, better than all the abstractions of a more technical theology, the biblical anthropomorphisms are capable of expressing, even if inadequately, the living and personal character of the divinity. Whether a question of images or concepts, we must always remember that our knowledge of God proceeds necessarily by *analogy* and not by *univocity* (qq.v.).

ANTICHRIST   This term designates a mysterious person, referred to by this name in the first two Epistles of St. John (1 John, 18,22; 4,3; 2 John 7). The concept is also found in the Apocalypse where the reference is less explicit, under the image of the "Beast" (11,7;13–17 *passim*; 19,19 and 20,20), and in St. Paul's Second Epistle to the Thessalonians (2,3 ff.) under the names "man of iniquity," "son of perdition" and "adversary." It seems that this person, who incarnates in himself the power of Satan, is going to appear at the end of time to lead an ultimate battle against Christ and the Church. The Parousia of the Saviour will accomplish his irremediable defeat. Tradition, as followed in the first text cited in St. John, is divided on the question whether it is necessary to see in this concept a particular person whose appearance would coincide with the end of time in the strict sense, or rather a figure capable of manifold partial realizations in the course of history (cf. St. Thomas Aquinas, *Sum. Theol.*, IIIA, q.8, a.8).

ANTINOMIANISM   Originally from the Greek *nomos*, meaning law, this term denotes the heresies or heretical tendencies which use the Pauline opposition of grace and the law (cf. Rom. 7–8 and Gal. 3) as a pretext for declaring that there is no longer any law a Christian need respect. St. Paul himself, anticipated and refuted these tendencies (Gal. 5,13 ff.). Antinomianism was upheld in the first centuries by certain Gnostic heretics, and later by the sectarians of the Middle Ages, and has been revived in certain extreme forms of Protestantism that take support from the exaggerated disparagement of works in the Lutheran preaching of salvation by faith.

APOLOGETICS   This name is given to that part of theology which is devoted to justifying the faith (positive apologetics) and defending it against attacks in which it can be the object (negative apologetics, or polemics). Apologetics has been a practice from the very beginning of Christendom, and the name Apologists was given to those Fathers of the first centuries (such as St. Justin Martyr) who devoted their writings to this end in the face of paganism.

Apologetics is used to demonstrate those religious truths which, while confirmed and enlightened by revelation, still remain accessible to the knowledge of reason applied to simple natural data, as is the case with the existence of God and the divine attributes. But apologetics would tend to defeat itself were it to pretend to demonstrate in the same manner supernatural truths, such as the Trinity or the Incarnation. What it can do then is to demonstrate their *credibility* (q.v.). The act of faith in these truths, contrary to the assent we give to truths that are demonstrable in the natural order, remains free, and cannot be posited except under the influence of divine grace. The result is that apologetics cannot bring us to supernatural faith, except in leading our reason toward a discovery of the moral obligation we have of accepting revelation. This discovery cannot be imposed on us except in a primary communication of the light of faith, urging our free acceptance. No room, then, is left for distinguishing, as two separate realities that would be joined, the external testimony that God would give us from His revelation, and that apologetics could establish by a strictly rational demonstration, and an internal testimony that would be supernatural, but at the same time independent from the objective reasons of apologetics. On the contrary, we must consider adherence to faith as the result of a unique testimony that is both internal and external, by which God leads us to the faith by using, *per modum unius*, rational motives of credibility advanced by apologetics and the attraction that his grace exercises directly over our will, which then moves us to give our consent by making us appreciate all their force. Consequently, there is no room either for a choice between an objective apologetic which could be centered on the fact of revelation, setting aside the spiritual needs of human subjects for whom it is destined, and a subjective apologetic that would encourage faith and be itself centered on these spiritual needs. Every apologetic that respects the course of faith and its threefold character (rational, free and supernatural) must be both objective and subjective, and at the same time must be perfected in an orientation toward prayer with which it must cooperate (*see* FAITH).

APOSTASY   In the strict sense, apostasy designates an abandoning of the faith on the part of a baptized member of the Church. This rejection can be made either by joining a non-Christian religion, or by professing doctrines contrary to faith (atheism, materialism, etc.). According to St. Thomas Aquinas, the heretic who still retains something of the Christian faith, is not properly speaking an apostate (*Sum. Theol.*, IIa-IIae, qq.11,12). Certain modern theologians like Suarez and Lugo, have nevertheless held that heresy, professed by someone who had formerly belonged to the Catholic Church is only a form of apostasy. Lugo points out that the censures are the same in both cases. In a broader sense, St. Thomas remarked that the word apostasy is also traditionally applied to the abandoning of religious life after profession, or of clerical life after reception of orders (*apostasia a religione, a. ab ordine, loc. cit.* q.12 a.2).

APOSTLE, APOSTLESHIP, APOSTOLICITY   These three terms
must be treated as a whole. The apostles in and through whom Christ
founded his Church, exercised a function, which remains for all time
fundamental in the life of the Church: the apostolate, which itself has
stamped the Church definitively with one of its essential marks, apostolicity.

The concept of the Christian apostle (in Greek, *apostolos*) had a
previous history in Judaism with the *shaliah*, a Hebrew term that passed
practically as such into Aramaic under the form *sheliah*. Both *shaliah*
and *apostolos* are terms derived from verbs meaning "to send." The
Hebrew *shaliah*, however, did not necessarily have a religious function.
But it is characteristic for the *shaliah* to be an envoy who, as the rabbis
say over and over again, must be considered an alter ego of the person
who sent him. The sender is supposed so strongly to be in the being of
the one sent that the result is that whatever the latter is doing will be
considered as an action of the former. For example, when Eliezer, the
servant of Abraham, chose Rebecca for Isaac, and when she had given
her consent, the marriage was concluded (cf. Gen. 24). During the
period in the beginning of Christianity, the term *shaliah*, in this very precise sense, was used especially to designate the representatives sent by
one local Hebrew community to another. On the other hand, the offi-
ciating priest was considered both as the *shaliah* of God to his people,
and the *shaliah* of the people to its God. Jesus adopted the term and
applied it to those who were to be most closely associated with his work.

At first, with the sending of the Twelve on their mission to Israel
(Matt. 10,1 ff.; cf. Mark 3,14 ff., and Luke 6,13 ff.), as with the sending
of the Seventy (Luke 10,1 ff.), there seems to be a question only of a
mission limited both in its duration and its object, as was the case with
the Hebrew *shaliah*. But after the Last Supper, in the discourse reported
by St. John, and even more decidedly after the Resurrection, we see that
the function of the Twelve is destined to last until the Parousia, and that
they are entrusted with the foundation of the new Israel that is the
Church. From the beginning, the number twelve, analogous to that of
the twelve patriarchs in the founding of ancient Israel, indicated that the
apostles were destined to play a role in the economy of the definitive
People of God. They are the foundation of the whole edifice, and from
them all further growth will come (cf. Gen. 49,28).

The discourse after the Last Supper manifests a renewed concept of
the apostleship Christ had in mind: "He who receives anyone whom I
send receives Me; and he who receives Me receives Him who sent Me"
(John 13,20). According to St. Matthew, this refers, in its application to
the Twelve, in a very special sense to what Jesus had said more generally

after having chosen and given them their commission (cf. Matt. 10,42). After the Resurrection, his words are even more explicit: "As the Father has sent Me, even so I send you. And when He had said this, He breathed on them, and said to them, 'Receive the Holy Spirit. If you forgive the sins of any, they are forgiven; if you retain the sins of any, they are retained'" (John 20,21–23; cf. Matt. 16,19 and 18,18). Thus, through the reality of the Spirit communicated to them in a very special manner, it can be said that what had only been a juridical fiction in the Hebrew *shaliah*, became a mystical reality in the Christian apostle: "All authority in heaven and on earth has been given to Me. Go therefore and make disciples of all nations, baptizing them in the name of the Father and of the Son and of the Holy Spirit, teaching them to observe all that I have commanded you; and lo, I am with you always, to the close of the age" (Matt. 28,18–20). The Pentecost account makes this obvious (Acts 2).

It may be noted on the other hand, according to St. Matthew, that what is given as such to the college of the Twelve had been promised personally to Peter at the time of his confession ("You are the Christ, the Son of the living God.") at Caesarea Philippi: "Blessed are you Simon Bar-Jona! For flesh and blood has not revealed this to you, but My Father who is in heaven. And I tell you, you are Peter and on this rock I will build My Church, and the powers of death shall not prevail against it. I will give you the keys of the kingdom of heaven, and whatever you bind on earth shall be bound in heaven, and whatever you loose on earth shall be loosed in heaven" (Matt. 16,16–20).

In a special way in St. John, it is evident that there is a very strict parallelism between the way in which the Father, in sending his Son, is present in him to accomplish his work in him, and the way in which the Son, sending the apostles, is in them. This may explain the expression of the Epistle to the Hebrews which calls the Son "the apostle and high priest of our confession" (3,1).

The primitive Church, while continuing in the Hebrew manner to call the community envoys "apostles," distinguishes those "who were reputed to be pillars" in the expression of St. Paul (Gal. 2,9), i.e., the group around Peter. At the same time, the Church was conscious of the "apostles" in the broader sense and, more generally, all the Church ministers as preeminently associated with the apostleship, and, because of this, they were also sent by the Spirit (cf. Acts 2; Phil. 2,25 or 2 Cor. 8,23).

In this regard some particular problems are posed by Matthias, Paul himself, Barnabas, and James, who was called brother of the Lord. Matthias, chosen by the drawing of lots among Christ's first witnesses (Acts 1,26) is considered without doubt as a part of the apostolic college, even though he was not chosen by name by Jesus. Inversely, Paul, who received his commission directly from the resurrected Christ (Gal. 1,11 ff. and its parallels in Acts), is considered an apostle in the strictest sense of the word, and lays claim to being on an equal footing with those whom he calls the superlative apostles (2 Cor. 11,5 and 12,11), even though he is not one of the Twelve. It has sometimes been wondered whether Barnabas, because of his very close association for a time with Paul's mission (cf. Acts 13,14), would not have enjoyed the same privilege. A very special case is that of James, first bishop of Jerusalem, and brother of the Lord, who for this reason had an exceptional authority (Acts 12,17; 15,13; 21,28; cf. 1 Cor. 15,7; Gal. 1,19; 2,9 and 12).

This immediately presents the problem of the association of the other ministries to the apostles, and then of their succession in these ministries. As founders and foundations of the Church the apostles certainly had a role that was impossible to pass on. The new Israel was founded by the Twelve, and it can be said that St. Paul was mysteriously added to their group as the one who was to become the primary instrument for uniting the converted pagans to the spiritual progeny of Abraham (cf. Gal. 3,6 ff.). The foundation was laid once and for all, and as St. Paul said, no one would be able to build again except on such a basis (1 Cor. 3,11).

On the other hand, the governing force of the presence of Jesus, the One sent by the Father, in those whom he himself sent, is permanent in the Church until the end of time, and is the justification for her apostolate, which is to spread over the entire earth and to all generations until the Parousia. It is clear that in the Church, according to the Gospel texts and according to that conviction from which she has never varied, it is always He who speaks and who acts. This could only be the case because the apostles believed that they were authorized to join to their number certain of those who had come to believe through them, in order that their work might be continued. In the lifetime of the apostles, as we see from the pastoral epistles, such was the case for those whom they set up as heads of the churches they founded (1 Tim. 3; 2 Tim. 1 and 2; Titus 1,5). These men could do no more than proclaim the message that had been entrusted to the apostles, but they did so with the whole reality of the Spirit communicated to the apostles and by them to the whole Church. After the apostles died, they continued to safeguard and to spread this message with apostolic authority and the reality of that communicated Spirit which is inseparable from it (cf. the epistle of St. Clement of Rome to the Corinthians, ch. 42). Today this is called the apostolic succession.

The apostles, however, had been given not only a charism of infallibility in the proclamation of Jesus' message about himself to the world, but one of positive inspiration which made them at least the equals of the ancient prophets. Since we are no longer to expect any new revelation, this properly apostolic charism has been replaced by the assistance of the Spirit in safeguarding everything which has been told to us about and for Christ by the apostles. This "safeguard" is furthermore something living, through the permanent reality of the Spirit, but it excludes any revelation that would be added to the deposit of apostolic faith (1 Tim. 6,20; 2 Tim. 1,14). As the First Vatican Council declared, the Holy Spirit has not been promised to the Church, to the popes or to the bishops "to reveal to them new truths to be manifested, but rather in order that, by his assistance, they might safeguard in a holy manner, and expound faithfully the revelation handed on by the apostles, the deposit of faith" (Const. *Pastor Aeternus*, chap. 4; D.B. 1836).

It is in this sense that the Church has not only been apostolic in her foundation, but remains so until the end of time. Apostolicity in this regard is only the steadfastness in the faith of the apostles, a steadfastness which is the permanent work of the Spirit who makes use of the instruments which Christ and those whom he joined to himself had set up once and for all. See St. Thomas Aquinas, *In Symbolum*, c. XII; *Quodlib.*, q.XI, a.19; *Sum. Theol.*, IIIa, q.64, a.2.

APOSTOLIC SUCCESSION   *See* APOSTLE, and BISHOP.

APPARITION   This term refers to a manifestation of God, the angels or the dead (not necessarily saints) that occurs in such a way that our senses perceive it. The Bible itself recounts numerous cases: for God, see among other texts Gen. 18; Isa. 6; Ezech. 1; for the Angels, Gen. 16,7–14; Judges 13,3–6; 2 Kings 24,16 etc.; for the dead, 1 Kings 28,8–21; Matt. 17,3 and 27,52–53. The apparitions of the risen Christ to the disciples, must be put into a special category. They are mentioned at the end of the four Gospels and recalled in a particularly important text of St. Paul (1 Cor. 15,5 ff.). Certainly all of these cases are not to be considered on the same plane. For example, the direct apparitions of God, generally in human form, obviously include an element of symbolic vision. On the other hand, the apostles insisted on the objectivity (which still leaves room for the mystery) of the apparitions of the risen Jesus. Even more important, we must distinguish between the various apparitions which are mentioned throughout the course of Church history. The Church never uses her authority to impose an instance of this type on our faith, beyond those expressly attested to in the Bible. At most, as in the case of the apparitions of the Virgin to Bernadette, the Church authorizes that a pious belief may be attached to it. Still, we are repeatedly cautioned against the only too human tendency to attach an exaggerated importance to happenings of this type, even in cases where there is every reason

to believe them to be authentic. On this point, see the very severe
teaching of St. John of the Cross, which is all the more important since
he has been declared a doctor of the Church particularly for his teaching
on the facts of mystical life (cf. *The Ascent of Mount Carmel*, bk.1,
chap. 16 ff.). Furthermore, whether it is a question of biblical apparitions or otherwise, the authenticity of the apparition does not guarantee
the objectivity of all its details. God, the angels and the saints can be
manifested to us, if such is God's will, by a simple supernatural
impression made upon our imaginations, as well as by the objective
presentation of a corporeal or material reality of miraculous origin to our
senses themselves. See St. Thomas Aquinas, *Sum. Theol.* Ia, q.43, a.7;
q.51, a.2; cf. q.83, a.8, ad 1um; and on the general problem, IIa-IIae, q.95,
a.4, ad 1um and q.174, a.5, ad 4um; and on the particular case of the
apparitions of the risen Christ, IIIa, q.54, a.1; q.57, a.6, ad. 3um.

APPROPRIATION   In theology, this word is used in speaking of the
three Persons of the Trinity, and denotes any particular attribution to
one divine Person of something that belongs in fact to all three Persons.
But because of particular sign or characteristic, it is thus attributed to
one Person. Practically speaking, appropriations come to be used when a
question of the divine actions *ad extra* (q.v.) are involved. Consequently,
it is very important to distinguish properly among the appropriations.
Some are hardly more than figurative expressions in which the truth
content is very tenuous, as in the work of Creation when we appropriate
the power to the Father, the plan to the Son, and the harmony of its
realization to the Spirit. On the other hand, while the Incarnation, from
the point of view of efficiency, is a work common to the three Persons, in
essence, the subsistence of Christ's humanity in a divine Person is proper
only to the Person of the Son. Between these extremes there are many
gradations. But there is, for example, no doubt that although our adoptive sonship is also more profoundly the common work of the three
divine Persons, it has its exemplar in the sole Person of the Son. Yet it
entails a filial relationship with the Father, who becomes our Father, and
the Spirit, who becomes ours as the substantial gift of the whole Trinity.
The meaning of appropriation cannot be exhausted within the simple
proprieties of language without emptying the heart of the Christian faith
of its meaning, i.e., our association, mysterious but real, with the Trinity's own life (see references in St. Thomas Aquinas on actions *ad extra*).

ARCANE   The expression *disciplina arcani*, contrary to current belief,
never belonged in the idiom of the ancient Church. It was coined in the
17th century by the Protestant Daillé to denote the relative reticence
the Church Fathers had in exposing to nonbelievers the details of the

Christian ritual, reserved solely for the participation of baptized members of the Church. As Daillé remarks, this reticence was not felt in early times, but only from the end of the 4th century on, when the Church was afraid of being invaded by a world that had ceased to be hostile to her, but which nevertheless did not possess the true Christian spirit.

ARIANISM The teaching of Arius, condemned in 325 at the Council of Nicaea, and again in 380–81 at Constantinople, according to which Christ could not fully be God. Arianism was a product of the unhappy combination of Stoic or Neo-Platonist theories on the Logos, which they considered to be a simple instrument of God in creation, with biblical assertions considered in such a way that these assertions were in fact emptied of their content. Consequently all who deny the divinity of Christ, regardless of the reasons, are sometimes called Arians. Let us note however that, among the partisans of Arius in following generations, some were simply preoccupied with not exposing themselves to the error in opposition to their own, namely, the pure and simple confounding of the Father and the Son, which is what certain modalist errors did (*see* MODALISM), such as the monarchianism of Marcellus of Ancyra. Most of them, called Semi-Arians, came closer and closer to the orthodox position, first in admitting that the Son is like the Father (*homoios*, whence the name Homoeans), and then even that he is like him in substance (*homoiousios*, whence Homoiousians), and ultimately by rallying to the definition of *consubstantial* (*homoiousios*) which completed the distinction between the three *hypostases*. On the other hand, the true Arians, under the leadership of Eunomius, became fixed in their affirmation that the Son is not even like the Father (*anomoios*, whence the name Anomoeans). *See* CONSUBSTANTIAL, and HYPOSTASIS.

ARISTOTELIANISM The teaching of Aristotle and his followers. Since the first theological debates in which Christian thought was induced to take a position on the teaching of Aristotle and his school, the Church held a correct estimation of the invaluable contribution brought by this philosopher to all serious thought, regardless of the errors or the insufficiencies for which he might be reproached. This is why, despite the fact that Plato's decided spiritualism made it easier perhaps for the early Christian thinkers to feel admiration for him, the Fathers of the Church did not hesitate to borrow widely from the rival system. Moreover, it should be remembered that the Platonist or Neo-Platonist schools, whose contemporaries they were, had themselves been the first to practice an eclecticism that was more or less a happy blending of the two inspirations. However, the Latin Middle Ages, under the predominant influence of St. Augustine, originally caused Aristotelianism to be relatively eclipsed in favor of Platonism.

The first effect of the rediscovery of Aristotle's authentic works, begun in the 12th century through the medium of the Arabs, was to accentuate this adverse reaction, through the insistence of certain Arab philosophers, such as Averroes, on theses that were manifestly incompatible with the Christian faith, namely, the radical denial of the immortality of the individual soul, and determinism. The rationalistic daring of certain of the first Christian thinkers, particularly Abelard, who tried to introduce the Aristotelian dialectic into theology, did nothing to lessen this mistrust. The work of St. Albert the Great and especially St. Thomas Aquinas triumphed over this mistrust, by showing the benefits that could be derived by building a scientific Christian theology from a very critical use of Aristotelian thought, once it was better known.

In this context, Thomistic thought accommodated in the Church not only the Aristotelian method of deductive, or more precisely, syllogistic reasoning, but also notably what is known as moderate realism (i.e., the certainty that our concepts give us true knowledge of the real, even though these concepts can be drawn from it only at the expense of making abstract the concrete experience of our senses). From this system we also derive an anthropological concept in which the soul does indeed appear as a substantial form—the form of the body—conforming to the teaching of the Bible, rather than Platonic ultra-spiritualism. Finally, we have a metaphysical outlook on the world, dominated by the distinction between a being in act and a being in potency, with the hylomorphism that is its consequence, i.e., the analysis of every reality within two components, form and matter.

ARMINIANISM   The teaching of the Dutch theologian Jacobus Arminius in the 17th century, which spread widely through the Reformed Churches despite his condemnation by the famous Dordrecht Synod. Arminianism was characterized first and foremost by the rejection of Calvin's teaching on predestination (*see* CALVINISM). But the effect of its success was to submerge completely all belief in the gratuitousness of salvation in many Reformed Churches, to the point of leading Protestantism, in great measure, from an exaggerated supernaturalism toward more or less Semi-Pelagian ideas (*see* SEMI-PELAGIANISM). This strengthened the tendency toward a Christian humanism, strongly tinged with rationalism, that became prevalent in the 17th and, especially, the 18th centuries.

ARTICLES OF FAITH, FUNDAMENTAL ARTICLES   The first expression is not found among theologians prior to the Middle Ages. Although St. Thomas Aquinas was not the first to make use of it, he seems to have been the first to give it a precise meaning. He declared that an article of faith is not simply any revealed doctrine, nor even any point of doctrine that has been the object of a solemn definition by the Church. Rather, it is a truth so distinctly revealed that it constitutes by itself a particular problem for the one who believes. Moreover, it must be for the believer the object of an explicit act of faith. Nevertheless, it is also essential to the concept of an article of faith that it be a particular truth seen as a part of the organic whole of revelation. (See St. Thomas Aquinas, *Sum. Theol.*, IIa-IIae, q.1, a.5 ff. and q.2, a.5; *In IV Sent.*, bk. III, dist. 25, q.1, a.1.)

Other theologians after St. Thomas Aquinas did not adhere to this strict definition, either because they reduced the articles of faith to the articles of the Apostles' Creed, or they extended the term to all the truths of defined faith (*de fide definita*). From this uncertainty of vocabulary flow in great part all the confused controversies about the so-called fundamental articles. Becoming current in the 16th century through the Flemish Erasmian humanist, George Cassander, the expression was aimed at designating a collection of truths on which agreement could be reached between Protestants and Catholics. Everything else was considered to be free opinion. Vehemently rejected from the beginning by both Protestants and Catholics alike, this system, under varied forms, has been revived many times by ecumenists, who expected a sort of compromise reunion. There is no doubt in one sense that among the articles of faith, even understood in St. Thomas's particularly strict meaning of the term, some, like the Trinity, the Incarnation, and the Redemption are more fundamental than others, such as those that refer to the Church and to the sacraments. In turn, the collection of the articles of faith is more fundamental than many defined truths which can touch on but one relatively secondary aspect of the faith. However, once the Church solemnly defined a point of doctrine, whether or not it is called an article of faith, or is fundamental, no longer can this point be argued against without one's leaving Catholic unity by doing so.

ASCENSION OF CHRIST   Simply mentioned in the long ending of St. Mark (16,19), and briefly described by St. Luke (24,50–53), the Saviour's Ascension is reported in all its details in the beginning of Acts (1,4–12), where we learn that it took place on Mount Olivet (near Bethany). With regard to the Ascension, two things are clear. The angels tell the disciples that although Jesus may still appear in exceptional circumstances (as in the case of St. Paul), he who is risen will never again appear on earth, except for the last judgment. However, we must not consider him to be separated from us, but rather as having gone to heaven to prepare a place for us, before he returns to take us back forever with him (John 14,3–4).

It is evident that the place called "the heavens" in Scripture where

Jesus is, while he awaits the Parousia, remains a mystery to us. What is sure is that this is where God reigns in all his glory, the same place where the angels are alleged to stand in his presence. Moreover, the Ascension is the expansion of the glorification of Jesus begun in his Resurrection. Since he no longer belongs to the present world, the world of sin and death, but belongs in his whole being to the future and everlasting world of holiness and life, Jesus can no longer be detained on earth. This is, it seems, the meaning of Jesus' words to the Magdalene, "Do not hold me, for I have not yet ascended to the Father" (John 20,17). Nevertheless, as the Epistle to the Hebrews says, he entered into the heavenly sanctuary (the immediate presence of the Father), as our forerunner (6,20), and he remains there always living to make incercession for us (7,25). Mark emphasizes that Jesus did not simply enter into the heavens, but that he sits at the right hand of God, illustrating that he is now, in all his being, as the Son made man, a partner in the divine sovereignty. This is what the prologue of the Epistle to the Hebrews emphasizes (1 and 2). By his voluntary humiliation and passion, the Son of God, clothed with our humanity, caused it to enter into divine glory, not only in the manner of the angels, but also to the point of associating it directly with the divine rule (this is found as well in the hymn of Philippians 2,1–11, with the insistence on the name that is above every name that had been given to Him).

The Ascension is in itself the ultimate accomplishment of Christ's redemptive work (cf. Eph. 4,8–10). Not only does he appear in heaven as our forerunner, but as one who involves us with himself to such a point that St. Paul says that God has "made us live together with Christ, and raised us up with him, and made us sit with him in the heavenly places" (Eph. 2,6; cf. 1,20 ff.). Further on, he says again: "For you have died, and your life is hid with Christ in God. When Christ who is our life appears, then you also will appear with Him in glory" (Col. 3,3–4).

We see then in what sense St. John has Christ say, "It is to your advantage that I go away" (John 16,7.). What follows in the text shows this immediately. This departure was the condition of the coming of the Spirit. Actually, in bringing together the texts of St. John containing Jesus' discourses after the Last Supper, with those of the Epistle to the Ephesians already cited, we can see what a strict bond there is between this "accomplishment" of Jesus' work represented by his Ascension, and the sending of the Spirit, which makes of them one sole body with him in the Church. As St. Paul further teaches, the Lord is "Spirit" (2 Cor. 3,17) i.e., the glorified Christ has become the receptacle of the divine Spirit. Furthermore, Christ is for us a new Adam, no longer simply earthly, but the "life-giving Spirit," since he ultimately reveals himself as the "heavenly man" (cf. 1 Cor. 15,45–49).

The pouring out of the Spirit in the Church by the glorified Lord is not merely a reverse counterpart of the Ascension. Rather, it is the fruit of it, since it constitutes the first fruits of our perfect association with the One who sent him to us from the heights of heaven.

In conclusion, it is evident that the Ascension of Christ, along with the promises it contains for us, which find their primary realization in the pouring out of the Spirit that follows immediately, is that to which tended his voluntary humiliation in the redemptive Incarnation. This is what the fourth Gospel expresses in such characteristic fashion, by seeing always in one perspective Jesus' mounting of the cross and his ascension in glory (cf. John 2,14; 8,28; 12,32–34).

ASCETIC, ASCETICISM   From the Greek *askesis*, which refers to any exercise, and particularly to those practised by the gymnasts. To the Greek Fathers, asceticism already had come to designate the effort a Christian must exercise in the battle waged against those things, both from within himself and from without, that oppose the realization of the ideal of Christian perfection as proposed in the Sermon on the Mount. The word appears to have been suggested by the sports metaphors that St. Paul, like the Stoics, did not hesitate to apply to spiritual life (see in particular 1 Cor. 9,24–25, which has often been compared to Matt. 11,12). The word ascetics, consequently, designates the theological science of this spiritual combat. The term asceticism is generally understood as the practices of self-denial involved in this science. In addition, the motivation behind these practices is often included in the concept. It may also be noted that modern terminology has included under the general term of ascetical and mystical theology, the theological study of the sum total of the problems posed by progress in the spiritual life. In uniting these two concepts, ascetical seems to be opposed to mystical, as human effort is opposed to the work of grace. This opposition, as has often been remarked, is not without risk. We should not conclude from this that human effort, in the Christian concept of the spiritual life, can ever be considered apart from the action of grace. This is the temptation that always threatens ascetics, i.e., those who practise ascetical exercises, and it was very much in evidence in former times, at the end of the 4th and at the beginning of the 5th centuries, with the Irish monk Pelagius, who was opposed by St. Augustine. Pelagius, actually, arrived at the point where he no longer saw in grace anything but the crowning glory given by God to ascetical effort.

Without falling into this extreme, those who became known as Semi-Pelagians, tended to see in grace and human effort two complementary aspects of spiritual progress. This is not the case. In the whole spectrum of spiritual progress, human effort cannot be efficacious or worthwhile, unless it relies entirely on grace through faith, the fundamental gift of grace. On the other hand, divine grace, however infinitely varied the forms of its action in the believer may be, never acts in him as a substitute for his own activity, but, on the contrary, it stirs action and marks it thoroughly with its own imprint. That is the mystery that St. Paul expresses when he says: "Work out your own salvation with fear and trembling, for God is at work in you, both to will and to work for His good pleasure" (Phil. 2,12).

It must be pointed out that the practices of Christian asceticism have somewhat literal equivalents in most religions. But what makes Christian asceticism different, are the motives behind it. It can be said that the seed of Christian asceticism is contained in the ideal of true poverty that developed little by little in Judaism, and found its best expression in certain of the Psalms: the ultimate believer here is described as one who is not tempted to put his confidence in any earthly good, but who relies on God for everything. This is the ideal behind the beatitudes as they are found in Luke 6 (still in a very Hebraic form) and in Matthew 5. It is evident from these texts that the disciple of Christ must detach himself from everything that belongs to the present world, in order to be ready to welcome the Kingdom of God, and, in a more profound sense, this voluntary deprivation entrusts him in faith to the unlimited generosity of God's love. With the development of monastic asceticism in the 4th century, this deliverance from the world, the flesh and one's self, was translated as poverty, chastity and obedience, which became the substance of the three great religious vows. But, these denials of self, as well as all of the other renunciations that follow, are never thought of in the Christian view as a condemnation of creation in general, nor even of the material world in particular. They merely bear witness to the absolute preference that is given to the Creator, in relation to every particular and limited good.

Because of this, Christian asceticism remains distinct from the forms of asceticism that are based on any sort of contempt for creation, as in Neo-Platonism, Manicheanism or Buddhism. During the medieval period, and then in modern times, Christian asceticism came to assume varying shades of emphasis. The Irish monks insisted especially on its penitential aspects. Later the influence of what is called the devotion to the humanity of Christ introduced the idea of sharing in his sufferings, and later still, of making reparation through a generous acceptance of suffering for the disloyalties of which he is the object. Finally, there were those who wished to substitute themselves for the sinners in order to ward off divine punishment from them. But since the doctrinal value is very variable in these secondary motivations, they can never replace the fundamental motivations of Christian asceticism as found in Scripture and in the tradition of the early Church. See St. Thomas Aquinas, *Sum. Theol.*, Ia-IIae, qq.14,69; IIa-IIae, qq.88,104,146,147,151,152,155,179–189.

ASEITY   Since St. Anselm, theologians have used the Latin word *aseitas* to express the fact that the existence of God proceeds from no other existence. To this negative aspect a positive aspect is necessarily joined: God is in himself his own reason for being. In other words, his existence is identical with his essence. In the fourth century, the disciples of Arius, confusing the Greek words *agennetos* (unbegotten) and *agenetos* (not-produced), concluded from this that divinity in the strict sense could only belong to the Father, and not to the Son. The Church Fathers retorted that the begetting of the Son was both inseparable from the Father's existence and in the same essence, which essence remained *agenetos* in him as in the Father.

ASSISTANCE OF THE HOLY SPIRIT   Modern theologians use this expression to distinguish the *general action* of the Holy Spirit in the Church in her definition and her proclaiming to the world of the Word of God, from *inspiration,* in the strongest sense of the word, which was the privilege of both the prophets, and even more so of the apostles. The assistance of the Spirit makes it possible for the Church, once the Word of God has been manifested, to bear fruits of intelligence and charity. It preserves the Church from entangling the Word in error, and guarantees, together with the general accuracy of the *ordinary magisterium* of the pope and the whole episcopate in teaching the divine Word, the *infallibility* (q.v.) of solemn definitions that the *extraordinary magisterium* may be led to make. This does not mean that the official doctors of the Church can ever be dispensed from having recourse to the permanent sources of the divine Word that have been manifested once and for all, i.e., the Holy Scriptures, enlightened by the whole of Catholic tradition. Neither does it mean that the divine Spirit replaces the normal use of their intelligence in this pursuit (this was not even true of the inspired writers). The divine assistance simply guarantees to the *magisterium* of the Church that it will never err positively in its proposal of the truth, although it does not give divine authorship, as is true of the Holy Scripture, to the formulas used to express this proposal, however authentic they may be. (*See also* INSPIRATION, and WORD OF GOD.)

ASSUMPTION OF THE VIRGIN MARY   On the first of November, 1950, Pope Pius XII, in the presence of a great number of bishops, and after consulting the whole Catholic episcopate, solemnly decreed that Mary was glorified in both her body and her soul at the end of her earthly life. This definition consecrated definitively the devout belief that had been expressed since Christian antiquity in the feast of the 15th of August, which was first celebrated in the Byzantine Church and from there spread to the whole Catholic Church. The deliberately very reserved terms of this definition, however, do not give any support to the more or less positive traditions that had surrounded this belief, nor do they accredit any of the various theological opinions with regard to the precise way that Mary's life on earth came to an end. Added to the treasury of revelation entrusted to the Church, which the Pope defined, is simply that Mary, because of her very special union with her divine Son, henceforth gives witness, as perfectly as possible, to the whole victory over death which Christ achieved for us. Similarly, the Immaculate Conception bore witness to the fullness of the victory over sin which the redemptive Incarnation accomplished and was itself to be the foreordained instrument of this Incarnation. (See the entire bull proclaiming this definition.)

The Assumption of Mary must *not* be interpreted, as it was by some Protestant polemicists, as a sort of apotheosis, nor, as some theologians of the Orthodox Church thought, as though it meant Mary's separation from the common lot of all mankind. On the contrary, this truth must be considered by Christians as a measure of the reality of the association of all of us with the victory over evil of our divine Head, and the assurance that we will share his glory to the extent that we shall have been made partners in his redemptive work through faith and love.

ATHEISM   A rejection or denial of God. Atheism is called practical when a person leads his life as if God did not exist and without actually troubling himself with His existence. Speculative or theoretical atheism occurs when God's existence is formally rejected. The reasons one might use to justify such a position can be considerably diverse.

Obviously, atheism goes hand in hand with materialism, which is a refusal to admit the existence of any reality beyond the material. Practically the same is true in certain radical forms of evolutionism where the term "spirit," however understood, is nothing more than the immanent product of the evolution of the material reality. In this case, even if one still consents to speak of "God," the word means only the ideal term of evolution. A more complex form of atheism is found in systems that actually do admit of an absolute but refuse to recognize anything of a personal character in it. In this instance, however, we have one of the forms of *pantheism* (q.v.) rather than true atheism.

Many apparent atheists are only agnostics, who do not think it possible to reach any conviction that is solidly based on a metaphysical reality. This attitude, which is particularly common today, can assume many different forms. It can be the result of practical atheism: i.e., one is persuaded that the existence of God cannot be proved because one has decided to lead a life that ignores his existence. It is possible, however, for some men whose moral behavior would seem to be in harmony with religious convictions, to declare themselves incapable of sharing these convictions, because of erroneous speculative grounds.

It can even happen that such men are, or believe themselves to be, positively irreligious because of a false concept of divinity. A typical example can be found in Feuerbach's atheism, which exerted such an influence on the thoughts of Karl Marx. Actually, for Feuerbach, the concept of God is nothing more than a confused projection of the fears of man in his comparatively primitive state of evolution, and more precisely, a result of the sum total of the prohibitions which are such a burden to his development. The denial of God would then be implied in man's whole advancement, and he could attain freedom only from the moment that he begins to be bold enough to reject God. In Marxist atheism, God and religion are comforting myths forged by the working classes for themselves as a sort of consoling dream ("the opiate of the people"). As the dominating classes become aware of this illusion, they organize systematically so as to assure their exploitation of the proletariat. In a manner analogous to the foregoing, Freud chose to see in religion the simple search for a sort of camouflage compensating for sexual appetite. These forms of atheism cannot be refuted without first recognizing that they aim at, and actually hit certain possible (and historically incontestable) deformations of religion among certain individuals or social groups. Such recognition is necessary in order to demonstrate that the true concept of God and authentic religion do not actually correspond to the idea fashioned of them from these faulty bases.

Atheism is a phenomenon appearing in all civilizations, although manifested particularly in times of cultural decline when it invariably goes hand in hand with an awakening of the grossest forms of superstition. Modern psychology has brought to light the fact that the depths of the human soul still remain instinctively religious, whatever the surface denials may be. The analysis of dreams, and the spiritual orientation observed in the poetic works of professedly atheistic cultured persons, illustrate that they still remain subject to psychological reactions fundamental to a spontaneously religious nature. Their atheism stems from a confused intellectual development, which, instead of facilitating the integration of these reactions into their conscious *psyches*, makes such integration extremely difficult, if not impossible. Nevertheless psychologists assert that these psychological reactions, which are at the very root of religion, are also the basis for man's whole harmonious adjustment to the totality of his experience in the world. The result is that atheism in man, far from being a sign of achievement and progress, inevitably shrouds or accompanies a tendency to neurosis. The atheist's return to God, then, seems to be a condition of his psychological healing process, while the return itself depends upon the acceptance of those conditions necessary for his recovery. It then follows that atheism is not in fact overcome by mere abstract reasoning, however correct that reasoning might be, but rather through an analysis of the atheist's conscience. He cannot lend himself to such an analysis, however, unless he has the desire to yield not only to an abstract truth, but also to the good demanded personally of him. The Delphic rule, "Know thyself," has great relevance here, as does Plato's formula, "You can be a philosopher only with your whole soul."

ATTRITION   Because of the subtle variations of meaning that this word has undergone over the course of centuries, it became, particularly during the Jansenist controversy of the 17th century, the occasion for impassioned discussions (although many theologians today would look upon the object of these discussions as having been ill-defined). Everyone, nevertheless, is in agreement that attrition is an *imperfect* contrition, in the sense that although it is sorrow for sin, the penitent does not have as his motive the love of God whom he has offended. But, obviously, this true sorrow, attrition, can only be experienced insofar as one has again effectively begun to love God. The Scholastics, however, generally concur on one point, namely, that efficacious penance presupposes both the penitent's contrition and the confessor's absolution. But in the 12th century, following Peter Lombard, there was a tendency to deduce falsely from this that absolution did nothing more than reaffirm what already existed. St. Thomas Aquinas, in opposing this opinion, emphasized that absolution effectively grants forgiveness, since every contrition presupposes either the sacrament, or a desire for the sacrament. Thus, contrition and absolution cannot be considered separately. Absolution presupposes contrition, which in return gives it its *form* (in the philosophical sense of the word). However, St. Thomas wrote, "If anyone comes to confession merely with attrition, i.e., not with fully *perfect* contrition, provided that he places no obstacle in the way, he does receive grace and the remission of sins in confession, once the absolution has been given him" (*In IV Sent.*, bk. IV, dist. 22, q.2, a.1). Certain theologians concluded from this that there were two possible ways to forgiveness: one, in which the sacrament of itself is not necessary, while *perfect* contrition is required; and, the other, including the sacrament, where only attrition is required. This thesis appears unacceptable since, on the one hand, forgiveness cannot be effective without real contrition, and on the other, the supposed addition of an objective reality such as the sacrament, and of a subjective reality such as attrition, cannot, without becoming totally absurd, be considered as the equivalent of another subjective reality such as contrition. St. Thomas meant that attrition, already the result of grace, draws us closer to the sacrament, by means of which the grace received turns attrition into contrition. This at least seems to conform most to the description given by the Council of Trent (Sess. XIV. chap. 4; D.B. 897–898).

In these views, contrary to what was the case in the controversies to which we alluded, it is quite clear that attrition cannot be thought of as a stable state of the soul, but rather as an intermediary state, in which the soul is already pointed toward contrition, without actually having attained it.

AUGUSTINIANISM The teachings of St. Augustine (354–430), who died as bishop of Hippo or of his followers. Incontestably a dominant force throughout the Middle Ages, St. Augustine's teaching first met strong and pertinent criticism on certain essential points by St. Thomas Aquinas. Since then the term Augustinianism has been reserved for those writers who have been unwilling to follow St. Thomas in his criticism, and who, despite this criticism, returned again to the points at issue. This was the case with several of the early initiators, forerunners and adepts of Protestantism, and later the followers of the Louvain theologians, Baius and Jansenius. It would be erroneous, however, to see only heresy or heretical tendencies in post-Thomistic Augustinianism. On the one hand, there are some theologians who have upheld Augustinian positions since St. Thomas, and to a certain extent in opposition to him, whom the Church herself has refused to condemn, however daring their views might have seemed (e.g., Giles of Rome, Thomassin, and even Noris, Berti and Bellelli). On the other hand, in the controversies over grace that developed in the 15th century, and especially from the second half of the 17th century on, theologians were often wrongly accused of exaggerated Augustinianism, even though they only kept precisely what St. Thomas himself had retained of St. Augustine's teaching.

In comparing Augustinianism and Thomism, the first issue is that the Augustinians, in considering man's primeval state, refuse to distinguish it from his *nature*: that which is necessary and sufficient to constitute him as a man. Considered in these terms, one either runs the risk of maintaining, as did Baius, that the gifts of supernatural grace belonged *necessarily* to man before the fall; or one tends, as did the Jansenists, to look upon fallen man as impaired, i.e., incapable of doing good acts without efficacious grace, that is, denying that man has freedom of will to choose between good and evil. However, even though we may feel we should go further than did St. Thomas, neither error prevents us from emphasizing that the fitness and harmony of grace in human nature was God's will in the beginning, or from emphasizing the relative impotence of nature in fallen man.

Another aspect of Augustinianism that is not quite independent from the positions taken regarding the problem of grace, is the concept, influenced by both Platonism and the Neo-Platonists, that St. Augustine had of the human soul. Contrary to the Thomists, St. Augustine maintained that it does not seem essential for the human soul to be the *form* of the body. As a consequence, it follows that he in no way believed that all of the soul's knowledge, even in this life, must necessarily be derived from the knowledge of sensible reality. He admitted that the soul could have a direct intuition of itself, and through this intuition the possibility of a knowledge of God, which did not need to be channeled first through the knowledge of the world, and the reflection on God that arises from it. Concomitant with this concept is the idea of an immediate illumination of the soul by God, which is necessary for all knowledge, even non-supernatural knowledge. From these inwardly directed aspects of Augustinian thought, it can easily be seen how it has never ceased to influence theologians who might otherwise have had little direct interest in the relatively extreme positions on grace that characterize the teaching of most Augustinian theologians.

AUREOLE   In English, this term is synonymous with halo, nimbus, and glory. In its theological sense, the aureole designates the accidental reward of a soul in heaven, consisting of a particular joy that is added to its essential beatitude (i.e., the beatific vision), and which is the joy of that perfection proper to the accomplishments of saints in their earthly lives as their own particular victory. Therefore, a distinction is made between the aureole of martyrs, virgins, and doctors. St. Thomas Aquinas adds that in each of these cases there is a different degree of perfection that corresponds to the personal merit involved.

AUTHORITY   The power to exact obedience. In Roman law, authority, whether the State's or that of the *paterfamilias*, was considered a *dominium*, that is, the holder of authority was considered to be the real possessor of its subjects. Christianity was to modify this concept profoundly, even with regard to civil authority. When St. Paul states that there is no other authority except that which comes from God (Rom. 13,1), his justification of civil authority actually involves two separate ideas (Rom. 13,4): the affirmation that the holder of authority is only a minister (a servant) of God, and that this ministry has been entrusted to him for the good of his subjects. St. Thomas Aquinas (*De regimine principum*) gives a very forceful development of the ultimate consequences of this principle, asserting that authority, even though in the hands of one person, still rests in the whole body politic. It therefore becomes illegal to exercise that authority in violation of the common good. However, the rebirth of Roman law at the end of the Middle Ages led nominally Christian states to disregard increasingly this teaching. The effect of this was so strong that in a number of modern treatises on ecclesiology, we find not only civil but even ecclesiastical authority defined as a *dominium* rather than as a *ministerium*. This deviation contributed in no small measure to the scandalous adulterations in the exercise of ecclesiastical authority during the Renaissance, as well as to the discredit brought upon ecclesiastical authority during the period of the Protestant Reformation. On the other hand, there is sufficient assurance in the pastoral epistles of St. Paul to Titus and Timothy that the authority of pastors in the Church is principally one of service. Since they are outstanding members of the flock over which they have been placed, they must, like Christ whom they represent, follow his example and conduct, by not domineering over those in their charge. (cf. 1 Pet. 5,3, and the entire context.)

B

BAPTISM Derived from the Greek *baptizō*, which means immerse, baptism designates the sacrament of Christian initiation in accordance with the primitive form of its rite.

In addition to the manifold ablution rites often called baptisms (cf. Mark 7,4), Judaism practiced a baptism of proselytes. It is possible that the Essenes or other Jewish groups, more or less dominated by the expectation of the Messiah, had already imposed this ritual on the Jews themselves, as a way of entering into the new economy of the expected Kingdom of God. In any case, it is what St. John the Baptist practiced with all those whom he publicly called to *metanoia*, i.e., a radical changing of one's spiritual state, which, more than a penance, was an act of faith in the coming of a new "world," the world of the Kingdom that he proclaimed as imminent (Mark 1,1–4).

Apparently it is in this same sense that Jesus baptized in the beginning of his ministry (John 3,22.26; 4,1–2), just as he had allowed himself to be baptized by John (Mark 1,9–11), thus actually bringing into reality the Kingdom that John was announcing. This was the reason for John's surprise that He who was to make the Kingdom a reality should himself have taken the course that was to be man's, and for Christ's insistence on leading the way himself for all who were to follow Him, thereby giving meaning to the Incarnation (Matt. 3,13–15). But the Fathers underlined how the manifestation of the Trinity, which accompanied the baptism of the Saviour, gives a portent of the transformation of this rite. From then on baptism centered on Christ and became no longer merely a baptism of water, but of the Spirit (i.e., the divine power of this Kingdom on high, which is nothing less than the communication of God's own life to men). It associates men not only with the work of the Son of God made man, but also with his very being itself.

Christian baptism is the fruit of the Saviour's passion, and in a sense, its extension. We understand, then, why Christ prescribes it only on leaving the earth, and how he sends his apostles to continue his work (i.e., the apostolic mission which he entrusted to them at this moment, bestowing on them the effect of this rite, although probably dispensing them from it; cf. Matt. 28,19).

Moreover, it is in St. Paul (Rom. 6) that we find the meaning of baptism expressed for the first time as an immersion (burial) in the death of Christ which permits us to come to life again in the new life of his Resurrection. By baptism, Paul said, we are a part of Christ, and more precisely of his cross (verse 5). Or again, as he said to the Galatians, "For as many of you as were baptized into Christ, have put on Christ." From this comes the opposition between the prior life, a life of the flesh for the pagans, or at least for the Jews a life under the law, and the life of the baptized, which is a life "in Christ," the life of the Spirit in us (Gal. 5,19; cf. Rom. 8), "mortifying the works of the body" and giving us in exchange life everlasting (cf. Rom. 8,13).

It is in St. John, that this predominant aspect of the new life of baptism is described as a rebirth, which is also a birth from on high (John 3,3-7). But it is no less clear in St. John that all the force of Christian baptism proceeds from the death of the Saviour (cf. verses 14-15).

These two complementary aspects of death and life, as the early baptismal liturgies of both East and West correctly emphasized, are bound to two fundamental systems of water symbolism, which were first developed in a supernatural sense in the Old Testament. The first is the symbolism of the living waters, source of life, the most significant symbol of what the divine Presence is for the people of Israel. The other is the symbolism of the waters of the flood, of the surge of the sea or of the great rivers, where the Leviathan dwells, the image of demonic power which, through sin, reabsorbs creation in death. The Genesis account, with its image of the waters of chaos, from which the Spirit who descends into them brings forth the first living beings (1,2.20), already seemed to have prepared the blending of these two symbolisms.

As a mystical death with Christ of those who pledge their faith to Him in a decisive act, baptism opens the door to a new life by sending into them the Spirit of God. From the very beginning, rites in which baptism found its complement were the imposition of hands and anointing, which more directly affirm this communication of the Spirit of the risen Christ, and the entrance into the fellowship of which the Spirit is the soul. Today we find this realized in the rite of the *consignation* (q.v.) with the Holy Chrism (*see* CHRISM) that is still a part of the baptismal ritual in the West, and which is completed by *confirmation* (q.v.). In the East, *chrismation* which is equivalent to confirmation is in principle never celebrated apart from baptism itself.

In the early days of the Church, a question arose as to whether baptism administered by heretics was valid. In Rome, particularly, the practice of admitting the validity of every materially correct baptism ultimately triumphed, as long as there was manifested sufficient intent to effect the intention of Church. St. Augustine gives proof of this, in saying: "Whether it be Peter or Judas who baptizes, it is always Christ baptizing" (*Tract. in Johannem*, in III, 3). Although in principle baptism of adults is always reserved to the bishop, as the head of the local community to which baptism introduces us, in the same context, every pastor of a parish is allowed to give baptism solemnly to children. Not only a priest, but also every layman, and even an unbeliever, in a case of necessity, could confer baptism validly and lawfully, always provided that they had at least the intention of doing what the Church does, and observed the minimum ritual that is required by the institution of the sacrament itself, namely, an ablution with water, accompanied by the words: "I baptize you in the name of the Father and of the Son and of the Holy Spirit."

As for who may be baptized, it is every man who, once having accepted the Christian faith, consequently has the desire to receive it. However, from the earliest times the Church allowed the baptism of children of Christians before they attained the age of reason, even though the practice itself did not become general until somewhat later. This permission is grounded in the faith of the Church that takes these infants as a charge before God, and particularly in the faith of those who bring them forth to be baptized, and who must take on the responsibility of bringing them up in this faith. It might be observed here that *Baptists* (or more exactly, Anabaptists, i.e., advocates of a new baptism) are those who reject as worthless any baptism given to an individual who is not yet personally able to make a profession of faith.

However, these peripheral cases which we have just cited must not, contrary to what is too often the situation, serve as a basis for a theology of baptism. This theology, on the contrary, must start out only from a completely normal case, i.e., baptism of a believing adult who is received publicly into the Church by her local head, in the presence of the community assembled for a special, solemn eucharistic celebration. Let us also observe that baptism by simple pouring, to which we are accustomed today in the West (unlike the East where baptism is always conferred by immersion, a practice that until recently was still the case in many regions of the West) is simply a reduction of the matter of the sacrament to its barest minimum. It is deeply regrettable that this has become customary, for it deprives the administration of the sacrament of a great part of its expressive power.

The traditional baptismal celebration, where the theological essence of baptism is clearly expressed is the Easter Vigil. Here baptism is given during the principal celebration of the Saviour's victory over sin and death. Baptism appears clearly in this celebration as the act by which the Church, in a single action, receives a new believer into the fellowship of the faith, and integrates him into the mystical Body of Christ, by welcoming him at the eucharistic table. Baptism, completed by confirmation, in conforming us to Christ in the mystery of his redeeming death, actually makes us into members of a whole priestly people. In this way, it leads us to the Eucharist, where this people, joined by common prayer in the unity of faith, and by the sacrificial offering, and fellowship in the resurrected Christ, becomes associated with this unique sacrifice of reconciliation and of thanksgiving, of which Christ is the priest.

It is in this sense that we can fully understand the baptismal *character* (q.v.), that is, the supernatural mark that baptism impresses forever on the one who receives it, making him a member of Christ. There immediately follows, unless obstructed by a positive forswearing of the true faith, a total purification with regard to *guilt* and *punishment* (q.v.) of faults committed prior to baptism. Although the *temporal punishments* for all mankind, that follow from sin, including *concupiscence* (q.v.), remain for us, there flows from the sacrament, together with *habitual grace*, a permanent title to receive, through the means Christ has set down, the *actual graces* that will be necessary for the new Christian's perseverance in the faith, and for his arrival at the fullness of holiness to which God has destined him. Because baptism is such a great gift, it has always seemed unrenewable. Consequently, a question has been asked from the earliest times regarding what happens to the believer who is unfaithful to this grace of his baptism and who loses it through *mortal sin*. From this question has resulted the conviction that, if he can recover this lost state of grace by a true *penance* (q.v.), this penance would not be the completely free grace that baptism was. While it is also, and for a stronger reason, only possible because of the pure generosity of God, it would be a grace that demanded and at the same time produced a *contrition*, which is painfully toilsome compared to the grace of baptism that has been thrown aside. (*See also* GRACE, and SIN.)

Although baptism is normally necessary for salvation, its absence can be made up for either by baptism of blood, i.e., martyrdom suffered by a believer who is not yet baptized, or baptism of desire, which presupposes faith and a desire to receive its sacramental seal, which only circumstances independent of the will of the subject prevent from becoming an effective realization. Regarding the expression, "second baptism," as sometimes applied to monastic or religious professions, it must not be taken literally. It simply means that this profession, by the radical penance it presupposes if performed under correct conditions, can restore baptismal innocence as perfectly as possible. (Cf. St. Thomas Aquinas, *Sum. Theol.*, IIIa, qq.66–71.)

BARTHISM The name given to the teaching of the contemporary Swiss-German Protestant theologian, Karl Barth. Rather close to certain aspects of *Calvinism* (q.v.), from which he is distinguished, however, by a greater radicalism, Karl Barth has given many Protestants, who had lost it, a sense of the Word of God as sovereign authority and source of all Christianity. However, he remains more or less the prisoner of a philosophical concept of the divine transcendence through which he denies that any institution can be the guardian of divine authority, or that any present reality of grace and salvation can belong ontologically to the believer. Nevertheless, after the primary phase of his teaching, these same principles led him to deny that the truth proclaimed by the Word could in any way be defined. His reaction against his former disciple Bultmann (who rejects all traditional doctrines as simple mythology) persuaded him, along with the development of his *Dogmatik*, to take hold in a more positive sense of a number of traditional dogmatic assertions (e.g., the Trinity, the Incarnation, etc.).

BEATIFICATION   Admission by the Church of the fact that a person who died in reputed sanctity can be considered as blessed, and as a result can become the object of at least local veneration. Until the Middle Ages, beatification was not distinguished from *canonization* (q.v.) except by the local limits of the veneration in question. At that time, sanction was dependent upon the power of the bishop. Since then, the Holy See has reserved this power to itself. Moreover, a distinction is still made between *formal* beatification, pronounced by the pope after a canonical process investigating the heroic nature of the virtues and the authenticity of the miracles; and *equipollent* beatification, which is a simple, tacit approbation of a *de facto* veneration given by the people. But formal beatification cannot involve in a strict way the Church's infallibility, since it is merely a temporary permission given to a local devotion, as shown by the fact that in the case of canonization the whole process must be repeated. *See* Benedict XIV, *De servorum Dei beatificatione et beatorum canonizatione* (Rome, 1747).

BEATITUDE   Beatitude is defined as the state of a being, gifted with intelligence and free will, once he has attained the sovereign *Good* (q.v.) to which he was destined. Since it is therefore the perfect happiness achieved by man upon reaching his proper goal, it is also the perfect union of happiness and virtue.

The philosophers have made an effort to distinguish happiness (i.e., the one thing that satisfies) from simple pleasure, which only momentarily satisfies one or another of our most superficial desires. In this sense then Plato contrasts *eros pandemos*, the desire for sensual pleasures, with *eros ouranios*, the aspiring to spiritual happiness found in reaching and possessing the Good. Aristotle was critical of this solution to the extent that it is connected with Plato's theory of Ideas, which exist by themselves, independently, and outside of the objects of the world of the senses. Aristotle believed that man finds beatitude in the operation proper to him, through reason, and, therefore, in the contemplation of truth. Particularly virtuous actions contribute to beatitude only insofar as they dispose or orient us to the fullness of this supreme activity. Material conditions themselves, although important, are only important to the extent that they make that activity possible or facilitate it.

The Stoics, on the contrary, made beatitude one with virtue, defining it as the perfect acceptance of the divine will in us, such as it is inscribed in the very nature of things. Plotinus developed the first synthesis of these theories by seeing in beatitude the fruit of the activity of our contemplative intelligence, insofar as it is applied to the Good alone, and that through this application we desire the Good (not that contemplation itself is the cause of this assimilation with the Good, but rather its result).

Biblical revelation begins by inculcating the idea in man that everything that makes up his happiness, beginning with the enjoyment of the physical goods necessary for a full life (what the Hebrew understands by the word *peace*), could not be assured to him in a stable fashion, except by the Creator of all good (cf. Ps. 1). One then proceeds to the idea that to live in His presence, in his service, just as this is the correct way toward an untroubled possession of these various goods, constitutes a higher good, for which all others can be sacrificed, and, if necessary, must be sacrificed (cf. Ps. 84). Whence follows a transition from the primitive idea that God blesses man by enriching him (cf. Gen. 49; Ps. 111), to the ultimate idea that the truly happy man, on the contrary, is the poor man, whose wealth is his living faith in the living God (cf. Ps. 126; Jer. 20,1–13).

These ideas are extended and enlarged upon in the evangelical beatitudes (Matt. 5,1–12; Luke 6,20–22). In St. Luke, they are asserted (in opposition to the corresponding maledictions) under the most paradoxical form, as the eschatological counterpart of a total deprivation accepted in this life. In St. Matthew, the need for an explanation makes itself felt in the spiritualization of poverty thus blessed. But, in both of these evangelists, the beatitudes find all their meaning only in the context of the sermon which they introduce (there is but one meaning behind all of them: they are not so many different beatitudes, but rather one unique and total beatitude seen under different aspects). Actually, it is the faith in the fatherhood of God that produces the evangelical beatitude in us, but only when this faith takes possession of our whole life. Recognizing in God this generous, creative and saving *love* (q.v.) which is his, we discover that for us true happiness is found in the filial life, which consists in living in this same love by which we are loved.

It is along this line of thinking that St. Paul analyzes the love of God communicated to men by his Holy Spirit, giving us an incidental definition of the beatitude which we expect, i.e., knowing God as we have been known by him (1 Cor. 13,12; cf. the entire context in relation to Rom. 5,5 and 8). The latter prophets had already developed the notion of this *knowledge* (q.v.): a knowledge which is a conforming to the recognized divine will, a conforming which is only found in an intimate union with God, of which his grace is the sole principle.

This is again specified even more profoundly in St. John, when he says that life, i.e., life which in its fullness is God's love communicated to His People, is to "know Thee the only true God, and Jesus Christ whom Thou hast sent." (John 17,3).

This beatifying knowledge, which is a reciprocal intimacy, a transforming union with the God of love, will bloom only in the Resurrection. This implies, along with a restoration and glorification of our entire being (body and soul) inside the transfiguration of the universe, our perfect union both with God and with all those whom he loves and calls us to love with him. Theologians call this accidental beatitude in contrast to essential beatitude, which is found only in the union with God.

Since St. Augustine, theology's endeavor has been to assimilate the best philosophical idea with these Christian concepts. By an analysis of happiness that owes much to Neo-Platonism, St. Augustine shows that God alone, known and loved, can give us in eternal life a love that satisfies and endures ("You have made us for Yourself, and our hearts are restless until they rest in You"). St. Thomas Aquinas (who very closely follows the *De Causis* of Proclus) returns to the Aristotelian notion of an essentially intellectual beatitude. But those who have reproached him for this, as if he were specifically disregarding Christian charity, have not observed the dexterity with which he modified the meaning of these borrowed formulas; incorporating in them all the values proper to the biblical notion of divine knowledge, along with Plotinus's concept of the sovereign Good as the ultimate object of contemplation (which, however, cannot evolve except through our assimilation with the contemplated object).

However, the Franciscan school, and particularly Duns Scotus, maintained that beatitude, even in its eternal realization, is rather the activity of the will which delights in the divine Good, than that of the intelligence which contemplates it. But the opposite insistence of the Thomist school, far from betraying an abstract intellectualism, simply emphasizes that the essential of true beatitude is the *perfect Being* who presents himself for our discovery, rather than that which causes us to adhere to that Being. In the same consideration of the transcendent objectivity of the sovereign Good, one finds the solution to the problem of pure *love* (q.v.). To believe that one would love God more, if one could love him without aspiring at the same time to beatitude, is to ignore the fact that this beatitude, before becoming our own, depends on God. God cannot be loved purely in any other way than by our willing all that He wills. Now our beatitude, which is found in this love, is precisely too essential an element to the divine will for us to be able to substract it, without contradiction, from this divine will, under the pretext of conforming to it more fully. The question of whether beatitude is only accessible in the hereafter, must be answered by saying that it is only known in its essential fullness from the moment that the faithful soul arrives at the vision of God. Consequently its accidental complement, as we have defined above, is only attained in the final and general resurrection. On the other hand, and this is essentially the very meaning of the evangelical beatitudes, once man orients himself efficaciously in his present life toward his everlasting goal through the theological virtues, he knows an undeniable foretaste of it in proportion to his progress in these virtues. The mystical experience is the highest realization of man's eternal goal, since, while one still remains within the shadows of the faith, the attainment in a sort of *chiaroscuro* of the everlasting Good (which hope already knows through charity) is such that even the most acute joys of the senses are totally unimportant by comparison. The testimony of the martyrs and those who, in one way or another, suffer voluntarily for Christ, assure us also that in the midst of the worst earthly ordeals of fidelity to the Saviour God, we can, paradoxically, be more deeply happy than at the zenith of any happiness of earthly origin.

See St. Thomas Aquinas, *Sum. Theol.*, Ia-IIae, qq.1 to 5.

BEING   Being, considered separately, cannot be defined, since it is logically the first concept which all others presuppose, i.e., being does not exist outside of the order of beings. Contrary to what Hegel thought, being is not a genus; being is transcendental, beyond every genus, since one cannot pass from a genus to the species that it includes except by adding a specific difference, and nothing can be added to being.

On the other hand, being is analogical (*see* ANALOGY). The other transcendentals are like different aspects of being itself: *Unity*, since every being exists insofar as it is undivided in itself, while the Supreme Being, God, is indivisible, not only physically—as is a created being—but metaphysically, since His existence is not distinct from his essence; *Truth*, not the conformity of our judgment to reality, but conversely the conformity of all things to the ideal type of their nature, according to how it is understood in the divine intelligence; *Goodness*, insofar as evil is always only a lack of being.

We call laws of being the first principles, i.e., the principle of non-contradiction: a thing cannot *be* and *not-be* at the same time; the

principle of identity: on the plane of essence, a thing is *what* it is, and on
the plane of existence, a thing is that which *is*; the principle of the
excluded third: a thing is or it is not; and, the principle of the equivalent
third: two things, identical to a third thing, are identical to each other.
To these is added the principle of causality, which is not applicable to
every being, but only to contingent beings: every being that could *not-be*
had a cause that makes it be. Today, philosophers also consider as a
principle of this type the principle of sufficient reason, enunciated for the
first time by Leibnitz. But in this theory Leibnitz arrives at a denial of
the possibility of any contingency, and therefore of all freedom, even in
God. We can, however, include this principle among the laws of being, if
it is formulated (as M. Verneau suggests) in the following way: being is
intelligible of itself, which does not mean that in its fullest meaning this
is necessarily so for man himself. (*See* St. Thomas Aquinas, *De Veritate,
De Malo, De ente et essentia.*)

BELIEF   When it is distinguished from faith, religious (or pious)
belief is merely an opinion that one can legitimately make one's own, in
proportion to the reasons that militate in its favor, but that no one can
impose on another, or even make his own belief equal to faith without
putting faith at least indirectly in danger. The supposition that it would
be more devout to admit all the beliefs which the Church, without ever
having sanctioned them, has never rejected, has no foundation. The
Church *de facto* tolerates many innocent beliefs of little foundation
simply because they are of such little importance that the trouble
invested in their formal condemnation seems out of proportion to any
real danger they represent.

BELLARMINISM   The teaching of St. Robert Cardinal Bellarmine
about the Church, and especially regarding the relationship between the
Church's authority and that of the State. According to him, the Church,
in its very definition, implies a divinely instituted authority, for it is "the
assembly of men united together by the profession of the same Christian
faith, and the participation in the same sacraments, under the authority
of legitimate pastors, chiefly of the Roman Pontiff, sole vicar of Jesus
Christ on earth" (*De Conciliis et Ecclesia,* bk. III, chap. 2).

Nevertheless, this authority, however august it may be, is directly
applicable only to spiritual things. However, the Church can intervene in
temporal things, but only when the salvation of souls requires it, and to
the extent that it requires it. Thus the pope himself cannot, according to
his ordinary jurisdiction, appoint or depose civil authorities, make civil
laws, or confirm or abrogate those which have been established by the
lawful civil authority. On the other hand, he can intervene extraor-

dinarily in all these areas, to the degree and according to the extent specified. This is called indirect power. Bellarmine was careful to specify that these extraordinary interventions, even when they appear to be lawful and necessary, are such only within strictly narrow limits. The ecclesiastical authority will not involve itself in this way except as a last resort, and if it should go so far as to prescribe the deposition of a civil authority, it will not be able to replace the civil authority, but must give free course in this area to the right of succession or of election (*De Potestate Summi Pontificis*, c. XII, t. VII, col.901).

Even those of the modern theologians who have sometimes regretted that Bellarmine seemed to put authority on an equal plane with faith and the sacraments, recognize on the other hand that his thought (without giving way at all to modern Gallicanism or Laicism) has dispelled the confusion of the Middle Ages, at least *de facto*, between the authority of the Church and the State.

BISHOP   From the Greek word *episkopos* meaning inspector or overseer. In Christian usage the term has come to refer to the chief ministers of the Church, who are considered to be the successors of the *apostles* (q.v.).

While the apostles were still living and exercising their office, it appears from the New Testament that the terms *episkopos* and *presbyteros* (from which we derive the word *priest*) were practically synonymous. They designated the heads of the local communities founded by the apostles, and they were appointed under apostolic authority to continue and direct these communities once the founding apostles were no longer there (cf. Acts 20,28 and Phil. 1,1). In certain places, such as Rome, if we may judge from the Epistle of St. Clement, something of this primitive identification of the two terms subsisted for rather a long while, together with the opinion that the body of presbyters always exercised its authority collectively. Elsewhere, as in Syria, with the Epistles of St. Ignatius of Antioch, we may observe that the bishop stood out most clearly from the body of local presbyters, even though they always remained at his side, and were inseparable from him. But in both cases, the Church through the persons of her local heads, showed from the beginning, in her manner of proclaiming the Gospel, celebrating the holy mysteries, and settling the most diverse problems that arose in her pastoral work, her intention to carry on the same apostolate of the apostles themselves; not that she could in any way modify what they had set down, but rather would maintain its permanent relevance to the everchanging spectrum of life. Soon, in fact, even though everywhere the numerous presbyters continued to be associated with the work of the apostolate, it also seemed that the principle of their authority and power was to be found in the bishop alone, who by this time was the head of each local church. When Ireneaus or Tertullian restricted the title of successor of the apostles to the bishop, a fact already implied a century earlier in the teaching of Ignatius, we see no one opposing them, or even having any idea that they were advancing something of a novelty. (Cf. Irenaeus, *Adv. Haer.*, III, iii,1; P.G. 7,848, and Tertullian, *De praescr.*, 32; P.L. 2,44, and Ignatius, *Ad Trall.*, II, 2; *Ad Smyrn.*, VIII, 1, etc.)

The fact that the apostolic succession is centered in the bishop, appears to be tightly bound up with the unity of the Church that his pastoral office was to guarantee, founded as it is in the unity of faith given to the apostles and, particularly, in the eucharistic celebration which makes the whole Church one body in Christ. (Cf. St. Cyprian, *Ep.* 66,8; *Ep.* 65,14; *Ep.* 63,13 and 14; C.V. 3(2),732,728,711–713, and St. Ignatius, *Ad Smyrn.*, VIII, 1.)

Nevertheless, the *communion* (q.v.) of the bishops among themselves is no less important, since it is due to this fellowship that all the local churches are one Church. If bishops or churches should withdraw from it, they would cease to be the Church of Christ, or to belong to Him (this is the theme of the *De Unitate Ecclesiae* of St. Cyprian, especially 5; C.V.3(1),213). On the other hand, it becomes increasingly clear that this unity of the successors of the apostles has its nucleus in the successor of Peter (*see* POPE): was it not Ignatius who said that the Church of Rome is "she who presides over charity"? (*Ad Rom.*, inscr.)

Thus the traditional image of the bishop takes form around the offices of doctor and pontiff, which are essential to the realization of the pastoral office that entrusted to him the flock which the apostles constituted on the cornerstone that is Christ. The unity of the Church is realized locally in the bishop, just as it is realized universally in the communion of bishops over which the bishop-successor to Peter presides.

Two major questions arise from these principles. The first is the relationship of the bishop with the Bishop of the Church who "presides over charity." The second is the relationship of each bishop in his own Church with the other "presbyters," the priests of second rank, who are associated with him.

To clarify the first point, the Church of the patristic era accepted both the collegiality of the episcopate on the one hand, and the general responsibility and correlative preeminence of the Bishop of Rome on the other. Although he may have had over a longer period of time more occasion to exercise his supremacy in the affairs of the Western Church rather than elsewhere, the least that can be said is that the claim of the Roman prerogatives, however precise St. Leo may have already been on this point, does not seem to have created any difficulty even in the East. The Middle Ages saw this state of balance that was as yet undefined become slowly modified. First of all, the schism between East and West (although the question of the role of the pope was not its primary cause) over the papal claims wrought a hostility through the fault both of the claims to autonomy of the patriarchs of Constantinople, and the blundering of the Roman envoys. Subsequently, the great schism in the West, which was produced by an apparent division of the papacy against itself, led the episcopate to assume the position of judge between the pretenders to the pontifical throne, and then led them to set themselves up as an authority in opposition to the authority of Rome. The bishops found themselves encouraged in this through the wishes of the temporal power to interfere in the affairs of the Church, since the kings and the jurisconsults were more ready to meet with bishops who could be easily made to submit to their power, than an independent power such as the papacy, which could slip from their hands. From this collusion, *Gallicanism* (q.v.) and similar movements arose. And these movements themselves, in turn, brought on justifications of the pontifical supremacy by the theologians of the Curia, who went so far as to exalt it in opposition to the power of the episcopate in its totality. Consequently this unfortunate tendency of considering the pope as somehow outside the episcopate, if not in opposition to it, was manifested on all sides.

The Vatican Council of 1870 contributed forcefully toward clearing up the situation, by giving a definition of pontifical supremacy which is now recognized by the whole Church, and which prepared the way for a new approach in an organic and positive relationship with the episcopate in general. The task of the Second Vatican Council, initiated as it was by the pope himself, was to restore the collegiality of bishops to its proper importance, because the definitions of 1870 are now part of the Church's official teaching, and not any longer in opposition to this supremacy, as shown by the facts. In line with the teaching of St. Gregory the Great and the practice of St. Gregory VII, the pope's role as sovereign arbiter is the best support of the entire episcopate, and the safeguard of its collegiate life and authority.

As for the second problem, it is certain that the complex origins of the monarchical episcopate and especially the strict connection it could not help but keep with the priesthood of second rank, aided for a long time in preventing a precise definition of their relationship. St. Thomas Aquinas, whose remarkable theological synthesis on the priesthood is constructed entirely on the power to celebrate the Eucharist (including in it the proclamation of the evangelical Word as inseparable from the sacramental consecration), concluded, with perhaps too unilinear a logic, that from the point of view of *Holy Orders* (*see* ORDERS) there is no difference between the bishop and the priest (even though a difference does exist from the point of view of *jurisdiction* (q.v.), and that consequently the consecration of a bishop does not belong to the sacramental order (cf. *In IV Sent.*, dist. 24, q.3, a.2, ad 2um). However, the opinion of theologians, encouraged more and more by the pontiffs themselves (cf. the Constitution *Sacramentum Ordinis* of Pius XII in 1947), seemed to have decidedly rejected this view which has been formally disowned by the Second Vatican Council. Doesn't St. Thomas himself provide the principle for the rectification of his views, when he further says that the priest of second rank possesses the eucharistic power in a participated manner (*ibid.*, dist. 13, q.1, a.1, ad 2um)? It seems necessary, therefore, in deference to all the elements of tradition, to maintain that it is only the bishop who possesses the sacramental order in its fullness; autonomously, however, he communicates essentially the same order, although in a necessarily subordinate manner, to those whom he makes his cooperators through presbyteral ordination.

See together with the Constitution *Lumen Gentium* of the Second Vatican Council, *L'Episcopat et l'Eglise universelle*, published under the editorship of Y. Congar, O.P. and B. D. Dupuy, O.P. (*Unam Sanctam* series, No. 39, Paris, 1962).

BLESSING   A prayer formula that has the purpose of bringing God's grace in a special manner to some object or person. Blessing in the strict sense is distinct from intercessory prayer because it supposes a special authority in the person pronouncing it, thus assuring to that extent the realization of the desire expressed. This distinction explains how the principal blessings are the object of precise liturgical prescriptions, and are generally reserved, depending on their importance, either to bishops, or to priests of second rank.

It is then necessary to distinguish between consecratory blessings, which refer to the consecration of a person or an object to the worship or the service of God, and those blessings which are destined to procure special graces for those who receive them, or who will use the objects to which the blessing applies.

Moreover, if we refer to the origin of Christian blessings, which is undoubtedly in the Jewish blessings from which the Eucharist itself was born, and if we examine the formularies of the blessings still used by the Church, we observe that all blessings are bound to a certain more or less direct consecration of the object of that blessing to the service or worship of God. The Jewish blessing (*berakah*) was always addressed to God in the form of an act of grateful faith in the goodness of the creative power and divine providence which, having produced the being or the object under consideration, still allowed us to make use of it. It always implied (often to the point of a categorical statement) in those who pronounced it, the disposition to use the object of the blessing only for the glory of

God. This is what St. Paul expresses when he says, "Everything created by God is good, and nothing is to be rejected if it is received with thanksgiving [i.e., blessing; *eukharistia* here is still the equivalent of the Hebrew *berakah*], for then it is consecrated by the word of God and prayer" (1 Tim. 4,4–5). We therefore completely disregard the meaning of Christian blessings if we implore them outside of the view of faith which leads us to consecrate ourselves more, through the object of the blessing, to the glory of God in the accomplishment of His will alone.

BLOOD   As we see from the commands given to Noah on leaving the Ark, blood was considered by the ancient Hebrews to be one with the soul (Gen. 9,4), i.e., life. This is the reason for the sacredness of blood, the prohibition against eating meat with blood in it, and all the rituals of purification by blood, recalled in the Epistle to the Hebrews (Heb. 9,18 ff.). The blood of Christ, shed in his passion, appears as that which washes and regenerates us, our life being thus returned to its author. This is the blood of the New Covenant, spoken of in the institution of the Eucharist through the allusion to the blood of the Paschal Lamb (*see* LAMB OF GOD). St. Ignatius of Antioch gave to this image its full Christian meaning, when he identified the blood of the eucharistic cup with the supernatural charity to which Christ gave testimony and communicated to us. On this is based the veneration of the Precious Blood of the Latin Middle Ages, all of which caused long polemical disputes. The Thomist theologians denied that one could appeal to any supposed relic, based on the principle that the bodily Resurrection and Ascension of the Saviour does not allow us to believe that anything of his humanity could have remained on earth (cf. St. Thomas Aquinas, *Sum. Theol.* IIIa, q.54, a.2, ad 3um).

BODY   Christian teaching concerning man's body is opposed to the different forms of dualism which see the origin of evil, and more particularly moral evil, in matter. According to the Bible, man was created by God with a body and a soul, and in the beginning his body, like his soul, was good. This teaching is clearly present in the two successive accounts of Creation given in the first chapters of Genesis.

It is a faulty interpretation of the New Testament texts on the *flesh* (q.v.) that prompts the incorrect belief of any disagreement on this point between the Old and New Testaments. What is true is that the influence of Platonist ideas on some theologians has sometimes led them to minimize the importance of the body in the composite of man, as if the body were united to the soul accidently. This is a particularly noticeable characteristic of *Augustinianism* (q.v.).

By further developing the Aristotelian theory of the soul as the "form" ·

of the body, St. Thomas Aquinas was able to vindicate biblical anthropology. He does not deny that the soul by itself is a substantial form, but he specifies that the soul is the "form" of the body, and very precisely of that body for which God has ordained it. Thus, along with the unity of the composite of man, the essential role played by the body is also safeguarded. In the same way, the holiness of marriage and procreation can be fully understood along the premises outlined in Ephesians 5,22 ff. Therefore, the New Testament views, which orient us not toward a bodyless life of the soul after death, but toward the hope of rising again with Christ, are respected (cf. 1 Cor. 15; Col. 2,12 and 3,1; Eph. 2,6). See St. Thomas Aquinas, *Sum. Theol.* Ia, qq.75–76.

BREAKING OF BREAD   After the first act of the liturgy of the Jewish meal on which was based the primitive eucharistic liturgy, the name "breaking of bread" was given to the Eucharist itself (cf. Acts 2,42). In all subsequent liturgies, the breaking of bread has been developed through rites and prayers that generally insist on the participation of all in the one bread (cf. 1 Cor. 10,17), and also, at times, on the death of the Saviour, although this developed at a later date. However, to counteract interpretations of this rite that involved a physical realism contrary to the very nature of the sacramental presence, the Church has insisted on the fact that the Christ present in the sacred species is no longer suffering. Completely present in each of the particles, he does not suffer any adverse effect, either from the breaking of bread, or from any other action affecting these particles (cf. the hymn *Lauda Sion*).

C

CABALA   From an Aramaic word (*qabbalah*) meaning "tradition." In Judaism, the term particularly designates an esoteric tradition of theosophical interpretations of the Scriptures. Its doctrine is formulated in the *Zohar* ("Book of Splendors"), which is attributed to a rabbi of the 2nd century, Simeon ben Yohai, but which seems in fact to be the work of Moses de Leon (13th century). Nevertheless, there is no doubt that the *Zohar* incorporates many prior traditions, some of which may date from the earliest days of Christianity. Whatever the case, Cabala proposes a doctrine of creation, by a successive emanation of *Sephiroth*, which combine the 21 letters of the Hebrew alphabet and the elements of the world they would represent. Its doctrine holds that evil is made possible by a mysterious "withdrawal" of God, bound up with creation, and reveals the chaos that is correlative to God himself.

We cannot avoid being struck by certain analogies between these doctrines and the teaching of the Gnostic systems of antiquity (*see* GNOSTICISM). Some have thought to see a kinship here with certain later Neo-Platonist speculations, but at least we can wonder whether the analogy, insofar as it may exist, does not proceed from common sources in Jewish gnosticism. In any case, it is from the Cabala itself that renaissance Neo-Platonism, in Pico della Mirandola, Giles of Viterbo, and Johann Reuchlin, sought for the inspiration that was to direct it more and more toward an occult theosophy. Combined with the naturalistic and magic physics of Paracelsus, at first by the theosophist-physician Henry Kunrath, author of the *Amphitheatrum Divinae Sapientiae*, and then by Jakob Boehme, the cobbler-philosopher of Görlitz, in the 17th century, as well as by Cambridge Platonism (Henry More, particularly), the cabalistic current of thought exerted a considerable, although often overlooked, influence on all of modern thought, especially in Germany and England, and particularly in the age of Romanticism. It also profoundly influenced religious thought among Catholics like Franz von Baader, Görres and his school, and Louis Bautain in France, and especially the Russian Orthodox, such as Vladimir Soloviev, Paul Florensky, and Sergei Bulgakov, as well as Nikolai Berdyaev.

CALVINISM   The teaching of the French Protestant theologian, John Calvin. Contrary to the belief of many Catholics who use the word "Calvinists" indiscriminately to designate all Protestants who call themselves "Reformed" or "Presbyterian" (the first term is used by French and German Protestants, and the second by British and American Protestants, although "Reformed" is also used in the United States), Calvinism is only one theological school in those Churches owing their origin to Calvin. Its original precepts remain somewhat constant only in the Reformed Churches of Holland. Strict Calvinism is distinguished principally by 1) the belief in a twofold predestination (i.e., a conception of predestination that supposes God predestines some to salvation and the rest to damnation in a manner that is positive, although in different ways, for both); 2) a relatively realistic concept of the sacraments, particularly of the Eucharist, although Calvinism looks upon the real presence as a virtual and dynamic presence, rather than as a presence that is substantial but accessible only through faith (the position admitted by orthodox Lutherans and Catholics alike); 3) a concept of the Church that is visible and defined not only by a dogmatic faith and correct celebration of the sacraments, but also by an organization Calvin believed he found in the New Testament, which is called presbyterian (*see* PRESBYTERIANISM); 4) a concept of the mutual independence of Church and State, which, when combined with the doctrine that civil magistrates must conform to the teaching of the Gospel as given by the Church, comes in fact rather close to Catholic teaching on indirect power, as found particularly in Bellarmine; 5) an acceptance of a natural theology, and a natural law, quite removed both from the Lutheran positions, and those adopted by the modern disciples of Karl Barth on these questions; 6) finally, and perhaps especially, a positive concept of sanctification that must, in the every day life of a Christian, be the sign of his justification, although this remains, according to Calvin, a pure transcendent reality that can be received only by faith alone, as Luther had taught. Proceeding from this point on sanctification, it is no exaggeration to say that Calvin brought Protestantism much closer to traditional Catholic concepts, and that he even contributed toward its involvement in an activism that so opposed the relative *quietism* of certain Lutherans, that it became at least *Semi-Pelagian* (qq.v.). This, moreover, was what happened with the *Puritans*, or the *Arminians* and other *Protestants* (qq.v.) whom Calvin would have doubtless condemned, even though they claim to follow his thought more or less.

CANON This word, which comes from a Greek term designating a ruler used in measuring, is applied in general by the Church to every solemn decision of Church authority (especially in a council). We will be concerned here more specifically with two uses of the expression: the Canon of Scripture, and the Canon of the Mass, and will refer the reader to the word *symbol* (q.v.) which was also called the ecclesiastical canon, or canon of faith, in the early Church.

The Canon of Scripture is the list of books recognized by the Church as inspired by God. The *inspiration* (q.v.) of these books is an objective fact. The canonicity, consequently, does not make inspired a book that was not inspired from the start (which would make no sense), but makes it recognized as such by the faithful through apostolic authority. This is the meaning of the famous quotation from St. Augustine: "I should not believe in the Gospel, were it not for the Church which obliges me to do so."

The recognition of the totality of inspired books that the Church, since the Council of Trent, proposes formally and exclusively as such to the faithful is a progressive process (Sess. IV, D.B. 784). The complete list is found for the first time in a letter of Pope Innocent I (401–417; D.B. 96). In fact, with respect to the Old Testament, it is the list of books which are found in the Septuagint Version, a broader list than the one given in the Hebrew Bibles. Because of this difference, and the state of flux that resulted, the books (or fragments of books) which appear only in the Greek Bible are called deuterocanonical. The Protestant Reformers, without completely rejecting these books, generally refused to recognize them as inspired. When Protestant Bibles contain them, they give them the name Apocrypha, which Catholics now reserve for what the Protestants themselves call the pseudepigrapha, and which everyone agrees should be rejected from the canon. The Protestants of that time were forced into this attitude by the exaggerated attraction on the part of the humanists for the Hebrew text alone; on the other hand, some of the deuterocanonical books embarrassed them because of the support they give to Catholic beliefs or practices, such as the prayer for the departed (cf. 2 Mach. 12,43–46).

Regarding the New Testament, early agreement was reached by the Church on the four Gospels, Acts, and almost all the Epistles. Agreement was slower with respect to the Apocalypse and the Epistle to the Hebrews. Generally, it can be said that in the Church, as in the synagogue before her, there was a core of books whose inspiration never caused any difficulty with regard to canonical acceptance. Others were added to this nucleus through a progressive consensus. Concerning the books of the New Testament, it is certain that the decisive criterion was their apostolicity. But this did not always mean that the Church's conviction was brought directly to bear on the identity of their authors. There were certainly cases in which the importance of the book's content was the decisive reason for concluding the apostolic origin and inspiration, even in instances where a certain doubt persisted in regard to the exact identity of the redactor, even when it was evident that he was not one of the apostles (as in the case of Mark or Luke).

The Canon of the Mass is the name given (at least since St. Gregory the Great, *Epist.*, lib. IX,12; lib. XIV,2; P.L.77, cols. 956 and 1305) to the most important prayer of the Mass, still to this day called *actio*, and later, when said in a low voice, *secretum*. The latter has led the texts since the Middle Ages to have the Canon begin only with the words *Te igitur*. A probably erroneous interpretation of the word *praefatio* also played its part, as if the formula bearing this name was only an introduction (in fact, *praefatio* here must undoubtedly be interpreted in the light of the word *praefari*, "say in a loud voice"). Whatever the case, from the solemn salutation that begins the preface to the concluding doxology that precedes the *Pater*, the unity of the prayer is unbreakable, and it is only in the preface that its major theme is unfolded: the Eucharist, in the sense of a thanksgiving, of a blessing, of a proclaiming of the *mirabilia Dei*. The *anaphoras*, which are the Eastern equivalents of our Canon, always include the preface as an essential element.

The Council of Trent (Sess. XXII, cap. IV, D.B. 942) explains that the Canon is made up of the words of the Lord, the traditions of the apostles and saints, and the pious institutions of the pontiffs. The question arises whether there was *one* formula for the Canon given by the apostles themselves, and it was thought successively that this had been found in various early texts, e.g., liturgy of the eighth book of the *Apostolic Constitutions*, liturgy of the *Apostolic Tradition* of St. Hippolytus, etc. But if the apostles themselves held to one particular formula, it is probable that it would have been universally imposed, but instead it is the variety of formularies that strikes us the closer we get to primitive times. Nevertheless, behind this diversity, there is certainly a schema which is found again and again in all the ancient liturgies, and which can be called apostolic. It flows out of the Jewish liturgy itself, such as Our Lord undoubtedly celebrated, while giving it a new meaning through the words reported in the First Epistle to the Corinthians and in the Synoptic Gospels.

Looking over the various Eastern anaphoras, and the analogous Western texts, five principal models of Christian eucharistic prayer can be found, three in the East, and two in the West, corresponding respectively to the great centers: East Syria, West Syria, Egypt, Rome and Gaul (to which Spain must be joined). But these five models can be reduced to three, if strict kinship is observed, on the one hand, between the Alexandrian and Roman traditions, and on the other, between the West Syrian and Gallican or Hispanic traditions (let us recall that the ancient liturgy of Spain is called the Mozarabic rite, and might better be termed Visigothic).

The East Syrian tradition (which is known to us both by the anaphoras of Addai and Mari, and that of St. Hippolytus) is clearly

archaic. It is a simple Christian transfer of the Hebrew blessing of the
cups of wine that ends the meal: (1) blessing of God, first of all, for
creation (represented by the fruits of the earth); (2) blessing his
redemptive work (centered for the Jews on their joyful entrance into the
promised land); this memorial of his past work leads to (3) a prayer, that
he might finish what he had thus begun, in the restoration of his People,
and in the advent of messianic times; (4) to come back ultimately to a
concluding doxology in which the initial theme of blessing reappears.
The formation of a Christian eucharistic prayer on this model presupposes a very early period, when Christians still assisted at the Jewish
synagogue service of prayers and readings, while they celebrated their
eucharistic meal in a special way, in formulas directly related to those of
Judaism.

On the contrary, the West Syrian and later the Gallican or Visigothic
traditions, on the one hand, and the Alexandrian and Roman on the
other, reflect a stage where Christians who now had an office of prayers
and readings distinct from the synagogue service (yet at the same time,
heir to the latter's forms), combined it with the eucharistic meal. This
being the case, the blessing for the knowing care of God, ending with the
Sanctus, which preceded the recitation of the *Shemah* (Deut. 6,4–9) in
the synagogue service, and the great prayer of intercession that followed
it (called *Shemone esre, Tefillah,* or *Amidah*) came to be combined with
the meal prayer in different ways. In Syria, an elaborate synthesis was
made of the two collections of prayers, and this was later imitated in
Gaul and Spain. In Rome, as in Alexandria, they remained content with
a juxtaposition of these different elements, without any attempt to do
away with doublets.

Under these conditions, the Canon of the Roman Mass, like other
prayers of the same type, brought together the thanksgiving for the
knowing care of the creating and redeeming God, with the intercession
that the whole People of God might arrive at perfection in God's
Kingdom, around a sacrificial memorial which now was that of the cross.
All Christian rites, such as they are observed today in the different
Christian Churches faithful to the Catholic tradition, bring to the heart
of the Eucharist the very words of the Lord which cause us to perceive in
it the sacrificial *memorial* (q.v.) of his glorious passion. All of them also
include what is called an *epiklesis* (q.v.) in the East, i.e., an invoking of
God to accomplish in us the same mystery that the Eucharist celebrates.

However, the liturgies of West Syrian tradition and of related traditions developed this epiklesis into a formal invocation of the Holy Spirit,
placed after the unfolding of the memorial prescribed by the Lord (a

development which is called the *anamnesis*), and insisted especially on the mysterious transformation of the bread and wine into the body and blood of the Lord. The Roman Canon, like the ancient Egyptian liturgy, while it includes two types of epiklesis, one before (*Quam oblationem*) and the other after (*Supra quae* and *Supplices*) the words of institution, mentions the transformation only in the first prayer, and does not invoke the Spirit in either of them. These divergences explain the medieval controversies on the consecration between East and West: does it come about in virtue of the *Verba Christi* alone, or by the epiklesis? The only answer that conforms to the whole of tradition and that is conscious of its origins, is that the consecration comes about by virtue of the words of Christ instituting the Eucharist, formally recalled by the Church in the heart of the invocation in which it yields to the power of the mystery it communicates (*see* CONSECRATION).

CANONIZATION The solemn act whereby the Church, in a definitive pronouncement, inscribes a servant of God in the catalogue of saints. As Innocent III specified, this decision rests on the authentication of the heroic practice of Christian virtues during life, and the accomplishment of miracles after death. Canonization, which for a long time was nothing more than a *beatification* (q.v.) extended *de facto* to the universal Church, has since the 12th century become reserved at least in principle to the Sovereign Pontiffs (*Decret.*, bk. III, tit. 45, c.I, of Alexander III, issued in 1170). This was definitively specified and confirmed by two decrees of Urban VIII on the 13th of March and the 2nd of October, 1625.

Canonization, which today is always preceded by simple beatification, like the latter can be either formal, following a regular process, or equipollent, by a pronouncement sanctioning a *de facto* veneration without the intervention of a canonical process. Prevailing opinion is that pontifical infallibility is involved in the pronouncements of canonization. But it is generally admitted that if this is a proposal of *divine faith*, it is not so, directly or explicitly. As to knowing whether the canonized person actually enjoys heavenly beatitude, it seems that no more than a certitude of *ecclesiastical faith* can be had (*see* ECCLESIASTICAL, and FAITH). *See* St. Thomas Aquinas, *Quodlibet*, IX, q.8, a.16; and Benedict XIV, *De Servorum Dei Beatificatione et Beatorum Canonizatione*, Rome, 1747.

Canonization was at first reserved to martyrs, then extended to confessors (i.e., in the early days, those who were the object of persecutions from which death did not actually follow), then to holy monks, and ultimately to all whose practice of Christian virtues appeared extraordinary.

CARTESIANISM   The teaching of the 17th century French philosopher, René Descartes. Cartesianism has had a troublesome influence on
modern theology, especially because of its revival of Platonist spiritualism under an extreme form, by developing out of thought and
extension two substances completely foreign to each other. Descartes,
furthermore, is the father both of modern scientific *rationalism* (that
tends to bring all learning into a mathematical type of knowledge) and
of *idealism*, making thought its own and eventually its only object. (*See*
RATIONALISM, and IDEALISM.)

CATECHESIS   A Greek word which means "to resound," to "awak-
en an echo," this name applies to the instruction given to those who
wish to accept the Christian faith, especially in order to prepare them for
baptism, and introduce them to Christian life. From earliest times, it
seems that catechesis has joined to the *kerygma* (the proclaiming of
the truths of salvation) a practical teaching of the life a Christian must
lead, as well as an explanation of the ritual in which he is to participate.
It will be noted that catechesis followed the rites, rather than preceding
them (as is clearly indicated in the catecheses attributed to St. Cyril of
Jerusalem, in his *Mystagogical Catecheses*, which explains the sacraments of baptism, confirmation and the Eucharist to the neophyte
who has already participated in the rites). One reason for this is that the
rites were celebrated then in such a manner that their celebration itself
spoke, while catechesis, far from pretending to furnish any abstract
explanation of Christianity, only proposed to shed light on its mysteries.
What is striking in what remains to us of this teaching is its concrete
character. Christianity is presented, above all, as a fact, the event of
salvation: the great fact of Christ and his cross. This event becomes the
fundamental fact of our life in the baptismal initiation and the eucharistic celebration to which it leads. From this point, all the details of our
existence are transformed by a morality that has no aim other than the
extension of the life of Christ in us.

CATECHISM   This name is given to Christian instruction, especially
by very simple questions and answers, as it was conceived for the children
of Christians who were baptized at birth and subsequently raised in the
faith. During the Middle Ages a number of manuals aiming at this goal
existed and they explained, along with the Ten Commandments, the
vices and virtues, the Lord's Prayer, the Creed (also the Hail Mary), and
the sacraments. Gerson, in particular, set himself this task. But catechisms were still primarily manuals for pastors or schoolmasters, rather
than books to be put into the hands of children. Luther must be given
credit for producing the first manual having widespread popular success,

with his Small Catechism (on the Decalogue, the Creed, the Lord's Prayer, the sacraments of baptism and the Eucharist, with an appendix on penance), and, later, its companion, the Large Catechism, for teachers. Admittedly and openly inspired by Luther's method, St. Peter Canisius edited analogous works, but of course completely Catholic in doctrine, which knew similar success. Later, the Council of Trent (Sess. XXV) ordered the redaction of an official catechism, to be realized by a commission appointed by Pius IV. The result of the commission's work was published simultaneously in Latin and Italian, by order of Pius V (*Catechismus ex decreto concilii Tridentini ad parrochos Pii V jussu editus*, Rome, 1566). However, this catechism, whatever its merit, received only a general approbation from the pope (and, of course, the authority of the Council still is little involved, since the book became a reality only after long deliberations). It is, then, neither a profession of faith, nor a symbolic book. The Church has never imposed any one particular text in this area. Nevertheless, in modern times, after having used diverse diocesan catechisms, the episcopates of certain countries such as Germany and, more recently, France, have agreed to prescribe common catechisms.

CATECHUMENATE   An institution of the early Church, whereby adults, as they became converted to the Gospel, were made ready for baptismal initiation. After a period of instruction in which those who were attracted to Christianity could become familiar with it through the teaching and the prayers of the first part of the Mass (still called the Mass of the Catechumens), they became formally inscribed as catechumens. That is to say, one had to give one's name to the bishop or his representative, which could not be done without having one or several sponsors who were themselves proven Christians (this gave rise to the custom of godparents). Then began a period of instruction and testing, which lasted for a variable time depending on the locality and the background of the candidate (in principle, this period covered several years). It began with a ceremony in which the Church took the catechumen in charge; a ceremony that has subsisted to the present day in the first part of the baptismal liturgy. The most common rites were the imposition of hands (sign of the Church's taking charge of the catechumen), the signing with the sign of the cross, the breathing with an exorcism (image of the divine Spirit, working from that moment to cast out the spirit of evil). To these ceremonies was added, in some churches, the placing of salt in the mouth of the catechumen as a symbol of preservation from all worldly corruption; a symbol that was to characterize his life from then on, and which would be made possible by the teaching he would receive. This teaching, the task of the catechists, involved something more than the precise dogmatic instruction that was to come later. This period was an initiation into Christian life and prayer, a period of probation. Upon completion of this phase, usually at the beginning of Lent, the catechumen could pass over into the upper rank of the "elect"—the "competentes," or *photizomenoi* (i.e., enlightened). They were again inscribed, but this time with a view to direct preparation for baptism.

Thus began a more formal initiation. Enlightened by all of the teaching found in the daily Masses of Lent, this stage culminated in the communication and explanation of the Symbol of Faith and the Lord's Prayer (*traditio symboli, traditio orationis*). New exorcisms, along with special prayers, led to this final preparation, in which, more than ever, catechesis was accompanied by a real apprenticeship in the Christian life. Graded examinations verified the manner in which the "elect" assimilated their instruction. Then followed the *redditio symboli*, in which they were called upon to publicly express in the church their newfound faith. This was customarily accompanied by an anointing with oil (called oil of the catechumens), impressing upon them the necessity of struggling with the spirit of evil so that they might remain faithful to Christ, through that strength which only Christ communicates. They were then ready to renounce Satan, and to make their personal commitment to Christ in the Church, after which they would receive baptism.

At least a vestige of these ceremonies is today still part of the baptismal liturgy (especially in the case of adults). Encouraged by recent liturgical reforms, in areas where the Church has most efficaciously resumed her missionary efforts, an attempt has been made at a revival of these rites together with a restoration of the catechumenate.

CATHOLICITY   Etymologically, this word is synonymous with universality. It is used in the creeds as one of the marks of the true Church, and, as the most diverse Eastern and Western Church Fathers show, it has been so from the beginning. Catholicity supposes a visible unity together with universality, which must be understood in contrast to the local churches that make up the universal Church, as well as to national, racial or social idiosyncracies; not that the Church refuses to adapt herself to them, but it is essential for her to reject every tendency to exclusiveness in them (cf. 1 Cor. 12,13; Gal. 3,28; Col. 3,11). A distinction is made between *de jure* catholicity, by which the Church is open to all men, and from the beginning has made herself all things to all men; and *de facto* catholicity, toward the full realization of that which her missionary endeavor is constantly devoted.

There has never been a precise definition of the catholicity of the Church on the part of council or pope. Theologically the notion has been worked out only in recent times, except for the Donatist contro-versy in which St. Augustine defined its importance. But little more than *de facto* catholicity was involved, as his celebrated formula taken up again by Newman shows: *Securus judicat orbis terrarum.* Reflection on the problem of ecumenism helped greatly because it resulted in pinpoint-ing, together with what distinguishes the Catholic Church from those that are not catholic, the fact that she is not only the Church that holds the truth, but also the Church in which this truth can and must be set forth in a manner that all men can accept. In this light, Father Congar came to define the catholicity of the Church as "the dynamic univer-sality of her unity: the capacity that her principles of unity have for assimilating, fulfilling, exalting, winning for God, and reuniting in him each and every man, every human value" (*Chrétiens désunis,* Paris 1937, p. 177). Perhaps one should insist no less on the unique capacity the Catholic Church has for harmoniously unfolding all the elements of the Christian message.

Another aspect by which ecumenical work has contributed toward enriching theologians' thought on this point, is the reflection on theolog-ical thought in the Orthodox Church in the 19th century, particularly under the influence of the Russian lay thinker, Aleksei Stepanovich Khomyakov. Together with exceptionable concepts, his school in effect set forth a definition of catholicity (in Russian, *sobornost*), in which the qualitative aspect is successfully emphasized: unanimity in love, ex-plained by the absolutely intrinsic bond existing between Christian truth and the communication to mankind, in the Church, of supernatural charity. Khomyakov himself was the first to recognize that this definition had at least been prepared within the Catholic Church herself, by the book of the German Johann Adam Möhler (*Unity in the Church,* 1825), and nourished by the thought of the early Church Fathers, whom Möhler was one of the first to rediscover in the 19th century.

CAUSE   Everything that explains that a being exists as it in fact is, is called its cause. God, the only being who bears in himself his own cause, is said to be his own cause (*causa sui*), which essentially means that he is the only necessary being, and that all other beings beside him are contingent. By the same reasoning, God is called the First Cause of everything that exists, all contingent beings ultimately depending upon the only necessary being. This does not prevent created beings from exerting a causality in relation to one another. But this is because God has created them precisely within these mutual relations, and not because he is himself subjected to any other causality but his own. Consequently, if God creates, it is never out of a cause that is foreign to himself: he creates contingent beings in such a way that they exist in causal relationships to one another. However, these are only *second causes*, and although they are undoubtedly real on their own plane, they are nevertheless always in a state of absolute dependence with regard to the unique First Cause.

Following the ancient philosophers, particularly Aristotle, St. Thomas Aquinas singled out five principal forms of causality. First, *material* and *formal* causality: the first individualizes the concrete existence of a being in which the idea or the concept specified by the second is realized. Then, there is *efficient* causality, i.e., the agent whose activity imparts a specific form to a specific matter. *Exemplary* causality is established by the model that the agent, supposing that it does not act out of chance, but according to an intelligible order, tends to realize. Similarly, the *final* cause is the end toward which its action operates.

This concept of causality is one which has been attacked most vehemently in modern philosophy, especially since Hume and Kant. The many prejudices this concept meets in the modern mind come from the fact that modern science, having undergone a technical orientation, was first oriented toward an exclusive investigation of the efficient causality of material phenomena. Today, when the word "cause" is used, there is a tendency to think of an "efficient cause." Therefore, the idea of a "final cause" takes on the appearances of a contradiction in terms, since it is conceived, without clear realization, as a sort of occult efficient cause which would result in distorting the function of the observable efficient causes. On the contrary, those who reject the idea of causality, while still pretending to give an explanation of the world, do not realize that they are only reintroducing under another name the very concept they think they have thrown off. (See the commentary of St. Thomas Aquinas on the *Liber de Causis*.)

CEREMONIES In the broader sense of the word, "ceremonies" includes all the external forms of divine worship. In the Age of Humanism and the Protestant Reformers, there was a tendency to broaden its meaning to include all the forms of private piety, even asceticism. Conversely, in a stricter sense, ceremonies are understood as everything that Christian practice has added in the Church to the essential rites of the Eucharist and the other sacraments. Still, one must be wary of a confusion that sometimes results from an exclusive consideration of the minimum required for the validity of the sacraments, and imagining, contrary to history, that our Lord, in the institution of the sacraments, would have given the weight of His authority only to this minimum, which is singled out in the abstract by theologians and canonists. In fact, the sacraments are deeply rooted in human nature and in tradition, through a maturation process in the Old Testament People of God, and it would be wrong and dangerous to wish to uproot the sacraments from their context.

As for those ceremonies that go beyond the minimum required for validity, St. Thomas Aquinas (*Sum. Theol.* IIIa, q.66, a.10), followed by the Council of Trent (Sess. VII, can. 13 and Sess. XXII, cap. 5,7 and 8; D.B., 856, 943, 945, 946), justifies them by the need to fully instruct the faithful on the meaning of what is essential, while at the same time awakening their devotion and respect.

It is evident that the Church alone is definitively the judge of what must be admitted, kept or suppressed among these elements, none of which by itself is essential. Generally St. Paul's opposition (particularly striking in his Epistles to the Romans and the Galatians) to the practice by Christians of the ceremonial ordinances of Jewish law, contrary to what some sectarians maintained, does not condemn either the sacraments in themselves, nor the collectivity of traditional ceremonies in the context in which they are found. Actually his opposition aims at the idea that the Christian faith, along with all that flows from it, would be insufficient of itself to obtain salvation. The ceremonies, therefore, cannot have any bearing on sacraments that are the precise sacraments of this faith, nor on what is prescribed or encouraged by the Church to enlighten or arouse this faith. On this issue, certain Protestants were opposed not only by the polemicists of the Catholic Counter-Reformation, but also by many Anglican or Protestant writers like the Anglican Richard Hooker, in the fifth book of his famous treatise *Ecclesiastical Polity*, published in 1597.

CERTITUDE   Certitude can be defined either objectively, as the quality of that which is certain, or subjectively, as the mind's conviction that objects are as it believes them to be. To understand many of the discussions, especially in modern times, that have been raised with regard to certitude about the truths of faith, we must be aware of the two different interpretations that can be given, according to the texts of writers in which it is found, to an easily ambiguous expression, namely, moral certitude. Some understand it to be a true and utter certitude, such as can be achieved in the area of moral truths, which are not usually demonstrable by a mathematical type of reasoning. But this must not be confused with what is commonly understood as moral certitude, and which in fact designates only a strong probability.

The Catholic faith is quite obviously opposed to all skepticism or agnosticism, which rejects the idea that any certitude could impose itself on man in any area whatsoever, and more particularly in religion. But it is also opposed to what is called *Fideism* (q.v.), i.e., the doctrine according to which no certitude in religious matters could be possible except the certitude of faith. This actually contradicts the categorical declaration of Holy Scripture. St. Paul says (Rom. 1,18–23) that all men can and ought to derive an elementary knowledge of God from a consideration of His works.

Isolating faith from reason, i.e., radically opposing the two, would be dangerous for faith itself. The most precise condemnation in this regard was formulated by the First Vatican Council (Sess. III, Const. *De fide catholica*, chap. 2, and can. 1; D.B. 1785 and 1806). The Council is no less strong in rejecting the intention to demonstrate in a purely rational way the truths that constitute faith, and which escape the scope of reason because of their supernatural character, and further (*ibid.*, chap. 4; D.B. 1795) defines this position in opposition to the different forms of *semi-rationalism* (*see* RATIONALISM). However, this should not be interpreted to mean that there is no fruitful cooperation possible between reason and faith. The Council sheds much light on this point in the preceding chapter of the same constitution. In particular, this is what occurs in the judgment of *credibility* (q.v.) that, without giving us the immediate certitude of faith in a purely rational way, leads us to recognize that it is reasonable to derive certitude from faith itself.

CHARACTER   The character, which means "imprint" or "indelible sign" is a participation in Christ imparted by the three sacraments of baptism, confirmation and holy orders. Because this participation is permanent, these sacraments may not be repeated. It is an assimilation to Christ of the one who received it, and more precisely, an assimilation to his priestly power. To this extent, it is possible, in different degrees, to take part in the worship of the Mystical Body, in particular the eucharistic celebration (either as a lay participant, i.e., a member of God's People, in prayer, in the offering, and in Communion; or as president of the priestly action, in proclaiming the word of the Gospel, and the eucharistic consecration; or, as is eminently the case for a deacon, as an assistant of this action). The character is a particular example of what is called *sacramentum et res* (*see* SACRAMENT). By itself it is distinct from grace, although it provides a permanent right to receive grace, and remains even when grace has been lost through a serious fault.

This doctrine, taught by Innocent III (D.B. 411) was formally defined by the Council of Trent (Sess. XXIII, chap. 4 and can. 4; D.B. 960 and 964). It follows, especially from the assertion of St. Paul with regard to baptism (Rom. 6,5), that by character we have been made "one sole plant" (*symphytoi*) with Christ in his death, and more generally from all the teaching of the New Testament on the consecration of Christians, which makes even of their bodies the temple of the Spirit, and on the People of God which is set up as a priestly people (cf. 1 Cor. 3,16; 6,19; 2 Cor. 6,16 and 1 Pet. 2,9).

CHARITY   *See* LOVE

CHILDREN OF GOD   *See* SUPERNATURAL ADOPTION

CHINESE RITES   The twofold problem of adapting traditional Christian rites to different forms of culture was raised in the 18th century and for a long time was subject to debate. To what extent can Christian rites incorporate forms or customs borrowed from pagan rituals? To what extent can the pagan rites themselves be admitted into Christianity and be "Christianized"? It has appeared that an affirmative answer could easily be given to the first question, as long as all danger of confusion was avoided. For example, the forms of ritual salutation long in use among the Chinese (e.g., keeping the head covered in deference to a superior) could be substituted for the customary forms even in the liturgy. On the second point, however, the answer would have had to be negative as long as the rites in question (essentially those connected with ancestor worship) seemed to be connected in the minds of people with their primitive meaning of adoration. On the other hand, once this correction is no longer in evidence (as in modern times when the Emperor of Japan declared that the rites of homage to ancestors should no longer be given definite religious significance), it seems possible to allow them and to give to them a Christian sense. We find in the Church's reactions to this particular problem the principle of a general solution.

CHRISM   Holy chrism is oil mixed with perfume. It is consecrated on Maundy Thursday by the bishops in the West, and by the patriarchs in the East. Chrism is used chiefly for anointing in confirmation (or chrismation). In some rites, such as the Roman, this anointing is anticipated by the *consignation* (q.v.) in baptism itself. We find in the New Testament such expressions as "it is God who has anointed us" (2 Cor. 1,21), or "you have been anointed by the Holy One" (1 John 2,20; cf. v. 27). But if it seems clear that the anointing in question is that of the Spirit, it is not clear that it is a rite that includes not only the imposition of hands, but also a material anointing (Acts 8,17). Nevertheless, early history shows that this rite was attested to by the Church as universally established. Even in the 2nd century, Theophilus of Antioch wrote: "We are called Christians because we are anointed (*chriometha*) with the oil of God" (*Ad Antolycum*, I,12; P.G. 6, col. 1041). The custom of mixing perfume (or perfumes) with chrism, although it may not be quite so early, goes back to ancient times. In the East, it resulted in giving the name *myron* ("perfume") to chrism. Undoubtedly inspired by the text in St. Paul about the fragrance of Christ that Christians must spread everywhere (2 Cor. 2,14–15), this mixture has served to distinguish chrism from the other oils used in the liturgy, such as the oil of the sick, or of the catechumens. In the 4th century the Fathers insisted on the sacred character of chrism, going so far as to set up a parallel between the presence of the Spirit in it, and the presence of the body of Christ in the Eucharist (St. Cyril of Jerusalem, *Cat. myst.*, III, 21; P.G. 33, col. 1092; cf. St. Gregory of Nyssa, *Disc. Catech.* 34; P.G. 45, col. 85 B).

St. Thomas Aquinas (*Sum. Theol.*, IIIa, q.72, a.4, ad 1um) believed that the use of chrism was imposed by Christ on the apostles. This was already the formal opinion of St. Basil (*De Spir. Sanct.*, 27; P.G. 32, col. 188). Alexander of Hales (*Summa*, IV, q.9, m.1), and less clearly, St. Bonaventure (*In IV Sent.*, dist. VII, a.1, q.2) believed rather that it was instituted by the Church. The Council of Trent gave no definition on this matter.

The manifold uses of chrism in the West—anointing the heads of bishops, consecration of altars, churches, and of sacred vessels, and even dedication or "baptism" of bells—were introduced by the Gallican liturgy in the Middle Ages. The only parallel known in the East is in the consecration of altars (the altar representing Christ). However, the Byzantine emperor (as the French kings in later times) received a special anointing with chrism at his coronation. These different customs came from a medieval imitation of Old Testament practices.

CHURCH   From the Anglo-Saxon word *cirice*, a root common to all Germanic languages, coming from the Greek word *kyriakon* (the house of the *Kyrios*, the Lord), or quite possibly from the expression *kyriake ekklesia* (the Lord's assembly). The *ekklesia* was the regularly convoked assembly (*ekkalein*) of the people, and is found in the Septuagint as a translation of a Hebrew word of similar origin, *qahal*, which referred to the assembly of God's People. On the basis of this fundamental concept of "the People of God," we shall see how the Church is successively described in the New Testament as the Fullness of Christ, the Body of Christ, the Apostle of Christ, and finally the Bride of Christ and Mother of the Faithful.

1. It is evident from the first books of the Old Testament that the People of God was constituted in its convocation by the divine word. Once this divine word had brought the *qahal* together, it made its voice heard by the people and set up the covenant between them and God. The word and the faith it aroused in those who listened to it were then ratified together in the sacrifice it had ordained. This is revealed for the

first time on Mount Sinai with Moses, when the Law was proclaimed (Ex. 19 ff.). Similarly, after the revival of the Law in the preaching of the first prophets, the *qahal* was again brought together under King Josiah for the promulgation of Deuteronomy, and the renewal of the covenant in the celebration of the Passover sacrifice (2 Kings 23). Finally, after the ordeal of exile, together with those who had come back from captivity and who were to rebuild both the Temple and the city, the people were again convened in a third *qahal*, in which the entire Old Testament Bible (probably the Pentateuch) was read to them. Again on this occasion the terms of their obedient faith were renewed in a prayer of the eucharistic type, which served as a prelude to the resumption of a sacrificial form of worship, in the consecration of the people to the requirements of the word (Neh. 8–10).

Throughout this entire succession of events (these solemn assemblies mark its most decisive phases), the *election* of Israel (q.v.) was made a reality by a progressive segregation, first from Egypt, then from the Canaanite tribes whose practices and outlooks it had more or less adopted, and finally, within Israel itself, as the faithful "remnant" that is singled out by its ordeal and the resultant deepening of its faith.

Moreover, as this "remnant" (*see* Amos 5,15; Isa. 4,2–3 and 11–16; Jer. 23,3; Ezech. 9,8 and 11,13) became progressively refined and appeared to be totally absorbed in the idea of the unique faithful Servant of the second part of the book of Isaiah, it becomes evident that the definitive People of God, whom the Servant will call together, will come, not only from the diaspora of Israel, but also from the elect gathered out of all nations (cf. in particular Isa. 49,4–6).

This becomes a reality in the New Testament, and it is in this light that the Church comes into existence as the People of God of the new and everlasting covenant. The choice of the Twelve in the Gospel marks the election of the final "remnant," and the fact that they are sent into the world after the Resurrection implies the realization of the words of the Deutero-Isaiah (cf. Mark 3,13–19 and the parallels, and Matt. 28,18–20). The Church, as the assembly of the People of God, is constituted by the preaching of the Gospel, and the faith that accepts this proclamation with "the Spirit and power" (1 Cor. 2,4 ff.). More precisely, the Church is built preeminently on the eucharistic celebration, for the saving death of Christ is here "announced" in such a way that all who partake of it, whatever their origin, become one in the dead and risen Christ (1 Cor. 10,16–17; Col. 3,11; Gal. 3,28). Thus baptism, which initiates us into the eucharistic celebration by making us part of Christ himself, for precisely this reason makes us part of the priestly people of whom the Jewish people were the forerunners (Rom. 6,1–11; 1 Cor. 12,13; 1 Pet. 11,9–10 with Ex. 19,6).

This aspect of the Church as the definitive People of God is fundamental to the Bible. And the eucharistic assembly of the New Covenant in the blood of the Saviour is principally the new and definitive *qahal*. This is why the Apocalypse describes the heavenly Church for us in terms of the eucharistic celebration of the Church on earth (cf. Apoc. 4, and 5, and particularly the hymns).

As an immediate result of this first aspect of the Church, there is a direct transition to what may be termed her final or eschatological aspect, and is best described in the following sentence from the Epistle to the Ephesians that completes the total vision of the development of the People of God: The Church is "the fullness of him [Christ] who fills all in all" (1,23).

2. To understand the complete meaning of the Church described as the *fullness of Christ*, we must weigh precisely the significance that this word "fullness" (*pleroma*) has for the apostle, when he uses it with reference to Christ. Christ is first of all the One in whom "the whole fullness of deity dwells bodily" (Col. 2,9; cf. 1,19.), i.e., in him we have the fullness of revelation and communication of God to mankind. This is made more precise in St. Paul's teaching on *mystery* (q.v.). The word "mystery" means that everything toward which the divine Word has pointed from the beginning of the Old Covenant is found revealed and given in Christ, namely, the realization of God's plan for all mankind (1 Cor. 2,6–10, especially verse 7). This plan is made known and realized particularly in the cross, understood in the light of the Resurrection, and in the association of all mankind in the Church with the risen Christ (cf. 1 Cor. 1,18 to 21,5). But this plan, identified in the saving cross, discloses for us the mystery of the depths of God (1 Cor. 2,10–12), or, more simply, the mystery of his most intimate life. And this is so because the cross is above all the revelation of the unique love (*agape*) that is the love of God (cf. Rom. 5,5–11).

If the mystery therefore communicates to us the fullness of God, by the same token the mystery of Christ reaches its fullness in the reconciliation effected among all men, Jews and pagans, as well as between man and God, "in his body of flesh, by his death" (Col. 1,26–27; cf. 19–23). Or, according to the Epistle to the Ephesians, it is accomplished by the summing up of the whole history of fallen mankind in Christ and his cross, but now restored to God's original plan "for the fullness of time" (1,9–10). Finally, the mystery reveals that "we may be filled with all the fullness of God" by the fact that since "Christ dwells in our hearts through faith . . . , we, being rooted and grounded in love [*agape*], may have power to comprehend with all the saints what is the breadth and length and height and depth, and to know the love [*agape*] of Christ which surpasses knowledge" (Eph. 3,17–19, and the entire context).

In this supreme vision, the Church appears as the fullness of Christ, who is himself the One in whom the "fullness of deity dwells bodily," because the mystery of the characteristic life of God in the communication of the *agape* is revealed to mankind and made a reality in the Church. This is what St. Thomas Aquinas explained, by bringing together the substance of traditional teaching in his *Explanation of the Symbol of Faith*, showing that in the Church the very life of the Trinity is extended from the Son of God made man to all mankind. (See *Exp. in Symb.*, a.9. The entire text is available with an excellent commentary in Congar's *Esquisses du mystère de l'Eglise*, Paris, 1941, pp. 59 ff.)

In St. John we find the Pauline concept deepened in the discourses after the Last Supper, with their intertwining themes of the new covenant of love, and of Christ's dwelling in us as the Father dwells in him through the Holy Spirit, especially in the vine metaphor, and the priestly prayer (John 15–17).

3. But this ultimate eschatological reality of the Church is anticipated in time by our incorporation in Christ, which is made possible for each of us through baptism and inseparably effected in us through the Eucharist. Insofar as she is the *Body of Christ*, the Church is a visible organism composed of men in whom different graces are manifested, although they are all given by one and the same Spirit. Consequently, in the earliest formulations of this doctrine, St. Paul began by introducing the image of the body as a metaphor of social unity, such as is found in the well-known fable of Menenius Agrippa (Rom. 12,3 ff.). But in the first Epistle to the Corinthians, it is clear that this is much more than mere metaphor. Here we see that the common spirit is the personal reality of the Holy Spirit, because this "body" of Christ, which is the Church, is realized through the sacramental participation of all through the Eucharist in his true body, crucified and risen for our salvation. "The bread which we break, is it not a participation in the body of Christ? Because there is one bread, we who are many are one body, for we all partake of the one bread" (1 Cor. 10,16–17; cf. 12,4 ff.). In other words, the Church finds its unity and reality in the body of Christ partaken of in the most real sense by means of eucharistic Communion. Moreover, as outlined in the captivity Epistles, this building of the Church in the context of time by means of the different ministries, and the different charisms that Christ has set up, leads to the perfect unity of all in the eschatological Christ. Thus it is truly the very body of Christ that succeeds in being built in all of us "until we all attain to the unity of the faith and of the knowledge [*epignosis*] of the Son of God, to mature manhood, to the measure of the stature of the fullness of Christ" (Eph. 4,11–13).

Moreover, as St. Paul explicitly tells us, this comes about from him who is the head, Christ, toward whom all things are directed, for it is from him that "the whole body, joined and knit together by every joint with which it is supplied, when each part is working properly, makes bodily growth and upbuilds itself in love" (Eph. 4,16). This other aspect of the Church according to which the body, through the intention and the operation of her divine head, has within itself what is necessary for its construction, leads to the consideration of the role of the *apostolate* (q.v.) in the Church, and at the same time the apostolicity of the Church herself.

4. The preaching of the Gospel "in the Spirit and power," and the celebration of the Eucharist wherein the Church finds her life and growth, actually depend upon the ministry which was both given and entrusted to it. The ministry makes up the Church, and at the same time it is she herself who exercises it. This ministry, i.e., this service of Christ, which is both the service of God and the service of the man in the preeminent Servant, is chiefly the apostolate, from which all the other ministries are derived. The apostolate is the mission given to certain men chosen by Christ (the Twelve and St. Paul) to preach the word of the Gospel in his name. Through this ministry, Christ sends them forth as he had been sent by the Father, so that whoever hears them, hears him, and whoever receives them, receives him, Christ, and in Christ receives the very One from whom he was sent. This ministry then goes hand in hand with the gift of the Spirit to the Church. But it does not accompany it from without. Precisely because the Spirit was first given to the apostles, it is through them that he is to be transmitted to others. This, however, does not prevent God, on occasion, as with St. Paul or in other instances recounted in the Acts of the Apostles (cf. the case of Cornelius and his household, 10,44 ff.), from pouring forth his Spirit freely so that the apostolic initiative cannot but follow. But only through union with the Twelve can even those graces of the Spirit, of which they were not the intermediaries, be preserved (cf. Gal. 2,2). Conversely, their power, just as it proceeds from the Spirit given by Christ, is designed for the spreading forth of the Spirit among men in the Church.

Nevertheless, the apostolate in the Church is an institution by which men who are the "foundations of the Church" are vested with the very authority of God, as the Gospel texts cited above formally declare, and act with full awareness of both the powers and the responsibilities their mission gives them.

According to St. Matthew's Gospel, it is evident that these powers are given in their fullness both to the apostolic college as such, and to the one person alone who had previously been set up as its head, and, simultaneously, as the head of the whole Church. Jesus tells Peter after his confession of faith at Caesarea Philippi: "And I tell you, you are Peter, and on this rock I will build my church, and the powers of death shall not prevail against it. I will give you the keys to the kingdom of heaven, and whatever you bind on earth shall be bound in heaven, and whatever you loose on earth shall be loosed in heaven" (Matt. 16,18–19). And after the Resurrection, it is to the whole apostolic group that Jesus says:"All authority in heaven and on earth has been given to me. Go therefore and make disciples of all nations, baptizing them in the name of the Father and of the Son and of the Holy Spirit, teaching them to observe all that I have commanded you; and lo, I am with you always, to the close of the age" (Matt. 28,18–20).

The Church has held that no one could replace the apostles as founders of the Church. However bishops, whom the apostles had appointed to cooperate with them in giving nourishment to the People of God, and to extend the Church throughout the world had now become their successors. The bishops have the permanent function of proclaiming the mystery and accomplishing its sacramental celebration, without which the Church would no longer exist in the manner willed and set down by Christ. The Bishop of Rome, from earliest times, acted as Peter's particular successor in guaranteeing the unity of the apostolic college and of the Church herself. Moreover, in 1870 the First Vatican Council defined that through the promise of Christ the pope is guaranteed the infallibility that the Lord had promised the Church when he defined his faith. Generally speaking, the entire college is similarly infallible, as is the entire body of the faithful in its permanent commitment to the Gospel which its pastors never cease proclaiming in the name of Christ.

Consequently, by this instrumental aspect, in which the Church is seen as Christ's minister, her apostolate communicates Christ to the world by his own power, as that of the Head acting through these members whom he willed to associate with his work of salvation. In this work, it is evident that the Church is one with Him to such an extent that when she acts, it is he who acts, despite the personal unworthiness that always to some degree characterizes those who are called to represent him. As St. Augustine said, "Whether it be Peter, Paul or Judas who baptizes, it is Christ baptizing." And similarly, from the eschatological point of view, the realization of which has been outlined since Pentecost, the Church, not only in her ministers who are bearers of an apostolate that surpasses them, but in all her members, is still one with him insofar as she is "the fullness of him who fills all in all." This is why the Church remains one despite the schisms of men, holy despite their sins, with the unity and the holiness of Christ and his Spirit.

5. However, through a final aspect that is revealed to us in the New Testament, and previously outlined in the Old Testament, it is clear first that the Church in her earthly progress remains very far from this ideal of unity and the tangible realization of her trust. But even in eternal life, although she will have become perfect insofar as she will be perfectly

united then with her divine Head, the Church will not be confounded in any way with him. Accordingly, she is today the Bride, and on the last day she will be revealed as the *Spouse of Christ*.

In the first place, there is no doubt that at the end of time the Church will be revealed as the "pure bride" about whom St. Paul tells the Corinthians, and whom the apostle hopes to be able to present to Christ as the Betrothed who is at last worthy of Him (2 Cor. 11,2). But what he tells them further on in the same Epistle leaves no doubt as to the gap he sees still subsisting between what they are by right, and what they in fact remain. To substantiate this, the Apocalypse shows the Lamb's Betrothed as coming down from heaven on the last day (21,2 and 9–10). Moreover, this is the same Church which has been built on earth little by little over the course of time. But in all the partial and temporary realizations of the Church in the course of history, the Fathers of the Church will hardly hesitate to apply to her what the prophets Osee and Ezechiel said of Jerusalem, who was destined to be the Bride of the Lord, although she endlessly prostituted herself through her infidelities. There is, however, this difference between the Church of the New Covenant and what she was under the old covenant; in the glorious Christ she now possesses all the glory to which she was destined, and her faith finds a realization of this glory, anticipated by the Spirit who already lives within her. This anticipation is made real through the saints, and most particularly through the Virgin Mary. Her Immaculate Conception is a primary realization of the perfect purity which the Church will completely attain in eternity, just as her Assumption foreshadows the ultimate victory over sin and death which will follow for the entire Body.

Nevertheless, when the eschatological marriage of the perfect Church is realized, in which her union with her divine Bridegroom is consummated, the consummation which brings their union to perfection, far from blotting out the distinction between the Church and Christ, will bring the collective personality of the Church to full flower, a realization still only roughly visualized in the communion of saints. In addition, this visualization was already so real, that in combining the Church's instrumental reality as Apostle of Christ with the view of the eschatological Church as Bride of Christ, tradition very soon gave her the title of Mother of the Faithful. This idea is implicit in the 12th chapter of the Apocalypse, which undoubtedly applies to the Virgin Mary as an image of the whole Church.

All of these complementary aspects of the Catholic teaching on the Church were developed through the tradition of the Fathers and theologians with admirable harmony, but without ever having been fully synthesized. The schisms and heresies at the end of the Middle Ages led to a special development of the doctrine of the hierarchical and authoritarian aspect of the Church. But since the 19th century, a need has been felt to complete this development, through a profound renewal of the teaching on the Mystical Body, insofar as it asserts the active participation of all the members in the life of the Head, and brings again to light the fact that external unity is only the manifestation and the safeguard of supernatural unity, the gift of the Spirit in Christ. From this, however, no conflict between an invisible Church, pure and holy, and one or some visible churches, soiled and corrupt, need necessarily arise, as Protestants view the idea. If we remain faithful to what St. Paul tells us about it, the mystery of the Church, the teaching on the Mystical Body, is precisely the mystery that is inherent within the visible Church, which is visibly one, but whose visible unity can still be explained only in the realities of faith that are ultimately invisible.

(See in Congar, *op. cit.*, the principal texts of St. Thomas Aquinas on the question; also, the Constitution *Lumen Gentium* of the Second Vatican Council.)

CHURCH GOVERNMENT   *See* AUTHORITY, and CHURCH

CIRCUMCISION   Circumcision seems from the very beginning to have had not only a hygienic purpose, as Herodotus claimed, but a religious meaning, namely, the consecration of life, and more particularly of virility. In Israel, with Abraham, circumcision became the rite of the covenant with the Lord that irrevocably marked the sons of Abraham as members of His People (cf. Gen. 17,9–14,23.27, and Ex. 12,14). As in Deuteronomy, the prophets emphasized that a circumcision of the heart, i.e., a consecration to God of the inner being, must accompany the rite for the Israelite to be acceptable to God (Jer. 4,4; Deut. 10,16 and 30,6). For this reason, St. Paul asserted that circumcision, which is valueless except as the preparation of a particular people for the coming of Christ, could no longer be included as a necessary element of Christian initiation without losing its unique significance (Rom. 2,27–28; Gal. 5,2–6; cf. 1 Cor. 7,19). He further said that it is in Christ alone that we have true circumcision (Phil. 2,2–3 and Col. 2,11–15). Certain modern exegetes have wanted to interpret these latter texts as referring to a rite peculiar to Christians (probably an anointing, accompanying baptism), but actually this is an erroneous interpretation. All theologians admit that circumcision, by virtue of the future merits of Christ, blotted out original sin. Their opinion is divided as to whether it conferred grace *ex opere operato*. St. Thomas Aquinas maintains that it does not (*Sum. Theol.*, IIIa, q.70).

CIRCUMINCESSION   In theology this term is applied to the mutual presence of the divine Persons in one another (cf. "The Father is in

Me and I am in the Father," John 10,38). This mutual presence is related to the unity of essence, and to the fact that the processions are immanent in the divine essence, at the same time orienting each of the Persons toward the other, in the very thing which makes Them distinct. It will be noted, from this latter point, that the Greek term *perichoresis* corresponds to the idea of a flow of life and of communication. (See St. Thomas Aquinas, *Sum. Theol.* Ia, q.62, a.5.) In Latin the forms *circumincessio* and *circuminsessio* both correspond to the Greek *perichoresis*. The immanence of the divinity of Christ in his humanity is also sometimes called circumincession.

CLEAN AND UNCLEAN   This contrast played a major role in the Old Testament; for example, animals were divided into these two categories (cf. Gen.7,2). One of the principal aims of Leviticus was to state its precise application. It is clear that the idea is deeply ritual, but we must still specify its significance. Cleanness and uncleanness (or purity and impurity, as the words are sometimes translated) are explained in relation to the possibility man has been given of communicating with the sacred, i.e., the domain reserved to God, and the special sign of his presence. The result is that one may be rendered unclean, that is, incapable of approaching God, either through imprudent contact with sacred realities, or through a contact with that which is most radically opposed to them. Actually, we may well wonder whether there is any other origin to the idea of the unclean than an alleged profanation of the sacred.

   With the correlative moralization of the sacred, and the sacralizing of the moral that is so characteristic of the work of the great prophets (beginning with the Mosaic Decalogue, and particularly explicit in Isaiah), cleanness or uncleanness are defined as compliance or noncompliance with the divine will. The further identification of this will with the Law inscribed by the Creator in the nature of things, and discerned by reason, finally led to the consideration of cleanness as consisting of the consciously preserved integrity of a created being.

CLERIC, CLERGY   From the Greek *kleros*, signifying "share" or "inheritance." From its use in the First Epistle of Peter (5,3), in which it is applied to the whole People of God, the word, from the 5th century on, was applied in a special way to all who were consecrated to the sacred ministry by either major or minor orders. Today it is used to include even those who have received tonsure. There is no doubt that the *apostleship* (q.v.) (i.e., the ministry of the bishops as the successors of the apostles, the priests who cooperate in their work, and the deacons who assist them) constitutes by divine institution a positive distinction in the

Church, which is extended to include all who are associated with the apostolate in a legitimate continuity. But it must be remembered that the purpose of this distinction is the service of the whole body of the Church. In addition, the laity (in Greek, *laos*), by the very fact of their baptism and confirmation, ought not to be considered alien to the Church and her priestly function, or to have only a passive role in it.

The word clergy refers to all those who are involved either in the ministry (i.e., clerics) of the whole Church or of a particular church. It can be noted that the former Church law extended the privileges of clerics to all the religious, even laymen, i.e., to all laymen living under a common rule approved by the bishop.

CLOUD   In the Bible, the paradoxically luminous cloud is one of the most characteristic symbols of God's presence among his People. The Israelites were led out of Egypt by a pillar of fire and a cloud (cf. Ex. 13,21 and 14,24); a cloud covered Mount Sinai at the moment when God spoke to the people through Moses (Ex. 19,16 ff.); it descended upon the tabernacle when it was set up (Ex. 33,9 ff.); it determined the movements (traveling) of the people (Ex. 40,34 ff.); and it entered Solomon's Temple at the moment of its dedication (3 Kings 8,10 ff.; cf. Isa. 6).

In the New Testament the use of a cloud in its figurative sense is apparent in the angel's words to Mary that the Most High was to overshadow her (Luke 1,35). And, at the Transfiguration the luminous cloud, in which Moses and Elijah appeared, enveloped Jesus (Matt. 17,1–8 and parallels; cf. 2 Pet. 1,17–18), thus manifesting the divine presence that dwelt in him. At the Ascension, the heavenly cloud received him, and we are to await his return in glory "on the clouds of heaven" (cf. Acts 1, 9 ff.; 1 Thess. 1,17; Matt. 24,30 and 26,24 and parallels). St. Paul tells Christians that the baptism of the Hebrews under the cloud and through the sea was the "type" of baptism he had given them (1 Cor. 10). In Christian theology and mysticism, following Origen, St. Gregory of Nyssa, Evagrius Ponticus, and the Pseudo-Dionysius, the cloud became the image of the *knowledge* (q.v.) of God toward which our faith leads us. It envelops all human forms of knowledge for us, although it is but another aspect of that inaccessible light in which God dwells, which we can only reach through Christ. (Cf. 1 Tim. 6,16; Pseudo-Dionysius, *Fifth Epistle*, P.G. III, col. 1073A.)

COMMUNICATIO IN SACRIS   This expression designates a special application of the *fellowship* (see COMMUNION) that exists among all the members of the Church in the fact of their participation in the same sacred realities, especially the sacraments. For this reason, this *communi-*

catio in sacris would be distorted if it were extended to heretics and schismatics, since they are separated from the Church. The application of this general rule must, however, be guided by the practice of the Church herself, which has always encouraged a certain tolerance in the case of baptized persons who, through no fault of their own, are outside the Church. Even if they cannot be admitted to the sacraments (except for exceptional cases), they can, as long as there is no proximate danger of scandal, be given sacramentals when they ask for them and, furthermore, under particular circumstances, they may be allowed to join in the prayer of the Church.

The question of participation by Catholics in the prayers and rites of non-Catholics is more delicate, but it may be permitted, within certain bounds, in cases where there is no fear of such participation being construed as a commitment to, or encouragement of, schism or heresy. It is the responsibility of the Church authority alone to define the limits of this participation in non-Catholic rites, according to the locality and the circumstances. In the case of Catholics and Eastern Orthodox, the Second Vatican Council has reopened the door to some wide measure of *communicatio in sacris*, which had been the general practice until the beginning of the 19th century.

COMMUNICATION OF IDIOMS   This expression, based on the Greek *idioma*, which signifies "property," is used in Christology to designate one consequence of the personal unity in Christ. One can, with certain reservations, that is, by avoiding any confusion between the natures that remain distinct, attribute to his divinity only what belongs to his humanity, and *vice versa*. (*See* St. Thomas Aquinas, *Sum. Theol.*, IIIa, q.16, and *Contra Gentiles*, bk. IV, chap. 39.)

COMMUNION   In the Christian context, the Latin word *communio* has two separate but closely related meanings that have passed into English. The first designates the participation of the faithful in the Eucharist through the eating of the consecrated species. The second, which may be more aptly expressed by the word *fellowship*, refers to the community life in the Mystical Body of Christ that is the effect of the Eucharist, and as St. Thomas Aquinas says, constitutes the *res tantum* (*see* SACRAMENT) in the Eucharist itself. Since the eucharistic celebration is essentially a meal, the Communion of the celebrant and normally of those in the congregation who are in a state to receive it, is an integral part of it. Communion supposes that the recipient has been baptized, that he has not been barred from Communion by an ecclesiastical censure, and that he is in the state of *grace* (q.v.). In effect it is the most significant act in which we affirm our commitment to the Church and our desire to participate more fully in the supernatural life. Normally, Communion should be received in its proper place during the celebration of Mass. Together with the enlightenment of our faith by God's word, Communion implies prayer, the offering of ourselves in our entirety to the divine will, and our union with the eucharistic sacrifice of which Communion is the completion. Even when Communion is given outside of Mass for valid reasons (as in the case of sickness), it cannot have meaning outside of the context of at least a spiritual union with the celebration from which it comes. The same must be said with regard to the devout practice of spiritual Communion by one who is prevented from receiving it sacramentally.

Normally, one should prepare for Communion (the principal preparation is, of course, the celebration that leads up to it) by an endeavor at personal preparation. The Church suggests the direction for us to take in the prayers provided for this purpose in her liturgical books. The same is true of the continuation of each individual's personal thanksgiving. This practice is particularly important so that our Communions do not become purely routine, especially when they are as frequent as it is desirable for them to be. But we must remember that the Mass itself is the fundamental act of thanksgiving (see EUCHARIST). Our personal thanksgiving can never be anything more than the flowering of the Church's Eucharist in us, as she unites herself with her divine Head in his unique sacrifice. This is why our thanksgiving should not, any more than the Communion which it follows, be assimilated only in the consideration of the personal gift of his presence that Christ accords us. Not only does he come to us in this way to complete our union with him in his sacrifice, i.e., the full accomplishment of the heavenly Father's will, but this union cannot be separated from our union with our brothers in Christ, namely those first of all with whom we are receiving Communion, those throughout the world in whose participation in the same bread along with our own, we are all made one, without forgetting all those who have died in Christ. The same Christ who becomes one with us in the eucharistic Communion also unites himself so inseparably with all that we would not really be united with him were we to ignore the union he established in himself among all of us. This explains why, without disregarding the necessity of recollection for a worthy celebration by all the faithful, the ideal celebration is not the most private one, but rather the most effectively public celebration that can possibly be realized. Communion makes the Church, and must make us live in the Church.

All of this is formulated concisely by St. Paul: "The cup of blessing which we bless, is it not a participation in the blood of Christ? The bread which we break, is it not a participation in the body of Christ? Because there is one bread, we who are many are one body for we all partake of the one bread" (1 Cor. 10,16–17).

In the ancient Communion rite all the faithful came before the altar. There they received in their right hand, which was crossed over the left, the species of bread, while the priest said, "The Body of Christ," and they communicated themselves. In the same way, the priest or the deacon gave them the chalice, saying, "The Blood of Christ." Later, in the East, the difficulty of giving Communion in the chalice to a large number of people, along with the fear of possible profanation, led to giving the two species together to the laity. In the West, from the 13th century on, this difficulty led to having the celebrant alone take Communion from the chalice, although they still retained the participation of the laity in principle by the distribution of a cup of unconsecrated wine. This is still included as part of the rubrics of the Mass as a manner of *purification* (q.v.), although the custom has actually fallen into disuse except in the ordination Mass.

It must be emphasized, however, that the chalice was not just denied to the laity, contrary to Protestant accusations against the Church, but to all communicants other than the celebrant (priests, bishops or the pope himself). This was not the result of an arbitrary decision of authority, but of a spontaneously established custom that the authority subsequently accepted. The same reasons that obtained here also resulted in the custom of having the priest place the sacred species directly in the mouth of the communicant in all rites, both Eastern and Western. The ancient Communion formula had survived only in the Ambrosian rite, until its recent restoration in the Roman rite, but the people's amen, however, is still prescribed not only in the Eastern rites, but in the Roman pontifical liturgy for the ordination Mass as well. Everywhere else, optative formulas of the type used in the Roman rite of yesterday have been added to the early formula: "May the Body of Our Lord Jesus Christ be the guardian of your soul (or your guardian, as in the pontifical) into life everlasting." The custom of the communicant receiving Communion kneeling was progressively introduced in the West and was ultimately sanctioned, despite the ancient custom that has survived in the East, of receiving Communion in a standing position.

The former eucharistic rituals emphasized the importance of Communion (fellowship) with the members of Christ as being inseparable from the Communion in his body. The eucharistic breaking of bread (*fractio panis*) underlined the participation of all in the same bread of which St. Paul speaks. In fact, in the present Roman rite, in which completely prepared small hosts are used, the use of the large host by the celebrant is merely a symbolic reminder. This is not true in other rites where the particles are actually distributed to the participants. In the

Roman rite, the mingling (*see* IMMIXTIO) of one of the fragments of the celebrant's host in the chalice is a vestige of an ancient rite in which the priests mixed a fragment of the host consecrated by the bishop in their own celebration as an affirmation of their fellowship with him. This fragment, borne by a subdeacon or acolyte was called the *fermentum*. The bishop himself usually mixed the *sancta* in the chalice. The *sancta* is the species remaining from a previous celebration, and was kept in the paten, a custom that has long survived in the solemn Mass where the subdeacon held the paten in his raised hand, covered by the humeral veil, before bringing it to the altar for the *fractio*. These rituals visibly asserted the fellowship and unity of the whole Church, and especially with the Roman pontiff, still recalled in the prayer *Te igitur* before the commemoration of the living, as is the fellowship with the deceased saints in the *Communicantes* that follows. The kiss of peace before the Communion, along with the prayers for peace among the faithful has the same significance.

Concelebration (q.v.), especially of the bishop with his priests, or the bishop of one locality with a visiting bishop, or the bishops meeting in council, asserted even more solemnly the catholic universality of the fellowship within the Church, based on common participation in the Eucharist. It is the main object for which it has been recently restored in the Roman rite.

This is also why the principal minister of the Eucharist, and particularly of Communion, is the bishop. It is by virtue of their very special association with the bishop in the presidency of the eucharistic assembly that all priests, and especially pastors in their respective parishes, are also ordinary ministers of Communion. Deacons, associated traditionally with the giving of the chalice in particular, are the extraordinary ministers of Communion who, in order to distribute Communion lawfully, need only the permission of the bishop or the pastor. In the absence of a deacon, canonists generally admit that lesser ministers, or in their absence, even lay people could also become extraordinary ministers in certain cases (particularly, to give *viaticum* to a dying person). In the early Church the laity were allowed to keep the Blessed Sacrament at home, so that they might take Communion themselves in the absence of a priest or a deacon.

Although Communion is primarily the eating of the bread of life spoken of in the sixth chapter of St. John's Gospel, we must not forget on this account that traditional teaching does not separate Communion from that other form of the bread of life which is the Church's proclaiming of the Word of God to God's People, such as in the first part of the Mass.

See the decrees and canons of the Council of Trent; Session XXI; and chapter VI of Session XXII (D.B. 930–937 and 944); and St. Thomas Aquinas, *Sum. Theol.* IIIa, qq.79–80. A decree of the Congregation of the Council, approved by St. Pius X on December 20, 1905, specified the conditions for daily Communion (D.B. 1981–1990) and he also approved on August 8, 1910, a decree of the Congregation of the Sacraments specifying the conditions for the admission of young children to Communion. The substance of this decree has passed into canons 88, 853 and 854, and its effect has been to admit children to Communion much sooner than had been the custom previously in the West.

COMPREHENSIVE   This term is applied to the knowledge which God, and God alone, has of his essence, and signifies that he knows it perfectly, and through it knows every real or possible being.

CONCELEBRATION   Although the words *concelebrare* and *concelebratio* came to be used in the broad sense as the collective celebration of the liturgy by the whole People of God gathered together, these terms were applied at an early date in a technical sense that restricted them to a eucharistic celebration in which several priests took part, and even more precisely, as a common priestly action. Forms of concelebration have varied over the course of centuries and still differ in their various rites. Evolution within the Church itself has tended to make the effective participation of the concelebrants, particularly in the consecration of the Eucharist, more and more evident. Thus in the early Roman rite, it was prescribed, as early as the *Ordo Romanus Primus*, that cardinal priests concelebrating with the pope have in their hands a part of the *oblata* (offered gifts), and recite in lowered voices the entire canon with the pontiff. A similar practice was introduced in modern times, first among some Eastern Catholics and then all the Slavs, both Catholic and Orthodox. Except in the rite of Lyons at the pontifical Mass on Maundy Thursday, concelebration had practically disappeared in the West until the Second Vatican Council. Although it had been kept in the pontifical for the Mass of the consecration of a bishop, between the chief consecrator and the newly consecrated bishop, it had been retained only in an equivocal form in the case of ordination to the priesthood. In the latter case however, it might be considered to be a genuine concelebration nowadays, since that seemed to be the intention of the Church, although most probably the 16th century editors of the rubrics were of another opinion. In the restored rite of concelebration in the Roman rite, the concelebrating priests say (or sing) together the central part of the Canon (from *Hanc igitur* to *Supplices*), while they distribute among themselves the other prayers (the *Mementos*, etc.).

It may be observed that outside of the Eucharist itself, concelebration exists in the sacrament of holy orders, particularly among the three consecrating bishops at an episcopal consecration. See St. Thomas Aquinas, *Sum. Theol.*, IIIa, q.82, a.2.

CONCUPISCENCE Etymologically, this word designates any strong desire. In its customary theological usage, it is restricted to a desire of the senses, particularly sex. This desire eludes reason and puts our nature in disorder. This explains why St. Paul and the other New Testament writers, connect, almost to the point of confusion, the *flesh* (q.v.) with concupiscence (Gal. 5,16–17 and 24; Eph. 2,3; cf. 2 Pet. 2,10 and 18; and 1 John 2,16), as well as concupiscence with sin (Rom. 6,12). It also explains why various theologians, such as Luther and later the Jansenists, restricting certain views of St. Augustine, had identified concupiscence with *original sin* (q.v.). The Council of Trent defined that concupiscence, as it appears in us today, is an effect of original sin, and subsists in us after baptism (even though baptism takes away original sin). Concupiscence is no longer a sin in the strict sense, but rather the inheritance of sin and a tendency toward it, which, however, grace permits us to resist victoriously (Sess. V., par. 5; D.B. 792).

CONFESSION *See* PENANCE

CONFIRMATION Called *chrismation* by the Christians of Spain, Italy and the East, confirmation is one of the seven sacraments defined by the Council of Trent (Sess. VII; D.B. 844 and 871). Its chief New Testament source is found in two texts of Acts, which explicitly attribute the gift of the Holy Spirit to an imposition of hands, administered by the apostles and received after baptism (8,5–25 and 19,1–6; cf. Heb. 6,3 and Gal. 4,4–6). We do not have any explicit evidence about the sacrament before the 3rd century, undoubtedly because it was always administered with baptism, as it is still done in the East. For this reason, we do not know when the practice of combining the anointing with holy chrism and the imposition of hands actually began. In present Roman ritual, the forehead is anointed; in the East the whole body, as is still the case in the Byzantine rite where anointing is even substituted for the imposition of hands.

The unanimous teaching of the Church Fathers is that confirmation or chrismation is a sacrament of the gift of the Spirit, the essence of the definitive seal of Christian initiation. For the Eastern ritual, see the texts of St. Gregory of Nyssa and St. Cyril of Jerusalem cited in the article *Chrism*; for the Western, Tertullian, *De Praescriptione*, XL, and *De Baptismo*, VI, P.L., t.2, col. 54–55 and t.2, col. 1206; St. Cyprian, *Epist.* LXXII, 1 and LXXIII, 21; P.L. 3, cols. 1046 and 1124.

In the West, since the Middle Ages, confirmation was separated from baptism in that it was still reserved to bishops, even though current practice allowed priests to administer baptism. Because of this, certain writers saw in confirmation nothing more than an ecclesiastical institution that some thought did not go back any further than the Council of Meaux in 843. St. Thomas Aquinas, on the contrary, adhered to its apostolic orgin (he even thought this to be true of the practice of anointing). However, since the most important texts of the Fathers on this sacrament remained unknown to him, St. Thomas saw in confirmation only a sacrament of the coming of age in the Christian life, just as baptism was the sacrament of supernatural birth (*Sum. Theol.*, IIIa, q.72, a.1). He did affirm that the Holy Spirit was given in it (*ibid.* a.7), to which he added, *ad robur*, according to a medieval formula that was later to be unfortunately interpreted in a restrictive sense, as if confirmation gave only the gift of strength. This gradual loss of tradition was more and more accentuated in the West, and at times confirmation seemed nothing more than a sort of transition from adolescence to adulthood. But the adulthood of which St. Thomas spoke must be understood supernaturally, and it belonged to any baptized person, once he was confirmed, even if in childhood. At most, it was a consecration to Catholic action.

A reaction finally set in which made us again recognize this sacrament as the completion of baptism, by which the putting off of the "old self" and putting on of the "new self" in Jesus Christ were expanded as the permanent gift of the Spirit. The *character* (q.v.) that the sacrament confers is actually an association with Christ as the anointed One of the Spirit, enabling the Christian not only to benefit from the transitory influences of the Spirit, but to become his living temple, since in this way he has been made an active member of the whole priestly people, which is the Church (see the biblical texts cited in the article CHRISM). The fullness of the early teaching on this sacrament is successfully expressed in the treatise *Life in Jesus Christ*, by the Byzantine theologian Nicolas Kabasilas, recently re-edited in a French translation by the *Editions de Chevetogne*.

The indecisiveness of the Latin Middle Ages previously explained was at the root of the first Protestant rejection of confirmation as a sacrament. Under the influence of the Alsatian Reformer, Bucer, they reintroduced it, however, (sometimes under the name "reception of catechumens into the Church") to mark the completion of the catechism preparatory to first Communion. Only the relative negligence of modern Catholics in this regard can explain the curious inconsistency which, in certain countries like our own, resulted in reestablishing the custom of giving Communion to young children, without any thought to advancing the reception of the final sacrament of Christian initiation in the same way. Confirmation, therefore, has come to be given, contrary to all of tradition after and not before first Communion.

CONGRUISM A name given to the system according to which grace is efficacious because it would adapt itself to circumstances outside the subject, as well as to conditions from within, in such a way that the free will of the subject consents to it (*congruentia* signifies fitness, propriety). *See* GRACE.

CONSCIENCE Theologically it is necessary to distinguish between the psychological conscience and the moral conscience. The first is the personal awareness of self that each being possesses from the very fact that he exists as a spiritual substance. The tendency that has developed, especially in our own time, to confuse the psychological conscience with the person itself has created all sorts of theological difficulties, chiefly in the study of Christological and Trinitarian problems (these problems are treated in the article JESUS CHRIST, and TRINITY). The moral conscience implies the psychological conscience, but adds to it the faculty of perceiving a moral obligation that is imposed as such on the person.

Thus, the moral conscience is a clearly observable fact in every human being, although it may be relatively obscured in inferior civilizations, or as a result of deficient upbringing. Moreover, it is quite necessary to avoid confusing the preciseness with which an individual (or group of individuals) may be capable of apprehending the moral conscience for himself, with the effectiveness with which it will eventually be manifested in him. The Old Testament uses the term conscience (*syneidesis*) only in a late passage in the book of Wisdom (17,10). But its reality is recognized in more concrete terms, such as *heart* (q.v.). (See 2 Kings 24,10 or Job 27,6; also the account in Gen. 4,12 ff., on Cain, which is so striking because of its description of a bad conscience, without even using the term). Matthew (6,23) speaks of the inner eye (cf. Luke 11,13).

The term moral conscience (*syneidesis*) comes from the Stoics, who believed it to be an instinct of preservation of the spiritual person, by which our practical reason (*hegemonikon*) is guided by the ordering Spirit of the world. The most religious among them, such as Seneca, saw in it explicitly the manifestation of a divine presence in us. The idea was so popularized that we see it expressed even by the poet Ovid (*deus in nobis*). The New Testament frequently mentions the conscience (especially St. Paul). St. Paul underlines its presence among the pagans, with whom conscience is a substitute for the Jewish Law to the extent that it is clear enough, and that they obey it (Rom. 2,11 ff.). However, with the

Christian, the conscience is enlightened by the Holy Spirit (Rom. 9,1).
Thus, he comes to identify it with faith (Rom. 14,23). The pastoral
Epistles particularly continually connect the two (cf. 1 Tim. 1,19, and
3,9). For the apostle, on the other hand, it is perfectly clear that the
judgment of conscience is obligatory even when it is in fact unenlight-
ened (cf. Rom. 14,20–23 and 1 Cor. 8 and 10,23–33).

The scholastics singled out two aspects of the conscience: 1) *synteresis*
or *synderesis* (a corruption of the Greek *syneidesis*), which they explained, as the Stoics did, as a personal effort that is essential for a person
to preserve his identity in striving to comply with his rational nature
(this is conscience as a faculty); and, 2) *conscientia*, i.e., the particular
judgment that an individual is led to make in each particular case. St.
Thomas Aquinas, following St. Albert on this point, considers *synderesis*
as the *habitus* of the first principles of morality, the most common of
which is that good things should be done. From this point the *conscientia* then makes its decision according to an explicitly or implicitly
syllogistic judgment in which the major is the first principle of *synderesis*
and the minor a practical judgment brought to bear by prudence on the
particular case. The intellectualism of this concept is less radical than it
might seem, for we must remember that for St. Thomas all practical
knowledge is rooted in an orientation of the will, which gives it its
impulse to act. However, the Scholastics of the Franciscan school
preferred to say that *synderesis* is connected with the profound desire of
the will that spontaneously orients us toward the properly known good.
In this regard, we speak of the *scintilla animae*, the spark of the soul, a
special faculty of the created spirit which continually draws it toward
God.

Whatever may be said about these controversies, we may observe how
the distinction between *synderesis* and *conscientia* permits us to resolve
the objections often leveled against the authority of the moral conscience
on the basis of uncertainties of fact; or of variations observed among
different human consciences, or in the same conscience in different
circumstances. However sure and immediate the profound movement of
synderesis can be, the particular decisions of the conscience depend upon
its perfect enlightenment. Consequently, it is a primordial duty of the
conscience itself to seek to be enlightened, which becomes easier as the
person complies more faithfully to its concrete injunctions. Therefore,
we must give equal consideration to the duty of obeying our conscience
and of enlightening it as much as we can. This implies that the
conscience, far from being opposed to the different authorities capable of
guiding it, recognizes and gives proper value to each of them. For the
believer, the data of faith in this respect have an unequalled importance.

The problem of freedom of conscience will be treated under the word FREEDOM. (See St. Thomas Aquinas, *Sum. Theol.*, Ia-IIae, q.19, a.5, and *De Veritate*, q.17.

CONSECRATION   A liturgical act whereby a being or an object is definitively appropriated to the worship and the service of God. The most eminent example is the consecration of the Eucharist. Every consecration, in the Christian understanding of the word, is an act of God by which he not only repossesses (in a manner of speaking) the world that the sin of creatures has alienated from him, but, moreover, makes it a sign of his presence and of his redemptive action. Consequently the principle of every consecration (and especially of the eucharistic consecration) is a divine statement whereby God asserts his plan, which we find in Christ's words that are recalled in the heart of all the prayers of consecration in the liturgical tradition of the Eucharist. However this recollection is not enough for the consecration to take place. It is essential that consecration be formulated in a prayer of the Church in which she asserts her faith in the divine Word and her expectation of the realization of the Word here and now. In this principle we may have the solution to a question that has divided Latin and Greek theology for a long time, namely, whether the eucharistic consecration takes place by virtue of the priest's reciting the words of institution, or by the *epiklesis* (q.v.), i.e., a special invocation asking that the divine Spirit effect the consecration. As the Byzantine theologian, Nicolas Kabasilas, in his *Explanation of the Divine Liturgy*, was one of the first to see it, the alternative thus formulated is a false problem: the invocation by the Church and the words of Christ mutually imply each other so that they retain all of their meaning (*see* CANON).

More generally, in all of the consecrations performed by the Church, we thus find a supplication addressed to God, reminding him of his promises and expressing the expectations of the faith of the Church: let them come to pass now that the moment has arrived!

A particular case is presented by the consecration to God that solemn vows represent. Does this not seem to be a step taken by man in order to make his own consecration to God himself? St. Thomas Aquinas states that although solemn profession is not a sacrament, it does contain a spiritual consecration of which God is the author, even though man may be the minister (*Sum. Theol.*, IIa-IIae, q.88, a.7, especially *ad primum*).

CONSIGNATION   The name now given in the Roman ritual to the anointing with holy chrism that is applied to the top of the head of a newly baptized person immediately after baptism. It is a promise and a foretaste of confirmation, from which it was not separated (perhaps not even distinguished) in the old baptismal rituals. Confirmation was then as one with the baptismal ceremony, as is still the case in the East.

CONSUBSTANTIAL   From the Latin *consubstantialis*, consubstantial is used to translate the Greek *homoousios* in the Nicene Creed, and signifies not only that the Son is specifically of the same substance as the Father (as may be said of different pieces of the same metal), but that together they have only one and the same concrete substance. After the First Council of Constantinople, this truth was admitted for the entire Trinity, including the Spirit. The doctrine of consubstantialism is opposed to subordinationism, according to which only the Father would, in the strictest sense, be God, and to ditheism or tritheism, according to which the Persons of the Holy Trinity would be separate gods.

CONSUBSTANTIATION   A theory generally held by the Lutheran theologians, following Luther. According to consubstantiation, the substance of bread and wine in the Eucharist would not of itself be changed into the body and blood of Christ, but would simply be present along with (*cum*) this substance (*in, cum, sub pane*). Many modern Lutheran theologians, while firmly maintaining the doctrine of the real presence of the body and blood of the Saviour in the eucharistic elements, prefer to maintain that the means by which this presence is possible are mysterious, without binding themselves to either consubstantiation or transsubstantiation, which the classical forms in the Catholic Church explain.

CONTEMPLATION   Considered as a pure view of truth in which the mind is at rest, contemplation was held in Greek thought (Aristotle as well as Plato, despite their very different conceptions of it) to be man's superior activity. The Fathers of the Church (St. Augustine no less than the Greek Fathers) derived many formulas from this basis, and from their own point of view held to the superiority of the contemplative over the active life, recalling the words of Christ to strengthen their arguments: "Mary has chosen the better part . . ." (Luke 10,42). St. Thomas Aquinas singled out the apostolic life, in which the superabundance of contemplation is communicated to others in such a way that they are made to contemplate in their turn, from what he called the mixed life (i.e., a combination of contemplation and action, which seemed to him to be inferior to the purely contemplative life, for him the highest form of life in the present). In eternity, contemplation will arrive at its perfection for all of the blessed, and it will subsist alone as the highest form of activity that man can ultimately attain.

In Protestantism today, and in many Catholic circles as well, these views are regarded as unfaithful to the Gospel and as the result of an unfortunate Hellenization of Christianity. There is some confusion here, however. The term itself and the theory of the contemplative life are not formulated in the New Testament, but undeniably stem from Hellenic thought. Before condemning the Christian understanding of contemplation and the contemplative life as a pure infiltration of paganism, however, it must be determined what the Church Fathers and the great scholastics understood by this "knowledge" of which contemplation is the full flower. Certainly, it is not the purely intellectual knowledge of Aristotle, nor the semi-esthetic knowledge of Plato (and to some extent the Neo-Platonists), but rather biblical *knowledge* (q.v.), that is, the knowledge of God as inseparable from his love, and of that love penetrating us entirely and reflecting on all creation and on all our fellow men. To oppose Christian contemplation with the charity exalted by St. Paul (1 Cor. 12) is to quarrel over words, since this contemplation is itself the flowering of charity and consists precisely of that which St. Paul gives in the same text as the characteristic of everlasting life: "To know (God) as I have been known" (v.12).

Another question raised in modern times has been the problem of knowing whether Christian contemplation should be considered as infused (i.e., as a pure gift of grace), or whether it can also be acquired by human effort (with, of course, the help of grace). It must be admitted that this manner of posing the question seems to be connected with a rather deficient theology of grace and human activity. Christian contemplation in the highest sense must be considered as a superior awareness of the activity of grace in us, and therefore not only is it infused, but it is connected with the higher *gifts* of the Spirit (*see* GIFTS OF THE HOLY SPIRIT). Nevertheless in the ordinary course of God's providence it is not the sort of miracle that an individual would not be psychologically ready to receive. On the contrary, it appears that it must be considered as a superior but normal fruit of the grace of baptism itself, with which it is given creatively.

See St. Thomas Aquinas, *Sum. Theol.*, IIa-IIae, q.179–182, along with the commentary on his teaching given by Fr. R. Garrigou-Lagrange in *Christian Perfection and Contemplation*, St. Louis, 1937.

CONVERSION Literally, a changing of direction. Conversion is used with reference to the act of a sinner who returns to God after having been estranged from Him (*see* PENANCE), or to the unbeliever who embraces the faith (*see* BAPTISM, and FAITH).

COUNCIL An assembly of bishops gathered to discuss and decide any problems present in the life of the Church. Councils may be *general* (called universal, or ecumenical, i.e., representing the *oikoumene*, the whole "inhabited" earth), *plenary,* in which the episcopate of a whole country is assembled (also called national councils), or *provincial,* where the bishops of an ecclesiastical province meet together. Today, canon law requires the metropolitan to convoke a provincial council at least every twenty years (can. 283). It reserves the convocation of plenary councils (with certain exceptions such as those made for the patriarchs of Syria and the Coptic patriarchs) to the Holy See, which presides over them through a legate (can. 281). Ecumenical councils must be convoked by the pope and presided over by him or his legates, and their decrees must be confirmed by the pope in order to be valid (can. 222 to 229).

A distinction must be made between the collective exercise of episcopal responsibilities, which belong to the Catholic episcopacy by their very nature, and councils that are an eminent but extraordinary form of this exercise. Moreover, as the Constitution *De Fide Catholica* of the First Vatican Council expressly states: "It is here that the holy dogmas of religion are defined with more depth, expressed with more fullness; that Church discipline is restored and more solidly established . . . that the bonds of members and head are strengthened, and the strength of the whole body of Christ is increased." (Mansi, t.51, pp. 31–32; it is surprising to note that D.B. omits this text.) This obviously applies in its strictest sense only to ecumenical councils, whose code of canon law reminds us that their dogmatic decisions are infallible (can. 1323, par. 2). In effect the same relationship exists between the whole episcopate and the pope, *mutatis mutandis,* as between St. Peter and the entire apostolic college (cf. Matt. 16,19 and 18,18), i.e., the same powers are entrusted collectively to the whole episcopal college and individually to its head. The effect of this is that the question posed since the Middle Ages and the Great Schism, as to whether a pope or a council is superior, makes no sense, since the council cannot exist without the pope, while all the bishops in the council are co-lawmakers with the pope. Moreover, it should be noted that conciliar decisions are always understood to be unanimous. A minority that would not go along with the majority truly representing the mind of the body of bishops in its entirety, would commit an act of schism. At the same time, a simply numerical majority could not outweigh the well-founded reservations of a considerable minority, not only because of its material importance, but also because of the representative quality of the opinions it would express on the true faith of the Church. In a case where such a situation might develop, we can reasonably assume that the pope would refuse to ratify a majority decision. Actually, since no council in history has in fact brought all of the Catholic bishops together, a council is definitively recognized as being ecumenical and therefore infallible, only by the *de facto* concurrence of the whole Church in its Catholic unity. In history there is no unique formula for this concurrence (there is no official list in existence of the councils which have in fact been ecumenical), but the explicit, or merely implicit, ratification by the first of the bishops is the simplest expression of it, and therefore the most certain. This is why canon law has come to require this formal ratification as a sign of validity for the decisions of future councils.

COUNSEL and PRECEPT   *See* ASCETICISM, LAW, and PERFECTION

COVENANT   A translation of the Hebrew word *b'rith*, originally meaning a sacred contract of partnership. All Semites believed themselves to be bound to their gods in this manner. But the covenant with Israel was, on the Lord's part, a free and sovereign initiative. It was the essence and fundamental content of God's *plan* (q.v.) which the Word revealed to Abraham, and which began to be realized at the time of the Exodus (cf. Gen. 12 ff., and Ex. 19 ff.). It was the covenant which was at the very root of the existence of the people as the *People of God* (q.v.). God showed himself to be faithful, demanding the *faithfulness* (q.v.) of the patriarchs in return. The prophets announced that this covenant, concluded on the foundation of the Decalogue, and already renewed in the spirit of its prophetic interpretation (cf. 2 Kings 22), had to give way to a new and everlasting covenant, to be written this time in men's hearts (cf. Jer. 31, and Ezech. 36–37). It was to these texts that Jesus alluded at the Last Supper when he instituted the New Covenant in his own blood.

CREATION   The act by which God gives existence to all being outside of himself. The knowledge of God as the Creator is attainable in principle by man's reason alone. In fact, although all religions have a rather well-evolved concept of it, the philosophers have never been able to define creation in a completely satisfactory manner, outside of biblical revelation. This is perhaps the most striking example of those truths of the natural order, which the fall and its consequences have obscured in man's mind to the extent that revelation was necessary to help him regain them. Either we see in effect the idea of creation being confused with an emanation by which the divine being itself would become diffused through its own gradual debasement, as is the case with Neo-Platonism, or, as with Aristotle, who followed the ancient Greek thinkers, the distinction of the world from its author would depend on the existence of prime matter which is independent of God's own existence. This second theory, inspired in certain schools of thought by Pythagoreanism, and even more crudely present in Manichaeism, is at the root of the dualistic ideas that look upon matter as the source of evil, and see in good and evil two independent and coeternal principles.

The biblical teaching on creation, as it is set forth in the first chapters of Genesis, is as far from *dualism* (q.v.) as it is from all of the pantheistic forms of *monism* (q.v.). In the Bible it is clear that God created everything that exists, the material and spiritual worlds as well, and that he created it from nothing (*ex nihilo*), which is understood to mean that nothing outside of him existed before the creation of the universe. But this creation is no longer to be thought of as merely an emanation of something which would actually be the divinity itself under another form. It is rather a being at once radically distinct from God, and yet owing everything, and above all its existence, to him.

Understood in this way, creation, from the creature's point of view, is a total dependence of contingent beings (i.e., of those beings who do not have reason for existence within themselves) upon God, who is considered the only necessary Being. According to St. Thomas Aquinas, it is to this extent that God is knowable by natural reason from his works, according to St. Paul in the Epistle to the Romans (1,18 ff.). Still following the Holy Doctor, we must distinguish between this ontological dependence of the creature upon the Creator, and the fact (which following St. Thomas is not demonstrable by reason) that creation had a beginning, as the Church believes, according to Scripture. Even if the world such as we know it had always existed, which does not seem unthinkable to him, it would nonetheless be created in the sense that its existence would not be any less contingent, since it depends upon God's free will alone. It follows reciprocally that creation cannot merely be reduced to the event that was the beginning of all things. It is a permanent situation in which the creature subsists at every instant, as well as at the first instant, and which makes it at all times the recipient of its being, a permanent gift of the Creator.

It is incontestable that the idea of permanent and total dependence of the creature upon the Creator is also very much a fundamental biblical teaching (see among others Psalms 103–104, vv. 27–29). On the other hand we should go off the track completely, were we to deduce from St. Thomas's rational analysis something which he himself never believed, namely, that the assertion that all things have a beginning can be disregarded in the teaching of the Bible. The resistance by other schools of Christian thought to the hypothetical assertion of the Thomistic school (that creation could have been eternal) came precisely from a fear of this false deduction. It would then logically follow that history would have no importance, either because one would imagine the unfolding events in the created world as a meaningless succession of everlasting changes, or because one would concede the perpetual existence of all things in the same state. Or else, there would be the idea of an eternal returning, or of cyclic history, which would only lead to a perpetual starting all over again. Therefore, it is essential in the biblical or Christian view of creation to believe that God created the world with a beginning. The finite succession of unfolding events constitutes an irreversible whole in a temporal existence, beginning with the original creation of free beings in a state of goodness, followed by their fall and their redemption. Both the redemption and the fall occurred once and for all time, a fact which would make no sense if the present universe had always existed, or if it had simply taken its place in the infinity of other universes.

This does not in any way prevent creation, on God's part, from being eternal, because God himself is not only eternal but immutable, and therefore does not begin by creating at a certain moment. What is true is that he eternally creates the temporal world. In other words, the world was not created in time, in the sense that there would be a "before" that preceded creation, but in the sense that time begins with creation itself.

If creation as revealed in the biblical view (which not only enlightens but supernaturally completes the truths on this point that are accessible to reason) cannot therefore be considered as eternal in the sense that it would have no beginning, there is no reason to set the doctrine of creation against every evolutionary or progressive idea of human and cosmic history. Since creation does not mean that in some way God would be more the cause of beings at the beginning of their existence than afterward, but means that he is their cause at every instant, there is nothing to prevent one from believing that this first causality only *progressively* reveals all of its possibilities. On the other hand, given the biblical assertion which is strictly connected with that of creation, namely, that God creates free beings in an historical "becoming" that has an irreversible direction, the hypothesis of a universe in progress is not only not contradicted by the dogma of creation but is evidently in positive harmony with the biblical presentation of this truth.

What Christian dogma must exclude first of all would be all immanent-ist evolutionism that would attempt to place the first cause of beings coming into existence only in the immanent power of cosmic reality, which would in that way thus be identified *de facto* with the divinity. This would be one of the forms of pantheistic monism which, as we have said, must be excluded by the very idea of creation. It was this idea, which certain religious and irreligious philosophies of the 19th century had so strictly connected to the scientific concept of evolution, particularly of animal species, that came to be considered suspect by a great many theologians. But confusion of the two ideas is by no means necessary.

The biblical notion of creation would also exclude any simplistic notion of progress that looks upon it only as a linear development in which each stage would be automatically superior to all the preceding ones merely by the fact that it follows them. The biblical schema of history certainly supposes progress, not only in the order in which beings make their appearance, as we see typified in the first pages of Genesis, but also from the first state of free creatures to their ultimate state. But the Bible asserts, conjointly with the freedom of creatures, the dramatic character of this progress: that divine Providence realizes their infallibility in one sense, but not without respecting their freedom even when it efficaciously comes to the aid of their defects.

It is by taking into account all these aspects of a very rich and complex truth that Christian thought on creation combines the assertions of revelation, the unquestionable certitudes of reason, and the progressively evolving data of science. We should be wary of extravagantly simplified antitheses, as well as too hasty agreement, which might risk soon being completely out of date.

A last point which it is important to emphasize is that creation must be considered both a principal manifestation of divine goodness, and a free initiative on God's part. To think of creation as necessary, in the sense that the *divine processions* are necessary in the Trinity, would be to confuse the world with God and reintroduce emanatism in place of creation. Asserted in the symbols of faith of the early Church, the dogma of creation was more precisely defined against the dualism of the Manichaeans by the Fourth Lateran Council (D.B. 428) and against the errors of modern materialism or pantheism by the First Vatican Council (Sess. III, Const. *De Fide Catholica*, D.B. 1782–1784 and 1801–1805). See St. Thomas Aquinas, *Sum. Theol.*, Ia, q.44–105, on the question of the possibility of conceiving of an eternal creation, in particular q.46, a.2 and 3.

CREDIBILITY   A property of the truths of faith. Although these truths cannot be demonstrated directly because their object is supernatural, it can be demonstrated in certain ways that these truths can and must be believed on the testimony of God (*see* APOLOGETICS).

CRITICISM   The particular meaning given to this word is the systematic activity of verifying the grounds for our various judgments. Textual criticism endeavors to verify the authenticity of the texts in question, and historical criticism to verify the authenticity of generally admitted facts. In the same way, philosophical or theological criticism is legitimately practised in verifying the arguments by which we attempt to establish or justify our beliefs. Although we must be wary of a spirit of systematic criticism that is merely a caricature of genuine critical spirit, which it too often hampers instead of helping, it would be a total error to oppose in the name of faith the spirit of criticism as such. In so doing, we would end up by confusing genuine faith with mere credulousness. In questions dealing with faith, the Church may certainly impose the rejection of certain ill-founded philosophical or theological conclusions. However, far from ever wishing to put aside the legitimate use of sane criticism, the Church merely warns those who practise it of the danger present in believing that some opinions are above all criticism, while the least one can say about them is that they are certainly not self-evident.

CROSS   A discussion of the theology of the cross will be found in the article REDEMPTION. Our object here is to speak of the traditional veneration given to the cross (either to relics of the true cross, or simple images of the cross with or without the corpus). This veneration, such as is found particularly in the great office of Good Friday, is currently called "adoration" of the cross. In what sense is this to be understood? All Catholic theologians agree that this is only *relative adoration*; it has Christ alone for its object, by means of an image which reminds us of him in the manifestation par excellence of his redeeming love. Neverthe-less, St. Thomas Aquinas expressly declares that the adoration of the cross is an adoration of *latria*, which can only be given to God; this is distinct from *relative veneration*, which is given only to images and relics. (*Sum. Theol.*, IIIa, q.25, a.4.)

Other theologians, especially in the wake of Bellarmine (*De Ecclesia Triumphante*, bk. II, chap. 25), are no less formally opposed to St. Thomas's opinion. Actually, it seems that St. Thomas expressed himself as he did because he was unaware of the very clear formula of the Second Council of Nicaea regarding the distinction between the different forms of worship (*see* ADORATION). But, his thought and that of Bellarmine are less far apart fundamentally than one might believe. Both thought that the honor given to the cross has, in fact, Christ alone for its object, and it is for that reason, and that reason alone, that the "adoration of the cross" is linked with the worship of *latria*, which can only be given to God.

CURSE   A formula that is the reverse of a blessing, in the sense that it is supposed to bring condemnation rather than grace to an object or a person. Deuteronomy, which insists so strongly on the choice open to man through the call to the divine covenant, shows us, after the crossing of the Jordan, a real liturgy of curses against sin, and blessings for faithfulness to the words of the covenant (Deut. 27,11–26, and all of chap. 28). The liturgy of the New Testament, however dominated it is by the saving blessing contained in Jesus' cross, expressly sees in it, along with the curse against the powers of evil (the reason for keeping the curse-psalms in the divine office), a curse against sinners impenitent to the end. It even contains, besides the exorcisms which are genuine curses against devils, certain curse formulas against those who would commit a sin of particular enormity without repenting of it (see in the *Roman Pontifical* the curse against whoever would cause a consecrated virgin to violate her vow).

D

DAMNATION The final condemnation brought against sinners who have refused to repent. Its consequence is that they are deprived of the vision of God. (*See* HELL).

DARKNESS Just as light is the sign of the divine presence, darkness, especially in Judaism and the New Testament, is the sign of the presence and the activity of the devil. The "power of darkness" is synonymous with the power of the devil (cf. Luke 22,53 and Col. 1,13). We see the beginnings of this idea in the "shadow of death" mentioned in Psalm 23,4. St. Paul uses the contrast between "sons of darkness" and "sons of the day" (1 Thess. 5,5), and describes arriving at the point of faith and baptism as a crossing over from darkness into light (Eph. 5,8 and 11), which is found again in the First Epistle of Peter (2,9). But it is in the Johannine writings that this contrast is constantly present. Proclaimed in the prologue (1,5), it is used as the thread of the Gospel (cf. 12,35 and 46). The same is true of St. John's First Epistle (cf. 1,5; 2,8 etc.), and the contrast certainly underlies all of the Apocalypse (cf. 9,2 and 16,10).

Since the light of God remains mysterious (compare the article CLOUD), a mysticism of darkness and light is inseparably involved in Christian spiritual tradition. It is found in all the commentators on the life of Moses: Origen, St. Gregory of Nazianzen, and St. Gregory of Nyssa, and figures most prominently in the writings of Evagrius Ponticus and the Pseudo-Dionysius. For if God is light in himself, this light so much surpasses ordinary light that it begins by putting us in darkness. Thus, as the Pseudo-Dionysius explains, the divine darkness is nothing other than the inaccessible light in which God dwells, as according to the First Epistle to Timothy (6,16; and cf. *Epist*. V of the Pseudo-Dionysius, P.G. 3, col. 1037A). Similarly, in St. John of the Cross, it is through the dark nights of the senses and of the soul that we throw off the deceptive brightness of the earth in order to attain to the contemplation of the divine light.

DAY The idea of a day that is to be preeminently God's runs throughout the Bible. It is the day on which God will manifest himself by destroying the powers that appear today to be freely opposed to his will in the world, through a judgment that is looked upon as the supreme act of his kingly authority. The prophets put Israel on its guard against the temptation of God's People to believe that this day would automatically be the day of their own victory over their enemies (cf. especially Amos 5,18). On the contrary, it is to be the day when God will reveal the commandments his People have transgressed, and the consequent punishment they have merited. More generally, every time faith is put to the test, we see a day of the visitation of the Lord, i.e., specifically, a day of his judgment. (cf. 1 Pet. 2,12). *See* JUDGMENT, and ESCHATOLOGY.

DEACONESSES   An order of women consecrated to a form of service in the Church, to which the New Testament alludes in Rom. 16,1 and 1 Tim. 3,11. Within the Christian community in the early centuries, they played a role somewhat analogous to that of the deacons, particularly with regard to the care of the poor, but also in the liturgy, especially the baptism of women. At an early date (in the 5th and 6th centuries), there was reaction against what was judged to be an encroachment on their part, particularly in their participation in the service of the altar. This, along with the gradual elimination of the custom of baptizing adults by immersion, explains why, by the end of antiquity, the order of deaconess had almost completely disappeared. The Syrian Churches were the most conservative in this regard, and even today the Maronites have retained a small number of deaconesses in women's monasteries. It must be noted that in the West as well, some nuns, such as the Carthusians, have kept certain rites in their consecration which are left over from the ordination of deaconesses, as well as some corresponding privileges, such as the wearing of the maniple.

   In the 19th century the Protestants, under the influence in Germany of Fliedner and W. Löhe, reintroduced deaconesses into their Churches, a custom which soon spread to many other Protestant and Anglican Churches. However, they are (except those under the "High Church" Lutheran influence of Löhe) more the equivalent of Catholic sisters of charity, than of their ancient counterparts.

DEACONS   Ministers who have received the first of the three major sacramental orders, and who, according to the etymology of their name, are the "servers" of the bishop or the priest, particularly in assisting in the celebration of the Eucharist. Although the words *diakonos* and *diakonia* were used in the New Testament in the general sense of "servant" and "service," there is no question that the texts of Philemon (1,1) and 1 Timothy (3,8–10.12.13) refer to a distinct order of "ministers" associated with the *episkopoi* and *presbyteroi*. It is generally admitted that the seven persons, including St. Stephen, appointed by the apostles, through the laying on of hands and prayers, to administer charity (especially in what was called the "serving at table"), were the first Christian deacons (Acts 6,1–6). However, the text does not call them *diakonoi,* and what follows seems to imply that they would in fact have a most important ministry of preaching. On the other hand, some have interpreted these seven persons as *presbyteroi,* rather than what were later to be called deacons. All one can say is that the early Church seems to have been overwhelmingly in favor of the first interpretation. Furthermore, it is incontestable that the deacons, especially archdeacons, in the early Church, as is the case in the East today, not only had the role given them in the *Roman Pontifical,* namely to preach (which covers the entire solemn proclamation of the Word of God in the liturgy), to baptize and to administer Communion subject to the bishop or the priest. They also had important administrative functions in the Church, especially with regard to its possessions and its works of charity, making them auxiliaries to the bishop, somewhat like our vicars-general today. A vestige of this was preserved until recently, where cardinal deacons in Rome were in fact not obliged to be ordained priests. This explains why we find that in the primitive Church some deacons were elevated directly from the diaconate to the episcopacy.

Although the Council of Trent (Sess. XXIII, can. 6; D.B.966) only mentions the *ministri* after the bishops and priests in the hierarchy, the testimony of tradition is so constant and unanimous that it is faithfully accepted that the office of diaconate is a divine institution, through the apostles, and is therefore a sacramental order. The Holy See has recently incorporated the commonly accepted doctrine of the matter and form of the ordination sacrament: the laying on of hands together with an accompanying prayer (D.S. 3860).

Although in the West today the diaconate is only conferred as a step in the preparation for the priesthood, in the East it is still a stable office, and it is not permissible for a priest to fulfill the liturgical functions of the deacon. The Second Vatican Council has decided in favor of the restoration of an analogous state in the West for pastoral reasons, i.e., as a help given to the priesthood by competent assistants who would be provided with sacramental graces, but who could also be dispensed from certain clerical obligations that it is judged necessary for priests to maintain.

In principle, Protestants have kept the office of deacon in their churches, although they are generally only laymen associated with the charitable works of the church, or, as in the Scandinavian countries, sacristans, who often have the additional duty of giving religious instruction.

DEATH   The Bible not only asserts with progressive clarity throughout the Old Testament, and with conclusive lucidity in the New Testament, that man is destined for everlasting life, but it precisely states that the introduction of death, in man's case at least, is contrary to God's plan. The Wisdom of Solomon expressly declares: "It is not God who is the author of death" (1,13), thus specifying that which was implied in the account of the fall (cf. Gen. 3,19). St. Paul is even more explicit: "As sin came into the world through one man, and death through sin, and so death spread to all men because all men sinned. . . ." (Rom. 5,12).

Contrary to Greek religious thought, that looked upon corporeal life as the result of a fall, and that the death of the body permitted the soul to be set free (cf. the play on words between *soma*, "body," and *sema* "tomb," used by Plato), the entire Old Testament considered death as a curse, and the immortality it hoped for assumed from the very first the whole man (cf. Isa. 38,18–19 and 26,19). The New Testament fully corroborates this expectation, and for St. Paul in particular, Christian hope is asserted as the hope of a resurrection with Christ, which is explicitly opposed to the mere hope of immortality of the soul (cf. 1 Cor. 15). This does not mean that survival of the soul is denied, but rather that the expectation of faith lies not only in this natural immortality, but in the reunion of all the faithful with Christ, in order that their total humanity, body and soul, might be reintegrated and transfigured (cf. 2 Cor. 5,1–10). The result is that the Christian, too, may desire death; not merely for the sake of death, but through it to perfect his union with the saving cross of Christ, and, from then to the consummation of a union with him, which, however, will find its apogee only in the general resurrection (cf. Phil. 1,20–23). This is what the authentic *acta* of the martyrs so admirably demonstrate, especially the letters of St. Ignatius of Antioch to the Roman Christians, who tried to persuade him to escape his ordeal of faith. His desire was obviously for a resurrection with Christ, and it seemed to him that there would be no better way to attain it than in death for Christ, which would in a sense repay Christ's death for him and complete his own union with Christ.

This is certainly the teaching that underlies the whole Johannine Apocalypse which reveals the ordeal of the martyrs as an imitation and a following of their Saviour, which leads them to the glory he had won for himself and for them in his cross. The Gospel of St. John looks upon Christ's glorification in such continuity with his cross that it systematically uses the term "raise up" to express both the torment of the cross and the glory of the Ascension (cf. 3,14; 8,28; 12,32). The sense of this connection of the two events has never been stated more explicitly or more strongly than in the Easter *troparion* of the Byzantine liturgy: "Christ is risen from the dead; by his death he has vanquished death, giving life to those who are in the grave." It is in this same sense that the Roman eucharistic preface of the cross establishes an identification between the tree of death of the cross, and the tree of life.

We shall see more precisely in the article REDEMPTION how the theology of the Church Fathers developed the dialectic of sin that produces death as a punishment, and of death which occasions the redemptive act; once sin has been abolished through this act, death will ultimately also be done away with.

DECALOGUE   A term meaning "the ten words," i.e., the Ten Commandments given in the text of Exodus (20,1–17) and repeated with minor variants in Deuteronomy (5,6–21), which represents the basis of all Mosaic legislation. Uniting our duties toward our neighbor with our duties toward God, the Decalogue remains for Christians as it was for the Jews, the basis of morality. Christ confirmed its authority and, at the same time, enlightened its meaning, by summing it up in the two commandments of love of God and love of neighbor (*see* LAW). St. Paul writes: "Owe no one anything, except to love one another; for he who loves his neighbor has fulfilled the law" (Rom. 13,8).

DECREE and DECRETAL   The name *decree* is particularly given to conciliar decisions on canonical matters. In a more general way, the collections of canonical decisions are called decrees. Similarly, *decretals* are papal letters stating the decisions of the Holy See.

DEIFICATION (or DIVINIZATION)   These expressions used by the Greek Fathers (*theosis* or *theopoiesis*) do not signify any notion of personal divinization of a Christian, but the certainty of the genuine reality of our *supernatural adoption* (q.v.), involving, as the Second Epistle of Peter says, our participation in the divine nature.

DEISM   A teaching widely held in the 18th century. Its chief originator, in the preceding century, was Lord Herbert of Cherbury. Rejecting, or confusing, all positive religions as so many childish thought-germs, deism only acknowledges an abstract divinity that presides over the natural order and is to be honored only through a life of conformity with that order. Voltaire was its great propagator in France. Claiming to oppose it in the name of the Gospel, Rousseau did little more than cloak deism in pious sentimentality.

DEMOCRACY   The word democracy means "government by the people." Throughout the course of its history, however, the term has been subject to wide interpretations and, consequently, various forms of democratic governments. These forms range from the *direct* democracy of ancient Greece (a vestige of which is found today in the small Swiss cantons); the elective parliamentary forms of *representative* democracy;

the *constitutional* democracy (of the United States); and, in a curious pleonasm, to the so-called "people's democracies" of the Communist satellite countries.

It can be seen, therefore, that juridical and philosophical interpretations given the terms democracy and democratic have often been diverse. This is why the Church has, in the past, reacted in varying ways in the face of democratic ideas. In the 19th century particularly, the tendency of theologians and Church authorities was to oppose democracy not simply out of concern for preserving the traditional institutions of Christianity, but because many philosophical theories at that time connected democracy with the implicit rejection of God as the source of all authority. Today, on the contrary, the Church has come to uphold democracy to the extent that it is identified with the defense of freedoms that are essential to the human being, especially religious freedom.

DEMONIAC   A person obsessed or possessed by the devil. *See* POSSESSION.

DEMYTHOLOGIZATION   An English translation of the term *entmythologisierung,* used by the German Protestant exegete and theologian, Rudolf Bultmann, who was closely associated with Karl Barth, but later broke with him on this particular point. According to Bultmann, all of the traditional idioms of Christianity, beginning with the Gospels and the entire New Testament, belong to a mythical form of thought that is radically unacceptable to minds shaped by modern science. This is especially the case in all statements that suppose an intervention on the part of transcendent influences or beings in the world's course, such as the dogmas of the Incarnation or the communication of the Holy Spirit.

Demythologization would substitute the traditional mythological elements of the Bible with an interpretation based on the existential attitude that it aims to produce in the Christian; an interpretation, therefore, distinct from traditional dogma. The philosopher Karl Jaspers has observed that with Bultmann's quite negative idea of *myth* (q.v.), as well as his concept of a world that is, in a radically deterministic sense, unified solely by science, Bultmann actually reflects a stage of thought that is left over from the 19th century, and which 20th century science can no longer hold.

In addition, the science of comparative religions makes it quite evident that what Bultmann considers typically mythical in the New Testament, namely, the intervention in this world of a God who radically transcends it, is, on the contrary, the farthest possible notion from the ancient myths, and is actually what exploded them. The great cosmic myths of

Hellenic religions, like those of the Far East, are in effect a vivid projection of the cosmic phenomena in their perpetual alternation. The Christian affirmation of a God who surpasses the world, and intervenes in it once and for all to produce a definitive alteration of reality, far from having to be dismissed as mythical, represents both the surpassing of the myths and of a strictly deterministic rationalism. We come back, therefore, to a good use of analogy in the sense defined by St. Thomas, in order to explain the real import of the Christian affirmations, and the symbolic element they contain, and not to an impossible dismissal of this element itself.

DEPOSING AND DEGRADING OF CLERICS   Although the Church considers that the sacrament of orders (i.e., major orders) creates an indelible character, she claims the right, for serious faults, to depose clerics and to reduce them to the lay state. This does not mean that their orders are completely taken away from them, but that they are forbidden to exercise them except in special cases; for example, giving the sacraments to a person in danger of death. Originally, the degradation of clerics was a liturgical ceremony in which the penalty was quite vividly illustrated through public removal of clerical insignia. Today, although the rite is still in the Pontifical, it is generally *edictalis* (by edict) and not *realis* (real), and merely increases the gravity of a simple deposition. (*See* can. 2298, ff.)

DEPOSIT OF FAITH   This term, from the Latin *depositum* which is a translation of the Greek term *paratheke* (literally, anything entrusted to one), is used for the first time in the pastoral epistles (1 Tim. 6,20 and 2 Tim. 1,14). The idea is also revealed in the words of Christ in St. Matthew (28,20): "Teaching them all that I have commanded you," in which it is clear that the reference is not only to a new life, but to the truths bound up with that life (even though the word itself does not appear in the text). In the word *paratheke* itself or in other terms like *paradosis* (*tradition*, q.v.), this idea is found again in all of the Fathers: a body of truths was entrusted by Christ to the apostles, and is kept, as a sacred trust by the Church, which can neither add to it nor subtract from it.

At an early date the *symbols of faith* (*see* SYMBOL) furnished a succinct formula for this deposit. But it was clear in early Christianity that this did not refer primarily to a series of formulas, but rather to a single truth, which was very rich and very much *one*, and which, although remaining unalterable in itself, since it was given in its entirety in apostolic times, was nevertheless capable of being defined through increasingly precise formulas. We find this stressed in the *Commonito-*

rium of St. Vincent of Lérins (P.L. 50; cf. especially col. 667 ff.). St. Vincent, in emphasizing that the Church changes nothing in the dogmas entrusted to her by Christ, and that she always takes the same dogmas in the same sense, is no less aware of the relative newness of the formulas used, for example, by the councils. But he explains that these new formulas, which generally arise out of the necessity to ward off misinterpretations of revealed truth, do nothing more than state with greater diligence (*diligentius*) what until then had simply been believed. Only in modern times has the idea been expressed that perhaps doctrinal *development* (q.v.) does not evolve only in the transition from the implicit to the explicit; it is possible to bring to light relatively new truths that, nevertheless, are so inseparable from the basic traditional truths that they actually are inspired by them (just as the Roman primacy must imply the doctrine of papal infallibility, or Mary's supereminent holiness, her Immaculate Conception). Therefore, these new truths can come to be declared truths of faith by the Church, and for that reason they belong to the deposit of revelation, even though they had not been formulated explicitly as such, or perhaps even proposed implicitly in the beginning.

Kindred, if not exactly similar, are those truths that, although they are not supernatural (i.e., belonging as such to the deposit of faith in the strict sense), cannot be denied without endangering the truths of faith themselves. Such is the case with natural truths like the immortality of the soul, or the validity of the first principles of reason. It is the Church's function to uphold these truths and to define them to the degree that to put them in jeopardy would run the risk of injuring the faith itself.

The distinction between the direct and indirect objects of the deposit of faith was formulated for the first time by St. Thomas Aquinas in the *Summa Theologica* (IIa-IIae, q.11, a.2), and more precisely stated by modern theologians, particularly following Gregory of Valencia and Bañez (cf. the fifth proposition condemned as erroneous by the decree *Lamentabili*, D.B. 2005).

DESCENT INTO HELL A statement of faith concerning Christ with regard to the period of time between his death and his Resurrection. It is formulated in this expression in the Apostles Creed. Scripture mentions the fact (1 Pet. 3,19), and the word "hell" in this context designates the general abode of the dead, which the Hebrews called *sheol*. St. Peter considers this above all to be the occasion for announcing the redemption to certain persons, but the view of the Church from a very early date has been that this mysterious sermon of Christ was an announcement of deliverance to all who before the coming of Christ had had some hope of redemption. Early iconography developed this theme symbolically by depicting the rising Christ as bringing Adam and Eve into everlasting life, as the representatives of a once fallen, but now liberated, mankind (cf. Matt. 27,52–53). See St. Thomas Aquinas, *Sum. Theol.*, IIIa, q.52.

DETERMINISM The teaching that denies man's freedom by claiming to explain everything in the universe through a chain of necessary causalities, leaving no room for the existence of human freedom, and even less for its intervention in the course of events. Certain determinist systems do admit freedom in God, but deny it in creatures (theological determinism). Others, while they admit God's existence, deny that he is free (metaphysical determinism). This was the view of the Stoics of antiquity and, in Renaissance times, the optimism of Leibnitz (which supposes that God must always choose the best possible alternative). However, most modern theories of determinism (physical, biological and psychological) simply reject the idea of God and see the world as an enclosed system in which everything is explained by the necessary interplay of unalterable physical principles. We must single out in this context the limited point of view of modern natural sciences, which strive to explain every phenomenon by constant and necessary laws. It is only a philosophical extrapolation, which, from a principle that is at first simply methodological (its application being limited each time to an order of particular phenomena), creates an *a priori* metaphysics that is extended to all reality, not only to that which is known at present, but to everything that is knowable or even possible. There is no strictly demonstrable transition from one to the other.

Obviously, Christian faith is opposed to any form of absolute determinism, since it would lead to a denial not only of man's freedom, but even the freedom of God. (On man's freedom, see canons 4 and 5 of the sixth session of the Council of Trent; D.B. 814 and 815. On divine freedom, see St. Thomas Aquinas, *Sum. Theol.*, Ia, q. 19 ff., and q.45.)

DEUTEROCANONICAL The term applied in present-day Catholic usage to the books of the biblical canon, or parts of books, which are only found in the Septuagint Bible (*see* CANON).

DEVELOPMENT There are two distinct but related developments in the Church, that of her institutions and that of doctrinal formulas. Even though the full extent of the development of the Church's institutions has not always been universally appreciated, it has never been the cause of serious difficulty because it is quite evident that no society could expand from a small group to worldwide proportions without its organization evolving to some extent. However, for a long time, and especially since the controversy with the Protestants, who accused the Catholic Church of deviating from the practices of the primitive Church, any idea of a genuine dogmatic development or even a simple doctrinal development in its most general form was viewed with a certain suspicion.

Newman's *Essay on the Development of Doctrine*, after meeting with a great deal of resistance, succeeded in being accepted once it was realized that it provided for the defense of dogmas only defined at the end of the 19th century (Immaculate Conception and pontifical infallibility). In the meantime, a new reaction brought about by the unbridled evolutionism of the modernists made itself felt. It has not always been kept in mind, however, either in mistaking Newman for one of the modernists, or in praising him, that the purpose of his essay was not to set down or to glorify the idea of development as such, but rather to bring to light the singular characteristics of the development of Catholic dogma.

Catholic dogma is developed organically in such a way that the same truth, far from being in any way altered by new definitions, remains the same, despite the changed circumstances and, more particularly, despite the appearance of questions that had not previously been asked.

Theologians today tend to go beyond those positions that hold that developments can only be made from the implicit to the explicit, and in no other way; i.e., only logically deduced *conclusions* (*see* THEOLOGICAL CONCLUSIONS) can become canon law, and all conclusions can come to definition. Instead, they acknowledge that only the Church, under the guidance of the Holy Spirit, can decide upon newly defined truths that are implied by those that have already been defined. In this connection, pure logic is only one of the decisive arguments, and not necessarily the chief one. We must add that merely multiplying dogmatic formulas does not necessarily imply progress. The Church Fathers, particularly St. Athanasius and the Cappadocians, emphasized that multiplying may become necessary because of the obligation to dispel the disastrous subtleties of the heretics, while at the same time there is the risk of obscuring the simplicity and the fullness of Christian faith that is present with incomparable purity in the teachings of Christ and the apostles. (See J. H. Walgrave, *Newman, le développement du dogme*, Tournai-Paris, 1957.)

DEVIL   Devils, or evil spirits, is the name given to the fallen angels. (For their general characteristics, *see* ANGELS.) When the word devil is used without further qualification, it usually designates their prince, Satan. It is essential to Christian belief that the evil angels were originally created in a state of goodness by God, and only became as they are now through a fall, the sole cause of which was the revolt of their will against God's. This was defined in the Fourth Lateran Council against the Manichaeans (D.B. 428). The book of Wisdom (1,24) tells us that death came into the world through the envy of the devil. The third chapter of Genesis shows us the snake, representing the devil, as the instigator of man's fall.

The Epistle to the Hebrews says that Satan had the power of death (2,14), from which Christ freed us by taking on our mortal flesh in order to achieve atonement for our sins. In a general way, the Bible assumes that idolatry is in fact devil worship (see the texts cited under the article ANGELS), and connects it with the devil's domination over the world, which Christ came to bring to an end. For this reason, Satan is called the ruler of this world, or more precisely, of this age, i.e., of the present dispensation (John 12,31; cf. 1 Cor. 2,6 and 8, and Eph. 2,2), or even the "god" of this age (2 Cor. 4,4). The Church Fathers generally interpret this as a fundamental domination of the evil angels over the material world, which, because of their fall and man's involvement with it, has degenerated into tyranny. Indeed, in the opinion of modern exegetes, it seems that this was the thought of St. Paul.

In opposition to the followers of Origen, the so-called *endemousa* Council of Constantinople, ratified by Pope Vigilius, defined devils as definitively damned (B.D. 211). Theologians explained this by saying that the angels' purely spiritual nature endows them with such lucidity that the first commitment of their will to evil is in itself definitive. It seemed to them that this single offense, which had such fatal consequences, could be nothing other than a sin of pride (i.e., the refusal to yield to God). Manifested chiefly through man's sins and death, the power of the devils in this world, as can be seen from the Gospels, seems to appear in a still more immediately visible way in diabolical *obsessions* or *possessions* (*see* POSSESSION). For further discussion, see St. Thomas Aquinas, *Sum. Theol.*, Ia, q.63–64, 109 and 114, as well as his *De Malo*.

DEVOTION   Substantial devotion is the act of the will whereby it gives itself fervently to the service of God. Accidental devotion is distinguished from it insofar as it is a joy of the intelligence and the will, brought about by the consideration of the divine perfection, and which does or does not affect the senses (cf. St. Thomas Aquinas, *Sum. Theol.*, IIa-IIae, q.82).

Any habitual practice of religious acts, characterized by a special object, or even the attachment to this practice, is called a particular devotion. We must distinguish in this regard the great devotions encouraged by the Church (devotion to the Blessed Sacrament, to the

Sacred Heart or to the Blessed Virgin, etc.) and the special forms that they have assumed in certain environments and at certain periods. Even when these forms are duly authorized, if only by custom, it is advisable not to give them an exaggerated importance that would put them on a plane with the most essential practices. On the other hand, the fact that one might not feel any attraction for a particular devotion authorized by the Church should not allow us to dissuade anyone who might be helped toward true piety from practising such devotion. In this regard, it is advisable to recall the very wise rules set down by the Council of Trent in its session XXV (D.B. 984 ff).

DIOCESE This word was first used for the administrative divisions of the Roman Empire, and around the 4th century began to be applied in the Church in Africa to a particular territory over which the local jurisdiction of a bishop was exercised. Until that time, the reference had been confined to local *churches* (q.v.). However, for a long time, the words parish and diocese were synonymous, and since the whole territory in which a bishop had jurisdiction continued to be called a parish, it happened that the word diocese was used where parish should have been used. The Eastern Church still prefers the word eparchy to diocese.

It is generally acknowledged that, although the pope is unable to dispense with the collegiate episcopate, since it is constituted by divine right, this is not the case with the form of their association. Therefore, since the territorial divisions between bishops did not exist from the beginning, they can be modified by the supreme authority. Today, in fact, canon law, in codifying a clause that was found in a decretal of Urban II in the 11th century, reserves to the Holy See all erections, modifications, divisions, unions and eventual suppressions of dioceses (can. 215).

DISPENSATION An act by which the competent authority suspends the obligation derived from a law in a particular case (can. 80). A dispensation must not be confused with *epikia* (q.v.), in which there is no intervention by a superior, or with the *abrogation* (q.v.) of a law. Whoever is competent to make a law may also allow dispensation from it, and this power can be delegated. It is accepted that neither the natural law nor the divine positive law can be the object of a dispensation.

DIVINATION A practice that seeks to uncover hidden knowledge, and, more particularly, to foretell future events. Since these practices are ordinarily not only tainted with delusion, but are connected with idolatry or devil-worship (i.e., magic), they were condemned in Deuteronomy (18,10–11). The early Councils renewed these condemnations for the same reasons.

DIVINE ASSISTANCE   This term was used especially during the celebrated controversies *Congregatio de Auxiliis* between the Jesuits and the Dominicans in the 16th century, with reference to the terms *grace* and *freedom*, to designate the supernatural help God gives to fallen nature. More generally, in a view of the Augustinians, it referred to the divine intervention that is implied in every act of knowledge (*see* ILLUMINATION) or of the will.

DIVINE ATTRIBUTES   These are the perfections of God, common to the three Persons, which, following what our reason tells us about him, flow necessarily from his essence. A distinction is made between *positive* and *negative* approaches to the divine attributes. The former, such as omnipotence, truth, goodness, intelligence, will, etc., are applied to God from what we know about his creation, except that all imperfection is removed. This is called the *via affirmationis*. On the other hand, by the negative approach we arrive at a knowledge of God by denying of him the imperfections or limits of created things, as when we say that God is uncreated, independent, necessary, simple, infinite, immovable, eternal, incomprehensible, ineffable, etc. This is the *via negationis*. There is a third way that is termed the *via eminentiae*, through which we recognize that God surpasses all that we can say about him. By definition, that last way defies any possibility of being formulated into proper attributes. The main question posed by the divine attributes is the relation they have to his essence. St. Thomas Aquinas, following the Greek Fathers, holds that it is only by a rational distinction, with a foundation in objective reality (*cum fundamento in re*), that they can be said to be distinct from God's essence (*Sum. Theol.*, Ia. q.13, a.12; *C.G.*, lib. I,c.35; *In IV Sent.*, lib. I, dist.2, q.1, a.3).

DIVINE CONCURSUS   See GRACE, and PROVIDENCE

DIVINE GOVERNANCE   See PROVIDENCE

DIVINE MONARCHY   By this is understood the basic principle of all Trinitarian theology, according to which not only do the three Persons have but one unique concrete substance, but they have only one principle, in the Person of the Father.

DIVINE PLAN   See PLAN

DIVINE PROCESSIONS   The divine processions refer 1) to the procession of the Son from the Father in the bosom of the life of the Trinity, and 2) the procession of the Holy Spirit from the Father in the

Son, or through the Son (expressions acceptable to both Latins and Greeks), or, as expressed in the *filioque* clause: from the Father and the Son. The *filioque* clause was accepted into the Creed by the West in the 11th century and became the cause of many controversies with the East. The *filioque* had first been introduced in Spain in the 6th century, even though the formula could already be found in certain Greek Fathers, such as St. Gregory of Nyssa. Primitive theology generally considered that the procession of the Spirit belonged to an indefinable mode because it had no analogy on the plane of creation, unlike the generation of the Son. St. Augustine, in the final pages of his *De Trinitate*, proposed a psychological analogy that would apply to both processions: the Son as the Word, proceeding by the mode of intelligence, and the Spirit as the spirit of love (cf. Rom. 5,5), proceeding by the mode of will. Accepted by all medieval Latin writers, this explanation has met with some favor in the East despite the *filioque* controversy. See St. Thomas Aquinas, *Sum. Theol.*, Ia, q.27 ff.; and also the articles MISSION, and TRINITY.

DIVORCE   On the basis of St. Matthew (19,9), the Church has with increasing forcefulness rejected any acceptance of divorce, i.e., the breaking of a valid marriage, except by the death of one of the parties.

The following are the only recognized exceptions to the indissolubility of marriage: 1) a marriage that has not been consummated, though a valid sacramental contract, may be dissolved by dispensation of the Holy See for some grave reason, such as impotence, or when one of the parties makes a solemn religious profession (or, prepares to take holy orders); 2) marriage between unbaptized persons, one of whom has become a convert, while the other refuses to join the Church or to live peacefully without offending God—this is called the Pauline privilege (1 Cor. 7,12–15); 3) marriage between unbaptized persons in which one becomes a convert and for the good of the faith it is deemed desirable to dissolve the marriage, even though the letter of the Pauline privilege does not apply (can. 1125).

DOCETISM   *See* INCARNATION

DOCTOR   From the Latin *docere*, this term refers to a person whose aptitude in teaching has been officially recognized. In St. Paul there are three lists of ecclesiastical offices in which the word doctor (*didaskalos*) is found (Rom. 12,7–8; 1 Cor. 12,28–29; and Eph. 4,11). Later, it was acknowledged that bishops are the doctors par excellence of the Church, although they may also seek the assistance of priests or even laymen who are endowed with sufficient knowledge. Among the saints, the Church therefore recognizes as doctors not only bishops but also eminent theologians who were not bishops. She also bestows the title of doctor on those theologians who were examined and who have taken the oath for that purpose.

DOCTRINAL CENSURE   A doctrinal judgment passed by the Church and implying at least some reproach. It may involve a simple proposition, a doctrine, a book or an article. We must know who the authority was that passed the judgment, how far it wished to go in the condemnation, and also the precise character of the condemnation in a case in which the censure is formal, i.e., constituting a real juridical decision or sentence, rather than a simple warning.

The censures passed by competent theologians, by whatever authority their knowledge gives them, are never of themselves vested with the public authority of the Church. This would still be true even if the theologian in question were a bishop or a pope.

Furthermore, there are all sorts of degrees between a condemnation formally declared in solemn terms by a pope or an ecumenical council involving the Church's infallibility and those declared by a Roman congregation after having obtained the pope's approbation *in forma communi*, or those which a local council or one isolated bishop might more or less solemnly declare. In the same way we must discern whether the censure is really dogmatic, i.e., bearing directly on that truth that is the object of the dispute; or whether it is merely disciplinary— prescribing what is fit to be taught or not fit to be taught at the time, without claiming to settle the dispute directly and definitively. We must also discern whether the censure is simply a matter of practical consideration, with the exclusive aim of reconciliation, or of other prudent considerations such as when the authority simply forbids the outward profession of an opinion or effectively prohibits the censuring of another.

As for the technical terms given to formally condemned propositions, at least three categories must be mentioned. They may censure an opinion because (1) by its very nature it is either heretical, proximate to heresy, suspect of heresy (or even seeming to be heretical), simply erroneous or rash; or, because (2) its formulation is equivocal, ambiguous, ill-sounding, offensive to the ears of the devout; or, finally (3) simply because adverse effects may arise from it: derision of religion, opposition to Church discipline, tendency toward schisms, subversion, sedition, or dangerous to good morals, etc.

It is apparent that every condemnation set down by the Church obliges, and obliges in conscience, but only to the extent and the manner corresponding to the particular censure. It is superfluous to add that no private person should take it upon himself to impose a censure beyond the degree of authority the Church herself intended to give it. An authority of lesser rank connot act in this way, in opposition to a higher authority, without committing a grave offense thereby rendering the censure illegal.

DOGMA The Greek word *dogma*, after having acquired the meaning of a juridical decision, came to denote the opinions of different thinkers, while still retaining a degree of authority. Today, the word refers to the truths defined by the extraordinary *magisterium* of the Church (i.e., the pope or an ecumenical council) as belonging to the faith of the Church. It must be remembered that even statements of authority if they do not refer to the content of the divine Word are not dogmas. On the other hand, the term dogma can be extended to include the truths contained in the Word of God as expounded by the ordinary *magisterium* of the Church, even though these truths have never been the object of a conciliar or papal definition.

It may be well to point out that even in the late Middle Ages theologians used the expression *article of faith* (q.v.) in preference to the word dogma, which is not found at all in St. Bonaventure. The term dogma was later used for both the content of heretical beliefs and the articles of Catholic faith. Since the Trent and Vatican councils, the sense which we have given it has become the rule.

The problem of the value of dogma as a statement of supernatural truth has been treated in the article ANALOGY. Let us be content here with saying that Christian truth is a truth that is very much a living unity of the mystery of Christ and a truth of unfathomable richness. The medium of communication of this truth to man being the Word of God, it finds its purest expression only in Holy Scripture, since God alone is its author, something that cannot be said of even the most solemn dogmatic formulas. But Holy Scripture itself can only be fully understood in the light of the living awareness of the Divine Word as a unity and a totality possessed by the Church. This awareness takes form through meditation on Scripture within the whole context of tradition, and is a gift that is constantly kept alive by the Holy Spirit. It is both as a statement of this supernatural awareness and as the means necessary for upholding it and disseminating it to the world in a meaningful fashion, that dogmas are both justified and required in proportion to the changing conditions under which the Church must uphold the unique truth that has been entrusted to her (*see* DEVELOPMENT).

DOGMATIC From the earliest days, this word has referred to intellectual activity and its results in reference to dogma. In the 17th century, it was used more particularly with regard to the central core of theology, in order to distinguish it from its subsidiary parts such as

positive theology, which aims at collecting and interpreting the documents of tradition without proposing a systematized explanation of
them.

DOUBT   The mind's state of uncertainty before making an assertion
of any sort. To counteract the semirationalism of the theologian Hermes,
the First Vatican Council defined that those who received faith through
the Church's teaching can never have a just cause for doubting it (Sess.
III, Const. *De fide catholica*, chap. 3, and can. 6; D.B. 1794 and 1815).
This does not mean that we cannot experience, without moral fault, the
forcefulness of certain difficulties, but that we must never find in these
difficulties an objectively sufficient reason for questioning our faith in
revelation as it has been proposed to us by the Church.

DUALISM   This term is used in reference to systems, like the Gnostic
heresies (*see* GNOSTICISM), which explain the world by two principles,
one good and the other evil, that are coeternal and independent.
Manichaeism (q.v.) is the strictest form of dualism. The roots of these
systems can be found in the opposition between light and darkness that
characterized the ancient religion of the Persians (Mazdaism). The
Bible rejects any dualism of this type.

DULIA   A Greek word, meaning "service," which denotes the character proper to the veneration given to the saints or to images and relics, in
contrast to the worship of *latria* ("adoration"), which is given to God
alone. *See* ADORATION.

EAST AND WEST Our intention is to discuss only the most obvious differences between the East and the West from purely theological and philosophical points of view. Our prime consideration here is the distinction commonly made between the Christian East and the Christian West; however, in this respect, certain observations should be helpful that deal with the more general differences between Western thought (understood as all forms of thought that have a common origin in the Mediterranean world), and the thought patterns originating in the great civilizations of the Far East, particularly India and China.

Regarding our primary interest, Christianity, we must be aware of the danger of oversimplification that tends to consider something to be typical of either the East or the West, or that singles out certain peculiarities as representative when actually they are merely anomalies. For example, it has been stated repeatedly that the spirit of Eastern theology is impregnated with Platonism, while Western theology is Aristotelian; that the East is mystical and the West, juridical. Such thinking totally disregards the fact that the classical theology of Byzantium always eyed Platonic thought with suspicion—a suspicion that grew throughout the Middle Ages. At the same time, Platonism has never ceased to have enthusiasts in the West, e.g., no school of religious thought is to be found in the East as deeply Platonic in inspiration as Rhenish mysticism. By the same token, the juridicism of Western canonists is inherited from the juridicism of Byzantium. Likewise, in its centralizing tendencies with regard to Rome, the West found little to envy in the autonomous character of the great Eastern patriarchates: the "New Rome" of Constantinople and, later, the "Third Rome" of Moscow. We must be especially wary of certain hasty and artificial syntheses of Eastern Christian thought that have been made recently, where it has become absorbed in a brilliant but special school, like that of the Slavophile movement in 19th-century Russia, and then contrasted with what are purely decadent forms of thought in the Latin West of the same period. Such syntheses run the risk of confronting the thought of men who at times are deep thinkers (although they remain primarily poets and enthusiasts) with nothing but an artificial conglomerate of everything that could have been said or written from the opposite side . . . by ignoramuses or half-wits.

We must begin by recalling that Christianity is Eastern in origin in the sense that it was presented in primitive forms of Semitic thought that became progressively Hellenized, although in turn this Hellenism in being Christianized underwent a complete transformation. The Greek Fathers, the majority of whom were actually Hellenized Semites, Egyptians, Syrians, or Asiatics, are not a parallel and independent source of Eastern Christianity, as compared to the Latin Fathers, who could be looked upon as the source of Western Christianity. The Latin Fathers (their most outstanding representatives being either Latin-speaking Africans like Tertullian, St. Cyprian and St. Augustine, or merely deeply orientalized Levantines like St. Jerome) are above all heirs of the greatest Greek Fathers, and the originality of their own development of Greek thought is hardly more appreciable than that manifested in turn either by those who wrote in Syriac from the 5th century on or by the Byzantines themselves in relation to the same sources. Again we must add that the great minds of both traditions, even for many years after the split of 1054 that, in principle at least, made the mutual alienation of Eastern and Western Christianity definitive, still remained open to the foremost thought, new or old, of each tradition. Even though St. Thomas Aquinas did write the treatise *Against the Errors of the Greeks*, and then produced the work that has undoubtedly become the most representative of Western theology, he also showed an inexhaustible curiosity and sympathy for Eastern theological tradition. Two centuries later, George Scholarios, the most powerful of the Byzantine theologians at the end of the Middle Ages, and for his part the most steadfast in opposition to what he looked upon as the errors of the Latins, was nevertheless an eminent expert in Thomistic thought as well as its convinced propagator in the East.

It is only after we have made these preliminary reservations that we can attempt, with circumspection, to describe what is original to Eastern and Western theological traditions.

The modern Western idea that the East had ceased to develop after the age of the great ecumenical councils of antiquity never had any basis in fact. Actually, the East's development over the course of the Middle Ages by no means weakened the triple biblical, liturgical and monastic stamp that had marked Christian thought and all of Christianity in the East as in the West in the period of the Church Fathers. On the other hand, the East never experienced the pessimism with regard to human nature and the world in general that was a result of African influence in the West; namely, Tertullian, and certain aspects of the anti-Pelagian thought of St. Augustine, in which we may discern certain survivals or resurgences of his early Manichaean and Neo-Platonist formation. By the same token, it did not experience the reaction against this tendency that began in the 13th century in the West and that became sharply accentuated with the Renaissance and modern secularism. Such a clear distinction as that made by Thomistic thought in the West between the possibilities of human nature as such (putting aside the fall and its consequences) and the perspectives that became open to it through its being freely called to the supernatural life, never became common in the East as it did in our own countries. Consequently, the idea of a proper stability of the human and cosmic order, subordinated to the supernatural order but not confused with it, was not implanted there. The East's Christian view of the world has remained in general more narrowly or immediately sacral and theocentric. A typical example of this is that in Eastern monasticism, although it did in fact fulfill all of the functions that have become specifically associated in the West with those religious who are called to the active apostolate, these activities never overcame their autonomy with regard to the chiefly contemplative ideal of ancient monasticism; nor, consequently, was monastic life divided in the East into a contemplative life turned completely away from the world, and a "religious" life that became more and more absorbed in it.

Furthermore, in the East, the fact of religious autonomy of the local churches and the principle of that autonomy caused an interreaction that resulted in an increasing development of that autonomy, at least on the national level, while in the West the ecclesiastical centralization around Rome continued to be accentuated both in fact and in theory.

And so the East is more inclined toward a detachment with regard to the present world and its Christianization, while the West tends toward a secularization of the ecclesiastical institutions themselves. The East's tendency is to ecclesiastical anarchy, together with a close and potentially dangerous connection between faithfulness to orthodoxy and a nationalism that is much more impregnated with Christianity than it is in the West, where it was non-religious from the beginning. On the other hand, the tendency of the West is to an exaggerated consolidation of authority, and even of every initiative in the hands of a religious authority whose finally triumphant assertion is coupled with its power, at least in its exercise, taking on a shape similar to that of the temporal powers.

This amounts to saying that the only real conflict between the Christian East and the Christian West is to be found in their congenital weaknesses and, consequently, in a certain narrowness of thought. Finally, they manifest, although by opposite paths, the same deficiency: either a Christianity of too spiritual an orientation that, under a veil of idealism, does nothing to raise concrete existence above the level of unregenerated nature—or a Christianity that is too much concerned with its immediate effectiveness, but that lets its missionary spirit degenerate into secularization. More precisely, we may say that there is either the illusion of an apostolate that believes that "heaven on earth" is too easily attained, or else an apostolate whose overly emphatic realism runs the risk in the long run of being confused with apostasy.

Nothing could spur us on more effectively to shun all attempts at an *a posteriori* systematization and justification of a Christian East or West artificially confined within their exclusive particularity: we may even say that to the extent that the two traditions cease their search for mutual encounter and reconciliation, they are indeed well on their way toward a unity in a common denial of each other's Christian authenticity.

If at this point we come to the distinction between the forms of thought that have emerged from a combination of Romanized Hellenism and biblical Christianity on the one hand, and those of the Far East on the other, we have to begin by taking note of the duality, indeed the undoubtedly irreducible multiplicity, of the latter. Essentially, we must make a distinction here between those forms of thought that come from India and those that have developed in China. Hinduism has known multiple philosophies that have one thing in common, namely, that against appearances, against the world of the *maya* in a state of perpetual becoming, they set a supreme reality in which all differences vanish. Yet they differ profoundly on their notions of this. This is so true that it is not easy to say whether primitive Buddhism, since it originated in Hinduism, is merely a refined form of this basic Hindu duality, or whether on the contrary it has actually broken through the maze of this teeming and confused mental universe to something beyond. In other words, is the *nirvana*, the emancipation for which the Buddhist longs, the pure nothingness judged preferable to every being, or is it rather (as the Christian philosopher Solovyev understood it) an heroic attempt to escape to a transcendence that until then was unknown to the traditional thought of India? No Indian specialist today would be rash enough to take a decisive stand for one or the other of these possible answers. All that we may state positively is that these various systems of thought that have come from India, whether or not they are judged to be orthodox, appear equally opposed to the activism of the modern West, but hardly less to the ideal of a cosmos transfigured by the divine Spirit that is presented by the most contemplative line of Christianity under the form that we consider Eastern.

As diverse as they are among themselves, the basic trends of Chinese thought are quite different from the Indian pattern. Taoism appears to represent a very particular sort of pantheism, in which dualist and monist tendencies are found paradoxically reconciled in a kind of cosmic vitalism and naturistic mysticism. On the other hand, Confucianism is essentially a rationalistic and social humanism, which has nonetheless been able to develop an ethic of personal relations that surpasses the greatest advances made prior to Christianity by the post-Socratic ethic.

Chinese Buddhism in turn has made a synthesis of these two diverse trends of the oldest Chinese civilization, while it has retained little more of Indian Buddhism than its asceticism of universal detachment and its ethic of pity. Above all, it is perhaps the best tradition of Sung art that reveals the astonishing possibilities of a religious contemplation of the world. They enrich the at once realistic and refined humanism already possessed by the Chinese soul. Under foreign influence, China was to modify its primitive sense to the point of making it unrecognizable. Here we certainly find ourselves confronted with a richness of thought and human experience that, however far they may also be from the various conclusions of thought and experience in the Christianized Greco-Latin world, seem much more in harmony with it than any of the Indian forms of thought. They seem particularly able to lend themselves to new expressions of the essentially positive attitude that is inherent in Christianity, both with regard to creation and concrete humanity—and much more easily than the religious philosophy of India. Although Indian thought seems no less capable of prodigiously enriching our metaphysics through the immense variety of its ontological meditations, it does not seem that it can ever be Christianized as long as it remains limited by its scorn for history and for the individual.

EASTER   *See* PASCH

ECCLESIASTICAL   This term is used for everything that formally pertains to the Church. An attempt has recently been made to introduce the neologism "ecclesial" in opposition to it, in order to designate that which pertains to the Church as a supernatural mystery. But it is to be feared that this would only favor the false notion, of Protestant origin, that places the invisible Church of the Spirit in opposition to the institutional Church. In reality, the visible Church *is* the Church of the Spirit despite her human weaknesses, and although she must constantly be revitalized by a spirit of reform and renewal, realizing more fully in her phenomenal reality what she could not for one instant cease to be in her essence.

ECSTASY   From the Greek word *ekstasis*, meaning a coming out of self, this word has come to designate in Christian spirituality an experience that transports the believer in God with such psychological violence that he momentarily loses the use of his senses, namely, all consciousness of external reality or of himself. The doctors of the mystical life, like St. John of the Cross, have insisted that the psychological phenomenon of ecstasy is in fact nothing more than a transitory maladjustment of our psyche to unaccustomed spiritual experiences.

According to them, ecstasy should normally disappear once the spiritual life reaches a higher plane. It may be well to add that the most ancient Christian authors who speak of ecstasy understand it not as a particular psychological phenomenon, but as the deepest aspect of the life of grace in us, according to which something St. Paul said is made a reality: "It is no longer I who live, but Christ who lives in me." (Gal. 2,20.) This seems particularly to be the case with St. Gregory of Nyssa.

ECUMENISM   Over the course of the last two generations we have given this name to every effort that has successively developed in the different Christian sects toward the reconciliation of divided Christendom. Beginning among Protestants and Anglicans, the ecumenical movement has shown from the outset a certain duality of orientation. With the first Life and Work Conference that met in Stockholm in 1925 under the influence of the Swedish Lutheran Archbishop Söderblom, it seemed that it would follow not only a pragmatist but a deliberately anti-dogmatic tendency, as if unity could be achieved by putting aside doctrinal and ecclesiological problems in the name of an opinion inspired by liberal Protestantism, and concentrating exclusively on a common endeavor at social Christianity. Nevertheless, when the first Faith and Order Conference met at Lausanne in 1927, under the particular inspiration of the American Episcopalian Bishop Brent, even though it brought together most of the participants of the former conference, it dealt on the contrary directly with problems of doctrine, sacramental practice and Church structure. In 1937 the two movements had two general conferences, the first at Oxford and the second at Edinburgh. After the Second World War, they met conjointly at Amsterdam in 1948 and founded the World Council of Churches, which had been anticipated since 1938 and outlined in provisional form in 1946.

From the beginning the participants in these meetings, along with most of the Protestant Churches and the entire Anglican communion, included representatives of the Orthodox Churches, with the exception of the Church in Russia. However, she too has recently become a member.

The Catholic Church, although sounded out at the start, has never been represented other than by observers, especially at the New Delhi conference in 1961. From Pope Pius XI's encyclical *Mortalium animos* in 1927, it was concluded by some that the Church condemned the movement, without reservation. Actually, what the Pope wished to denounce was its misinterpretation of unity as a purely social action, which would put doctrinal or ecclesiastical questions in the background and actually deliberately discard them, as Söderblom seemed to do in his inaugural address in Stockholm in 1925. The Pope also wished to state precisely, from the beginning of this or any other movement for Christian reunion, that for Catholics there can be no question of constructing or rebuilding a unique Christian Church, since it already exists in the traditional Catholic Church and cannot cease to exist. It should be observed that the Orthodox East, and even those who from the outset took part in the meetings of the ecumenical movement, had held from the very beginning an exactly analogous position and warned that they would agree to be present at the sessions only to bear witness to their own faith and not to enter into any discussions on any possible compromise in this area, or with reference to the profound nature of the Church. Moreover, Pius XI was far from being disinterested in the problem of bringing separated Christians together. He was to demonstrate this particularly in his forceful encouragement of the efforts made by Catholics, such as the Benedictine Dom Lambert Beauduin, to not only keep pace with Protestant, Anglican and Orthodox inquiries and exchanges in this direction, but to actively promote studies and prayers in the Catholic Church with an aim to restoring unity to divided Christendom. Consequently, under the inspiration of the Abbé Couturier at Lyons; the Dominican house of studies, Istina, which began at Lille and was then developed in Paris; the monastery founded by Dom Lambert Beauduin at Amay in Belgium and later transferred to Chevetogne (widely known for its periodical, *Irénikon*); as well as many other individual and collective endeavors, a Catholic ecumenism took shape on its own. It was independent of the ecumenism of Protestant and Anglican inspiration, but in close contact with it. From this preparatory stage meetings gradually took place, followed by a Catholic Conference on Ecumenical Questions, which was private in character but given formal authorization by the Holy See; finally, the Secretariat for Christian Unity was created officially by Pope John XXIII with the German Cardinal Augustin Bea, S.J., at its head, assisted by Msgr. Willebrands the Dutch prelate and theologian who had previously been the founder of the Catholic Conference.

This quite sketchy account brings to light a fact that at first sight is quite disconcerting, namely, in the beginning the ecumenical movement in the non-Catholic world took the form of more or less official organizations, while in Catholicism it was at first the product of the initiative of a few individuals. Actually, outside of the center of Catholicism, ecumenism has always gone far beyond the organizations themselves, and even today they are far from being all-inclusive.

It is necessary to recall these elementary concepts so that we may be able to answer the question which alone interests us here: What can the theological principles of a Catholic ecumenism be? Its first principle ought to be that the Catholic Church is not one Church among others that can, with respect to the unity that is to be recreated among Christians, lend herself to substantial modifications. On the contrary, we must believe that she is the Church willed and created by Christ, and that only in her heart can today's dismembered Christianity again find the unity that this Church would be incapable of losing. However, this does not mean that in order to accomplish this unity, all Catholics need do is wait for and encourage the dissidents to return to and assume their position in a Church in which nothing would therefore be modified. Indeed, the Catholic truth and unity of the Church are a divine gift to her, which men who make up her membership must work unceasingly to put into a better light and to make more evident in her daily life. Truth and unity are not to be kept as a static gift, but as that talent about which the Gospel parable speaks. The task of the men to whom it was entrusted is to make it bear fruit through their efforts. Undoubtedly the promise of the *assistance of the Holy Spirit* (q.v.) that the Lord has given his Church will keep her from ever altering the Christian faith of which she is the agent. In the apostolic hierarchy and the sacramental celebration of the Christian mystery that is entrusted to it, the Word made flesh remains forever present among His people, along with his unfailing power of sanctifying mankind. But the Church, in her most exalted as well as in her most lowly members, does not remain less human because of our fallen humanity, which is in the process of recovery. It follows that the assurance she has of never losing for herself, or for the world, either the faith or the spiritual realities which are its object, does not prevent her from being in perpetual need of reforming herself in everything that depends upon the actual faithfulness of men to respond to these gifts of grace.

When heresies and schisms are produced, they are not only caused by the error and the obstinacy of schismatics and heretics, but also by the inadequacies of the faithful members of the Church themselves, by the scandal that their inconsistency can cause, or quite simply by their laziness in fulfilling their responsibilities. Schismatics and heretics often begin as Catholic Christians who are particularly sensitive to some essential aspects of the truth or of the Christian life, which the masses of the faithful or responsible authority itself have dangerously allowed to run to seed. Too exclusive an attachment to what they themselves have rediscovered will result in a separation more or less tinged with error, which sufficiently clear-headed reformers and certainly those of deep personal holiness would have been able to avoid. But, even in this case, the duty of faithful Christians, and especially responsible churchmen, should not be limited to negative condemnations, even when they are proven to be really unavoidable. In a manner faithful to the fullness of authentic tradition, they should be accompanied by an effort to restore those elements of the truth which the dissenters have unfortunately come to detach from that tradition in order to oppose it, which, in the end, will eventually defeat their purpose. Truth, like goodness, is a fullness and therefore a living orthodoxy could never be limited to opposing one denial with another.

Do we not observe, as is the case in the Church of the East and to a lesser degree in Protestantism, groups of Christians separated from Catholic unity who nevertheless have not only *not* declined and rapidly disappeared but actually, over the generations, been able to retain in their membership something of an authentic Christian faith and life, even to communicating this to others? There is at least a probability then that those Christians who in principle have remained faithful to the Catholic faith have still not made the necessary effort to emphasize to the required extent certain aspects of this faith or its vital consequences, to which the dissenters had been sensitive and to which their descendents (their converts) remain specifically attached.

The fundamental endeavor of Catholic ecumenism should therefore be: 1) to take cognizance of these just *desiderata*; 2) to distinguish them carefully from the erroneous conclusions the dissenters have come to draw from them; and, 3) with the help of such an analysis, to supply the Church herself with a positive response, in conformity with all the requirements of the true faith. This task supposes an effort among competent Catholics to be informed, and to manifest a critical sympathy with humility in charity, which requires not that they become less Catholic but much more Catholic than they are at present; not only in principle, but in practice. In this way, they will prepare the way for all Christian souls of good faith, remaining outside Catholic unity, to not only be able to recognize and accept this unity without having to deny anything to which they are rightfully attached, but also to discover in it the only complete and lasting fulfillment of their desires, in the fullness of that unique body into which Christ wishes to gather all of his people. This explains the importance for Catholic ecumenism, of movements like the biblical movement or the liturgical movement, or of a renovation both of the doctrine and the reality of the episcopacy, and of the effective role of the layman in Church life. Such renewals, since they make the Church in her concrete life more consonant with her essential and permanent reality, multiply and deepen the possible effectiveness of her direct efforts to reconcile separated Christians, which could not otherwise lead to anything substantial or lasting.

ELECTION   From the Greek *eklegein*, meaning "to choose," this word in biblical and theological language ordinarily means the choice that God makes of his people. In the Bible this concept is strictly connected with the idea of the *covenant* (q.v.). While the divine covenants known among other Semitic peoples suppose a reciprocal choice of the people by their God, and of the God by his people (this second aspect easily predominating), the prophets insist upon the fact that it is God alone, freely and sovereignly, who has chosen his people. There is no other reason for this than the mystery of his wholly gratuitous love (Deut. 4,37; cf. Isa. 41,8 ff.). It is the same idea that is found again in the New Testament when Jesus said to those about him: "You did not choose me, but I chose you. . . ." (John 15,16).

It is in reference to this election of the people, and because of it, that the idea of an election proper to certain individuals was introduced: Abraham, the father of the people (Neh. 9,7) is the preeminent example. But the notion may be extended to include certain personalities who do not belong to the chosen people, but who have a providential role to fulfill in their regard, as in the case of Cyrus (Isa. 45, esp. 4). In the New Testament the same is true; the apostles were the first to be chosen (Luke 6,13; cf. Acts 1,2 & 9,15). But this election also separates that part of Israel that has faith in the Gospel (Rom. 11,7), and all believers whatever their origin (cf. Rom. 8,33; Col. 3,12; 1 Pet. 1,1 & 2,9; Apoc. 17,14 with the texts of Matt. 20,16 & 22,14). However, in the New Testament, if the election of individuals comes about through a connection with the Church and their belonging to her, or their ministry within the Church, the Church herself is the "chosen people" depending upon an election that belongs first of all to Christ, the "Chosen One" of God (Luke 23,35). This is probably a vague recollection of the book of Enoch, which under the influence of the Servant songs (Isa. 42,1 and 44,1–2 in particular) had already designated the Son of Man by this term. The only text, on the other hand, in which this word is used with reference to the faithful and their judgment by the Son of Man is in the synoptic apocalypse of Matthew (24,22 ff; and paralleled in Mark 13,20 ff.).

St. Thomas Aquinas makes a distinction (following Eph. 1,4–5) between election, as a primary act of love, and predestination which follows it, as an act of intelligence (*Sum. Theol.* Ia, q.23, a.4). See the article PREDESTINATION for the questions that this distinction raises.

Election is still used in the theological sense to designate the choise made by the will in a human act, enlightened by the practical intelligence, of a particular means to achieve an end (cf. St. Thomas Aquinas, *Sum. Theol.*, Ia-IIae, q.13, a.1.)

Finally it will be noted that election by a vote of the community is used in the Acts of the Apostles with reference to the choice of the Seven (6,5) and that for a long time election in different forms was used for choosing a bishop (popular election under the control of neighboring bishops, later on election by the priests of the city, and then by the cathedral chapter). The present-day form for the election of the pope (by the vote of the cardinals) is the most interesting survival of this ancient practice.

EMINENCE   This term is used in theology to designate the method used in speaking of God: after first attributing to him the perfections that are encountered in creatures, and then denying that they can be applied to him such as they are, we come back to assert them, but in a necessarily mysterious sense. St. Thomas Aquinas describes this as an *analogy* (q.v.) of proportionality.

EMMANUEL   A Hebrew name meaning "God with us," and applied to Christ by Matthew (1,23) in reference to the prophecy of Isaiah (7,14).

ENCYCLICAL   A public letter addressed by a pope or a council to all Christendom. In fact, an encyclical, despite its name (which means "universal"), may be aimed at a very specific audience, e.g., the encyclical of Pius XI, *Mit brennender Sorge*, addressed to German Catholics on the question of Nazism. But even in that case it had a certain universal import. The content of encyclicals as such does not have the guarantee of pontifical infallibility insofar as the pope does not express there the intention of giving a definition, in accordance with the conditions expressed by the First Vatican Council. However, it goes without saying that the universality of these documents as an expression of the ordinary *magisterium* gives them a special degree of authority.

END   That in which a being or its action terminates; therefore its final cause whereby its being is defined, considered under the aspect of tendency (the objective end, prescinding from the fact of whether one is conscious of it or not), or of intention (the subjective end, of which one is conscious). In this context, a further distinction must be made in an action between the end sought by the conscious agent himself (*finis operantis*), and the end intrinsic to the action (*finis operis*).

God could have no other end but himself, all orthodox theologians maintain, but it would be childish to see any egoism in this statement, since he is *pure act*, and therefore pure creative generosity. The love he manifests in his creation is all the more generous because he would lack nothing if he had not created, and creation adds nothing to him, even though it freely demonstrates his sovereign generosity.

As for man, since his ultimate end is that which gives meaning to his whole life, moral law has to be based entirely on an orientation toward this end, which is nothing less than the full realization of man's being. This is tantamount to saying that it is God himself who is the only ultimate end of man, as the fullness of being and the fullness of all things. But for man, to be conscious means to know God and, therefore, to love him above all things. This would be true even if man were not called by God to a supernatural knowledge and love, i.e., to a participation through grace in God's own knowledge and love. From this we can say that man, by virtue of his own nature, is disposed to everything that God will choose to communicate to him of himself; thus the gratuitous call to the supernatural friendship of God, although it infinitely extends the possibilities inherent in human nature, does so consistently with this nature. Grace surpasses nature in such a way that it brings to it an unhoped for fulfillment, but not as though it were imposing some compulsion or deformation upon it. This is what theologians develop from the notions of *image* (q.v.) and *likeness*. The image of God is inscribed in the very nature of man, and constitutes for man the basis for a participated likeness.

This concept of the last and ultimate end surpasses and unifies what are commonly called the last ends: *death, judgment, paradise* and *hell* (qq.v.). *See also* ESCHATOLOGY.

These different concepts permit us to grasp the sense in which St. Thomas sees the cause of causes in the final cause (*De Veritate*, q.28, a.7). It is only in this that we uncover the meaning of each being. See St. Thomas Aquinas, *Sum. Theol.*, Ia, q.6; Ia-IIae, qq.1 to 5, 91 to 94; *Contra Gentiles*, 1, III, cap. 1 to 63; *In I. lib. Ethic.*, lect.1. (*See also* CAUSE, and BEATITUDE).

ENERGY   In Christian antiquity, at the time of the controversies raised by *Monophysitism* (q.v.), this word served to define, in the theological sense, the will in Christ as a concrete action. *Monoenergism* (q.v.) was therefore a mitigated form of *Monothelitism* (q.v.), according to which the faculty of willing, in the humanity of the Saviour, although distinct from his divine will, would nevertheless have received all of its activity from it.

Later, particularly with the Byzantine theologian Gregory Palamas in the 14th century, the divine energies were set apart as divine qualities that were uncreated but at the same time capable of being shared, in contrast to the divine essence, which cannot be shared. Strictly speaking, this distinction risks introducing a real ontological fission into the divinity itself, which is obviously unthinkable. However, in the minds of those who proposed it, it was only a way of expressing the fact that the divine grace effectively makes us sharers in the divine nature (cf. 2 Pet.

1,4), without our thereby becoming God himself (*see* GRACE, and GLORY).

EPIKIA   From the Greek *epieikeia*, meaning "understanding clemency," the word defines the principle, admitted in canon law, according to which a dispensation can be presumed when the authority cannot be reached and there is every reason to believe that the authority would grant such dispensation.

EPIKLESIS   A Greek word meaning "invocation." It is applied to liturgical prayers which beseech God, and more especially the Holy Spirit, to consecrate the eucharistic elements. These prayers were the object of lively controversies between East and West. *See* CANON (*of the Mass*), and CONSECRATION.

EPISCOPACY   The function and dignity of a bishop.

EPISCOPATE   This term designates the body of bishops, or the length of time during which a bishop exercises his office. *See* BISHOP.

EQUIVOCITY OF BEING   The concept according to which the being of God is so absolutely different from that of a creature that nothing of this creature may be truthfully transposed to him. If such a concept is admitted religious agnosticism becomes unavoidable.

ERROR   A false judgment and, by extension, the incorrect assertion it contains. Since the principle of every error is complex, it can happen that we are in no way able to rectify our erroneous judgment, due to circumstances beyond our control. This is what is called *invincible error*, and we have explained the extent to which it may erase our culpability in the actions that stem from it in the articles on CONSCIENCE and GOOD FAITH. We must also mention *common error*, in which the faithful assume that a priest enjoys a power of jurisdiction that he does not in fact have; for example, celebrating marriages or hearing sacramental confessions. Since the time of Innocent III, for the good of souls the Church has decided in these cases to supply the necessary jurisdiction (canon 209).

ESCHATOLOGY   From the Greek *eschatos*, which means "last," this word signifies the knowledge of the ultimate realities, e.g., the divine judgment and the Parousia of Christ. By extension, although not without a certain misuse of language, it is applied today to these last realities themselves.

Eschatology is the object of the Jewish and Christian writings that are called Apocalypses, the most eminent being the New Testament book of this title attributed to St. John. It is common to this type of literature to make use of figurative expressions, and the primary eschatological problem is to know how to fittingly interpret these images. The error of the *Millenarians* (q.v.) of antiquity was to interpret literally; for example, the thousand-year reign of Christ and his people that will precede the final battle, or the more or less symbolic descriptions of the happiness of the elect. Errors of this type are no longer found today except among some of the sects that even Protestants do not regard as really Christian. However, in this context two forms of more subtle errors are currently to be found.

The first uses the term *realized eschatology* to describe itself. By this is meant that since apocalyptic literature in general is dominated by the coming of the awaited Messiah and since this coming has already been realized in the person of Jesus, nothing more is to be found underlying the apocalyptic images than a symbolic description of the spiritual transformation already realized by Christ in the Church. The other error, which is that of certain Protestants generally influenced by the theology of Karl Barth, places the realization of the eschatological promises so completely in the future that it is unwilling to acknowledge any current objective reality of our salvation as an effective sanctification of believers by the divine grace beginning in this life.

It is easy to say that the truth is to be found halfway between these two errors, but much less easy to determine with certainty what has already been accomplished in the eschatological expectation, and what is still to come. However, we can say that during the earthly life of Jesus, in his divine person made flesh in our common humanity, the world to come is found to coexist with the present age. Today in his resurrected and ascended Being, the world to come has, in a sense, absorbed the present age. In the Church which is his body, however, and to which he sent his own Spirit, the world to come is already here under the appearances of the present age, which perdures somewhat in the same way in which it did in himself before his passion. His Parousia will bring us, in turn, to that state into which he has preceded us. Such seems to be the perspective of the New Testament, as present-day exegetes generally agree it should be interpreted. But the reality of the Spirit's presence in us, which in a fashion causes us to anticipate in a special way the eschatological realities, even though it has assuredly unmistakable signs, still remains the ultimate object of faith and, therefore, profoundly mysterious. For even stronger reasons, the same is true in regard to the final revelation of the Kingdom of God. All that we are certain of is that sin and death will be no more. But we do not know when or how that will be realized, and Christ himself has put us on guard against the temptation to look for the obvious answers to these questions, while maintaining the need to live each moment, not only of our own personal history but of that of the whole universe, as if it were to be the last (cf. Matt. 24, 36–50).

We sometimes hear it said, even by Christians, that this conception deprives our present life of its value. This is a completely erroneous view that disregards the Gospel's very explicit assertion that the eternal judgment will be passed on us in accordance with the realization of the divine love which we shall have accomplished in our daily life (cf. the parable of the judgment in Matt. 25,31 ff., in the immediate context of the foregoing passage). We must say, rather, that the perpetually imminent eschatological perspective is that which communicates an incomparable intensity to each moment of the life of the Church and of the Christian, since it must always be lived as if it were not only the last but the decisive moment of our lives.

ESSENCE   A being is specifically what it is because of its essence, its formal element. Nature is the same, viewed in the dynamic aspect, as a principle of action. Any essence that does not contain any intrinsic contradiction is possible. But this logical possibility is not transformed into a real possibility unless a cause exists that is capable of realizing the essence. For all contingent beings (*see* CREATION), effective existence depends, ultimately, on the only necessary Being, God. Contrary to what it is for him, their existence is not identical with their essence. The Thomists maintain that this distinction is not only logical but real, since they particularly rely on the reasoning of St. Thomas Aquinas, according to whom the identification of essence with existence is perfect only in the perfectly simple being (cf. St. Thomas Aquinas, *In lib. Boëtii de hebdomad.*, 1. II). Duns Scotus held to the opposite opinion, which was fully systematized by Suarez (*Metaph*, disput. XXXI, sect. 1, n. 13). The Thomistic position seems to have the advantage, since it safeguards the radical distinction between the infinite being and limited beings in order to make the absolutely unique relationship of the Creator with creatures much more intelligible.

ETERNITY   Existence without beginning or end which belongs to God alone. The scholastics set it apart from the *aevum* (from the Greek *aion*), which is eternity shared by those creatures called to supernatural beatitude. Contrary to the divine eternity, which is a changeless present, the *aevum* does not exclude change. Centered in God for what is essential in their beatitude, angels, like the blessed, can nonetheless experience successive thoughts and volitions. This notion of the *aevum* emphasizes the difference between the Greek idea of eternity and the biblical and Christian concept. It implies, in effect, quite a different connection between eternity and time. In Greek thought, eternity and time cannot possibly be reconciled. The two notions can be said to characterize two universes parallel to one another. Eternity is a characteristic not only of immutable, but of purely ideal realities. Time belongs exclusively to the world of matter and of change. If man belongs at once both to time and to eternity, it is through two different and distinct parts of his being that are associated only because of the fall: body and soul. The temporal being can no more reach the eternal than he is able to proceed from it in any way. But, on the contrary, in the biblical and Christian view, the time aspect of the creature follows not from the fall, but from creation by the divine eternity. And it is the battlefield of created freedoms, whereby they might reach the divine eternity. This is how God himself can descend into time, not through a fall but, quite the opposite, by a supreme condescension of love. Reciprocally, that which has taken shape in time and reached eternity will not in any way be abolished there, but rather will be immortalized. See St. Thomas Aquinas, *Sum. Theol.*, Ia, qq.9 and 10, 53 and 63.

EUCHARIST   The word Eucharist comes from the Greek *eucharistia*, which can be translated as "thanksgiving," and is used in the New Testament to translate the Hebrew term *berakah*. Although *berakah* is a thanksgiving pronounced over everything by pious Jews, it is not an egocentric thanks. It is primarily an exultant act of faith and homage to the divine Word, not only as a revelation, but as an event in which God makes himself known. It is a confession of the Name of God, i.e., of his nature revealed in the realization of his plan of love for men, and particularly in regard to his people. In the restoration of the divine meaning of all things, it is therefore a consecration of man to the acknowledged will of God. The *knowledge* of God (q.v.), in the sense of the prophets, becomes a reality in it, as a commitment to his will, a conforming to that which he is and wills to be for our sake. Particularly in the solemn blessing that concluded their meals, the Jews "gave thanks" for their food as a sign of the goodness of the Creator who communicates his own life to us, and for the promised land that produced the food, a sign itself of the salvation he assured his people when he brought them to live there in his knowledge. It is this rite and this prayer that our Lord made his own in order to express both the definitive gift of true life to the people of God in his body, which he gave up to the cross, and the door to the eternal Kingdom through the acceptance of this same cross as the acknowledged sign of the new covenant sealed in his blood.

The Eucharist, therefore, gives full meaning to the cross, and in the cross to the whole life of the Word made flesh. At the same time as it reveals this meaning to us, it involves us in the response of faith to the love it manifests for us. For the memorial of the first covenant in the blood of the Paschal Lamb, it substitutes the memorial of the new and everlasting covenant in the blood of the true Lamb whereby, in his footsteps and with him, we arrive in the presence of his Father, who has become Father to all of us.

It is in this fundamental context that the Church's unity is realized: the eucharistic celebration appears primarily as the act in which the Church receives the gifts of God that constitute her as God's people. Its significance is seen in her surrender to God in the footsteps of Christ and in her commitment to his cross. It is in this sense that St. Paul says that every time we take this bread and drink of this cup, we "proclaim the Lord's death until he comes" (1 Cor. 11,26). This supreme profession of faith through the will of Christ allows the Church to penetrate the mystery of his cross.

As a *memorial* (q.v.) the Eucharist makes known to us, in the very being of him who is its substance, the whole content of the mystery of the divine will. This same mystery, acknowledged, confessed and accepted in this way, gives us access to God himself through the Eucharist. Through it, the act of salvation not only reaches out to include us in its scope, but is actually appropriated to us. It is in this sense that the Eucharist is the sacrifice of the Church, a sacrifice renewed day after day in the liturgy, although its reality is only that of the cross, offered once and for all for the salvation of the world. The reconciliation thus effected between the Father and man in the flesh of the body of his Son (Col. 1,22) is made ever present to us.

We see then that the sacramental aspect of the Eucharist as the gift of God in Christ cannot be opposed to Christ's sacrifice, which lives on in us, permitting us to "complete in our flesh what is lacking in Christ's afflictions for the sake of His body, that is the Church" (Col. 1,25). It is by the gift of God in Christ crucified, and only by that gift, that we offer ourselves to him, that is, to his holy will for the accomplishment of his love in us. Moreover, this sacrificial aspect is expressed directly in the eucharistic prayer, but since it follows from remembrance and the invoking of the words of Christ: "Take, eat, this is my body . . . Drink, this is my blood . . . Do this as a memorial of me . . ." it is directed toward Communion, in which the sacramental aspect is immediately in evidence although it is only the consummation of the sacrifice.

The real and objective presence of the gift of God in the body and blood offered on the cross, received and accepted by God in the Resurrection and communicated to men in the sacrament, far from being opposed to the memorial character of the whole Eucharist, is what makes this memorial not merely a human remembrance, but a divine sign, living and efficacious. And the gift remains inseparable from the memorial, and indistinguishable outside of it, because it is always still the same gift: not an ordinary partial or limited gift, but the gift of the whole of God's love, which was given to us once and for always on the cross, but which we shall receive here on earth for evermore.

As the presence of the *mystery*, i.e., of Christ and his cross, in the *thanksgiving* by which the Church receives both Christ and his cross, as a *memorial* which God himself has given us so that we may unceasingly *re*-present it to him, and as a *sacrifice* of which Christ remains forever both the offerer and the victim, although he associates us with him in his twofold role, the Eucharist is finally *Communion* (q.v.). That is, in nourishing us with the living bread, with the unique bread that has come down from heaven to give life to the world, Communion gathers us up into this body of his flesh in which Christ reconciled us all with his Father, and at the same time reconciles us with one another, uniting us all in him. It is in this way that the Church is built on the Eucharist, as the body of Christ through which we become members of Christ (cf. John 6; Col. 1,22; 1 Cor. 10,17).

Let us add that just as the Church did not wish to separate the eucharistic celebration from the service of the reading of the Word of God, since the mystery communicated to us in the Eucharist is the same one that is proclaimed to us in the Gospel, we cannot receive it with the faith it requires unless we nourish this faith just as regularly with the divine Word. This is why tradition constantly presents the preaching of the Gospel and the eucharistic celebration to us as two inseparable tables at which the bread of life is given to us.

Against the Protestants, who deny or minimize the real presence of the body and blood of the Saviour in the Eucharist, the Council of Trent defined this presence as real and substantial, and effected by a conversion of the whole substance of bread into the body, and the whole substance of wine into the blood of Christ. But, although it recalled that this conversion is called *convenienter et proprie* transsubstantiation, the Council did not propose any particular theological explanation of it. Against the same adversaries the Council again defined the sacrifice of the Eucharist as not only a sacrifice of praise and thanksgiving (in the restricted sense that Protestants understand it, namely, the simple expression of our gratitude for what Christ had done for our sake), but as a truly propitiatory sacrifice, in specifying its unity with the sacrifice of the cross: "for it is one and the same *hostia* (i.e., victim), and it is the same who offers himself today through the ministry of the priests, who had offered himself previously upon the cross, the only difference being the mode of the offering." The context shows that it is now a question of an unbloody sacramental oblation, since the physical, bloody oblation is not renewed nor is it renewable (see Sess. XIII and XXII (D.B. 874, 877, 883 ff., 938–940, 948–951). Cf. St. Thomas Aquinas, *Sum. Theol.*, IIIa, qq.73–83. *See also* CANON, COMMUNION, MEMORIAL, MASS, PRESENCE, SACRIFICE, and TRANSSUBSTANTIATION.

EVIL   In contrast to Greek thought, which always tended to look upon matter as the origin of evil, and, to an even greater extent, *Manichaeanism* (q.v.), which went so far as to make evil a positive principle coeternal with good, biblical revelation asserts the goodness of all beings, both spiritual and material, since they are a creation of the absolutely perfect God (cf. Gen. 1). This is why Christian theology accepted the definition of evil given by Plotinus (*Enneads* VIII, 1, ch. 2; cf. III, 3, ch. 5), namely, that it is only a *privation*, the simple absence of good. As such, evil is never positively willed by God, theologians say, but only permitted, always with a higher good in mind, of which evil is the inevitable counterpart. Thus, the imperfection inherent in every finite being is always only the existential condition of such a being, which is good in itself insofar as it exists.

But this metaphysical problem of evil is compounded by a religious and moral problem, in which it is not just a question of the fact of limitation and simple imperfection in a created world. On the one hand, it is a question of suffering and death, especially of the innocent, in a world that we maintain was created by an all-powerful and all-perfect God; and, on the other hand, a question of sin. The account of the fall in the third chapter of Genesis manifests the fact that man has had to suffer and die as a result of sin, a fact the Epistle to the Romans (5,12) states more precisely: "Therefore as sin came into the world through one man and death through sin, and so death spread to all men because all men sinned." A twofold tendency is revealed throughout revelation in this regard, namely, to look upon every evil suffered as punishment for a sin (cf. Ezech. 18, in which the principle of responsibility and of personal punishment is asserted); and, to place in a prominent position the mystery of evils that strike the innocent as well as the guilty despite this principle (cf. all of Job, and Luke 13,1–5). The solution is proclaimed in the idea that the suffering of the righteous man is salvific in relation to the unrighteous themselves (the theme of the songs of the *Servant* (q.v.) in the second part of the book of Isaiah), and, finally, that it thereby becomes the means of the manifestation and supreme realization of the divine *agape* in the world of sin (cf. Rom. 5, and Phil. 2).

Origen was the first Christian thinker to show that the problem of evil in this form is essentially the problem of a world of created freedoms. By creating the world, God accepts the possibility of sin, of which suffering and death will be the consequences. But, the consequences themselves open up the way for possible redemption. This is the profound thought that animates the ancient liturgical texts, which see in the tree of the cross, planted through sin, the saving love that will ultimately flower into the tree of life that will bear the fruit of the resurrection.

Nevertheless, Origen certainly goes too far in wishing to see in the shortcomings of created wills the only source of inequality among creatures. Without going so far, St. Augustine in his struggle against Manichaeanism still tends to see in every evil *sive culpa sive poena:* "either a fault [of the free creature] or its punishment." St. Thomas Aquinas accepts the principle but reduces its application to the world of voluntary beings.

In short, it must be said that the religious and moral problem of evil is a problem inevitably caused by the creation of a world of free wills joined in a mysterious solidarity, which for them is the beginning of their introduction to the supernatural society of the communicated divine love. The suffering and death of the innocent that result become the means by which the redemptive love is reintroduced and manifested, thus giving to sinners themselves the way to return to God and, therefore, access to the generosity of the love of God despite the momentary failing of their freedoms. This problem cannot, therefore, be resolved by any purely speculative answer, but rather by the fact that God himself, who permitted the existence of a world in which there is a seemingly inexplicable reign of suffering and death and sin, took upon himself the preeminent scandal of the cross in order to save sinners and do away with sin. See St. Thomas Aquinas, *De Malo; In II Sent.*, dist. 34–35; *Contra Gentiles*, bk. III; *Sum. Theol.*, Ia, qq.48–49, and IIIa, qq.41, and 46–49.

EVIL ONE   *See* DEVIL

EVOLUTION   Etymologically, this word means an unfolding, a process of opening out something that is contained in or implied by something. Modern scientists have used it in particular to designate from the many verified facts in paleontology and biology, the progressive manner in which animal species appear to emerge from other species, and gradually to develop new characteristics. In this regard, we have to differentiate the scientific hypothesis of evolution, and the very different theories that have come to be identified with it. The majority of contemporary scientists tend to admit that if evolution is not an immediately evident fact, it is at least a practically unavoidable hypothesis. If we refer to what was said in the article CREATION, we shall be easily convinced that there is nothing in the fact or the hypothesis that is opposed in general to the idea of a God who is the creator of all things, or in particular to the idea of a direct creation of the *soul* (q.v.). What is opposed to this, however, are those metaphysical theories that claim to interpret evolution either as a simple reduction of mankind to an animal state devoid of an intelligent and free soul, or as a more general reduction of spiritual reality to matter in such a way that the existence of the spirit would be implicitly or explicitly denied. The reluctance on the part of theologians to admit even the possibility of evolution is due, not only to a sort of mental sloth, but rather to the fact that in the thinking of the recent past, which is still prevalent, too many scientists themselves connected their theories of evolution with the unacceptable theories we have just recalled.

EXEGESIS   The explanation of a text, especially of Holy Scripture. There is a twofold aspect in biblical exegesis: philological and theological. Theological exegesis could not do without the help supplied by philological studies (examination of manuscripts, establishing of texts, enlightenment of its meaning through the resources of linguistic, grammatical, stylistic, historical studies, etc.), without inviting the foolhardiness that Church Fathers and theologians since Origen have constantly censured, and which has been the object of particularly important declarations by recent popes (especially the encyclical *Divino Afflante Spiritu* of Pius XII). On the other hand, since the prime object of the Scriptures is to present the Word of God to us—the Word that is addressed to the People of God and only kept alive among them—the most scientific interpretations of Scripture run the risk of superficiality, and even of missing the point entirely, either when they separate it from the study of the whole Christian tradition, or when they prescind from the directives of the living *magisterium* of the Church.

   We should completely misinterpret the foregoing considerations were we to conclude from them that there could be, on the one hand, a purely philological exegesis, and on the other, a theological exegesis. Since Scripture is a unity, there is only one authentic exegesis that is both scientific and religious, nourished by scientific research, and enlightened by the testimony of the Church under the safeguard of her hierarchy. The spiritual exegesis recommended by all of Christian tradition must not be interpreted as an ordinary allegory that would be freely superimposed outside of the historical meaning of the texts. On the other hand, a literal exegesis that is not concerned with the development and the unity of the great themes of revelation that make up the profound unity of Scripture itself, would be doomed to superficiality, and even to misinterpretation of the immediate grammatical sense of the texts. True spiritual exegesis, through its submission to the text seen in proper perspective, brings the Spirit gradually to light. It avoids seeing anything in a text that does not have any objective connection with it, but it comprehends what it is that makes up their continuity and profound unity (*see* ALLEGORY). Refer to the above-mentioned encyclical of Pius XII.

EXISTENTIALISM This name refers to different systems of thought that give a certain primacy in philosophy to the consideration of concrete existence over abstract essence. We must admit that the manner in which their proponents understand the words essence and existence is not only quite different from the classical understanding of these terms, but also variable and even contradictory. It is not very easy to determine what they have in common except, perhaps, their concern for the historical and psychological aspect of human reality. In the recasting to which he submitted his outline of Thomism, Etienne Gilson came to consider St. Thomas Aquinas as the existentialist par excellence, since St. Thomas maintained that *pure act* must be interpreted as an inexhaustible source of power. But such views are quite far removed from those of existentialists like Heidegger, or even more so, Jean-Paul Sartre, for whom man's essence resides either in his existence or else proceeds from it (which, for its author, seems tantamount to saying that there could be an essence in a being only insofar as it lived freely). This position ends up by simply putting aside the problem of God, or excluding him by giving to man's activity an almost divine freedom that becomes definite in contrast to a world totally devoid of meaning. The theistic, if not Christian, existentialism of Jaspers, and even the thought of Gabriel Marcel (who no longer wishes to be called an existentialist, since the term has become primarily identified with the theses of Heidegger and Sartre) are quite different. They both construct a philosophy on existence, in that they begin from a reflection upon the concrete existence of man. But this brings Jaspers to a philosophy of love and transcendence, and Marcel to a philosophy of faithfulness and of the person, who comes to meet God not only as pure transcendence but as the Supreme Being "who gives me to myself to the extent that I give myself to him." It can therefore be seen that it would be quite futile to make a blanket judgment with regard to the philosophies that call themselves (or are called) existentialist.

Nevertheless, in order to understand what they all have in common, we must refer to the influences that they all have undergone: first, Kierkegaard, the Danish Protestant thinker of the romantic period, and his reaction against the rationalistic essentialism of Hegel (who reduced being to the thought that thinks itself), and then the phenomenology of Husserl, which brings all thought down to an analysis of the concrete awareness in the intentional relation whereby it focuses on its object.

The most positive forms of existentialism represent a development of certain trends that Augustinianism first suggested to Christian thought, to meet God in the reflection of man's awareness of himself. And even the most negative forms are not without having considerably enriched our vision of the drama of human consciousness separated from God, thereby supplying ample material for an apologetic that focuses on contemporary man's characteristic situation.

EX OPERE OPERATO   This expression denotes the mode of action of the sacraments and signifies that they act as divine acts, by the power that is proper to them, namely, that which God conferred upon them in Christ. They are contrasted with our actions, which act *ex opere operantis*, or with those actions of the Church in which God is not involved because of his Word, such as the sacramentals, which act *ex opere operantis ecclesiae. See* SACRAMENT, and SACRAMENTAL.

EXORCISM   A rite and formulary used conjointly for the casting out of devils. The Catholic liturgy, particularly the pre-baptismal ritual, and in a general way all of the blessings of natural elements, include many exorcisms. Exorcism was not only practiced by Christ and his apostles, but when they were first sent forth on their mission it is stated (Mark 3, 15) that they were sent out "to preach and have authority to cast out demons." Jesus himself, in the parable of the strong man and the stronger man who takes possession of his goods (Matt. 12, 23–30 and parallels), describes his own mission as being fundamentally an exorcism. We must understand this in the context of the idea, underlying the whole New Testament, according to which the *world* through *sin* has fallen into the *slavery* of the *devil* (see the words in italics). Redemption, from this point of view, is therefore the deliverance by which Jesus takes us from the power of God's enemy in order to reinstate us in the divine Kingdom. There is then nothing surprising about the fact that exorcism appears in the Christian liturgy to be the prelude or the other half of all consecratory rites, beginning with the baptismal rite.

There are, moreover, two kinds of exorcisms. The first are correctly those that precede baptism (or other consecratory blessings), and which can be performed, should the case arise, by any priest or even by any minister who has received the order of exorcist. The others which pertain to the case of extraordinary diabolical obsession or *possession* (q.v.) are today reserved by law to an experienced priest designated by the bishop (can. 1151 and 1152).

Along with the prescribed formulas, exorcisms usually include the laying on of hands, to which insufflation is sometimes added, illustrating the fact that it is through a communication of the Spirit of God that the evil spirit can be cast out.

EXPERIENCE   The act of testing or having tested any reality. Can we speak of a religious experience, as has been done particularly by the psychologist William James? Although it has at times been denied, we must recognize that the most certain Christian tradition has done this, undoubtedly beginning with the writings attributed to the monk Macarius (end of the 4th century), who did not hesitate to speak of the experience of the inner man. But we must specify from the outset that there can be no question of likening this experience to what is understood by the term "experiment" in modern science. The spiritual experience, first of all, does not lend itself to detached objectivity; we cannot have a religious experience unless we involve our entire selves. Nor can it be reproduced at will: the more profound and authentic it is, the more it remains suspended in the gratuitousness of God's action in us. With these reservations, we may certainly admit the idea of religious experience in Christianity.

Furthermore, it is necessary to discern precisely what the object of this experience is. It is well understood that this cannot be God as he is in himself. To believe this would assuredly make us succumb to an *immanentism* (q.v.) for which the very idea of a religious experience has been reproached by various schools. What is accessible to our experience is never anything but the echoing of God's action within us, which is exerted directly upon our soul. Nevertheless, in the mystical experience (*see* MYSTICISM) it seems that we do arrive at such a transparency of the effects of grace on the soul that to a certain extent we can speak of an experience of God. On earth this experience undoubtedly cannot arise completely out of the *chiaroscuro* of faith, but it is the daybreak, or at least the dawn of what will be everlasting beatitude when we shall see God as he is (cf.1 John 3,2; 1 Cor. 13,12).

EXPIATION   An action capable of appeasing the divine wrath caused by sin. The Christian idea of expiation has its direct origin in the notions bound up with the Jewish liturgical feast of Yom Kippur, and the fundamental treatment of the theology of expiation is the Epistle to the Hebrews which is a Christian commentary on this Old Testament feast.

Essentially, the primitive rite of expiation was the presentation by the High Priest in the holy of holies of the blood of a bull and of a ram which he placed on the *kapporeth*, the cover of the Ark (translated as the "mercy seat" or the "propitiatory," whence the identification of propitiation with expiation). The modern use of the word has tended more and more clearly to give it the meaning of a punitive reparation for sin. But this does not seem to have been the biblical meaning, which was rather a purification from sin and a reconciliation with God whom this sin had offended, through a new consecration of which the shedding of *blood* (q.v.) was the means. In fact, even in the Old Testament, the intercession of either Moses (Ex. 32,30) or Aaron (Wis. 18,21–25) seems to have been closely connected with expiation. It is in this way that the Targum, on the other hand, interprets the expiation of the Servant of the Lord in the texts of the second part of Isaiah. The Epistle to the Hebrews develops this line of interpretation by showing us Christ as the Intercessor insofar as he offers the definitive expiation (7,25 and 9,4). But it is undeniable that the intercession for sinners appears in that case to be connected in turn with the Intercessor's offering of his own life.

EXTREME UNCTION   *See* ANOINTING, and ANOINTING OF THE SICK

F

FACE The image of God's "face" is a metaphor that the Bible uses to express his special action in the world. Thus, God says to Moses, "My face shall go with you . . ." (Ex. 33,14). More particularly, God shows his face to his people in the sense that he makes himself personally known to them, and they can know him in a completely different way from the manner in which other people know him (cf. Deut. 4,37 or 2 Sam. 17,11). However, man cannot see God's face (Ex. 33,20; Judges 13,22), not only because man is a sinner (cf. Isa. 6,5), but also because no creature can bear its brilliance (cf. the seraphim in Isaiah's vision, who veil their own faces in the presence of the Lord). And yet the nostalgia of this vision runs throughout the Old Testament (Ex. 33; Ps. 42,3, etc.). In the New Testament St. John says, "No one has ever seen God; the only Son, who is in the bosom of the Father, he has made him known" (John 1,18). The account of the transfiguration shows us, in effect, the whole manhood of the Saviour shining with divine *glory* (q.v.). The Epistle to the Hebrews says that Christ is the very stamp of the divine nature (Heb. 1,3), and St. Paul shows us that in beholding the glory of the risen Christ, we are called upon to reflect this glory in such a way that we may be transformed into the likeness of the Lord who is the Spirit (2 Cor. 3,18). He also says that, although we now know God as through a glass, we are called to know him in the way that we have been known by him, "face to face" (1 Cor. 13,12). The Apocalypse declares that the servants of God and the Lamb "will see his face" (22,4), and the first Johannine Epistle explains, "we shall be like him, for we shall see him as he is" (3,2). *See* VISION, and KNOWLEDGE.

FAITH The supernatural virtue that brings us to accept revealed truths of the Word of God as revealed to us by him. The Christian idea of faith is therefore correlative with the notion of the divine Word (*see* WORD OF GOD), and thereby includes two aspects that are inseparable. Faith is a personal trust in God, which is expressed through the acceptance of what God has revealed. It is therefore essential that faith, as a response to the content of this Word, be an intellectual act, rooted in the will that God has invited to love and obey him. The opposite of faith is not then simply the absence of belief, but rather *sin* (q.v.). This is revealed in the third chapter of Genesis in reference to man's fall. Sin results from man's preferring the evidences of the senses rather than the promises and exigencies of God, i.e., the sight and taste of the forbidden fruit in preference to the promise of life or death that God has made. On the other hand, Abraham is the father of believers because he gave his consent to the divine Word, which caused him to abandon all his human security for a promise that was to be realized only in the future. The Bible states: "And he [Abraham] believed the Lord; and he reckoned it to him as righteousness" (Gen. 15,6; cf. all of chap. 12). This twofold aspect of faith is marked in Hebrew by the twofold series of words designating faith, built either on the root *batah*, expressing trust (as in the last verse quoted), or on the root *aman*, expressing steadfastness (whence truth), as in this verse of Isaiah: "If you do not believe [*ta'aminu*], you shall not remain steadfast [*te'amenu*]" (Isa. 7,7).

From the beginning faith has relied on signs, and for Israel its principal sign was the deliverance from Egypt, the exodus into the promised land celebrated at each feast of Passover (cf. Ex. 12). For this reason, the immediate object of Israel's faith was the *covenant* (q.v.) that God made with his people. But all Old Testament progress is directed towards a deepening of the perspectives of this covenant, emphasizing that the ultimate object of faith is still to come. This is made definitively specific in Israel's great trial of faith: its destruction and the Babylonian captivity. From this it is apparent that the object of the promises inherent in the faith is not the whole people, but the *remnant* (*see* CHURCH) of this ordeal. This is brought to light in the teaching of Isaiah on faith: on the one hand, he supposes that faith in God is absolutely distinct from any trust in tangible realities, even though they are considered to be God's gifts; and on the other, that faith thus purified lives on in an effective obedience of our whole life to his word. Jeremiah then reveals the notion of a new covenant that will be engraved in the very heart of man, and which Ezechiel describes as a real resurrection of the People of God who have passed through the ordeal of death (cf. Jer. 31 and Ezech. 37). The second part of Isaiah then makes allusion to the figure of the faithful Servant, bearer of Israel's faith, who will realize the plans of the divine Word in the mystery of his innocent suffering, and who will not only bring back God's People, who for a long time had been unfaithful, but will extend to every nation the promises made to Abraham and his descendants (cf. Isa. 49,1-6 and 52,13 to 53,12).

In the New Testament Jesus begins by making faith in God, as a King who will establish his Kingdom over all the earth, blossom into faith in the Father whose will it is to adopt all of us as his children (cf. the Sermon on the Mount in Matt. 5,1 ff. and Luke 17 ff.). In this way, he answers the expectations of the *poor* (*see* POVERTY), who according to the piety of the psalms are the principal "faithful": those who put their trust in God and in God alone. Moreover, since the divine Kingdom finds its realization in Jesus himself, the Son and Servant, Jesus reveals himself little by little as the "Word made flesh" (prologue of John) not only in what he says but in what he does and above all in his cross. Therefore, as the Son of God who has come into the world to die for us, he himself becomes the definitive object of faith.

It is in this light that the faith, which is the faith of the nascent Church (see the first chapters of Acts), is fundamentally a faith in the Resurrection of Jesus, i.e., in the consecration God gave to his death as the principle of salvation for all who believe (cf. 1 Cor. 15).

Thus, it is apparent that the faith of the New Testament is bound up with hope (which has as its object our final participation in the Resurrection of Jesus as the ultimate accomplishment of the promises of God), and with charity, i.e., with the communication by the Spirit of God himself of this supernatural love, of which God has revealed the principle to us by the cross of his Son (Rom. 5,1–8), and which the Spirit pours into our own hearts (*ibid.*, v.5).

It is in this context that St. Paul (*ibid.*, v.1) proclaims faith as the principle of our *justification* (q.v.). He explains this by opposing faith to the *law* (q.v.), which was both a symbol of a preparatory economy that has now been superseded by its own fulfillment and a command given to man to realize certain definite prescriptions in order to be pleasing to God. But the Gospel, on the contrary, proclaims to man the pure *grace* (q.v.) of God through which he is saved and which, through charity, imbues him with the principle of the surrender of his whole being to the divine *love* (q.v.) that surpasses all law (cf. Rom. 4–5 and 7–8 with Gal. 3).

In the course of time, the Church came to clarify her teaching on faith against the successive errors of the Pelagians and Semi-Pelagians, then against the Protestants, and finally against the modern forms of rationalism or irrationalism that are equally contrary to the proper balance of an authentic faith.

Against these first errors, which minimize the role of grace in our salvation in order to emphasize man's own endeavor, the Church, following St. Augustine, proclaimed that faith which receives the grace of justification is itself the gift of grace, and that it is still from grace that all efforts proceed that effectively bring us to faith. Even more so, perseverance in the faith once received, and particularly final perseverance, is a grace that must be asked for in prayer (Council of Orange, can. 5,6,7 and 10 in particular; D.B. 178–180 and 183).

Against the Protestants, on the other hand, it was defined that faith is not merely a blind trust: trust in God is inseparable from the belief in the truths that his word makes known to us, and which is solely the Church's function to define. In the second place, if faith justifies us, it does not do so without God's love, which is the principle of good works and without which faith would be dead (Council of Trent, Session VI, cap. 7 and can. 9,11–16; D.B. 799, 800, 817, 819, 821–826). At the same time, the Council of Trent reminds us of the fundamental truth of the New Testament: salvation by faith need not be opposed to the necessity of the sacraments, particularly baptism, since it is precisely in the sacraments, and first of all in baptism, that faith takes possession of divine grace as a gift to the believer himself (cf. Mark 16,16 and Rom. 6). On the other hand, it emphasizes that the object of faith is not at all primarily or immediately *our* salvation, but rather Christ and his work, from which our own salvation will follow if we remain faithful to him.

Finally, the first Vatican Council made several definitions against the rationalists and the irrationalists, which were aimed particularly at those who, like Hermes in the 19th century, tended to turn the commitment of faith into a purely rational act in which grace would not intervene, or who, like Günther, thought that once faith was received as a grace the succession of dogmas could be demonstrated purely by reason. But these definitions were also directed against those who, disagreeing among themselves (like the Fideists and particularly the school of Lamennais), wanted to exclude every rational element from the faith. In consequence, the Vatican Council defined that the act of faith was simultaneously a supernatural (depending entirely on grace), a rational (justifiable by the exercise of reason, and lending itself to rational investigation provided that the mystery is respected), and a voluntary act (i.e., in which the commitment of the intellect, while it is solicited by grace and encouraged by reason, remains the object of a personal and free decision). See Sess. III, Constitution *De Fide Catholica*, chaps. 3 and 4, with the corresponding canons, in D.B. 1789–1800 and 1810–1820.

Consequently, two major problems for Christian theology arise. The first is the *object* of faith. This object is defined by numerous propositions, which the Church works out according to the questions posed to her by the basic themes of the Word of God. But as St. Thomas Aquinas emphasizes, in full faithfulness to Holy Scripture, the object of faith nevertheless remains one, for it is not in the formulas themselves but beyond them, in the mystery of God revealed in Jesus Christ. St. Paul admirably shows us how this mystery is made one for us in the contemplation of the cross of Jesus (cf. 1 Cor. 1,17 to 2,16, and Eph. 3), which reveals to us the depths of the mystery of God (cf. St. Thomas Aguinas, *Sum. Theol.*, IIa-IIae, q.1, a.2 ad 2um, and *De Veritate*, q.14, a.8, ad 1um).

The second problem is the *subject* of faith. The act of faith is an act in which the intellect perceives through reason, by signs which God proposes to it, that it is morally good to believe what the Church presents to us as being the Word of God. Nevertheless, it adheres to it only because the will, attracted and solicited by grace, gives its consent. But we would delude ourselves by a fantastic and very false idea were we to imagine this intellectual perception (*see* CREDIBILITY) as preceding the gift of grace or the influence, if not the decision, of the will. If the will needs the intellect in order to make its decision to believe, then the intellect has no less need of the will's virtuous acceptance of the good proposed to it by God in order to recognize its indispensable value. In fact, the intellect can no more reach a decisive judgment, nor the will the decision itself, without the light of faith given by grace, which light is at the same time strength for the will. In the reasonableness, freedom, and supernaturalness of the faith, it is not a question then of imagining three distinct and somewhat superimposed acts, but of the mystery of a single act in which our intellect and will act with equal fullness and in concert under the influence of grace. See St. Thomas Aquinas, *Sum. Theol.*, Ia-IIae, q.62, a.113; IIa-IIae, qq.1 to 16; Commentary *In Sent.*, bk. II, dist. 26–28 and bk. III, dist. 23–25; *Contra Gentiles*, bk. I, chap. 6 and bk. III, chaps. 40, 102 and 104.

FAITHFULNESS   The faithfulness of God, expressed in Hebrew by the term *emet* (literally, "truth"), is a fundamental concept of Scripture. It generally accompanies *hesed*, "mercy" or "loving kindness," emphasizing in this way the fact that divine grace, although sovereignly free, is completely steadfast (cf. Ex. 34,6). Whence the sureness of the covenant God made with his People: He concluded it freely and sovereignly, and it will never be he who will fail to keep it. God's faithfulness requires the faithfulness of man, which means both man's perseverance in the faith and his obedience, which will permit him to persevere. It is in this light that Osee presents the ultimate union of God with His People as a marriage in mutual faithfulness (Osee 2,22). But the Deutero-Isaiah, in the Servant songs, looks upon this faithfulness as being realized only in a singular figure despised and rejected by men (42,18 ff., and 52,13 ff. in particular).

The New Testament, under the influence of the words of Jesus himself, pictures Jesus as the faithful Servant whose faithfulness bears witness to that of God and induces man's faithfulness (Mark 10,45 and par.). He is the faithful witness (Apoc. 3,14) in whom all of God's promises have their "yes" or "amen" (2 Cor. 1,20). This is also why He appears as the merciful and faithful high priest who goes before us to the throne of God (Heb. 2,17). Through Him, we shall be made faithful until death (Apoc. 2,10). Thus, at an early date, the word "faithful" also came to designate the followers of Christ (cf. Acts 10,45; 2 Cor. 6,15; Eph. 1,5).

FALL   The event in which spiritual creatures, first the angels and then men, lost along with the friendship of God certain gifts with which He endowed them when He created them. The idea of the fall is to be found in many religions other than Judaism and Christianity, but in no others is it so clearly distinct from creation itself. Particularly in the forms of religious thought evolving out of Platonism, it is because the intellect could not continue in the contemplation of abstract truth that it fell into the material realm, and thus man finds himself in his present bodily state. Biblical teaching, however, is formal: Everything in the beginning was created by God, matter and spirit both, and the fall has nothing to do with bodily existence *in se*. The fall is the consequence of a profoundly spiritual act whereby *some* created spirits were unfaithful to their Creator. This is what the first chapters of Genesis teach us with perfect clarity, although the forms of expression used are veiled in symbolism. Thus, the order that was willed by the Creator, through which the faithful created spirit would have illumined matter itself by making it an instrument of praise, was replaced by a profound disorder in which the spirit gone astray associated the material world with its own failure, by claiming to make use of it as a sovereign master. All of this has the ultimate effect of rendering the created spirit the slave of matter.

What the Bible tells us about the fall is centered about the fall of man himself. That it is bound up with a previous fall of intelligences superior to his own seems clear according to the Genesis account. However, we have but very little data on this other primary fall. Theology tends to define the sin of the angel as a sin of pride in that he wanted to put himself in the place of God. In this sense the origin of idolatry may also be explained, whereby man turns away from the Creator to adore those creatures that surpass himself. The fallen angels, however, would not have incited man except by inspiring the desire in him to regard the goods of this world as sovereign master, after their own example. Thus, the sin of mankind, although pride is behind it, was in the beginning a sin of selfish desire for goods that were immediately perceptible to the senses, which is opposed to faith in the Word of the sovereign God (cf. Gen. 3,1–4).

Therefore, the fall is expressed by a darkening of the whole world, in which the spirit of man in particular becomes alien to God. It is a universe that, instead of helping man to raise himself to God, has become a weight and an obstacle that separates him from God, even though the origin of that fault is within the conscience of man. It is very difficult to specify to what extent the fall is reflected independently of man in the material world, although St. Paul in particular seems to admit that this world is itself in a state of enslavement from which man will not be freed until the last day (cf. Rom. 8,22). In man, theologians distinguish the loss of the supernatural gifts that are inseparable from grace, from the loss of preternatural gifts, which together with grace brought nature to perfection in the beginning, but without which grace can still be recovered. *See* SIN.

FATALISM   From *fatum*, meaning "fate," the term is used for every form of thought whether religious or not that abolishes human freedom, and even divine freedom, by attributing all events to an impersonal necessity. *See* DETERMINISM.

FATE   A Greek concept according to which everything, and especially the course of each man's life, would have been previously determined by an impersonal law superior to that of the personal gods. From their point of view, the Stoics saw in the concept a law immanent in the universe, the *fatum*, which they at times referred to as the will of God, but of a God who was often merely a figure of this law. All Christian thought spurns this idea of fate since it is tantamount to a denial of human and divine freedom. It was reintroduced, however, under the form of a heresy in the errors on *predestination* (q.v.). In the early days of Christianity and again in the Renaissance, the neo-pagan ideas on fate against which Christian thinkers fought were often connected with astrological fatalism, as if the unalterable influence of the stars determined everything. *See* DETERMINISM.

FATHER   First asserted in connection with Israel (cf. Jer. 31,9; Ezech. 16; Osee 11,1–11; Isa. 63,15–16 and 64,7), and then more particularly with regard to the righteous man (Wis. 2,13 to 3,12), the fatherhood of God that was promised to all men in the Sermon on the Mount (cf. especially Matt. 5,45) becomes the principal object of the Good News of salvation. Its reality is asserted in the Gospel by the possibility of becoming like God, and the call made to all men to become like Him in the *love* (q.v.) that is His. The revelation of this love is His own preeminent revelation. It will be noted that Deuteronomy had already implied that the divine fatherhood would be extended to Israel to the point that it would bear the mark of God's holiness (cf. Deut. 14,1–2).

The revelation of the New Testament, however, is not simply a feasible extension of this privilege to all men, but the deepening of the concept of the fatherhood of God itself. This no longer appears as merely a possible aspect of God's relationship with his creatures, but rather as the most intimate revelation of the very nature of God. This is what is accomplished in the revelation of Jesus as the preeminent Son; either as just *the* Son (Mark 13,32), or as the "beloved" Son (i.e., according to the Hebrew usage of this term, the Only-Begotten Son; cf. Mark 1,11 and par.). Finally, in a major text of Matthew and its parallel in Luke (cf. Matt. 11,25–27 and Luke 10,21–24), the fatherhood of God appears as the object of the reciprocal and completely unique *knowledge* (q.v.) that the Father and his Son have of each other. Thus, side by side with the assertion of our not nominal but real adoption, inscribed as it must be in a transformation of our whole life by this love that is God's, the Gospel reveals to us the perfect and transcendent realization of the divine fatherhood in God's relationship to the One whom he sent to bring us this grace of graces.

St. Paul sheds light on the connection between these two fundamental notions. For him, God has sent his Son, who took on our human condition (that of men who had fallen because of sin) that we in turn might become a part of his sonship. As the Epistle to the Galatians says: "But when the time had fully come, God sent forth his Son, born of woman, born under the law, to redeem those who were under the law, so that we might receive adoption as sons. And because you are sons, God has sent the Spirit of his Son into our hearts, crying, 'Abba! Father!' So through God you are no longer a slave but a son, and if a son then an heir" through Christ (Gal. 4,4–7). Therefore, the work of the Son made man is to free us by His cross from the state of slavery to which our sins have brought us (cf. Gal. 3,13), so that in exchange we might be given a share in the sonship that is proper to him. At the same time, St. Paul specifies that this comes about through baptism, in which we literally put on Christ (Gal. 3, 27–28). The gift of the Spirit, which involves us in the "inheritance" of God, namely, the possession of everything that is proper to him and that he communicates to the Son as his Son, realizes in us the extension of the divine sonship. (Cf. a parallel text, in which this time everything begins from the gift of the Spirit in order to end up in the sonship communicated in the Son: Rom. 8,14–17.) It is in this light that St. Paul again applies to Christ the title of firstborn Son, which had originally been given to Israel (cf. Ex. 4,23 with Rom. 8,29). The Epistle to the Colossians shows us how the eternal Son, destined from before the beginning of the creation of the world to be the firstborn of creation (1,15), became so in fact through His Resurrection, which established him as the firstborn among the dead (1,18).

For St. John, who wished to fully bring out the absolutely unique character of Jesus' sonship, and who speaks of God as *His* Father from all eternity, the name "Son" is reserved for Jesus, and he calls him explicitly the "Only-Begotten Son" (John 1,4–18; 3,16–18; cf. 1 John 4,9). He only calls men the "children of God," while emphasizing: "See what love the Father has given us, that we should be called children of God; and so we are" (1 John 3,1), just as the Johannine Gospel declared: "For God so loved the world that He gave His only Son, that whoever believes in Him should not perish but have eternal life" (3,16). The great discourses at the end of John's Gospel can be considered as a development of the theme of the major texts of Matthew and Luke (quoted above) on the reciprocal intimacy, based on a unity without counterpart, between the Father and the Son, and on the similar unity the Son has willed to establish between him and us so that we might be associated with his sonship (cf. especially John 17,22–23).

We then see that if the liberal Protestant theologian Adolf von Harnack was not wrong in summing up the essence of the Gospel as the proclamation of the divine fatherhood, he was completely mistaken in reducing it to an assertion that was independent of every dogmatic belief concerning the nature of Christ. Far from being merely a significant image of the natural relationship of every man with God, this fatherhood is first of all the most supernatural assertion possible about the divine nature. And, this assertion can in no way be separated from the revelation of the supernatural character of the Saviour's personality. It is the Son's coming into the world that reveals to us that this love, which is the heart of the divine life, makes God the Father in an absolutely proper though transcendent sense. The extension of this fatherhood to us, in the redemptive Incarnation of the eternal Son, and through the communication of God's Spirit as its culmination, is therefore the grace par excellence, a grace that becomes meaningless if we reject the dogmatic assertions of the apostles with regard to Christ. This is what was to be shown so admirably by the Greek Fathers of the 4th century, and particularly by St. Athanasius of Alexandria in the controversy against *Arianism* (q.v.). It was one of the major arguments of Athanasius against Arius and his disciples, who denied the full divinity of the Saviour, that the evangelical assurance of the reality of our adoption effected in Christ would be reduced to a metaphor of no real import if he were not himself, in the strictest sense, the Son. Still more profoundly he showed how God is the Father in a sense which, in contrast to human fatherhood, creates a very imperfect simple image of that which has its realization only in him: a life that is realized completely in the fatherhood, in the total communication of one's self. (See Athanasius' three books *Against the Arians*, P.G. 26). In this regard, we can see how wrong certain adepts of contemporary theology are when, out of pseudo-scientific considerations, they claim to eliminate the divine fatherhood from Christian preaching by declaring that it is only a "survival of the neolithic age."

See St. Thomas Aquinas, *Sum. Theol.*, Ia, q.33 and IIIa, q.23.

FATHERHOOD   The active relationship of a father toward his son. Its essential element is the communication of the father's own life. As Scripture has emphasized, and the Fathers of the Church (especially St.

Athanasius) specify in connection with the Arian controversies, the heavenly Father is the only father in whom this quality is not secondary and transient, but fundamental. Every other fatherhood, whether physical or spiritual is, therefore, merely an approximate image of His own (cf. Matt. 23,9 and James 1,17).

FATHERS OF THE CHURCH This name is given to the early theologians, most of them canonized, who were the first to define and explain the Christian faith and, in particular, to those who prepared the definitions that the early councils brought to bear against the first great heresies. If we do not separate their individual works from the collective synthesis to which they so forcefully contributed, their testimony, insofar as it is in agreement and does not represent individual opinion, is the most important factor in Christian tradition outside of Holy Scripture. Their almost immediate proximity to the Scriptures gives them a very special authority to interpret it theologically, i.e., to extract from it the fundamental themes of the Word of God, and to assure us of their authentic meaning.

All of this remains true, even when it is acknowledged that their exegeses could reflect the historical or philosophical deficiencies common to the writers of antiquity. Actually, their interpretations were often filled with information that remains extremely valuable because of their knowledge of certain facts about the beginnings of Christianity, which we could otherwise know only in part or not at all if we were obliged to rely only upon biblical evidence. And their familiarity with the Greek language as spoken at the time right after the New Testament was written is frequently very enlightening. Their testimony thus understood is not any more affected by their possible scientific errors, than it is properly measured by their personal genius even when this is most evident.

Actually, thinkers can be found in every age who equal their intellectual prowess and who individually gained a superior authority in the Church through their special qualifications as doctors (e.g., St. Thomas Aquinas). But most characteristic of the authority of the Fathers were their unique qualifications as witnesses to the faith of the primitive Church and as spokesmen for the faith in its first clash with differing opinions and with heresy. Many of the heretics were victims of their own inability to distinguish between the true Christian faith and opinions analogous but actually foreign to the tradition of Christianity. This also explains why, although the Church rejected certain tentative opinions of some of the Fathers, she acknowledged the authentic value of the opinions of these thinkers in matters that were not affected by their shortcomings. This is especially true of Origen, who, despite some errors, is of unequaled importance because of the enlightenment of his exegesis and his precise statements of Christian positions in the face of contemporary pagan thought. To a certain extent this even remains true in the case of writers like Tertullian, who fell into momentary formal heresy, or of authors like Theodore of Mopsuestia, who undoubtedly contributed to the formation of future heresies.

A distinction is habitually made between the Greek and Latin Fathers, and, we must add, the Eastern Fathers who wrote in Syriac. But we must be on our guard against too rigid a separation between genuinely different traditions that would correspond to these linguistic differences. In a general way, the early Greek Fathers, until the beginning of the 5th century, were the direct ancestors of most of the Latin Fathers. Some of the Latin Fathers were hardly more than popularizers of the thoughts of their forebears; e.g., the greater part of the works of St. Ambrose and a considerable portion of the works of St. Jerome stemmed from Origen. Even the most original among the Latins, notably St. Hilary and St. Augustine, are no less obligated to the Greek Fathers. The well-defined distinctions that we are sometimes tempted to make between the Latins and the Greeks are only possible if we retain only the particular opinions of these Latin Fathers, and neglect the evidence they themselves gave of the uninterrupted tradition that bound them to the Greeks. A typical example is the so-called Augustinian theology of the Trinity, which is in fact only a one-sided development of personal reflections added by St. Augustine to a collective account that faithfully follows the most common trend of Greek patristics. It is quite true that the Latin Middle Ages tended to draw from St. Augustine, and therefore contributed to his isolation from the whole of prior tradition. Still, we must consider the curiosity that was very much alive for a long time during the Middle Ages with regard to what could be learned from the Greek Fathers. And, it cannot be denied that the religious and theological rebirth of the 12th century, as in Carolingian times, owes much to them. As for the Syriac Fathers, they are of particular interest because their Semitic language was so close to the Aramaic spoken in the time of Christ. But it must not be forgotten that most of them were rather late writers who, in fact, depended heavily on the Greek tradition. A certain number of them, furthermore, not only knew Greek, but practically wrote interchangeably in the two languages.

The precise determination as to which of these latter writers we can call Fathers seems rather useless, since we are concerned not with creative genius, but rather with the collective evidence given about the Church during her primary period of formation. Therefore, when the Latins speak of St. Bernard as the last of the Latin Fathers, or the Easterns look upon Gregory Palamas as the last of the Greek Fathers, they confuse the undeniable importance of the representative doctors of their times with the characteristic quality of the Fathers as witnesses of Christian antiquity.

FELLOWSHIP   *See* COMMUNION

FIDEISM   The error of those who want to remove every rational support from the *faith* (q.v.). Fideism was particularly widespread in the 19th century as a reaction against the excesses of rationalism. Anti-fideist propositions had to be subscribed to by Louis Bautain, although it does not seem that he actually ever was a fideist. This was, however, the case with various *Traditionalists* (*see* TRADITIONALISM), notably Bonnetty. See D.B. 1622–1627, 1649–1652, as well as the Const. *De Fide Catholica*, chaps. 3 and 4, of the First Vatican Council (Sess. III; D.B. 1789 ff.).

FIRE   To the Hebrews, fire was the principal theophany; particularly, it seems, the fire of lightning on Sinai. God appeared to Moses for the first time in the burning bush (Ex. 3), and it was during another fiery theophany on the mountain that the Ten Commandments were given and the covenant concluded with the people (Ex. 19; cf. Abraham's covenant, Gen. 15,17). The pillars of fire and cloud had manifested God's guiding and protective presence during the Exodus (cf. Ex. 13,21), and descended upon the tabernacle when it was erected (40,34). Also, we find Deuteronomy declaring: "For the Lord your God is a devouring fire . . ." (4,24). The prophets have similar visions (Isa. 6; Ezech. 1; Dan. 7). But it is clearly evident here that this "fire" is a mysterious reality, an expression of the "jealousy" of the God of transcendent holiness (cf. Deut. 4,24 and 6,15) who cannot tolerate man setting himself, or anything else, as His equal. Undoubtedly, the idea of a judgment by fire came from this (cf. Isa. 41,15 f.; Soph. 1,18; Mal. 3,2 and 19). But, as in the vision of Isaiah (6), the same divine fire can, as it consumes, become purifying.

In the New Testament, the fire of the judgment appears first as the primary eschatological image. The Second Epistle of Peter speaks of the present world as destined to perish by fire (cf. Matt. 3,10–11; 5,22; 13,10, etc. with 2 Pet. 3,7,12). In the same way, the ordeal by fire seems destined to prove or refine the apostolic work (1 Cor. 3,15), the faith, and the whole life of the faithful (1 Pet. 1,7 and 4,12–17). The Apocalypse again connects the image of the judgment by fire with the fiery theophanies (1,14; 15,2; 19,12; 20,10 f.). But Pentecost, recalling Sinai, describes the descent of the Spirit as a new fiery theophany, this time filling men with the divine presence (Acts 2,3–4).

In the Roman liturgy, the mention of the last judgment by fire concludes the exorcism blessings in which the divine Spirit is called upon to drive out the evil spirit.

All of this imagery expresses both the transcendence of the divine holiness and love, and the purification and transfiguration it requires of man before they can in some way be communicated to him. *See* HELL, and GLORY.

FLESH   In authentic Catholic tradition, the use of this word as implicitly opposed to "spirit" does not signify the body as opposed to the soul. "Flesh" (or "flesh and blood") in biblical language refers to the creature (soul as well as body) left to itself without the Spirit of God coming from on high to sustain it (cf. Gen. 6,3). It is in this same sense that St. John uses this expression, when he says "the flesh is of no avail" (6,64). But with St. Paul, another idea is added to the traditional notion: man's natural perversion due to sin. Sin is obviously not to be confused either with man's being a creature, or with his corporality. But, unhappily, it is shown in a preference accorded to the selfish desire for immediate pleasure, rather than in a preference for obedience to the Word of God, which incites us to a faith that would reunite us with the invisible God (cf. Phil. 2,6–8, and Rom. 7,7–20).

Thus, through sin the flesh becomes the slave of the spirit of evil, and on the one hand appears not only as alien to the Spirit of God but positively opposed to it (Rom. 8, 5–13 and Gal. 5,12–24), and on the other hand, without in any way being confused with the body, it becomes characterized by the disorder of its natural desires (cf. Rom. 7,24, and all of ch. 1, especially from verse 24). This is why St. Paul speaks of pommeling his body and subduing it, lest after preaching to others he himself should be disqualified (1 Cor. 9,27). But Christian asceticism, of which he gives one of the first formulas in this text, never means a struggle with the body that would aim only at shedding or getting rid of it, as can be the case in the forms of asceticism inspired by Neo-Platonism or Buddhism. Rather, the struggle itself aims at reconquest and transfiguration. And it is not the human soul, considered as though it were essentially pure, that will be capable of this transformation. On the contrary, since it is the soul that sinned while the body was merely its instrument, it is the soul itself that has the greatest need for salvation. Only the Spirit of God, by freeing the soul from the enslavement of its desires, can restore the body along with the soul to the ultimate glory for which God destines the whole man (Rom. 8,10–11).

FOREKNOWLEDGE   The divine foreknowledge is merely God's knowledge, considered in its priority in relation to the existence of created things. But this logical priority must not be interpreted as if it involved a priority in time, which would reduce the universe to pure determinism. God is not in time, nor is he before time (if we understand this "before" in a temporal sense, which obviously has no meaning). God is beyond time, in the sense that his eternal action sustains all things in being without the action itself, which measures the progression of created activities, being subject to time. See St. Thomas Aquinas, *Sum. Theol.*, Ia, q.14 ff.

FORGIVENESS   Forgiveness on the part of the one who has suffered an offense of some sort is the act of allowing the person responsible for it to go free. The Bible, particularly the New Testament, sheds light on the singular generosity of the forgiveness of God, who not only does not require any prior reparation from the guilty person before bringing him back to His friendship, but takes upon Himself the act of reparation itself, so that the sinner may be effectively restored to this friendship and the sonship for which God has destined him. St. Paul underlines this as the utmost manifestation of the *love* (q.v.) that is characteristic of God (Rom. 5,5–8; cf. Ps. 103). But since God's forgiveness has as its primary and chief effect our being restored to the shared possession of his love, it cannot become real for us unless we forgive our brothers as we have been forgiven (cf. Matt. 6,14–15 and 18,15–35). *See* PENANCE, and REDEMPTION.

FORM   According to the philosophy of the Scholastics, *form* in all things is opposed to *matter* as that which determines what would otherwise remain pure undefined possibility. Therefore, form is that which constitutes being, as well as that which gives it its intelligibility. The doctrine of form and matter is called hylomorphism (from the Greek *hyle*, "matter," and *morphe*, "form"). *See* MATTER.

In the theology of the sacraments, a distinction is therefore made between the sacramental matter, which is the reality taken from the world of the senses and made into a sacramental sign, and the form of the sacrament, which is found in the divine Word that impresses on this sensible reality its supernatural significance.

FREEDOM AND FREE WILL   Freedom in a being with a will and reason is opposed both to outward constraint and to any inner necessity. The free will is more precisely the faculty that exercises this freedom, and by which a being has a choice of action.

The account of the creation and the fall of man in the first pages of Genesis obviously supposes this freedom. The same may be said of the biblical exhortations that are particularly characteristic of Deuteronomy:

". . . I have set before you life and death, blessing and curse; therefore choose life" (Deut. 30,19). Furthermore, the prophets already underlined the fact that this fundamental freedom in man is seriously hampered by the fact of such deep-rooted sin that man needs to be saved not only from an external captivity, such as Israel knew in Egypt, but from an inner and even more serious enslavement. The prophets, in weighing the seriousness of this inner slavery, even said: "Can the Ethiopian change his skin, or the leopard his spots? Then how can you do good, anchored as you are in evil?" (Jer. 13,23).

The most striking description of this slavery from which man's will needs to be freed is given by St. Paul in the Epistle to the Romans: "For I do not do the good I want, but the evil I do not want is what I do" (Rom. 7,19). St. John went so far as to say: "The whole world is in the power of the evil one" (1 John 5,19). In the face of this situation the Gospel appears as a proclamation of freedom: "If you continue in my word, you are truly my disciples, and you will know the truth, and the truth will make you free" (John 8,31–32). For St. Paul's dialectic on slavery and freedom see the article SLAVERY.

This sense of the Gospel, as a restoration of man to an original freedom that had been lost through sin, was so in evidence among the first Christian thinkers that Origen went so far as to be unwilling to admit any other differences among created beings than those that result from the exercise of their respective freedoms. Against the Manichaeans, for whom evil in the world in general and in man in particular was simply the product of matter and corporeal existence, St. Augustine (*De Libero Arbitrio*) shows that the root of all the evils from which man now suffers is in the disobedience of his free will, which has been paralyzed because of his disobedience. The later assertion of Pelagius that the possibility for good resides inalienably in our nature and never depends on anything other than our free will, to which grace is simply the finishing touch, brought St. Augustine to take up again and considerably develop the consideration of the present weakness of our free will, acknowledging in his *Retractationes* that until then he had not really touched the core of the problem. In this way he was able to develop especially that aspect of our liberation through grace: freedom in relation to the enslavement of sin.

The medieval thinkers who took up this theme devoted themselves with increasing preciseness to determining to what extent our free will is in fact diminished by sin, and in what way it is regenerated through grace. St. Bernard's treatise *De Gratia et Libero Arbitrio* is one of the most remarkable in this regard, since it asserts that in salvation everything is from God and from his grace, although in the regenerate sinner everything is no less from him, i.e., from his free will. But it was

St. Thomas Aquinas who was to arrive at the most satisfactory synthesis, first the metaphysical problem of freedom in relation to necessity in creatures, and then the theological problem of being freed from the enslavement of sin.

For him, as for Aristotle, free will is the common product of reason and will, but more precisely it is the act of the will judged by the intellect, rather than a simple deliberate judgment. Only in God is the understanding of good immediate and total, and it is inconceivable that his will could swerve from it, which is why in God alone freedom and necessity go hand in hand. In man, on the other hand, although his will cannot positively will anything other than good, his intellect immediately grasps only particular goods, none of which is the absolute good. Therefore, the will is determined toward a good that seems best to it, not in itself, but in connection with a concrete judgment in which the intellect's discernment is not itself independent of the inclination of the will. Although it may perceive that a particular good attracting it is not consistent with the perfect good, since this perfect good is not directly accessible to it, the will does not have the power to impose itself necessarily on the intellect. On the other hand, every determination taken by the will constitutes the principle of a *habitus* (q.v.) that makes the ulterior determination toward the objective good easier or more difficult. In particular, once the free will has consented to the preference of a particular good over the pursuit of the sovereign good even if it remains capable of good impulses, it cannot, without the special help of grace, reorient itself in a lasting way toward this sovereign good. But, the created will is naturally incapable of being constant in the pursuit of the sovereign good, since it always pursues it only by means of particular goods among which it is always free to lose itself. Nevertheless, once our will has submitted to the entreaties of grace, if it brings our intellect to the supernatural contemplation of the sovereign good, as in the case of the beatific vision, the will can no longer be detached from it. This is true of the blessed, in whom, as in God, freedom has become one with necessity. Without attaining on earth the perfect coinciding of the two, it is possible to conceive of a help of grace so powerful and a providence so special that every present possibility of sin could in fact be averted. This perfect coinciding is eminently true of the Blessed Virgin Mary, and could be the case with others less perfectly holy. But in any case, final perserverance for all who are still on the road to eternity remains a grace that must be sought through prayer. On the other hand, contrary to the fallen angels who are lucidly and forever fixed in evil, the determination of human wills on earth is never made with such clarity, and it is always possible that grace will preserve them from such a determination.

See St. Thomas Aquinas, *De Veritate*, q.24. Many of the most essential points are taken up again in the *Contra Gentiles*, bk. 1, chap. 88 and bk. III, chaps. 73, 89 and 148, as well as in the *Sum. Theol.*, Ia, qq.19,63 and 83, and Ia-IIae, q.109.

Nominalist theology, in losing sight of the radical transcendence of the creative and redemptive act as being not made up after the way of a human action, as though both belonged to the same plane of being, produced a real rebirth of Semi-Pelagianism (all the more so since the formularies of the Council of Orange remained practically unknown in the Middle Ages). Against this tendency, as long as one remained within the confines of this thought, the only possible reaction was a fatal opposition between grace and free will. This is what happened with Luther. His insistence that a sinful man's justification is pure grace, implied that the free will had no part in it, and his polemic with Erasmus led him to even deny the existence of any free will in man after the fall, whether he is enslaved by sin or remains purely passive under grace. Calvin went still further, and taught a divine predestination to perdition that was strictly parallel with predestination to grace and to salvation (*See* PREDESTINATION). In contrast, in the first generation of Protestantism, among those who, like Zwingli, refused to follow this path, we saw the rebirth of a teaching that was not only Semi-Pelagian, but almost purely Pelagian (*see* PELAGIANISM, and ZWINGLIANISM). The Council of Trent's reaction to these different errors was to assert that the free will has been weakened, and even inclined towards evil by the fall, but has not altogether disappeared (Sess. VI, the Decree *De Justificatione*, cap. 5; D.B. 793; cf. canon 5; D.B. 815), any more than we are not saved without it, since it clings to and cooperates with grace (*ibid.*,) cap. 5; D.B. 797; cf. canon 4; D.B. 814). Against the idea that supposes grace to be efficacious and that therefore the justified man cannot lose it, see also canon 23 (D.B. 833).

When Baius and Jansenius made these same errors they were again condemned by St. Pius V (see D.B. 1001 ff.) and later by Clement XI (1216 ff.).

Nevertheless, the reconciliation of grace with freedom remained an object of very lively debate among Catholic theologians, particularly in the controversies *de auxiliis* that took place under Clement VIII and Paul V from 1598 to 1607. The Jesuits, following Molina and his system, which was called *scientia media* (*see* SCIENCE), maintained that in clinging to grace the free will acted of its own full initiative, since grace is only efficacious by virtue of the divine foreknowledge with regard to the determinations of the created will, without being the cause of these determinations. The Dominicans, following Bañez, asserted on the other hand that grace, which is efficacious *per se*, produces the cooperation of the free will by virtue of a physical predetermination. The outcome of the controversies was to forbid both sides to present the contrasting opinion as heretical. However, it must be admitted that the very notion of physical *predetermination* (*see* PREDESTINATION) seems unfortunate, for in its wish to safeguard the notion of grace as being efficacious *per se* (as Thomistic as it was Augustinian), it tends to compare the action of God and that of man, as if they were able to operate together as a sort of composite on the same plane (which is a misunderstanding of Thomistic metaphysics). But on the other hand, how can the theory of *scientia media* avoid making the divine will depend upon a created cause, which would even more directly destroy the transcendence of God? It seems best to recognize that in this question there is a mystery that cannot be penetrated, since we must be satisfied with saying that God, as Creator and Saviour of our freedoms, acts in us in a manner that surpasses all explanation.

Quite different is the problem of civil freedom, especially in its connection with the profession and practice of the faith by individuals themselves, and insofar as they belong to a social (political) body. St. Augustine had already enunciated the principle, firmly set down by St. Thomas, that no one can make his commitment to faith under duress, but only out of a rational conviction (St. Thomas Aquinas, *Sum. Theol.,* IIa-IIae, q.10, a.8). Does it therefore follow that civil authority has to abstain from all intervention in the domain of religion? Since the principle behind every just law is its conformity with the exigencies of reason, no State could lawfully take any measure that would impede either the preaching or the profession of the authentic Christian faith. But, on the other hand, is it necessary, positively or exclusively, to promote its maintenance and development? In principle it is, but this principle can and indeed must be controlled by many concrete circumstances, as is the case of a mixed society where this support in fact would simply provoke animosity against Catholics and even revolt against the Church. St. Thomas does not hesitate to go further and say that the rites of infidels may be lawfully tolerated, either for the good that they themselves may derive from them, or to avoid the evil that their suppression would cause (*ibid.,* a.11).

More generally, this freedom must be safeguarded to allow for personal commitments to the faith, and must also be safeguarded through legislation in all matters that are essential to the fulfillment of the individual. This would include respect for an erroneous conscience, because error as such could not be the subject of any law, since an erroneous conscience imposes its law subjectively. Therefore, the person who finds himself in such a state must certainly be left free to follow the dictates of his conscience as long as he does not disturb the consciences of others or the public order. Understood in this way, freedom of conscience is certainly an indefeasible right (*See* CONSCIENCE).

The condemnations the Church issued in the last century against certain claims of an ideal of freedom (cf. the *Syllabus* of Pius IX, D.B. 1700 ff.) aim either at the claim of individual freedom that would reject the very principle of any authority at all, or at the assertion on the part of the civil authority that it could impose laws without concern for the *natural law* (q.v.) or the positive divine law (resulting from revelation), or the ecclesiastical law, or, finally, the assertion that man could not be subject to any other obligations than those resulting from human reason.

G

GALLICANISM   From the name formerly given to the Church of France, the Gallican Church, this word has come to denote a school of thought that for a long time had its chief proponents among the French theologians, canonists and, in a more general way, lawyers. The term was widened to include analogous tendencies, even when they had little or no connection in fact with Gallicanism. Even in France, distinctions must be made among several simultaneous or successive forms of Gallicanism that were far from agreement on all points.

The first form of Gallicanism was a royal one through which the jurists, particularly those of King Philip IV and his successors, sought to justify the intervention of the French kings in Church affairs by relying on two arguments that were most difficult to reconcile: first, the juridical fiction that the king is an heir of the Holy Roman Empire, and therefore heir to the semi-ecclesiastical prerogatives conceded to the emperor and given to him through his coronation; and second, the revival of the Roman law, with its theory of the *imperium* as a *dominium* (*see* AUTHORITY) of the prince over his subjects, and even including its notion of the emperor as the *pontifex maximus* (a title which the first Christian emperors continued to use for some time). In union with this royal Gallicanism, or rather using it as a pretext, the bishops tended to protest against the encroachments of the pontifical Curia on their own prerogatives or what they interpreted as such. This tendency resulted in a theological and canonical theory on the superiority of the body of bishops over the pope, particularly when meeting in council, which took strength from the schism that during the 14th and 15th centuries set up rival pretenders to the pontifical office. In the 17th century it took shape in the four famous articles of the assembly of the French clergy in 1662, in which we may say that royal Gallicanism took shelter behind the theory of an episcopal Gallicanism. But from the beginning of this century, in the theories of Richer, the syndic of the Sorbonne, we observe the definition of a Gallicanism that was no longer only episcopal, but presbyteral. This in its turn put a check on the bishops' authority, through the authority claimed in a similar way for priests of second rank, particularly pastors, which was held to be of divine origin, as the successors of the seventy disciples sent out by Christ, like the apostles themselves, on their mission (cf. Luke 10,1–17). In the 18th century a parliamentary Gallicanism appeared in which tendencies toward a Church government that was half-oligarchic and half-democratic came to the fore. These tendencies put their imprint on the civil constitution of the clergy voted by the national assembly of the Revolution.

Without realizing it, Napoleon dealt the death blow to traditional Gallicanism by dealing directly with the pope in the reorganization of the French Church, and particularly by asking him to revamp the distribution of the dioceses and, if necessary, forcing the prelates of the former sees to resign. In spite of the fact that the organic articles tried subsequently for a certain restoration of royal Gallicanism, it was doomed to only a brief and artificial survival. The Vatican Council marked the end of episcopal Gallicanism. Nevertheless, it was not to be the theses of extreme *Ultramontanism* (q.v.) that would triumph over it. More recently, the calling of the Second Vatican Council, with all of its renewal of Church doctrine, brought to light the error that was still present in wishing to simply oppose the authority of the pope and the authority of the episcopate, as if there could be a Catholic espiscopate that was not centered around the pope, and as if the pope were not himself the first of the bishops and the principal guardian of episcopal authority. *See* COUNCIL, BISHOP, and POPE.

GENERATION The action whereby the living communicate life to the being that is born of their union. The question was raised very early as to whether in human generation the parents could be said to beget the soul as well as the body of their child. This theory was maintained by Tertullian in a particularly artless form (*see* SOUL). St. Augustine held to it as well, but in a more delicate way, safeguarding the spirituality of the soul and its immediate dependence upon God, along with concern for explaining the transmission of original *sin* (q.v.). However, this tradition did not continue. St. Thomas Aquinas taught the creation and infusion of the soul by God when the body is ready to receive it. However, since matter for him remained the principle of individuation, and each soul is the form that is proper to the body which it is to inform, it can be said that because of this bias, he did not exclude every type of spiritual heredity. See St. Thomas Aquinas, *Sum. Theol.*, Ia, qq.76,90,99.

GIFTS OF THE HOLY SPIRIT Evidence that the Holy Spirit is given to us as the penultimate gift of God is found in the New Testament (cf. particularly Acts 2,38 and 10,45). But from the very beginning it has been evident that this gift was manifested in all sorts of particular gifts which St. Paul, especially in chapter thirteen of the First Epistle to the Corinthians, enumerates in proper order, asserting the primacy of the gift of charity over all the others, even the most miraculous.

The Fathers developed the idea that the Spirit is the gift of God in us because, in the Trinity itself, he is the substantial gift that the Father makes to the Son, and through which the Son gives himself to the Father. It is from this notion that St. Augustine derived the idea that in God the Holy Spirit proceeds by love, and the Son by intelligence (cf. the connection established between the Spirit and the communication of love to our own hearts in Rom. 5,5). Peter Lombard goes so far as to purely and simply identify the uncreated gift of the Spirit with charity. The reaction of St. Thomas Aquinas was not to minimize the importance, much less the reality, of the gift of the Spirit, but to assert the fecundity of that gift within us. Therefore, he distinguished the divine Spirit who has been given to us, from the created grace by which He adapts our natures to the divine life. This grace flourishes in us through the supernatural virtues (which, by definition, are infused) of faith, hope and charity, as well as by other infused virtues which supernaturalize merely natural virtues, by impregnating them with the impulse of charity itself. He also thought that there must be added to these virtues, which supernaturalize man's modes of acting so that the communication of the Spirit to our being may be perfect, entirely new and divine modes of acting which fully deserve the title of gifts of the Holy Spirit. It is through them that the words of St. Paul most superlatively become a reality: "It is no longer I who live, but Christ who lives in me" (Gal. 2,20), and again, "For all who are led by the Spirit of God are sons of God" (Rom. 8,14). According to a tradition of patristic exegesis that St. Thomas systematized with skill and profundity, he found in Isaiah (11,2–3) not only the enumeration of these gifts, but, as he believed, also the principle for unifying and grading them: the gifts of wisdom, understanding, counsel, fortitude, knowledge, piety and fear of the Lord. Thus the "gifts" form a supernatural framework through which the Spirit moves us from within, by conforming us to the very mode of His own action.

Among the commentators on St. Thomas, John of St. Thomas, especially, developed this teaching in the last tract of his *Cursus theologicus*, of which he was himself the editor (In Iam IIae, q.68). See St. Thomas Aquinas, *Sum. Theol.*, Ia, qq.37,38; Ia-IIae, qq.57–70, 109–111; cf. *In IV Sent.*, bk. I, dist. 17, and *Quaestio unica de caritate*.

GLORY   In Scripture, particularly when referring to the glory of God, this word does not mean a flattering opinion or the honor accorded to someone, as it does in our modern usage. From a term signifying "weight," the biblical *kavod* stands for a self-evident reality. It is in this light that the manifestation of divine power in the drowning of the Egyptians in the Red Sea is proclaimed in these terms: "And in the morning, you shall see the glory of the Lord" (Ex. 16,7), in the same way creation bears witness to his glory: "All the earth shall be filled with the glory of the Lord" (Num. 14,21). Nevertheless, since a storm was the preeminent manifestation of the power of the God of Sinai (cf. Ps. 29), the expression "glory of the Lord" very soon denoted primarily the fiery manifestation of the presence of God, as in the pillar of fire (compare the text of Exodus quoted above). It is in this manner that Ezechiel describes the vision of this glory (ch. 1; cf. Isa. 6). It is also in this sense that Moses asks the Lord to show him His glory (Ex. 33,18), and we are told that the glory consecrated the tabernacle (Ex. 29,43 and 40,34; cf. the account of the consecration of the Temple by Solomon, 3 Kings 8,10 ff.). The prophetic visions of the future Jerusalem are dominated by the splendor of the glory of the Lord who will set himself up as king (cf. Isa. 60,1; 62,7, etc.). The Servant songs announce the paradox that this glory will shine upon all nations from the work and the person of the humiliated Servant (Isa. 49,3).

In the New Testament this glory, which is the shining forth of the power and *holiness* (q.v.) of God, is revealed as the light emanating from a life that is *love* (q.v.), and that will make itself known in Christ's passion. Glory accompanied his birth (Luke 2,9), showed itself at his baptism by the opening of the heavens (*ibid.* 4,21), and was manifested particularly at the Transfiguration (*ibid.* 9,28 ff.; cf. 2 Pet. 1,17 ff.). These were the forerunning signs of the "coming of the Son of Man in His glory" (Matt. 24,30; cf. Mark 8,38), but the manifestation in the Transfiguration is explicitly connected with his approaching passion. In St. John, Jesus begins to manifest his glory in the sign wrought at Cana (John 2,11), but it is mainly in delivering himself over to the cross that he looks for his glorification by the Father. (Compare John 17,1: "Father, the hour has come; glorify thy Son that the Son may glorify thee.") He will enter into this glory, which was given to him before the creation of the world (17,24), through his Resurrection (cf. Luke 24,26 with Acts 3,13). From then on he is the "Lord of Glory" (1 Cor. 2,8), and St. Paul, who introduces this expression, explains to us how the glory of Sinai was only a shadow of what is manifested in the risen Christ (2 Cor. 3,10; cf. 4,6). To Christians, then, he promises that they will reflect the glory of the Lord with uncovered faces, shining from the risen Christ, in such a way that they are "changed into his likeness from one degree of glory to another, for this comes from the Lord who is the Spirit" (2 Cor. 3,18). Actually, the Spirit appears as the instrument of glorification. (He is the Spirit of glory according to 1 Pet. 4,14; cf. 2 Cor. 3,8. See HOLY SPIRIT.)

According to St. John, the Spirit will glorify Christ through his disciples (John 16,14), and the "fruit" they bear (the fruit of his passion, cf. *ibid.* 12,24) will glorify the Father (*ibid.* 15,8). Following this line of thought, the whole Apocalypse shows us the martyrs, who are witnesses to Christ in his passion, finding in the Spirit their own glorification that is as one with the definitive exaltation of the glory of God (cf. especially Apoc. 15). The book concludes with a vision of the heavenly Jerusalem, as the "Bride of the Lamb," coming down from heaven clothed in God's glory (Apoc. 21 and 22). It is in this way that the promise made in the Johannine Gospel becomes a reality: "That they might see my glory," and again, "The glory which thou hast given to me, I have given to them" (John 17,24 and 22). The verse of Isaiah (42,8; and 48,11), "My glory I give to no other," comes to mind. Is this simply denied by the New Testament? Not at all, for God's glorification of man in Christ, contrary to what Adam's wayward pride had sought, and far from being opposed to the unique glory of God, simply completes its radiance, which is once again revealed to be the radiance of the *agape*. This is the theme of the great hymn of Phil. 2.

If we try to grasp what is essential in this mysterious reality of the divine glory as it is expressed in all the texts, it appears to be a paradoxical communication of that which renders God's absolute transcendence as not only metaphysical, but indissolubly sacral and ethical. Its expression is light, both visible and invisible, as extended throughout material creation itself, but especially reflected by creatures of a higher order, as the angels. (See the vision of Isaiah 6 with the seraphim, who seem to be a condensation of this spiritual fire that is released by divine embers.) It achieves its perfection in the *knowledge* (q.v.) by which those beings who are in God's *image* (q.v.) reflect his own light back to him. Whence the glorification (expressed in the *Sanctus* of the same vision), which is simply the divine glory recognized by those who are called to a life in its contemplation. This is what is expressed so beautifully by the introductory prayer of the Sanctus in the synagogue liturgy, a prayer that is the primary source of all Christian eucharistic prefaces.

All of this is faithfully expressed, although in more abstract form, in the Thomistic theology of the divine glory, of the glorification of the elect, and of the supreme glorification of God in his work that is its ultimate consequence. Everything God does can be done for no other end than his own glory. And yet this glory is perfect in itself. From the moment that it pleased God to create, therefore, his creatures could not reach fulfillment except by glorifying him. Intelligent creatures, particularly, find their *beatitude* (q.v.) in the vision of the divine essence communicated to them by the light of glory. Succeeding the obscure light of faith in eternity, this is, however, only the full flowering of grace through which we live with God in love in this life, even though we do not yet see him. The vision of the divine essence in the resurrection will be reflected in the body itself, and in a certain manner through the whole sensible universe, which has been made spiritual and immortal. Other theologians, like the Byzantine Gregory Palamas (heir to the thought of the Cappadocians), balk at this assertion, and make a distinction between the vision of the essence itself, maintaining that it is inaccessible to any creature, and the vision of the glory, considered as a simple radiation of the uncreated divine "energies" by which God makes himself known in and to his creation. In fact, it does not seem that the divine simplicity can tolerate a real distinction between the essence and these uncreated energies. Nevertheless, the introduction of this distinction into Byzantine tradition is only a questionable way of stating an essential element of biblical tradition, upheld by St. Gregory Nazianzen and St. Gregory of Nyssa against the rationalism of the second generation of the disciples of Arius: the radical incomprehensibility of the divine essence. Even though St. Thomas Aquinas speaks of a vision of the divine essence in glory, he emphasizes the fact that creatures cannot comprehend it. On the other hand, the light of glory for St. Thomas is created, like grace in this life (of which it is the full flowering in eternity), in the sense that it is a quality impressed upon the soul by the divine essence. But its precise purpose is to adapt the soul, as much as it can be adapted, to this vision that causes the soul to really see God in a real union with him, but does not thereby make gods out of us, anymore than it permits us to comprehend the unfathomable mystery of God in himself. Thus, these two great Christian traditions, starting out from different points of view that seem to be in conflict point by point, actually constantly parallel what they intend to affirm. See St. Thomas Aquinas, *Sum. Theol.* Ia, q.19, a.3; q.26 and q.65, a.2; Ia-IIae, q.3. Regarding Gregory Palamas and his influence on Eastern tradition, see Jean Meyendorff, *Saint Grégoire Palamas et la mystique byzantine*, Paris, 1959.

GNOSIS   *See* KNOWLEDGE

GNOSTICISM   In the 19th century historians gave this name to a series of sects in the early Christian centuries that had the common claim of offering their adherents a *gnosis* (*see* KNOWLEDGE) that was superior to that of orthodox Judaism or Christianity, although they borrowed many doctrines and practices from both. But it must not be forgotten, as it too often is, that the words *gnosis* and *gnostic* during this period were in no way the exclusive property of those heretics, but rather the common possession of the Christians and Jews from whom they were taken. In fact, the orthodox writers who fought against those whom we call Gnostics today emphasize that in their opinion they were only pseudo-

Gnostics (the formula is even found in the title of the work written against them by St. Irenaeus).

These heresies had two things in common: 1) the assertion of a radical dualism between the world of matter and that of spirit, as well as between the higher principles governing them; and 2) the pretended revelation of a series of emanations and combinations that, beginning from a good God and a principle of evil (more or less strictly identified with matter), would have produced the present world. These systems vary, especially in the details of their explanations of the second point (the chain of "aeons," as they were generally called). In common with many other forms of Hellenistic religiosity, the Gnostics prided themselves on an esoteric tradition which those among them who called themselves Christians claimed to have originated with Christ as the revealer of their meditations. But even those only admitted an apparent incarnation, destined to bring only the "spiritual men" back to their original home, a super-cosmic *Pleroma*, through the revelation of this *Pleroma*, while those who did not accept it were rejected as being hopelessly "*psychikoi*," i.e., endowed with merely an animal existence.

Made famous especially in the rival systems of Bardesanes, Valentinus and Carpocrates, with whom Marcion has been connected because of his dualism (although he did not find it necessary to propose a series of aeons, but only an evil Demiurge identified with the God of the Old Testament, in contradistinction to the Father-God of Jesus), Gnosticism, in its primitive forms, had practically disappeared by the end of the 3rd century. But, it does correspond to certain tendencies of the fallen human mind toward a more or less puerile and pretentious esotericism, which did not vanish with the ancient systems. *Manichaeanism*, a new form of *dualism* (qq.v.), with its successors the Cathari and the Bogomils, and various medieval sects like the Beghards or Brethren of the Free Spirit, and later the different forms of esotericism and occultism of the Renaissance, as well as those that abounded in the Age of Enlightenment as a reaction to, or in singular alliances with, its rationalism, are approximate equivalents of primitive Gnosticism. Today it is found again in occultism, which has remained little changed, in theosophy and all of the forms of spurious orientalism of which it is a type. Many sects about which we may wonder how much they have retained of Christianity, such as the Jehovah's Witnesses, are equivalent to the most crass forms of the old Gnosticism. Here we again find, along with supercharged but more puerile than profound explanations of the world, the claim to a higher knowledge that is reserved to a few initiates, the tendency toward dualism, and very often the inclination toward complete separation between an ethereal spirituality and a complacent morality that frequently accompanied Gnosticism among the ancients.

Without becoming members of any of these sects, many Christians retain certain tendencies toward the fanciful and superficial theologies of certain groups, betraying within the Church herself the persistence of these shortcomings of religious reflection and of the spiritual ideal. There is no earthly end to the struggle against these shortcomings.

GOD Modern thought, particularly since the 18th century, has been affected by an attempt at first to make the idea of God appear irrational, and then as an artificial and, in effect, accidental product of a human thought still in its infancy. This is the thesis of all materialistic philosophies, and particularly that of Marxism. If such were the case, the idea of God in an adult society would die out like all outmoded illusions. We must underline the fact that recent developments both in the history of religions and depth psychology agree in acknowledging that the idea of God is, on the contrary, a primitive notion of the human consciousness, irreductible to anything else, and ineradicable. Atheism appears not only as a secondary phenomenon of civilizations in decline, but as a superficial phenomenon that is contradicted by the deepest unconscious reactions among even those who imagine that they have outgrown the idea of God, or who think they have rid themselves of it.

It must be said that even before the idea of God emerged clearly and distinctly, man's primitive consciousness is shown to have been deeply religious, insofar as it was unified in spontaneously considering every experience as dominated by a reality of the sacred, a reality at once immanent and radically transcendent. This spontaneous reaction of the human soul confronted with the universe is primary in the sense that it seems absolutely primitive; that is, there is no historical genesis of the idea of God, properly speaking, but only of the diverse and more or less elaborate representations that can be made of it. Furthermore, it is at all times the fundamental reaction of the conscience and seems to be eliminated only through the disintegration of the conscience. This disintegration is a fact present in all civilizations in crisis, but it never reaches the roots of the subconscious. Whenever this disintegration does happen, therefore, it is always a sign of man being at odds with himself to such an extent that the situation cannot persist without resulting in a tendency toward individual and collective neuroses.

The still obscure apprehension of the sacred is determined by what have been called its hierophanies. It may be said that they determine man's awareness of God, who is present in all things, but who commands and controls all things through the things themselves and through man's relationship with them. The most important of these hierophanies is the sky (the "heavens") which encompasses the universe and rises above it to an inaccessible height. The notion of the divine transcendence evolves from this fundamental religious symbolism. The sun expresses the divine as the source of light and life. To this heavenly source, the moon and the waters of either the rains or the seas are associated (or opposed) as expressions of a second sacredness that is deeply involved in the world's development, and which is, furthermore, ambivalent. In this hierophany, man finds in effect both the symbolism of creation (the mother-waters) and the symbol of the chaos to which the wrath of the heavenly powers is perpetually threatening to return it. Finally, the earth is the most immediately maternal symbol of a fecundity with which the universe is associated, although its primary source remains "on high."

In all primitive religions, the related myths in which the dynamism of these hierophanies is manifested emerged from substantially the same rituals, although they may be understood on numerous levels depending upon the state of the development of religious reflection. They are the rituals of the new year, or the renewal of vegetation, in which the divinity appears as the One who gives life and brings death, the creator and at the same time the judge and savior. With these may be connected the journey rites (in which the journey is always the return to the divine origin) and even the ascension rites (associated with the sacred tree). But the most important myths and rites are connected with meals. Therefore, as a constantly renewed awareness of not only what our life is in its unceasing dependence upon the divine, but also of the fact that there is nothing more divine, if we may say so, than the communication of life, the communion banquet, naturally associated with marriage rites, is the unfailing origin of all sacrificial notions.

However, through all of the myths we observe a perpetual tendency to confuse certain ideas, a tendency that is bound up with a process of progressive degeneration. This process, furthermore, is in almost every instance a conscious one, and takes the form of the "golden-age" myth, i.e., it is believed that in the beginning man's relationship with the divine was much more intimate. In fact, the rites themselves are always vivified by some cryptic hope of regaining this original communion. But its loss is undoubtedly reflected in the fact that creation and the fall are ordinarily superimposed to such an extent that they can never be perfectly differentiated. Beneath this primary misunderstanding, there is another universal confusion between the salvific coming of the ritual god and his own fall. There is so much confusion that the rites themselves easily slip into magic, that is, man is no longer quite sure whether it is still really a God worthy of the name that is taking possession of him, or whether it is he himself who is endeavoring to take possession of God in these rites. Undoubtedly, the root of all atheism is in this idea of a God that man's hypertrophic awareness of himself wants to dominate, and who for that very reason is no longer God. It is the inevitable prelude to the thought that the only God in this world is man himself. Concomitantly, the hierophanies we have mentioned become vulgarized until they turn progressively into autonomous "powers," and this results in polytheism. God's image is broken into pieces and pulverized until the powers become anonymous, and man sees nothing more in them than natural forces that have lost their sacred character, and over which he believes he himself can be master. From practical atheism, through magic, we arrive at the rational atheism of all humanistic civilizations.

But to these processes of the decomposition of religion, two often contrasting factors are opposed, which are always much more strictly connected than one would believe at first sight, and sometimes even aptly conjoined. One is prophecy, which appears in those who are called founders of religions, and who in general are simply religious reformers. The other is rational and critical thought in its most positive elements. In the masses, or at least in a spiritual elite, the prophets revive the easily dormant but never dead sense of the God of heaven. Man never stopped believing in this transcendent, unique God, although he had ceased to have any contact with Him when he became absorbed only in heeding the "powers" bound up with the activities peculiar to the stage of development of a particular civilization. It was the sun for those who remained gatherers, the moon for those who had already begun to hunt, the fertilizing waters for the first pastoral peoples, mother earth for the first settlers who engaged in agriculture, and then nothing less than man's action, once he became master of his own dexterity. For their part, the wise men, or the simple seekers of wisdom who became the philosophers, salvaged the age-encrusted intuitions of the "heavenly" God by scraping off the overlay of centuries from them through the use of a new-found reflexive intelligence.

Moreover, as was evidenced in Israel, on many occasions the prophets made forceful use of rational reflection to dispel the illusions of idolatry. The great promoters of an inventive rationalism claimed to be, and actually were, moved by an inspiration of some sort (cf. the "*daimon*" of Socrates). But even on these higher levels the same confusion was found. These inspired men ended up in frantic flight away from a world deprived of its sacred character (the best example is that of the Buddha), without being able to discover any countenance in the divine mystery. Otherwise they only managed to summon forth the faces of common idols, still only sparkling masks, such as the sun-God of the reformer-pharaoh Akhenaton. And if they did have an inkling of the obscure vision of the inaccessible, their disciples soon made it materialistic, as with the fire-worship of the followers of Zarathustra, along with the shadow of progressive contra-divinization of darkness that reached its completion in Manichaeanism.

If, like Plato, the philosophers do reach the pure idea of the Good,
they are tempted to look upon it as nothing more than an idea merely
extracted from reality. And if, like Aristotle, they do reemphasize the
real, their God is only the immovable Prime Mover of this world, which
is its highest sphere and does not include an infinite beyond. Ultimately
their criticism destroys its object, and reason merely acknowledges the
absence of God, which rapidly brings us, if not to a formal denial, at least
perhaps to an even more paralyzing agnosticism.

It is in this context that the experience of Israel, through biblical
revelation, comes into full relief and takes on all of its meaning. At first
sight, the worship of the God of Sinai seems to be only a revival of the
most primitive and unpolished hierophanies, namely, the God of heaven
manifesting himself on earth, especially on the mountains amid flashes
of lightning. But it was there that the burning bush was, for Moses, the
place where the ineffable *Name* was disclosed and entrusted to man. And
down from this mountain-top, with its veil of luminous clouds, He came
again with the Decalogue, the principle of a *plan* (q.v.) that was to be
revealed little by little as the vehicle whereby the progressively revealed
face of God was to be made known to man. "You shall be holy, for I
the Lord your God am holy" (Lev. 19,2) is the leitmotiv gradually
defined by the prophets until it is finally stated precisely by Him who is
much more than a prophet, "You therefore must be perfect as your
heavenly Father is perfect" (Matt. 5,48).

The biblical God is the supreme "God of heaven" who does not dwell
in any house made by man (Acts 7,48; cf. Isa. 66,1). But at the same
time it is God who, freely and sovereignly, makes himself a fellow-
traveler with lost and wandering man in order to bring man back to
Him. His holiness reveals a new face, more perfect and more severe in its
stringent demand for overwhelming justice than anything that had been
imagined. But this holiness is even more present in his *hesed*, the
incomparable loving kindness and the tireless compassion, which the
Gospel tells us will flourish forever in the *agape*, the creating and saving
love. It is a love that not only gives and is itself purely a gift of perfect
and unmeritable grace, but actually gives itself completely and without
return. The new and everlasting hierophany is the cross, but a glorious
cross that accomplishes all of the most ecstatic hopes of "natural" man's
ascension in a divine condescendence that, if it is indeed an exinanition
without parallel in all the sufferings of any imagined savior-gods, does
not involve a fall or a decline. The Resurrection and the glorification of
this Son of Man, the only true Son of God, is in no way a reparation for
the cross through some *deus ex machina*, but rather the full flowering in
heavenly glory of the love that was revealed through it on and to this
earth.

Thus man's history takes shape under the guidance of the God of revelation, and in that history His true face is revealed through the human characteristics of Jesus of Nazareth. There is no more confusion and, in principle, man will no longer fall back into his former ignorance. He has finally reached the eternal, not by doing away with the broken and tangled threads of his history, but because divine intervention straightens out and disentangles them. Creation has recovered its true meaning as God's first gift. The fall is explained not as a contamination of higher realities through an equivocal compromise with a matter incapable of salvation, but rather as an infidelity on the part of those creatures who were closest to the Creator; it first beclouded their minds, and then caused them to sink into material realities that they vulgarized further, instead of enlightening them. On the other hand, the free and generous descent of saving love takes on its true meaning as a love that prepares the re-ascent of the saved, not as a flight into the extracosmic night of a Buddhist *nirvana*, but as the ascension of man and the assumption of the whole universe into the hitherto inaccessible light of God.

Nevertheless, we should not conclude from this that the revelation of the God who has himself spoken to us, and who came down from heaven and made himself one with us, that we might be one with him, dispels all mystery. In a sense, it is perfectly true to say that the hidden God revealed himself first as hidden and mysterious, far beyond anything man could imagine or conceive about him.

Neo-Platonism, which seems to be a condensation of the most religious of diverse schools of Greek philosophical thought, although it was not without a somewhat diffuse and indirect biblical influence, had taught with Plotinus the necessity of a conversion and purification of the spirit in order to arrive at, or at least to approach, in ecstasy, the One in whom fullness is found. But Christian thinkers, even those closest to Plotinus, such as St. Augustine or even more so the Pseudo-Dionysius, teach that this ecstasy must not only bring us back to our innermost selves, but must make us escape ourselves (St. Augustine), and even that it is beyond the One of Plotinus, such as we can conceive of it in the total night of all our concepts and all our images, that the true God is encountered (Pseudo-Dionysius). And above all, it is not we who can ever reach out to him in this way, but rather it is he alone, in his grace, who can carry us off with him into this inaccessible light where he dwells.

As St. Gregory of Nyssa says, far from being the world, or the self, seen purely in their ultimate depths, God is like an abyss of such transcendent light that paradoxically always puts us in ever greater darkness the more he plunges us into it, without our being able to delude ourselves into thinking that we have ever reached its center. Undoubtedly, he is not completely unknowable to us, for all creation speaks to us of him. St. Bonaventure says that we find the traces, the vestiges of His passage everywhere. Our soul itself is his image, and this image has been illuminated by the divine model through the immediate light of his own Face, since the Word of God has assumed our flesh in order to speak to us from the closest vantage point. But this amounts to saying that all the knowledge that we can formulate about him, according to his own Word in the creation in which It was made flesh, is only analogical (see ANALOGY). In other words, the most we can say about him directs us toward a knowledge of him only if we realize its insufficiency at the very moment of our assertion of it. And the supereminent significance that all our inadequate assertions thus assume clears up the darkness of the night only to the extent that he himself brings us to the heart of this night.

Therefore, the constant paradoxes of the faith. It is God the Father, Son and Holy Spirit who is not three but one, and even more of a unity than the One of Plotinus. In this everlasting fecundity of His inner life, he has no need of his creatures, and yet they exist by virtue of a free and incomprehensible superabundance of this love which is his own life. It is this love that creates them, adopts them in the eternal Son, and makes this adoption fully effective in the communication of the Spirit: thus, what proceeds from Him, who is fully sufficient in himself, must come back to him. And it is not for the purpose of some sort of sublime annihilation, but for these mysterious nuptials of the Lamb in which the Church will be perfect in the consummation of her union with Christ, and in her, each soul-child of God in the Only-Begotten Son. The Word, eternally uttered in the silence of the Deity, will in that way sum up a many-sided Wisdom in His unity, without dissolving that Wisdom in it. It is according to the plan of this Wisdom that what was realized by God in time, and will be completed when time is no more, was conceived by God from all eternity.

Therefore, the Word in which God has revealed himself to us is the word of the supreme Mystery. Disillusioned as they were with a rationalism that was destroying itself, the men to whom the first announcement of the Gospel was to be made, as a victory over the world in which they were enslaved, were insatiable for mysteries. But the mysteries of a dying paganism were only the artificial secrets of artificially revived primitive rites, or the false depths of obscure formulas that cloaked, without substantially modifying it, a religious thought that was dying out. The Christian mystery is above all the mystery of Christ. This is a unique fact, central to history, in which the unknown and unknowable God surrendered himself to us, according to a plan of love which he kept in his heart from the beginning, but which he alone, and in his own time was able to reveal in this way. And the mystery of Christ, which takes form in the mystery of the cross, brings us to the mystery of God: the mystery of this everlasting love, which was manifested in time, is that He *is* in the eternity of his Trinitarian life. Christian thought will shed light on man's groping toward this revelation, or rather it will light the way for man's chance not only to encounter the Word, but rather to confide in the coming of that Word to him, towards which he was attracted by an instinct whose mysterious source he did not yet know. St. Augustine throws light on the Platonist quest for the Good through the corroboration of the Gospel, and finds the object of this search to be a happiness that is both lasting and satisfying and which only the perfect Good can give (*see* GOOD). Later, St. Thomas Aquinas follows the five convergent ways that Aristotelian metaphysics discloses to him. He shows how all of them end up in the postulation of one unique, necessary Being, through all of the uniquely contingent realities our senses provide for our intelligence to grasp.

The moderns, like Newman and those after him, deepen the new discovery of the personal Being that Christian experience has indelibly marked on even the most laicized rational conscience. They endeavor to prepare man to hear God speaking to him in Christ more immediately, by inducing him to listen thoroughly to what He has already told him in his own conscience.

All this effort to refine and to insure the progress of the quest of the intelligence for faith undoubtedly benefits from the examination of the intelligence itself in the light of faith. Nothing shows this better than an argument of St. Anselm, so justly debated, and yet so thought provoking. The idea that the perfect Being has in his own perfection the demonstration of his existence would undoubtedly be only a pleasant dream were this perfection merely an abstract idea. But for an intelligence which starts out from faith in its quest, it becomes a luminous certitude.

In the clarity which the human mind never attained before biblical revelation in its quest for a rational explanation of the meaning of creation in general and our own existence in particular, we can as it were experience this supernatural help that the Word of God brings to man's reason, a reason beclouded and weakened by the fall. This supernatural help is described in particularly clear terms by the First Vatican Council. But its opposite can be observed in the twofold temptation to which man's mind can be subjected when it looks at revelation. On the one hand, it is the error of *Fideism* (q.v.) that claims to render greater homage to faith if it purely and simply substitutes faith for reason. On the other hand, it is the error of all the imperfectly Christianized rationalisms that claim that they can thoroughly penetrate the truths of faith about God through reason, to the extent that they turn them into purely rational truths. In fact, the first attitude results in making the truths of faith truths that the mind cannot assimilate, while the second denatures and volatilizes them by believing that it sheds light on them.

Without committing herself to any particular philosophical system with regard to the problem of God, the Church accepts everything of the philosophical thought of every age that constitutes a rational approach to the mystery of God. Faithful to the analogy of being, she excludes both agnosticism, which claims any assertion about God is equivocal; and the various forms of Gnosticism, which are under the delusion that it is possible to know, as an object of this world, One who by his essence transcends this world. In the same line of thought, the only theological efforts that the Church recognizes as valid are those that, faithful to the analogy of faith, strive to put the mystery in proper perspective once it has been revealed. There is no question here of dispelling the mystery, but of preserving the apprehension of it through faith that does not in any way contradict reason, but which, under the influence of grace, allows itself to be transported beyond all the limitations of our minds and of the world itself from which God took us in creating us. See St. Thomas Aquinas, the entire *Contra Gentes*, and the first 26 questions of the *Summa theologica*, Ia.

GOOD   In the *Philebus* (20d) Plato defined the Good (in Greek *agathon*) as the perfect (*teleiotaton*), sufficient in itself, and the object of all who know it (this second aspect is called the sovereign Good). In the *Republic* (VI, 509b) he said, on the other hand, that everything that we know receives from the Good, not only the quality of being known, but also existence and essence. This text contains germinally some of the most important developments of Neo-Platonism, and through both the Pseudo-Dionysius and St. Augustine it had a considerable influence on all Christian theologians. We may add to this two other famous formulas from the *Republic*: "The divinity is essentially good . . . it is the cause of everything that is good" (II, 379a and b). However, the manner in which Plato explained these formulas became the basis for the metaphysical dualism that attributes evil to matter.

Aristotle (*Nicomachean Ethics*, bk. I, c.1, n.1) kept the definition of the Good as that which everyone desires, but discarded the Idea of the Good as engendering essence, existence and knowledge (i.e., the quality of being known), and only retained a Good immanent in being itself. Plotinus accomodated the Platonist theory in his conception of hypostases: the Good being the same as the transcendent One, from which Intelligence, the universal Soul, and the manifold and changing world proceed by turns.

The Bible, of course, does not give us a philosophical analysis of the Good, but the Old Testament formulates two essential assertions. God is good, of a unique goodness that manifests itself above all in his steadfast love (cf. the great Ps. 136: "O give thanks to the Lord for he is good, for his steadfast love—*hesed*—endures forever"). God, on the other hand, made everything, and everything that he made, the material world and the created spirits that inhabit it, is good, of a goodness that in the beginning was unmixed (Gen. 1). Evil thus appears above all as that which sets itself against the divine will, i.e., the rebellion of created wills against it (cf. Gen. 3). Inversely, the Law, which is the expression of the divine will, is what is best in the historical world (cf. Ps. 119).

The New Testament develops this teaching by the evangelical assertion that "no one is good, but God alone" (Mark 10,18 and Luke 18,19). Above all, it is evident here that the transcendent goodness of God is his creating and saving love (*agape*), a love of unlimited generosity, just as the goodness that is attainable for spiritual creatures is to believe in this love and to be united with it (cf. Matt. 5,43,48; Rom. 12,8; Gal. 6,2).

As wary as the Pseudo-Dionysius was of the teaching of the Neo-Platonists, he fashioned out of it a profoundly biblical systematization by identifying the Good in God with transcendent love, source of all good in all beings including matter. He thus gave a different sense to the formula of the *Timaeus* (29c), "God is without envy," (*aphthonos*) than Aristotle had attributed to it, namely, that all beings can participate in the divine goodness insofar as they tend toward it, although God himself is not concerned with this. He maintained rather that God manifests his transcendent goodness by calling all things to an existence that participates in his own. This is not a degradation of God's Being, but the free act of his love. In the same way, St. Augustine saw in the goodness of God the cause of all being and of the fact that every being is good insofar as it *is*. See EVIL.

St. Thomas Aquinas, contrary to Plato and the Neo-Platonists, maintained that the Good is identical with being, in God as in His creatures, and that the justification of being is prior to the justification of Good, distinguishing the Good from being by its character of desirability (*appetitabilitas*). He agreed with them, on the other hand, that on the plane of causality the justification of Good becomes prior to the justification of being. As for matter, St. Thomas says that if prime matter, insofar as it is not act, is not absolutely good, it becomes good through participation in the form that makes it exist in concrete beings. God, then, is supremely Good. He is the only Good who is good *essentially*, and he is the sovereign Good insofar as his goodness is the source of all desirable perfections. In creatures goodness, like being, is only participated. But insofar as they *are*, beings are good (contrary to the Manichaeans, there could not be any being which is evil by nature). Moreover, against Origen, St. Thomas admits that there are, by the will of the Creator, degrees in the goodness of beings. Their diversity arises at first from creation, and not simply from their fall. Nevertheless, creatures are all capable of perfecting themselves by their actions if they remain governed by the divine goodness. God, in this regard, is the cause of evil only insofar as he permits it, since evil is never a total corruption of the Good, but only the deprivation of a particular good, permitted by God in view of a greater ulterior good (*see* EVIL). See St. Thomas Aquinas, *Sum. Theol.*, Ia, qq.5,6,13,44,47–49,65,103; Ia-IIae, qq.55,85,98; *Contra Gentiles*, bk. I, chaps. 37–47; bk. II, chaps. 41,45; bk. III, chaps. 7,9–12,17,18,20,21.

The Manichaeans, who saw in evil a principle independent from the Good and identified with matter (something the Fathers had already condemned in the Gnostic heretics), were again condemned on this point by Eugenius IV (D.B. 706–713). John XXII, on his part, condemned the 28th proposition taken from Eckhart, which seemed to deny the divine goodness. The First Vatican Council confirmed these decisions in a vast synthesis on the goodness of God as the source of the free creation of the universe and of the raising of man to the supernatural order (Sess. III, Const. *De Fide Catholica*, cap. 1 and 2; D.B. 1783,1785,1786).

GOOD FAITH   Theological good faith is distinguished from juridical good faith. The first is an erroneous conviction that is exempt from all moral culpability. The second is an erroneous conviction that depends on a juridical basis, whether this is recognized by the law itself or simply accepted by jurisprudence. Thus, the two can exist simultaneously, but also one without the other. Theological good faith presupposes not only a totally involuntary and even unconscious inadvertence to the fact that one is ignorant of or has forgotten a moral obligation, but also the absence of indirect consent, i.e., in regard to the causes of the error inasmuch as they depend on us. Good faith excuses us from all grave culpability (St. Thomas Aquinas, *Sum. Theol.* IIa-IIae, q.10, a.1). However, we must remember that even though good faith does dispense from all fault those whom it maintains in error, it does not exempt those who could disabuse them of their error, and who should at least have a charitable obligation to do so.

GOSPEL   The Gospel, according to the meaning of the Greek word *euangelion*, is primarily the "Good News" of salvation proclaimed and realized by Christ. Secondarily, it is each of the four inspired books in which His words and deeds are recorded according to St. Matthew, St. Mark, St. Luke and St. John.

Although the word *euangelion* was already used in secular Greek, its use in the New Testament hinges explicitly upon its use in the Old Testament, and in particular from the proclamation of the deliverance and the return from captivity in the second part of Isaiah (cf. Isa. 52,7, quoted in Rom. 10,15; and Isa. 40—especially v.9—of which the first part is quoted in Matt. 3, Mark 1, and Luke 3). In the words of Jesus, the Gospel is above all the proclamation of the Kingdom of God (Mark 1,15). But it can be said (and this seems to be the meaning of Mark 1,1) that the Gospel is Jesus himself, for in him the Kingdom is present (Matt. 12,28). The Kingdom of God, in effect, as Jesus describes it in the Sermon on the Mount, is but one with our adoption by the Father, but this becomes a reality only through the sending of the Son (cf. Matt. 11,25–30, and Luke 10,21–24).

The Church, and especially her apostles, has the fundamental task of the proclamation, *kerygma* (cf. the short ending of Mark, and 1 Cor. 1,21), of the Gospel, whose heralds, *kerykes* (cf. 1 Tim. 2,7), the apostles are. For the Church, the Gospel becomes centered on the Resurrection of the Saviour (cf. the beginning of Acts, and 1 Cor. 15,1–5), which implies the *Parousia* (q.v.) of the Lord Christ and our own resurrection (cf. 1 Cor. 11,22–28).

Therefore, the Gospel proclaimed by Christ may not be separated from the Gospel of which Christ is himself the object. Actually, the Gospel finds its unity in what St. Paul calls the *mystery* (q.v.) that particularly signifies Christ's cross as the ultimate secret of the wisdom of God. In this mystery, at the end of a human history that has seen his saving intervention, God reveals his whole plan by revealing and communicating to us the most intimate aspect of his own life: his love (cf. 1 Cor. 2,7 ff.; Col. 1,26 ff.; Eph. 3,3 ff.).

This proclamation of the Gospel mystery is inseparable from its effective communication to the faith through the sacramental signs. Thus, St. Paul can tell us, "We proclaim the death of the Lord," each time we eat the bread that is the communion in his body and drink the cup that is the communion in his blood (cf. 1 Cor. 11,26 and 10,16). The reality of what the faith thus receives through a sign is also attested to by the Spirit in such a way that the *kerygma* brings with it what St. Paul calls "a demonstration of the Spirit and power" (1 Cor. 2,4). This demonstration, as revealed in the First Epistle to the Corinthians, is not accomplished only, or even chiefly, by the extraordinary gifts of the Spirit, but above all by the charity that He communicates, and which is the end of all the other gifts (1 Cor. 13).

We see, then, how the Gospel is proclaimed by the Church and by Christ, as a reality inseparable from its proclamation, and a proclamation inseparable from its already communicated reality. This communication, certainly, can only be arrived at by faith. But, in the gift of the Holy Spirit, the faith grasps its signs, which are not only its certain pledges, but already the first real fruits of the Kingdom (cf. 2 Cor. 1,22 and Eph. 1,14, with Rom. 8,2 and the entire context).

Finally, we see that the proclamation of the Gospel is not merely the communication of certain ideas; it finds its living unity in the person of the Saviour and in his works, and it is, in him and in the Spirit, the major event of human history, which, through the Church, becomes the major event in the life of each one of us.

GRACE   The theology of grace is a particularly noteworthy example of a doctrinal development within the Church that, although it reached its completion quite late, nevertheless only expresses and defines fundamental realities that have been consciously lived from the beginning. *Gratia* is the Latin translation of the Greek *charis*, previously used in the Septuagint version of the Bible to translate the Hebrew *chen*, meaning a favor accorded to someone. In the Old Testament, the favor God shows to his elect is generally accompanied by an almost motherly compassion (*rahamim*), and is manifested first of all in his loving kindness (*hesed*) and then in his faithfulness (*emet*), as in the particularly important text of Exodus (34,6).

In the New Testament, the word *charis*, pregnant with all of these associations, is used by St. Paul particularly to designate the totality of the new economy established by Christ on the basis of the forgiveness accorded to sinful mankind through Christ's death. But this negative aspect is paired off with a positive aspect that is not separate from it, namely, the adoption that makes us children of God in the risen Christ through the Spirit. It is in this way that the Epistles to the Galatians and especially to the Romans oppose grace and the law, i.e., the forgiveness requiring a justice to be realized by man as a basis for his relations with God is opposed to a forgiveness gratuitously given by God in Christ, from which flows a life based on "God's love poured into our hearts through the Holy Spirit which has been given to us" (Rom. 5,5), in contrast to a life limited in its ideals to the realization of the precepts of the law (cf. Rom. 5–6 chiefly, but also 7–8, and Gal. 5, and also 3). In these great Pauline texts, in which grace is objectively opposed to the law, the same opposition is expressed subjectively in justification by faith as against justification by works (*see* JUSTIFICATION). In the Synoptic Gospels, the word *charis* is not found, and in the Johannine Gospel it appears only in verse 17 of the prologue. But we may say that the "gift of God" referred to in the conversation with the Samaritan woman has the same meaning, while the Sermon on the Mount, with its proclamation of the divine fatherhood and of the filial life that is to be its fruit, gives the principle of this economy of grace as described in Romans 7,25, and elaborated in Romans 8.

Therefore, the content of grace in the New Testament is what God gave us in giving us his Son, and more precisely the gift of the Spirit himself by whom we become sons in the Only-Begotten, the forgiveness of our faults thus being confirmed by our renewed adoption. The development of the doctrine of grace is essentially a development within the definite notion of the need we have for God to give us this gift in order to lead us to salvation, and also the notion of the reality of this grace in us, which, as St. Paul emphasizes, does not come from us (cf. Eph. 2,8). The primary purpose of this development was to refute two series of errors. The first arose from exaggeratedly optimistic views about the actual possibilities of human nature that were held at the beginning of the 5th century by certain ascetic followers of Pelagius. On this occasion, St. Augustine showed himself to be the preeminent doctor of grace in the early Church. In the 16th century the Protestants strayed in the opposite direction into an exaggerated pessimism, which was refuted by the work of the Council of Trent. Between the two errors, however, St. Thomas Aquinas, who was even then aware of the danger that certain narrow presentations of St. Augustine's thought might produce, had effected a synthesis that was to furnish an answer to the Protestants, and later even to the similar but more subtle errors of Baianism or Jansenism, as well as to the opposite errors of certain Christian humanists.

Pelagius not only destroyed the notion of original sin, but reduced grace to the mere forgiveness of actual sins, and a better knowledge of the divine law, along with a help given to the will to facilitate what was still possible anyway for every man through his own natural powers. St. Augustine's argument against Pelagianism found criticism, however, from those who, while agreeing with his rejection of Pelagianism, felt Augustine was too far removed from the formulas taught by the ascetics of the East, such as St. Gregory of Nyssa, regarding the cooperation (synergism) of our free will with grace. This attitude was especially true of the ascetics gathered around Cassian in the area of Marseille. They taught that the response to grace, and even the search for God prior to conversion, depend at the very least upon our effort alone, as well as upon our perseverance in grace thus received. (This, in the 16th century, was called Semi-Pelagianism.) St. Augustine answered with newly detailed propositions, and by correcting some of the formulas that he had previously used, which he conceded could have been misinterpreted. The essential argument of his teaching against Pelagius was recognized by the

Council of Carthage in 418 and approved by Pope Zosimus (D.B. 101–108). In 431, in a letter addressed to the bishops of Gaul, Pope St. Celestine I made this argument even more expressly his own. To it were joined a series of specific quotations (which must have been put together by St. Prosper of Aquitaine, D.B. 128–142, in what is called the *Indiculus de Gratia*). Finally, in 529 the Council of Orange (confirmed by Boniface II) formally condemned the Semi-Pelagians in very similar terms (D.B. 174–200). Nevertheless, it must be observed that the canons of this council were soon forgotten and were not rediscovered until the scholarly research of the Renaissance, so that many a medieval theologian made use of many formulas that were more or less tinged with Semi-Pelagianism, without suspecting that they had previously been condemned by the Church.

This fact certainly contributed to the ambiguities of the Protestant controversy. The Reformers, with just concern for restoring St. Paul's teaching on grace as St. Augustine had developed it, undoubtedly fell into exaggerations in the opposite direction (i.e., a denial of all freedom to man after sin, a denial at times even of all reality of grace in the forgiven sinner, etc.). On the other hand, their errors were more than a little corroborated by the often very incompetent formulas with which their opponents, in their desire to be orthodox, answered them. It was necessary to wait for a rediscovery of the teaching of both St. Augustine and St. Thomas before the whole question could be brought into focus in a really satisfactory manner. This was to a great extent the work of the Council of Trent (Sess. V and VI; D.B. 787–843). However, excesses of naturalistic optimism among many Catholics, who were affected by the ideas of the Renaissance, again produced reactions within the Church of a calcified and exaggerated Augustinianism, first with the theologian Baius of Louvain (in the second half of the 16th century), and then with Jansenius, Bishop of Ypres (whose principal book, *Augustinus*, appeared only after his death in 1638). The errors of Baius were condemned by St. Pius V in the Bull *Ex Omnibus Afflictionibus* (1567; D.B. 1001–1080). The errors of Jansenius were first condemned in five propositions singled out by the Apostolic Constitution *Cum Occasione* (D.B. 1092–1096) of Innocent X (1653), and then again, along with the developments added to them by the Oratorian Paschase Quesnel, in the Bull *Unigenitus* of Clement XI (1713; D.B. 1351–1451). In the meantime, however, many propositions of some extreme anti-Jansenists had also been condemned by Alexander VII, Innocent XI or Alexander VIII. (These will be found under Nos. 1101–1145, 1151–1216 and 1289–1290 of D.B., where, in some editions, by an inexplicable confusion, they are presented as errors of the Jansenists themselves or the Baianists.) Finally, we may point out the *"De Auxiliis"* controversies that were carried on under Paul V regarding the Jesuit theologian Molina's system on grace. Molina was primarily attacked by the Dominican Thomists of the period, and the controversies on this delicate subject (D.B. 1090) ended up with both sides being prohibited from treating one another as heretics.

This very complex situation resulted in some clear assertions by the Church, although she refused to make any pronouncements on the lesser points. Primarily, grace is necessary not only to sustain our adherence to it through faith, when this adherence has been accomplished, but it is necessary to effectively prepare us to achieve this faith. As it is, grace prepares us for our return to God, from whom we have gone astray because of *original sin* and our *actual sins* (*see* SIN). An adherence to grace is also grace itself; as it is a grace to persevere in grace throughout our lives. These assertions resulted primarily from the condemnations of Pelagianism and Semi-Pelagianism, and their essentials were implicitly (and on many points explicitly) renewed in the teachings of the Council of Trent. On the other hand, against the Protestants, Baianists or Jansenists, the gift of grace does not suppose either that we were previously deprived of our freedom on account of original sin and its consequences, or even that in our forgiveness and regeneration God's action was purely and simply substituted for our freedom. Far from annihilating our freedom in any way, grace restores it. Consequently, in the forgiven and regenerate sinner, faith, charity and all the other virtues are gifts of God in the fullest sense, without being alien to the one who possesses them. As St. Paul said, it is God who creates our will and our action in us (Phil. 2,13), but this is so little opposed to the need we each have of working personally for our salvation, that St. Paul's assertion is given to explain to us how we can and must accomplish it (*ibid.*, v.12).

This is found with an equally remarkable balance and fullness in St. Thomas's teaching on grace. The article NATURE describes what our nature is in itself, as set down by Aquinas, together with the already supernatural state to which it had pleased God to raise it in the beginning, and the fallen state in which it found itself since original sin. We shall limit ourselves here and merely state that for St. Thomas grace in the forgiven and regenerate sinner is a new quality permanent in itself, in the manner of a *habitus* (q.v.), but accidental and not substantial (*see* ACCIDENT, and SUBSTANCE). It is a pure and free gift of God, whereby he adapts us to a profoundly mysterious, but nonetheless real, participation in his own life (following the formula of the Second Epistle of St. Peter 1,4, which declares that we have been made sharers in the divine nature). St. Thomas specifies that this grace, insofar as it is something that God creates in us, is distinct from the Holy Spirit (against Peter Lombard, for whom grace was merely the Spirit of God in us). He maintains that the Holy Spirit is actually given to us as an uncreated grace. But if a created effect were not also present with the Holy Spirit in us, as the mark on us of the divine gift, there would be no effective giving of the divine life to man, and the presence of the Spirit in us would be nothing more than that of an inert thing in an inanimate receptacle. Obviously, nothing would be more contrary to all that Scripture tells us of the life of grace in us.

This *habitual* grace, whereby we are sanctified in the very depths of our being, blossoms forth in the different *infused virtues* and the *gifts of the Holy Spirit* (q.v.). But, far from thereby dispensing us from the necessity of a special grace by which God would intervene in each of our holy actions (*actual* grace) so that they might actually be holy, habitual grace demands it. Habitual grace does not in any way establish an autonomous mode of being in us, from which an analogous mode of acting could result. On the contrary, in place of our prior sinful dispositions, it sets up an inclination to act only in dependence upon, abandonment to, and conformity with, God's own action in us.

On the other hand, all grace that sanctifies us (*sanctifying* grace)— although it is true that it sanctifies us only in taking possession of our being and our will—does so of itself, and not through any sort of supposed autonomous action on our part, or even our mere consent. This is what is expressed by St. Thomas, who said that grace is of itself *efficacious*. But this must not be understood to mean (contrary to the Baianist or Jansenist tendency) that grace suppresses our freedom or is substituted for it. Quite the contrary, it only regenerates our freedom. How can this be understood? This is the great mystery that St. Thomas does not attempt to fathom, although he clarifies it admirably by showing how God's action upon us for our good is absolutely different from the action of all created other instruments since He is the Creator and, more precisely, the Creator of our freedom itself (*see* PROVIDENCE, and PREDESTINATION). However, it must be admitted that the notion of a grace that could be called *sufficient* for salvation, without being *efficacious*, is not found in St. Thomas. Although it does not merit censure on that account, nevertheless we must add that such an idea could not have been proposed by St. Thomas without departing from the principles of his entire synthesis on the subject.

Finally, let us give some particulars of vocabulary. Following St. Augustine, we have distinguished *gratia operans*, which acts in us to move our will (although our own will does not yet act), from *gratia cooperans*, to which the justified sinner freely adheres. As for the term *gratia praeveniens*, it was used by medieval theologians in opposition to *gratia subsequens*, according to which the successive effects of grace in us are considered. In the language of modern theologians the word no longer designates the priority of an effect of grace in relation to another effect, but rather the priority of grace itself in relation to its effect. The texts of the Council of Trent call *gratia excitans* the grace that strives to save us from sin, and *gratia adjuvans* that which is focused directly on inducing our free acts (St. Augustine simply said that grace is *excitans* and *adjuvans*). These are two forms of what St. Thomas would have called *gratia operans*, which would be called *gratia praeveniens* today.

In the articles NATURE and SUPERNATURAL the problems posed by the relationship between nature and grace are discussed. The article MERIT deals with the question of the connection between merit and grace. See also St. Thomas Aquinas, *Sum. Theol.*, Ia.-IIae, qq.109–114; and IIIa, qq.48–49; cf. q.62; and, on the distinction between uncreated grace and created grace, see IIa-IIae, q.23, a.2.

A last distinction remains to be explained. All the forms of grace we have discussed so far are graces *gratum facientes*, that is, the immediate effect upon those who receive them is to bring them into the friendship of God. In this they are opposed to the graces *gratis datae*, i.e., the extraordinary gifts (gifts of miracles, prophecy, etc.) that may be given to an individual for the benefit of the entire body of the Church, but which do not sanctify the individual himself, at least not directly. St. Paul points out, in the 12th and 13th chapters of the First Epistle to the Corinthians, the transcendent superiority of grace, *gratum faciens*, over even the most extraordinary graces, *gratis datae*.

GUILT   This term is used with regard to the defective state in which a sinner finds himself as a result of his *sin* (q.v.), and in opposition to the *punishment* (q.v.) that must be its consequence and its compensation (*reatus culpae* and *reatus poenae*).

H

HABITUS　According to St. Thomas Aquinas, a *habitus* is an inclination in proportion to which our nature finds itself well- or ill-disposed in relation to itself or to another being. These *habitus* are then entitative, like health, or simply operative, like the virtues. The state of grace is a supernatural entitative *habitus*, which in the powers of our soul corresponds to those operative supernatural *habitus* that are the infused *virtues* (q.v.). It is evident then that we must avoid confusing *habitus* with those merely automatic habits through which, as soon as they have been established, we act almost without realizing it, and in such a way that our responsibility is thereby more or less impaired. *Habitus*, on the contrary, St. Thomas says, make us act *firmiter, expedite, delectabiliter*, that is, in a manner that involves us more deeply and more spontaneously in the healthy pleasure that we derive from an activity that is connatural. See St. Thomas Aquinas, *Sum. Theol.*, Ia-IIae, q.49 ff.

HAGIOGRAPHY　This word literally means "the description of the saints," or better, of their holiness. The only hagiography that conforms with the spirit of the Church in saints' canonization is one that respects the essential hierarchy between grace *gratum faciens* and the graces *gratis datae* (explained under the word GRACE). This is true of the oldest and most reliable of the *Acts of the Martyrs*, the official accounts of the trials and sentences of the martyrs. But it is far from being the case with many more or less popular biographies, where the marvelous, often conceived in a most puerile fashion, is preferred over perfection in faith and charity. Yet, it is the orientation and the efficacious tendency toward this perfection that alone constitute Christian holiness, while these extraordinary gifts themselves have no other meaning than to arouse our faith and our love.

HAND OF GOD　This vivid expression, used many times in the Bible, especially the form, "A mighty hand and an outstretched arm" (cf. Ex. 6,1; 15,6 and 12; Deut. 26,8 etc.), signifies God's intervention in human history, which accompanies his Word, and by which he carries out his judgments on those who refuse him their faith, while he sets his people free.

HEALING　Throughout the Gospels, it is undeniable that sickness, even when due to immediate and purely natural causes, appears as a consequence brought down on man by sin. Certain sicknesses assume the appearance of real signs of the devil's domination in the world (*see* POSSESSION), but even when this is not the case, it is clear that Jesus heals sickness just as he forgives sins, and manifests by both actions his removal of men from Satan's power in order to bring them back to his Father (cf. Luke 13,16). It follows that prayer is recommended not only to help the sick bear their ordeal in a Christian way, but that they may be cured, if it is God's will (cf. Matt. 10,8; Mark 6,56; Luke 5,15 etc.). The references to anointing the sick in the New Testament are expressly aimed at this objective (Mark 6,13 and Jas. 5,14). Finally, with the saints as with Christ, the gift of healing (mentioned many times among the charismatic gifts of the Spirit; cf. Acts 4,22 and 30; 1 Cor. 12,9,28 and 30) appears as an especially noteworthy sign of divine favor (cf. Acts 5,15 and 19,12).

To prayerfully expect the healing of the sick who have received the sacrament of anointing is, therefore, perfectly normal, even though we accept in advance that the decision to manifest its spiritual effectiveness, whether tangibly or not, is God's alone. The same is true in a more general way with regard to prayer for the cure of a sick person, the petition addressed to the holy servants of God that they might help in obtaining it, or pilgrimages to holy places that seem to have been particularly singled out by God because of the relative abundance with which this sign has been given to us in these places. As long as all of these practices are done with a faith that is resigned to God's ultimate decision, whatever it may be, far from being considered superstitious, they are certainly praiseworthy, and follow the example of so many cases of this type in the Gospels, in which we see Christ praising the faith that is expressed by them (cf. in particular the case of the woman in Matthew (9,21) whom we might otherwise easily be tempted to accuse of superstition).

All of this explains why the Church, in the processes of beatification or canonization, attaches such great value to miracles of this type.

HEART, HEART OF MARY   *See* SACRED HEART

HEAVEN   English is one of the very few languages where a distinction exists between the dwelling place of God, *heaven* (Anglo-Saxon *heofon*), and a word referring to the upper atmosphere, *sky* (from Old Norse, a cloud or a cloudy sky).

In any case, heaven (or the heavens) in primitive religious symbolism has always designated not only God's dwelling-place, but his superior manifestation, namely, that of an inaccessible power that dominates all others. In Israel, the assertion that the Lord is the God of heaven signifies in a more or less miraculous manner that his presence cannot be captured and grasped by men (Isa. 66,1–2 and Acts 7,48–50). The Apocalypse describes heaven as the place where the immediately manifest presence of God is praised by the angels and saints (chaps. 4 and 5). The Gospel accounts of the Ascension express the conviction that the risen Saviour is now associated with the Kingdom and power of God (Mark 16,19–20; Luke 24,50–51; Acts 1,4–11). Finally, St. Paul presents the risen Christ as the heavenly Man whose image we are called to bear, just as we bore the image of the earthly Adam (1 Cor. 15,47–49). These interpretations are sometimes presented as if this vision were narrowly bound up with an archaic concept of a universe of tiered zones, as in the cosmological theories found in Aristotle or the astronomer Ptolemy. In fact, despite the inevitable inadequacies of language the biblical writers, when speaking of "heaven" in a religious context, indicate that they understand by it a place of paradox, not accessible to man or to any creature (cf. 1 Tim. 6,16), but a place from which God can, without ever "leaving" it, intervene everywhere and at the same time bring to it whom he will (cf. 2 Cor. 12,2). In this sense, heaven is like a place beyond the visible world, while the world is suffused with it. (Cf. St. Thomas Aquinas, *Sum. Theol.*, Suppl. q.69, a.3.) Let us note, however, that if St. Thomas admits with some reservations the theories of the ancients about the existence of an empyreal heaven (i.e., a heaven made of igneous and subtile matter, beyond the material world to which we belong), he emphasizes at the same time that it is a question of a hypothesis that is based only on the authority of Strabo, the Venerable Bede, and St. Basil (St. Thomas Aquinas, *Sum. Theol.*, Ia, q.61, a.4).

HELL   A translation of the Latin word *infernus*, which means "the place below," it has come to designate the abode of devils and damned souls. In the Christian sense, the Greek term *Hades* has a wider meaning, corresponding to the Hebrew *Sheol*, the general abode of the dead. However, the word used in the Bible that corresponds most closely to our notion of hell is *Gehenna*, a metaphorical term designating a valley near Jerusalem where it seemed rubbish was burned. The Jews had used the term to designate the place where the worm does not die, and the fire does not go out, and to which the damned are sent (Isa. 66,24; cf. Jude 16,21). The term is found again with this meaning in the Gospels (Matt. 5,22–29; 18,9; Mark 9,44). The furnace spoken of in Matthew (13,42–50), the fire described in Matthew (18,8 and 25,41; cf. Jude 7), the pool of fire and sulphur referred to in the Apocalypse (19,20; 20,9 and 15; 21,8), the place of torment in Luke (16,28) and the Tartarus in the Second Epistle of Peter (2 Pet. 2,4) all seem to refer to the same reality. Against certain theologians, like Origen, who seemed to cast some doubt upon the final character of God's judgments, the formula of faith of Damasus, the Fourth Council of the Lateran, the Second Council of Lyons, and the Council of Trent (Sess. VI, can.25), simply using the Gospel terminology, asserted that damnation as well as salvation is eternal. The Synod of Constantinople in 543, approved by Pope Vigilius, more explicitly defined the perpetual nature of the punishment of the damned (D.B. 211). The Second Council of Lyons defined further that those who die in a state of mortal sin go immediately to hell (D.B. 464). Besides, theologians almost unanimously admit that the punishment of hell does not consist merely in *damnation* (q.v.), but also in a positive punishment, which the worm and the fire metaphorically designate. Everything else on this profoundly mysterious question is only speculation, which the Church has never accepted. See St. Thomas Aquinas, *Sum. Theol.*, Suppl., qq.69,70,86,97–99; cf. *ibid.* Ia, q.21, a.4, ad 1um.

HELLENISM   The culture proper to the world of Greek antiquity. A distinction is to be made here between the purely Greek Hellenic culture of the great classical period (6th to 5th centuries B.C.), and the Hellenistic Age that was practically coeval with the beginning of Christianity, and in which Hellenism had become imbued with many foreign elements, notably Eastern in origin. In the articles ABSOLUTE, ARISTOTELIANISM, PLATONISM, MYSTERY, and SOUL, the chief elements of Hellenism that succeeded in affecting the development of Christian theology are discussed.

HERESY   From the Greek *hairesis*, which means "choice," this word, after having been taken simply as a synonym for schism (from *schisma*, "a division of opinion"), was at an early date used by the Church to designate separations from the common doctrine of faith resulting from a grave and unyielding doctrinal error. The first heresies seem to have been those of the various *Gnostics* (*see* GNOSTICSM). It is necessary to distinguish between *formal* heresy, an action by those who deliberately contradict a truth defined by the Church, and *material* heresy, simply inadvertence or ignorance of Church definitions. In judging heretics themselves, there is also a distinction between the heresiarch (i.e., the person responsible for originating the formal heresy) and his sectaries, who may have been deceived by the reputation of a generally revered teacher, and even by the piety of the one who subsequently fell into heresy. Therefore, we have to distinguish between those who belong to the first generation in which a heretical sect was established, and those who are born into it, and who, consequently, have little or no means of knowing the true Church and her teaching. As a result, the application of censures regarding heretics should be handled delicately, and even considered individually depending upon the particular case. For obvious reasons, our judgment in regard to their conduct should reflect this thinking.

It should be noted, also, that heresies—especially those that show a singular capacity for outliving their founders and propagating themselves long after by producing certain manifest signs of God's grace—generally rely upon a correct perception of certain truths or aspects of the truth that too many Christians, even responsible clergymen, have previously neglected. An individual does not ordinarily become a heretic except when his enthusiasm for the truth he recognizes brings him to disregard other truths that are no less essential to the integrity of the faith. But we have to admit that he should often be excused from such errors due to the negligence and inactivity of theologians, as well as Church authorities, who should have been the first to recognize and reestablish truths that, for the moment, are obscure. It is, therefore, an error to believe that the Church has truly triumphed over a heresy once it has discovered and condemned it specifically. She has effectively overcome it only when her theology and her practice have reintegrated into Catholic faith and life that which is authentically true, even though poorly evolved, in the heresy in question; thereby restoring to Catholic unity those Christians who had been deceived through no fault of their own.

HESYCHASM   From *hesychazein*, "to be at peace," the word is used of a school of spirituality that originated in the ancient monastic tradition of Sinai, although it developed during the Middle Ages on Mount Athos. Its theologian was the 14th-century Bishop of Thessalonica, called by the Byzantines St. Gregory Palamas. The essential point of this school is a yearning after the contemplation of the *glory* of God (q.v.) in Christ, through the quieting and unification of one's whole being in a constant prayer dominated by the invocation of the *Name* of Jesus (q.v.).

HIERARCHY   Apparently this word made its appearance in Christian vocabulary with the Pseudo-Dionysius, two of whose major works are *Celestial Hierarchy* (divisions that exist among the angels) and *Ecclesiastical Hierarchy*. It is frequently argued that this notion of hierarchy simply denotes his absorption in the notions of the heirarchy of being of Neo-Platonism, particularly those of Proclus. This is an egregious error. If Proclus speaks frequently of *taxis*, i.e., of the immutable order that exists among the different parts of the universe, and the different beings that correspond to it, he ignores "hierarchy" completely and it is an utter misinterpretation to believe that the

Pseudo-Dionysian hierarchy is simply a facsimile of the Neo-Platonist *taxis*. In fact, the Dionysian hierarchy is essentially a communication through which all those who have received something from God must communicate it to those who are not as well-favored, inasmuch as they cannot keep the graces given to them without sharing them. This, therefore, is quite different from the Neo-Platonist *taxis*, which is the product of a simple degradation of being, and in no way the result of a free generosity of a love it does not know. Moreover, it is essential to the view of the Pseudo-Dionysius that each member of the hierarchy directly participates in what he calls the divine thearchy of the three divine Persons, regardless of the level he starts from and whether or not with the help of those superior to him. Finally, on this basis, he tells us explicitly that the one who responds faithfully to the overtures made to him, even though he should be in the lowest rung of the ecclesiastical hierarchy, can be raised to a level of holiness, of perception of the divine realities and life in God, in keeping with the lofty gradation of the heavenly hierarchy itself.

This analysis is not merely concerned with specifying Dionysius' thought, but also with throwing light on the sense in which the Christian view of the Church and the universe is hierarchical. It is undoubtedly hierarchical, provided it is not forgotten that "hierarchy" must not be understood as simply an immutable order, but, rather, a generous communication. All order of life in God himself and in the universe or the Church, as arranged by him, has no other meaning than to prepare for this communication.

In view of this, the hierarchy of ministries in the Church is merely a hierarchy of services, ordained with a hierarchy of holiness in view; a holiness that, finally, has no other principle than God's freedom, on the one hand, and, on the other, the extent of each personal response to His ultimately inexplicable generosity.

If we keep this concept in mind, it is evident that hierarchy, in the traditional sense of the word, is not simply composed of authorities, i.e., of bishops within the Church, or even of the different ministers ranked according to their respective orders. It is extended to the whole body of the faithful. It is not merely a static order of dignities and functions within this body, but, rather, the communication of life made by the members to one another, and the fellowship in this life that is its purpose.

HISTORY From the Greek *historia*, which means simply a "description" (a sense that has been retained in natural history), the word has come to mean more specifically the description of events that mark the lives of people and of mankind as a whole, as well as an inquiry into the causes that may explain the sequence of events. By extension, the word has more recently come to designate this development of human facts in itself. It is a new tendency of human thought, actually, to stress that aspect of human life that is in a state of perpetual transformation. The idea of progress is a particularly popular expression of this, but even those who are averse to admitting that it is the real key to human history, are just as concerned about history's possible meaning. Furthermore, the idea of progress, as well as the more specific idea of a sense of history (a notion that Marxism, in particular, has propagated in our own day) seem to have originated in Christianity. It was Christianity, actually, that introduced the idea of a decisive event, the Incarnation, into Western thought; an event that gives meaning to everything that went before, and prepares for a new and definitive future. Before it, Greek thought knew only the idea of a primitive golden age, followed by a sempiternal decline or, perhaps through Eastern influences, as in Stoicism, the idea of an eternal return in which all things unceasingly pass through the same cycle of birth, development, decline, death and rebirth.

However, it is only with the Renaissance that a real science of history based on *criticism* (q.v.) of documents and facts took shape. Its application to the documents of Christianity at first caused a scandal, particularly because many of those who gave themselves most brilliantly to it in the 19th century, did so with rationalist prejudices and, in the name of a so-called objective criticism, tended more or less consciously to justify these prejudices. But we may say that progress itself in the application of historical criticism has tended to bear out these devious apologetics disguised as the science of history. Is this to say that the science of history alone can establish the truth about the fundamental facts of Christianity? It does not seem so insofar as certain of these facts are essentially supernatural, and therefore only accessible to faith, like the Resurrection of the Saviour. But history, as a critical science, can establish, on the one hand, the inadequacy of historical explanations that would eliminate the data of faith; and, on the other, the accord between what faith tells us and what we can know with certainty about the facts accessible to science.

As for the philosophy of history, which posits the question whether history has a particular sense, Hegel, in the 19th century, tried to construct it on an idealistic and rationalistic basis. He thought it possible to evolve an idea by which the immanent dialectic alone would explain the complete unfolding of history. For him, ultimately, this idea was the modern State organizing all human activity so that in it would be realized, in a rational way, everything promised by the notion of God, which in turn was a simple premonitory figure of the ultimate idea. Bringing the same dialectic down to the level of materialism, Marx focused on the Socialistic State as the next to the last stage of evolution, i.e., once the State had fulfilled its role of freeing man from economic slavery it was to be succeeded by the perfection of Communist mankind.

Quite obviously, these different philosophies of history are only attempts to transpose Christian eschatology in materialistic or rationalistic terms. They put us on guard by the very fact that no philosophy, if by that we understand a purely experimental and rational science, can, in fact, express the sense of history. The Incarnation, in spite of sin, has made it possible for us to realize man's call to divine sonship, and does not allow for a total sense of human history to subsist that would not be profoundly supernatural. It follows that the problem of the sense of human history is a specifically theological one and that the views regarding the Kingdom of God, as revealed in the Gospels, must dominate its solution. See ESCHATOLOGY, KINGDOM OF GOD, and PAROUSIA.

HOLINESS Holiness (or sanctity) is synonymous with sacredness (see SACRED), although the term has come to imply a moral aspect through a consideration of the personal character of the Godhead. It is one of the major teachings of the great prophets, particularly Isaiah, that divine holiness is manifested especially in justice. Spiritual creatures, then, are made holy to the extent that their will conforms to the holy will of God through faith and obedience (Isa. 6). In Christianity, holiness is therefore one and the same with the perfection of charity (see BEATIFICATION, and CANONIZATION). In the New Testament all Christians are called holy (i.e., saints) by virtue of their baptism (cf. 1 Pet. 1,15), just as Jesus, to whom baptism assimilates them, is the "holy one of God" (Mark 1,24; Luke 4,35; John 6,39). And, just as the angels are traditionally called "saints" (cf. Mark 8,38), the Apocalypse gives this title to the blessed, especially martyrs (cf. Apoc. 5,8; 11,18; 13,7 etc.).

HOLY OILS The use of oil as a fortifying embrocation or lotion, and as the excipient of different perfumes, is at the root of its religious symbolism. In the Old Covenant the custom of anointing kings particularly signified that the strength they needed to govern human affairs came from on high (cf. the anointing of Saul by Samuel, in 1 Kings 10,1 ff.). The priests and, more particularly, the high priests were also anointed (cf. Ex. 29,7 and Lev. 8,12). Finally, in the case of Elisha we are told of the anointing of a prophet (3 Kings 19,16). It is from this early symbolism, and the royal anointing in particular, that the idea of the Messiah comes, i.e., the idea of the preeminent Anointed One; the One in whom the divine Presence will be manifested, and who will act with heavenly power to establish God's own Kingdom on earth. The name Christ is merely the Greek translation of the Hebrew term *mashiah* ("messiah").

It is to signify our sharing in the messianic anointing of Jesus that the holy oils have become an element of Christian liturgy. The first and most important of these oils is chrism, scented oil (called *myron*, "scent," by the Greeks) with which new Christians are anointed after their baptism (*see* CONFIRMATION, and CHRISM). With it may be connected the oil used in the prebaptismal anointings that symbolize the strength we must receive from God in order to wage combat with the forces of evil, a combat that must culminate in a profession of Christian faith. In the West it is what is called the oil of the catechumens, which, with chrism, is consecrated in the West by all bishops in a special Mass on Maundy Thursday. In the East, in principle, the consecration of chrism on this same day is reserved to the patriarchs.

Quite different from these oils is the oil of the sick. It is used for the sacrament of the *anointing of the sick* (q.v.) and is related to the very ancient use of oil as a medication, which is founded on the fundamental notion of oil as a source of strength. In the West this oil is also consecrated at the Pontifical Mass of Maundy Thursday (not, like chrism and the oil of the catechumens, after the Communion, but before the doxology of the eucharistic canon, at which point, in the early days, blessings of the fruits of the earth and their products took place). In the East the priests bless it before each administration of the sacrament.

HOLY SCRIPTURE   This term is understood to mean the sum total of books that the Church formally acknowledges as directly inspired by God (*see* CANON). These books obviously constitute the most fundamental statement of the *Word of God* (q.v.), and from the fact that they must be thought of as having God himself for their author, they are an absolutely privileged statement of that Word. This does not mean, contrary to Protestant belief, that they may be reliably interpreted, either without the intervention of the Church, or without the Church herself having to refer, for that purpose, to any other document. The Word of God, in effect, is a living reality, which no text, however sacred, could preserve independently of those who hear it. Consequently, we are always certain of being able to keep the Word of God in its authentic expression, and also in its true sense, only by virtue of the promise made to the Church of a permanent *assistance* (*see* ASSISTANCE OF THE HOLY SPIRIT) of the same Spirit who has inspired the Scriptures (*see* INSPIRATION). Moreover, since this assistance makes it possible always to read this text in its true sense, it could no more dispense with recourse to the sacred text than it could dispense with a recourse to the life of the truth of the Word of God evidenced in the body of God's

People, which constitutes *tradition* (q.v.). As is explained in greater detail in the article TRADITION, we should look upon Scripture and tradition not so much as two complementary but independent sources of truth, but rather as Scripture constituting the kernel of tradition, from which it cannot be separated in order for it to be understood, while at the same time, tradition itself takes shape only in a scriptural context.

It is these different considerations that make it possible to understand that, for all the theologians of the Middle Ages, as well as for the Fathers of the Church before them, theology is essentially an explanation of Scripture, which must not only always start from the sacred text, but must always return to it. The anti-Protestant polemic has contributed not a little towards obscuring this focal point. But it is very important not to forget that a theology that would disregard it definitively would for that very reason cease to be a Catholic theology in the traditional sense of the word, and especially in the sense described by St. Thomas and the great Schoolmen of the 13th century.

Nevertheless, it is not primarily as a source of scientific theology that Scripture is given to the Church: it is as the source of life inseparable from truth. Revealed truth, in effect, was not revealed to us to satisfy our curiosity, but to lead us to salvation. And it is in the form that God himself has given it in Scripture that it is immediately and most eminently suited to do this. Here again, however, Scripture must not be separated from the whole of tradition, and especially liturgical tradition. For, since Scripture is the primary deposit of the Word of God addressed to the People of God, it is in the midst of this people especially, where they are prepared to hear God speaking to them in order that they might devote themselves to the exigencies of that Word and to open their hearts to its promises through prayer and sacrifice, that we will find ourselves ready to listen to it as we should. Consequently, since Scripture has always served as a basis for the liturgical celebration, it is in a deep absorption in the liturgy, not merely in a bookish way, but in a truly vital manner, that we will have the best chance of hearing God as he wishes to be heard.

See St. Thomas Aquinas, *Sum. Theol.*, Ia, q.1.

HOLY SPIRIT   The Spirit of God (in Hebrew *ruah*, which, like the Greek *pneuma* and the Latin *spiritus*, means first "breath," and more particularly, "life's breath") appears in the Old Testament both as the power that inspires the prophets and causes them to speak in the name of God Himself, and as the power that accomplishes the works of God through men as works that bear his own mark. (Cf. Ex. 15,20; 2 Esdras 11,25 ff.; 1 Kings 10,6; and 3 Kings 18,22 with Judges 3,10; 6,34; 11,29 etc.) Finally, the priestly document of Genesis shows us the Spirit moving over the chaos to draw the organized world out of it, just as the Word was at the beginning (Gen. 1,2). The same relationship between the Spirit and the Word is found again in the prophecy of Ezechiel on the dry bones; they take on flesh and stand up under the operation of the Word, and then the Spirit breathes on them and they come to life again (Ezech. 37).

However, throughout the Old Testament the distinction between the divine Spirit and the angelic spirits sent by God does not always appear very clear. Even the evil spirit who takes possession of Saul can, on occasion, be called the "spirit of God" (cf. 1 Kings 18,10). Nevertheless, a direction is already taking shape in which the Spirit signifies the very presence of God in man, either in regard to the Messiah in the great text of Isaiah (11), or with regard to the whole renewed People in the text of Joel, which Peter uses to explain Pentecost (Joel 2,28–32, quoted in Acts 2,17–21), or in the expectation of a new Passover revealed by Isaiah (63,7 to 64,12).

In the Synoptics the Spirit is introduced as the author of the virginal birth of Jesus, both by Matthew and Luke (Matt. 1,18; Luke 1,35). John the Baptist proclaimed that the One to come after him would baptize "in the Spirit and fire" (Matt. 3,11 and par.; cf. John 1,33). The Spirit, furthermore, visibly comes down upon Christ at his baptism and remains with him, while the Father's voice makes itself heard (Matt. 3,16 and par.; John 1,32), and it is God who sends him into the desert to fight against the devil (Matt. 4,1 and par.). Jesus himself says his mission is to cast out the spirit of evil by the Spirit of God (Matt. 12,28 ff.), and makes a pronouncement in this regard on the inexpiable sin, which is the sin against the Spirit. Finally, He promises his disciples that the Spirit will inspire them when they will have to bear witness to Him in facing men's hostility (Matt. 10,20 and par.).

But it is St. John who describes the complete revelation of the Spirit's role to us as an essential note of Jesus' last conversation with His followers. They are to rejoice that Jesus is on the eve of leaving them, for his departure to the Father will result in the Spirit's coming down to them (John 16,7). The Spirit will be among them as another Paraclete (understood as one other than Jesus), i.e., as an advocate who both defends and counsels his client (John 14,16–26). It is the Father himself who will send the Spirit through the intercession of the Son (John 14,17; cf. v.26), but it is also the Son himself who will send Him (15,26) on behalf of the Father, for He is the Spirit of truth who will remind them of everything Jesus had told them, who will teach them all things, and who will glorify the Father in taking what is the Son's in order to make it known to them.

For St. Paul, the relationship between the Son and the Spirit is described in quite similar terms, but with the specification that it is by the gift of the Spirit that the reality of our adoption by the Father is made manifest in the Son (Rom. 8,14–17; cf. Gal. 4,6–7). According to John, baptism must be a new birth, or a heavenly birth, of water and the Spirit (John 3,8). In the same way, St. Paul draws a parallel between the life of the natural man, who is merely flesh, and the life of the new man in Christ, who is "Spirit" (cf. Rom. 7–8 and Gal. 5,16–22). Just as in the Fourth Gospel, Jesus, having risen from the dead, breathed on this disciples and communicated the Spirit to them, thus also in St. Paul, it is apparent that the risen Jesus, who has become the "Life-giving Spirit" (just as Adam was only a "living spirit"), communicates the Spirit (cf. 1 Cor. 15,45 and 2 Cor. 3,17–18).

As a matter of fact, the gift of the Spirit at *Pentecost* (q.v.), which follows the Resurrection, and at which time He comes down to the Church gathered together in prayer with the same signs of theophany (the rushing wind, and the flames of fire) that had marked the first covenant on Sinai commemorated on that day, had been the consecration of the Church; at the same time the Spirit had given the Church the task of bearing witness to the Resurrection to all peoples (cf. Acts 2). The extraordinary gifts that had accompanied the descent of the Spirit (speaking in tongues, miracles, etc.) awakened the enthusiasm of the first Christians. But in his First Epistle to the Corinthians St. Paul insists upon the fact that the only essential gift, and the purpose of all the others, is charity (cf. 1 Cor. 12 and 13). For St. Paul the most characteristic gift of the Spirit is what he elsewhere calls "the *agape* of God [i.e., the *agape* proper to God] poured out into our hearts by his Spirit" (Rom. 5,5).

The Church of the patristic age was torn for some time between the illuminist tendency dominating in the *Montanism* (q.v.) of Tertullian, which advocated living a perpetual Pentecost in an artificial prolongation of the miraculous manifestations of the Spirit; and a rationalistic tendency, following Arianism, that would reduce the Spirit to a communication of a principle of higher life, which is not God himself. This is the Macedonian error (from its originator, Macedonius). The First Council of Constantinople, confirming the definitions of Nicaea on the Son and his full divinity, condemned it, and at the same time asserted the divinity and the personality of the Paraclete in terms that have passed into the Creed used today in most of the eucharistic liturgies of both East and West.

The last controversy involving the Holy Spirit was when the East reproached the West for having added the *filioque* ("and from the Son") to the Creed after the phrase taken from St. John (15,26) in respect to the Spirit, "who proceeds from the Father." It is to be noted that the Greek Fathers, such as Gregory of Nyssa, already knew the formula "and from the Son," and that the formula "who proceeds from the Father by the Son" (a possible translation of the *filioque*) was as common in the East as in the West. The first controversies arose, therefore, out of the unilateral introduction (begun in Spain around the 6th century, it seems) of the new phrase, rather than on a doctrinal basis. But as a result, the East, always preferring to emphasize the Persons of the Trinity rather than the abstract nature in their view of the Trinity, tended to look upon the *filioque* as an indication of the Latins' imperfect appreciation of the personal role of the Spirit. The answer of many a medieval theologian in the West, which was designed to mollify their scruples, namely, that the Spirit proceeds from the Father and the Son as from one sole principle (*tamquam ab uno principio*), seems rather to have aggravated them by appearing to be a supplementary indication of an imperfect personal distinction between the Father and the Son himself. Therefore, it would be better to say, according to the ancient and beautiful formula of Pope Dionysius (in his letter to his namesake of Alexandria, in the 3rd century), that the Spirit proceeds from the Father in the Son, and returns with Him to the Father.

Another theological controversy affecting only the West, found St. Thomas Aquinas in opposition to Peter Lombard's disciples, who declared that the Spirit was purely and simply one with grace and charity (*see* GRACE). In the articles EUCHARIST and EPIKLESIS we have already spoken of the problem of the role of the Spirit in the Eucharist, and in the articles INDWELLING OF THE DIVINE PERSONS and GIFTS OF THE HOLY SPIRIT the problem of the Spirit's presence and action in us is discussed. See also the article CONFIRMATION, which is the sacrament of the Holy Spirit. On all see St. Thomas Aquinas, *Sum. Theol.*, Ia, qq.36 to 38.

HOPE   Among the theological virtues, hope comes between faith and charity. It can be defined as an expectation of attaining eternal life, i.e., the fullness of the knowledge and the love of God, founded on his own assistance (cf. St. Thomas Aquinas, *Sum. Theol.*, IIa-IIae, q.17, a.2). In the Old Testament, its perspective becomes gradually dominated by the hope for the *Kingdom of God* (q.v.) that will become a reality in the coming of the *Messiah* (q.v.). Although the word *hope* itself does not occur in the Gospels (in Greek, *elpis*), it is undeniable that the Synoptics are dominated by the expectation of the Kingdom of God, which is specified in the Beatitudes, by the promise of a share in it for those who, as the sons of the heavenly Father, will have faith in his plan to adopt them through his Son whom he sent them. In St. John, and particularly in Christ's discourses after the Last Supper, the object of hope becomes more explicitly the faithful's entrance into that reciprocal intimacy of the Father and the Son to which the Spirit will lead them.

But it is in St. Paul that we find, to a certain extent, an *ex professo* treatment of hope. Not only do the Epistles to the Thessalonians and to the Corinthians (cf. especially 1 Cor. 15, and 2 Cor. 4,16 to 5,10) give the Resurrection as its object, seen above all as our full association with Christ in the state of glory which he has now reached, to the point that the Apostle can say, "Christ is our hope" (Col. 1,27), but it is also St. Paul who gives hope its place between faith and charity, throwing light on its specifically Christian meaning. (The same triad is found again in Rom. 5,1–2 and 5; 1 Cor. 13,13; Gal. 5,5–6 and 17; Eph. 1,15; 3,17; Col. 1,4). In this regard, it is interesting to note that other Pauline texts identify hope either with the expectation of the resurrection and life with Christ (Phil. 1,20), or with confidence in God's promises (Eph. 3,12). Finally, in the place of hope, the texts associate patience in present trials with faith and charity (1 Tim. 6,11).

From this latter point of view, namely, the connection between patience and hope, we can say that the Apocalypse, even though it does not use the word hope either, is the book of Christian hope.

However, there are no traditional theological developments of hope that can compare with those dedicated to faith or charity. Its inseparability from faith and charity was nevertheless underlined in the controversies with the Quietists (*see* QUIETISM). Even today, one of the most urgent problems facing Christian thought is to give a greater emphasis to the definition of supernatural hope in the context of the different hopes harbored in the modern world. It is certain that Catholic truth implicitly rejects any possible confusion between the realization of Christian hope and the effect of a natural endeavor toward human progress. The Messianism essential for Christian hope cannot be replaced with a type of secularized Messianism of either technical advances or political ideology. But to what extent can Christians welcome the human hope for a better world that would be achieved by man himself? This hope must certainly be encouraged insofar as it is in harmony with the capacity for anticipating Christian hope that is characteristic of charity, which charity, in order to manifest itself, must make use of every concrete means at its disposal. In this context this is an aspect of the Christian witness that is necessary for every age, particularly for our own. But, to the extent that the desire for temporal progress would claim that the forces of man alone (even aided by grace) could arrive at the specific object of Christian hope—even a part of this object (that cannot be detached from the object itself)—such as the definitive victory over sin, death or suffering, the marriage of the two concepts would become suspect. Today, therefore, Christians have the very particular obligation of a lucid charity imposed upon them.

See St. Thomas Aquinas, *Sum. Theol.*, IIa-IIae, qq.17–22, on the classic questions concerning hope; and, on Quietism and hope, D.B. 1227–1233 (the condemnation of Molinos by Innocent XI), as well as D.B. 1327–1338 (condemnation of Fénelon's *Maxims of the Saints* by Innocent XII).

HUMANISM   This word appeared during the course of the 19th century to designate the work of the humanists, and later the general outlook they shared. The word *humanist* itself at first meant simply a scholar who concerned himself with humane (i.e., profane) letters, as opposed to a man dedicated to divine letters, i.e., Holy Scripture. But very soon these words began to imply (beginning in the Renaissance) first the philological and historical methods that permitted a revival of the study of ancient literature in general, and then a state of mind bound up with the use of these methods, an outlook that was essentially critical and positive, i.e., appertaining to the facts. Humanism finally became a conception of man and the world marked by its optimism concerning the capabilities of human nature, and a claim for its right to a full and free development. Today, humanism as a quest for the total fulfillment of man's nature has come to be opposed to any asceticism that would seem to maim or curb it, and to every assertion of any transcendence that would claim to judge man in the light of whatever surpasses him. It is in this sense that Sartre's *existentialism* (q.v.) lays claim to being a type of humanism (just as Marxism had already been put forth as the only humanism) following Feuerbach in its assertion that man could be himself only once he had definitively left behind the idea of a divinity upon which he depends.

It is enough to cite the successive definitions given to the word humanism to see that no simple answer can be given to the problem of what the Christian attitude towards humanism should be. If it is a question of the philological and historical methods of humanism, the Church can have only a positive reaction, as long as their limitations are acknowledged. As to the meaning of man himself, of his fullness, and of the value in the eyes of God of the full development of his original nature, it is obvious that this can take on a completely Christian sense, as long as it is not confused with any form of too facile an optimism that would not recognize either the actual reality of the fall or the consequent need for giving up certain things even with restoration and fulfillment in view. But, if humanism is taken in the sense of man's claim to autonomy in regard to God, it is obvious that it becomes irreconcilable with Christianity. However, we must learn a lesson from this antireligious humanism, and ask ourselves whether, in fact, certain inadequate presentations of the Gospel have not contributed toward giving the false impression that it would maim human nature.

HYLOMORPHISM   From *hyle* ("matter") and *morphe* ("form"), this name is given to the Aristotelian-Thomistic teaching according to which every reality of this world can be analyzed in an intelligible form and a matter that concretely individualizes it, although it itself receives its being distinct from form. It is indeed important to note that "matter" in this case represents a pure potentiality that has little in common with the physical reality that modern science recognizes under this term. Similarly, "form" in this context in no way designates merely an outward appearance, which in some way envelops the reality, as it is commonly understood today, but, rather, the intelligible reality in a very real sense.

HYPERDULIA   This word is used to designate not the worship of *adoration*, but the veneration of *dulia* (q.v.) that is given preeminently to the Blessed Virgin Mary in preference even to the angels over whom her personal share in the mystery of the Incarnation exalts her.

HYPOSTASIS   A term used in Greek theology to designate more particularly the three divine Persons as opposed to the essence that is common to them. This distinction was the work chiefly of the so-called Cappadocian Fathers, St. Basil, St. Gregory of Nazianzen and St. Gregory of Nyssa. For a time it was a source of difficulty for Latin theologians because, etymologically, *hypostasis* corresponds to the Latin *substantia*, already used to translate the word *ousia*, i.e., "essence," in the Creed. The Greeks, for their part had an aversion to the Latin *persona*, since it originally designated an actor's mask. This caused them to see the danger of *Sabellianism* (q.v.) in the use of this word as if the Father, the Son and the Holy Spirit were not three distinct Subjects in God, but only three roles played by the same unique divine Subject. Finally, agreement was reached on the equivalence of person and hypostasis in Trinitarian theology.

HYPOSTATIC UNION   The phrase is used of the union of the two natures, human and divine, in the unity of the Person or hypostasis of the Son. Against the Nestorians (*see* NESTORIANISM), the Council of Ephesus defined this union to be without confusion of the human nature with the divine nature in Christ. Against the Monophysites (*see* MONOPHYSITISM), the Council of Chalcedon, for its part, asserted the subsistence of the human nature despite its inseparable union with the divine nature. A theological formula had to be found that would allow a reconciliation between these two complementary assertions. This was the work of the theologian Leontius of Byzantium, who explained that the human nature of the Saviour was *enhypostasized*, i.e., it subsisted personally in the Person of the eternal Son. It is this union without parallel that is called the hypostatic union. The consequences for the humanity of Christ resulting from this are discussed in the article JESUS CHRIST.

ICON From the Greek *eikon*, meaning "image," this word has come to refer specifically to the sacred images in use in the East, especially in Greece and the Slav countries. Following the iconoclastic controversy that was brought to an end by the Second Council of Nicea, the icon itself came to be considered both as witness to the Incarnation, and as a means of expressing our veneration of the saving God and his grace through the reverences made to the liturgical representations of Christ and his saints. In addition, iconography, chiefly in churches, came to be organized and conceived as an anticipated symbolic representation of the eschatological world in which all things will be, as it were, invaded by the manifest presence of God's *glory* (q.v.). The result was a particular kind of sacred image. It would, however, be completely wrong to say that its style has been "frozen" or at least stereotyped, since through the ages and from country to country it is constantly in a state of renewal with a variety equal to that found in secular art. Disregarding the periods of decadence, the icon has kept through all of these transformations its deliberately symbolic character, eschewing realistic representation and, in the most varied ways, always alluding to the final transfiguration of the universe.

It is worth noting that despite certain tendencies toward a sympathy for iconoclasm, which appeared in Charlemagne's empire and served to reduce the role of iconography in churches to a mere ornamental and didactic one, Romanesque painting (and even sculpture) has visibly translated, in a holy image, the same sacred sense that is so striking in all Eastern Christian iconography. But the naturalism and expressionism that was to triumph in Gothic art prepared the desacralization of religious art in the West, which was to be continued by a deliberately secular treatment of religious subjects from the Renaissance on. It is nonetheless curious to note that Baroque art attempted to refashion a religious iconography that would express the theme of divine glory. But, in most cases, it accomplished nothing but the precipitation of the secularizing of Christian themes through its notion of the glory of the saints and of Christ as a pure pagan apotheosis. Despite praiseworthy attempts to pull religious art in the West out of the stagnation in which it was ultimately destroyed in the 19th century, and even despite the success of a vaguely sympathetic curiosity that the art of the icon is experiencing at present among us, it does not seem that artists, and clergymen even less, understand today, any more than in the past, the doctrinal and spiritual significance and value of the icon.

IDOLATRY   Literally "worship (and therefore adoration) of images." The term came to designate every act of *adoration* (q.v.) directed to a creature instead of to the Creator. It is pointless to dwell at any length on the radical condemnation by the Old Testament of the worship of adoration given to images, and more generally, of every adoration of any being whatsoever other than the God who revealed himself to Israel on Sinai (cf. the second part of the first prohibition of the Decalogue according to the Septuagint division followed by the Vulgate, or the second prohibition according to the division of the Protestant versions of the Hebrew text). For the prophets, particularly Osee, idolatry is a form of adultery (in relation to the covenant founded upon the Decalogue, which he likens to a real marriage between God and his people). Thus idolatry becomes the supreme sin. Reciprocally, sin, such as it is described in the third chapter of Genesis, is shown to have been from the beginning a latent form of idolatry: the preference of a creature and its allurements to the Word of the Creator.

Like the faithful Jews before them, Christians were primarily brought to suffer martyrdom because of their refusal to sacrifice to idols, thus proclaiming the uniqueness and transcendence of God. But we should not conclude from this, either in the case of the first Christians or of the Jews, that for them idols were merely images empty of reality or content. On the contrary, for both, idolatrous worship did contain a reality, but a demoniacal one: the adoration of those sacred powers who are in revolt against the one and only Creator, namely, the devils. The forms used by the prophets to describe the gods who are nothing but nullities, and similarly described by the apostles (1 Cor. 10), must certainly not be taken in the sense of a mere rationalistic denial, but, rather, as their immediate context often shows, as a declaration of contempt and derision: compared to the true God, the "false gods" are but nullities. But this does not mean that their baneful reality is not manifested in their real hold over those who follow them.

For the Jews, however, the worship given to Jesus from earliest Christian times appeared to be an idolatry (and the same was true at a later date for the Muslims). The doctrines of the Incarnation and the Trinity, of course, dispel this error: when we adore the Son made flesh, it is ultimately his divine Person that receives the honor given to his humanity subsisting in it. Besides, the Incarnation itself in no way causes the divinity to lose its transcendence, as is shown by the fact that the Father, who is the source of the whole Trinity, does not become incarnate and, as most of the Fathers say, could not do so. It was, it seems, as a reaction against the Christian belief in the Incarnation that the Jews came to rid their sanctuary of every image, even those that were not the object of worship. Recent archeological discoveries, as in the synagogue of Dura-Europos, actually show that the Judaism that was contemporary with the beginnings of Christianity did not yet have this aversion, which apparently came about through a slow process. From this discovery we are inclined to think that even the primitive Christian liturgical iconography must have developed in continuity with an analogous Jewish one. Let us also recall that the Decalogue's prohibition never prevented Israel from using cultual representations like those of the cherubim that surrounded the Ark of the Covenant (cf. Ex. 25,18–20). We may add that these ancient Christians, just as those of the East today, were always very strict in their application of the prohibition against images of the Divinity itself, only allowing representations of the humanity of the Saviour and of the saints. Similarly, the worship given to the Virgin and to the saints is radically distinguished from *adoration* (q.v.; *see also* DULIA), for it is only an honor given to the work of grace in them and, to that extent, reverts ultimately to God alone. Actually, we must acknowledge the decline in religious imagery over the course of the Latin Middle Ages (in particular the belated appearance of representations of God the Father that Christian antiquity would have repudiated with horror and, more generally, imagery's evolution in the direction of naturalism and sentimentalism). This fact certainly contributed to many of the deformations in piety (when it did not already express them). On the other hand, undoubtedly more serious was the exaggerated and excessive development of a devotion of a superstitious tendency to Mary and the saints, which, rather than extolling the marvels of divine grace in them, was capable of causing the unique role of Christ as mediator of this grace to be obliterated. The Protestant reaction to condemn all veneration of saints as idolatry, and even every use of sacred images in worship or devotion, is explained by these deformations. But, as the further evolution of Protestantism shows, this itself runs the risk of leading men to lose sight of the realism of the Incarnation and the reality of the work of divine grace in us.

IGNORANCE   In the article GOOD FAITH we have seen in what way ignorance of a precept may excuse its transgression. It will be noted, however, that the censures with which the Church brands certain trangressions are not *ipso facto* removed through an ignorance that causes sin to be subjectively avoided. On the other hand, we call *invincible ignorance* the state in which a person, despite his efforts to know the truth, finds himself, because of circumstances, in such a situation that he is unable to discover the Catholic faith and accept it. For such an individual the fact that he does not become a member of the Church would not constitute a positive fault. But this does not resolve the problem of knowing how he may be saved either from his own sins, or, supposing he had not committed any that were serious, from original sin. This question will be treated in the article SALVATION OF UNBELIEVERS.

ILLNESS   *See* HEALING

ILLUMINATION   This word was used among the first Christians either of baptism itself or of the initiation into the fullness of the Christian faith that accompanied it. Later, in the language of the mystics, it came to denote a state in which, once sinful tendencies had been overcome through purification, one opens himself to an authentic awareness of the truths of the faith, a phase that is a preparation for the higher stage of union with God. But the great mystics who propagated this very suitable distinction were the first to point out that it is indeed good to be wary of a too strict acceptance. No purification of the soul is possible without the prior illumination of faith. Reciprocally, this purification cannot be deepened within us without a development of the illumination itself. Finally, purification on earth is never so perfect that relapses into former sins are not always to be feared, or that we may not fall into new and more insidious sins, like certain sins of pride which hardly threaten any but the mystics themselves.

IMAGE OF GOD   Genesis tells us that God made man "in His image and likeness" (1,27). Although the second account of the creation does not use these terms, it gives their full sense by showing that man is called to life by a direct intervention of God, who breathes His own breath of life into him (2,7). The New Testament, on the other hand, calls Christ "the likeness of God" (2 Cor. 4,4), or more precisely, "the image of the invisible God" (Col. 1,15), while it insists upon the fact that we are called to bear the image of Christ as the heavenly Man (1 Cor. 15,49) at the end of time, and to be now transformed in his image by reflecting it as in a mirror (2 Cor. 3,18).

St. Irenaeus was one of the first theologians to synthesize these notions, applying the conception of God's image in its fullness to the Son of God made man, and, as a consequence, the secondary realization of this divine image to the whole man, body and soul. Influenced to a certain extent by Platonism and its ultra-spiritualism, the Christian School of Alexandria, following Origen, applied the theology of the image to the Word, on the one hand, and to the human soul, on the other. This theology was combined with the Platonist notion of the divine likeness that man must acquire in order to know God, dependent upon a progressive detachment from the bonds of matter. At about the same time, the master of Neo-Platonism, Plotinus, developed the idea of the image that is latent in us and that we must restore by removing all impurities from ourselves; but by doing this, we do nothing but return to an original identity with God, restored in us to the extent that we return to the primordial One.

Whatever role these elements (which are heterogeneous to the biblical notion) played in later theological developments, it is very remarkable to see the cautious, but efficacious, way in which the Fathers corrected them in order to adapt them to the developments of Christian thought. This is particularly notable in St. Gregory of Nyssa. He also speaks of restoring in us this image, saying that it cannot be lost but has only been obscured by the accretions of sin. Nevertheless, he does not do this without specifying, following the text of the Second Epistle to the Corinthians that we have quoted, that the image of God in us is one that is formed as in a mirror, in such a way that no purification could give it back to us without the renewed presence of God within us through the fact of the Incarnation. We find the same thing in Evagrius Ponticus, who, moreover, adapted the idea that Origen had previously proposed of seeing the image of God in us in the *nous*, i.e., in what is most purely spiritual in the soul, or, as he himself puts it, most purely intellectual (which must not be taken in the modern sense of the word, but in the sense of a conscious being, including both the ideas of consciousness and conscience). This was taken up again by many later mystics who spoke of the "depth" of the soul whereby it does not cease to be one with God, or of its "spark," or again of its "acumen." It was subject to new and very rich, if sometimes rash, developments among the Rhenish mystics, and especially Eckhart. In quite an opposite sense, the spiritual tradition that emanated from the Pseudo-Macarius insisted upon the image of God as appearing in the transfigured or finally glorified Christ, with the correlative that it must, in man himself, illuminate the body by a reflection of the soul impregnated with the divine Presence.

In the tradition of St. Augustine, still another conception of the divine image in man is developed, at times at the expense of the foregoing, at times in more or less successful syntheses with them. This notion is clearly psychological. It sees in the "memory" (understood as the permanence and the continuity of the consciousness) the image of the Father, that of the Son as Word in the intellect, and that of the Spirit as love in the will. This image, engraved in the creation of the soul, would be animated in a restoration of the living likeness, lost by sin, in supernatural knowledge and love by which grace flourishes in us. Let us note here that most of the Fathers agreed with St. Augustine's distinction between the image which is natural to the soul and can only be obscured, but not erased, by sin, and the likeness which assumes a participation in God's own life that supernatural grace alone can communicate to the righteous. This rather forced opposition between image and likeness does not correspond with a distinction that is already found in the text of Genesis (1,27, cited above), in which this is merely a pleonasm used to underline the reality of the image. It does respond, however, to an intention that is certainly biblical, i.e., of asserting man's destiny to a likeness with God that implies a true kinship, as well as the possible loss of this effective relationship, without, however, man ever being able to lose God's promise of such a relationship.

On the idea of image as applied to Christ, it may be said that St. Thomas Aquinas took what was essential to the Alexandrian idea of a perfect likeness in connection with sonship, by detaching it from any subordinationism (*Sum. Theol.*, Ia, q.35). Furthermore, his theology of the divine image in man systematizes the Augustinian theory by felicitously completing it, e.g., by the idea that to the image proper to the soul there are joined divine vestiges in the body, as in all material creation to which it is bound (*ibid.* q.93). But he does not mention the New Testament idea of man being in Christ's image. It must be said, in regard to a tradition that involves such diverse aspects, that the biblical notion of image is evidently so rich that it is difficult to present a strict systematization that would unite all of its aspects. But it is undoubtedly in relating it to the notions of sonship and adoption that we shall again grasp its most essential elements.

IMAGES   See ICON for the material images used in worship or devotion, and IMAGE OF GOD for the theological and spiritual notions.

IMITATION   In Judaism, the theme of imitation of the great figures of Israel already underlies all of the Midrash exegesis, which seeks to transfer their experience to every believer. This is found again in the Epistle to the Hebrews (6,12; cf. all of chap. 11). St. Paul, on several occasions, does not hesitate to give himself as an example to be imitated by his disciples (1 Cor. 4,16; 11,1; 2 Thess. 3,7 and 9; 1 Thess. 1,6). But through this imitation of himself, he leads them to the imitation of Christ: "Be imitators of me, as I am of Christ" (1 Cor. 11,1). The essential meaning of this latter imitation is set down in the second chapter of the Epistle to the Philippians, in which the Apostle makes the implicit contrast between Christ's obeying the Father even to the cross in the *agape* manifested toward his brothers, and the example of the selfish and rebellious covetousness of Adam. This is what the First Epistle of Peter synthesizes in saying, ". . . Christ also suffered for you, leaving you an example, that you should follow in his steps" (1 Pet. 2,21). This latter text shows a concern for combining the general idea of imitating Christ with the directly evangelical idea of following him. (Cf. the call of Jesus, many times repeated: Matt. 8,22; 9,9; 19,21 and par.; John 1,43;

12,26; 21,19.) This idea of "following Jesus" is particularly developed by St. John (8,12; 10,4,5 and 27; cf. 13,36 and 37, in which there is a clear allusion to the imitation of His death). It will be noticed that the medieval book *Imitatio Christi* was translated into German as *Nachfolge Christi*, i.e., "following of Christ." It is very important never to dissociate the two ideas, for we certainly cannot copy Christ as it were from without, and purely on our own, but only follow in his footsteps, in order to be led by him in the way he has revealed to us. It is in this sense that the imitation of Christ has legitimately become a major theme of Christian asceticism.

Nevertheless, St. Paul does not speak only of imitating Christ, but of imitating God (Eph. 5,1). He specifies that the essence of this imitation must be sought in the *agape* that Christ manifested toward us, and through which our life becomes that of a son of God. This brings us back to the basic teaching of the Sermon on the Mount in which the meaning of the divine sonship, which is the essential point of the proclamation of the heavenly Kingdom, is revealed in the realization in ourselves of the same love that God shows toward men; whence the final exhortation: "You therefore must be perfect as your heavenly Father is perfect" (Matt. 5,48). This is only a repetition and a deepening of the exhortation of Leviticus, "You shall be holy for I the Lord your God am holy" (19,2 etc.). Indeed, the Jewish law was already to be interpreted in some way as signing the members of God's People with the divine Name that was revealed to them.

This Jewish and Christian notion has sometimes been compared to the Platonist conception that we must imitate God, or more exactly, restore our likeness to him, in order to know him. The analogy is not without some import, for the biblical notion itself is based on the idea of the image of God in which we were created and that Christ is to reform and perfect in us. But two basic differences must be mentioned. The likeness assumed by Platonism between God and man originates entirely in the deep spirituality of the soul. Its restoration is the result of human endeavor, which the divine knowledge would follow as its effect. In the biblical view, the likeness is much more dynamic: it is ultimately in the faculty of loving in the way God loves that it fully blooms. Besides, it is not so much our endeavors to restore the likeness of God within us that make us able to know him, but rather his gratuitous revelation, especially in the redemptive Incarnation, that will permit us to reproduce in ourselves the traits of the heavenly Father by following his eternal Son, Christ. *See* KNOWLEDGE, and IMAGE OF GOD.

IMMACULATE CONCEPTION This privilege of the Virgin Mary was only defined in 1854 by Pope Pius IX. Protestant theologians, and even some theologians of the Orthodox Church, consequently denounced it as an innovation that had no basis in Scripture or ancient tradition, understanding it as an attribution to the Virgin of a native quality that would place her outside of the children of Adam, and remove her from the universal need for salvation, a condition that Christ alone could meet. This confusion should be dispelled by the pontifical definition (D.B. 1641) that declares that this is a question of a singular grace accorded by God "in view (*intuitu*) of the merits of Christ Jesus, Saviour of the human race." Still more precisely, what is defined is not that the parents of the Virgin, by an inexplicable miracle, did not give her a human life that was corrupted in Adam, but rather that "at the first instant of her conception," by virtue of the express grace, "she was preserved from every stain of original fault" (*ab omni originalis culpae labe praeservatam immunem*). In other words the Immaculate Conception, in the sense in which it was finally defined by the Church, does not mean in any way that the Virgin would not have needed the same salvation as we as sons of Adam, but, as the Bull *Ineffabilis Deus* says again, she was saved, on the contrary, in an especially wonderful manner (*sublimiori modo*), by reason of her very particularly close bond with Christ the Saviour.

In order to have a full grasp of this point of Catholic doctrine, and at the same time understand how it can be the object of such persistent misunderstandings, we must recall in a few words the history of the expression *immaculate conception*. The certainty that Mary, by reason of her unique role in salvation history, in which she was called to be the Saviour's own Mother, had been sanctified in a manner proportionate to this vocation is evident in the first Christian texts concerning the Virgin. This is, in particular, the meaning the Church has always recognized in the Angel's greeting her as *kecharitomene* (in Latin, *gratia plena*) in Luke 1,28 (*see* MARY). From the high Middle Ages, the Byzantines were to concretize this conviction of the Church in a feast of the Conception of Mary in which she was addressed as immaculate (*achrantos*). The idea evidently came from the biblical accounts concerning Jeremiah (chap. 1), or the Baptist (Luke 1), in which those whom God selects for a mission of particular importance, in relation to the coming of the Messiah, are shown to be sanctified within the womb of their mother. When the feast in question, along with this expression's first application to the Virgin herself, began to spread in the West, the question was soon raised as to the sense in which it should be interpreted. As is seen from St. Bernard's letter on this point to the canons of Lyons, a fear arose that the conception of the Virgin by her parents as immaculate would be interpreted to mean that she did not need to be saved. This explains why, shortly after, St. Thomas Aquinas, while formally teaching Mary's sanctification from her mother's womb, remains reticent concerning the expression *immaculate conception*. Actually, Duns Scotus was the first to declare formally that the Immaculate Conception ought to be understood not as an exemption for the Virgin from the transmission of the original fault in the transmission of life itself by her parents, but rather as a sanctification that began at the moment of this transmission in such a way that the grace of Christ preserved her from ever having to exist in an unregenerated state, however short that might be thought to be (*Scriptum Oxoniense, In IV Sent.*, lib. III, dist. 3, Q.1). Despite these specifications, and because all theologians had not yet accepted them, the popes until the 18th century, in order to dispel any misunderstanding or possibility of misunderstanding, insisted on the use of the expression "Conception of Mary Immaculate" in preference to the "Immaculate Conception of Mary" (even to the exclusion of the latter). If in the long run they were to canonize this expression, it would, evidently, only be on the condition that it be understood in the sense defined above, namely as a realization in Mary of the salvation of which her Son is the source, beginning from the first instant of her conception. Again, it is indeed necessary to specify that this definition in no way means that Mary would have been brought to the fullness of perfection from the very first, but simply that she was from the outset preserved from every actual harm of the original fault. As for the objection as to how Mary could have benefited from the grace of Christ before he was conceived, it must be answered that her case is only the most eminent of all the graces of the Old Testament, which, since the justification of Abraham, were all preparatory to the coming of Christ, and given *intuitu meritorum Christi*.

IMMANENCE   It appears that we owe the first use of this word, as opposed to *transcendence* (q.v.), to the Thomists of the 17th century, who employed it to designate any activity of which the term is not outside the agent (like thought), as opposed to one where the term is outside of him (like the building of a house). But, in a short time, the pantheistic philosopher Spinoza was to give it a more radical sense, defining immanence as the activity that finds its complete explanation within the subject. In that way immanence, by definition, would exclude transcendence. The ambiguity resulting from this in modern philosophy explains the existence of many interminable theological controversies both at the end of the 19th century and in our own century, chiefly because there was no exact agreement existing about the words used. For a number of those thinkers who were dubbed modernists (*see* MODERNISM), and for the liberal Protestants, the insistence on the principle of immanence amounted practically to an exclusion of the possibility of any *revelation* (q.v.), or of anything properly *supernatural* (q.v.). Religion, therefore, would consist entirely in the religious feeling itself, and it would be senseless to look for something beyond, in an objective reality of God, that would be transcendent to man himself. Or at the very least, following the clearcut opposition set up by Kant between *noumenon* and *phaenomenon* (*see* ABSOLUTE), God and the divine realities in their transcendence would totally elude the grasp of our minds. What we say about them would not have any other value than a symbol, a symbol of our religious experience only and of nothing beyond it. Different, at least in intention, was the method of immanence advocated by Maurice Blondel at the same period. On the contrary, his desire was to open a breach in the philosophies that, following Spinoza, Kant and Hegel, claimed that human thought could make no assertion of any religious reality that would surpass it. Blondel, in *L'Action* (Paris, 1893), attempted to show that a sufficiently complete analysis of the human mind, if it is not improperly separated from man as a whole, could not allow it to be shut in on itself. It ought on the contrary to dispose it first to acknowledge the existence of a God to whom all moral life must be referred, then to accept, should the occasion arise, the more intimate communications that God proposes to us. A certain ambiguity as to the use of the word "supernatural," by which Blondel designated both the simple existence of God and his revelation and everything connected with it, made no small contribution toward causing the orientation of his thought to be misunderstood. This thought, which by intention was most orthodox, is specifically opposed to the radical immanentism that was to attract more and more of the modernists in the wake of the very philosophies that Blondel had wanted to combat. The long and often confused controversies that ensued at least brought back into prominence this twofold truth that had been traditional in the Church since St. Augustine, namely, 1) that not only the consideration of the physical world, but also that of the human soul as well, must lead philosophical reflection to the assertion of a transcendent God, and 2) that the experience, particularly of sin and death, but also the simple discovery of the unlimited character of human aspirations, must ready man to welcome supernatural revelation, without being of itself able to prejudge either its necessity or its content.

IMMANENTISM   A tendency to understand the *immanence* (q.v.) of God or of his action in us in such a way that it would, in fact, exclude the reality of his *transcendence* (q.v.). *See also* MODERNISM.

IMMENSITY   Used in theology of the presence of God in everything (*praesentia immensitatis*), stemming from his almightiness, which is limited by nothing. Consequently, everything that exists, exists and is maintained in being only by his action.

IMMERSION   Baptism (the word itself means "immersion") was administered primitively by complete immersion in water. At a very early date it was admitted that a simple pouring (infusion) of water on a part of the body (preferably the head) could be substituted. Certain sects (like those who are called Baptists or Anabaptists) generally refuse to admit that this equivalence is well-founded. It is important, however, to underline that still today in the East, while the validity of baptism by pouring is acknowledged, baptism by immersion is always practiced whenever possible, particularly in the case of infants. The same was true in the West throughout the Middle Ages, and it was still the case in the beginning of this century in many regions of France. The contrary custom that became established, even if it does not influence the validity of the sacrament, incontestably causes it to lose a great part of its expressive power. It has undoubtedly contributed to the spreading of an incomplete conception of the sacrament, as if the ablution of sins were all there was to it or at least its essential element, and not the death to a fallen mankind that makes ready a resurrection with Christ.

IMMIXTIO   A term referring to the mingling of one particle of the host with the precious blood in the chalice. It is done in the East in order to give Communion under the two species together. It must have been introduced in the West at first to make consumable the species of bread, which had been kept for some time, and later it was taken as a symbol of the Resurrection.

IMMOLATION   A decisive act whereby sacrifices were generally performed by putting the victim to death. In modern eucharistic theology, as a reaction to the Protestant tendency to see merely a *memorial* (q.v.) of a past sacrifice in the Eucharist, and not an actual sacrifice, there has been abundant argument as to whether (and, when this is admitted, in what sense) Christ is immolated anew during the Mass. Some Counter-Reformation theologians, like Lugo, went very far in this direction, as if the separate consecration of the body and blood of Christ at least tended to produce a new immolation of the Saviour. More recently there has been a very lively reaction against these speculations. M. Lepin, P.S.S., made an effort to show that the *oblation* (*see* OFFERTORY, and SACRIFICE), i.e., the offering of the victim, constituted the essence of the sacrifice, and for the Mass to be a true and real sacrifice according to the expressions of the Council of Trent, there was nothing more to look for than the renewal of this offering by the Church (see *L'idée du sacrifice* *d'après les théologiens depuis l'origine jusqu'à nos jours*, Paris, 1926). Father de la Taille put forth a more complex view, according to which the essence of the sacrifice would indeed be the oblation, while the intervention of sin would require the immolation in order for the oblation to be effectively accomplished. The sacrifice in the Mass at present would therefore be an actual renewal by the Church of the sacrifice that was immolated once and for all. (See Father de la Taille's *Mysterium Fidei*, Paris, 1921, and *Esquisse du Mystère de la foi*, Paris, 1924). Since then the reinstatement, particularly following Dom Vonier, of the traditional Thomistic teaching on the Eucharist as a sacrament of the passion, in which we participate really but mysteriously, without it being possible or necessary therefore to begin it again materially (cf. St. Thomas Aquinas, *Sum. Theol.*, IIIa, q.79, a.5 and 6), caused these discussions to lose a great part of their value concerning the Eucharist itself. What they preserve in regard to the nature of sacrifice in general is discussed in the article SACRIFICE.

IMMORTALITY   *See* SOUL, and RESURRECTION

IMMUTABILITY   A divine attribute by which God is placed above any possibility of change. In Christian thought, this must not be understood as an absence, but rather as a superabundance of life, as the Epistle of St. James explains by saying: "Every good endowment and every perfect gift is from above, coming down from the Father of lights with whom there is no variation or shadow due to change" (1,17). It is in this sense that St. Thomas Aquinas sees God alone as *pure act* (*see* ACT). The biblical notion expressing the entire religious content of the divine immutability is that of *faithfulness* (q.v.).

IMPASSIBILITY   The absence of "passion," in the philosophical sense of the word, i.e., of passivity in regard to any external agent whatsoever. This quality belongs above all to God insofar as he, as *pure act* (*see* ACT), is the source of all being. We need go no further to see that this quality should not be interpreted as a form of indifference, or as an inertia that would, in fact, be the extreme opposite. Against the heresy of *Patripassianism* (q.v.), which held that the Father himself underwent the passion of the Saviour, early theology underlined the fact that although the Son alone, insofar as his divine person took on a human nature, became passible as a result of the Incarnation, this passivity pertained only to his human nature in the condition in which he received it from us. Since his Resurrection the glorious Christ has become impassible in his humanity as well as in his divinity. As a particular consequence of this, his real presence in the Eucharist, and the sacramental renewal of his passion that it produces, must not in any way be understood to mean that Christ is able to suffer all over again (*see* PRESENCE, and SACRIFICE). From another viewpoint, following Clement of Alexandria, the early Christian ascetical writers were quite willing to adopt the Stoics' idea of impassibility (in Greek, *apatheia*). However, the notion these Orthodox writers had, beginning with Clement, must not be interpreted either as a lack of sensitivity, or as a form of indifference. *Apatheia*, as they saw it, is the victory over the sense impressions that have gained ascendency over our fallen sensibility. But this victory is nothing more than the result of the divine *agape*'s dominion over everything within us that might attempt to thwart its command, and, consequently, its own flowering in our whole being. They themselves take pains to state, however, that it would not be possible for us, even through this victory, to reach a true impeccability on earth.

IMPECCABILITY   A quality that belongs only to the saints in glory; they can no longer sin because from this point on their will is totally and definitively identified with God's will. St. John asserts both this impeccability to which the Christian is destined once he belongs to Christ through faith and baptism, as well as the fact that we remain capable of sinning, and even of committing positive and more or less serious offenses as long as we are still on earth, when he says: "We know that anyone born of God does not sin" (1 John 5,18; cf. 3,6,9), after having declared in the same Epistle, "If we say we have no sin, we deceive ourselves, and the truth is not in us" (1,8).

Only Christ was impeccable in the strictest sense of the word, from the beginning of his earthly life, because he was the Son of God made man. It is well worth noting on this point that the Synoptic Gospels do not even hint at any trace of a consciousness of a state of sin, or of a possibility of sinning on his part, even when they state in strongest terms his consciousness of his Sonship. His own statement in St. John does no more than underline the impression that they had already conveyed: "Which of you convicts me of sin?" (8,46). This radical absence of sin in One who made himself one with sinners in order to free them from their sins is the object of the most deliberate assertions of St. Paul (2 Cor. 5,21), of St. John (1 John 3,5), and of St. Peter (1 Pet. 2,22).

In the case of the Blessed Virgin Mary, the Church, after some hesitation (even among those Fathers who were most convinced of her supereminent holiness, like St. Cyril of Alexandria) reached the conviction that the divine grace that preserved her from every effective trace of original corruption from the first moment of her conception (*see* IMMACULATE CONCEPTION), also kept her free from any taint of actual sin in this life.

On the impeccability of the blessed, see St. Thomas Aquinas, *Sum. Theol.*, Ia q.62, a.8; Ia-IIae, q.4, a.4; and on that of Christ, *ibid.*, IIIa, q.15, a.1; and on that of Mary, *ibid.*, IIIa, q.27, a.4.

INCARNATION   The act by which the Son of God made humanity his own by assuming the body and soul of man. The term goes back to the Greek *sarx*, meaning *"flesh"* (q.v.), and it was inspired by the words of St. John: "The Word was made flesh" (1,14). In the early days of Christianity, the *Docetists* (from the Greek *dokein*, "to seem") looked upon the Incarnation as being only an illusion. This assertion was common among the heretical Gnostics of the first centuries (*see* GNOSTICISM). It is based on a pessimistic notion of the "flesh," and the material world as well, that was very popular in pagan antiquity. However, the ambiguity of the word *flesh* in Greek always caused the Greek theologians to prefer the word *enanthropesis* to *ensarkosis*, the former designating more explicitly the idea of "becoming man." We see in fact that the Arians, as early as the 4th century, while denying the genuine divinity of the Son of God, also explained his incarnation as if his preexisting heavenly being had taken the place of the soul in the humanity of Jesus. More subtle was the subsequent error of the theologian Apollinaris of Laodicea who explained that the divine Word in Jesus took the place of the *nous*, i.e., that which is most spiritual in the soul, that by which every soul is related to God. The numerous forgeries that the Apollinarists committed, particularly under the name of St. Athanasius, who had defended the Catholic faith against the Arians after the Council of Nicaea first condemned them in 325, gave their doctrine credence in many orthodox circles. It was the source of the Monophysite error (according to which there is but one nature, *physis*, in Christ), and, as a reaction to it, of Nestorianism (according to which the two natures, divine and human, would be juxtaposed in him, more than truly united). *See* MONOPHYSITISM, and NESTORIANISM.

The Patriarch of Constantinople, Nestorius, in his zeal to get rid of the Monophysitism of the Apollinarists, went so far as to deny that Mary could be called Mother of God (*theotokos*), and he described the Incarnation as if the humanity of the Saviour were simply the temple of his divinity, and the union between them but a higher form of that produced by grace in all Christians. The Council of Ephesus, held in 431 under the presidency of the Patriarch of Alexandria, St. Cyril, canonized the text of a letter of his to Nestorius, in which he justified the title of *theotokos* given to Mary in a spirited expression of the union of the two natures, divine and human, in Christ. However, the anathemas that Cyril appended to his letter, and which seem not to have received the same conciliar approbation, contained formulas that could have been read in a Monophysite sense. This resulted in a spirited resumption of the controversies. They seem to have come to an end in the act of union of 433, at which time the accord of the episcopate of the East, up to then divided, was achieved. We find these formulas stated: ". . . union of two natures . . . union without mixture . . . as for the evangelical and apostolic expressions concerning the Lord, we know that theologians regard those which unify as referring to the one unique Person, and those which separate as referring to the two natures" (D.S. 250–264 and 272–273).

But after this agreement, the monk Eutyches, relying on the formula the false Apollinarists had attributed to St. Athanasius (namely, "one nature of God, the incarnate Word"), claimed to see in this the formula itself of the Cyrillian teaching canonized by the Council of Ephesus. A second council at Ephesus in 439, held under such irregular conditions that it was to be styled the "Robber Council," upheld him. Pope St. Leo opposed it in a letter addressed to the Patriarch Flavian of Constantinople, with the formula: "one sole person, in two natures." And a new council, held in Chalcedon in 451, canonized this formula, asserting that "each of the two (natures) has preserved its own manner of being (*idiotes*) . . . coming together with the other in but one Person (*eis en prosopon kai mian hypostasin*)" (D.B. 148).

The theologian Leontius of Byzantium explained this formula by saying that the nature (*ousia*) simply marks the idea of being, and the person (*hypostasis*) that of a being existing in itself. Normally, each human nature exists in itself and thus has its own proper person, but, he maintained, the human nature in Jesus Christ is "enhypostasized" in the Person of the divine Word. The Second Council of Constantinople, in 553, followed him in saying that the divine Logos united himself in the flesh, "*kath'hypostasin* (according to the *hypostasis*) so that there is but one *hypostasis* or only one *prosopon*" (D.B. 217).

Since Monophysitism persisted in latent forms in Monoenergism and Monothelitism (qq.v.), Pope Martin I and the Constantinopolitan theologian, Maximus the Confessor, took up the fight again. Under the influence of Pope Agatho, the Third Council of Constantinople put an end to these debates in 681 by finally canonizing the doctrine expounded by the latter: "two wills . . . two energies . . . in no way contrary, but the human will following . . . the all-powerful divine will and in submission to it" (D.B. 291).

Such are the definitions that the Church was brought to make on the mystery of the Incarnation. It goes without saying that this left many problems on which theologians are not in agreement. In the first place, it must be remarked that most of the Christians of Eastern Syria, clinging to the traditions of the School of Antioch that Nestorius represented, have never accepted the Council of Ephesus in which they thought they saw a condemnation of the full human reality of the Saviour. Nevertheless, these Churches, which thereafter were called "Nestorian" seem not as a whole (perhaps, Nestorius too) to have ever completely adhered to the harmful conclusions that can be drawn from the formulas of Nestorius, and which were the cause of their rejection. Inversely, attachment to the doctrine of St. Cyril led the Coptic Church of Egypt, and the Churches of Western Syria (called Jacobites for the theologian Jacob Baradaeus, who died 578) and of Armenia, to reject Chalcedon, although their Monophysitism, for the most part, is merely a verbal one. In the Catholic Church herself, as in the Orthodox Church of the East, the harmonization of the complementary assertions necessary to the truth of the Incarnation, which supposes both the integrity of the two natures and the reality of their union, continues to our own day to provoke unrest and opposition.

More particularly, the attention that the modern mind has brought to the psychological reality of humanity has led some theologians, like Günther in the 19th century, to wonder whether Christ, from a metaphysical point of view, while having but one Person, the divine, could not be considered as having been provided with an autonomous "personality" on the level of human psychology. This point, among others in his teaching, was to be condemned by Pius IX in 1857 (D.B. 1655). Other theologians, in a more subtle fashion, have since tried to revive the use of the formula *assumptus homo* (the exalted man) to assert the full reality of the humanity of Christ, while opposing it to the idea of a man only adopted by divinity with which it is commonly identified (following the eighth anathema of St. Cyril, D.B. 121). Msgr. Gaudel and Msgr. Amann subscribed to this view, in which they were preceded, with fewer distinctions, by the Franciscan Déodat de Basly, and followed on the whole by Fr. Galtier, S.J. They were most strongly opposed by Dom H. Diepen, O.S.B., as well as by Msgr. Parente, who held that Christ is not *one* man determined apart from the substantial appropriation of his humanity to the Person of the Word. Such a prudent judge as Fr. H. F. Dondaine, O.P., was of the opinion that, "We are not sure that either of these two systems, that of the *assumptus homo* and that of *substantial appropriation*, succeeds in supplanting the other" (*Revue des sciences philosophiques et théologiques*, 1951, p. 611.).

Quite a different question was raised in the Middle Ages by the Franciscan School, following Duns Scotus: whether the Son of God would have become incarnate even if there had been no fall to repair.

They answered in the affirmative (D. Scotus, *Lectio Parisiensis, In IV Sent.*, 1. III, dist. 7, qq.3 and 4). After having admitted the likelihood of the hypothesis in his *Commentary on the Sentences* (dist. 1, q.1, a. 3), St. Thomas Aquinas finally pronounced himself categorically against it (*Sum. Theol.*, IIIa, q.1, a.3). It is a fact that not only the Bible and all of ancient tradition never envisaged this hypothesis, but, moreover, they seem to exclude it by the insistence with which they accentuate the idea that the Incarnation had for its purpose the salvation of fallen mankind. Those who insist upon the necessity of the Incarnation for the greater glory of God do not seem to realize, on the other hand, that it would then be necessary *a fortiori* to uphold the preliminary necessity of creation (which is certainly inadmissible; *see* CREATION). As for the idea that the Incarnation would be necessary for the supernatural association of mankind with the divine life, by the gift of adoptive sonship, it seems to rest on a confusion between our participation in the son-life, and the Incarnation itself—precisely the seed of the Nestorian error. When the Fathers say that God became man so that man might be divinized, they take care to specify the limits of this parallel, and they explain their formula in relation to the necessity of now reuniting a mankind estranged from God in order to bring it back to him. But if the divine condescendence of the Word on our behalf (they speak of this when they treat of the primitive plan of God to adopt man) is for them presupposed by the redemptive Incarnation, in no way does it seem, in their view, to have had to result in the Word's becoming incarnate even if sin had not come into the world.

See St. Thomas Aquinas, *Sum. Theol.*, IIIa, qq.1 to 26. It will be noted that his two most noteworthy contributions on the problem of the Incarnation are the interpretation he gives of the *capital* grace of Christ as the fullness of sanctifying grace and the source of all the particular graces of the elect, and his notion of the humanity of Christ, considered as the *conjoined instrument* of his divinity for the accomplishment of the work of redemption.

In the article REDEMPTION, the effect of the Incarnation of the Son of God on mankind in general is discussed.

INCREDULITY and UNBELIEF   *See* AGNOSTICISM, APOLOGETICS, ATHEISM, and SALVATION OF UNBELIEVERS

INDEFECTIBILITY   By this term, theologians attribute the fact that the Church, even if she can endure, internally as well as externally, severe assaults from the powers of evil, could never succumb to them. This is what is asserted in Christ's words to St. Peter, saying that the gates of hell (i.e., the diabolic powers) will not prevail against her

(Matt. 16,18 and par.; cf. Luke 12,32 and Matt. 28,20). The *infallibility* (q.v.) of the Church, in her doctrinal definitions, is a particularly important consequence (and at the same time, a condition) of this indefectibility.

INDEX   The name given to a list of books that in principle are forbidden to be read because of the danger to faith and morals that such a reading could present. Drawn up at first by a special Roman congregation (the Congregation of the Index), this list is now within the competence of the Holy Office. The listing of a book in the Index is not of itself an absolute condemnation of what it teaches, but a caution against the dangers it may present. For this reason, the Index allows more or less broad dispensations, depending upon the usefulness that the books mentioned may yet offer, as well as on the ability that their possible readers have of standing fast against the errors and wrong impulses that could result.

INDISSOLUBILITY OF MARRIAGE   *See* DIVORCE

INDULGENCES   Today this word is understood to mean a remission of the *temporal punishment* (*see* PUNISHMENT) due to a previously forgiven sin, a remission granted by Church authority by virtue of the power of the keys. It may be either plenary or partial. This remission is generally granted in connection with a prayer or a special act of piety determined by the authority granting it, and it presupposes faith in the communion of saints, through which everything we do to bring us closer to God mysteriously benefits from the assistance afforded us by the merits and prayers of the whole Church, and especially by those of her holiest members. To have a proper understanding of indulgences, it is necessary to recall that they were introduced as an equivalent mercifully granted by the Church authority to the rigorous penances imposed by the early Church, namely more or less lengthy excommunication coupled with very harsh penitential practices (fasting and different kinds of abstinence). This is the origin of the reference to the number of days connected with the granting of an indulgence. This number no longer has more than a symbolic character, expressing the respective importance the Church attaches to the different practices she indulgences. To avoid abuses that might easily creep into the use and interpretation of indulgences (and these were at least a determining cause of the Protestant Reformation), the Church has progressively restricted the power to grant them that had been conceded to bishops and other prelates. At the same time, she did away with all granting of indulgences that were connected with any sort of money gifts. It is acknowledged that an indulgence gained may not be applied to another (especially a dead person), except by way of *suffrage*, i.e., intercession.

INDULT   The name given to a permanent dispensation granted by the Holy See in relation to a canonical prescription that otherwise would be imposed on the beneficiary of the indult in question.

INDWELLING OF THE DIVINE PERSONS IN US   Formally expressed by Christ in John (14,23): "If a man loves me, he will keep my word, and my Father will love him, and we will come to him, and make our home with him," this notion is constantly assumed by the texts of the New Testament, particularly St. Paul's, which consider Christ or the Spirit as being habitually present in the souls of the faithful in grace with God, even in their whole being. Compare St. Paul's comment to the Corinthians: "Do you not know that your body is the temple of the Holy Spirit within you?" (1 Cor. 6,19; *see* TEMPLE). In the article GIFTS OF THE HOLY SPIRIT, the special way in which it seems that this notion is to be applied in this context is discussed. Let us say here only that the presence of the divine Persons within us as a result of grace is quite different from the presence of *immensitas*, by virtue of which God is everywhere. This is a special presence marked by the particular "knowledge" God has of the righteous, the personal love which he accords them, and which is manifested in return by the knowledge and love we receive from him. This presence constitutes a real consecration (as the temple-figure shows), and it conforms us to Him who dwells within us: through it the image of God, which we are by nature, becomes a participated likeness (*see* IMAGE OF GOD).

    The indwelling of the divine Persons is to be understood in connection with the whole theology of the divine *mission* (q.v.) in us. It is established in us (in principle, permanently) by baptism and confirmation, but it is renewed and maintained by Communion, in which the sacramental presence of the body and the blood of Christ is itself only a means of intensifying the presence of the Godhead within us.

    See St. Thomas Aquinas, *Sum. Theol.*, Ia, q.43.

INERRANCY OF HOLY SCRIPTURE   A consequence of *inspiration* (q.v.), referring to the fact that since the sacred books have God himself as their author, they could not teach any error in a positive way. At times people have attempted to reduce this privilege of biblical inerrancy to the mere domain of religious truths. It is true that Scripture was not inspired by God to teach us astronomy, chronology or the like, but rather to lead us to salvation. Nonetheless, religious truth cannot be removed from the whole of human and cosmic reality without becoming artificial. Consequently, to say that biblical inerrancy bears directly on the religious objects that are the proper objects of revelation, could only result in the fallacious consequence that every biblical assertion of which we do not immediately see the religious character could not in any way be guaranteed by inerrancy. We must certainly invert the wording of the question and say, on the contrary, that every biblical assertion for which the inspired author holds himself accountable must have some connection with revelation in such a way that it is guaranteed by inspiration, even if that connection is not obvious to us. On the other hand, this does not mean that every apparent assertion that can be thought to be present in an isolated scriptural text, or even less, one that is deduced from it by logic, actually does fall under this guarantee. If God chose to speak in human terms, then it is indeed certain, on the other hand, that he did so within the terms that are those of all human language. When we say, for example, that the sun rises, we are merely using a current form of expression, and no one could rationally accuse us of error under the pretense that the primary sense of this expression implies a mythological notion of a physical phenomenon. Nor could anyone criticize the sacred writers for being erroneous when they use analogous modes of speech, nor could anyone claim to take them strictly literally on the pretext of their inspiration and in the name of the necessarily consequent inerrancy. The only scientific method that allows us to specify with some certainty what is or is not covered by biblical inerrancy in the apparent assertions of the text, is an historical exegesis that attempts to determine exactly what the biblical authors were focusing on in their teaching, by distinguishing it from what pertains merely to the modes of expression proper to their surroundings and their age. As we are reminded in Pius XII's Encyclical *Divino Afflante Spiritu*, it is notably in this context that determining the *literary genre* (q.v.) to which a passage belongs plays such an important role, for a truth set down in a poem, for example, is not presented in the same form that could be expected in a treatise on systematic theology. However, the fact remains that the exact determination of what a biblical author does or does not teach is always a delicate problem on which the best specialists may not agree. In addition, in those scriptural assertions where the meaning is not obvious, only the Church can assert definitively what must or must not be considered as the object of an assertion with the guarantee of inspiration. Yet, it is only very rarely that the Church does determine what must be held definitively in such a matter. More often she merely limits herself to setting down some rules of prudence that must be observed, as long as a question does not seem ripe for a solution.

INFALLIBILITY A privilege granted to the Church's teaching on matters of faith and morals, whereby she can never teach error in this area. This privilege refers especially, although not exclusively, to the solemn definition of a disputed point of doctrine that the Church may be brought to make. Its chief and most general effect is the assurance to us that once we have placed ourselves under the Church's tutelage in order to receive God's Word from her and to grasp its true meaning, we can go wrong only through an error or a weakness of our own, and not of the Church's, since she is the spokesman of Christ, her divine Head. The Church's infallibility in this regard is only a consequence of her indefectibility, i.e., of Christ's promise that he would perpetually assist her by his invisible presence, so that the forces of evil could never prevail against her, and, more precisely, that the teaching she gives in his name would remain always his teaching (cf. Matt. 28,20 and 16,18; Luke 10,6; cf. Matt. 10,14 and 20).

Infallibility, as such, belongs to the whole Church. For it is all her members who live the truth within her, and the object of the witness to that truth is indivisible from the totality of her membership. But infallibility is especially manifested in the decisions the Church authorities may be called upon to make for the safeguard of this witness, and it is manifested in proportion to the respective importance of the authorities in question, and the circumstances attendant to the formulation of their decisions. Sometimes the infallibility of the hierarchy is called *active*, and that of the faithful, *passive*, since it is the hierarchy that officially proposes the truth that the faithful are called on to believe. But this formula runs the risk of being misinterpreted. On the one hand, simple adherence on the part of the faithful to the Catholic faith is certainly in no way a purely passive thing, but, on the contrary, the object of an essentially free and therefore personal activity (*see* FAITH). Furthermore, all within the Church have the duty of bearing witness to the Catholic faith and of participating actively in its life and in its mission (this is the basis of Catholic action). On the other hand, the bishops themselves, when they proclaim and, should the occasion arise, define Christian truth with apostolic authority, are reflecting the faith of the faithful.

Nevertheless, it pertains to them alone to carry on the work of the apostles as official teachers of the truth, although they may require the assistance in this task of priests of second rank who are accountable to them, and, more generally, in view of certain qualifications which they recognize, of all the faithful to the extent that they judge it advisable. And, perhaps most important, whenever a serious doubt about a particular point of doctrine is raised in the Church, it is the function of this official teaching of the body of bishops to clear it up. The methods it may follow are manifold. Customarily, the guarantee of a doctrine's truth is assured infallibly by its ordinary teaching in the unanimity of the episcopal *magisterium*. But, should the case arise, this *magisterium* can assume the extraordinary form of a solemn definition stated in a council, with the guarantee of infallibility, since a council, through the voiced unanimity of her responsible hierarchy, represents the whole Church. Following the celebrated definition of the First Vatican Council, the same must be said of a similar definition made by the pope alone, provided he is clearly acting in his function as supreme pastor and universal doctor; in this case he of necessity enjoys the infallibility that belongs to the Church as a whole (D.B. 1839).

As the same constitution, *Pastor Aeternus*, adds further on in the same paragraph, it follows that decisions of this kind made by the pope are unalterable of themselves, and not by virtue of some future assent given to them by the Church (*ex sese et non ex consensu Ecclesiae*). In connection with this, in no way does this mean (as certain controversial-ists thought they could maintain) that the pope, acting in this way, either would not have to take into account the conscience of the Church, or would be infallible independently or differently from her. The opposite is the case. He is infallible insofar as he is the principal interpreter of the conscience of the Church, and the supreme responsi-bility he exercises has the effect that the infallibility Christ assured his Church in general finds its particular application in the pontiff.

INFINITE   That which is not finite, that has no limits, either known to us, or even possible. In the full sense of the word, then, the term refers only to God. Philosophers, on the other hand, discuss the question of whether there can be real infinities (and not merely virtual ones) in the sphere of creation. St. Thomas Aquinas appears to believe that there can be, in the sense that he admits that the universe could have been created from all eternity, which would suppose at least an infinite time *a parte ante* (*see* CREATION). But if the question is not posed with regard to an infinite number of simultaneous creatures (which would be meaningless, every number being by definition either finite or non-existent), but in relation to creatures without number, St. Thomas does not think that such a real infinite can exist in the many (*Sum. Theol.*, Ia, q.7, a.4). Whatever may be the answer to these rather subtle questions concerning creation, it does not seem that the absolute infinity of God was admitted in Western thought apart from biblical revelation. For the Greeks, the infinite was confused with the indefinite, the *apeiron*, and, as such, it only had reference to matter; not as some sort of perfection, but rather as the source of all imperfection. On the contrary, the idea of a positive infinite, resulting from the limitless transcendence of God, from the fact that he is of a plenitude without possible or conceivable limitations, even though it is not technically expressed in the Bible, certainly follows from it, and has been accepted in all of Christian thought. It is very typical in this regard to observe the contrast between Neo-Platonist philosophy, which most closely approaches the notion of the infinite through its idea of the One, i.e., of the divine perfection transcending every particular determination, and the thought of the Christian theologian who made the widest use of Neo-Platonist notions, the Pseudo-Areopagite, for whom God is beyond the One itself. (Cf. *Mystical Theology*, V; P.G., t.3, col. 1048A, and *Divine Names*, XIII, 3, *ibid.*, col. 981A.) See also St. Thomas Aquinas, *Sum. Theol.*, Ia, q.7.

INFUSED KNOWLEDGE   Theologians distinguish in Christ, in contradistinction to his beatific vision, an *infused natural knowledge*, which is extended to all the objects concerned through his role as Redeemer, although it does remain limited; and a *natural knowledge*, which developed like our own and is subject to the same limitations.

INFUSION   In baptism this term refers to the method of conferring the sacrament through the simple pouring of water over the body of the person being baptized, instead of completely immersing him in baptismal water. The *Didache*, VII, 3, already declared this practice to be valid. Through St. Cyprian we know that it was common in his day in the case of sick people. St. Thomas Aquinas stresses its validity while admitting its limited use, since, as he says, the custom of immersion is the most common (*Sum. Theol.*, IIIa, q.66, a.7). We may regret that in recent times in the West the situation has been reversed in that baptism by infusion has become practically the only method used. *See* BAPTISM, and IMMERSION.

INHABITATION   *See* INDWELLING OF THE DIVINE PERSONS IN US

INHERITANCE   The lawfulness of the principle of inheritance, by which the goods of parents are passed on after their death to their children, or in their absence, to the next of kin, is deduced from the fact of the handing on of life, which ought normally to be carried on in the circumstances under which it is lived. We shall not broach the question of the limitations in which this right may be extended or restricted.

INNASCIBILITY   The quality of being independent of birth. In the Trinity, it is a quality pertaining to the Father alone, and one which theologians in the Arian controversy were brought to distinguish, as His exclusive characteristic, from the uncreated (but not necessarily unbegotten or un-produced) character that pertains to the three divine Persons in common.

INNOCENCE   The state of one who has never sinned, like Adam before the fall, or of one who has been reestablished through an exemption from all sin, whether actual or original, as through baptism, although in this latter case the exemption does not extend to all the consequences of sin (*see* BAPTISM).

INSPIRATION   In the most accurate sense of the word, such as it is understood today by theologians and in the documents of the *magisterium* of the Church, divine inspiration pertains exclusively to the text of Holy Scripture, which means that it must be looked upon as having God himself as its chief author, or, in other words, as being the Word of God not only in its content but even in its expression. It is generally admitted that the charism of inspiration itself belonged to the apostles in a permanent fashion. But the Church recognizes only the canonical writings of the two Testaments as the actual documents presenting with certainty the result of such an inspiration.

Judaism, in a very special sense, already had a belief in the inspiration of the Holy Scriptures, in relation to the Old Testament. Similarly, from the outset, the Church admitted this belief with regard to the New Testament as well. But it was only in contemporary times, when the problems of textual or historical criticism were brought into sharp focus that the Church came to define this inspiration. She did so at the First Vatican Council, in these terms: "The Church holds the Books of Scripture as sacred and canonical, not in the sense that being composed by human industry alone, they would then have been approved by her authority, nor just for the reason that they contain revelation without error, but rather because they have God for their author since they were written under the inspiration of the Holy Spirit and were transmitted as such to the Church" (Sess. III, Constitution *De Fide Catholica*, chap. 2; D.B. 1787).

For a proper understanding of this text, we must be aware of the errors at which it was directed. The first error considered inspiration as nothing more than a subsequent guarantee granted to the Holy Books by the Church in canonizing them. This was especially the opinion expressed at the time of the Council itself by the theologian Daniel Haneberg, who subsequently abandoned it. This error would have justified a charge leveled by Protestants against the Catholic Church, namely, that she places herself above the Word of God instead of submitting herself to it. Such would indeed be the case if the Church claimed that a text were the "Word of God" simply insofar as it was approved by her, and not because of an intrinsic quality that she would recognize in it, thereby submitting to the authority of the text, rather than imparting her own authority to it. The second error confuses inspiration with a quality that is merely its consequence in the recounting of revelation, i.e., *inerrancy* (q.v.). If inspiration were nothing more than that (as was held by other theologians, like Jahn), it would actually no longer be possible to ascertain what distinguishes the inspired Word from the simple infallible definitions of the Chruch (*see* ASSISTANCE OF THE HOLY SPIRIT).

Since the Council, the Modernism controversies, and in a more general way, the development of biblical studies, have provoked numerous discussions aimed at specifying the exact nature of this inspiration. Although St. Thomas Aquinas never treated this question *ex professo*, certain incidental remarks of his have played a great role in it, and especially this formula that is found several times in his work: "God is the chief author of Scripture, but man is his instrument." By the same token, resort has been made to the distinction he makes in regard to the gift of prophecy, between revelation, which directly communicates new truths to a prophet, and inspiration, which disposes his whole being to receive and to communicate the truth (cf. *Sum. Theol.*, IIa-IIae, q.171, a.1, ad 4um). Although these discussions have not yet achieved a complete answer to the question, it seems that they have produced a certain consensus, of which certain elements have been embodied by recent popes in their encyclicals on Holy Scripture (especially, the *Divino Afflante Spiritu* of Pius XII). The chief points seem to be the following: 1) the inspiration of the sacred books not only exempts them from any error in the teaching of revealed truths, but, even if it does not imply that everything they teach is the product of an immediate revelation, it does imply that God wanted these books in their entirety to be his Word, i.e., not only do they say the truth, but they do so in a manner that he has judged to be most suitable to lead us to salvation (in other words, inspiration involves not only the ideas expressed, but their expression as well); and, 2) inspiration uses the sacred writer as an instrument, not in the sense that he merely writes under a form of automatic dictation, but in the sense that the use of his intellect and his will in weighing and choosing his expression is guided and fecundated by divine influence. This influence in no way suppresses the human reality of the writer, but rather mysteriously exalts it. (Compare the close analogy, found in all of Christian tradition, between inspiration, and the Incarnation: the Word becoming "flesh," i.e., "humanity," in the biblical sense of the word in both cases, respects the reality of this exalted humanity). *See* WORD OF GOD.

INSTINCT This word is used of any obscure knowledge leading to a sure apprehension of truth that is beyond or apart from a clear perception of the reasons behind it. It is in this sense that we speak of animal instinct. Similarly, although in a different way, the influence of divine grace in every act of faith causes us to adhere to revealed truth through a supernatural instinct, in the sense that however good the reasons for believing may be, they of themselves do not obviate the divine truths. It is when these truths become self-evident to us that we shall have left *faith* (q.v.) behind in order to enter into the state of *vision* (q.v.).

INTELLIGENCE   The faculty of understanding the truth, or the fact of understanding it. Intelligence is defined by St. Thomas Aquinas, following Aristotle, as an *adaequatio rei intellectus*, which we may translate as the intellect's adhering to or even identifying with its object. In this operation, the concept, and for a stronger reason its verbal expression, is not purely and simply the truth, even if it is true that in doing so it does not exhaust it. This fundamental realism of the intelligence could not be dismissed without our falling into a skepticism that would empty all adhesion to the beliefs of the Christian faith of its meaning. Therefore, we understand that the Church, without binding herself to any system of philosophical thought, recommends the teaching of St. Thomas and more or less radically condemns (as she did in the Encyclical *Pascendi* at the time of the Modernism controversies) any system of thought in which its idealism would succeed in denying or in casting doubt on the fact that the intelligence can ever grasp an object that transcends it, or express the knowledge it derives from it in formulas that truly define it.

INTENTION   The sacraments are in no sense magic actions, and theology therefore teaches that on the part of the minister conferring the sacraments the intention to confer them is necessary for their validity, as well as the intention of receiving them on the part of those who approach them. Nevertheless, since the ministers themselves function only insofar as they are specifically ministers of Christ and the Church, in order that the sacrament administered by them be valid, it is enough that they respect its matter and form prescribed by the Church in the name of Christ. As long as they do not formally state an intention contrary to that of the Church, it must be supposed either that they positively maintain the intention of the Church, or that she supplies it *de facto* when it is lacking in the minister. On this point, see St. Thomas Aquinas, *Sum. Theol.*, IIIa, q.64, a.8. This doctrine explains why the Church has not thought it possible to recognize the validity of orders bestowed in the Anglican Communion, because it seems that the modifications introduced into the ordinal at the time of the Reformation expressed a positive intention of no longer doing what the Catholic Church intends to do by ordination (Apostolic letter *Apostolicae Curae* of Leo XIII, of September 13, 1896; D.B. 1966).

INTENTIONALITY   A characteristic of knowledge, and, more generally, of all of human psychology, that causes knowledge to be directed toward an object that transcends it. Modern phenomenology, following Husserl, has shown how a consideration of this intentionality is essential for any understanding of the act of knowing. Whence the undeniable artificiality of philosophical idealism.

INTERPRETATION   In the article EXEGESIS we have already treated the particular problems related to an authentic interpretation of the Word of God such as it is found in its preeminent expression, Holy Scripture. It is hardly less important to understand the exact nature of the problems posed by the interpretation of the documents of the whole of Catholic tradition in general, and especially the interpretation of the texts themselves, whereby the living *magisterium* of the Church actually specifies for our time the interpretation the Church gives of this Word, of which she is both the docile servant and the permanent and only ultimately authorized witness.

On the first point, everything that has been said about the necessarily critical and scientific character of a thorough exegesis of the texts of Scripture is applicable to the texts of tradition in general. But we must add this one specification of particular importance: Since Scripture alone is inspired in the strict sense of the word (*see* INSPIRATION), it is not enough just to ascertain the sense of a particular traditional text, but it will be necessary in addition to specify in each case what is the exact extent of the authority it may be fittingly acknowledged to have, in order that some evidence having theological worth may be derived from it. In this regard, the concordance of different documents of tradition is evidently what creates the greatest presumption in favor of a doctrine not yet defined. As for the most solemn definitions themselves, it must never be forgotten what canon 1323, par. 3, formally declares, namely, that they are to be interpreted in the strictest sense, since what is defined in these documents is only that which manifestly appears to be what the authority intended to define. Consequently, the romantic idea that one would be more faithful to authority were one to overestimate its assertions, is nothing more than infidelity to its formal intentions. Finally, when it is a question of documents of the living *magisterium* other than definitions, it is necessary to determine exactly, according to their form and context, what they prescribe or advise, and to what extent, in what manner, and on whom precisely they are enjoined. For example, from the fact that the *magisterium* recommends that future priests be taught a particularly solid and balanced system of theology, it cannot be concluded that the same *magisterium* vouches for each and every thesis in the system. Nor from the fact that it forbids a questionable doctrine to be taught publicly, may we conclude that it forbids competent theologians from making an effort to extract what partial truth such a doctrine may nevertheless contain. More generally, we should never be quick to suppose that the authority has intended to put an end to a discussion between theological schools, as long as that is not clearly evident from the very terms it uses.

INTUITION   An immediate knowledge, such as that which is proper to vision. Theologians ask whether the soul can have an intuitive knowledge of itself or of God. Thomistic theology, following the philosophical position inspired by Aristotle, rejects both possibilities. As the form of the body, the soul knows itself only through reflecting upon its sense knowledge, and it is in this same way that it arrives at a knowledge of God. *Augustinianism* (q.v.), however, admitting a direct intuition that the soul would have of itself, is prepared also to admit a certain intuition of God in the mirror of the soul, which is made in his image, and is constantly illuminated by him. We could not say that this latter position has ever been directly condemned by the Church. However, it is equally clear that it harbors the ever-present danger of either of illuminism (i.e., an illusion as to the actual possibilities we have communicating with God without passing through some intermediary, whether of the world or of human society), or of *ontologism* (q.v.), i.e., a confusion between the created being and the uncreated being, which would easily develop into pantheism.

ISLAM   The religion of the disciples of Mohammed, founded on the *Koran* and its accompanying tradition. Through its origins, Islam is connected both with Judaism and Christianity. Its members look upon themselves as descendants and heirs of Ishmael and, therefore, of Abraham (cf. Gen. 16 and 21). Its monotheism is a hardened form of Jewish monotheism; it acknowledges that Jesus is at least a prophet, and has even retained some noteworthy traces of a singular veneration for the Virgin Mary. Nevertheless, it is clear that Mohammed, on the one hand, confused Christian belief in the Trinity with polytheism, while what he kept of Christianity is influenced by Docetism (*see* INCARNATION), since he looks upon the crucifixion and the Incarnation itself only as illusions.

J

JESUS CHRIST "Jesus, the Christ" (or the "Messiah," i.e., the One whom God has anointed to be the realizer, and not only the perfect forerunner of his plan for the salvation of the world). For Christians, this basic profession of Christian faith has become, as it were, the fully explicit name of the Saviour. According to the words of the Epistle to the Hebrews, he is "the pioneer and perfecter of our faith" (12,2); in other words, the One who both engenders that faith in us and realizes its content for us. Indeed, he himself constitutes that content. The theological problem of Jesus is then the central problem of theology, and Christology is, so to speak, the core of all Christian theology. A *priori* it seems that two approaches to this problem would be possible and legitimate; either we begin from Christ's humanity in order to attempt an analysis of what there is in this humanity that brings us to acknowledge his divinity, or else we start from his divinity and deduce from it what the humanity he assumed must have been. The first approach would be an apologetic one, and it would lead us to faith via the path of *intellectus quaerens fidem*, whereas the other would be in the realm of theology proper, as *fides quaerens intellectum*. Actually such an opposition would correspond only with a completely abstract view of the mind, one that would intentionally ignore the ways God himself has outlined for us to be led to him through Christ, and especially for him to come to us in Christ. From the moment we make the mistake of isolating Christ from the history of salvation, of which he is the center and, as it were, the instigator, we run the risk of creating warped notions about him through an arbitrary simplification. Rather than shed light on the mystery of Jesus (insofar as that is possible or necessary), these notions would seem merely to add more insoluble problems. In fact, the preparation for Jesus's coming into the world, both in the providentially oriented events that make up sacred history, and in the prophetic enlightenment of a whole series of human minds who, themselves, may not be isolated from this history, is the prelude necessary for any faith that is to reach its full flower in Jesus Christ. It is when we allow ourselves to be guided in this way by God's intervention (which was directed from the beginning toward the appearance of the Saviour) that we can then, through an understanding of God's plan as realized in Christ, arrive at some understanding of what he is himself. It is this twofold approach, developed in the order just mentioned, that alone can keep us from simply juxtaposing along side of an apologetic that endeavors to reduce the act of faith to the mere process of human reasoning, a theology that would give way to the illusion that it is capable not only of putting itself on the necessary supernatural plane, but even on the level of God himself. In this way, at the same time, we can avoid the otherwise practically insurmountable hazard of separating Christ from his work, or (which amounts to the same thing) his work from its effect on us, on mankind and on the world.

It may be said that Christology is indeed constantly threatened by two errors that came to light simultaneously in *Nestorianism* and *Monophysitism* (qq.v.). The first explains Jesus as an ordinary man, thus making it no longer possible to admit the reality of his divinity, while the second, by pretending to follow in a strictly logical way the implications of his divinity alone, understood in a human way, makes it impossible to take his humanity seriously. These errors can be avoided only through submissively following the course in which God chose to reveal himself to us; he leads mankind toward the divine encounter where he will make himself fully known by giving himself to man in as perfect a way as possible. In this light, the Old Testament is by no means merely a sort of preparation for the Gospel, and which became outdated the moment the Gospel was given to us, but rather the only permanent way to bring us to accept the Gospel without misapprehensions and ultimately unsolvable enigmas. This is why the Church has never ceased to read it, to inspire her prayer from it, and to teach it as the genesis of her own faith and of the faith she imparts, a faith that could be none other than her own.

Let us note from the start that the name "Jesus" itself means "salvation." Since the Gospel emphasizes the importance and the providential significance of this name, we must begin by recognizing the need for salvation so strongly felt in the Old Testament, shedding light, as it does, on mankind's natural presentiments. As the deepening of the basic experience of the Passover, in which Israel was adopted by God through her deliverance from Egypt, was to bring to light in the meditation of the succeeding prophets, mankind has a need of being saved, since it is now in a state of *slavery* (q.v.) (see especially Isaiah 40 ff.). The manifestation of this slavery culminates in *death* (q.v.), a death that is inseparably physical and spiritual, which demonstrates our separation from the source of *life* (q.v.) that is God. But its origin is *sin* (q.v.), a rebellion of the free creature against its Creator, and, for man in any case, a preference given to immediate enjoyment rather than to the promises of the divine Word (cf. Gen. 3). Therefore, in every sin there is a tendency to put oneself in God's place. But quite far from being the emancipation hoped for, its effect is merely the slavery in which Satan (*see* DEVIL) holds us through the *flesh* and the *world* (qq.v.). For the prophets, idolatry was the immediate outcome of this slavery, as it was also the result of the consent, implicit in all sin, that is given to the diabolical pride that brought creatures to the point of wanting to take the place of the Creator. Yet, while the service of God results in life, the worship of idols only engenders death. (Compare also the last two parts of the book of Isaiah.)

Deliverance from the slavery that, through sin, the powers of evil have brought to rule over the world, despite its having been entirely created by God, will be achieved on the preeminent day of God, in which he will show himself to be the *Redeemer* by the reestablishment of his *Kingdom* (q.v.) over the rebellious world. The *Messiah* (q.v.), i.e., the King anointed with heavenly power in order to assure the establishment of this Kingdom by conquering all who oppose it, will come to crystallize all the hopes of Israel in his expectation. But despite the prophets' centuries-long endeavor to raise the hopes of Israel above and beyond merely earthly perspectives, the expectation of the Messiah in the popular mind at the time of Jesus did not exceed a desire for a primarily political deliverance, and ran the risk of being reduced to the expectation of a victorious king, an undoubtedly providential personage, but one too often conceived of in very materialistic terms. This explains the evident paradox in the Synoptic Gospels: Jesus is very soon greeted with the title of Messiah which he, in fact, refuses to accept. On the contrary, he directs the thoughts of his listeners to the mysterious *Son of Man* (q.v.) in the vision of Daniel (7), i.e., to a figure whose humanity does not prevent it from appearing completely supernatural from the outset, both in its person and in the realization of its work, namely, the founding of a kingdom that is most truly God's. And when he directly urges his disciples to acknowledge him as this mysterious Son of Man, he does not do so without combining with his supernatural characteristics the not only human, but mysteriously humiliated, characteristics of the *Servant* (q.v.) of the Lord described in Isaiah (53). Thus He states: ". . . the Son of Man came not to be served but to serve, and to give his life as a ransom for many" (Matt. 20,28). Yet it is only before the Sanhedrin, when the high priest, adjuring him to say whether or not he claims to be the Messiah, gives death as the possibility of an affirmative answer, that He replies by what will later be understood as an affirmation. It is, however, primarily an assertion of the completely supernatural character of his kingship, made at the very moment when he deliberately hands himself over to the ignominious death of the faithful Servant: "You have said so. But I tell you, hereafter you will see the Son of Man seated at the right hand of Power, and coming on the clouds of Heaven" (Matt. 26,64).

In the light of the Resurrection (and of the glorification of the humiliated Saviour it asserts, which will reach its full flower in his ascension to the right hand of the Father and in the spreading forth of his Spirit, God's own Spirit, among his people), the disciples will acknowledge and proclaim the true messiahship of Jesus. As St. Paul describes it in the hymn of Philippians (2), it is opposed, trait for trait, to the usurped kingship and to the fantastic equality with God that the first man, inspired by Satan's deceit, had sought in vain. This is, in fact, the kingship of the *agape* (q.v.), of that divine love that is asserted in the New Adam, in the heavenly Man (cf. Rom. 6 and 1 Cor. 15), as the creative and saving generosity that never shines so supremely as it does in the fullness of his obedience and voluntary humiliation. It is in this way that Jesus's death destroyed death itself along with sin, and made him the *Lord* (q.v.). This title, which the first Christians gave him and by which they designated the definitive establishment of his kingdom in his return in glory (*Marana tha,* in Aramaic: "Lord, come"; cf. 1 Cor. 16,22 with Apoc. 22,17 and 20), means that they recognize in him not only the Anointed of the Lord, but God himself manifested to us in his supreme kingship in the dead and resurrected Jesus.

This is what is first made explicit in the meditation of the primitive Church on the Sonship of Jesus and our own. Primitive paganism used and misused the expression "*Son of God*" (q.v.), but they saw in it nothing but a metaphor that asserted that an extraordinary man was gifted with supernatural powers. (Cf. the exclamation of the centurion at the foot of the cross, Matt. 27,54, and Mark 13,39.) In Israel, on the contrary, the use of this name in relation to the People of God already signified a solicitude, a covenant without analogy between God and herself (cf. Osee 11,1–11). But, in the Sermon on the Mount, it was evident that Jesus was offering to every man, as the preeminent Gospel—the essential *good news* of salvation—the perspectives of an adoption much more perfect than anything until then imagined. As St. John says further on, man in this context was not merely called to a nominal adoption but to one that was very real (1 John 3,1), since it was to reproduce this divine life, the life of the Father, in the *agape* that is His alone, that he was invited. Behind the announcement of this grace, the disciples were now grasping the meaning of the words or attitudes of their Master, which clearly implied that they were finding realized in him in a unique fullness this sonship which he was inviting them to accept in the faith as God's greatest gift. Did he not call himself simply "the Son"? And did he not go so far as to say: ". . . no one knows the Son except the Father, and no one knows the Father except the Son, and anyone to whom the Son chooses to reveal him"? (Matt. 11,27; cf. Luke 10,22.) It is again St. Paul who brings out the implications of this in a text which, like the one in Philippians, seems moreover to be prompted by a confession of faith of the Church: "For you did not receive the spirit of slavery to fall back into fear, but you have received the spirit of sonship. When we cry, 'Abba! Father!' it is the Spirit himself bearing witness with our spirit that we are children of God, and if children, then heirs, heirs of God and fellow heirs with Christ, provided we suffer with him in order that we may also be glorified with him." (Rom. 8,15 ff.; cf. Gal. 4,5 ff.)

But it was primarily St. John who was to reveal the unique intimacy with God, acknowledged as the Father, that is represented by the unique sonship of Jesus, which, he emphasizes, is a sonship to which we are introduced by His redemptive work, which was accomplished in the cross and is being completed by the outpouring of the Spirit in us. (Compare, along with the assertion of the prologue, 1,18, the discourses after the Last Supper.) He felt ultimately that this full sense of Jesus's sonship could not be expressed except in showing him to be the very Word (q.v.) of God made flesh, the Word that was with him from the beginning, through whom God created all things, in whom everything he created has life, and who is nothing else than God himself.

We can no more look upon the confession, "Jesus is the Lord," as a simple equivalent of a pagan apotheosis, to which from the outset it is formally opposed (cf. 1 Cor. 8, and the beginning of 12), than we can find the key to this formula in the philosophical speculation of Hellenism on the Logos, such as it is presented and explained in the prologue of the Johannine Gospel. In this text it is really simply the end result of the whole process of the progressive revelation of God to Israel, and it was not separate from a more and more intimate approach of the personal presence of the One who revealed his Name (q.v.), i.e., his divine reality, by preparing little by little the realization of his plan (q.v.), namely, not a nominal but a real adoption of mankind, delivered from the slavery of the enemies of God in his definitive Kingdom. In Jesus, in what he said, but at the same time in what he did (and especially in his cross), in what he is, God shows himself definitively to us and, in so doing, gives himself that we might be recreated in an eternal life that is not only our human life freed at last from sin and death, but his own divine life. Here we have what St. Paul had already pointed out as the great mystery (q.v.) of the divine wisdom, i.e., of the realization in Jesus, and Jesus crucified, of his plan for us, namely, the mystery of our redemptive adoption in which the most intimate mystery of the life of God is uncovered and delivered—the mystery of this love that he has revealed on the cross as uniquely his own, with the result that St. John for his part can sum up the whole of the revelation of Jesus in saying: "God is love" (cf. Rom. 5,5 ff., with 1 John 3,16 and 4,16).

The first thing that is emphasized by this progressive discovery and

this paramount vision of Christ in the New Testament, is the impossibility of separating authentic Christology from soteriology, i.e., the
faith-knowledge of Christ, and the recognition of the basic fact that he
is the Saviour and the nature of this very clearly defined salvation that he
willed to bring to us. This could not invalidate the speculations of the
Fathers and the resultant definitions on the two natures and the one
person of Christ. They became necessary precisely to keep the image of
the Saviour from being distorted by metaphysicians who were of an
inspiration foreign to the thought of the Church. What is characteristic
of the Fathers, in their answers to the heresies of Gnosticism, Arianism,
or later, Monophysitism and Nestorianism, is their refusal to discuss the
problems raised in the abstract, and their constant concern for bringing
the thinkers who had strayed back to the essential consideration in
Christ of the One who saves us by making us the children of his Father
through the victory over our sin and our death that he alone was able to
achieve. It is the same reason, or the same spiritual instinct, which later
brought St. Thomas Aquinas so decidedly to dismiss as not only foreign
to the letter of the Word of God, but foreign to its spirit, even those
speculations which at first sight seemed so appealing, such as the Scotist
idea of an Incarnation that would have come about even without sin.
Once, indeed, that we admit in principle a divorce between Christology
and the salvation of humanity within this body of Christ that is the
Church, there are no longer any idle questions that may be discarded *a
priori*, as, for example, knowing if the divine Word could not just as well
have become incarnate in some creature other than man. In addition, we
lose sight of the fact that everything that is revealed to us in Christ, and
especially about Christ, is revealed within the perspective of salvation to
which God wills to lead us, and not merely to satisfy any purely rational
curiosity.

If these considerations prevent our knowledge about Jesus from being
dissipated in some sort of abstract metaphysics, they no less also dispel
the even more insidious tendency that appeared for the first time in the
Middle Ages, and found its full development in the so-called liberal
Christologies of modern Protestantism, namely, a reducing of this same
knowledge to a simple problem of psychology. Indeed, to suppose that
Jesus could be explained as an ordinary man, setting aside faith's
assertions about his work and his person, is not only foreign to the Word
of God, but is in flagrant contradiction with what is most essential in the
Gospel. It is once again in the Middle Ages that it came to the surface in
certain ambiguities in the devotion to Christ's humanity. This devotion
came to give such importance to sentiment and the imagination that the
faith itself was threatened. Sooner or later, such a devotion would
inevitably lead to a view of Christ in which the divine would appear as

nothing more than the ideal of perfection that could be readily conceded
to exist in a human nature conceived of exclusively within the lines of
our own experience. Furthermore, the perfection in question would run
the great risk of being nothing more than the perfection of the idea that
a man from a given environment and a given age has of himself. In that
case, if we should try to rediscover in the Gospel a figure whose
perspectives are quite different from its own, it would be inevitable that
we would attempt to alter it in accordance with an alien model that we
would suppose to be more "true." All of our efforts in this regard would
be in the name of a philosophy that would perhaps never be more
narrowly subjective than when it would hide behind a scientific critique,
to which, furthermore, it had dictated its own prearranged conclusions.
Actually, it was simply the progress made in the truly objective exegesis
and historical criticism of the Gospels that gave the mortal blow to these
psychological reconstitutions of an artificial Jesus. All that was left for
the liberal ministers and the modernist writers was their flattering image.
But even in many areas of more orthodox Protestantism, as well as
among Catholics who are imprisoned in the prejudices of their age, there
remains a whole series of false problems like that of *kenosis* (q.v.) in the
sense that it was understood at the beginning of the century, and more
generally, the numerous attempts to describe the consciousness of Jesus
in modern terms. It would be hoped that the various systems of depth
psychology that showed us the impossibility of an exhaustive description
of any human consciousness, would help us to rediscover a necessary
respect for the mystery inherent in the consciousness that was Jesus'
during his earthly life.

Once again this in no way means that it would be unwarranted for us
to attempt to shed light through psychological considerations on the
only knowledge of Jesus given to us by faith—a faith rooted in a history
in which it perceives what surpasses mere human history. There is no
question that the teaching of the Bible and of Catholic tradition on Jesus
allows us to make firm assertions with regard to what his psychology had
in common with ours as well as to what is superior in it to ours. Jesus
assuredly thought, felt and willed like a man since he took upon himself
all of our humanity save sin. To deny or minimize this is to go back to
the error of the Docetists who wanted to acknowledge merely the
semblance of man in him. But this humanity was not only perfectly holy
(which should already be enough to cause us to be extremely prudent
about trying to imagine his reactions in the light of our own), but its
holiness was the incomparable holiness of the Son of God made man, of
the Word who was made flesh to save man and to "divinize" even his
flesh, as the Fathers say. It follows, therefore, in the consciousness of his
mission, that his awareness of his unity with God could not find any

analogy in our own experience. From this flows a transfiguration whose exact definition escapes us. It arises from the inevitable spreading out of this consciousness of unity with God to those aspects of his consciousness that, in the abstract, could bring it nearer to our own. The great Schoolmen generally admitted that because of this, during his earthly life, there resulted for Jesus a paradoxical superposition of a state of *viator* and a state of *comprehensor*; in other words, a beatific vision at the summit of his soul, but which was kept from penetrating his whole being because of the solidarity he willed to maintain with us. To refuse to admit something of this order in the Saviour does not seem possible without emptying of their reality those metaphysical assertions that the faith obliges us to uphold against all who, in the name of metaphysics, tended to empty the biblical assertions themselves of their content. To claim to define with greater precision the condition and the working of His consciousness would be to fall again into the subjectivism of that psychology without mystery that once believed it could reach the very depth of the secret of the divine incarnate Person, but has had to renounce its claim even to plumb fully mere human personality.

See St. Thomas Aquinas, *Sum. Theol.*, IIIa, qq.1 to 59.

JUDGMENT   In the theological sense, the judgment of God is the final act whereby he settles forever the fortune of free creatures. In accordance with the biblical notion that sees judgment and its execution as the supreme act of kingly power, the destruction of the power of evil, which in the present world seems to hold the divine power in check, will accompany the judgment, or rather is not separate from it. It is what is already clearly seen in the texts of the prophets about the *day* (q.v.) of the Lord, and what is taught by Jesus in the parables of the judgment (cf. Matt. 25), as well as in St. Paul (2 Thes. 1 and 2 and 1 Cor. 15,24-28, and the last part of the Apocalypse).

From this general (or last) judgment, there must be distinguished a particular judgment, that is, one that affects each man at the moment of his death, according to the words of Hebrews 9,27. At that moment our ultimate destiny is fixed, depending upon the outcome of our time of trial that has come to an end. However, not all the consequences of this judgment are in evidence before the general judgment. In particular, even if some of the elect have finished their earthly purification and consequently are now able to be admitted to the beatific vision, they could not share in the full glory of the Lord in their resurrected bodies (except in exceptional cases, like that of the Blessed Virgin Mary). (See St. Thomas Aquinas, *Sum. Theol.*, Suppl. q.69 ff.)

There is a particularly important problem connected with judgment: Who is our judge? On the one hand, the Gospel of St. John does say,

"The Father judges no one, but has given all judgment to the Son" (5,22), but it also states, "For God sent the Son into the world not to condemn (judge) the world, but that the world might be saved through Him" (3,17). This apparent contradiction is resolved by another text in the same Gospel: "And this is the judgment, that the light has come into the world, and men loved darkness rather than light, because their deeds were evil" (3,19). In other words, the essentially salvific coming of the *agape*, of God's love for men, itself lays down the judgment, according to whether it is accepted or not. Accepted, the *agape* transports us beyond all judgment; refused, by that very fact it lays down an inexorable judgment. See St. Thomas Aquinas, *Sum. Theol.*, IIIa, q.59.

JURISDICTION   The faculty of exercising pastoral authority in the Church. According to different modalities, it belongs properly to the pope, and to the other bishops. Pastors themselves enjoy an ordinary (i.e., stable) jurisdiction, although it is delegated by the bishop. Every priest of second rank, particularly in absolving penitents, requires a jurisdiction delegated by the bishop. The pastor, like the bishop, may delegate to whomever he will the necessary jurisdiction for the celebration of a particular marriage. The source of all jurisdiction in the Church is in the *apostleship* (q.v.), which today is committed solely to the care of the bishops.

JUSTICE   In theology this word is susceptible to different interpretations that must be distinguished. In the narrowest sense of the word, justice consists in rendering to each person his due, i.e., that to which he has a *right* (q.v.). Thus the virtue of justice is the *habitus* (q.v.), which inclines us toward the realization of this basic moral duty. The so-called duties of justice are those that stem from it and, in this context, following St. Thomas, *religion* itself is made to fall under the heading of justice insofar as it causes us to give God the honor due him. (See *Sum. Theol.*, IIa-IIae, qq.57–122.) From this viewpoint, in which justice and right correspond, a distinction is made between *distributive* justice (regulating the participation of different individuals in the goods which are at the disposal of society as a whole), and *commutative* justice (regulating the relations between individuals themselves, or the particular institutions which may, from this point of view, be likened to individuals within the body social). (*Ibid.*, Ia, q.61.)

When we speak of the justice of God toward his creatures, it would only be a question of distributive justice, since God is himself the source and perpetual possessor of all the goods which we can have, so that, as St. Augustine says, when he rewards our merits, he is only rewarding what are his own gifts (*Ep.* 194,5,19; P.L. 33, col. 880). This justice of

God metes out to every creature what it deserves according to its own nature, and to free creatures who are called to a life of supernatural friendship with God, it assures the full flowering of their total being, corresponding to their faithfulness to the graces received (*see* MERIT).

But the Bible, and the language of theology in its wake, have taken the word justice (or righteousness) in a sense which absorbs the foregoing realities, and goes much further. The justice of the righteous man, in this sense, is the state of conformity of his moral being to what God expects from him. The Old Testament therefore brings us to see righteousness, in a primary phase, as the compliance of one's entire life to the *law* (q.v.) given by God as the expression of His will. Yet, in the Gospel, Jesus says to his disciples: ". . . unless your righteousness exceeds that of the scribes and Pharisees, you will never enter the kingdom of heaven." (Matt. 5,20.) The whole Sermon on the Mount sheds light on these words by showing how we must pass first from a negative notion (not to do what God forbids) to a positive notion (to do all that he commands); secondly, from an outward notion (doing the commanded act) to an inward notion (on the one hand, committing one's whole conscious will to it, and on the other hand, looking upon the purely internal act of this commitment, when the occasion arises, as just as capable of merit or demerit as an act which is actually externalized); and thirdly, from a minimalist notion (merely to respect commutative justice, and insofar as it is one's concern, distributive justice) to a maximalist notion (to practise, beyond justice strictly understood, all the requirements of charity, i.e., of the *agape* of which the heavenly Father gives us the perfect model). With regard to this new justice, St. Paul, like Christ himself, says that far from abolishing the old law, it actually fulfills it (cf. Matt. 5,17 with Rom. 13,10). Nevertheless, under another aspect, treated in the articles ABROGATION and LAW, we shall be able to say also that the Gospel, insofar as it is the Gospel of *grace* (q.v.), abolishes not only the law of the Old Testament but every law conceivable.

This New Testament righteousness can be man's only as the fruit of the particular grace of *justification* (q.v.), produced in us, as the Council of Trent says in explaining St. Paul, by God's own justice, "not the justice by which He himself is just" (spoken of above), "but that whereby He makes us righteous" (Sess. VI, Decree *De Justificatione*, chap. 7; D.B. 799).

JUSTIFICATION   In the theological sense of the word, it is that operation whereby God makes us righteous through the *justice* (q.v.) of which the Gospel speaks, or the effect in us and for us of this operation. It is in St. Paul that this notion, in its active aspect (in Greek, *dikaiosis*) or its passive one (*dikaioma*) is brought to light especially in the Epistles to the Romans and the Galatians. To this justification introduced and applied by the Gospels is opposed the idea (which is seen threatening behind the error of the Judaizing Christians who wanted to keep to the practice of the Jewish law as it had been) of a justification which would have man himself as its author through his works, i.e., what he would get in fulfilling the law. The justification in the Gospels however, St. Paul says, is a gratuitous one (Rom. 3,24) stemming from God's own justice (cf. Rom. 1,17) and therefore the justice it confers upon us still remains his justice (cf. Rom. 3,22). This justification then comes to us by faith (Rom. 5,1; cf. Gal. 2,16), faith in the God who is just and who justifies (Rom. 3,26), and it is precisely those who until then could be looked upon as ungodly (Rom. 4,5), which is eminently the case of the pagans themselves (Gal. 3,8), whom he justifies. As for the faith whereby we receive justification, it is the faith of Christ (Rom. 3,22; cf. Gal. 2,16), i.e., the faith which leads us to be justified in him (Gal. 2,17), justified in his blood (Rom. 5,9). The fifth chapter of the Epistle to the Romans sheds light on this latter verse by showing us the cross of Jesus as the root of our justification, just as the sin of Adam had been the root of our sin. We must further see it in connection with the following chapter, where St. Paul shows us how it is through baptism that the faith takes possession of God's gift, which brings us justification insofar as we are baptized (i.e., immersed) in his death, "so that as Christ was raised from the dead by the glory of the Father, we too might walk in newness of life" (v. 4). The whole context shows how justification by faith in the grace of God in Christ, quite far from excusing us from living in the holiness of Christ, requires and enables us to do so.

It is, however, to be believed that the possibility of a misunderstanding in this regard did not at all appear absurd to the primitive Church, since the Epistle of St. James insists on the fact that a faith whereby one would think he could be justified without good works resulting from it would be only illusory. Going back to the example of Abraham to which St. Paul, in the Epistle to the Romans, referred in order to shed light on the text of Gen. 15,6: Abraham "believed the Lord, and He reckoned it to him as righteousness" (cf. Rom. 4), St. James categorically draws the conclusion from it that Abraham himself, and every man like him, is justified by works (2,21 and 24). In saying this he seems to put himself in direct contradiction to Rom. 4,2 and 3,20 (cf. Gal. 2,16). Actually, he does not do so, for 1) the works that he speaks of are precisely all those which proceed from the faith, and 2) he only speaks of them as a test of a truly living faith, the opposite of a dead faith, i.e., merely an abstract belief without any connection with the person of the believer (cf. the whole context in his Epistle).

Consequently, we can understand that, despite St. James's words, St.

Thomas Aquinas himself did not hesitate to hold that we can and must say, not only that we are justified by faith, but that we are justified by faith alone, insofar as for us nothing else could be a principle for a justification received from God as a pure grace (cf. the commentary he gives on 1 Tim. 1,8). Nevertheless, the Protestants, following Luther, as a reaction against some only too real deviations in contemporary piety which ran the risk of blotting out this primacy of the faith beneath a multiplication of external practices and which were not without their influence on many assuredly deficient theological treatises, came to misinterpret this unique role of faith. They thought that not only were external works therefore useless for justification, but that the restoration in us of a positive holiness as well, and particularly the infusion of charity into our hearts by the Holy Spirit, had nothing to do with it. Especially, under the influence of the nominalist views in which he had been formed, Luther had trouble separating the idea that grace received by faith is supreme in the work of our salvation, from the quite different idea that no subjective change on the part of the justified person is essential to his justification. This is forensic justification, i.e., it remains outside us, as if the cloak of Christ's merits merely covered us over, without transforming us. The grace of justification is then reduced to a judiciary declaration, absolving the sinner but not regenerating him. A reading of chapters six and eight of the Epistle to the Romans should have clearly demonstrated that this was not the authentic thought of St. Paul. Calvin realized this so well that, while keeping in principle to the Lutheran theory of justification, he declared a positive sanctification of the whole life of the Christian to be inseparable although distinct. But, through this division, he introduced the hazard of combining a purely juridical notion of justification with an at least Semi-Pelagian notion of sanctification; sanctification would become an activity in which man again seems to take the initiative in a more or less autonomous fashion, while the essential action of grace is first produced not within him but outside of him. Calvin himself would certainly not have accepted this consequence of his system, but it nevertheless came to light in the different forms of *Puritanism* (q.v.) that followed his system, especially in the English-speaking world. Or else, when sanctification is made to be more strictly connected with the grace of justification itself, as is the case in the pietistic notion of conversion (*see* PIETISM), there is a tendency to look upon it purely as a miraculous and instantaneous change, going so far as to imagine a subsequent impeccability in the believer.

It is against these various errors, either fully developed or clearly in germ at the time, that the Council of Trent in its sixth session set forth a particularly detailed and delicately worded doctrine of the different aspects inherent in justification. It put an end once and for all to the doctrine of a twofold justification first proposed by Seripando. This teaching held that to an extrinsic justification by the merits of Christ alone, there would be joined a subjective justification, as it were, an internal complement, but one which, in itself, would remain bereft of ultimate value in the eyes of God. In conformity with the much more unified conception of St. Paul, the Council affirmed that there is only one justification, which comes entirely from the merits of the crucified Christ alone, but which is realized in the positive justification that grace engenders in us, the principle of good works that will be its fruit and, immediately, the principle of charity that is inseparable from the state of grace. To illustrate this synthesis, the Council made use of the distinction, then current in the schools, between the different types of causality that act in concert, declaring: "The final cause of this justification is the glory of God, of Christ and eternal life—the meritorious cause, his well-beloved Only-Begotten Son, our Lord Jesus Christ, who, while we were his enemies (cf. Rom. 5,10), because of the great charity with which he loved us (Eph. 2,4), by his most holy passion on the wood of the cross merited justification for us and made satisfaction for us to God his Father—the instrumental cause, the sacrament of baptism, which is the sacrament of faith, without which no one has ever obtained justification—finally the sole [against Seripando] formal cause, the justice of God, not that by which he is righteous, but that whereby he makes us righteous, i.e., in having received the gift from him, we are renewed in our own spirit (*spiritus mentis nostrae*), and not only are we deemed righteous but we are justly called righteous, and we are righteous, receiving righteousness in us to the extent that the Holy Spirit ascribes it to each according to His good pleasure (1 Cor. 12,11) and according to each person's own disposition and cooperation" (Decree *De Justificatione,* chap. 7; D.B. 799).

See St. Thomas Aquinas, *Sum. Theol.,* Ia-IIae, q.113.

K

KENOSIS   This expression comes from the Greek *ekenosen eauton* ("he made himself nothing," or, more exactly, "he emptied himself"), used by St. Paul to designate Christ's voluntary impoverishment in the Incarnation (Phil. 2,7). The question arises: Does the Pauline text speak of a diminution of the humanity of the Son of God, or of a diminution involving his divinity itself? In fact, among the theologians of antiquity who showed tendencies toward *Monophysitism* (q.v.), we may already point to a compensating tendency to refer *kenosis* to the divinity itself, since otherwise their exclusive consideration of the divine nature in Christ would inevitably end up in pure Docetism (*see* INCARNATION), according to which the Incarnation was only apparent. The same tendency to admit a *kenosis* of the divinity itself in the incarnate Son is developed even more in our own day, chiefly among Protestants or Anglicans dominated by a notion of person that is more or less identified with the psychological consciousness. Whereas St. Paul is obviously referring to the fact that Christ assumed a passible, mortal condition, and went so far as to make himself obedient even to the cross, they intend to look upon this as a suspension in him of the divine omnipotence and omniscience, thus confusing the person of the incarnate Word with the psychological consciousness it was able to have of itself in the soul of Jesus during his earthly life. Behind these clearly deviating speculations we may also rediscover a certain influence of the Jewish *Cabala* (q.v.), according to which creation would already suppose on God's part a manner of contraction in himself whereby he would make room outside of himself for a being other than his own, and especially for freedoms other than his. If these vivid expressions are not bereft of all worth insofar as they indicate the unfathomable generosity of the divine *agape* as shown in creation, and even more so in the redemptive Incarnation, we can nevertheless take them literally only if we misunderstand the transcendence of God. By the fact that a created being is only analogous and not univocal in relation to the divine Being, it is not added to it, and therefore could not cause any necessary diminution in God. The *kenosis* of the Incarnation need not be sought anywhere else than in the fact that the Son of God, obviously remaining what he is through all eternity, in order to save fallen mankind does no less than assume not only its creature-state, but even the state of a suffering and mortal creature. It is in this way that the divine love saves us by realizing that obedience which the pride of sin has resisted.

See St. Thomas Aquinas, *Contra Gentiles*, bk. IV, chap. 28; *Sum. Theol.*, IIIa, qq.33 and 34.

KERYGMA and KERYGMATICS   From the Greek *keryx*, which denotes a herald charged with official proclamations. The word is used, according to the Synoptic Gospels, the Acts, and St. Paul, to designate the preaching of the Kingdom of God (Matt. 4,23), of the penance (*metanoia*) that must be its consequence (*ibid.* 4,17), of Jesus' messiahship (Acts 8,5), and finally, of the mystery of his cross (1 Cor. 1,23). The *kerygma* then is the proclamation by the Church, as sent by Christ (*see* APOSTLE), of the salvation-event that finds its accomplishment in Him. For this reason, any theology that aims directly at putting the essentially salutary import of the Christian message into relief is called *kerygmatic* (in contrast to a theology concerned purely with speculation). We may say that every theology that is faithful to the meaning of the divine Word that it explains is to that extent *kerygmatic*.

KINGDOM OF GOD, KINGDOM OF HEAVEN   The Greek word *basileia*, generally translated "kingdom" in our versions of the Bible ("Kingdom of God" in Mark and Luke; "Kingdom of Heaven" in Matthew, through a typically Jewish periphrase), often also involves the concept of a "reign." Actually this does not refer to a particular "domain," but rather to a temporal world economy. The "present world" in the view of the Jewish apocalyptic writings which Christ accepted, because of the fall not only of man but of the "powers" which dominate the world, is a "world" in which God does not reign in the sense that his name is not hallowed there (i.e., acknowledged to be the only holy One) nor is his will done. The "world to come," on the other hand, by the all-powerful judgment to be accomplished in it, will set up God's Kingdom (or Reign) over the rebellious "powers" who will have been conquered and unseated. Once Christ has appeared, however, the Kingdom of God is present, even though this presence is not yet within us, but merely "in our midst," and evidently in his person (cf. Luke 17,21). The result is the paradoxical co-existence of the "present world" and the "world to come." However, this co-existence is not a peaceful one, but results in this inexpiable struggle ending on the cross, where the "powers" crucify the Lord of glory (cf. 1 Cor. 2,8). This apparent victory, however, is in reality their irremediable defeat (cf. Col. 2,15).

From then on, in the risen Christ, the Kingdom of God has supplanted the diabolical kingdom. Consequently, it seems that in those who belong to Him through faith and baptism, there is produced a counterpart of what was in him during his earthly life; the "inner man" belongs to the Kingdom of God, while the "outer man" is still subjected to the "powers" (cf. 2 Cor. 4,16). If we are faithful to Christ, his victory will be our victory: "If we endure [i.e., suffer with him], we shall also reign with him." (2 Tim. 2,12.) From this comes the idea of an intermediary Reign of Christ, which at least underlies one text of the Synoptics or of St. John (cf. Matt. 13,41 and John 18,36), and which we find explicitly in St. Paul (1 Cor. 15, 24–28). Contrary to the Reign of God, which will be established by a transcendent intervention of God at the end of time (see DAY, JUDGMENT), the Reign of Christ is spread for the faith with the Church. Its triumphal culmination will be at the *Parousia* (q.v.). But then it will be absorbed in the Reign of the Father.

We see then how the parables which express a growth of the Reign (or rather, in this case, it is better to say Kingdom) are applied to this Reign of Christ in the Church, preparing the Kingdom of God which remains completely eschatological (see ESCHATOLOGY).

KNOWLEDGE   The idea of a salutary religious knowledge, and more precisely, a knowledge of God (in Hebrew, *dahat*; in Greek, *gnosis*) occupies an important place in the Old Testament, in Judaism, in the New Testament and in the whole theological and spiritual tradition of Christianity. It has here a very rich, but at the same time well-defined, sense, and it is extremely important to understand exactly what is meant by it. Many manuals, even Catholic ones, remain encumbered by the notion that in Christianity *gnosis* is a product of the heresies that were called "Gnostic" (see GNOSTICISM). In this heretical context, *gnosis* would spring from an elaboration of a notion that is traditional in Greek religious (i.e., pagan) thought. But both the texts and the facts belie this. In the first place the word *gnosis* is never found in ancient Greek religious thought as designating any philosophical knowledge whatsoever (the technical term is *episteme*), or even a religious knowledge of any special importance. The word took on this sense in Greek (pagan) texts only in the Alexandrian literature of the 2nd or 3rd century of the Christian era, where it undoubtedly arose from Jewish and Christian sources. Actually the Septuagint translation used the word *gnosis* to convey the meaning of the Hebrew *dahat*, and thus for the first time gave this Greek term a definite religious connotation. The heretics who were called Gnostics took over the term, with this meaning, either from the synagogue or from the Church. When the Christian theologians of Alexandria, such as Clement or Origen, proposed a Christian *gnosis*, whatever relations they may have had with the "Gnostics" in question, they in no way borrowed the notion or the term from them. In their use of it they were merely complying with the established usage, and following the tradition in the Church of men, notably St. Irenaeus, who were the most energetic opponents of these heretics.

In the Bible, the knowledge man can have of God always hinges on God's knowledge of man. This is what St. Paul, in expressing and summing up a long tradition, conveys in the ideal, "I shall know [God], even as I have been known" (1 Cor. 13,12). But this knowledge God has of us is not a passive one. To say that God knows someone means that He is concerned about him, that He singles him out through a choice that is a particularly pure and tender love. This is the way that we are told He knows Abraham (Gen. 18,19), and that He says to His people, "You only have I known of all the families of the earth" (Amos, 3,2). It is to those whom He knows in this way that He makes himself known. To Moses, as the guide of the people who are to be His own, He reveals His name (Ex. 3,14). Consequently, to know God is to respond to this divine initiative, to comply with his plan, that is revealed to us inseparably from his name, in his law, which has for its aim precisely to implant in us as it were the mark of this sacred Name (cf. Ex. 20). The knowledge of God therefore grows in this obedience wherein, as Isaiah was to show better than anyone else, the faith in the God who has spoken to us is of necessity continued. It is thus that "the earth shall be full of the knowledge of the Lord as the waters cover the sea," when the Messianic times come (Isa. 11,9). But our conforming of ourselves to God depends, therefore, on his communicating himself to us, a communication that will result in a union of God with us that can only be compared with the union of marriage: "I will betroth you to me forever," says the Lord to his people in Osee, and He adds, "I will betroth you to me in faithfulness; and you shall know the Lord" (Osee 2,19 and 20). Let us recall here that in Hebrew the word "know" is used precisely to designate the union of husband and wife (cf. Gen. 4).

After the prophetical books, the Wisdom literature developed a specifically Israelite concept of wisdom, as the knowledge of the paths man must follow which is the fruit of reflective experience enlightened by the divine Word. Subsequently, the apocalyptic literature extended the still earthly dimensions of this notion to a completely supernatural revelation of the mysteries of God's design in history. This design will be revealed to all in the latter days, but even now God allows his chosen servants to see it imperfectly (cf. all of chapter 2 in Daniel, and particularly, vv. 29 and 30). In the Judaism of early Christian times, "knowledge," therefore, in the casuistry of the rabbis, became the discernment of the way that man must follow in order to be pleasing to God, while among those who expected the imminent coming of the Messiah, as at Qumran, their meditations produced a concept of knowledge as the advance understanding of the ultimate realization of God's plan in the world.

In St. Paul, consistent with all of these already deeply established currents of thought, "knowledge" is centered entirely on the Supreme Mystery, i.e., the mystery of Christ and his cross seen both as the key to all Scripture, and to the history of each man and of the entire universe. This knowledge (*gnosis*, or *epignosis*, which emphasizes, it seems, the renewed awareness of all things in Christ) is for the apostle a gift, a supereminent charism of the Spirit (cf. 1 Cor. 13,2 and 12,8). But it is also a knowledge in faith of the divine Wisdom revealed to believers in the Mystery of Christ (cf. 1 Cor. 2), a knowledge of the divine will that supposes that man will commit himself to it (Eph. 19), a knowledge of the Mystery of God that is Christ himself and, more precisely, "Christ in us, the hope of glory" (Col. 1,27 and 2,2), and this knowledge is finally "to know the love (*agape*) which surpasses all knowledge" (Eph. 3,19; cf. the conclusion of 1 Cor. 13).

St. John (who does not use the word "knowledge" but very frequently the verb "to know") showed clearly that "to know the only true God and Jesus Christ whom he has sent" is everlasting life (John 17,3), which is found by entering into this very intimacy that exists between the Father and the Son (cf. all the conversations after the Last Supper). However, he only developed a theme that already existed germinally in the saying reported by Matthew and Luke: "No one knows the Son except the Father, and no one knows the Father except the Son and any one to whom the Son chooses to reveal him" (Matt. 11,27; cf. Luke 10,22).

For the Fathers, along this same train of thought, Christian knowledge was properly the deepening in the consciousness of the Church of this truth of life that is the Mystery of Christ, contemplated through Scripture; a deepening in the light of living tradition, maintained in the Church chiefly in the celebration of the liturgy, and under the continued influence of the Spirit. This knowledge is unfolded in each person with "God's love poured into our hearts by the Holy Spirit" (Rom. 5,5) in mutual conversation. On this point all agree, St. Clement, Origen, and St. Irenaeus, regardless of whatever direction their reflections may take. What does differentiate the Alexandrians, especially Clement, is not any influence of the Gnostic heretics in this respect, but rather the insistance on the propaedeutic role that Greek philosophy may play in regard to this knowledge. Making use of these philosophical preliminaries, together with the dawn of the first scientific exegesis (i.e., one in which history and philology held greater and greater sway) did no more than create a tension that risked splitting religious knowledge in two. On one side was a theology that, because of the struggle against the rationalizing heresies, was for the first time impelled to accentuate its technical character, and on the other, there was mysticism. This latter term after having simply referred to the knowledge of the Mystery of Christ through the Scriptures and then in the sacramental life of the Church, was applied, after the Pseudo-Dionysius, to a *pati divina*, i.e., it designated what St. Gregory of Nyssa had already called the "perception of the presence," or the Homilies of the Pseudo-Macarius, the "experience" of God living in us. But in all of these authors, this always referred to both the reading of the Scriptures and to the sacramental life, as the ways in which the Mystery of Christ is disclosed to us as the mystery of God himself coming to live in our souls. Chiefly through Evagrius Ponticus and Cassian, the traditional sense of *gnosis* (or in the West, *scientia*) was maintained, and it reunited the religious knowledge of God in Christ that is proper to the Church, as an indivisible whole transcending all possible approaches to it (from the simple faith of the newly baptized, up to the mystical experiences in which one sees as it were a foretaste of the beatific vision). This is what the great monastic tradition continually upheld in both the East and the West. From St. Augustine on, however, a different vocabulary tended to be introduced, which called the living knowledge of the divine realities in Christ *sapientia*, rather than *scientia*, using the latter term for moral or theological reflection. One meets with this again in the explanation of the different *gifts of the Holy Spirit* (q.v.) up to the time of St. Thomas Aquinas. Authentic Thomism, on the other hand, held that there can be no theology "as a science" except in the light of faith (which was particularly emphasized by Cajetan in the 16th century). To this we must add that the notion of the object of faith as the mystery of God revealed in Christ (see FAITH) in Thomism preserves the fundamental principle of unity of all religious knowledge in Christianity. More complete treatment of this question will be found in the articles CONTEMPLATION and MYSTICISM.

KORAN   The collection of Mohammed's preaching, which constitutes the sacred book of Islam. The collection itself was only determined definitively after the death of the prophet, but there is general agreement on the authenticity of the texts that compose it. The article ISLAM describes the teachings that characterize it.

LAMB OF GOD, PASCHAL LAMB In the fourth Gospel (1,29 and 36) John the Baptist refers to Christ as the "lamb of God." The rest of the phrase, "he who bears," or "takes away the sins of the world" (the Aramaic *natal*, like the Latin *tollere*, even more than the Greek *airein*, contains both the idea of *bearing* and *taking away*) implies a reference to Isaiah (53,7; the still living lamb being led to the slaughtering place is an image of the Servant who substitutes himself for sinners and *bears* the weight of their sins). The expression also refers to the paschal lamb in Exodus (chap. 12; the victim that was sacrificed to *take away* or remove a curse). Actually, as we see from John 19,36 ("A bone of Him shall not be broken"), the first Christians must have identified the two images with their respective meanings of substitution and propitiation. Isaiah's image of the lamb is found again in Acts 8,32, and the Exodus concept reoccurs in the First Epistle of Peter (1,19). But the two are more or less intermingled in the many texts of the Apocalypse, which take up the image again (chaps. 5 ff.). Primitive Christian art made frequent use of this representation. After the *In Trullo* Council of 691, the East abandoned its use in art, but it survived for a much longer time in the West (witness the famous "Mystical Lamb" of Jan van Eyck exhibited today in a chapel of the Ghent Cathedral).

LANGUAGE Since Christianity depends upon God's Word being expressed in the words of man, the language in which it is directly expressed as well as the languages into which it can be translated pose a series of theological problems that have not yet been sufficiently dealt with. Hebrew became the basic medium of revelation through a providential preparation disposing it to receive, as it were, the stamp of divine inspiration. As a correlative to the idea of an inspiration of the Septuagint Greek translation, commonly held by the Jews of Alexandria, there was an analogous process for the language which was to become that of the New Testament. This explains the Jewish aversion, lasting until the present day, to accepting a language other than Hebrew as a liturgical language (despite thoughtlessly made and reiterated assertions to the contrary, neither Aramaic, which was the vernacular in the time of our Lord, nor any other language afterwards has ever been accepted in Jewish worship, except for explanatory paraphrases of Scripture, the *targumim*, or secondary prayers), as well as the early Church's attachment to *Koine* Greek. The progressive replacement of Greek by other languages, like Latin, Syriac, Arabic or Slavonic, was done in the liturgy only through a genuine recasting of these different languages, which in some cases was more or less successful. This recasting imparted to them certain equivalences of typically Hebraic expressions, or of New Testament Greek, which was the first language to undergo a strong biblical impregnation. From this we see how desirable it is for a theologian to have a grounding in the sacred languages, as well as the necessity, in translating the Word of God, or the prayers of the Church which closely adhere to it, of working out an idiom that sufficiently refashions the common languages in order to communicate to them, not only in vocabulary but in style, a genuine equivalent of the languages in which the inspiration was directly formulated, or of those, like Latin in the West, that bear the age-old mark of Christian thought and prayer.

LAST AGONY To an extent, the Greek word *agonia* is used in English to refer to any particularly tragic struggle, with the idea of anguish and extreme pain attached to it. In many modern languages (English, as well, when the word is coupled with the adjective "last") it stands for the death struggle. From an early date theologians have been debating the question posed by a text in St. Luke (22,44), namely, in what sense can Jesus be said to have been in a state of last agony? Some Gnostic heretics maintained that there was only the semblance of the death struggle as well as for every other humiliating aspect of the Incarnation. Without going quite as far as the Gnostics, some theologians of a *monophysite* (q.v.) tendency held that the Saviour could only have suffered a physical and relatively superficial agony. On the other hand, the *Nestorians* (q.v.) and those who have been tempted to adopt their views, like many modern Protestants, see nothing specifically different in Christ's agony, either physically or psychologically, from that of any other human being. Without claiming to dispel the mystery, every balanced Christology, out of reverence both for the unity of Christ and for the reality of his two natures, must resist both temptations. It seems that we have then to maintain not only the physical reality of Jesus' agony, but its psychological aspect as well. But at the same time, we may not lose sight of the fact that during his suffering he still retained the permanent presence of the beatific vision in the depths of his soul. The fact remains that at the supreme moment of his sacrifice, the reality of his Incarnation, in a nature similar to ours in its present state, kept this vision, in a special way, from radiating freely throughout his whole humanity. Contemporary psychology has uncovered for us the many areas in which our psychological life operates, and therefore helps us to revere this mystery, if not to comprehend it. (Cf. St. Thomas Aquinas, *Sum. Theol.*, IIIa, q.9 ff.)

LAW   The law is generally defined as a prescription of authority. But Greek thought had already concerned itself not only with a definition of lawful authority, i.e., as the only authority capable of imposing genuine laws, but also with defining the conditions which these laws must satisfy in order to be recognized as such. In that way, not only can a tyrannical authority, with no foundation other than brute force, not make laws worthy of the name, but authority itself risks losing its legitimacy, even if it were legitimate in the beginning, to the extent that the laws which it makes veer away from what law must be. The meaning of the distinctions so strongly expressed in Sophocles' *Antigone* became the object of deepened analyses in Plato and Aristotle, and then among the law specialists of Hellenic and Latin antiquity, and these analyses were revived in a revision by canonists and theologians. This basis enabled St. Thomas Aquinas to arrive at one of the most masterful systematizations of his work. A distinction is therefore made between *eternal* laws and those which are merely *temporal*; between *natural* laws (which arise from the nature of things) and *positive* laws, which result from the positive and free will of a lawmaker. All *natural* law comes from God, as author of nature; but among the *positive* laws, we must still distinguish those that come from God, i.e., from revelation, those that come from the authority instituted by him in the Church, and those that come from lawful civil authorities.

But before going more thoroughly into these distinctions, it is important to specify what the law of the Old Covenant was, and how its notion and reality were not abolished but fulfilled in the New Covenant, according to the words of our Lord in the Gospel of St. Matthew (5,17). Although there is no Greek word other than *nomos*, "law," to translate the Hebrew word *torah*, it is clear that this latter term has a sense in the Bible that does not exactly coincide with *nomos*, even in the most highly evolved Greek thought, and it certainly goes far beyond it. Whether we refer to the Decalogue or the more ceremonial laws that followed it, the imparting of the *Torah* to Moses on Sinai as reported in Exodus (20) is not separate in the Jewish view from the revelation of the divine Name that the same Moses received on the same mountain some time before (cf. Ex. 3). This is the chief reason why the term *Torah* is used of the Pentateuch as a whole. It follows that for the godly Israelite the *Torah* is not so much a juridical prescription, even one deeply penetrated by rationality as is the case in the most exalted concept of Greek law, but a gift of grace, in virtue of which the adoption of the People of God becomes effective in the sense that the People are called to bear the stamp of the Name of God, i.e., as a reflection of what He himself is. It is through a development of this basic theme of the Jewish law, correlative to a development in God's own revelation, that the Gospel can be presented as its fulfillment, much more than its abolition. Indeed, from the Sermon on the Mount, the evangelical law of love appears as the consequence of the supreme "good news": not only is it God's will to act as our Father, but it is His will to make us his sons by the grace that is brought to us by (and especially in) the Only-Begotten Son made man. This is what is so evident in the substitution of the formula: "You therefore be perfect as your heavenly Father is perfect," for the well-known formula of Leviticus, "Be holy as I am holy." For more details on this point, see the article ABROGATION OF LAWS.

It is in this light that the Thomistic theology of law assumes its full meaning. The *eternal* law is primary and must be understood as "the disposition (*ratio*) of the divine wisdom, according as it directs all acts and movements" (*Sum. Theol.*, Ia-IIae, q.91, a.1). The *natural* law is the "divine ordering of the rational creature toward his final end, which is imprinted on human nature and perceived in the light of reason" (*ibid.*, q.94, a.2). The *positive* divine law, while it sheds light upon and strengthens the prescriptions that flow from the natural law, expressly directs man toward his supernatural end, which is revealed and at the same time made accessible to him (*ibid.*, q.91, a.4). Human laws, whether they be ecclesiastical or civil, could then be only particular applications, made for the good either of Church society or civil society, and by the competent authority in each case (*see* AUTHORITY), in order to assure, according to human reason, that the two preceding laws will have all their effect according to circumstances of time and place (*ibid.*, q.94, a.3 and 95, a.2). When these human laws correspond to this definition, they oblige in conscience. However, the civil authority may never validly prescribe anything but external actions, its domain being restricted to these, while Church authority itself may prescribe internal actions only to the extent that they are intrinsically bound up with external actions within her sphere (*ibid.*, q.91, a.4). Opinion is divided with regard to the question posed by modern moralists as to knowing whether authority may ever prescribe purely penal laws, i.e., ones which would not oblige in conscience (except in complying with the known sanction in the case of non-observance). *See* PUNISHMENT. See also St. Thomas Aquinas, *Sum. Theol.*, Ia-IIae, qq.90–108.

LAY, LAITY, LAYMEN   We may use the word *lay* in reference to everything that pertains properly to God's People (Gr. *laos*, "people"). Laity refers either to the state of laymen, i.e., of those members of the Church in general in contradistinction to those who have a particular ministry in the Church, or to the totality of laymen taken together. In the modern use of the term this contradistinction has been crystallized to the point that the term "lay" has come to be used in the sense of neuter with regard to religion (i.e., secular). This is merely the inverse side of a deformation that has brought us to look upon the *clergy* (q.v.) as if they alone make up the Church, and on those who take vows in religion as if they alone are religious. In reality, the laymen in the Church are full members of the body that she constitutes, and through the sacraments of Christian initiation they have received an indelible consecration that is maintained and developed by the other sacraments, especially the Eucharist. The particular consecrations that the various ordinations constitute must not, therefore, be considered as causing one to leave the laity, but rather as an adaptation to a special ministry in and for the whole body of the Church on the part of those who are already completely a part of that body through baptism and confirmation. This is so true that a person who would receive orders without having first received Christian initiation could not be considered to be validly ordained. It would not even be enough to say that the laymen are indeed members of the Church, but only passive members, for faith is already the product of a free act, and charity even more so. What is true is that faith is imparted to us, together with its object, only through the apostleship (q.v.), which is exercised in the Church first by the successors of the apostles—the bishops and their various assistants, starting with priests of second rank. But in the mere witness to the faith of his baptism that every layman must give, there is a true association with the apostolate of the Church. And baptism, together with confirmation, which constitutes the fullness of Christian initiation, introduces every layman to a genuine participation in the principal priestly act of the Church: the eucharistic celebration. The Fathers of the Church generally specified this participation by saying that it included as essential elements participation in prayer, in the offering, and in fellowship (*see* PRIESTHOOD). The share in the apostolate and the priestly activity of the Church on the part of a simple layman is therefore always dependent on the apostolic ministry, but it is no less real, and to that extent it is a truly active ministry. This is the basis of what is called Catholic Action today; it effectively unites the laymen with the apostolic hierarchy, according to modalities which it leaves to the bishops to determine, as those responsible for the common activity of the whole body. Furthermore, the consecration of baptism and of confirmation, sustained and developed, as we have said above, chiefly through the participation in the Eucharist, and extended in the sacrament of marriage, makes it possible for laymen to consecrate every aspect of their lives. This consecration asserts itself in a supernatural adaptation of all the activities that are natural to the goal of the Church as the fullness of Christ, accomplishing itself in all of her members. The performance of earthly tasks, as well as the procreation and upbringing of children, is shown as the path for the flowering of charity throughout the world: both the praise and confession of the creating and redeeming God and the fulfillment of his plan in man and in the world. In this regard, the particular consecration through the *vows* (q.v.) to practice certain evangelical counsels, which constitutes the "religious" life in the technical sense of the word, is only one way of fulfillment, through the use of superior means, of an ideal of evangelical perfection. Its sole principle is charity, and therefore it is the ideal of every lay Christian. On the one hand, a vow consecrates a person only with a view toward a fuller realization of the charity to which all must strive. On the other hand, the spirit of *poverty* (q.v.), which is, as it were, the soul of "religious" vows, obliges everybody; even those who have not taken a particular vow to practice the counsels are in no way thereby dispensed from being inspired by this spirit insofar as it is necessary in order for them to realize efficaciously the perfection of charity within the circumstances of their own lives. *See* VOCATION.

On this question an extensive documentation, along with a personal synthesis, will be found in Yves M. J. Congar, O.P., *Lay People in the Church*, Westminster, 1957.

LAYING ON OF HANDS   Used particularly in the sacraments of order (cf. 1 Tim. 4,14; 2 Tim. 1,6) and of confirmation (cf. Acts 8,18), this rite is generally understood, for this reason particularly, to be the handing on of a gift or of a power. It would seem that primitively it implied taking possession, and from this concept came the idea of admission to a social body. These two latter senses seem to have been what was behind the priest's laying his hands on the victim in the various sacrifices of Leviticus (1,4; 3,2; 4,4), and also, coming obviously from the foregoing, the sense of the imposition of hands on the levites themselves (cf. Num. 27,15–23). It will be noted that the directly sacrificial gesture of the laying on of hands at the *Hanc igitur* of the Roman rite was introduced at the end of the Middle Ages.

LEGALISM   A deformation of the spirit of Christianity that caused both the divine grace, which is the principle of the Gospel, and charity, which is its fruit, to be misunderstood. Furthermore, it reduces or tends to reduce religion to mere observance of a law that can be formulated in definite precepts, and, more particularly, in precepts regarding merely outward behavior. The positive assertion of the Sermon on the Mount and the polemic of St. Paul against the Judaizing Christians (particularly his Epistles to the Romans and the Galatians) demonstrate the permanent danger of legalism and its basic error. *See* LAW, and ABROGATION OF LAWS.

LENT   A period of forty days (Latin, *quadragesima*) reserved for the preparation for Easter, and marked by the ultimate preparation of the catechumens who are to receive baptism on that day. Since the 4th century there has been a tendency to make it a time of penance and renewal for the entire Church, along with the practice of fasting and abstinence. Although this practice has remained quite strict, at least in principle, in the churches of the East, it has been more and more relaxed in the West. But the Church still invites us to make of this season a spiritual retreat, where the endeavor at meditation and prayer, schooled by the liturgy, must be sustained by an effort of personal mortification; its extent, beyond this minimum, is left up to the individual. We may note that the East observes a second Lent, of medieval origin, as a preparation for the feast of Christmas. Western monastic congregations have an analogous custom in the practice of a more rigorous abstinence at the outset of autumn.

LIBERALISM   This name is given to all of the systems which attach particular importance to freedom, whether political or religious. But, granting the great variety of meanings modern man has given to the word "freedom," these systems may correspond to very different tendencies. In France, particularly in the last century, the name "liberals" was given to those Catholics who refused to bind their Catholicism, unlike Joseph de Maistre and Louis de Bonald, to a purely authoritarian notion of society. In Protestantism, the term "liberalism" denotes quite another thing. It refers to a school of thought of which the German romantic thinker Schleiermacher can be considered the first source of inspiration at the end of the 18th century. This school wanted to react against the deistic rationalism (*see* DEISM) that was reducing religion to an ethic dominated by an abstract idea of God. But their justification of religion is only a justification of religious feeling, and they saw in belief only the expression of this feeling, bereft of any capacity for truly defining any transcendent religious object. Consequently, they preached that the believer is free to formulate his religion as he understands it, without feeling himself bound by any dogma. With Albert Ritschl, at the end of the 19th century, Protestant liberalism attempted a revival through a stricter analysis, and thereby to come closer to some doctrinal formularies, either evangelical or traditional. For Ritschl and his successors, these must not be considered as criteria of truth, but simply as value criteria. In this way it will be possible to return to the traditional expressions and to speak, for example, of the divinity of Christ; however, the meaning will simply be that the figure of Christ, such as it is found in the Gospels (and independently of their historical value), expresses for us the religious values that we attach to the divinity. This liberalism has its most remarkable expression today in the theology of Paul Tillich who maintains that all religious statements are merely symbols. Although they are essential for the full flowering of religious life, the question of their objective cognitive value appears meaningless to him. Behind all these forms of religious thought we again find the opposition (which was explicitly behind the thought of Schleiermacher) made by Kant between the *phaenomenon* (the only possible object of our knowledge) and the transcendent *noumenon* (which would remain inaccessible to us). The thought of Rudolf Bultmann seems at first sight to escape this framework, since it is directed toward seeking beyond the dogmatic assertions, in their immediate purport reduced to the elements of mythical thought (*see* MYTH, and DEMYTHOLOGIZATION), the expression of the religious man's existential situation. But it expresses no less than any of the others the same process of substituting simply a religious philosophy penetrated with agnosticism for the assertions of the divine Word, while it remains even more superficial than the analysis of Tillich in his transposition of the meaning of these assertions.

LIBIDO The name given by Sigmund Freud to the fundamental impulse of all psychological activity, which according to him is of a sexual nature. The psychologist Carl Gustav Jung, a disciple of Freud, broke with him over this point particularly, although he nevertheless continued to use the term to designate the tendency that underlies our whole psyche. But he maintains that the sexual impulse, whatever positive importance it may have, is only one of the major aspects that this libido may assume, as for example the aggressive impulse pointed out by Alfred Adler in his study of the inferiority complex. There is nothing in this idea of a vital tendency—rooted as it is in our corporeal nature, and furnishing a physical basis for the construction of our personal life—that is necessarily opposed to traditional Christian anthropology. The contrary, in fact, is true, if with Jung we admit its essential polymorphism, and more especially, the real possibility of raising all that it implies to the authentically spiritual sphere.

LIFE Together with light, life appears throughout the Bible as a characteristic of the true God. While false gods are only dead idols, He is the living God, the God who gives life (cf. Gen. 2,7; Jer. 2,13 and 17,13; Ps. 36,10). Life in this context belongs to Him in a very special way (cf. Gen. 9,3–4, and Lev. 17,10–12). Nevertheless the life of God is of such a sacred fullness that man cannot see it without dying (cf. Ex. 33,20 and Judges 13,22). Yet, God makes his intention of coming to man known so that this will no longer be the case; instead, man may come to Him in such a way that he will find in Him, on the contrary, a new and superabundant life (cf. Ex. 24,11). This is possible only for God's elect whom he purifies for that purpose (cf. Isa. 6,5–7). Thus, the righteous man will be with God as a fruitful tree by the waters (cf. Ps. 1). From the Old Testament on there is a progressive revelation of the view of a new resurrected life that regenerated man will lead with God (cf. Isa. 26,19). It is in this way that the image of the living waters appears as the sign of the life imparted by God's presence among his People (cf. Ezech. 47,1–12). In the New Testament it is evident that faithfulness to the New Covenant from the outset is the principle of the only true life (Matt. 7,14; 18,8), eternal life (Matt. 19,16 and 29, and par.). Similarly, for St. Paul, the righteous man will live by faith (Rom. 1,17, quoting Heb. 2,4). But the life of a Christian may no longer be centered on himself, but rather on the One who died for him, Christ (2 Cor. 5,15), as St. Paul will reiterate: "It is no longer I who live, but Christ who lives in me" (Gal. 2,20), and again, "For me to live is Christ" (Phil. 1,21).

But it is St. John who shows life to be the supreme sign of God, and His supreme gift in us. It could be said that in the fourth Gospel, life becomes, as it were, the equivalent of what the Kingdom of God was for the Synoptics. It is in the divine Word that life is, and this life is one with the light of men (John 1,4). Whoever believes in the Son, who is that very Word, will have everlasting life, and God so loved the world that he gave his Son that the world might have this life (*ibid.*, 3,15 and 16). In those who will believe in him, a spring of living water will gush forth for eternal life (4,14). He will give them the bread of life, which is himself, and which more precisely is his flesh given for the life of the world and on which they are to be fed (*ibid.*, ch. 6). Finally, he is himself the truth (i.e., the divine reality) and the life (*ibid.*, 14,6). St. John's First Epistle specifies that this life abides in love, in this very love of which it may be said that God is love (1 John 4,7 ff.).

The life in question, for St. John, results from a new birth whereby we are made children of God (cf. 1 John 5). It is a heavenly birth, a birth of water and the Spirit of which Jesus spoke to Nicodemus (John 3,3 ff.). This idea is connected with a similar one in St. Paul, when he speaks of a renewed life (Rom. 6,4) of which the Spirit of life is the principle (cf. Rom. 8). It is, indeed, the hidden life with Christ in God that from now on is our life, and which will be shown in its fullness only when He appears (Col. 3,3–4). The Apocalypse develops these views in showing life as the eschatological gift promised to the witnesses of Christ in his death (cf. 2,7; 7,17; 21,6; 22,1,2.14.17.19).

LIGHT   Whether or not it is expressly associated with fire, the image of light is used in the Bible as the principal symbol, together with life which is inseparable from it, of the divine nature (see FIRE, GLORY, and LIFE). As we have already said, the divine glory is represented in the Bible as a luminous radiation. Reciprocally, we should begin by saying that material light itself was taken by the Hebrews as the proper manifestation of the glory of the Creator in the heart of the physical world. This is illustrated, for example, in Psalm 18(19), which looks upon the sun as the symbol of the presence of the Creator shining throughout His work. Psalm 103(104), another sun psalm, says (v.2): "Thou . . . who coverest thyself with light as with a garment." The *knowledge* of God on the part of creatures gifted with intelligence is looked upon simply as a higher form of this light. In the vision of God in Isaiah (6), in which light and fire are symbols of the divine presence, the *seraphim* (i.e., literally, "the fiery beings") and their proclamation of the divine holiness, appear as personifications of this light. This is also true for the *hayoth* (the living creatures) and the *ophanim* (the ocellate "wheels" of the divine throne) in the vision of Ezechiel (1), and again in that of chapter 4 of the Apocalypse. This is why the law, which permits us to know Him, is the lamp of the divine light (cf. the second part of Psalm 18 (19); Psalm 118 (119),105; Isa. 2,5, and many other texts). The salvation of the righteous is presented as an irradiation of light (Isa. 9,2; 42,6; Mich. 7,8; etc.). The heavenly Jerusalem will be aglow through the presence of God in her and the knowledge of God that will be possible for His People by His presence. On the other hand, *sheol*, where the dead live away from God, is but darkness (Dan. 12,3), just as the day of judgment, however luminous for all in principle, will only be darkness for the ungodly (Amos 5,18). The book of Wisdom, in its recalling of the plagues of Egypt, emphasizes that the Egyptians remained in darkness while the Hebrews were in full light (17,1–18,4).

However, this light is deeply mysterious; not only does its fiery character make it unbearable to the eyes of mortals (*see* VISION), but it appears to them only in connection with the *cloud* (q.v.).

Just as the faithful Servant was called "the light of the nations" (Isa. 42,6 and 49,6), and God himself, "the sun of righteousness" (Mal. 3,20), the appearance of Christ is greeted in the canticle of Zacharias as the coming of the dawn to give light to those who sit in darkness and in the shadow of death (Luke 1,78–79). The healings of the blind frequently recounted in the Synoptics are certainly seen in that context as signifying the Messianic work. The transfiguration shows Jesus shining with this same heavenly light that Moses and Elijah (who reappear) had contemplated on Horeb, and he becomes the source of the luminous cloud of the divine presence into which he introduced his disciples (Matt. 17,2–8 and par.).

But it is St. John who develops this theme fully. We may sum up his presentation of the work of Christ—in His people, throughout the Apocalypse; in Himself, throughout the Gospel—by the title of a small work of the Qumran community (and it is clear that this community represents a Jewish spirituality closely akin to many of the characteristics that will be part of the specifically Johannine spirituality), "The Combat of the Sons of Light and of the Sons of Darkness." This opposition had soon become an expression familiar to Christians as we see from St. Paul (1 Thess. 5,5; cf. the contradistinction he makes between darkness and light, every time he speaks of conversion in Col. 1,12; Eph. 5,8–9, etc.) and St. Luke (Luke 16,8, in which it is "the sons of this world" who are contrasted to the "sons of light"). But in St. John, Jesus spoke of himself as the "Light of the World" (John 8,12 and 9,5). His redemptive Incarnation is described in these terms: "The light shines in the darkness, and the darkness has not overcome it" (ibid., 1,5). On the other hand, this light is connected with the divine life (q.v.) in the communicative brightness with which it is identified (ibid., 1,4). Those who act according to truth (see FAITHFULNESS), i.e., the divine reality, come to the light; while those whose works are evil, flee it (ibid., 3,19 ff.). Believing in light, one becomes a son of light (ibid., 12,36).

In the Apocalypse we see the martyrs (i.e., the witnesses to this light) garbed with resplendent (in Greek, lampros) linen, and the heavenly city in which they are called to live for eternity is illuminated with the light of the immolated lamb to whom they have borne witness (cf. 15,6 and 21,23). There, Christ proclaims himself to be the "bright morning star" (lampros, again; 22,16).

The first Johannine Epistle shows that to "walk in the light" is to practice the agape (the love so proper to the life of God that it defines that life) even in this world, in the midst of men, our brothers, so that we demonstrate that we are in fellowship with the God who is light (cf. 1 John 1,5 ff., and 2,8–11).

Thus, while the First Epistle to Timothy recalls to us the typically Jewish assertion that God "dwells in unapproachable light" (1 Tim. 6,16), the First Epistle of Peter sums up the vocation of the baptized in these terms: "God called us out of darkness into his marvelous light" (1 Pet. 2,9).

In Christian tradition, baptism is then conceived as the supreme illumination. Following the great text of 2 Cor. 3,18, "And we all, with unveiled face [in contradistinction to Moses who had to cover himself with a veil before he presented himself before God], reflecting the glory of the Lord, are being changed into his likeness from one degree of glory to another; for this comes from the Lord who is the Spirit" (cf. ibid., 4,6), the ideal of Christian mysticism (q.v.) is defined in a transforming contemplation of the divine light that emanates from the Saviour, just as

Christian *beatitude* (q.v.) will be defined in the perfection of this contemplation and transformation. St. Thomas Aquinas ultimately describes the development and the definitive full flowering of grace in us as a passing from the still obscure light of faith to the light of glory. (See *Sum. Theol.*, Ia, q.106, a.1, ad 2um; q.12, a.5, ad 3um and a.13; also IIa-IIae, a.173, a.2.) Byzantine mysticism, such as the systematization of Gregory Palamas, sees even more explicitly in earthly contemplation (a prefiguration of the heavenly One) a transfiguration of the soul and the body itself by the divine light shining forth from the glorified humanity of the Saviour.

LIMBO   From *limbus*, which in Latin refers to the hem of a garment. Since the thirteenth century, the word has come to be used of an intermediary place and state in which are found for all eternity those who, like infants who have died without baptism, would not have attained redemptive grace, but would not, on the other hand, be guilty of any personal fault. Following St. Thomas Aquinas (*In IV Sent.*, bk. II, dist. 23, q.11, a.2, and dist. 45, q.1, a.2; cf. *De Malo* q.5, a.2 and 3), most modern theologians tend to admit that although these persons are deprived of supernatural beatitude, not only would they not have any positive suffering, but they would enjoy natural happiness. The Church has never made any pronouncement on this question.

LITERARY GENRES IN SCRIPTURE   In general, the term *literary genre* is applied to the particular type of literature to which every book belongs, in relation both to the type of knowledge that it is intended to impart, and the methods it uses for this purpose. As the Encyclical *Divino Afflante Spiritu* of Pope Pius XII strongly emphasized, the careful consideration of the type of literature to which each book of Scripture belongs is essential for the forming of a solidly founded exegesis. The message of a poem can certainly not be understood in the same way as a doctrinal tract, nor can a historical account be read in the same way as a fable. Still, even when we speak of historical books, we must know what concept of history the author had and, in particular, we must avoid attributing to books written some two thousand years ago the same intentions that we should expect to find in modern historians. The importance of this study can be seen particularly in the application of the principle of biblical *inerrancy* (q.v.), which itself results from the doctrine of *inspiration* (q.v.). The fact that the biblical authors were exempt from all error must naturally be understood with regard to what they actually meant to teach. But this may not be specified if we do not understand exactly what their own viewpoints were. Only an exact definition of the literary genre in question can clear up this point. For example, when it is a question of literary genres that are characteristic of the ancient Eastern literatures, in which the role of symbolism is very different from that which is ordinarily found in modern literature, we would be completely misled were we to attempt to make use of methods of interpretation that are only valid in modern criticism.

LITURGY From the Greek *leitourgia*, which means properly a public service (generally rendered by an individual to the community). The word was first used in the East for the eucharistic celebration (and remains so today as the equivalent of our word *Mass*). In modern times it has come to be used in the West for the public prayers of the Church taken as a whole, together with the sacramental celebration that is inseparable from it. The canonists of the nineteenth century tended to restrict the use of the term to the official text prescribed by Church authority for this purpose. But, in the wake of the contemporary liturgical movement, the Encyclical *Mediator Dei* rejects this narrow juridical and purely external notion, and defines the liturgy as, "the public worship which our Redeemer, as Head of the Church, gives to the Father, and also the worship given by the society of believers to its Head, and through Him to the eternal Father; in a word, the integral worship of the Mystical Body of Jesus Christ, i.e., of the Head and of its members."

From this definition and from the entire text of the encyclical in which it is found, we may conclude: 1) that the liturgy is public worship; 2) that this worship is given to the heavenly Father, and its priest is fundamentally Christ; 3) that all the faithful are associated with him, in a hierarchical manner of course, i.e., in the body of the Church according to the way in which the Redeemer himself distributed the various functions within that body; and, 4) that this worship has Christ (living sacramentally in the Church) as its immediate object, as well as its primary subject; and Christ, since he associates his People with him, makes their homage ascend to the Father in this worship.

In this view, the sacraments reassume their organic place in coordination with the *Eucharist* (q.v.), and this celebration is restored to the center of every worship celebration as the fulfillment of the homage that the creature renders to the Creator, and especially the children of God to the Father who willed their adoption through his divine Son. The teaching aspect of the liturgy as the Word, and the aspect of its gift of grace as the administration of the sacraments, are thereby not overlooked but, rather, reintegrated within the chief aspect to which the others are all directed: the response of sacrificial adoration in the communication of God's *agape*, that is made by the whole supernatural society constituted by this very communication itself.

LOCUTIO   This Latin term refers to certain words that, at times, contemplatives believe to be addressed to them from heaven, either by God himself, Christ or the saints. Without denying that objectively there can be a grace from God given to certain souls in such phae-nomena, the tradition of the doctors of the spiritual life, and St. John of the Cross particularly, puts us on guard against the too facile persuasion that, even in the rare cases where this could be genuine, the experience must necessarily be supernatural, in a way that our subconscious would play no part in it. And even when this might be the case, say the same authors, it would be completely erroneous to suppose that such graces are among the highest, dangerous to become attached to them, and positively wrong to seek them out or even to harbor a desire for them within oneself. (On this latter point in particular, see St. John of the Cross, *Ascent to Mount Carmel*, II, 8th part, chap. 20.)

LOGOS   This Greek word has come to designate the divine Word when speaking of his personal fullness, i.e., of the eternal Son of God. Various ancient philosophies, Stoicism and Neo-Platonism, had a notion of a Logos that was intermediary between God in his transcendence and the world (either, as with the first case, a sort of subtle fire communi-cating life to the whole universe, or in the second case, a divine exemplar, a model imprinting itself on matter to give it form). This concept has colored the essays of Christian theology on the divine Logos since the Apologists. And it seems that the Apostle John himself more or less referred to notions of this type that his hearers might have had, although he was not truly influenced by it because his own concept in substance is completely biblical. This was not the case for the first Fathers, notably St. Justin, or for Origen. Although they did stand their ground fairly well, they indicated a certain tendency toward *subordinationism* (q.v.), and, what is more serious, a tendency to reduce the Word to the simple role of instrument in the act of creation or in creation's salvation. The Arian heresy only developed the logic of this trend by in fact reducing almost completely the Christian Logos to the conception that the pagan philosophies had been able to evolve of their Logos. It was the task of St. Athanasius, and the group of theologians whom we call the Cappadocians, to reestablish on a scriptural basis, clarified by the whole of tradition, the full divinity of the Logos. They showed how Christ's saving and creating role is only an extension of his eternal existence in God "with the Father," according to the phrase in the prologue of John.

LORD   A title given to God in Jewish tradition. In order to avoid the profanation of the divine Name, it came to be substituted for it, and ultimately became synonymous with it. Thus the Jews retained the custom of reading *Adonai* when the tetragrammaton YHWH was found in the Bible, to the point that the Massoretic text gives this tetragrammaton the vowels of the other word (hence the erroneous modern reading Jehovah, which is nothing more than a barbarism). The Greek Septuagint Bible, however, always uses the Greek *Kyrios*, translated by the Vulgate as *Dominus*. With this in mind it is not surprising that the most typical manifestation of the belief of the writers of the New Testament in the divinity of Christ is the use of this word in His regard, as is seen particularly in the great text of Philippians (2,1–11).

Certain exegetes of the 19th century attempted to deduce from this a Hellenistic religious influence on the first Christians, particularly the emperor worship, since the emperor was given the title *Kyrios* in precisely this divine sense. But a closer examination of the texts shows that if the first Christians were indeed aware of this, they merely drew from it an opposition between the Lordship of Christ and the lordship falsely attributed either to the pagan gods in general or very especially to the divinized emperor. This is illustrated particularly in the First Epistle to the Corinthians (8,5–6). In fact, as we saw from the text of Philippians cited above, it is the Resurrection of Christ, and the vision of the divine victory over the "powers" who are enemies of God and of man that the Resurrection represents, that brought Christians to see in Jesus the Son of God in fullness, and therefore to attribute to him, as they did to his Father, the title *Kyrios*.

LOVE   The very rich and diverse meanings of this word, particularly in its religious and Christian use, do not lend themselves to a simple definition. Let us note first of all that the pagan philosophers of antiquity had distinguished between two forms or aspects of love, namely, the love of desire, where we are drawn to an object simply out of a desire for our own personal benefit, and the love of benevolence, which on the other hand causes us to wish for the well-being of the object of our love. Without necessarily excluding every aspect of self-interest, they emphasize that true friendship only exists where the love of benevolence predominates. Friendship goes even further, however, and requires not only reciprocity, which implies that the one loving is at the same time also loved, but also both a passive and an active communion, which consists in a mutual possessing and giving.

Furthermore, it is important to note certain peculiarities of vocabulary in both Greek and Latin, which are more or less connected with the foregoing distinctions, although the two do not necessarily overlap. The Greek language has three words for love: *eros*, which refers especially to the desire that draws us toward the good (this desire, as in Plato's "heavenly love," could still be extended to include a completely spiritual good); *philia*, which is friendship, in that it is a love of individuals, in which some element at least of unselfishness enters out of consideration for the other person; and *agape*, which denotes esteem or preference rather than passionate attachment or personal intimacy. Latin also distinguishes between *amor* (rather indefinite, but involving an element of passion), *amicitia*, which implies reciprocity and communion, *dilectio*, which is principally delight in another, and *caritas*, which is every generous love.

It is worth noting that in following the Septuagint Greek translation of the Old Testament, the New Testament uses *agape* (later the Latin versions used *caritas*) to denote both God's love for man, and the love He wishes to inspire in us (both toward Him and our brothers), even though this term was the least developed (or used) from the point of view of philosophical reflection. For the biblical concept of this love is perhaps the most striking notion of revelation, in that it cannot be found anywhere else, even in the most exalted religious ideas of pagan thought.

In the Old Testament, the revelation of the love of God for his creatures (*ahabah*) must not be separated from the revelation of his *rahamim* (lit. *bowels*, i.e., compassion), or from his *hesed* (mercy, loving kindness), as developed particularly in the prophets Osee, Jeremiah and Ezechiel. The love of God for Israel is the fundamental notion. It is bound up with the notion of the *covenant* (q.v.) which God freely concluded with his people, and which does not depend upon some quality inherent in this people (cf. Deut. 9) but only on the divine mercy. The prophets Osee (see especially chap. 11) and Ezechiel (23) compare it to the boundless love that a man may have for a woman who does not deserve it, but who, despite everything, is made worthy by the greatness itself of that love of which she is the object. However in previous texts it is more usual that it be expressed in the image of the fatherhood of God, which is bound up with this gratuitous, creative, merciful love by which God loves his own (cf. Ex. 4,22; Deut. 22,6). In return, it is also the love he expects from them, a unique love that is expressed predominantly for Israel in the *shemah*, i.e., the text of Deuteronomy (6,4), which begins: "Hear, O Israel: The Lord our God is one Lord; and you shall love the Lord your God with all your heart, and with all your soul, and with all your might." Love of neighbor, i.e., of those with whom one lives, especially the Israelites, but the visiting foreigner as well, was also emphasized: "You shall love your neighbor as yourself" (Lev. 19,18; cf. Ex. 22,20–24 and 23,4–5,9). Amos, and later Isaiah, insisted upon justice toward men as the first rule by which those who believe themselves to be righteous before God will be judged by him. The way is thus prepared for the strict connection between the two commandments of love that Christ made in the Synoptic Gospels (Matt. 22,37; Mark 12,30; Luke 10,27). But we must wait for the New Testament to see this connection established, and justified in an unequalled deepening of the notion of the fatherhood of God.

The summary of the law, with its bringing together and identification of the two commandments of love, actually can only be understood in the context of the Sermon on the Mount (Matt. 5 ff.). From this text we see that the whole soul is involved in this teaching on the fatherhood of God, which is inseparable from the announcement of this adoptive but nevertheless real sonship, to which all men are called. It is the whole message of the Gospel, the Good News. God is Father in the super-eminent sense that he gives life and that he gives it freely and generously to those who in no way deserve it. He does this as the Creator who does not look for anything of worth in us to attract him, but who is himself the source, the unique source of all worth, and more simply of every being. We are called to be his sons precisely in that we are called to live in his image. Just as he gives and forgives, gives himself with abandon, without seeking any return other than the gift itself, so must we reflect this image of him within us.

St. Paul saw the confirmation of this essential assertion in Christ's own cross, "God proves his love toward us, because, while we were yet sinners, Christ died for us" (Rom. 5,8). As he insists here, it is possible, perhaps, with some difficulty to find one righteous man who would give his life for another righteous man, but the fact that God gave the life of his Son for sinners is the sign of an unparalleled love. For St. Paul, our adoption, or better, our sonship, is manifested in that we too become capable of loving in the same way. It is the supreme gift poured into our hearts by the Spirit of God (Rom. 5,5; cf. 1 Cor. 13), who is the Spirit of the Son, and therefore of that sonship which he communicates to us (cf. Rom. 8,15 ff.; and Gal. 4,5 ff.). It has been rightly pointed out that in St. Paul this love, as it exists in us, is almost always directed toward our neighbor (whence the tendency to use simply the word *charity*, when *fraternal charity* is actually meant). This is obviously because for the Apostle, even though this love has been transferred to us, it still remains God's love, i.e., that by which God loves, a love of which he is first cause. Our own response to this love is faith, but faith operates in charity (Gal. 5,6). And yet, as St. Paul himself states, in loving everything that God loves as God loves it, we still love him as the primary object of our love (cf. Rom. 8,28; 1 Cor. 2,9 and 8,3; Eph. 6,24), and his Christ with him (1 Cor. 16,22).

It can be said that St. John makes a synthesis of all these notions by placing them at the heart of a real theology of charity. St. Paul had previously described the God of the Gospel as the God of charity (2 Cor. 13,11). St. John takes the ultimate step and tells us that God is love (1 John 4,16). For him as for St. Paul, God manifested this love preeminently in giving his Son to the world "in order that whoever believes in him should not perish, but possess eternal life" (John 3,16). For all eternity the principal object of this love is the Son (John 3,55). The Father loved him before the foundation of the world (John 17,24), and just as the Father loved him, so the Son also loved us (John 15,9). Thus, the Father "sent his Only-Begotten Son into the world, in order that we might live through him" (1 John 4,9). And we have life because we are made capable through the Son of loving as we have been loved, ". . . Love is from God, and everyone who loves is born of God . . ." (1 John 4,7). Witness the words of Christ to his own: "I give you a new commandment, that you love one another; that, just as I have loved you, you also love one another. By this all men shall know that you are my disciples, if you have love for one another" (John 13,34–35). And He specifies what love he means when he says: "Greater love has no one than this—that one should lay down one's life for one's friends" (John 15,13).

Thus, St. John is no less insistent than St. Paul that it is the reality of our love for our brothers that certifies the authenticity of the divine sonship, of the presence in us of the love that is proper to God (1 John 3,16–18). St. John, however, is even more explicit than St. Paul, first that this love in us, as in God, must be concentrated on the Son (John 14,21–23, and 16,27), and then that ultimately there must be a response of love to that love itself by which we are loved: "We love because he first loved us" (1 John 4,19). Although St. John proclaimed more vigorously than anyone not only that God first loved us, but that the love in question is so proper to Him that it cannot be distinguished from his life or his being, it was also John who described most perfectly this return to God of the love which comes from him. Finally, we should underline two final characteristics of God's love in St. John. The first is its strict connection with "knowledge" in the biblical sense of the word, i.e., intimacy, or reciprocity in a love that is a conforming and a union (cf. John 17). The second is the paradox of love that gratuitously saves the sinner who is open to receive it, but inexorably condemns those who have closed the door to it. Compare the statement, "God so loved the world . . ." with its apparent opposite, "It is not for the world I am asking" in John 17,9 (cf. 1 John 2,15: "Love not the world . . .").

The great task of theology is the effort to make a synthesis of these statements of revelation with the best of Greek thought: either the heavenly love (*eros*) of Plato, or Aristotle's concept of friendship as a mutual communion in a love that is above all the love of benevolence. This had led certain historians, particularly among Protestants like the

Lutheran Anders Nygrén, to reproach the Fathers and the Schoolmen for having submerged the originality of the Christian *agape* in a philosophical religiosity, in which God's grace would be reabsorbed into human *eros*. This objection disregards the fact that St. Gregory of Nyssa and St. Augustine have shown perfectly how *eros*, the desire even for the most purely spiritual goods, must be transcended, and to arrive at this it must be disclaimed and cast away before it is ultimately realized in the revelation and communication of God's love. In the same way, the Thomistic synthesis, in order to apply the Aristotelian notion of friendship to the concept of charity, transfigures it, by showing God's creative and redemptive friendship, and man's assent in faith to this communication, which wrests man from the limits of his nature and leads him to full flower in grace.

This brings us to the essential problems posed by love-charity. The first problem is that of the relationship between supernatural charity and natural desire that a spiritual creature has for his own good. This desire itself is not condemned by revelation. However, when its assertion is separated from obedience to God and to the obligation of morality, i.e., when it is so opposed to this obedience that it is itself set up as an absolute, it is certainly contrary to revelation. This is the root and consequence of sin. On the other hand, the desire inhering in human nature for good will find its own legitimate fulfillment possible in acknowledging God, not only as the sovereign Good for every rational nature, but as the source and end of this love that is His life to which he wishes to associate us. For the sinful man, the effective acceptance of this supernatural destiny will presuppose a dying to one's self, but this is the way to final salvation. Restored by and in God's love, man learns from that love to love himself in a proper way, i.e., not as an absolute end, but as a filial image of the Father, which itself can only exist in the light of the Father's love. The result is that man can no longer love himself except by loving his neighbor as himself, and by loving God above everything else, or more specifically, as the source and purpose of every lovable being.

This does not mean that creatures cannot be loved except as a means of reaching God. They are themselves loved by him, and in this love of his, personal creatures especially become subordinated but substantial secondary ends of the love that God has poured into our hearts. In this order of charity, God remains evidently supreme. Our own spiritual good (insofar as it is identified with the doing of God's will, a task for which we are primarily responsible) comes next, and it is followed by the spiritual good of our neighbor, inasmuch as it is inseparable from our own and can outweigh our own material good, even, in extreme cases, to the extent of being called upon to sacrifice our own life for another.

As for the question of knowing whether love-charity must ultimately be disinterested to the point where, to use St. Paul's word, we would wish to be *anathema* for our brothers' sake, or where, according to a hypothetical supposition of Clement of Alexandria (found again in St. Teresa of Ávila), we would prefer the sole accomplishment of God's will even to our own eternal salvation, the question itself is ambiguous. If by disinterested we understand that love-charity must love God for himself and in himself (and, within proper perspective, other personal beings in the same way in him), certainly it must be disinterested, i.e., unselfish. In this sense, the purity of love is in direct proportion to its degree of disinterestedness. But the assertion of St. Bernard, that pure love is its own reward, shows well that it is only by a unique division and opposition that the real good and well-being of the one who loves could in this way be separated from its love. It is simply in loving a proper object as it should be loved that one's own good is realized, to the extent that to formally exclude this realization would be to go counter to the purest love. Actually, we would not love God (nor his People) as he wishes, if, on the pretext of loving him more deeply, we were opposed to our own good, or simply pretended to be totally disinterested in it, since it is an essential aspect of his own love to desire our good, and to want us to welcome it.

Consequently, love-charity will not suppress nor in any way fight against our natural affections, provided they are healthy, i.e., that they respect the fundamental order of charity. Rather, it will transfigure them, although this transfiguration may require many painful sacrifices.

Finally let us point out a theological problem that was debated by the Schoolmen (*see* GRACE). Peter Lombard had established an identification between the gift of the Holy Spirit and grace and charity. Without following him completely, Duns Scotus admitted also that sanctifying grace and charity are the same thing in us, although he did distinguish them from the gift of the Holy Spirit. St. Thomas Aquinas, like St. Bonaventure, made a distinction between the gift of uncreated grace (or charity), which is the Holy Spirit himself; the created gift of sanctifying grace that makes us suitable for union with God; and charity that is the fruit of this union in us, whereby we share effectively in a love that is proper to God, a love that is hypostatized in him in the procession of the Spirit. (See St. Thomas Aquinas, *Sum. Theol.*, Ia, qq.20 and 37; IIa-IIae, qq.23–46.)

LUTHERANISM   The basic principle of Lutheranism is found in the assertion that *justification* (q.v.) is the work in us of the grace of God alone, received by faith alone (*sola gratia, sola fide*). As Luther expressed it in his spiritual works, like his great *Commentary on Galatians* (cf. especially III, 13), or the *Little Catechism*, this principle can be understood in a fully orthodox sense. But in his polemic against the Catholic theologians and through the use that he makes of the nominalist notion (*see* NOMINALISM), according to which creatures become clearly defined and differ from one another only through their actions, he came to identify this assertion with one of a completely forensic justification, i.e., a justification that remains extraneous to any change that would be brought about in us. As we see in his *Commentary on Romans*, and even more so in his *De Servo Arbitrio*, not only does he then deny that works are in no way essential for salvation, but he explicitly excludes from them the presence of charity restored in us through grace. In other respects, this first principle of his teaching, which Melanchthon had called the material principle, is closely connected with what this same systematician calls his formal principle: the sovereignty of the Word of God. Here again, very frequently, Luther's expressions merely convey (indeed, excellently) the traditional idea that the divine Word is the principle of all of Christianity, as the communication of the Spirit of God to our minds. It is not only a communication of thought, but a salutary event, in which revelation is inseparable from an infallible and saving intervention of God in the history of man and the world. But again, a one-sided polemic brings him to confuse this basic assertion with a reduction of the Word of God to the text of Scripture alone, isolated from the Church which proposes it to us, indeed opposed to her, and consequently to reject any connection between Scripture and tradition.

Another and secondary element of Lutheranism is the invitation given to Christian princes to assume the role of the bishops, who are judged to be faltering in their duty to effect the Reformation. This ended up in a complete domination of the Church by the State, and ultimately in an absorption of the Church into a presumably Christian State.

Nevertheless, Lutheranism in its development is set off from the other churches that emerged from the Protestant Reformation by various traditional elements that it preserved faithfully enough, at least up to the Thirty Years War. These included a realistic doctrine of the sacraments (especially the real presence in the Eucharist), and a liturgical practice that often kept very close to that which remained of the best in medieval practice, although accentuating certain of its exaggeratedly penitential deviations. In the 19th century, at first under the influence of certain Lutherans in Germany, in a reaction against the tendency of the Prussian kings to fuse and obliterate the characteristics of Lutheranism under the influence of the *Reformed Churches* (q.v.), Lutheranism not only revived these primitive aspects of its practice and doctrine, but tended to make them reassume their traditional value through a more or less explicit return to the primitive Church. This movement, began by Löhe and Klieforth in Germany, Horning in Alsace, Louis Meyer in Paris, Schartau in Sweden, and in a certain sense Grundtvig in Denmark, has become very widespread in our own day. It is one of the most important factors in the ecumenical movement, although it exists in a somewhat permanent state of tension with the tendency to revert to the most anti-Catholic aspects of the Lutheran teaching on justification or the Word of God. (This tendency is expressed particularly in the theological works of the Swedish bishop and theologian, Anders Nygren; that of his colleague Gustaf Aulén expresses a much more delicate and conciliatory orientation.) Some especially notable and influential manifestations of this relatively Catholic renascence in contemporary Lutheranism are the liturgical and ecumenical work of the German community of Berneuchen, as well as the liturgical restoration of the recently reunited Lutheran Churches of the United States (undoubtedly the most remarkable of all the Protestant liturgies in use today, both because of its theological and pastoral value and its profoundly traditional character). We must also mention the rebirth of monastic life that, after having been foreshadowed in Löhe's *deaconesses* (q.v.), has developed today in a more pronounced sense, especially in the Darmstadt community.

M

MAGIC A distortion of religion in which man strives to gain control over the divine power, through rites and formulas, in order to use it to his own liking. By an unavoidable consequence of this fundamentally debased concept, this inevitably implies that it will be used in an evil sense. Far from being a primitive form of religion, as certain ethnologists thought, like Sir James Frazer in England, or Hubert and Mauss in France, magic is evidently a secondary and parasitical phenomenon connected with religion. It seemed to originate at a moment in the development of civilization when man became aware of his relatively autonomous power (probably at the time of his passing from a nomadic to a sedentary state, and in correlation with agricultural techniques). His attention then turned away from the heavenly hierophancies, symbols of the inaccessibility of God, toward the powers of the earth, which he came to worship in such a way that the will to dominate went hand in hand with idolatry. This is why the prophets of Israel looked upon the cults of the "golden calves" not only as unfaithfulness, but as devil worship, arousing the most turgid instincts.

The question may be asked as to whether magic must be considered as simply a marginal deformation of the most varied religions, or as a genuine religion that was distorted from the start. In fact, in its popular forms, for which the name witchcraft is generally reserved, it is evidently a combination of practices that have survived from ancient religions and have been more and more reshaped, although it has also drawn from and distorted the rites of Christianity themselves. In its more intellectual forms it is ordinarily allied with occult syncretisms (*see* OCCULTISM), in which more or less questionable ancient cults are artificially revived, while the originally distorted aspects that may have been present in them are deliberately accentuated. The age of the Renaissance, like the last days of pagan antiquity, showed a singular multiplication of these practices in various circles, not all of which were popular.

Simultaneously there also appeared a claim to exercise against this essentially distorted black magic, a white magic, which boasted that it acted upon nature to uncover its hidden resources, but, in this case, for the good of mankind. This can be seen in the works of writers like Marsilio Ficino, Pico della Mirandola and Paracelsus. The figure of the wizard Prospero in Shakespeare's *Tempest* illustrates this tendency. We may wonder whether the ideal of modern technology, with the vaguely Promethean ideology that so often continues to pervade it, is not the more direct heir of this white magic than it might seem at first sight. The fact that it characteristically declares itself to be harmless no more exempts it from a formidable ambiguity than the same claim did for its fanciful Renaissance originators. Once man claims to compel nature to bend itself to his own designs, without any longer making any reference to any transcendent law, is he not falling back into the basic error of magic: the will for power freed from any respect for God as master of the universe, and in fact, tending to enthrone man as sovereign master?

Two questions suggest themselves with reference to the resurgence of the practice and the undeniable spread of magic during the Renaissance. The first is to what extent did the repression they instigated actually bring into being, through an actual collective suggestion, the very thing they were trying to eliminate? The "witch hunt" undoubtedly accentuated the evil it wished to dispel. But it is questionable that it was solely responsible for its existence. Research by specialists in contemporary folklore has shown effectively that magic has persisted even in modern times, a fact which would hardly seem believable, were irrefutable proofs not to be had. The second question that comes to mind is that of the exact nature of these practices: are they not merely the empty fancies of the neurotic, or do they actually enshroud certain obscure phenomena, undoubtedly intermingled with a great deal of fraud, but which are not entirely reducible to it, and, if that is the case, would it be necessary to admit the possibility, in certain cases at the very least, of an intervention of the devil himself? The bull of Innocent VIII, *Summis Desiderantes*, dated December 9, 1484, which gave full inquisitory powers to the Alsatian Dominicans, Krämer and Sprenger (who were soon afterward to publish their *Malleus Maleficarum*, which was to become, as it were, the "witch-hunter's handbook"), has been rejected as unauthentic by various modern historians because of the affirmative answer it gives to the last two points. It is in no way certain that it is, but if it is authentic, it is difficult to state positively the extent to which pontifical authority is itself involved in the ostensibly categorical expressions it contains.

MAGISTERIUM OF THE CHURCH This expression has only recently been admitted to theological vocabulary. The reality of the concept, however, is as old as Christianity itself. It means, in effect, the function that pertains to the Church, and particularly to her apostolic hierarchy, i.e., of perpetually proclaiming the Word of God in his name and with his authority, and of defining its meaning whenever necessary. In the article APOSTLESHIP the biblical bases of this notion are discussed. If it has come into clearer relief in modern times, it is because of the need we have today of specifying how the Church can and must at all times correct the errors resulting from an individual claim to interpret freely either Scripture (in the case of Protestantism) or the Catholic tradition itself (in the case of Modernism). The basic objectivism of the ancients impelled them to insist upon the objective rule of faith given in Scripture which cannot be separated from the whole of tradition. The subjectivism of modern times has made it necessary to insist on the fact that this objectivity of the traditional and revealed data of faith would be reduced to nothing if any individual could give whatever meaning he wanted to it, instead of its interpretation belonging to the body of the Church itself to which and for which the divine Word was given, and especially, within this body, to those members who are responsible for the whole in virtue of their apostolic charge. Whence the idea developed particularly by Cardinal Billot, S.J., according to which Scripture and tradition are the remote norm of faith, and the living *magisterium* of the Church the proximate norm. This must be understood in the sense that it pertains only to the Church hierarchy to propose and to define authoritatively the sense in which Scripture and tradition must be understood. But those who would imagine that the Church authority is therefore free to propose whatever doctrine it chooses without having to refer and submit to any objective norm, and that it would be within its rights were it to bend any text of Scripture or tradition to its own meaning through a forced interpretation, would completely misunderstand this distinction. The papal *magisterium* itself has specified this many times, particularly in the Encyclical *Humani Generis*, published by Pius XII, August 12, 1950, which declares that the Lord "has entrusted to the *magisterium* the whole deposit of faith, i.e., the Holy Scriptures and divine tradition, so that it may guard it, protect it and interpret it," as well as in the Encyclical *Munificentissimus* of the same pope, given November 1 in the same year. Let us point out the explanation given by Msgr. Parente in the name of the Holy Office in *Osservatore Romano*, February 9–10, 1942, with regard to the condemnation of two contemporary works. Among other reasons, they were proscribed because they upheld "a curious identification of tradition (the source of revelation) with the living *magisterium* of the Church (the guardian and interpreter of the divine Word)." The proper grace assured to the *magisterium* is by no means the grace of substituting a new revelation for what has been once and for all revealed, but, quite on the contrary, the grace of never wandering or allowing the faithful to wander from its true meaning. It goes without saying that the hierarchy itself, so that it can give this interpretation, must not only refer back to the objective monuments of revelation and its traditional interpretation, but make use of all the human means that are at its disposal in order to sift out its meaning. The divine assistance guarantees that it will never distort the profound sense of these sacred documents for the Church; but this by no means dispenses it from a painstaking research into this sense, without which it could not elucidate its riches. It follows that the importance placed more consciously today on this regulating role of the living authority could no longer justify an overturning of the theological method defined by St. Thomas Aquinas (that the supreme *magisterium* of the Church speaks to us today more than ever in the role of a model), particularly in the first pages of the *Summa Theologica:* begin with the Word of God in Holy Scripture in order to explain it rationally, in the light of faith (i.e., in considering the totality of tradition, under the permanent regulation of the living authority). According to the excellent phrasing of Cajetan, therefore, the hierarchichal authority, in relation to the revealed truth in the Word of God, becomes understood as a *ministra obiecti,* which means that for the faithful it is a *regula* of their profession of faith, but is itself *regulata* and *mensurata* by the Word of God as expressed in Scripture, and inseparable from the totality of Catholic tradition (*Commentarium in Sum. Theol.,* IIa-IIae, q.1, a.1, par. 10 and 12; cf. also q.2, a.6.).

The *magisterium* is divided into ordinary and extraordinary, the second comprising either the definitions of the ecumenical councils or the *ex cathedra* definitions that the popes might pronounce. Infallibility guarantees categorically all the definitions made by the extraordinary *magisterium.* It also includes everything that is taught unanimously by the ordinary *magisterium* of the whole episcopate in union with the sovereign pontiff. In order to specify the authority attached to a document of the ordinary *magisterium,* compare the indications stated in the article INTERPRETATION.

MAN   The biblical and Christian notion of man has been described in the articles BODY, FLESH, SOUL, and SPIRIT, as distinct from the Greek, and especially the Platonic, notion with which it is too often confused. It is in the first chapters of Genesis that we find man's relationship through his body with the material universe from which it was taken, and the no less strict relationship of his soul (i.e., of the breath of life within him) with God himself. The very positive notion the Bible gives us, further-more, about the creation of matter along with its very strong sense of the oneness of creation in general, and man in particular, is in much better accord with Thomist anthropology, inspired as it is by a profoundly rethought Aristotelianism, than with Augustinian anthropology, which has remained deeply Platonist or Neo-Platonist. In the Thomist view, the soul does appear as a substantial and therefore immortal form, but as the *form* of the body, and very precisely of that body which is its own. Thus the oneness and the deep holiness of the human composite are effectively safeguarded.

In this context, sexual life, the union of man and woman and its fecundity, are capable of assuming a fully positive sense in spite of sin, which has come to blur the question. Similarly, there are material tasks man is called to fulfill in the universe, to organize it in accordance with the full development of his own life, both as an individual and as a member of society. Finally, his view of eternity cannot be reduced solely to the beatitude of individual souls who would find their intimacy with God only in personal reflection. Without at all endangering the values of an interior personal life, there follows the necessary consideration of the one and total destiny of all of saved mankind in the final resurrection, wherein all individual beatitudes are completed and assumed in the unity of the whole Christ, Head and body, who gathers together and concentrates in himself an integrally transfigured universe.

It is in this light that we must understand the opposition often stated by St. Paul (and particularly developed in the fifteenth chapter of his First Epistle to the Corinthians) between the earthly man that *Adam* (q.v.) was, and that we were, following him, at the beginning of our lives, and the heavenly man that is the resurrected Christ, which we in turn must become. He takes up this idea again in the Epistle to the Ephesians when he describes, as it were, the future vision of mankind attaining its full development in the Church: "When we all attain to the unity of faith and the knowledge of the Son of God, to mature manhood, to the measure of the stature of the fullness of Christ" (4,13).

MANICHAEANISM   The error of Manes (or Mani) originating in the 3rd century of the Christian era. It combines elements of heretical Judaism and Christianity (in the sense of *Gnosticism*, q.v.) with a basis of Mazdaean (*see* DUALISM) and Far Eastern ideas (particularly Buddhism). Its chief characteristic is a radical metaphysical dualism, supposing a principle of good (the principle of the spirit and of light) that is in unending struggle with a principle of evil (the principle of matter and darkness). We know Manichaeanism especially from the numerous writings of St. Augustine, who combatted it after he had severed his connections with it (his first document opposing it is *De Moribus Ecclesiae*), but recent discoveries have permitted us to acquire first-hand knowledge about its earliest manifestations, and its founder. Under different forms (*Cathari, Bogomils,* etc.), Manichaean ideas, reviving the oldest tendencies that had already been present in the heretical *gnosis,* were a perpetual threat to the Catholic faith in the Middle Ages. It has been correctly pointed out that they played a role in a certain false spiritualism that marks a whole section of Court literature, especially among the troubadours of Southern France.

MARIOLOGY   A name given in modern times to theological studies devoted to the Blessed Virgin Mary. It will be noted that the development of mariology came later in the West than in the East, although there has been a growing tendency in the West for it to take the regrettable form of an excrescence separated from the rest of theology. On the contrary, in the great Eastern tradition, it is in the most consistent union with Christological, soteriological and ecclesiological meditation that the reflection in the faith on Mary, and the veneration that the faithful have pledged to her, have been pursued. In order to keep mariology from turning into a kind of sentimental and unhealthy Gnosticism in which piety toward Mary would risk deteriorating into superstition, it is desirable that the West effect a reintegration (from which, unhappily, we seem still quite far removed). Then, the devotees of Mary will no longer imagine that to render her the veneration which she is due must be translated as accumulating definitions of more or less well-conceived privileges, by which she would seem to be placed more and more outside of a humanity common to all Christians. On the contrary, mariology will reach full flower in acknowledging in Mary the supereminent perfection to which all mankind is called, in proportion to the intimacy and the proximity of an individual's union with the Person and the work of the one Saviour.

MARRIAGE   An institution of the natural law, creating a stable union between man and woman—the foundation of the family—raised by the New Testament to the sacramental plane. It is admitted that the indissolubility of marriage is a principle of the natural law, but that a positive prescription of divine law was necessary to make it fully clear (cf. Gen. 2,18 ff., and the comment in Matt. 19,3–12). Groundwork for the notion of the sacramentality of marriage was laid down in the fact that the union of man and woman already served in the Old Testament as a symbol of the union of the Lord with his People. Compare the use of this image by the prophets Osee (Osee 2,4 ff.) and Ezechiel (ch. 16), and the traditional interpretation in Israel of the *Song of Solomon* and of Psalm 44(45). St. Paul, in the Epistle to the Ephesians, goes further and shows in the union of marriage a true realization between man and wife of the love of charity of which Christ gave the supereminent example in delivering himself over to the cross for the Church (5,22 ff.). With this idea as a basis, and in connection with the formula that St. Paul uses ("This is the great mystery [in Greek *mysterion*, translated into Latin by *sacramentum*], and I take it to mean Christ and the Church." (v.32)), in the Middle Ages, in both West and East, marriage is ranked among the sacraments in the strict sense, i.e., the seven signs of grace that are considered to be efficacious by virtue of their being instituted by Christ. Even in the first centuries, we see Christians being urged not to contract a union without the approval of Church authority (cf. Ignatius, *Letter to*

Polycarp, 5,2). Tertullian writes as if the union contracted before a priest, and with his blessing, had become the universal rule (*Ad Uxorem*, II, 9; P.L. 1, col. 1302). Ambrose specifies that the ceremony includes the *velatio* as well, i.e., the giving of a veil to the bride (*Epist.* XIX, 7; P.L. 16, col. 984). In 886, Pope Nicolas I indicated to the Bulgars what rites were then followed by the Latin Church: the *sponsalia* (the exchange of promises), the *subarrhatio* (the ring by which the man binds himself to his fiancée), then during the course of the eucharistic celebration, the *velamen* and the *benedictio*, and finally the crowning (of both bride and groom). It is rather painful to observe that all of these rites, given as those of the Latin Church in the *Responsa ad Consulta Bulgarorum* (chap. III; P.L. 119, col. 980), are today faithfully kept by the Churches of the East, while the ritual of the Roman Church has lost those that are most significant. This is undoubtedly because the scholastic theology of marriage as a sacrament was developed at a time when the West was revivifying the notion of Roman law, and marriage came to be whittled down to merely the contract between husband and wife. It is from the same origin, also, that the modern Latin theory undoubtedly comes, stating that the spouses themselves are the sole ministers of the sacrament, and that the priest, when he does intervene, only plays the role of a witness, assuring the publicness necessary for the contract's validity. In this case, the nuptial blessing, given in the course of the eucharistic celebration, seems to be secondary, and it is not surprising that it is easily dispensed with. The viewpoint of the East, endorsed by the Eastern code of canon law, on the contrary, maintains that the sacramentality of marriage consists in the consent of the bride and groom together with the blessing that the priest is normally appointed to give them. These differences of interpretation show well that the theology of marriage as a sacrament has not yet been thoroughly developed and that it could not be developed without taking into consideration all the aspects of a tradition that, itself, is much broader than that which is currently taught in the West.

As for the morality or the spirituality of marriage, it stems from the biblical texts that we have called to mind. It was synthesized by St. Augustine in the formulation of what have subsequently been called the benefits of marriage, and which he enumerates: *fides, proles, sacramentum* (*De Nuptiis et Concupiscentia*, lib. I, cap. 17). We may understand them as the faithfulness of the bride and groom to their common involvement, the procreation of children and their upbringing, and finally the mystery of the conjugal union in the light of Christ's union with the Church. However, it is undeniable that he retained a certain exaggerated pessimism towards the physical union itself, by admitting that it can never take place without sin because of the disordered state that results from concupiscence: *nunc ergo sine isto malo esse non potest, sed non ideo malum est* (*Contra Julianum*, III, 53). St. Thomas Aquinas refutes him on this point in observing that since our corporeal nature was instituted by a good God, it is impossible to say that anything that involves the preservation of that corporeal nature and its inclinations is universally bad (*In Lib. IV Sent.*, dist. 26, q.1, a.3). In a general way, we may say that it is impossible simply to set the Christian doctrine of marriage against a teaching that exalts virginity consecrated to Christ. On the one hand, actually, Christian marriage derives all of its dignity from what it is in its total, indissolubly physical and spiritual reality, namely, a participated image of the union of Christ with the Church in charity (cf. the text of Eph. 5 cited above). On the other hand, consecrated virginity is worthwhile only because of its being very precisely consecrated to this latter union, through the ascetical renunciation of marriage itself. The superiority, in principle, of virginity over marriage therefore stems completely from the generosity of the sacrifice consented to from the outset, but it has meaning only within the same charity between God and man that marriage expresses and that it also realizes, if in another way.

Nevertheless, the dignity of marriage is found only in its single realization, and it is because of this singleness that its sign has value. This is why the primitive Church, although it fully admitted the validity and lawfulness of second marriages (after widowhood; cf. 1 Tim. 5,14), never acknowledged in them the dignity of a first and single marriage. In the West today, the nuptial blessing is still only given in first marriages, and the East has retained the ancient custom of reserving the *velatio* and the crowning to them also. Let us recall that in both canon laws the fact of one's having been married more than once constitutes an impediment to major orders (cf. 1 Tim. 3,2). See St. Thomas Aquinas, *Sum. Theol.*, Suppl. qq.41 to 68.

Let us recall also that the full sacramentality of marriage, already asserted by the Council of Lyons in 1274 (D.B. 465), was reasserted against the Protestants at the Council of Trent (sess. 24; D.B. 969 ff.). It is the same council that prescribed that in the future all clandestine marriages were to be considered invalid, i.e., marriages where the mutual consent was not made the object of an agreement "in the presence of the Church" (*ibid.*; D.B. 990 ff.). Nevertheless, theologians maintain that this obligation has only Catholics in view and that marriages contracted by baptized non-Catholics can be both valid and sacramental without this condition.

MARTYRDOM Coming from the Greek word *martys*, which means "witness," this term, at least since the Apocalypse of St. John which uses it frequently, has come to designate the principal witness given to Christ by Christians who accept death out of faithfulness to their Saviour. As we see from certain episodes in the books of Maccabees, Judaism already had called attention to the value of the witness borne to the faith by fidelity even to the extent of torture and death. But the idea developed by St. Paul, that baptism "engrafts" upon us the likeness of the death of Christ, and the sense of the Eucharist as a sharing in his risen life through the communion in his body broken for us and his blood shed for us on the cross, incomparably enhances the meaning of Christian martyrdom. It will appear as the perfect association of the Christian with the cross of the Saviour, in the supreme act of a charity nurtured in us by the sacramental participation in the great mystery of faith. The epistles of the martyr St. Ignatius of Antioch develop the idea that martyrdom shows in some way the reality of the eucharistic presence on which the Christian's faith is nourished. The *Martyrdom of St. Polycarp*, for its part, describes for us the death of this other bishop-martyr as the consummation of a supreme Eucharist. Whence, the belief, constantly attested to from Christian antiquity, of a presence of Christ, as victor over death, becoming manifest in those who die in order to stay faithful to him. We could even say that here we have the first example of what will be called the mystical experience. This also explains why martyrdom undergone by a catechumen was looked upon as the equivalent of baptism: did not the faith of the catechumen obtain here immediately the reality of this "engrafting" on Christ in his death that, according to St. Paul, is the substance of baptism? The preparation for martyrdom by the free renunciation of the goods of the world is one of the first forms of Christian asceticism that was to lead to monasticism. If the question were raised as to the usefulness of these renunciations for those who would not in fact be called to martyrdom, we would emphasize actually that they were undergoing a sort of voluntary martyrdom, capable of reaching the same consecratory value as the bloody martyrdom, even though it was itself unbloody. It is in this way that the monastic life, once martyrdom ceased, became its equivalent for the Church, which otherwise would have run the risk of becoming secularized after the Peace of Constantine. For all of the foregoing reasons, we can understand without difficulty that martyrdom was the first path to heroic sanctity canonized by the Church, and has served as the basic type for Christian holiness.

MARXISM   The teaching of Karl Marx, which finds its major expression in his book *Das Kapital* (first edition in German, 1867). The theory of Marx is opposed point for point to the idealist dialectic of Hegel, but in spite of that, it is a reverse reflection in a materialist mirror, and in fact defines itself as dialectical materialism. In it, man is nothing more than the product of an exclusively material nature. He will, however, from the beginning of his existence tend to be in conflict with that material nature in order to ultimately emancipate himself from it by gaining control over it.

What is more particularly our concern here is the way religion is explained within this theory. The whole evolution of mankind is understood in Marxism as being dominated by problems resulting from the production and consumption of the goods necessary for life. The classes and their struggle originate in the fact that the possessing minority tends primarily to keep the greater part of consumer goods for itself by controlling the means of production. Manual laborers, therefore, find themselves placed in a situation of alienation in which those who ought to benefit from the humanization of nature of which they are the instruments do not profit from their work or its fruits, and become in fact the property of the possessor class. It is in this context that religion should be born as the frustrated proletariat's consoling dream. The working classes would, therefore, conjure up another world in which they could find after life the compensation for what has been denied them in the present. The possessor classes would seize upon this illusion in order to organize it for their own profit; thereby keeping the proletariat in subjection, lulling to sleep the class instinct that would otherwise incite them to rebel. It is in this way that religion would become the opium of the people by fostering in the proletariat that resignation whereby capitalism keeps them enchained. Once they become aware of the illusion of which they are victims, along with the birth of their class consciousness in their struggle for liberation, and with the socialist organization which will rise up from the ruins of capitalism, religion will disappear together with the conditions that had engendered it.

This basically negative view of all religion did not keep Marx from acknowledging Christianity's historic role in the awakening of the proletarian consciousness, both by its exaltation of the poor and by its proclamation of a future kingdom of righteousness. But these two intuitive concepts were to find themselves paralyzed by the preaching of a resignation necessary to achieve this final kingdom, combined with the expectation that it was to come about by a divine initiative. Consequently, in one sense Marxism proposes to realize the Messianic ideal by substituting class consciousness for resignation and the class struggle for the awaited action of grace. The proletariat then become, as it were, the equivalent both of the Messianic community and the Messiah himself; its dictatorship, to be established by force, will fulfill the role of the eschatological coming awaited by Christianity. There is no Marxist equivalent that goes so far as the transfiguration of the whole universe around regenerated man, but it is united expressly with a truly demiurgic technological ideal: mankind, emancipated from all of its historical subjections, through its entry into the properly communistic stage that is to follow the socialist State (fading away in proportion to its own success), will enter into a definitive mastery over the physical world. This aspect of Marxian theory is allied with a notion of God developed by Feuerbach, in which God is merely the expression of the limits that man believes are imposed upon him by the nature of things. Putting aside the idea of God is then the necessary correlative to man's gaining control of his own destiny, and to his liberation from all of his alienations by overcoming and even mastering nature.

These few notations show well the complexity of the sources of Marxism, from which its creator was able to compose a work of an undeniable synthetic power: scientistic materialism, a demiurgic inspiration of technological civilization, a profound intuition of the historical and social reality of the human consciousness, and a political and social claim nurtured by a simple transposition of Judeo-Christian Messianism —the union, precarious no doubt, but brilliant and clever, of all of these elements explains the success with which it has been able to elicit great fascination. A number of intellectuals believed that they had finally found here the synthetic conception of the world to which modern man had been aspiring without being able to attain it until now, while the masses believed that they had discovered in Marxism a new Gospel which would assure them, together with their material deliverance, of a moral liberation.

Any criticism of Marxism, and particularly any criticism that one would wish to give from the Christian point of view, supposes, for it to be effective, that we begin by doing justice to those elements of truth that it contains. This is not easy to realize without succumbing to its fascination, or by giving the impression that we hold all the cards by drawing a deformed caricaturization of its assertions. The first point that we must plainly admit is that if the Marxist analysis and criticism of religion do not apply to authentic Christianity, they nevertheless do capture accurately the deformation of religion that is already noticeable in many modern forms of Gallicanism, which reduce the Church to merely an instrument of the domination over the consciences of people at the hands of a State that is, in fact, profoundly irreligious in inspiration. A *fortiori*, the same thing must be said with regard to certain attempts to justify a religious organization of mankind by systems of political thought inspired by the *positivism* (q.v.) of Auguste Comte. More generally, it is the entire religious policy of modern States, who wanted to use the Church without accepting or recognizing either her freedom or the transcendence of Christianity, that is found to be under question. In this regard, Marxism only brings to light and denounces the materialism underlying the orientation of a capitalistic civilization that in fact does not accept any other law, any other ideal than the quest for material profit. On the other hand, as soon as Marxism sets itself up as a liberator of mankind with regard to such forms of oppression, we can and must reproach it for riveting itself to the narrowly materialistic presuppositions that it underlines, and for its refusal to even entertain the idea that it is these very presuppositions that above all must be discarded. From this fact, which has been only too well proved in our own day by the Marxists' attempt at building a socialist community, it can do no more than substitute for this insidious oppression of human consciences, a systematic oppression camouflaged in the most illusory of liberations. Indeed, once the individual's transcendence with regard to the physical universe and society, as well, is no longer acknowledged, but on the contrary is found to be denied in principle, there can no longer be any question of any liberation that would be anything other than a decoy. This latter criticism is at least as relevant to Feuerbach's analysis as it is to the postulates proper to Marxism.

We must further point out the correctness of the Marxist intuition as to the historical character of mankind, including the acknowledgement, on the one hand, of the inseparability of the individual's salvation from the salvation of society as a whole, and, on the other hand, of the cosmic dimensions that this problem of salvation must take on as a consequence of the fact of mankind's being rooted in physical nature. But it must be maintained that the problem of human history cannot be resolved as long as there is disregard for both the spirituality inherent in each individual and the supernatural destiny of mankind. It follows that in Marxism we must reject, 1) the Promethean notion that mankind is to achieve fulfillment by excluding any reference or submission to any transcendent intervention whatever; 2) the reduction of the aims of an individual to those of a society defined solely by economic realities; and, 3) the degeneration, following from this, of the Judeo-Christian notion of a Messianic community into the genuine apotheosis of a social class (which alone, it wrongly claims, has the power to realize the goal of the species, and, still worse, to be itself that goal). This makes it impossible for Christians to entertain the fallacious hope that the Marxist dialectic can be Christianized by going beyond it; it is essential to its own premises, once they are accepted, that it be set against any possibility of that kind. For Christians, there could be nothing beyond Marxism other than a theology of history that returns to the roots of all the realities concerned by restoring to them at the starting point their dimensions that have been overlooked. Unfortunately we cannot say that this work has yet been seriously undertaken. Some particularly interesting suggestions, however, may be found in Jacques Loew, O.P., *Journal d'une mission ouvrière*, Paris, 1959; Madeleine Delbrêl, *Ville marxiste, terre de mission*, Paris, 1957; as well as in the two volumes of P. Gaston Fessard, S.J., *De l'actualité historique*, Paris, 1960, even if we cannot follow him in all of his criticism of so-called leftist Catholics, nor in the totality of his own historical dialectic.

MARY   At a very early date, in addition to the apostles' association with Christ's work, the Church understood that Mary, Mother of the Saviour, presented another, properly feminine, kind of association with the work of salvation, which, if it is possible, was even more intimate. Her spiritual as well as physical motherhood of the Son of God made man is its principle. Her virginity, which was very soon acknowledged to be of exceptional integrity and significance, was understood both as the condition and the effect of this singular predestination in the plan of salvation.

The Gospel according to St. Matthew seems to see in the virginal birth of Jesus the sign of the fact that he is God with us: not an ordinary child of men, but the Son of God made man (cf. Matt. 1,20–22). St. Luke describes the Annunciation by the angel in such a way that Mary plays, as it were, the role of the New Eve at the side of the Second Adam. The faithful angel calls her to faith just as the serpent had called Eve to unbelief. Thus the obedience of the one is the answer to the disobedience of the other: agreeing to be the "handmaid of the Lord" by her self-denial, in contradistinction to Eve's will to usurp the place of God by yielding to covetousness. Behind this contradistinction we have an inkling as to how Mary's virginity, her denying herself any immediate satisfactions, prepares her to be the Mother not of a life polluted at its source, but of the "holy One" who will be the source of the new life. At the beginning of this Gospel of the poor, Mary is, as it were, the living image of this supernatural fecundity of the faith that puts its expectation in God alone. It is noteworthy that it is again Luke, in Acts (1,14), who underlines Mary's presence in the midst of the Church that awaits, in prayer, the coming of the Spirit. In turn, the Johannine accounts evoke a figure of Mary, first of all, in the vision of Apoc. 12. It would indeed seem that if the woman who appears in the sun, her head crowned with stars and the moon beneath her feet, is not purely and simply the Virgin, but rather the Church, it would in any case be the Church as represented by the Mother of a unique male Child, the victor over the serpent, who is obviously the Messiah. That amounts to saying that if the woman represents the Church, it is first in Mary that the Church is seen. It would perhaps be most exact to say that the woman here is the Church of the Old Covenant giving birth through Mary to the Messiah, and with him to the whole Church of the New Covenant. In the Johannine Gospel, Mary is present at the beginning and at the end of her Son's public ministry. At Cana, she appears as the one through whom we come to Jesus, just as it is through her that he came into the world, and, just as in St. Luke she was the very example of that obedient faith with which we are to receive Christ, now she expressly urges us to that faith: "Do whatever he tells you" (John 2,1–12). At the cross, she is the image of faithfulness in following Christ into the depths of his trial and by God's express will she thus becomes the Mother of those in whom his death engenders life (John 19,25–27).

From all of these texts, the meditation of the Church is prompt to arrive at the certainty that in Mary, through faith, the mankind that Jesus came to save was, from the outset, freely associated with the redemptive work that he alone could accomplish. Whence the conviction that Mary is the Mother of the Saviour both spiritually and physically, and in him Mother of his whole Mystical Body. This is also the origin of the title of the New Eve that the Fathers gave her, following St. Irenaeus, and the acknowledgment of her motherhood of grace in which her physical motherhood of the Son of God is broadened to include all Christians. By the same token, her virginity consecrated to Christ is understood as the supereminent example of the supernatural fecundity of such self-denial accepted in the obedience of faith. And so Mary becomes, as it were, the perfect image of mankind's commitment to the saving work of which it is the object. As the supreme "handmaid" of the Lord by the side of the unique "Servant," the Church sees in her the fullness of the faith by which she is to live, the perfection of Christian intercession in complete correspondence to redemption. To this is added the certainty that in her supernatural motherhood her virginity has found a full flowering, exempt from any blemish. In this way, the victory in her of grace over sin and death anticipates from the beginning of salvation everything that the whole Church will attain in the end. Mary is, therefore, more and more clearly defined in the Christian consciousness as the perfect maternal realization of the vocation of mankind, foreshadowing and preparing what will be the perfect realization for the Church in the latter days of her marriage with Christ. *See* PERPETUAL VIRGINITY OF MARY, IMMACULATE CONCEPTION, and ASSUMPTION. For a complete conspectus of the data of tradition concerning Mary and the veneration given to her by the Church, cf. the Marian Encyclopedia edited by Father du Manoir, S.J., under the title *Maria* (Paris, Ed. Beauchesne).

MASS The name given in the West to the eucharistic service, called simply *leitourgeia* (i.e., the preeminent "service") in the East. The word itself comes from its concluding formula, *ite missa est,* which was simply a form of dismissal in the beginning. We also use the term "Mass of the catechumens" to designate the first part of the service to which for a long time the catechumens were admitted, even though they were excluded from the second part, the "Mass of the faithful." Many Eastern liturgies still include a formula of dismissal of the catechumens before the Eucharist proper begins. As explained in the article EUCHARIST, since this Eucharist is essentially the response of God's Word elicited by that Word itself in those who receive it, the connection between the service of readings and prayers and the eucharistic service is organic. In fact, Christian tradition has always looked upon them as inseparable in principle. Furthermore, in the Old Testament, we already may see the *qahal,* i.e., the assembly of God's People, regularly including after the proclamation of the divine Word a sacrificial celebration that both seals its reality on God's part and consecrates its acceptance on the part of the people (cf. Ex. 19 to 24 and 4 Kings 23). The *qahal,* in which the people were reconstituted after their return from exile, already included in the place of the covenant sacrifice a prayer of the type of the *berakah,* which is the germ of what will become the Eucharist (cf. Neh. 8 and 9). To the synagogue service of biblical readings, which developed into the Gospel proclamation, the Christian Church added the ritual meal *berakah,* opening with the blessing of bread and closing with the blessing of the last cup, which Jesus transformed at the Last Supper into the Eucharist of his body broken and his blood shed for the accomplishment in us of this "good news" of our reconciliation with the Father through his cross. In this way, the Mass, in which the New People of God listen to the definitive Word of God and commit themselves to it in the sacramental enactment of the reconciliatory sacrifice, becomes the constitutive assembly of the Church. This is the origin of the insistence on the duty that every Christian has of taking part in Mass, particularly on Sundays and greater feasts (cf. can. 1248).

MATERIALISM   The teaching that maintains that there is no reality other than matter. In the atomism of Democritus, later revived by Epicurus, a first attempt can be found at an explanation of the universe from a materialistic point of view. Stoicism itself could be considered a form of materialism, despite the very great importance it attaches to the spirit (*pneuma*), since it considers this *pneuma* to be a kind of subtle fire. But the groundwork for modern materialism was more immediately laid down by the Neo-Aristotelian school of Padua at the end of the Middle Ages, with the formal denial of the immortality of the soul made by its most prominent teacher, Pomponazzi (cf. the condemnation of the Lateran Council in 1513; D.B. 738). The school of Gassendi introduced an analogous doctrine in France in the 17th century, and it was developed in the most radical fashion in the following century by a group of philosophers, such as Helvetius and Holbach, who were opposed by both Voltaire and Rousseau. The 19th century saw the acme of materialism's claim to be scientific under the form of a determinist mechanism that boasted of an integral explanation for the life of the spirit. Actually, this modern materialism, despite its "scientism," is much less a philosophy than the simple refusal to philosophize. Strictly speaking, nothing can be seen in it other than the confusion brought about habitually between a methodological principle of modern science (limiting itself in its study of sensible appearances to establishing their relations—especially those that are mathematically measurable) and a metaphysical principle (rejecting as inconsistent everything that is not reduced to these appearances). But simple recourse to mathematical abstraction, which no physical science can overlook, destroys the materialist postulate at its root, since every abstraction goes beyond the purely material fact. Moreover, the simple evolution of modern scientific theories on matter, in fact, no longer even allows the statements of materialism to retain a semblance of significance, since all the sense qualities whereby 19th-century science thought matter could be defined, and which seemed to be primary and indestructible to those scientists, now amount to purely subjective impressions; their objective substratum is no longer conceivable except in terms of mathematical relationships between these impressions themselves. Marxist materialism was the first to hold this mechanistic materialism up to ridicule. But, for its part, the dialectical materialism of the Marxists is hampered by a basic ambiguity that becomes more and more evident in the evolution of Soviet thought. Either it actually admits of a genuinely creative dialectic leading to the emergence of realities that cannot be condensed to the realities from which they have evolved historically, in which case it is no longer truly materialistic; or else it persists in its intention to be materialistic and therefore nullifies the distinction of which it boasted: namely, that every strict materialism of a mechanistic type begged the question, and involved an inherent contradiction. Actually, modern materialism is most frequently nothing more than an unthinking materialism, which is satisfied with avoiding critical thought by a basically irrational prohibition of the consideration of everything that is not reduced to material progress; or else, it is, rather than a genuine materialism, a type of pantheistic monism that refuses to admit its real nature.

MATTER   Philosophically, matter could be defined only as pure potentiality with regard to the *forms* (q.v.) that it may receive, and without which it would have no concrete existence. Greek philosophy, which never reached the height of an idea of God as *pure act* in the strongest sense of the term, looked upon matter as preexistent to the work of the demiurge by which concrete beings come to be. But since it does not exist independently from the forms, and once it is acknowledged that all contingent beings are therefore created, it must also be acknowledged that matter is created in them. Here the question arises as to whether every created being, insofar as it is by no means exempt from passivity, must be called material. This is what is admitted by St. Bonaventure, who held that the human soul, and even angelic creatures, are composed of matter and form; God the Creator alone being above this distinction. To this St. Thomas Aquinas answers that if the created intellectual being is in some sense in potency, he is so only insofar as his existence is distinct from his essence. However, this distinction in him is not between matter and form but interior to the form itself. (Cf. St. Bonaventure, *In II Sent.*, 3,1,1,1, concl. 3a; Ed. Quaracchi, t. II, p. 91, and 17,1,2, fund. 5; *ibid.*, p. 414; with St. Thomas Aquinas, *Sum. Theol.*, Ia, q.50, a.2 and q.75, a.5.)

Scholastic theology has made use of the matter and form distinction to explain the Christian sacraments, looking upon the sensible sign as the matter, and the words which determine its content as the form. Strictly speaking, this distinction, which was first introduced for the Eucharist, is applied to certain other sacraments (e.g., penance and marriage) only in a rather forced manner. It is well, finally, to note that modern thought customarily uses the word matter to designate in general the objects of sense experience. It is in this context that Descartes defines it as *extended substance*. Modern *materialism* (q.v.) went on from there, believing that it could dispense entirely with the spiritual (defined by Descartes as *unextended substance*). But, even more than the Kantian criticism of the objectivity attributed to time and space, the evolution of the concepts of modern physics has, as it were, done away with the Cartesian notion of extended substance. This amounts to saying that the matter to which materialism would reduce everything is nothing but a word that no longer frames any definite or definable object.

MEDIATION OF CHRIST   St. Thomas Aquinas defines a mediator as one who conjoins and unites. It follows that according to the words of Timothy: "there is one mediator between God and men, the man Christ Jesus" (1 Tim. 2,5). This mediation, in effect, is proper to Christ as man, but as a man endowed with the fullness of grace, which is his because of his divinity (cf. *Sum. Theol.*, IIIa, q.26, a.2). This quality, on the other hand, fits Christ alone *simpliciter et perfective*, because of him alone may it be said: "God was in Christ, reconciling the world to himself" (2 Cor. 5,19; quoted by St. Thomas Aquinas, *ibid.*, a.1).

MEDIATION OF MARY While maintaining and explaining that Christ is the unique Mediator, St. Thomas Aquinas points out that in a less strict sense there are many mediators, namely, all who, like the prophets and priests, cooperate *dispositive vel ministerialiter* in the union between men and God, effected by Christ alone. In this sense, evidently, we can acknowledge that Mary, together with all the saints, is also a mediatrix in virtue of her intercession, although her mediation is supereminent from the fact of her divine motherhood and the very special union with the Mediator that it presupposes. This is why the Holy See has recently responded affirmatively to the request of those who asked for an office and a Mass under the title of "Mary, Mediatrix of all Graces." However, it must be emphasized that in order to avoid any confusion with the proper and incommunicable function of the Saviour, the authorities refused to allow the phrase "mediatrix with the Father" (annoyingly inspired by 1 John 2,1) to be applied to Mary in the Collect of this Mass. Instead, they required the following to be said: "Lord Jesus, you who are our Mediator with the Father, you have constituted your Mother and ours, the B.V.M., as our mediatrix with you," etc.

MEMORIAL This word, introduced into the formulas of the institution and consecration of the Eucharist, translates the Hebrew *zikaron*; it was used in Protestant polemics to uphold the view that there was no actual presence of the sacrifice of the Saviour in the Eucharist, but only a recalling of the unique sacrifice of the cross. The examination which a contemporary exegete, Jeremias (a Protestant), devoted to the notion of *zikaron* in the Bible has established in the most decisive fashion the basic error of this distinction. The biblical *memorial*, and especially the memorial of the covenant, far from being opposed to the real presence of what it recalls, actually supposes it. To be still more exact, rather than our being able to set off the memorial of a sacrifice against an actual sacrifice, it is proper to a memorial, according to the whole of biblical and Judaic thought, that it constitute itself as the supreme sacrifice: an objective reality that makes both the redemptive grace present for us and, on this basis, presents us to God in such a way that we are assured of being pleasing to him. Max Thurian's *L'Eucharistie* (Neuchâtel-Paris, 1959), may be consulted to examine the import of this rediscovery. On the other hand, we may point out that a study of the introduction of the explicitly sacrificial notions into the liturgical texts of the Eucharist shows positively that they developed from the *anamnesis* formularies, i.e., from the explicitation of the memorial.

MERIT Merit is the right that one has to a reward. When it is a question of a strict right, we speak of *de condigno* merit; when it is a question simply of appropriateness, it is *de congruo* merit. The concept seems to have been introduced into theological usage by Tertullian. But the idea of a judgment of God, corresponding to the good or the evil done by man during his life, not only for us sinners, but for every created being, is understood as a supernatural grace. Whence the principle that grace (which is itself the principle of all the merit we can have) could not be merited. As St. Augustine says, God, in crowning the merits of his saints, ultimately only crowns his own grace. This is why St. Thomas Aquinas says that we merit everlasting life *de condigno*, by grace acting in us, while, in regard to our free will, this merit could never be anything else than *de congruo*, insofar as the free will, by the power of grace itself, adheres to that grace. From this explanation we see that merit is therefore (and solely) a proportion set up by God between free beings and the gifts that he destines for them. But this does not make these gifts any less gifts; it makes them effective gifts that do not remain external and, as it were, foreign to us, but that become effectively ours, without in any way thereby ceasing to be radically God's and God's alone. We will note further that grace, being given to us for our own sanctification, does not allow us to merit *de condigno* its own growth or full development in glory except for ourselves. Only Christ, by virtue of his grace as Head, coming from the hypostatic union of the divinity with his humanity, has been able to merit for all the elect *de condigno*, and not only the development of grace in them, but even its acquisition. However, the righteous may contribute *de congruo* to this acquisition and development of grace in their brothers, insofar as they are in the divine friendship and God is therefore disposed to answer their prayers. But, even for himself, no one on earth may merit final perseverance in grace, at least *de condigno*, for perseverance in grace has no other cause than the cause itself of grace: God's good pleasure. Finally, we must again specify that grace makes our actions meritorious through the outpouring of charity in us, i.e., that love which is God's own love poured into our hearts by his Holy Spirit (Rom. 5,5). See St. Thomas Aquinas, *Sum. Theol.*, Ia-IIae, q.114.

MESSIAH, MESSIANISM   A Hebrew word meaning "anointed" that was translated into Greek as *Christos* (from which our word *Christ* comes). In Christ's time, the Messiah was the figure in whom the popular religious aspirations in Israel were concretized. These aspirations were united under the name Messianism.

In the Old Testament the word *Messiah* was applied to all those (priests, prophets, or kings) to whom God had imparted something of his power and authority, symbolized in the rite of anointing. But this word is used preeminently of David and of the kings of his line who followed him and who were expected to pursue or restore the work of rebuilding the People of God, a work that had once belonged to David. Because of this, kingship in Israel seems to be the heir of a whole notion, more sacred than political, that reflected the kingship idea present for some time among all the Semitic peoples. But from the outset, by the rite of anointing and the significance this took on in Israel, the notion was transfigured. Samuel at first looked upon the Israelites' desire to have a king like the nations surrounding them as a repudiation of the Lord, their sole King. Under divine inspiration he ultimately consented to their request; the Anointed One of the Lord, however, would reign only as the sign and the instrument of the one divine Kingdom (cf. 1 Kings 8 and 9). The Psalms show us how this figure of the Messiah-King became the prefigurement and the outline of an ideal King who would realize definitively the Kingdom of God on earth (cf. especially Ps. 2, 7–8, and Ps. 110).

Nevertheless, in Christ's time we see well how in the popular imagination this figure, together with the exaltation of the expectation of the divine Kingdom, tended to become obscured by the representation of a king who is quite earthly in the forms of his kingship, although he still would assure the deliverance and the political revenge of a people oppressed under foreign domination. This explains Christ's reticence when either the crowds or his disciples themselves applied this title to him (cf. Matt. 16,20). There is no text other than John 4,25 ff. in which he appears to accept it before his passion. Yet there is no question that Jesus' consent to the triumph that was given to him on Palm Sunday (Matt. 21,9 and par.) in a certain sense implies his acceptance of the qualification of Messiah. But the interrogation before the Sanhedrin and his response to the High Priest's charge to declare whether or not He is the Messiah shows well that he accepts this title, even at this moment, only on the condition that his messianic kingship be understood as the supernatural reign of the *Son of Man* (q.v.), combined mysteriously with the supreme humiliation of the *Servant* (q.v.), to which his very answer delivers him. It is with this meaning that the first Christian preaching proclaimed that Jesus was made Lord and Christ by the Father in his Resurrection after having been crucified by men (Acts 2,36).

We must add that the Qumran texts have given evidence of the fact that at least certain Jewish groups were awaiting a Messiah, i.e., an Anointed One, who would be more priest than king. It is probable that this view is at the basis of all of the Epistle to the Hebrews' teaching on Jesus' priestly role.

METAPHYSICS   The title given to the treatises of Aristotle that come after his *Physics*, i.e., the description of nature (*physis* in Greek), and that deal with being as such and the principles that shed light on this notion. The term came to be applied to *first* philosophy, i.e., the science of being as such and of its first causes. See St. Thomas Aquinas, *In Metaph.*, *prooemium*, and bk. IV, lect. 1 and 5.

MILLENARIANISM, MILLENNIUM   The enigmatic period of a thousand years spoken of in the Apocalypse (chap. 20) is called the *millennium*. During its course Satan is to be put in bondage after a primary resurrection limited to those who were faithful until death to Christ. Thereafter there will be a second struggle with the Devil, his definitive defeat, and the universal resurrection and judgment. Millenarianism is the heresy or the heretical tendency that first appeared in the early Christian centuries, although it reappears frequently throughout the history of Christianity. The millennium is represented with such literalism that it falls back into the forms of earthly messianism rejected by Christ. It is usually combined with a belief that the millennium is already at hand or is at least imminent. There is Millenarianism in the *Everlasting Gospel* of Joachim of Floris (d. 1202), the 13th-century Cistercian abbot, and his announcement of the imminent coming of the reign of the Paraclete (already proclaimed by the Montanists in the 3rd century). The influence of this book and of Joachim's fanciful ideas made itself felt on all of the movements of the "Spiritual Franciscans," which were run through with an anarchical illuminism. A number of modern sects (Adventists, Jehovah's Witnesses, etc.) are revived forms of this illusion.

Confronted with these fancies, it is not so easy to explain what the author of the Apocalypse wished to express by the idea, or rather the image, of the millennium. This difficulty explains why the East, where Millenarianism had been particularly worrisome, was very slow to admit the canonicity of this sacred book (it will be noted that in several Eastern liturgies the public reading of the Apocalypse is still avoided today). We may say that by and large two opinions are shared by theologians and exegetes. The most widespread is the one developed by St. Augustine in the *City of God*, and most of the theologians of the Middle Ages rallied to his view. It looks upon the millennium only as an image of the Church (or of Christendom), in which the Kingdom of God is found to be inaugurated, before the judgment and the final restoration of all things. The difficulty with this interpretation is the first resurrection spoken of by St. John. Some consider that it refers to baptism, others to the anticipated association of the saints (particularly in heavenly glory) with the Kingdom of the resurrected Christ. Except for the great Protestant exegete Dodd and his school (which for that reason is called inaugurated, or realized, eschatology), most modern exegetes tend to look upon this only as a forced interpretation of the texts. But they themselves are not in agreement as to the exact meaning that should be assigned to this first phase in the eschatological Kingdom of Christ, which strictly speaking would nevertheless not be final, since struggles (indeed the decisive struggle) were still to follow. An ingenious interpretation was proposed by Fr. Féret, O.P., which stated that it must be understood as Christendom, not in the merely sketchy form that was known in the Middle Ages, but rather in the broader and truly universal form that should be the goal of the Church's mission in this world. Something analogous can be found in the earthly hope of a unification of world-wide civilization in Christ held by Teilhard de Chardin and his followers. To this we may object, not without reason, that the sacred writer does not seem to understand this period as a development immanent in history, but rather as a primary transcendent intervention of God that either, as in the Augustinian interpretation, is one with the appearance of the Church, or else pertains to the Parousia of Christ at the end of time. While discouraging simplistic explanations of a Millenarianist type, the Church has never made any pronouncement on this question, and it seems difficult at present to do so with reasons that are absolutely compelling.

MIRACLE   The Christian notion views miracle not only as an action that is out of the ordinary, beyond the forces of created nature, but as a "sign" of God (it is always this latter word that St. John uses in speaking of Jesus' miracles; cf. John 2,11). Traditionally, as was the case in Israel, miracles are connected with prophecy, as explained in the article WORD OF GOD (q.v.), considered as an intervention by the Creator in the history of the world. The essential miracle, according to the teaching of the apostles, is therefore Christ's *Resurrection* (q.v.), considered as the principle of the renewal of the whole of creation resulting from the redemptive Incarnation. All other authentic miracles have therefore to be considered as forerunning signs of this, or else as anticipatory pledges of its spread over the whole of regenerated mankind, indeed over the whole surrounding universe. In such a view, miracles are understood much less as a violation of natural laws than as the appearance within the heart of the present economy of a new world economy, for which the present dispensation is merely a preparation. The difficulties the miracles create for minds steeped in scientific *determinism* (q.v.) are not therefore of another order than those resulting from a belief in the freedom of man and the freedom of God creating and impregnating it. In fact, the Christian miracle is by no means the introduction of a disorder into the created universe, but rather the introduction of a higher order.

MISSION   In the theological sense of the word, the temporal procession of a divine person is called a mission. For the particular divine

Person, this mission is nothing else than his eternal procession, but this procession viewed as having now a temporal term. In other words, only the Persons who proceed (the Son and the Spirit, excluding the Father) can be sent (*missae*); on the other hand, their mission does not constitute any change in their eternal being, but rather in the created being to whom they are made present. Thus the Son and the Spirit are sent invisibly by grace *gratum faciens* (*see* GRACE) insofar as they become the object of supernatural knowledge and love in the soul. They are on the other hand sent visibly, the Son as author of sanctification (in the Incarnation), and the Spirit as the manifested gift of sanctification. These missions, furthermore, are respectively suited to them, to the Son insofar as he is associated with the Father as the very principle of the procession of the Spirit, and to the Spirit insofar as he proceeds from the others as love. This is the teaching developed by St. Thomas Aquinas in his *Commentary on the Sentences* (bk. I, dist. 14–18 and dist. 37, q.1, a.2) and, more briefly, in *Sum. Theol.* (Ia, q.43). It is merely a synthesis of the gospel teaching on the sending of the Son by the Father (cf. Matt. 15,24 and Luke 4,18 and 43, etc., together with numerous passages in St. John, particularly in chapter 17) and on the sending of the Spirit by the Father and the Son (cf. John 14,26 and 15,26), clarified by theological meditation on the *divine processions* (q.v.). See the article APOSTLE for the intimate connection between these divine missions and the mission of the Church herself.

MODALISM   An ancient error (particularly of Sabellius) revived by modern Unitarians (*see* UNITARIANISM), who refuse to see in the Father, Son, and Spirit persons or subjects that are eternally distinct. They look upon them only as modalities in which but one divine subject is manifested.

MODERNISM   The generic name given to a series of errors condemned by the Church at the beginning of this century, particularly in the Encyclical *Pascendi* of St. Pius X in 1907 (which had been preceded in the same year by the Holy Office's Decree *Lamentabili*). Their common characteristic is an attempt at a cursory adaptation of traditional doctrines to the modern mentality that actually more or less gravely distorted these doctrines. We may single out: 1) a biblical modernism, whose chief representative was Alfred Loisy, and which, in the name of a historical criticism run through with scientistic apriorities, questioned the authenticity of the evangelical facts about Christ and ultimately the inspiration of the Scriptures themselves; 2) a philosophical modernism, whose tendencies more or less came to light in the works of George Tyrrell, S.J., that undermined any idea of a defined revelation at its foundation and, more generally, even the notion of a

supernatural intervention of a God transcending the human consciousness (this is what has been called immanentism). Although
modernism set itself against liberal Protestantism by its positive appreciation of the role of the Church in Christianity, it incontestably depended
upon it for these two points. (See D.B. 2001 ff. and 2071 ff.) The
Encyclical *Humani generis* of Pius XII recently recalled that all of these
characteristically baneful tendencies of modernism have not ceased to be
influential and dangerous. This caution, however, did not prevent the
same pope from insisting many times on the necessity of resuming, on
more solid grounds, the work of confronting the traditional doctrine with
the certain notions of modern historical sciences, and in a general way,
with all the positive elements of contemporary scientific and philosophical research.

MONARCHIANISM   The Trinitarian heresy of Marcellus of
Ancyra, which forced the notion of the *divine monarchy* (q.v.) to the
erroneous conclusion that the other Divine Persons would be only a sort
of extension of the Father.

MONISM   The term applied to any system that exaggerates the
oneness of reality to the point of absorbing man in the world or the world
in God. Monism, consequently, tends either toward *materialism* or
pantheism (qq.v.).

MONOENERGISM   A mitigated form of Monophysitism, acknowledging only one energy or activity in Christ. Proposed to the Monophysites of Alexandria in 633 by the Patriarch Cyrus as the ground for a
possible agreement, the opposition of the monk Sophronius (who
became patriarch of Jerusalem in 634) soon caused everyone to abandon
it. *Monothelitism* (q.v.), however, was to result from it.

MONOGENISM   By this word is understood the fact that mankind
would wholly and entirely descend from one unique first human couple.
This is evidently the literal sense of the Genesis account of the creation
of man. In the presence of certain doubts of palaeontologists as to the
single origin of present-day mankind, a few theologians held that the
biblical assertion of the unity and spiritual solidarity of mankind, in its
fall as in its salvation, could be maintained even in the hypothesis where
it would originate not from one but from several human couples, who
appeared on earth in different places and at different times in the
evolution of the species. The Encyclical *Humani generis* of Pius XII
cautions insistently against too facile an acceptance of such a theory,
since there is nothing in the present stage of science that seems to
demand it.

MONOPHYSITISM   A teaching which states that, from the Incarnation, there would be only one nature (in Greek, *physis*) in Christ, the divine nature that would absorb the human nature in itself. Although the threat of this doctrine was already present among the followers of Apollinarius of Laodicea, this teaching grew as a reaction following the condemnation by the Council of Ephesus in 431 of the Patriarch Nestorius who, on the contrary, tended simply to juxtapose the two natures in Christ. Set down by the monk Eutyches and supported by Dioscorus, Patriarch of Alexandria, it was based upon certain ambiguous formulas that St. Cyril of Alexandria had borrowed in the preceding controversy, without knowing their exact source, from the false Apollinarists (e.g., "one sole nature of God the Word incarnate"). While at first it seemed to have been victorious in the irregular "Robber Council" of Ephesus, this new heresy was condemned at the Council of Chalcedon (451), which solemnly approved the opposite teaching taught by Pope St. Leo I. But Monophysitism survived, either in the mitigated, almost purely verbal form of Severus of Antioch, or in adulterated forms, like *Monothelitism* or *Monoenergism* (qq.v.). The present Coptic Church of Egypt, the Syrian Jacobite Church (after the name of the theologian Jacob Baradaeus, Bishop of Edessa, who died in 578), and the Church of Armenia have never recognized the Council of Chalcedon and to that extent are considered Monophysite. But the reasons for their rejection of this Council arose out of their reaction against Byzantine imperialism rather than out of a really heretical faith.

As a tendency to lose sight of the reality of the Incarnation through destroying or disregarding the truth of the humanity of Jesus, Monophysitism is limited to no specific historical period. This is particularly the temptation of the ardent (if unthinking) devout, just as *Nestorianism* (q.v.) is a temptation of theologians threatened by rationalism.

MONOTHELITISM   An aftermath of *Monophysitism* (q.v.), Monothelitism (from the Greek *thelema*, will) maintains that there is only one will in Christ. The Patriarch Sergius of Constantinople was its originator. Employing a simply unwieldy formula used by Pope Honorius in his desire to effect a reconciliation, Sergius held that there is no will in Christ other than the will of his divine person. The Ecthesis of 638, promulgated by the Emperor Heraclius, attempted to enforce it. If we are to believe the account of St. Maximus, Pope Honorius died after learning of the misinterpretation that he had unwittingly helped to create; and Maximus, backed at the Roman Council of the Lateran in 649 by his successor St. Martin I, ultimately succeeded in having the Third Council of Constantinople (680–1) define the duality of wills, divine and human, in Christ, as well as the free submission of the latter to the former. (*See* the formula in the article INCARNATION.) A paradoxical aspect of this controversy, which played no little part in obscuring the issue, is that some Nestorians, beginning with Nestorius himself (following Theodore of Mopsuestia), despite their inadequate notion of the personal unity of Christ, had also spoken of a unique will in Christ, by which they understood simply the constant accord of his humanity with his divinity.

MONTANISM   The error of Montanus, originating in Phrygia at the end of the 2nd century. Montanus and other followers claimed direct inspiration by the Holy Spirit and emphasized a renewal of the charisms of Pentecost that were supposed to attest to the fact. This was combined with a frenetic expectation of a supposedly imminent *Parousia* (q.v.) and a moral rigorism. At the end of his life, Tertullian was to fall into this error. With it can be connected certain later errors that also proclaimed an imminent reign of the Spirit, such as the *Everlasting Gospel* of the medieval Cistercian abbot, Joachim of Floris together with the inspiration that the most frenetic "Spiritual Franciscans" drew from it, or in modern times certain sectarian *Revivalist* movements (*see* REVIVALISM), and especially those that call themselves Pentecostal.

MORTIFICATION   A term used of all those ascetical practices that, by weakening our natural lives at present tainted by sin, have no other aim but to help us conquer sin so that life may be supernaturally restored in us. Their meaningfulness follows essentially from the Pauline concept of our union with Christ's cross in baptism, which becomes the principle of our union with the power of His Resurrection (cf. Rom. 6, together with Rom. 8,17; 1 Cor. 4,8; 2 Tim. 2,12 and especially 2 Cor. 4,10).

MOTHERHOOD OF MARY   Against Nestorius, the Council of Ephesus (431) defined that the Blessed Virgin Mary could and should be called Mother of God (in Greek, *Theotokos*; in Latin, *Dei Genitrix*), since the humanity of the Saviour did not have a person distinct from that of God the Son. Cf. the text of the letter of St. Cyril of Alexandria, called *Kataphlyarouse*, approved by the Council (D.S. 251).

MOTIVE OF THE INCARNATION   *See* the last paragraph of the article INCARNATION

MULTIPLICITY   The multiplicity and the diversity of the present universe were understood by certain Fathers, Origen in particular, as a consequence of sin. It seems that here there was a confusion between division and multiplicity (cf. Origen's formula *ubi peccatum, ibi multi-*

tudo). St. Thomas Aquinas upheld quite the opposite, namely, that a harmonious diversity, and therefore a certain inequality, in creation is by its very nature a better expression of the infinite richness of God than any sort of uniformity (cf. what St. Paul himself says about manifold— literally "multicolored"—wisdom in Eph. 3,10). The exegete Cullmann has well underlined that the development of God's plan throughout the Bible seems to go from a disconnected multitude through a call given to a particular people, then to a "remnant" within this people, then to a unique "servant" abandoned by the remnant, toward a supernatural unity that will then be embodied in the multitude, and the multitude itself will become the fullness of this unique Person, without however being suppressed in Him.

MYSTAGOGY   Borrowed from the language of the mysteries, where it means the introduction of the uninitiate to the knowledge and the effective celebration of the mysteries, this term was used currently by the Fathers to describe the baptismal initiation, and, upon its completion, the introduction to the eucharistic mystery. Cf. the *Mystagogical Cate- cheses* of St. Cyril of Jerusalem or the *Mystagogy* of St. Maximus the Confessor. *See* MYSTERY.

MYSTERY   This term, which merely means secret or a reality kept or to be kept secret, already had a technical religious use in the piety of pagan Hellenism. In this context it designated properly the rites of certain religions into which outsiders could be initiated, rites like those of Eleusis in Greece in the classical period, or later others, understood (indeed, remodeled) after this pattern, namely, the mysteries of Serapis, Attis, Adonis, or Mithra. Through borrowing the images and the technical terms proper to these mysteries, the term itself came to designate metaphorically any object of knowledge that requires a pains- taking initiation, whether this object be religious or not. Finally, particu- larly in Egyptian Hermeticism, it came to be applied more specifically to the initiation into secret doctrines whose revelation was considered salutary. But we must underline that in this case the mysteries in question are no longer rites but ideas, even when the claim is made a posteriori that their expression is prefigured in some ritual symbol or other.

The question has been asked as to the extent Christian use, and particularly the theological use, of the word *mystery* depends upon this usage, or rather these pagan usages, which are more or less prior to Christianity. It seems today completely certain that St. Paul's notion of the Christian mystery is in no way indebted to them. As introduced and described in chapter 2 of the First Epistle to the Corinthians, the mystery has its source not in the mystery religions of antiquity, which had yet to know their expansion and popularity, nor still less in the quite literary mystery of Hermeticism, which comes very much later, but in the Bible, and more specifically in the apocalyptic and wisdom books. A comparison between this text of St. Paul and that of chap. 2 of Daniel makes this evident. The Pauline mystery is actually the secret of God's wisdom, i.e., of his design with regard to the history of the world and more particularly for its salvation, a secret unknown even to the angelic "powers" that dominate the present world; God reveals it when he wills and to whom he will. Inaccessible to the wisdom of men for whom it is only foolishness (see chap. 1 of the same Epistle), scandalous for the Jews themselves who refuse to go beyond the merely preparatory revelations, the mystery of salvation is essentially the cross of Christ, whereby the "powers" in revolt against the Creator are ousted from their domination and believers find their deliverance.

This is what the Epistle to the Colossians develops in explaining how "the mystery hidden for ages and generations, but now made manifest to his saints" (v. 26) is the reconciliation worked in all things with God, in the body of his Son by his death, which has wrested us from the power of darkness and brought us into the Kingdom (see the whole first chapter). Thus the mystery is ultimately "Christ in you, the hope of glory" (v. 27). The Epistle to the Ephesians achieves a deepening of this notion by showing within the Church herself, wherein Jews and pagans are reconciled, the fulfillment of the mystery of the divine will (1,9), "the plan of the mystery hidden for ages in God" (3,9), where the whole extent of the divine charity is revealed in a knowledge that surpasses all understanding (3,18–19).

Moreover, the Fathers of the Church, particularly the Alexandrians, borrowed the symbolical application, which Philo had been the first to use, of the terminology of the pagan mysteries in order to express the uncovering of the deepest sense of the Scriptures. But for them, and especially for Origen, this initiation into the mystery is very precisely the uncovering of the Pauline mystery as the key of the whole Bible: Christ, his cross, together with all its consequences in the formation of the Church, understood as the focal point of the whole of revelation and of the whole of sacred history from which it is inseparable.

Finally, in a third stage, toward the end of the 4th century, the Fathers underlined that this mystery of Christ in us, our hope of glory, is the substance of the Christian sacraments, and they came to apply this same terminology, coming from the pagan mysteries, to the Christian initiation itself: to baptism and confirmation, considered as the introduction to the Eucharist, and in the Eucharist itself, to the share, together with the whole Church, in the mystery of the saving cross. Whence the title

Mystagogical Catecheses given by St. Cyril of Jerusalem to his explanation of the baptismal initiation, and, later, that of *Mystagogy* that St. Maximus the Confessor applied to a meditation on the eucharistic liturgy.

It follows from all of this that the Christian mystery owes nothing to the mysteries of paganism, although it could be correctly understood as a fulfillment of the obscure presentiments that appeared either in these pagan mysteries or even more in the religious philosophies, like that of Hermeticism, that had taken on the use of their symbols. Actually, in these various philosophies, religious mankind was seeking a solution to the problem of death, a union with the divinity that would draw life out of death. But the mysteries of paganism were never more than a simple projection of the fecundity of cosmic life, ever dying and being reborn, just as their gods were only mythical personifications of the powers of earth and the heavens. The Christian mystery, on the contrary, is the saving event accomplished once and for ever by the transcendent God's free descent into the circle of human life, and his pledge to die because of sin in order to do away with our sin in his death and to impart to us the life of his Resurrection, a life that from now on is immortal. Our initiation into this mystery, by faith in the evangelical word, and baptism that unites us to Christ, before we can take part, anointed with his Spirit, in his reconciliatory sacrifice, is neither merely a semi-ritual, semi-magic consecration under the supposed beneficent influence of "powers" that remain of this world, subject to the alternations of death and life, nor a symbolic introduction into an esoteric philosophico-religious knowledge. It is the entry into the divine secret of the creating and saving love: God made man and mortal in order to save man by imparting to him His own life, the only truly everlasting life.

Later, the development of the liturgical year, and in particular of the Feast of Christmas and all that it involves, details this essentially paschal mystery of the Saviour's death and glorification. It will lead us step by step from the preliminaries of His passion to His Ascension and the outpouring of the Spirit on all flesh, before joining with it, together with the recalling of the Nativity, the anticipation of the Epiphany, i.e., the definitive manifestation of Christ in the world. In this way we come no longer to speak of the mystery of Christ but of the mysteries of Christ. Finally, the word will experience a twofold extension of its meaning in order to designate either the different sacramental rites that make us share in the unique mystery, or the different truths about God that this mystery reveals to us, particularly the Trinity. But it is still true that, properly speaking, there is but one Christian mystery: that of the cross, wherein it is the mystery of God that is revealed, the mystery of his intimate life, of the love that is, as it were, the soul of that life and which was imparted to us in Christ. In revealing himself, he makes himself accessible to us, as the mystery of our life originating from this lifegiving death, through the whole sacramental order, but above all in the eucharistic celebration. The sacraments of initiation are directed to this celebration, and it is from it that there is diffused, so to speak, all the power of the consecration of our lives and our deaths in the other sacraments like marriage or the anointing of the sick. On all of this, see the eighth chapter of L. Bouyer, *Rite and Man: Natural Sacredness and Christian Liturgy* (Notre Dame, Ind., 1963).

MYSTICISM   Today this word habitually designates any experience, true or supposed, of God's uniting himself directly with us. In a broader sense it refers to everything that surrounds the subject understood in this sense. Thus we have come to compare the Christian mystical experience with the apparently analogous experiences that can be found either in the Neo-Platonism of antiquity or in religions like Hinduism or certain forms of Islam, not to mention the experience of Buddhism (although we may wonder whether it is actually a religious experience, since in orthodox Buddhism God, or the gods, plays no role). A step further and we come to look upon mystical experience as having nothing specifically Christian about it, indeed as a foreign element introduced into Christian tradition, originating from Neo-Platonist or, more generally, oriental influences. It is in this light that Friedrich Heiler in his book *Prayer* (New York, 1932) contrasts the type of mystical prayer that he judged to be extra-biblical with prophetic prayer. Anders Nygren in his book *Agape and Eros* (Philadelphia, 1953) goes so far as to view mysticism as a form of religious experience that is not only extra-biblical but anti-biblical, because it proceeds from a love of God that is no more than man's desire to possess God, instead of the love of God that reveals to us the divine Word as the pure generosity of God coming to man.

All these views are merely the successive results of a notion of mysticism that began to be sketched in the Middle Ages and developed in the contemporary period; it was looked upon merely as a peculiar psychological experience, isolated from its object that transcends the consciousness of the one experiencing it and ultimately imagined to be independent of this object. Nothing, however, is further from such a notion than what the ancients called mysticism, or more precisely mystical theology. The history of the term is enough to demonstrate this fact.

First of all, "mysticism" in the beginning was understood in connection with the *mystery* (q.v.). In Hellenism, while mystery in the religious sense simply designated rites that were not disclosed to the uninitiated, *ta mystika* was used of the rites themselves or of ritual objects, and *oi mystikoi* referred to the initiates themselves. However, neither in Plotinus nor in the other Neo-Platonists, nor among the adherents of the religious philosophy of Hermeticism, did these words ever refer to a particular religious experience. The only example of the word in Plotinus is to designate a hidden interpretation (let us recall that *mystikos*, in Greek, has precisely this meaning) of a myth. The notion of mysticism (or mystical theology, in the sense of a mystical knowledge of God) first made its appearance among Christian authors. And if it is true that the first to have popularized it was the Pseudo-Dionysius, a writer strongly tinged with Neo-Platonism, it is all the more remarkable to note that he does not use it to designate anything which he would owe to Plotinus or his followers, but rather to designate what is most traditionally Christian in his writings. After Clement and Origen, who used the adjective mystical to refer to an interpretation of Scripture that demonstrated the Pauline mystery of Jesus and his cross, there were the Fathers of the following century who added to this first use an application of the term to the interpretation of the Christian ritual, as imparting to us the reality of this mystery. The Pseudo-Dionysius in effect, following St. Gregory of Nyssa in particular, understood mystical theology as knowledge of God revealed in Christ through meditation on the Bible, and encountered in the liturgical celebration, a knowledge that is both a union and an assimilation (*see* KNOWLEDGE). For the whole of Catholic tradition, this has remained the sense of Christian mysticism (the only mysticism to which the name properly belongs, since it is actually never applied to other religious experiences except by modern scholars of comparative religion who transfer the appellation to experiences in other religions that seem to offer more or less analogous psychological characteristics). Every religious experience that surpasses both sense experience and intellectual speculation inevitably does present certain common traits, owing to the make-up of the human soul. Yet the most perceptive historians and psychologists of religion acknowledge that, if we do not abusively misrepresent the most varied religious experiences by refusing to consider the object that defines their *intentionality* (q.v.), these analogies should not be the source of confusion, like those attempted by the different forms of *occultism* (q.v.) or by syncretisms (Aldous Huxley's *Perennial Philosophy* would offer a typical example of this today) that are too facile.

On the contrary, a comparative study like the one made by Rudolf Otto (in his book *Mysticism East and West*) between Shankara, the most apparently personalist Hindu "mystic," and Eckhart, the Christian mystic who at first sight seems the closest to pantheism, sheds light on the root difference separating them: between a person-to-person union and an abolition of the person within an impersonal deity. The most recent and still more penetrating studies of R. C. Zähner (*Mysticism, Sacred and Profane,* Oxford, 1957) are even more clear on this point.

Understood in this light, we see that Christian mysticism, as is so strongly affirmed in the work of St. John of the Cross, the doctor par excellence of mysticism in modern times, is by no means composed of ecstasies, visions, and other extraordinary psychological phenomena. As luminously shown by Fr. R. Garrigou-Lagrange, O.P. in his book *Christian Perfection and Contemplation* (St. Louis, 1937), even in its most exalted states, mysticism is only the full flowering of the grace of baptism, prepared by meditation on the living faith of the gospel, nurtured by sacramental practice, and developed by a whole life devoted to the requirements of divine charity poured into our hearts by the Spirit. In a word, just as the Christian mystery according to St. Paul is nothing else than "Christ in us, our hope of glory," authentic mysticism is only the Christian experience that the same Apostle expresses when he says, "It is now no longer I that live, but Christ lives in me" (Gal. 2,20).

MYTH In today's popular vocabulary, myth is understood only as a simple fable without any real content. However, modern history of religions looks upon the myth, following the distinction made by Plato between *mythos* and *logos*, as a form of synthetic thought expressed in natural symbolisms, which rather than being opposed to purely logical thought actually completes it. In this regard, any statement of mysterious truths cannot purely and simply exhaust the content of mythical thought and its spontaneous forms of expression, even if it is obliged to judge them critically. The Bible uses myths constantly, but it gives them a depth and purity of content that is quite new.

NAME   A word that gives expression to the being of a substance, and more particularly to that of a person. In the primitive notion, especially among the Semitic peoples, to reveal a name implied a certain communication of the being itself. This is the reason for the importance attached in Ex. 3 to the communication of the name proper to God to Moses. Only the consonants of this name (YHWH) were ever written out, and, so that its profanation might be avoided, men were to refrain from pronouncing it. Although its probable meaning is that God is inexpressible, the communication of this name was looked upon as a free gift, the basis of the covenant. The *Law* (q.v.), given at the same time on the same Mount Horeb, was interpreted as a genuine assigning of the divine Name to the people whom it had acquired for itself. Because of this, it not only became its real property, but it bore within it a reflection, or stamp, as it were, of the divine reality. Whence the leitmotiv of Leviticus: "Be holy as I am holy." The same notion appears again in the Sermon on the Mount where the revelation of the name Father (i.e., the divine Fatherhood) is explained for those to whom it is made that it is in a real sense possible for them to become children of God. In this instance, we have the formula: "You therefore be perfect as your heavenly Father is perfect." (Cf. Lev. 19,2 together with 11,44 and 20,7; and on the other hand, Matt. 5,48.)

Understood in this way, it is evident that the Name of God is an expression of his mysterious but real presence among his People. When Solomon dedicated the Temple, he prayed that the Name of God would remain within it (cf. 3 Kings 8,16 and 29). Thus it is understood that one of the most remarkable ways in which the first Christians expressed the divinity of the Saviour was to consider Him as being not only the Word of God in general, but more specifically, the divine Name; in other words, the Word in which He reveals Himself. (Cf. particularly the *First Epistle of Clement of Rome*, 59,3, and probably *Didache* 10,3.)

The name Jesus, on the other hand, with its meaning of Saviour, is the object of veneration as we can see from Acts 3,16 and 4,12 and Phil. 2,10 (cf. Luke 1,31); i.e., to invoke the name of Jesus with faith is to be assured of divine help, and to give it supreme homage is to glorify God. This is the origin of the custom of concluding the liturgical prayers with this name, as well as of the whole mystical sense that the tradition of the Hesychasts (*see* HESYCHASM) attached to the incessantly repeated invocation of the Name of Jesus, and the ultimate convergence of every prayer in this sole Name.

Again it is this significance and power connected to a name that explain the custom of giving a new and holy name to the baptized. This, moreover, was already the case in the Bible for all persons consecrated to God in a special way. (Cf. Gen. 17,5; 32,28, etc., and Apoc. 2,17.) The same is true for a name given at the time of monastic profession (in the East, in order to emphasize that this profession is merely the full flower of the one grace of baptism, the monastic name is generally chosen with the intention of retaining the initial of the baptismal name).

NATIONALISM   If we understand by this word (and there is at least a tendency to do so in our own days) the attribution to a particular nation of a historic quality or mission in such a way that the furthering of this nation's particular interests is set up as an absolute, nationalism becomes a real idolatry and must be condemned as such. This is what is behind pontifical condemnations like the one against the *Action Française* movement in France, and even more so, the condemnation of Nazism in the Encyclical *Mit Brennender Sorge* of Pius XI. In this instance, however, the error of extremist nationalism went hand in hand with *racism* (q.v.).

NATURAL   That which pertains to nature as such. The distinction made in the article *nature* (q.v.) between the different senses in which human nature is to be taken according to Christian authors applies equally to this adjective.

NATURALISM   In the theological sense, it refers to the tendency to do away with the reality or the importance of the *supernatural* (q.v.).

NATURAL LAW   In effect, the natural law results from reason alone, while civil or religious positive law, since it can never go contrary to the natural law, adds to it divine prescriptions defined by a lawful *authority* (q.v.) that always originates in God. It will be noted that the terminology used by St. Thomas Aquinas puts all of the detailed prescriptions, resulting from the first principles *ex rerum natura*, under the *ius gentium*, which he looks upon as part of the positive law; while in modern times they would be considered, along with the principles themselves, to be part of the natural law (cf. *Sum. Theol.*, Ia-IIae, q.57, a.3, ad 3um; qq.94 and 95).

NATURE   Historically in Catholic theology this word has been used with two different meanings that it is important not to confuse. Generally, among both the Latin and Greek Fathers, and especially in St. Augustine, man's nature is properly his native state. Consequently, if we consider it before the fall, it is man endowed with the gifts of the divine Spirit; whereas if we have man's present state in view, it is not only man reduced to the state of a creature, but man weakened and corrupted by his sin. On the other hand, beginning with St. Thomas, when we speak of human nature it is understood in a metaphysical and not in a historical sense, i.e., what constitutes man as such, putting aside the question either of his elevation to the supernatural state or his fall. It has not always been pointed out sufficiently that even though St. Thomas hypothetically admits that man could have been created in the state of pure nature, he expressly rejects the idea that this actually ever was the case. After the Renaissance, and partly as a reaction against the exaggerated pessimism of certain extreme Protestants or Augustinians, an opinion was sometimes expressed to the effect that the fall was not truly capable of impairing human nature as such, since a nature cannot be anything else than what it is. This is a curious sophistry that confuses nature abstractly defined with nature as it exists concretely in individuals.

In speaking of God, it goes without saying that the distinction between nature in the sense of a native state and nature as equivalent to metaphysical essence does not apply. Nature and essence, on the other hand, are practically synonymous: nature is essence considered as the principle of activity.

In the modern period, and particularly in Romantic philosophy, there has been a tendency for the word nature, as applied to the totality of the cosmos, to regain the meaning *physis* that it had in the thought of the first Greek philosophers: i.e., to designate the living unity of the world looked upon as a vast organism. From Franz von Baader through Teilhard de Chardin, many Catholic thinkers, as well as those Protestant and Eastern Orthodox thinkers who were influenced by Schelling, attempted to give a Christian interpretation to this idea. The vagueness that has always characterized it has made no small contribution to the periodic debates that such endeavors have stirred up.

NATURISM   In its occasional philosophical or theological use, this word designates a tendency toward a nature *mystique* (the word nature being taken in the last of the senses treated in the article of that title).

NEIGHBOR   In the Gospel, the word neighbor refers specifically to those with whom we have the opportunity of having personal contacts: whence the expression "Love one's neighbor." (Cf. the summary of the Law in Matt. 22,39, citing Lev.19, and its parallels, as well as the parable of the Good Samaritan which underlines that our neighbor is not the one who is the first to do good to us, but rather every man to whom we are given the opportunity to do so spontaneously: Luke 10, 25,37.)

NESTORIANISM The error of Nestorius, Patriarch of Constantinople, who was condemned by the Council of Ephesus of 431. Nestorius held that the divinity would be present in Christ's humanity merely in the way it was present in the prophets, although more perfectly. The salient point of the controversy was the refusal to accept that Mary be given the title Mother of God (in Greek, *Theotokos*). This tended at least to give the impression that there were not only two natures in Christ but also two distinct persons, even though Nestorius himself does not seem to have wished to go that far. His position was only the ultimate materialization of a tendency noticeable in the whole theological school of Antioch, and particularly with Theodore of Mopsuestia who antedated Nestorius, that looked on Christ primarily as a perfect man upon whom the divinity was thought to be, as it were, superimposed. This went hand in hand with the historical and psychological realism that had always distinguished this school as a reaction against the metaphysical and mystical orientation of the Alexandrians. From this was to come the later condemnation of even the memory of Theodore at the Second Council of Constantinople in 553.

Actually, for many of the Nestorians (and Monophysites as well) their heresy appears to have been merely verbal, or at most it represented a still unformed state of thought, i.e., they upheld the Nestorian formulas because they looked upon their proscription and the blanket condemnation of a whole respectable school as Byzantine imperialism leveled against a brilliant local Church. The East Syrian (Nestorian) Church was quite soon cut off from the Empire by invasions, but for a long time afterward it underwent a considerable missionary development that extended as far as India and China. It is represented today only by a few thousand Christians of Mesopotamia (Iraq); the majority (called Chaldeans) returned to the Catholic faith by being reunited with the See of Rome. The Nestorian tendency, however, remains a permanent temptation of Christian thought. It can be seen operating in many schools of Protestant thought, like *Barthism* (q.v.), and even in certain trends of Catholic theology in which the legitimate wish to respect history and human psychology at times falls into a sort of naturalism. This is why we ought not to be surprised if these various groups sometimes show themselves to be somewhat hasty in clearing Nestorius entirely of the charges brought against him by the ancient Church.

NIGHT The paschal night on which God delivered his People (cf. Ex. 12), which was in this way changed into light for them (cf. Wis.

17–18), became the symbol of the salutary test through which Christians will find salvation. (Cf. "the night when Jesus was betrayed," 1 Cor. 11,23; the night that came at the moment of His death, Matt. 20,45 and parall.; the night He rose, Matt. 28,3.) St. John of the Cross, especially in his *Dark Night*, makes this the central theme of his description of mystical trials.

NOMINALISM   The teaching of those philosophers who refuse to see any objective reality in the distinctions that we make between beings and that are expressed in the names we give them. Nominalism dominated most of medieval thought from the 14th century onward, following the Franciscan William of Ockham, and was somewhat later to be revived in the teaching of Gabriel Biel (who had a great influence on Luther). The disappearance of the very idea of stable *essences* or *substances* would result (along with other dire consequences for theological thought) in a necessary confusion between beings and their activity. Consequently, in man's relationship to God in the economy of salvation there would no longer be room for any alternative other than a confusion between God and man (semi-Pelagianism, even pure and simple Pelagianism, which tended toward pantheism) or else a radical extrinsicism that would totally separate God's action and the action of man. Actually, the nominalist theologians rallied to positions of the first type, although they admitted as hypothetically conceivable, if the tradition of the Church were not against it, a forensic justification, i.e., one in which man would be saved by God alone without, however, being in any way changed in himself. Reacting against what was at least a *de facto* Pelagianism into which they were consequently to see a great many of their contemporaries fall, the Protestant Reformers (Luther especially, maintaining as he did the intellectual universe accepted by his teachers) had no other out than to admit this notion of justification, despite the fact that it was so foreign and opposed to the whole of that biblical teaching which they professed in principle. But even before this time, nominalism had reduced Trinitarian theology either to tritheism or to modalism. The growing disfavor with which this type of thought would be viewed in the Church is therefore easily understood.

NON-CONFORMISM   A term applied by Anglican jurists to all (and particularly to the extreme Protestants) who refused to comply with the Thirty-Nine Articles of faith of the Anglican Communion and with the use, prescribed by Parliament, of the Book of Common Prayer.

NON-JURORS   A name given to the royalist and "High Church" Anglicans who refused to take the oath of allegiance to King William of

Orange and Queen Mary after the fall of the Stuarts. By their expulsion, the tradition that they represented was to be almost wiped out within the Anglican Church until the Oxford Movement.

NOTHINGNESS   Nothingness is the absence of being. When we say that God created everything from nothing, we simply mean that he created without any preexisting matter or anything else that pre-existed creation. Strictly speaking, we should not even say that God "pre-exists" his creation, for preexistence cannot properly be understood except in a temporal sense: the beginning of time coincides precisely with creation. Nevertheless, certain modern thinkers, more or less inspired by Origen, have wished to explain created freedom by a distinction between a pure and simple nothingness (which they call *oukonic* from the Greek absolute negative) and a simply undetermined nothingness (called *meonic* from the hypothetical negative). This is the case particularly for Russian philosophers or theologians like Berdyaev or Fr. Sergius Bulgakoff. But we do not see how this *meonic* nothingness (i.e., the possibility of being what one would want to be, without God being involved in any way in what one will actually be) is conceivable, unless it is considered as a being that is independent of the being of God even in its essence. This, then, would come down to a radical dualism (or more exactly a pluralism) practically falling back into polytheism.

NUMBER OF THE ELECT   The incontestably common thesis in all of tradition as to the small number of the elect stems especially from two Gospel texts: Matt. 20,16 (repeated in 22,14): "Many are called, but few are chosen," and Luke 13,23–24 (parallel to Matt. 7,13, but more strict), on the great number of those who will not enter into the Kingdom. Nevertheless, the tendency of the Jansenists to interpret these texts even more strictly provoked a counter-reaction. What we can say with the greatest certainty is that the Gospel texts do not so much focus on eternal life as on the access to that life through effective conversion. We cannot conclude with certainty that in eternity itself a greater part of mankind will be damned, even though it does not seem that most men are concerned about it. As to what will ultimately happen, only God knows, and it seems also in this regard that Our Lord's command not to judge is most relevant (Matt. 7,1). See St. Thomas, *Sum. Theol.*, Ia, q.23.

NUPTIAL BLESSING   A blessing given to a woman following the marriage promises. It consecrates the union of bride and groom and its fecundity with reference to the teaching of St. Paul on their love, which is to be looked upon as the sacramental mystery of the love of Christ and the Church consecrated to the cross (cf. Eph. 5,25 ff.). It will be noted that the blessing can be received only once; this emphasizes the super-eminent value that Christian tradition places upon single marriages, even though it does admit the lawfulness of a second marriage after one of the parties has died (*see* MARRIAGE).

O

OBEDIENCE   The Christian import of obedience is brought out particularly in St. Paul's description of Christ's death as an act of obedience to the Father in contradistinction to Adam's disobedience, the result of his refusal to believe in the divine Word (Phil. 2). This idea is behind Christ's being called the preeminent *"Servant"* of God (q.v.). Moreover, in the beginning of the Gospel of Luke (1,38; cf. the Magnificat, 1,48), we see that Mary declares herself, in the same sense, to be the "handmaid" of the Lord; and in the beginning of the Gospel of John (2,5), she says: "Do whatever he tells you." In the Prophet Isaiah can be found the first explicit connection between faith and obedience, to the extent that for the Prophet both ideas are practically inseparable. In monastic or religious vows, obedience is looked upon as the giving up of one's own will by committing it totally, in the faith, to the divine will.

OBJECT   The object is distinguished from the subject as that which gives the subject's act its *intentionality* (q.v.). A distinction is made between the *material* object, which is the actual end of the action whatever the intention of the subject may be, and the *formal* object, which is an object insofar as it is formally intended by the subject.

OBLATION   *See* OFFERTORY and SACRIFICE

OBLIGATION   A distinction is made between an obligation that binds in conscience and that therefore must be the object of a free commitment, and compulsion, which tends on the contrary to suppress freedom.

OCCASIONALISM   The name given to the doctrine that refuses to see in what is ordinarily regarded as the real efficient cause anything more than a mere occasion on which a certain effect is produced. As an example, there is a general tendency in Protestant theology, especially strong in Calvinism, to reduce the sacraments to mere occasional causes of grace. More generally, all the inadequate theologies of creation tend to this extent to do away with all secondary causes, and to maintain that no other really efficient causality subsists than that of God. By this route we arrive at the most radical occasionalism.

OCCULTISM A characteristic common to many syncretistic forms of religious thought since the Renaissance. It claims to make a synthesis of the superior teachings of all the great religions by means of a hypothetical secret tradition that runs through and reunites them all. Modern occultism resembles the *gnosticism* (q.v.) of antiquity. Moreover, it appears to have some historical connection with it in the sense that its initiators, like Paracelsus in Germany or Robert Fludd in England, were certainly inspired by Alexandrian Hermeticism, which is bound up with it, and the Jewish Cabala, which is derived from it. Either these figures had some first-hand knowledge or else they were familiar with the popularization of gnosticism by Renaissance philosophers or scholars like Marsilio Ficino and Pico della Mirandola in Italy, or Reuchlin in Germany. This blend of confused thought has never ceased being reshaped, although it has been more impoverished than enriched over the course of recent centuries. It has not only inspired many writers from Shakespeare and Milton to Victor Hugo and Rilke, but has also captured more than once the interest of authentic philosophers. This was the case of the Cambridge Platonists (especially Henry More), or of the brilliant *illuminati* such as Jakob Boehme. It was particularly through him (as well as through the Masonic circles with which the 18th-century rationalism of the "philosophers" was to enter into a curious association) that occultism influenced 19th-century German idealism (particularly that of Schelling) and later Russian philosophy (e.g., Solovyëv and Berdyaev). Wavering between metaphysical dualism and a vitalistic monism or pantheism, occultism continues today to have an influence among some thinkers, tormented with religious aspirations, whom prejudice or routine keep away from ecclesiastical Christianity. It presents itself under crude forms like the philosophy of Annie Besant and Mme Blavatsky, or under more refined but scarcely more solid forms, like the different mystico-philosophical systems of Rudolf Steiner (which he called anthroposophy), René Guénon, Aldous Huxley, and F. Schuon. In these more recent forms there has been an attempt, although hardly successful, at a renewal by the infusion of a popularized Hinduism, generally of a strongly mediocre caliber (except perhaps in the case of R. Guénon, a narrow but disciplined thinker, who had a real knowledge of the classical philosophies of ancient India).

OFFERTORY The Mass rite in which the bread and wine that the faithful offer are placed on the altar for the purpose of their consecration and the Communion that follows. The exact meaning of this rite is delicate to specify, and its reemphasis in the contemporary liturgical movement is at times accompanied by incomplete or clearly erroneous explanations. The idea that by this rite we offer ourselves to Christ so that he may then offer us, and our whole life as well, with himself to God his Father is in effect basically ambiguous, and it does not seem that we can accept it as such without relapsing into some form of *Pelagianism* or at least *Semi-Pelagianism* (qq.v.). Actually, in the Mass there is only one oblation, or sacrificial offering, namely, that of Christ himself to his Father. This oblation, furthermore, is not distinct in itself from the one that he consummated once and for all on the cross. It is only its sacramental representation. Moreover, this is what is signified by so many secondary rites in all Catholic liturgies, which specify that the action performed at the offertory has value or makes sense only in its relationship to the cross. The cross is first recalled in this rite, but it becomes mysteriously present only later by virtue of the *consecration* (q.v.).

On the other hand, every sacrifice is a sacred meal in which man, in preparing the food that he himself provides, realizes that his life proceeds utterly from God and in return accepts the fact that he belongs to Him, freely and voluntarily. Placing the elementary foodstuffs of our life on the Christian altar implies the same acknowledgment. But the effective giving of our whole being to God is accomplished only by Christ and his cross, and because of his sacramental presence and his sole and unique sacrifice; this presence is not realized by any initiative of man, but only by the will of the Saviour. Expressed at the Last Supper in the words of the institution of the Eucharist, it is his will alone that imparts all value and reality to the action of Christ's ministers who are sent by him to accomplish among us what he has ordained.

OMNISCIENCE   The knowledge of God. It encompasses not only all reality, but everything that is possible. God *knows* in the unity of his own essence and every other being by the very fact that it is proceeds from that essence. God alone possesses and can possess omniscience; even the soul of Christ did not know with infused *knowledge* (q.v.) except all of those things that are related to the salvation of creatures. See St. Thomas, *Sum. Theol.*, Ia, qq.14 and 15; IIIa, qq.9 to 12.

ONTOLOGISM   A name given to philosophies, like that of Rosmini in the last century, which hold that since every created being is only a communication of the divine Being, all human knowledge implies an immediate knowledge of God himself. The danger with ontologism is that it runs the permanent risk of falling into pantheism by confusing being in general with the being of God himself. This is the reason for the condemnation by the Holy Office decreed in 1861 (D.B. 1659–1665) of ontologist propositions that are in the very least subject to misinterpretation. St. Anselm's "ontological" argument, which maintains that merely to reflect upon the perfect Being would allow one to conclude with certainty as to its existence, is generally considered to be tinged with ontologism in the sense that if it is supposed to have the force of a conviction, it presupposes a preliminary identification of this perfect Being with the idea that we are able to have of It.

ONTOLOGY   The science of being, which is the basic concern of metaphysics or general philosophy.

OPERATION   The principle of action in a given nature. In this regard, the idea of a theandric (i.e., God-man) operation, taken in its strictest sense and applied to Christ, betrays at least a tendency toward *monophysitism*, or in any case toward *monoenergism* (qq.v.). The idea, furthermore, seems to have been invented by Patriarch Sergius with this error in focus. It can nevertheless be taken in an orthodox sense, as seems to be the case in the writings of the Pseudo-Dionysius and other authors who made use of it after him, when the aim is simply to designate by it the performing by Christ of human actions in which his divinity is revealed, as is the case of all the actions that are the product of his *capital grace* (see this expression at the end of the article INCARNATION).

OPINION   Subjectively, an opinion is knowledge that is not certain. The term is also used in an objective sense to designate the thought (that may even be subjectively certain) of an author whose arguments do not appear absolutely convincing in general, i.e., to the extent of compelling universal assent.

ORDERS, ORDINATION   Holy orders is one of the seven sacraments recognized by the Church; it consecrates and enables a baptized Christian to fulfill the functions of a bishop, priest, or deacon (*see* BISHOP, PRIESTHOOD, and DEACON). The so-called minor orders, which have varied over the course of the centuries and still vary in the different local Churches, do not go back to an institution by Christ or the apostles and are considered to be merely sacramentals. This is the case in the Latin Church today for the orders of porter, reader (or lector), exorcist, acolyte, and even subdeacon, although the subdeaconate is sometimes considered a major order because of the obligations of celibacy and the recitation of the divine office that it entails today in the West. It is not, however, a form of the sacrament of holy orders. Since sacred orders bring with them an indelible *character* (q.v.), they may not be repeated. In the article SACRAMENT we shall see the place of orders in the totality of the sacramental economy, and in the article APOSTLE the common origin of all the orders. Ordination is the rite that confers the different orders (the Apostolic Constitution *Sacramentum Ordinis* has specified that its matter is the laying on of hands, accompanied each time by a particular formula defining the particular order that is being conferred). We shall see further in the articles BISHOP, and PRIESTHOOD what is entailed by the question of the connection between these two orders, and consequently the problem of knowing whether the episcopate constitutes a distinct sacramental order. The Council of Florence decreed that orders is a sacrament in the strict sense (D.B. 701), a doctrine that had already been held in common agreement for a long time by Greeks and Latins. Against the denials of the Protestants, this doctrine was defined with still more precision by the Council of Trent (Sess. 23; D.B. 959–968). See *Sum. Theol.*, Suppl. qq.34–40.

ORTHODOXY   Literally, right opinion. The word is traditionally used in the Church for the profession of the authentic Christian faith as defined and taught by the Church, in contradistinction to heretical or erroneous opinions. The Eastern Church separated from Rome espe-cially claims this title because of its faithfulness to the definitions of the ancient Church prior to the separation. But she herself remains in agreement, at least in principle, that orthodoxy and *catholicity* (q.v.) are notes of the true Church and cannot be separated.

P

PANENTHEISM   See the end of the following article

PANTHEISM   A philosophical doctrine that confounds God with the world, at least in the sense that in admitting the perfect *univocity* (q.v.) of being, it makes no distinction between God's being and that of the world. God then is merely the world considered in its unity and totality. The greater number of the philosophies of India, the Neo-Platonism of Plotinus and his followers, and in modern times the philosophy of Hegel may be looked upon as different forms of pantheism. As a tendency, pantheism appears whenever the divine transcendence is disregarded or minimized. This is the case in all forms of idealist *monism* (q.v.). Although it is less inevitable, the danger does exist in the different ontologist systems (*see* ONTOLOGISM). We must not, however, be too hasty in calling pantheistic every system that lays strong emphasis on God's immanence, particularly in his spiritual creatures. If with this assertion, the system keeps in balance a no-less-resolute assertion of the transcendence of God, however close its formulas come to the formulas of pantheism, the system could not be accused of it. This is particularly the case of *Augustinianism* (q.v.) in its orthodox forms. At times the term *panentheism* (literally, which see "all in God") is given to systems like the thought of the Rhenish mystics such as Meister Eckhart, or that of Malebranche, or again certain modern forms of Russian Orthodox theology, like that of Fr. Sergius Bulgakoff. The word would also be applicable to many expressions of St. Paul ("that God may be everything to everyone," 1 Cor. 15,28).

PARACLETE   *See* HOLY SPIRIT

PARADISE   This term comes from a word of Persian origin that passed into Greek and served to translate the Hebrew *eden*. Both words designated a pleasure garden (cf. Gen. 2,8 and Apoc. 2,7). Paradise is therefore understood as being simply the setting in which mankind had been created at the beginning, i.e., the conditions in which man would have been destined to live had he been faithful to his Creator's plan. Consequently, it also came to designate man's reinstatement with regard to his original destiny. It is in this light that we must understand the words of Our Lord to the good thief: "Today you will be with me in paradise" (Luke 23,43), and what St. Paul says of his own delight in "paradise" (2 Cor. 12,4). In these expressions paradise designates the present and future sojourn of the blessed (*see* BEATITUDE, ETERNITY, and LIFE).

PARISH Originally the words *parish* and *diocese* were interchangeable, both of them designating that part of the flock of the faithful entrusted to the pastoral responsibility of a bishop and his priests. Later, within each diocese, a smaller section of the faithful and of the territory where they lived came to be assigned to a priest who was delegated by the bishop for this particular pastoral responsibility. It is this subdivision in the episcopal diocese that is given the name parish today. Its center is the parish church where, together with the solemn Eucharist uniting all the people of God around their pastor, the other sacraments are celebrated, particularly the sacraments of initiation. Here the word of God is publicly taught and, in principle, the public prayer of the Church brings the parochial community together.

PAROUSIA A Greek word meaning "presence." It came to be used to designate the coming of Christ, and especially his definitive, eschatological coming. The expectation of the Parousia, as the realization of the Christian hope, is clearly characteristic of the whole New Testament, particularly the Epistles to the Thessalonians, the First Epistle to the Corinthians (chap. 15), and the whole Apocalypse (the last chapters). Here this expectation appears to refer to an impending event, one which from one day to another has every chance of being witnessed (cf. 1 Thess. 4,15–18). This is an extension, as it were, and an accentuation of the imminent expectation of the Messiah's coming that was so widespread in Jewish circles of the time. But the assurance of the definitive victory over the powers of evil, already won in principle in the Resurrection of Christ, at first tended to bring this expectation to its height. Paradoxically, while it would appear, according to the words of the Saviour himself, that we are to expect his coming at any hour like a thief in the night (Matt. 24,43 and par.), God alone knows the hour and the moment, and our certainty that the ultimate events have already been accomplished on the cross and in the Resurrection of Jesus should prevent us from being disappointed by their apparently unrealized expectation. However, beginning with the age of Constantine and the establishment of the Church in this world, there arose the danger of indifference about the Parousia and of replacing this expectation with the hope of individual immortality alone. In this there is a serious gap in the spirituality and the thought of too many Christians. According to the words of the Master that we have just recalled, even though we do not know the exact moment of the Parousia (and *because* we do not know it), not only must we keep ourselves ready at every moment to meet it, but our hope, in the light of the resurrection of both our body and our soul and of all the faithful together, can rely only on the coming of the Lord that is to renew the whole universe.

PASCH   Originally the Pasch, or Passover, was undoubtedly a Semitic feast of the spring return of vegetation (a factor in all primitive civilizations), but by the providential coincidence of its celebration with the deliverance from Egypt, it became for Israel the *memorial* (q.v.) of this deliverance (cf. Ex. 12, and 4 Kings 23,21–23). As its English name would indicate, it is generally supposed that the word itself comes from *pasah*, "to pass over" in the sense of "to spare" (cf. Ex. 12,23), because the Lord passed over the houses marked with the blood of the lamb immolated by the Hebrews and did not strike them with His plagues. Later, with this idea of the Lord's passing over so that he might redeem his People from bondage, there was connected the idea of the people's own "passing over," which He was to bring about later in leading them out of Egypt toward the promised land where Israel, in the house of his God, would be, as it were, in his own house.

Thus in the religious thought of Israel, Passover, with the memorial that is the focus of its celebration, recalls the typical redemptive intervention whereby God saved and reconstituted his People. Since Passover and the saving exodus became inseparable, the return from exile was described as a new exodus, a new Passover (cf. Osee 2,16 ff.; Isa. 63,7 ff.). In the New Testament St. Luke describes the announcement of Jesus' death to the disciples at the Transfiguration as "His departure [*exodos*] which he was to accomplish at Jerusalem" (Luke 9,31; cf. John 13,1, which speaks of His passing from this world to the Father at the moment of Passover). It is probable also that the image of the slaughtered lamb in Isa. 53,7 contained a paschal reference from the beginning. Again, St. Paul describes the saving passion of Christ by saying: "Christ our paschal lamb has been sacrificed" (1 Cor. 5,7). Thus for Christians the paschal celebration becomes the celebration of the death and resurrection of the Saviour; while the Jewish Passover and everything that it had signified for the Jews in the first covenant is the major source for the Christian interpretation of the passion. Even in the First Epistle of St. Peter we see the theme of baptism being superimposed on it, and at a very early date baptism was preferably celebrated on the paschal night. Having passed over from this world to his Father through the cross, Christ transports us after Him; no longer merely from a material Egypt to a no less material promised land (although both were already full of spiritual allusions), but "from the dominion of darkness . . . to the Kingdom of his beloved Son" (Col. 1,13), which is one with the entry into the sharing in "the inheritance of the saints in light" (v.12).

Thus the *mystery* (q.v.) of Christ, as explained by St. Paul and as celebrated by the whole liturgy of the ancient Church, is the paschal mystery, i.e., the one that was accomplished on Passover, which the Christian Passover commemorates, and which constitutes the definitive Passover of the new and eternal covenant. The *Parousia* (q.v.) of Christ, finally, is described in turn as the definitive accomplishment of this Passover in eternity (cf. Luke 22,16 and Matt. 26,29).

As in other Germanic languages, the English word Easter, although originally designating the pre-Christian Teutonic spring festival, at a very early date came to translate the *Pascha* of the Christian missionaries and has all but supplanted the term pasch.

PASSION   In all traditional texts the word passion is taken not in the modern psychological sense of an irresistible impulse of the affective order that diminishes and practically abolishes the control of the rational will, but in the metaphysical sense, namely, as an action undergone by the subject considered in contradistinction to an action of which he is the agent. St. Thomas in this sense makes a distinction between passion understood *communiter* (i.e., merely receptivity) and passion understood *proprie*, which is the reception in a subject of a *form* (q.v.) that entails the disappearance of a contrary form. This kind of passion can be found only in corruptible beings, since it is a real alteration of what they were. In an even stricter sense St. Thomas says that passion *propriissime* is understood as an alteration that contradicts the subject's natural tendencies. In the first sense, the soul in man is passive, particularly in the act of cognition, with regard to the object of its knowledge (*Sum. Theol.*, Ia-IIae, q.23, a.2); while in the second (and third) senses, it could not be passive *per se* but only *per accidens* insofar as it is the form of the human composite, made up of matter and spirit. It is then, to be precise, the sense appetite that is passive (*ibid.*, q.22, a.1 and 2).

The word passion is used in this sense to designate the sufferings and death of the Saviour. Although he is impassible in his divinity, he made himself passible even in the second and third senses defined above by taking on the flesh of our humanity in the state in which he received it from us sinners, although he did not in any way participate in our sin (Rom. 8,3). How this passion is salvific for us is discussed in the article REDEMPTION. We will limit ourselves here to trying to specify how and to what extent Jesus was made passible and suffered positively. On the first point, it seems that we must maintain with all of Christian tradition that Christ, by the fact of the personal union of his humanity with divinity, did not cease possessing even on the cross the beatific vision at the summit of his soul, although he voluntarily kept this vision from flowing over into the sensory powers of his humanity. On the other hand, even if he did not undergo, as is obvious, every possible kind of suffering, his passion remains incomparable, by the particularly painful character of death on a cross and by the circumstances in which it took place (the incredulousness of the Chosen People, the betrayal or denial of the disciples, etc.), by the very peculiar intensity of the senses in his innocent being, and finally by the fully and lucidly voluntary character of his acceptance of the passion. These two apparently opposite aspects of Jesus' passion are both clarified with equal precision by St. Thomas Aquinas (*Sum. Theol.*, IIIa, q.46, a.5 to 8).

PASSOVER   *See* PASCH

PASTOR   In American English this word refers to one who has the pastoral responsibility of a parish, by virtue of a stable delegation (which is called *ordinary*) of a part of the powers of a bishop. In the beginning, parish and diocese were practically interchangeable in scope, and the bishop directly exercised the powers considered today to belong to the pastor, but with the help and counsel of the assembly of his priests (i.e., the *presbyterium*). Later, as dioceses grew larger, they were divided into different parishes, and the chief priests no longer acted in constant association with the bishop for the whole of his diocese, but rather were entrusted respectively with a part of it that became the parish as we know it today. It follows that the heads of these parishes must be considered true pastors (i.e., shepherds), on which account canon law has gone so far as to assure their stability and even their irremovability, although they still may act only in union with the bishop and with respect for his orders.

PASTORATE   The function and office of a pastor (Latin for "shepherd"). The shepherd image was common in Semitic antiquity to describe the function of the leaders of the people. It is found again with this sense in the Bible (cf. Jer. 10,21). But the fact that the leaders insufficiently realized what this title ought to imply (cf. the same passage in Jer.) led the prophets to reserve it for the Lord. It is he who will make himself the true shepherd of his People, leading them, defending them, furnishing food for them, caring for sheep wounded by the misdeeds of wicked shepherds (cf. Ezech. 34, as well as Jer. 23). The New Testament directly recalls these prophecies in the parable of the judgment in Matt. 25,31 ff. But Jesus' assertion in the Synoptics that he has been sent for the lost sheep of Israel (Matt. 15,24), the fact that he called those close to him his "little flock" (Luke 12,32), and, perhaps especially, the parable of the lost sheep (Luke 15,4–7), all this prepares us for the assertion in the Gospel according to St. John: "I am the good shepherd," as well as for the whole development of the theme that follows with regard to His work (chap. 10). Drawing a connection between this text and the great prophecies of Jeremiah and Ezechiel recalled above gives at least some hint as to the Saviour's divinity. Heb. 13,20 and especially 1 Pet. 2,24 ff. apply this image directly to his redemptive work and more precisely to his Resurrection, which is seen as the principle of the deliverance of man who has been rescued from the captivity of the powers of evil.

The apostolic mission, in the person of Peter, is described as an association of men with this pastoral function (cf. John 21,16). From this point, 1 Pet. 5,1 ff. develops the duties of the apostles and their co-workers, and most particularly the duty of placing themselves at the service of the flock over which they have been set in charge (cf. Eph. 4,11).

The pastoral role of the pope and the other bishops sheds light on the meaning of all of their powers as leaders, doctors, and pontiffs: they serve the faithful, just as they serve God, in order to bring them to live the life that God willed to communicate to them in his Son. Priests, and chiefly pastors of parishes (who have a stable and locally determined care of souls), share in the powers of the episcopate to the full extent necessary to cooperate in its pastoral function. Conversely the pastoral duty and its exercise must not then be understood in pragmatic or empirical terms, but as strictly depending upon the theological reality of the gifts given to the ministerial hierarchy in order that it may guarantee to the whole flock of the Church the share in this "gift of God" that is the essence of the gospel.

PATERNITY   *See* FATHERHOOD

PATRIARCHATE   The function and office of a patriarch; or that section of the Church over which a patriarch has jurisdiction. The early Church very soon saw her dioceses being grouped into more or less homogeneous regions in which the bishop of a see that was particularly illustrious (usually because of its more or less directly apostolic origin) quickly enjoyed a special superiority over the other neighboring bishops. It is these bishops, endowed with a special authority (not always too easily defined), who have come to be called patriarchs. Besides Rome, the Church of Egypt experienced quite early a similar centralization around the bishop of Alexandria, to such an extent that he very soon came to act almost as if he were the only bishop of Egypt in the strict sense and that his colleagues were little more than auxiliaries. A similar, if not quite as extreme, situation obtained in Antioch. The restoration of the city and see of Jerusalem, together with the prestige that was very soon attached to it, contributed to brake the canonical expansion of the influence of the patriarchate of Antioch, although the patriarchate of Jerusalem never extended its *de facto* authority beyond its immediate suffragans. Finally Constantinople, claiming the title and office of "New Rome," instigated and encouraged the efforts of its bishops to obtain the patriarchate, even to the extent of claiming an "ecumenical" authority, i.e., one which in principle would extend to the whole inhabited earth. Ancient Rome was never willing to acknowledge it in the strict sense, although in fact it did accept the gradual recognition of the patriarch of Constantinople's preeminence over the other patriarchs.

Roman canonists generally teach that the patriarchs' power is only a delegation of the power proper to the Holy See, as is the case with every power granted to one bishop over other bishops. Eastern canonists always had the tendency to look upon this power as one surrendered for the common good to one individual by the body of bishops concerned. Actually, after the split between East and West, the patriarchs, who grew in number in proportion to the *autocephalies* (i.e., groups of relatively independent local Churches) to which they corresponded, have come more and more to govern in conjunction with a permanent synod representing the other bishops. We may perhaps consider the two theories, Eastern and Western, as being complementary rather than contradictory.

PATRIPASSIANISM   The erroneous doctrine, primarily of popular origin, which held that the Father himself underwent the passion on the cross. This doctrine goes hand in hand with errors like *Sabellianism* (q.v.) that confuse the divine persons.

PAULINE PRIVILEGE   This term is used properly of the possibility of the dissolution of the marriage of two non-Christians when one of them becomes a convert and the other no longer wishes to live peacefully with his spouse (cf. 1 Cor. 7,12–16).

PEACE   In the biblical sense of the word, peace is not only the absence of strife, but life in its fullness, which is found only with God and within his friendship (cf. John 14,27 ff.). This is also the import of the blessedness promised to the peacemakers.

PELAGIANISM   The heresy of the monk Pelagius (355–c.425), who denied any transmission of original sin and any alteration of the possibilities innate in human nature that would have been its consequence, thereby minimizing the necessity and efficacity of divine grace. According to him, grace does no more than enlighten man with regard to his end and reward his efforts toward it. First enunciated by an ascetic who through preoccupation with his ascetical endeavors was led to lose sight of the importance of heavenly grace, this heresy, with Julian of Eclanum, ended up by a certain justification of sensuality—a strange, but foreseeable turnabout (once the integrity of the present state of human nature was advertised in this way). St. Augustine led the battle against Pelagianism, and it was condemned particularly by the Councils of Carthage (418) and Orange (529), as well as by a very important letter of Pope Celestine I in 431, to which was added the *Indiculus de gratia*, a collection of Augustinian texts collected, it seems, by St. Prosper of Aquitaine.

Pelagianism, which corresponds with a deep-rooted tendency in the human mind, had numerous revivals (caused in part, furthermore, by certain excesses in St. Augustine's reaction). One of these is called today Semi-Pelagianism. It was present particularly among the monks of Gaul and was to give rise both to St. Celestine's letter and to the condemnations that were reiterated at Orange. The Middle Ages, which on the whole were unfamiliar with these latter condemnations, gave in only too strongly to Pelagian tendencies, at least in practice, but often also in theory. This was not one of the least reasons for the Protestant Reformation. In the climate of humanism, the reaction against the Reformation also included much Semi-Pelagianism, if not downright Pelagianism, which was again condemned in the moral theology of the "laxists." (See the condemnations of Alexander VII and Innocent XI in D.B. 1101 ff. and 1051, wrongly presented in certain editions as referring to the errors of the Jansenists, while they were actually leveled at the errors of people who were not precisely of the same opinion.) It would be naïvely optimistic to suppose that this outlook is extinct when naturalism, so widespread today even among sincere Christians, both Protestant and Catholic, gives it so much encouragement.

PENANCE   From the Latin translation of the Greek *metanoia*, which in the Bible signifies a sinner's conversion (literally, a change of mind), penance designates a whole series of internal and external acts of reparation for the sin committed and the resulting state for the sinner.

The sacrament of penance brings the sinner the grace he needs for repentance at the same time that it ratifies his return to grace, both with the Church and with God. Its basis is in the power of the keys given to the apostles, and particularly to St. Peter, in the Gospel text: "I will give you the keys of the kingdom of heaven, and whatever you bind on earth shall be bound in heaven, and whatever you loose on earth shall be loosed in heaven" (Matt. 16,19; cf. what was said to all the apostles in Matt. 18,18, as well as John 20,23.) The principle has been naturally admitted and applied from apostolic times, but the ways and means of its application have varied very much over the years, which causes difficulty in any study of the sacrament of penance or of penance in general. A radical difference in this connection has always been felt between sins committed before baptism and those committed afterward. For a man who comes to the faith, the reception of baptism, together with the involvement in the faith that it implies, has always been acknowledged to be a total remission of sin and of its consequences (*see* BAPTISM), to have a gratuitousness and fullness that cannot be equalled. Yet, because of the new gravity that sins assume, since they now imply at least a practical denial of the faith of baptism, it was immediately deduced that these sins could not be remitted without an even more burdensome penance. In fact, in the primitive Church, there was an almost universal tendency, based on a strict interpretation of Heb. 10,26 ff., to reject definitively from the communion of the Church those who became guilty after baptism of particularly scandalous sins (apostasy, murder, or adultery). However, in the sub-apostolic generation, we see a reaction against this rigorism in the *Shepherd of Hermas:* the Church calls these sinners to repentance by offering them the possibility of being restored to her communion, on the condition that they admit their fault and accept proportionate reparation. At first this opportunity was given only once, as an exceptional second anchor after baptism, but later it became possible to repeat this penance. This was then required no longer merely for particularly scandalous faults but for all grave faults, i.e., whatever is directly opposed to charity (*see* the end of the article SIN), even when they were not public at all. As a result, instead of being public, penance tended to become secret, and this became more and more the case once it was broadened in scope to include even venial faults, those "daily sins" about which St. Augustine speaks. Moreover, it was admitted that sins could also be taken away by a completely interior penance, which would result in a return of the fervor of charity that is weakened but by no means dead in the sinner. This evolution, which was to lead to the practice of the sacrament of penance as we know it today, was achieved particularly under the influence of Irish monasticism (7th–8th c.) and the penitential practices it produced, such as giving penances graded according to one's faults in the form of more or less severe ascetical practices. Since penances remained very exacting, they were to be the origin of *indulgences* (q.v.), i.e., pious works (prayers, pilgrimages, etc.) considered as the possible equivalent of the traditional penances, provided that they are knowingly carried out within the context of the

Communion of Saints in which the generosity of better or more-advanced Christians comes to the aid of those who are weaker or beginners in the faith.

Throughout this whole evolution, the official act of priestly reconciliation was looked upon as the sanction given by the Church to the penance performed and to the *de facto* restoration of the penitent, through his effective *contrition* (q.v.), to God's friendship; his readmission into the fellowship of the Church was to be its seal. Contrition, however, is possible only on the basis of faith in divine grace, which is manifested for Christian sinners in the power of the keys entrusted to the Church. In contradistinction to the Pelagian views, which hold that grace comes only as a reward for repentance and conversion, it became clearer and clearer that for the repentant sinner reconciliation with the Church is itself the efficacious sign of this grace, to the extent that contrition could not be perfect without at least the desire to receive it. St. Leo was one of the first to formulate this with full clarity: "Without the supplications of the priests, there is no remission of sins. By reconciliation with the Church, on the contrary, we obtain re-entry into God's favor. In this great act, Christ indeed continually intervenes" (Epist. 108). From this source may have come the application of the word *absolution* (q.v.) to ecclesiastical reconciliation, and a decree of the Fourth Lateran Council in 1215 obliged all the faithful to present themselves at least once a year to their own priest (*proprio sacerdoti*) to receive absolution from him if they had sinned gravely (D.B. 437). Also at this period, the requirement of fulfilling a penance after the reception of absolution became general. Only grave and public faults that still involved a formal excommunication entailed a solemn penance, which was terminated by a public reconciliation. However, there was an increasing tendency to separate this from absolution in the internal forum, to which was reserved the value of a sacrament in the strict sense.

Concurrently with this development, the confessor's obligation of confessional secrecy became more and more strict (cf. D.B. 438, in the same decree of the Fourth Lateran Council cited above), and the penitent's freedom to choose the confessor of his choice became consolidated. Hence the modern canonical provisions that not only no longer prescribe confession *proprio sacerdoti*, but tend in practice more and more to separate the exercise of jurisdiction in the internal forum from that of the external forum, and among other things, to prevent religious superiors from being at the same time the ordinary confessors of their subjects.

Since by and large East and West evolved similarly in regard to penance, both on the level of practice and in the elucidation of doctrine, the first difficulties were raised by the Protestants. From the beginning Luther maintained the assertion of the power of the keys entrusted to the Church and the practice of penance, although he never made any explicit pronouncement on its sacramental reality. However, despite sporadic survivals, the practice was quickly abandoned by Protestantism as a whole, and the theology that had been developed by the Schoolmen was more or less violently combatted. The Council of Trent, reiterating and giving greater precision to the obligations set down by the Lateran Council, in its fourteenth session (D.B. 894–906 and 914–925) underlined particularly the sacramentality of penance, the efficacity of sacramental absolution in reconciling us with God, together with the correlative necessity of an integral confession in order that the absolution be valid. On the other hand, it insisted on the biblical bases of penitential satisfaction, under one form or another, that the Church had always required for the reconciliation of sinners. On all of this, see St. Thomas Aquinas, *Sum. Theol.*, IIIa, qq.84–90 (the last of St. Thomas's writings), and the Supplement of the *Summa*, qq.1–28. Supplementary particulars will be found in the articles ABSOLUTION, and CONTRITION.

In various places, modern Protestants have tended to reintroduce some practice of confession. But this is not always connected with a rediscovery of the biblical bases of sacramental penance, but often only with a concern for encouraging and facilitating spiritual direction or merely the purely psychological effects of admitting one's faults. It should be noted that it too often happens that Catholics themselves confuse these secondary aspects of confession with what is essential, i.e., the sacrament itself. It is also true that the sacrament, as history shows, must never be isolated from penance as a whole, as a reparation for sin through an inward renewal. By necessity this renewal is bound up with an ascetical effort that the sacrament actually makes fruitful, rather than being able to dispense with it.

PENTECOST   Originally a harvest feast, Pentecost (or the Feast of Weeks, occurring on the fiftieth day after Passover, whence its Greek name *Pentekostes*) came for Israel to commemorate the covenant of Sinai (cf. Ex. 19,1–6 and Ex. 23,16 as well as 34,22). Marked by the same fiery manifestation of the divine Presence, the first Christian Pentecost was the day of the manifest descent of the Spirit, consecrating the Church as the New People of God and inaugurating its missionary expansion (cf. Acts 2). The Christian liturgy celebrates it as the fulfillment of the paschal resurrection of the Saviour in the communication of the Spirit, by which communication the Church becomes the Mystical Body of the One who has risen. It is therefore also the completion of the revelation of the Trinity that is celebrated. This is in particular relief in the Byzantine liturgy, although the Latin liturgy introduced the Trinity celebration in the Middle Ages as a conclusion to the octave of Pentecost. In this way, in the gift of the Spirit that anticipates the eschatological hope for us all, the Church celebrates in advance the final consummation of all things in the accomplished unity of her own people and her whole task in which God, according to St. Paul's phrase, will be everything to everyone (cf. 1 Cor. 15,28). In English this feast is also called Whitsunday.

PEOPLE OF GOD   As we saw in the article CHURCH, the notion of a particular people whom God has chosen and shaped is the primary basis of the notion of Church, not only in its preparations in the Old Testament but also in the working out of the concept by the writers of the New Testament.

PERFECTION   In keeping with the Sermon on the Mount (Matt. 5,48), Christian perfection can be nothing other than the perfection of charity: by this perfection the reality of our divine sonship is definitively asserted. Hence, there can be no question that this inclination toward perfection, far from being an optional thing for a Christian, is essential to his faithfulness to his calling. But in conjunction with this truth perfection must be considered rather as a goal toward which we must not cease striving, even though it can be arrived at, even in the case of the saints, only at the end of our present life. Before that, perseverance in the state of grace, with most rare exceptions, is only the object of hope. The state of perfection could then be spoken of only in a relative sense. It is in this light that we have come to speak, following Evagrius Ponticus and the Pseudo-Dionysius in particular, of a state of perfection that represents the summit of spiritual progress attainable in this life, after a primary phase of purification from sin and an intermediary phase of illumination with regard to the positive spiritual realities, which are truly assimilated only in a final stage. Yet the spiritual writers themselves who originated this schema were the first to stress that purification is never achieved, even in the highest stages of spiritual evolution, and that there is no one who cannot fall, if only through the temptation to spiritual pride. No one, undoubtedly, can ever flatter himself that he has become totally immune to a fall. In a still more relative sense the state of perfection (with *adquirenda*, i.e., "to be acquired," being understood) designates the religious state defined in the threefold vow to practice the counsels (poverty, chastity, obedience), as so many solid means of effectively preparing ourselves for this perfection of charity, which is the only perfection in the strict sense. Similarly, it is said that the episcopate is an acquired (*adquisita*) state of perfection, but in the sense that it requires the one called to this state to come close enough to it that he may be able to perform worthily his task of leading others to perfection.

The objection made to these different expressions, particularly by Protestant theologians, provided that we take into account the essential subtleties involved in their usage by the writers approved by the Church, is without foundation. Actually it is undeniable that they were always used in the Church and that they have the sanction of Holy Scripture itself, not only in the Gospel according to St. Matthew in the capital text cited at the beginning, but also in St. Paul. (Cf., among other texts: Phil. 3,15 and Col. 1,28 and 4,12, even without 1 Cor. 2,6, where it is possible that St. Paul uses the expression only with a hint of irony directed at the Corinthians who were too easily boasting about it.) On all this, see St. Thomas Aquinas, *Sum. Theol.*, IIa-IIae, qq.184 ff.

PERPETUAL VIRGINITY OF MARY   At a very early date we see the Church formally adopting the belief in the perpetual virginity of Mary, explicitly rejecting the interpretation of the Judaizing sects, like the Ebionites, who looked upon the brethren of the Lord mentioned in the Gospel (cf. Matt. 12,46 and 13,55 with their parallels, as well as John 2,12; 7,3,5.10) as having been children born of Mary and Joseph. In fact, without formally saying so, the evangelists seem quite persuaded to the contrary, since although they name as brethren James, Joseph, Simon, and Jude (Matt. 13,55), they explicitly distinguish the mother of James and Joseph from the mother of Jesus (cf. Matt. 27,56 and Mark 15,40). This is why the first Protestant Reformers, Calvin and Luther, solely on the basis of Scripture held to the belief in the perpetual virginity of Mary, even though the error of the Ebionites was repeated up to the 4th century by the opponents of monastic asceticism, like Helvidius and Jovinian.

But the Church teaches still more precisely that Mary remained a virgin during childbirth itself, i.e., it in no way constituted a violation of her virginal integrity. (Cf. what St. Leo says in the 4th paragraph of his *Epistola Dogmatica* to Flavian; D.B. 144.) We must indeed distinguish this assertion from the Docetist error. Refuted in particular by St. Ambrose (one of the first to hold explicitly to the virginity *in partu*), this error stated that Jesus merely passed through the body of the Virgin without really becoming flesh. (Cf. St. Ambrose, *Expositio in Lucam*, bk. II, par. 57; P.L. 15, col. 1655A; also his *De Institutione Virginis*, chap. 8; P.L. 16, cols. 234 ff.)

PERSEVERANCE   The article GRACE deals with what is relevant to the problem of perseverance, and particularly final perseverance, in the state of grace.

PERSON   Person is generally defined by traditional philosophies as a spiritual substance. Theologians prefer to say more precisely that it is the subject of the actions (or the *suppositum*) of such a substance, for reasons that will be made clear in what follows. The word comes from the Latin *persona*, which refers to the mask worn by the actors of antiquity in playing their parts; this is also one possible meaning of the Greek *prosopon* that, however, primarily designates the face. The use of these words in the sense just defined comes from Christian theological usage, i.e., Trinitarian theology, and then the theology of the Incarnation. It was first applied to the Persons of the Trinity. When in the second phase of the Arian controversy it proved necessary to define how the Father and the Son, and then the Holy Spirit, are distinct among themselves within the unity of one sole essence or substance (in Greek: *ousia*), Greek theology used the word *hypostasis*. Etymologically this would rather correspond with *substantia*. However, since *substantia* is practically synonymous in Latin with *essentia* (already the usual translation of *ousia*), and in order to avoid inextricable confusion, when they did not simply use *hypostasis* (written as we have just done in Latin characters), *persona* was substituted for it. It had already been used, particularly by Tertullian, to designate the Persons of the Trinity. The drawback was that the ancient sense of *persona* could also simply suggest modalistic interpretations (*see* MODALISM), as if the divine persons were merely masks, or at the most faces (*prosopa*) assumed, depending upon the instance, by one sole divine Person in his relations with us. Finally, at the cost of previous definitions, the term was nevertheless to become accepted for want of a better one. Consequently, following the definitions of the Councils of Nicaea and Constantinople on the consubstantial unity of the Father, the Son and the Holy Spirit, it became the norm to speak of their distinct Persons in the unity of one sole essence, substance or nature.

From this point, Trinitarian theology was brought to define the three divine Persons by the relations that distinguish them within the unique nature common to them without division; the Son is distinct from the Father by the active relation of fatherhood or the passive one of sonship, and the Spirit by a procession that is generally called the ineffable mode (*see* TRINITY). In Christology, the same notion of person is used to express the unity of Christ as the union of two natures, divine and human, united without confusion in the one divine Person (*see* INCARNATION).

This latter definition of person by relation (from Trinitarian theology) was not without its consequences on the general reflection about the very concept of person itself. It can be said that Christian thought is divided between two tendencies: one, which is more dynamic, tends to see relationship or at least the possibility of relationship in every person, created as well as uncreated, as essential; the other would tend to reserve this characteristic to the divine Persons, and to see in the created person only a spiritual subject that of itself does not imply an interpersonal relationship. We may say that the first tendency prevails when considerations of a supernatural order are dominant in the definition given of the created person, while the second prevails when we keep to a philosophical point of view, dominated either by the Aristotelianism or Platonism of antiquity.

See St. Thomas Aquinas, *Sum. Theol.*, Ia, qq.27–43 (especially q.29).

PERSONALITY   Modern usage tends to distinguish between personality and person, reserving for the first word what corresponds to the psychological principles that characterize person, which in turn is defined as a metaphysical reality. This distinction is certainly well grounded up to a point, in the sense that the definition of person cannot be reduced merely to psychological considerations. But we cannot conclude from this that there is a radical contradistinction to the extent that person and personality could be opposed without emptying person of its concrete reality. This is why the Church has shown herself more than reticent with regard to the attempts of certain modern theologians to attribute to Christ a human personality while maintaining the unicity of his incarnate divine Person. This is one of the points aimed at by the Brief of Pius IX, *Eximiam tuam*, addressed on June 15th, 1857, to the Archbishop of Cologne regarding the books of Anton Günther, in the paragraph referring to his doctrine of the Incarnation (cf. D.B. 1655).

PHILOSOPHY   A term used by Socrates, quoted by Plato, who claimed not to be a wise man but a friend (and therefore a seeker) of wisdom (*philosophos*). The word came to designate the effort of man's reason, left to its own devices, to explain the reality of his total experience. The specialized sciences (mathematics, physics, or the natural sciences) gradually became separated from philosophy, and it is generally admitted today that philosophy properly entails the study of problems that are called metaphysical (i.e., of general philosophy), namely, of the first principles of every being: logic, as a study of the principles of all knowledge; ethics (natural morality), to the extent that it can be rationally deduced from the principles of human nature;

psychology (except in its metaphysical part, which is called rational psychology), as the science of the soul, and sociology in turn both tend to develop into autonomous sciences.

If we define philosophy in this way, we must acknowledge that all reflection on any problem, as long as it tends to return to the most general principles that inspire it, could not be exempted from being a type of philosophy. In particular, theology (if the intention is for it to be anything other than a simple repetition of traditional formulas of which only a strictly grammatical explanation would be furnished, and if it is a reflection on divine revelation) implies, whether it wants to or not, a philosophy as an auxiliary science. Even in its most energetic refusal to admit this, under the vain pretext of not risking to contaminate the Word of God through merely human thoughts, as is eminently the case today in the Protestant theology of Karl Barth, it does nothing in reality, and could do nothing, but make use of an implicit philosophy. The implicit character of the philosophies necessarily involved in theologies that claim to ignore philosophy and to do without it, actually simply makes them its prisoners by preventing them from criticizing an instrument whose existence they may well refuse to acknowledge formally, although they could not dispense with it without ceasing to think coherently.

In that case, how are we to look upon the connection between theology and philosophy? The first point that must be acknowledged is that revelation, the basis of every Christian theology, if it neither imposes nor implies a particular type of philosophy, certainly excludes certain philosophies and does not allow the acceptance of any except conditionally. It is obvious that a materialistic philosophy, denying the existence of a God who transcends matter, could not be utilized by any Christian theologian. It may be less evident, but easily discovered upon reflection, that a philosophy of radical idealism, denying that we must see in our ideas any reality that transcends our mind that thinks them, is also impossible to reconcile with the Word of God, which without doubt proposes to inculcate in us assertions of transcendent truth. Besides, if it is historically averred that Christian theology has taken a great deal, in turn or simultaneously, from the great Aristotelian or Platonic systems of philosophy (to say nothing of Stoicism, to which its development certainly owes a great deal), an attentive examination shows that there is no thesis that it has been able to accept without more or less grave danger until it had subjected it to a rigorous criticism and a more or less exhaustive reinterpretation. To give but one example, if Thomism seems purely and simply to have borrowed *hylomorphism* (q.v.) from the philosophy of Aristotle, it did not do so without profoundly transforming it, as the Thomist definition of the human soul suffices to show: a substantial form, and as such immortal.

If philosophy is in principle a purely rational and natural knowledge, the objects of its study are so closely connected with man's ultimate end that the fall could not but profoundly disturb the innate capacity that man possesses of knowing them. Hence the conjectural and groping character of any philosophical study, and the actual impossibility, which the history of philosophy shows, of reaching in this area a solid system of truths that would be immediately accepted by all minds. We have only to think of a notion like creation; even though theologians agree that in principle it can be demonstrated in a purely rational way, this notion has never been clearly defined outside of revelation. Hence the secondary but nonetheless very important role of revelation in confirming and shedding light on truths, even of a natural order, that was so correctly underlined by the First Vatican Council (cf. D.B. 1786). In the face of modern rationalism, the Church has insisted more than ever on the weakness of the exercise of human reason left to its own devices (cf. the allocution of Pius IX, *Singulari Quadam*, of December 9, 1864, particularly D.B. 1644).

It follows that if it is true that in principle there cannot be a philosophy (any more than a mathematics or a physics) that is specifically Christian, in the sense that its principles or its conclusions would come from revelation alone and not from reason working on natural facts, actually there is a Christian philosophy in the sense that there are philosophical principles and conclusions that have never been clearly elucidated except by minds whose reflection was guided and stimulated by revelation. With regard to the *philosophia perennis,* as in the case of any human science, which is always subject to growth and eventual rethinking, it remains true that there could be no question of bringing an exclusive and definitive formulation to a standstill. The Church has never intended and could not intend anything of the kind. But it is her prerogative to divert the minds of the faithful away from systems of thought whose principles and orientations seem little or not at all compatible with revealed truths, and on the other hand to encourage the study and the utilization of philosophical systems whose vitality and productiveness have been proved through the positive assistance that they have provided for the development and explanation of Christian truths. For this reason these systems also seem capable of bringing together and pointing up the best in purely human thought. It is in this sense that the Church recommends the study and the employ, by those who have or will have the burden of teaching, of the philosophy developed by St. Thomas as an instrument of theological research. This recommendation, moreover, does not condemn any of the other paths of philosophical research traditionally pursued within the Church, since they also have given proof of their productivity. Nor even less could she exclude anything that is positive in the *adquisita* that new philosophical research can or could eventually bring to the treasury of human reflection even though it were pursued outside the Church.

PIETISM   From the title of Philipp Jakob Spener's work *Pia Desideria*, the name was given to a whole religious movement in German Protestantism in the 17th and 18th centuries, for which the groundwork had already been laid in Arnd's *True Christianity*. Desiring to escape from the more and more abstruse controversies between the partisans of Lutheran doctrinal orthodoxy and the proponents of an already rationalist Christianity, the first pietists concentrated on an affective piety that was directly inspired by Franciscan mysticism and the *Imitation of Christ*. The essential point in their conventicles (which grew on the fringes of the official Protestant Churches) was in cultivating a life of intimacy with Christ, showing itself in warmth of feeling and a life wholly impregnated with charity. Later, particularly with Count von Zinzendorff and the new impetus that he brought to the community of the Moravian Brethren who had taken refuge on his lands at Herrnhut, it became dominated by the ideal of a sudden conversion to a living faith in Christ the Saviour. In this whole movement, there was the great danger of confusing the most profound religious experiences with more or less artificially induced outbursts of emotion. But despite this it is impossible not to see through the whole history of the pietist movement the resurgence of a very authentic current of evangelical spirituality. It returned to Luther's assertions on salvation by faith what was most positive in them, and more than once, as with the two writers of the most popular German hymns, Paul Gerhard and Tersteegen, actually attained a genuine mysticism and holiness. But the flight from doctrinal problems remains pietism's congenital weakness and in fact laid the groundwork for Schleiermacher's liberalism, which isolated religious sentiment from the transcendent objects of faith. German pietism experienced an original extension in British Wesleyanism (q.v.).

PIETY   The gift of piety, in the Thomistic synthesis of the spiritual life, in the service of charity not only perfects the virtue of religion (seen as the form of justice toward God), but also every practice of the virtue of justice. Just as our duties toward God are raised to the highest perspective of a supernatural filial relationship, our relationships with others are transfigured in the light of our brotherly fellowship within the divine charity poured into our hearts by the Holy Spirit (cf. Rom. 5,5; see

St. Thomas Aquinas, *Sum. Theol.*, Ia-IIae, q.68, and IIa-IIae, q.80 ff.). The virtues of filial piety and piety toward fatherland are more special; they are annexes of the virtue of justice, but the influence of the same gift gives them a specifically Christian coloring (*ibid.*, q. 101).

PLAN   The idea of a plan of God centered in the formation of a People that is truly his own completely underlies the Word of God. It is associated with the revelation of the divine Name in Exodus (chap. 3), and the notion becomes explicit in the books of Wisdom. The wisdom of God is in fact his creative and redemptive plan (*see* WISDOM). For St. Paul, the essential element of this plan is in the *mystery* (q.v.) of Christ and his cross. The notion of a divine plan is behind the idea of *providence* (q.v.) through which, as St. Paul says again, "for those who love God all things work together unto good" (Rom. 8,28).

POLITICAL GOVERNMENT   *See* AUTHORITY, and STATE

POLITICS   From the dialogue of Plato and the treatise of Aristotle bearing this name, politics is properly the science and the art of organizing and governing the "city" (in Greek, *polis*). The formal object of politics is the temporal common good of mankind, but since this good is concretely inseparable from the pursuit of man's supernatural end, every political action, for the Christian, must receive a rectification and a higher inspiration from his faith. The requirement of justice will not thereby be diminished, but rather specified and extended to include a requirement of charity. If it can be lawful, in complex situations involving changing realities, for different Christians to follow in accordance with their particular lights different political orientations, they must do so with respect for those higher principles that it is the Church's function constantly to recall to them. Yet it is not within the Church's scope to become involved in temporal questions that do not directly concern her, except in the light of the relationship that they always have to man's last end. See St. Thomas Aquinas, *De Regimine Principum.*

POLYGENISM   A hypothesis of certain modern scientists who maintain that mankind may have originated not from one but from several human couples, appearing in the evolution of the human species in different places. *See* MONOGENISM.

POLYTHEISM   A simultaneous belief in several gods. The 19th century had somewhat tended to look upon polytheism as *the* primitive form of religion, monotheism being only a tertiary stage, following an intermediary stage called henotheism, i.e., worship reserved to a national or tribal god who subsequently would be looked upon as the unique God. This schema has even been offered as an explanation of the religion of Israel, the God of Moses having first been the local god of the Sinaitic tribes. As a general rule it is today in the process of being completely abandoned. If the thesis of primitive monotheism, held by Fr. Schmidt (a member of the missionary Congregation of the Divine Word and a celebrated anthropologist) has not rallied all minds behind him, it is generally admitted that the original apprehension of the sacred is that of one reality, behind the totality of human experience. Polytheism then would correspond only to a later breakdown of this experience through the growing complexity of civilization, and the monotheisms that subsequently appeared would only be a thought-out return to the facts of primitive experience.

PONTIFICAL MONARCHY   We use this term in referring to the fundamental principle of the establishment of the Catholic Church, according to which the supreme authority in the Church belongs to the Sovereign Pontiff. Nevertheless, this principle by no means excludes a collegial authority in the body of bishops (i.e., those in communion with the pope). Proof for it is found in the explicit statement of the Code of Canon Law that the Ecumenical Council itself enjoys supreme power over the whole Church (can. 228; cf. this canon and what is said of the power of the pope in can. 218 ff.).

PONTIFICAL PRIMACY   See the following article

POPE   From a Greek diminutive for "father," which in the early Church was used either for all priests or especially for certain bishops like the patriarchs, in particular the patriarch of Alexandria, this term has become preeminently the title of the bishop of Rome, considered as the focal point of Catholic unity and the visible head of the Church. From earliest antiquity we see the Church of Rome actually claiming for her bishop, as successor to St. Peter, this particular office within the heart of the episcopate of the universal Church. The theology of the papal office is therefore bound up on the one hand with a theology of the powers proper to St. Peter in the apostolic college, and on the other with the theology of the apostolic succession in the episcopate. On the first point it is interesting to observe how the evolution of New Testament exegesis, even in Protestant authors like O. Cullmann, tends today to come back to positions that have always been those of the Church of Rome. In other words, it is evident from the teaching of the Gospel according to St. Matthew that the same apostolic powers that were given collectively by Christ to the Twelve, Peter included, were also conferred by Him on

Peter personally. The efforts made for such a long time by the biblical criticism of liberal Protestant inspiration to demonstrate the inauthenticity of the verses "Thou art Peter, and upon this rock I will build my Church, and the gates of hell shall not prevail against it. And I will give thee the keys of the kingdom of heaven; and whatever thou shalt bind on earth shall be bound in heaven, and whatever thou shalt loose on earth shall be loosed in heaven" (Matt. 16,18–19) are themselves an implicit attestation of the fact that this phrase can be interpreted only in the sense traditionally admitted in the Church. But those arguments employed to deny that Jesus could have pronounced this phrase (founded on the supposition that the notion of Church was a later one) can no longer be seriously held. The idea that the Church, i.e., a New People of God, was to take the place of the ancient people did not come after Christ, but was already clearly present germinally in the apocalyptic movements that preceded his coming, like the Qumran community. What remains then is the problem of Peter's succession.

This problem in turn is twofold. First, there is the question of apostolic succession in general. Those, like Cullmann himself, who balk at the idea of apostolic succession in general do so because of a preconceived idea that in calling the bishops successors of the apostles, we would disregard the essential New Testament conviction that the apostles had a founding role, a role that could not be assumed by any one else after them. But as we have already said in the article BISHOP, the traditional sense in the Church of apostolic succession does not in any way mean that the bishops would have the power to undo and redo at whim what the apostles had accomplished once and for all, but rather that they are there to maintain what the apostles had done, and to maintain it not as a dead relic but as an ever-living reality of the same Spirit.

This brings us to the second aspect of our problem: the Petrine succession itself. If it was essential for the apostolic community and its ministry, as the foundation of the whole life of the Church, to be a community in which the same powers and the same responsibilities are inseparably entrusted to all together, and to one of them in particular, it seems inevitable that the community that will therefore be the successor of the primitive apostolate, in the precise sense just defined, should preserve the same initial structure. In fact, just as we see that in the ancient Church the bishops in general claimed apostolic succession, without this seeming to cause any problem, we also see the bishop of Rome claiming for himself a succession to Peter's particular role. In fact, his office in the universal episcopate is exactly as Peter's was in the midst of the apostolic community depicted in the New Testament. If what Cullmann says about the conflicts between Peter and Paul, indicated in the Epistle to the Galatians, is right (Gal. 2,11 ff.): namely, that the importance attached by St. Paul to the fact that Peter seemed not to contradict what he himself was doing, actually attests to the unique role which he acknowledged in Peter, the same thing must be said of the friction that can be observed on occasion in the ancient Church between local bishops and the bishop of Rome. To begin with, there was the episode of the discussions over the date of Easter and Irenaeus's insistence that Pope Victor not condemn the Asiatics on this point. We may look upon this only as an acknowledgment of the capital importance a papal decision had in the eyes of all the bishops at that time, as well as the immediate conviction of the popes that they were justified in principle in intervening in the affairs of local churches other than their own. As a matter of fact, by the 5th century, we see a pope like St. Leo I claim powers at least as extensive as those that were defined and acknowledged the Sovereign Pontiffs by the First Vatican Council. Despite numerous appeals made to Rome in antiquity by the other churches we never see the pontifical doctrine formulated elsewhere with such precision. It is indeed remarkable that this claim on the part of St. Leo, even in a universal council like that of Chalcedon where the Orientals were in great majority, seems not to have raised any difficulty nor to have created any suspicion with regard to the Roman claims (on the contrary, the letter of Leo to the Council was greeted with the unanimous acclamation "Peter has spoken").

The difficulties raised against the assertions of the power of the popes, as defined in the First Vatican Council in 1871 in the Constitution *Pastor Aeternus* (D.B. 1821–1840), seem to involve two types of confusions. Either we imagine that the universal authority, immediate and ordinary (D.B. 1831), attributed to the pope would imply a destruction of the authority proper to the bishops over their local churches, or else we believe that we must understand the assertion that the dogmatic definitions of the popes are irreformable *ex sese et non ex consensu ecclesiae* in the sense that the pope could define whatever truth he wanted without taking into account the sentiment of the universal Church (cf. D.B. 1839). But a thorough reading of the conciliar text, especially when it is enlightened by the discussions among the Fathers on the sense to be given to these words, and in addition by the letter addressed by Pius IX himself to the German bishops in approving the interpretation they had given of the definition (cf. D.S. 3117), does not allow us to understand it in his way. The immediate authority of the pope over the whole Church is exercised with, and not in contradistinction to, that of each bishop over his own church (cf. the characteristic text of St. Gregory the Great quoted in D.B. 1828). And if it is said to be an ordinary authority, that does not mean that it would be substituted for the authority proper to ordinaries of places, i.e., of the local bishops, but that the cooperation of episcopal power and of the power proper to the pontiff is constant (this furthermore in no way means that the pope may intervene or must intervene at every moment in the usual course of life proper to each diocese). As for pontifical definitions, it goes without saying that they can have bearing only for what is or is not the faith of the Church, since it is expressly stated in the conciliar text that the infallibility enjoyed by the Sovereign Pontiff when he is brought to pronounce these definitions is "precisely the one which the divine Redeemer willed to provide His Church, when she defines a doctrine concerning faith or morals": *Ea infallibilitate pollere qua divinus Redemptor Ecclesiam suam in definienda doctrina de fide vel moribus instructam esse voluit* (D.B. 1839).

Consequently, if the pontifical definitions are proclaimed irreformable *ex sese et non ex consensu Ecclesiae*, this simply means that they derive their official force not by virtue of a further confirmation that the Church, in one form or another, would be called juridically to give them, but at the instant that the pope makes them *ex cathedra*, which is, as the council says, "when he exercises his responsibility as pastor and doctor of all Christians, in virtue of his supreme apostolic authority." These last words evidently refer to that authority which he has in order that the faith received by the Church from the apostles be preserved in the Church; it is an authority that he exercises along with the whole episcopate and within it, but with his own power, should the case arise, to make if necessary decisions affecting the whole body, since he, like Peter among the apostles, is able to exercise alone the powers that also belong to all taken as a whole. *See* APOSTLESHIP, BISHOP, CHURCH, INFALLIBILITY.

POSSESSION   This word is used of the phenomena of diabolical influence that seems completely to dim the autonomy and responsibility of the subject, in contradistinction to obsession, which merely diminishes them. *See* DEVIL.

POTENCY   Following the basic distinction of Aristotelian metaphysics, every being is either in act or in potency, potency itself being merely a capacity of passing into act, and this passing being motion. God alone is pure act. Since every other being depends radically on His being, everything is done by His potency and there is nothing that it cannot produce, except when this would imply a contradiction in its definition, in which case it simply could not be. It is in this sense that God is called omnipotent, all-powerful. The potency (or power) belonging to him is not passive (which would be opposed to the definition itself of pure act);

it is, on the contrary, a pure activity. See St. Thomas Aquinas, *Sum. Theol.*, Ia, q.25, in particular a.1 and 3.

POVERTY   Although the Old Testament teaches the basic goodness of all creation and sees as a consequence a positive blessing from God in the peaceable enjoyment of its goods (see, for example, the blessing of the Jewish patriarchs, the sons of Jacob, in Gen. 49), it very soon became evident, once the Israelites had been set up in Chanaan, that riches became for them, as for other men, the occasion for idolatry, and at the same time for an unfair distribution of goods among their brothers. Hence the curses pronounced by Isaiah against those who put their trust in their goods (cf. chap. 5) and his assertion, repeated by Osee, that God will take His gifts away from His People so that they will again seek Him out, that He will be the object of their search and not the cosmic powers that they have worshiped in order to obtain their favor (cf. Osee 2). Hence the figure of a prophet like Jeremiah who is seen as the man who has given everything up in order to be faithful to his God (cf. chap. 16), which lays the groundwork in the second part of the book of Isaiah for the image of the Servant. He is not only a poor man, but the outcast of all the people. It is in this light, and particularly in the Psalms, that a spirituality of the poor man will grow, representing him as the preeminent believer, because he has nothing else but the Lord in whom to place his trust.

The poverty that Judaism already exalts in the Messianic expectation, and which is eminently embodied in St. John the Baptist, is a voluntary stripping of the self of all things, grounded in faith, with the purpose of living by faith. It ultimately assumes a directly eschatological aspect: one frees oneself from the bondage of the present "world" so as to be ready to welcome the "world" to come, and even so as to go out to meet it in the desert, as into a new Passover. The fact that the prophets applied these paschal images to the Babylonian captivity and to the revival that followed it laid the groundwork for a desert spirituality, i.e., one centered around a casting off of the world's adornments and a life alone with God. This supplied the framework for an exaltation of poverty (*see* PASCH).

In conjunction with the proclamation of the Kingdom of God, the Beatitudes then introduce the Sermon on the Mount as a call to liberation from the evil powers' kingdom of the damned. They keep us in bondage through our idolatrous attachment to earthly goods. Only by our becoming detached from these goods will we become committed to the regenerating power of the *agape*, the Father's love.

In this biblical and evangelical poverty can be seen the root of the whole of Christian asceticism. In monasticism, the defined framework of a threefold self-denial in poverty (in the narrow sense of the word, i.e., the giving up of all personal property), in chastity (understood as a renunciation of the possession of one's own body), and finally in obedience (the renunciation of one's own will), is only the complete explicitation of all that poverty in spirit implies in the Beatitudes. (Cf. Matt. 5,3–12, and Luke 6,21–26; the first expounds on the starker text found in Luke which is in a form closely related to the prophetic formulas and particularly to those of Isaiah.)

POWER OF THE KEYS   *See* ABSOLUTION, and PENANCE

POWERS   This word (Greek, *exousiai*) is used by the Scriptures of the angelic beings insofar as they are considered to be the rulers of the cosmos (*see* ANGEL, and DEVIL).

PRAISE   A form of disinterested prayer in which we come to God to express to him simply our joyful gratitude, in the faith, for what he has done in the work of creation and redemption.

Praise is the perfection of contemplative prayer. It marks the beginning on earth of what will be the foremost activity of the blessed whose beatitude will proclaim, as perfectly as is possible for creatures, the glory of God. In the Psalms and canticles of the Bible every prayer of a man who is on the road to his fatherland converges in praise. The Eucharist is the preeminent realization of Christian praise, not only because it is centered in the unity of the work of creation and redemption, but because it is its fruit: the great act of gratitude in which the creature who is saved in Christ praises Him for the grace He has brought him and, in so doing, is associated with the perfect praise, with the definitive glorification of the Father that He has accomplished. *See* EUCHARIST.

PRAYER   Man's conversation with God, especially to implore His gifts. Specifically Jewish and Christian prayer, of which the model is given to us in the biblical psalms and the liturgical prayers, in particular the *Eucharist* (q.v.), is distinct from all the others in that it is essentially a response to the Word of God. Its principle then is faith in this word. Hence the confession of this faith that is always, explicitly or implicitly, its first step. On this basis, prayer developed first as a meditation on and a praise of God's wonders. The awareness of belonging to His People, which is the uppermost object of His works, will give to this fundamental prayer of the Jew and the Christian the coloring of a joyous gratitude and a trusting abandonment to the beneficent will of God, which is properly eucharistic. But, with a spontaneous movement, the consideration of what God had done for his People in the past led them naturally to implore Him to continue His work in us now, and to bring it to its definitive completion. Hence the new sense assumed in this context by every truly Christian prayer of petition.

Following the schema of the Lord's prayer, it is first of all the prayer that God's name be hallowed (by this "recognition" of faith accomplishing itself in us and in all men), in such a way that His will be done on earth, today the abode of sin and unfaithfulness, and His kingdom definitively set up. It is only then, and in the interior as it were of this full realization of God's plan, that we will ask for ourselves, as trusting sons, for physical and spiritual food, which is necessary for us each day, that is to say in constant dependence upon the heavenly Father; the taking away of our past faults and their present consequences; the defense against future temptations and the final triumph over the power of the enemy. Just as contemplation in faith, which is the primary stage of every Christian prayer, must be centered on the saving mystery of Christ and his life-giving cross, the petition to which this contemplation is normally extended must flower forth into an insistent plea that there be accomplished fully in us and in the world this mystery that is the mystery of the whole Christ, in whom all things must be reconciled with his Father, in such a way that God finally will be all in all. Hence the vast collection of intercessions in the Great Litany after the praise of all the salvific mysteries, and the supplication for deliverance from all evils. With the request, finally, that the divine charity be completely poured out into our hearts, we realize that Christian prayer can never be reduced to a selfish preoccupation with our own welfare alone, and especially that we cannot ask for forgiveness for ourselves, the principle of all divine graces, without our thereby committing ourselves explicitly to forgive our brothers and to love them as we wish to be loved by God.

When we see Christian prayer in these broad and unifying perspectives, false problems are dispelled of themselves. In the first place, it is evident that the contradistinction set up by certain philosophers, like Kant, between a pure prayer, which is simply the lifting up of the soul to God, and an inferior prayer, that is selfishly absorbed in petitioning, no longer has any sense. In contemplating the love of God as it is revealed to us in his efficacious Word, we do no more than ask that his will be done in us and by us as we beseech him. Indeed, there is no longer any room for opposing a disinterested prayer of pure love, as the quietists did (*see* QUIETISM), to an interested prayer, where everything is resolved in the view of the immeasurable love with which God loves us, and within which, in some way, he wills that we love him, which supposes that we love all that he loves, including our own salvation, provided that it is as he loves it. Similarly, the opposition that certain historians had wished to set up, following Friedrich Heiler and his book on *Prayer* (New York, 1958), between a prophetic, biblical prayer which would be that the will of God be done, and a mystical prayer of Hellenic origin which, according to him (see the discussion of this opinion in the article MYSTICISM), absorbs us in God, finds itself outmoded when we acknowledge the personal character of God. Hence the absolutely transcendent value of the personal relationship that He wills to establish between him and us; only within this relationship do the other problems, whether they concern us or the whole world, assume their genuine significance.

As for the question raised by the phrase of Jesus in his priestly prayer in St. John, "Not for the world do I pray" (17,9), to resolve it we must recall that the *world* (q.v.), for St. John, does not stand for creation as a work of God, but for its present state as being subject to the power of sin. We do not pray then for the world, in the sense that we could not pray for the maintaining of its present economy, which is essentially rebellious and fallen, but we pray for the salvation of the world, just as "God so loved the world that he gave his Only-Begotten Son, that those who believe in him may not perish, but may have life everlasting," as the same St. John says (3,16). Finally the central problem of the efficaciousness of prayer is cleared up in the consideration of everything that has just been said, by the fact that, while remaining suspended from the all-powerful will of God alone, his Word reveals to us that he has made a world of free creatures in order to associate them with the realization of his plans, so that he has, as it were, suspended their fulfillment, to a certain extent, to make it depend upon the supplications that we would raise to him for that purpose. Therefore, far from looking upon the efficacy of prayer as if it should modify God's plan, we must conceive it as an integrating part of its providential fulfillment. On all of this, see St. Thomas Aquinas, *Sum. Theol.*, IIa-IIae, q.83.

PREACHING   A basic function of the Church, normally exercised by the bishops and their co-workers, the priests of second rank, which consists in proclaiming with authority the Word of God. *See* KERYGMA.

PREDESTINATION   In the strict sense, the eternal and infallible plan by which God decides effectively to bring to salvation those whom he wills. In a broader sense, we speak of predestination in relation to our receiving every particular grace. Contrary to what many people, whether Christians or not, imagine in our own day since various heresies with regard to predestination have been condemned, there is nothing heretical in the notion itself. Actually that there is predestination must be held as true by every Catholic as a truth of faith taught formally by Holy Scripture and expressly confirmed by unanimous theological tradition, supported by various acta of the magisterium. This is the express teaching of St. Paul: "And those whom he has predestined, them he has also called; and those whom he has called he has also justified" (Rom. 8,30; cf. 1 Cor. 2,7 and Eph. 1,5 and 11). St. John, without using the word, unquestionably teaches the same doctrine, particularly when he has Christ himself say: "No one can come to me unless the Father who sent me draw him" (John 6,44; see the whole context).

These texts were recognized as conclusive not only by St. Augustine but also by St. Thomas Aquinas; and those Catholic theologians who were most careful to safeguard the reality of human freedom, like the Jesuit Molina, never dreamed of rejecting the reality of predestination, even when they took care to explain it in a way that made the broadest possible concessions to the opposite point of view. After a declaration of the Council of Orange, which presupposed predestination without using the word itself (D.B. 196), the Councils of Quiercy (in 853, against Gottschalk) and Valence (two years later against John Scotus Erigena), while condemning exaggerated doctrines on this point, specified that predestination was an article of faith (D.B. 316 and 322). The Council of Trent itself, compelled to condemn the still graver error of the Protestants who taught both the possibility of arriving at a certitude that one is predestined to salvation and an equally positive predestination of the damned to their damnation (see Sess. VI, decree *De Justificatione*, particularly D.B. 805, 816, and 827), was no less clear in stating that no doubt could be allowed as to the fact itself of the predestination of the elect, however mysterious that remained. (Cf. D.B. 805, in connection with 797 and 801 which assert most strongly that our salvation comes entirely from the sole grace of God, without the possibility of intervention by any consideration of merits that are anterior to this.)

What we have just said suffices to show that the whole problem and difficulty in the doctrine of predestination arises when we ask what the situation is, not for the elect and the saved, but for the damned and reproved. On first sight we might be tempted to deduce from the words of Scripture that there is a strict parallelism between the two cases. Do we not find texts like the following in the Old Testament: "The Lord hardened the heart of Pharaoh" (Ex. 9,12)? And does not St. Paul himself, in citing the text of Jer. 18,6, say: "Is not the potter master of his clay, to make from the same mass one vessel for honorable, another for ignoble use?" (Rom. 9,21.) Yet it is certain that these texts may not be isolated from other texts that state most categorically individual freedom and responsibility, like Ezech. 18. What must we conclude then, if it is not that God himself is assuredly the Creator of our freedom, not only in a general way but in the sense that we would have no power of making any decision either for good or for evil unless he positively willed this power in us, with all of its consequences? Moreover, he wills our good, as he wills every good in an absolute fashion and merely tolerates a limited evil as the inevitable condition of a greater good. This is the whole meaning of that other biblical notion of the divine forebearance that St. Paul calls to mind some few lines further on after the passage just quoted (cf. Rom. 9,22).

The best light that can clarify this mystery to some extent comes from a profound remark of St. Augustine that St. Thomas was to develop as fully as possible: if God creates in us "to will and to work," according to another phrase of St. Paul (Phil. 2,13), he is the author of all good in us, and this above and beyond our own consent to grace; while every evil that we commit, and especially our refusal to open our hearts to him, is never more than a deficiency in our cooperation with his will. Moreover, since this evil has merely a negative reality, it is only in us insofar as we are limited beings, and not in any way from Him who is both Being and Good. It does not therefore follow that our consent to grace would be a forced act or that it would be any less our own than our refusal. Quite the contrary. On the one hand, since God is the author of our own freedom, it is as a free motion toward the good that he moves this freedom when he does so; and, on the other hand, since the good act is an entirely and solely positive act, and the evil act a deficient one, even though we act under the influence of a purely gratuitous grace we still act much more positively than when we do evil. It follows that if Scripture speaks of predestination to grace or to final salvation, it never speaks of a parallel predestination to evil or to damnation. If the Council of Quiercy consented to follow Gottschalk or Scotus Erigena, as well as other Christian authors, in speaking of a predestination of the ungodly to death, it did so only by specifying at once that this does not mean, nor could it, that God predestines us to evil, but only that he has fore-knowledge of evil; on the other hand, there is unquestionably a predestination to receive the grace of salvation (cf. D.B. 321 and 322). On all this, see St. Thomas Aquinas, *Sum. Theol.*, Ia, qq.23 and 24.

The fallacious parallelism that causes a duplication of the predestination of the elect by an equally positive predestination of the reprobate was adopted by Luther and Calvin only because they disregarded this fundamental principle. At the same time, the humanist tendency to assert human autonomy was hardly less harmful to the notion, so essential to Christianity, of the gratuitousness of salvation. Hence the controversies that ensued after the Council of Trent; they ended up in exaggerations that reproduced either the Protestant heresy, as in the case of certain Jansenists, or the heresy of Pelagius, with certain theologians or moralists that were called laxists. They caused the appearance of two great new systems that were on opposite sides in the controversies *de auxiliis* (mentioned in the article FREEDOM). Both claimed to give explanations of the traditional doctrine as recalled and justified by St. Thomas. One was that of the Dominican Bañez, known as the system of physical predetermination (or premotion); it explains the adhesion of human freedom to efficacious grace by the creation of an *entitas fluens* that leads man's freedom to coincide with the will of God for its own good, since the will of God can have no other determination than its own quite spontaneous determination. The other is that of the Jesuit Molina, known as the system of *scientia media*; this *scientia*, or knowledge, is the knowledge that we suppose God to have with regard to the free decisions of creatures. This would result in His granting, in a free and sovereign way, his efficacious grace to some and not to others, but in anticipation of the merits that they would acquire by their free adhesion to this grace. This latter solution is particularly attractive and ingenious, but it raises the apparently insurmountable difficulty of somehow placing the cause of a divine decision in a reality that is in some manner independent of God himself. How then can the principle of absolute transcendence of the divine Being in relation to the being of a creature be safeguarded? On the other hand, it is hard to deny that the notion of a physical predetermination put forward by Bañez, even though his intention was to maintain this transcendence, introduces a confusion between the plan of action of the primary cause and that of the secondary causes. Besides, the *entitas fluens* that he speaks of seems to have an equivocal being, and we could not acknowledge its reality on the plane of the creature without reducing his freedom to a simple *flatus vocis*. If the Church ultimately has held back from condemning or approving either theory and has merely forbidden those who hold them to treat their opponents as heretics, we can consider then that it is preferable not to claim to clarify such a mystery to any greater extent than St. Augustine or St. Thomas considered possible.

PREFACE The first part of the great eucharistic prayer, concluding with the *Sanctus*. The word must not deceive us. It is not a preliminary that is more or less secondary in relation to the eucharistic celebration proper. Quite the contrary, it is the expression of its fundamental theme: "thanksgiving," i.e., the Church's confession in praise of the *mirabilia Dei* that are the object of her faith, and above all of the saving mystery of the cross. It indeed seems, moreover, that the word preface in this context is connected with the sense of *praefari*, which is not so much "to say before" as "to say in a loud voice," i.e., "to proclaim." *See* EUCHARIST.

PRESBYTERIANISM From the Greek *presbyteros* (elder), from which our word priest (*see* PRIESTHOOD) is also derived. The word is commonly applied to the organization of the Church as conceived by Calvin, insofar as it gives its leadership to assemblies of "elders" who are elected by the laity, and among whom the ministers have only the function of presidents.

The same word is used for such extreme forms of *Gallicanism* (q.v.) as that of Richer, the syndic of the Sorbonne, in the 17th century or that of the Bishop of Pistoia, Scipione Ricci, in the 18th, according to whom all priests in the care of souls are to be considered the successors of the seventy disciples, partaking in the authority of the bishops, themselves the successors of the twelve apostles.

PRESENCE   God's presence everywhere, in the sense that the existence of all things is constantly and entirely dependent upon his will and his power, even though nothing could contain him, underlies the biblical idea that he is "in heaven." (Cf. Stephen's discourse in Acts 7 and especially vv. 48 and 49, quoting Isa. 66,1–2.) This is what theologians call his presence of *immensitas*. On this point see St. Thomas Aquinas, *Sum. Theol.*, Ia, q.8.

Israel already had an idea of a special presence of God among His People, manifested by the luminous radiance of the *Glory* (q.v.). It was revealed on Horeb-Sinai, first to Moses alone (Ex. 3), then in view of the whole people on the mountain (Ex. 19), before descending upon the tabernacle (Ex. 40,34 ff.), and then later dwelling in Solomon's Temple (3 Kings 8,10 ff.). From the rabbis this special presence received the name *Shekinah* (from the verb *shakan*, which means "to dwell under a tent," like that of the tabernacle). For the New Testament writers, this *Shekinah* is now set up in the manhood of Christ. This is the sense of the Transfiguration account in the Synoptics (Matt. 17,1–8 and par.), and v. 14 of the prologue of the fourth Gospel.

But Christ himself, as the Church was convinced from the beginning, is mysteriously but really present among his People every time they come together for the eucharistic celebration. This presence of the risen Christ is centered in the elements of the eucharistic meal, consecrated as his body and blood (cf. particularly 1 Cor. 10,16). Moreover, this sacramental presence of the body and blood of the Saviour supposes two other modes of presence among his People. The first is his permanent presence in those who exercise the function of the *apostolate* (*see* APOSTLE) in the Church: first the apostles, their successors the bishops, and their coworkers the priests, insofar as they were sent to speak and act not only in the name of Christ, but in such a way that the words and acts that he has commissioned them to say and to perform remain his words and his acts. This presence, connected with the apostolate of the Church and upon which the Church is founded, together with the efficacious proclamation of the Gospel, makes possible the properly sacramental presence that brings to us the essential content of this gospel: the whole reality of the mystery of Christ in us, being but one with the One who died and rose again for our salvation. But the sacramental presence of the body and the blood of Christ has no other aim than to be received by the members of the Church assembled so that from then on they will live "in Christ Jesus," as St. Paul says so often, and that they be made the "Body of Christ" through the participation of all in the one bread (cf. again 1 Cor. 10,17). Thus, through the Spirit, it is from now on He himself who lives in us: our own bodies become the temples of the Spirit (cf. 1 Cor. 6,19 and 3,16.17). In this way the eschatological presence that will visibly put "God in us" (1 Cor. 15,28) is prepared for.

The mystery of this presence of Christ in his People, in many closely connected aspects, is therefore inseparable from the fulfillment in them of what St. Paul considers as the preeminent "mystery": the cross of Christ extended in his Resurrection, the outpouring in us of the Spirit, and thus our incorporation into Christ, inseparable from our association with his cross and its life-giving strength (see MYSTERY). This presence of the mystery of the cross in the eucharistic celebration, connected with the personal presence of the Saviour, and, by this celebration, encircling and penetrating the whole life of the Church and that of every Christian, is as it were the heart of the whole sacramental order. As the contemporary exegete Jeremias has shown (even though he is a Protestant), the idea is rooted in the Jewish biblical and liturgical notion of the "memorial," which was never conceived as a simple psychological memory aid, but rather as the means of a presence, attained only by faith, but no less real despite that, of the divine event that it "represents," in the strongest sense of the word. It is in this way that baptism, according to a text of St. Paul, grafts us on to the "likeness" of the death of Christ (cf. Rom. 6,5), so that we are made capable of communicating in the reality itself of his body and blood in the Eucharist, and of proclaiming the Lord's death until he comes (1 Cor. 11,26) not only in words but in act.

It can be said of the mystical experience that it is only the experience of this presence in us of Christ and his mystery, realized in a faith that has taken possession of our whole being through charity (see MYSTICISM). St. Thomas explains this special presence in the righteous as being the presence of the object of knowledge and love in the knower and the lover, through this knowledge and this love shared by those by whom He knows and loves himself. See Sum. Theol., Ia, q.43, a.3.

This is one of the problems that contemporary theology, in particular the school inspired by the Benedictine Dom Odo Casel in Germany, has most meditated: namely, that of the sacramental presence of Christ and of his mystery in the Church through the sacraments. The explanation of *sacramentum et res* in the article SACRAMENT deals with the most traditional theological notions, particularly the views of St. Thomas with regard to the solution of this problem. On the problem of the presence of the body and blood of Christ under the eucharistic species, *see* TRANSUBSTANTIATION.

PRESENTATION IN THE TEMPLE This title is given to two feasts of the liturgical year: that of the second of February which celebrates, together with the *purification* (q.v.) of Mary, the presentation of Jesus, and that of the twenty-first of November, which celebrates Mary's own presentation in the Temple. The first of these feasts commemorates the event related in Luke 2,22 ff.; it looks upon this event as the first sign of the "encounter" (whence the Greek name *Hypapante* that is also given to the feast and that has this meaning) of God with his People in the Mediator. The feast of November 21 has its origin in accounts belonging only to the apocryphal gospels, but the Church has simply retained their symbolic overlay expressing the idea that Mary was herself the first Temple of the Word Incarnate, just as all are also called to become.

PRETERNATURAL That which is beyond nature. The word is used to designate the gratuitous gifts, but not supernatural in the strict sense, that God originally accorded to man and that he lost through sin, like the domination of reason over concupiscence and exemption from sickness and death. See St. Thomas Aquinas, *Sum. Theol.*, Ia q.94 ff.

PRIESTHOOD The function or character of the priest. We cannot analyze the notions of priesthood that are proper to Christian revelation without unraveling a fairly complicated question of vocabulary. Judaism had its priests, the descendents of Aaron. The Greek term for priest was *iereus*, to which the Latin *sacerdos* corresponds. The high-priest (*archiereus*) was their leader. But with him and the representatives of the great priestly families in the Sanhedrin there also sat the *presbyteroi* (literally, "elders") representing the layfolk, as was the case of the leading body in every synagogue. New Testament usage reserves the title priest (*iereus*, or rather *archiereus*) to Christ, specifying that he is not a priest according to the order of Aaron, but according to that of Melchizedek, i.e., a priest who has received his orders directly from God (cf. Heb. 5,5 ff.). This is the central teaching of the Epistle to the Hebrews. Nevertheless through the association of the People of God with Christ in His body which is the Church, the writers of the New Testament say that the whole People of God has become an effectively priestly people, in a much more profound sense than that which had been claimed for the Jewish people (cf. 1 Pet. 2,9, quoting Ex. 19,6; see also Apoc. 1,6; 5,10; 20,6). As for Christ's ministers within the Church, this title is never used in their regard in a special way, although St. Paul does describe their ministry in formulas that are most specifically priestly (cf. Rom. 15,16).

At the same time, the ministers who were in authority over the Churches founded by the apostles (in the following generation some would be set apart from the others as bishops, who were looked upon as their successors in the pastoral function exercised in its fullness) received the title of *presbyteroi*. This has passed into English, the other Germanic languages, and French as well as the word "priest" or its equivalent.

However, as early as the (first) Epistle of St. Clement of Rome, we see the word *iereus* always being used of the whole body of the faithful, while the term *archiereus*, or preeminent *iereus*, refers to the president of the eucharistic assembly, namely, the bishop or the "presbyter" acting in his stead, who has the role of representing the Head of the Church, Christ (chap. 40). This usage quickly became universal. All of patristic literature considers *iereus* (or better *archiereus*), translated into Latin by *sacerdos*, to be a title proper to the liturgical-episcopal function of presiding over the Eucharist. Furthermore, the title is given to the *presbyteroi* only insofar as they themselves can preside over the Eucharist in the bishop's stead, when he is absent or prevented from doing so. With the proliferation of local parishes, what had been the exception practically became the rule. At this time the term *iereus* or *sacerdos* came to be habitually used not only of the bishops but also of the *presbyteroi*, although pains were frequently taken to specify that they are only *iereis* or *sacerdotes* of second rank. Consequently, in current usage, the terms *iereus* and *sacerdos* became equivalents, as it were, of *presbyteros* (latinized, *presbyter*), resulting in the directly priestly sense that our word "priest" has come to assume.

From this brief examination of the evolution of word usage, it seems that the traditional view of the Christian priesthood emerges naturally. In the full sense of the word, there is but one priest for Christians, and that is Christ considered above all in his saving passion. But with his priestly character and function, i.e., the fulfilling of the properly sacred functions, all the members of his Mystical Body are associated. And so in this way the layfolk, i.e., the members of God's People, every one of them, are all priests in Christ. The Fathers tell us that this is made clear in the eucharistic celebration by the fact that they pray a prayer that is integrated with the properly liturgical prayer, that they offer, and that they take Communion. From this stems the priestly aspect of the whole life. The Jews already had some idea of this, but it is enhanced for the

Christian in that everything he does "in Christ" consecrates the reality to God. Nevertheless, like the spread of the Church and the maintaining of her union with Christ, this is realized only through the apostolic ministry (*see* APOSTLE). Insofar as this ministry is exercised in bringing together the eucharistic assembly, its presidency, and the eucharistic consecration worked in the name of Christ the sovereign priest, the ministerial function of the bishops and of the priests (*presbyteroi*) as their co-workers is therefore a priestly ministry (or, if this expression is preferred, a ministerial priesthood). The object of this essentially sacramental ministry (*see* SACRAMENT) is precisely to extend in unity the sanctifying power of the one priesthood that remains Christ's own to all the members of his Body. *See also* APOSTLE, and BISHOP.

PROBABILITY, PROBABILISM, PROBABILIORISM, EQUI-PROBABILISM

The quality of a proposition which can reasonably be accepted as true without conclusive demonstration. In the area of morality the question is whether one can act according to a merely probable opinion with certainty of conscience. Moralists agree that one cannot transgress the law, where it is certain, on a simple probability of fact. For example, if I see something move in a thicket and my judgment is that it is probably an animal rather than a man, I still cannot fire at the risk of committing murder. This is what is meant by saying that we cannot act with certainty of conscience on a simple probability of fact when the law is certain. On the other hand, the moralists whom we call probabilists will say that one can act in good conscience once it is seriously probable that the law permits it (this is what is called probabilism of law, which is founded on the juridical adage that a doubtful law no longer obliges; the whole question is whether a simple probability against the law suffices to make it doubtful). The probabiliorists, on the contrary, say that the law must remain obligatory if it is not more probable that it does not oblige, rather than the contrary. The equiprobabilists require at the very least an equal probability in favor of the two opinions for the law to become doubtful and for one then to be able to dispense oneself from it. Each of these three notions is freely held in the Church; she has condemned only the tutiorist theory which held that one should always follow the law, even though doubtful (cf. D.B. 1293). In practice, however, every confessor, whatever his personal opinion on the matter, must leave the penitents free to make use of a reasonable probabilism in their own conduct.

PROFESSION OF FAITH

A public act by which one makes the faith of the Church one's own, such as that which a person who is to be baptized is called upon to make. Episcopal consecration has always carried with it a new profession of faith, that is still more solemn and more detailed, representing the obligation that the bishop-elect has of being now not only a believer but a teacher in the faith. A simple renewal of the baptismal profession of faith was also introduced later in the liturgy of priestly ordination for priests of second rank. *See also* SYMBOL OF FAITH.

PROGRESS   The idea that the history of the world in general and of mankind in particular is inscribed in a line of ascending progress is certainly not only reconcilable with the data of revelation but in complete accord with it, as has already been explained in the article EVOLUTION. We must even add that it is through Christianity that this idea was introduced into human thought, since the ancient Greeks tended rather to look at the history of the world as a gradual downhill process. However, according to the biblical schema of the Fall and the Redemption, progress does not follow a continuous line, but rather supposes highs and lows. Moreover, it is not the simple product in some automatic way of some impulse that is immanent in the course of history, but supposes the divine redemptive intervention. Finally, without denying either the reality or the value of modern mankind's technical progress, a possible ambiguity in its moral and spiritual effect must certainly be recognized from a Christian point of view. More generally, it seems that the general view of history, which is that of the Bible and of the whole of Christian tradition, is that of a correlative development of the forces of evil and the forces of good until the final judgment of God that alone will assure the definitive triumph of good over evil in separating them (cf. the parable of the weeds, Matt. 13,24–30 and par.).

As regards the life of an individual, the Church Fathers, following St. Paul (cf. Phil. 3,12 ff.) described the normal Christian life as a progression, although it can alway entail relapses. Following Evagrius Ponticus in particular and the Pseudo-Dionysius, three chief phases are singled out. In the first (*via purgativa*), the soul chiefly unburdens itself of sin and its traces; in the second (*via illuminativa*) it deepens within itself in a more positive way the divine teachings with which it becomes more and more in accord; finally in the third stage it reaches, or at the very least approaches, a firm union with God (*via unitiva*).

PROPERTY   Roman jurists defined property as a right to use and to abuse what one possesses. Christian theologians allow and even justify some private property as the material basis for personal freedom and family stability, but they endeavor to define its limits in line with the requirements of justice and charity. St. Thomas Aquinas does not hesitate to say that the goods that some men possess in superabundance should be used, by natural law, for the feeding of the poor.

PROPHET AND PROPHECY

The word prophet does not seem to come from *phaino* and to mean "he who shows in advance," as many of the ancients and medieval writers believed, but rather from *phemi*, therefore meaning "he who speaks for" another. The Greeks, in fact, used the word to speak of the oracles themselves that gave advice rather than making predictions. In Israel, the prophet is simply one who speaks in the name of God, whether to express His demands or His promises (*see* WORD OF GOD). Contrary to 19th-century exegesis that, under the influence of Protestant a priori arguments, systematically opposed the prophets to the priests, it is generally admitted today that prophecy in Israel is of priestly origin. The first prophets seem to have belonged to communities that served the sanctuaries and the most ancient prophecies to have been the *toroth*, i.e., oracles given on the occasion of the offering of sacrifices connected with celebrations. Furthermore, even among the later prophets, many belonged to the priestly caste, like Jeremiah or Ezechiel; in any case, their prophecies remained clearly connected with worship, as the account of the calling of Isaiah so well shows (chap. 6). The common object of all the prophecies in Israel is God's design for his People. It is to this extent that the prophets are turned toward the future and that their prophecies always contain an element of prediction. But it is less a question of predicting particular events than of giving a positive direction to the people's advance toward the fulfillment of the divine plan in which it would come to full flower; this advance would be ruined were it to yield to the temptation to go against that plan. Moreover, the continuity in the prophecies of the most diverse prophets and the general conformity of the history in which they are inscribed to the global vision that emerges from their oracles, as Jewish and Christian theologians have always pointed out, constitute one of the most striking signs of the supernatural authenticity of their inspiration. This was already underlined by Ezechiel, in contradistinction to the lying oracles of the false prophets (cf. chap. 13).

In the New Testament, John the Baptist appears as the last and foremost prophet, because he proclaims as immediate the ultimate realization of God's plan that is to be accomplished in the Messiah whom he will acclaim (cf. Luke 1 and 3, with par. to the latter chapter in Matt. and Mark). Jesus himself, moreover, seems also to have been acknowledged as the preeminent prophet in the sense that all the preparatory prophetical statements find their conclusion and their definitive accomplishment in him (cf. Acts 3,22 and 7,37 as examples of primitive preaching, using with regard to Jesus the words of Deut. 18,15 on the prophet promised by Moses). This explains why prophecy seems to have ceased after the Christian Apocalypse. It will be replaced by the apostolic teaching, which is limited to spreading and deepening the teaching of Jesus. On the prophetic charism, see St. Thomas Aquinas, *Sum. Theol.*, IIa-IIae, qq.171–174.

PROTESTANTS The name Protestant was given to the disciples of the Reformers who entered into conflict with the Church in the 16th century because of the *protest* made by the princes, and the cities that followed them, on April 19, 1529, at the Diet of Speyer, against the will manifested by the Emperor to repeal the concessions that had previously been granted. Except for this purely historical definition, it is not easy to give a formula that clearly expresses the essence of Protestantism. We have only to cite two equally representative contemporary Protestant theologians. According to Karl Barth, Protestantism would be defined by unflinching faithfulness to the biblical Word of God; yet for Paul Tillich, the Protestant principle would be the refusal of any necessary intermediary between God and the believer, which would explicitly include the rejection of any authority attributed not only to the Church but to the Bible or the historical Christ as well. In fact, the more Protestantism develops, the more it appears that it rests on a complex of antagonistic principles. Although it came out of a reforming movement within the Catholic Church—one that in the beginning, in its intent at least, wished only to restore the Church by bringing her back to her own sources—Protestantism did in fact come to stand in opposition to the Church out of motives that did not keep essentially to this plan, indeed that roundly contradicted it. Melanchthon, who attempted the first systematization of Luther's work, said that there was, at the starting point of the Reformation, a formal principle (the sovereign authority of the Holy Scriptures) and a material principle (justification by faith in the sole grace of God). Both of these principles can be perfectly understood in an orthodox fashion, and in fact they have been asserted in every age by theologians who were most representative of the Catholic tradition. However, when Protestants began to draw from these principles consequences manifestly opposed to Holy Scripture itself and to the whole of tradition, a reaction set in within the Catholic Church to add complementary explanations of these assertions, which could be looked upon as correctives. The more or less absolute contradistinction made between Word of God and Church, and in particular between Word of God and Tradition, naturally provoked a re-enforcement of the theory and the practice of the authority of the Church, not in opposition to the authority of Scripture, but in order to prevent its true sense from being distorted. By the same token, the assertion of justification by faith in terms that come down to denying the importance of good works as a necessary consequence of a salutary faith, brought about within the Church a defense of good works. And the assertion of the sovereignty of grace in the work of our salvation, understood as if it made any effort on our part—indeed, any transformation worked in us by grace itself—useless or vain, produced as a reaction among Catholics a spirited reassertion of human freedom, preserved and encouraged to act rightly and not eliminated by salutary grace.

Moreover, in Protestantism itself there soon developed multiplying internal divisions, even to the point of rejecting the principles that had been set down in the beginning. Or else—which is perhaps still more serious—a metamorphosis of these principles ended up by giving them a sense both totally heretical with regard to traditional Catholic faith and hardly less opposed to what the first Reformers believed and intended, even though they themselves, without realizing it, had laid the groundwork for these consequences of their thought or actions that would have horrified them. As a result a free enquiry, which no longer recognizes any objective criterion, rejects every notion of a revelation of which the Bible would be the written evidence; while a more than Pelagian optimism about man's nature gets rid, first in practice and then in theory, of any idea of a supernatural grace that man would need to be saved.

How could it happen that deeply orthodox religious principles could first be turned against the Church and her tradition, and then, very soon, turned round against themselves as well? We ask ourselves this same question that Protestantism constantly asks of Protestants who are willing to see things as they are and to reflect on them. It seems that the historical answer must be not that the Reformation was too daring, but rather that it lacked lucidity. In recognizing the inadequacy of certain practices and certain forms of thought that were present in the Church of the time, Protestantism was unable to criticize them profoundly enough to arrive at the true root of the evil, while at the same time preventing the tree that it had wanted to cure from being uprooted. Medieval Christianity, when the Reformation set in, not only suffered from real corruptions that provided the occasion for the Reformation, but also from a profound intellectual decadence poorly disguised within the brilliance of dialectical virtuosity, and counterbalanced, but not corrected, by a fervor that slipped more and more into an irrational sentimentality. The result was a profoundly divided spiritual world, where the individual simply set himself against the Church or any organized society; where the Church herself, as she was, seemed cut off from her historical bases, and the world seemed separated from God. The Reformers were but slightly, if at all, aware of this disintegration, of which they were the first victims. With their frequently negative interpretation and elaboration of their own principles—which in another intellectual or spiritual atmosphere might have proven most fruitful— they evoked from the disintegration its final consequences instead of the remedy they sought.

The value of these principles, however, remains such that spiritual reawakenings in Protestantism constantly renewed its most positive aspects by opposing this disintegrating process the Reformers themselves had begun to cause. But such revivals either deteriorated into a pietistic sentimentalism opposed to all intellectuality, which in turn merely caused reactions of a negative intellectualism, or else, more or less consciously, the revivals returned to a Catholic tradition partially detached from its deformations or caricatures. The result is the more and more evident tension in Protestantism between a literalistic fundamentalism, clinging desperately, and most often vainly, to conservative formulas that serve as a support for a sincere but narrow piety, and a rationalism or liberalism that is incapable of retaining anything of the faith of the Gospels, beginning with the principles that cause it to justify the rejection of Catholic tradition. Between these two, particularly in the best of the ecumenical movement, there is emerging a desire that painfully ploughs its way toward a reinterpretation of the most substantial Protestant principles, in a sense that would no longer be basically anti-Catholic. Thus, however paradoxical it may seem at first sight, the best of Protestant inspiration seems to have no chance of arriving at any other conclusion than a reintegration within the Church it had once abandoned. So that this process might succeed, it is to be hoped that a Catholic *ecumenism* (q.v.), truly informed and solidly doctrinal, will facilitate the analysis of the positive elements in the Reformation movement by separating them from the purely negative and decadent elements that are the legacy of the Middle Ages, and then furnish proof through the facts that these positive elements can have within the Church the full flowering that they have never found outside her.

PROVIDENCE   Divine Providence is distinguished from simple *foreknowledge* (q.v.) by the fact that it adds to it the divine will; without its decision and efficaciousness nothing would be produced, since all existence, by the fact of *creation* (q.v.), is dependent on the existence of God, and more precisely on his will. The problem of *predestination* (q.v.) is itself only a particularly illuminating consequence in relation to God's elect of this providence that infallibly governs the course of all things. That providence, understood in this way, is one of the most fundamental truths in the biblical view of things, is what the prophets constantly proclaim (cf. particularly the contradistinction made between God and idols in the second part of the book of Isaiah), and what the Wisdom books come to explain in a manner that can be called classic.

The divine Wisdom, as defined for example in Proverbs 8 and the parallel texts of the other Wisdom literature, is precisely the plan, contained in God from all eternity, with regard to the "becoming" of creation, which plan will be infallibly realized by the sole power of His will.

Under these circumstances, it is evident that the twofold problem raised by providence is that of evil and the freedom of creatures. The only biblical solution is that which brings the two problems together to the point of making them one. The mere capacity for evil results from the limit introduced into every created being by the very fact of its creation. This capacity becomes a reality by the fact that created freedom exists only through being able to oppose itself or not to the divine will. But, since the magnitude of the Creator is never better asserted than when he reveals himself as the Creator creating freedom, his sovereignty is asserted by the fact that the freedoms which he created, however real they may be, would ultimately be incapable of standing in the way of his plan of love. He has foreseen and made all things to serve him under any circumstances, whether they oppose his will insofar as he has made it known to them, or comply with it. Consenting willingly to his plan brings them beatitude, while being opposed to it, if their opposition becomes unyielding, ends up in their damnation; this merely supplies the occasion for the full realization of this same plan with regard to the elect, by respecting to the end these freedoms that are immersed in their own perversity in spite of God. Thus theologians will be led to distinguish between what God permits in view of a greater good and what he wills positively, as that good itself. Here again, to allay certain misunderstandings that are merely the products of an erroneous fancy, it is well to repeat what was said about foreknowledge and which is eminently applicable to the case of predestination. The use in all of these words of prefixes like *pre-* or *fore-* does not indicate an anteriority in the temporal sphere, from which one could draw the conclusion of a simple determinism in the interior of the world, effectively reducing creative freedoms to naught. Since God is not in time, nor properly speaking anterior to time (which would be a contradiction in terms), but transcendent to time, even though his action is immanent in the becoming of the temporal creature, the anteriority that these prefixes obviously claim for Him must be understood in the sense that he is the transcendent source of the created being, a source, strictly speaking, that is perpetually contemporary to this being. In that way, far from suppressing freedom in any way, the foreknowing and provident God is the very source of freedom. See St. Thomas Aquinas, *Sum. Theol.*, Ia, q.22 ff. and q.103 ff.

PRUDENCE   Defined by Aristotle as the virtue of practical reason directing human actions in accordance with truth, prudence (in Greek, *phronesis*) is considered as one of the four cardinal *virtues* (q.v.). St. Thomas shows how the supernaturally infused virtue of prudence regulates our actions within the context of the supremacy of charity over our whole life. The gift of counsel (*see* GIFTS OF THE HOLY SPIRIT) perfects its work by creating in us a special docility toward the influences of the divine Spirit. See St. Thomas Aquinas, *Sum. Theol.*, IIa-IIae, q.47 to 56.

PSALMS   The Psalms and other hymns of the Old Testament, by the very fact that the Church uses them as one of the most essential elements of her prayer, acutely pose some of the major problems in the interpretation of the Old Testament in the light of the New, and more especially the problem of ascertaining in what sense the New Testament fulfills the Old Testament without abolishing it. Many of the circumstances to which the prayer of the Psalms refers could tend to make us think that this prayer is outmoded for Christians: e.g., its constant concern for Jerusalem or for the Israelite king, or again for Temple ritual, and more clearly still some of the sentiments expressed, like the desire for conclusive vengeance on the oppressors of the People of God, or of a salvation that is not merely spiritual, but merged, as it were, into the life of the present. But such conclusion could be reached only by confining ourselves to a narrowly literalistic exegesis to which the Church has always been opposed; in this, she does no more than follow the constant tradition of the synagogue, and before it, the use made in the Old Testament itself of the most ancient expressions to designate the newest realities. Indeed, two points are capital if we are to retain from Holy Scripture that understanding, which is and always was the Church's, of this People of God to whom His Word has always spoken as a living word.

The first point is that it is the same God who speaks to us, announcing the same plan, from the first page of the Bible to the last. The second is that revelation is progressive in the sense that the whole extent of this plan, as well as the concrete details of its realization, are revealed only progressively. This progress—that of a sound pedagogy—is both a progress in revelation (but only under the two aspects just recalled, otherwise it would no longer be a question of the same revelation, but of successive and conflicting revelations) and a progress in those to whom it is destined, since revelation itself encourages their progress and is unfolded accordingly. Consequently, the continuous use of the inspired prayers is explained by the continuity of the same basic plan and the need for never losing this plan from view, otherwise the actual progress made, or the correlative analysis of its meaning, would remain up in the air, as it were, and would become incomprehensible.

Moreover, we shall have in turn to recognize the necessity of transposing, on account of the final revelations (or rather of the ultimate Revelation in Christ), many concrete details that date from its first expression. In this way, Jerusalem appears as the type of the Church, the King as that of the Messiah, and the Temple sacrifices as that of the cross. But also, the struggle with the forces of evil for that final and conclusive victory of God's power, which brings salvation, and a total salvation to his People in the eschatological event of the Resurrection, inspires the transposition of the expressions which at first did not grasp the meaning of this combat, except as an earthly battle, even though its supra-terrestrial undercurrent could already be seen. In this way, the expectation of final beatitude will see some of the early expressions of a hoped for salvation only as imperfect and temporary images.

We would give in to a false spiritualism were we to reject these traces of past stages in revelation. Truths as basic as the conflict between the kingdom of Satan and the Kingdom of God, or the incarnation of the final blessedness of the elect within a completely regenerated cosmos would simply vanish into thin air if we were to do away with the continuous links that connect the full flowering of a deeply historical revelation with its primary roots. On the contrary, if we retain these links, we can avoid all artificiality, provided we understand that the evangelical revelation did not simply succeed to this preparatory revelation, but actually arose out of it: it is out of the patriotism of Jerusalem that the notion of the Church could be born; out of the theorizing on royalty or the Temple that all Christology and the whole theology of the Redemption could be formulated; and out of the wars of Judah that emerged the essential truth of the *spiritual combat* (q.v.). Above all, the most eschatological hopes are rooted in the concrete hope of the Hebrews; this fact alone can keep the former from completely evaporating into some sort of disembodied abstraction.

PSYCHOLOGY   Literally, the science of the soul. Together with scientific psychology, which endeavors to arrive at a positive and precise study of the functioning of the human soul in its present state, we must recognize the place of a properly philosophical psychology, which analyzes the metaphysical status of the soul in relation to God and to the world of bodies, and very particularly to that body which is its own. It is generally called rational psychology. A theological psychology must extend this analysis in accordance with the perspectives open to man by his supernatural destiny as it results from the Word of God. This is the task to which are dedicated all of the treatises *De Anima*, which are so numerous throughout Christian tradition. We must emphasize the possibility of renewal offered them by the development of the so-called depth psychologies, which reemphasize the inexhaustible richness of the life of the soul and our inability to reduce it to what it is not, or separate it from the whole cosmos.

PUNISHMENT For St. Thomas, since every sin is essentially a disorder, punishment is what reestablishes that violated order. Punishment for sin is threefold: 1) remorse is the punishment that man, as a rational being, inflicts on himself by the fact that he departed from reason; 2) human law will inflict upon him a punishment that corresponds to the social order which he violated; 3) finally, the divine law reserved for him a punishment that corresponds to the violation of the universal order. The chief question about punishment that St. Thomas asks is whether punishment can remain due after the fault itself has been taken away. His answer is that punishment is diminished by this fact but not abolished, at least under the form of making a reparatory satisfaction. Hence the distinction between *eternal punishment* due to grave sin and remitted by absolution, and *temporal punishment* that penance, in its subjective and personal aspect, must acquit. On all of this see *Sum. Theol.*, Ia-IIae, q.87, especially articles 1 and 6.

In all modern moral systems, as well as in the development of law, a tendency has arisen to allow only a medicinal punishment. It does not seem deniable, actually, that a major object of punishment must be the moral rehabilitation of the guilty person. But there still remains the question of whether such rehabilitation can have any meaning outside of an objective moral order and its necessary reparation by the man who has violated it.

PURGATORY While admitting that there are only for each of us two ultimate destinies, in themselves irrevocable and fixed from the moment we leave our earthly lives (and in accordance with those lives), Christian antiquity was in agreement in thinking that those who end their existence on earth in a state of grace, but without being entirely purified by penance from the traces of their sin, have still to rid themselves of these vestiges through a supreme test before they can attain beatitude. This is what many ancient writers felt was the meaning of the possibility of being saved "only as through fire" of which St. Paul speaks (1 Cor. 3,15). Since the thought of the East on this subject (although they too prayed for the dead) seemed to the West to be less precise than their own, they were asked (and this was obtained without great difficulty) to subscribe to clear declarations on this point such as those found in the profession of faith of Michael Palaeologus at the Council of Lyons in 1274 (D.B. 464), or in the decree of the Union of Florence in 1445 (D.B. 693). The doctrine was reiterated against

Protestant denials at the Council of Trent (Session XXV, D.B. 983), but without being made any more specific. The notion proposed by St. Catherine of Genoa, who thought that the fire of purgatory was nothing else than God's love, burning us to the extent that it had not yet succeeded (and so that it might succeed) in enflaming us, has consequently nothing heterodox about it. See the supplement to the *Summa Theologica*, qq.70 ff., as well as the appendix of the Padua edition.

PURIFICATION   The action of making clean what is no longer clean. Two traditional uses of this term pose a problem. The first is the purification of Mary, treated in the article *Presentation in the Temple* (q.v.; cf. Luke 2,22). The second is the use of the word in the liturgy for the ablutions of the sacred vessels after they have been used in the Eucharist (*see* ABLUTION), so that nothing of the sacred species remains. In both cases there could be no question of any uncleanness, either in the birth of the Saviour or in the remains of the eucharistic presence. But, also in both cases, we find the imprint, as it were, of this very profound Jewish idea that since man is unworthy of any contact with the divine, there is for him the presumption of uncleanness each time such contact takes place. This is why the woman's contact in childbirth with the creative power of God, and even, for example, the contact of the reader with the sacred books, were thought to make them unclean. With this meaning, the rabbis will speak of a book as soiling the hands when they wish to assert that they are speaking of an inspired book. Beneath this apparent paradox, we must perceive the certitude that nothing created is unclean, but that it is always by a more or less formal sacrilege that creatures become so.

PURITANISM   The name given to the belief of the Congregationalists, or Independents, of whom Cromwell was the champion, because of their claim to enforce a rigid moral discipline. The name was also applied to the partisans of the same religious ideas in New England.

Q

QUIETISM   A doctrine or tendency according to which, in the highest mystical states, the soul would have merely to abandon itself quite passively to repose (*quies*) in God. The accusation of quietism was leveled by turns against many people engaged in following the spiritual life, such as the medieval Byzantine Hesychasts, or in more recent times in the West against Molinos, Malaval, and especially Madame Guyon and Fénelon in the 17th century. Fénelon's *Maxims of the Saints* was condemned for various formulas that lent themselves to this interpretation. However, it is at least questionable whether these interpretations actually corresponded to the real intentions of the author.

R

RACISM   The name given to a doctrine that exalts one human race above the others to the point of attributing to it exclusively all real rights. Racism is generally connected with anti-Semitism, transferring the idea of the Chosen People to peoples other than the Jews, and grossly materializing it. It was condemned in the Encyclical *Mit Brennender Sorge* of Pope Pius XI.

RATIONALISM   This name is given to every doctrine that exaggerates the powers of human reason either by claiming to exclude any possibility of revelation or by minimizing its possible import. The First Vatican Council underlined the fact that, although revelation could not contradict any authentically rational statement, it does uncover for us truths that surpass the reaches of reason; while reason itself, on the condition that it allow itself to be illumined by faith, can contribute to some extent toward clarifying these truths (Session III, Constitution *De Fide Catholica*, chap. 4, espec., D.B. 1796 ff.). The need for these definitions made itself felt not only because of rationalist attacks against the faith of the Church that came from the outside, but also from the fact of erroneous doctrines held on this point by Catholics themselves (commonly called semi-Rationalists). Among these doctrines we should first mention that of Georg Hermes (1775–1831), who claimed to demonstrate the authenticity of revelation in such a way that the light of faith played no part in our adhesion to it. He went so far as to say that every Christian who had arrived at an adult stage in his intellectual development should suspend, as it were, the exercise of his faith in order to give revelation an adhesion that would be purely rational. In exactly the opposite direction, Anton Günther (1783–1863), who strenuously opposed Hermes on this point, was equally censured for having held that once the faith of the Church was accepted, it became possible to demonstrate its articles in a purely dialectical fashion. See the condemnation of the first by Gregory XVI in 1835, D.B. 1618–1621, renewed by Pius IX in 1846, D.B. 1634 ff., and of the second, also by Pius IX in 1857, D.B. 1655 ff.

REALISM   A doctrine according to which truth is in things before being in the intelligence, in such a way that knowledge is an *adaequatio rei et intellectus*, in the sense that the intelligence adapts itself to the object rather than the contrary. Platonism presents an extreme form of realism by supposing that the ideas of our mind have an objective existence that is completely independent of the mind, and which is the basis of all of our judgments. The doctrine of Aristotle, at least in the way in which St. Thomas Aquinas understood it, is more delicately shaded. It admits that ideas have no existence outside of our mind, but that the concepts that the mind forms of things are there in potency, in such a way that they permit us to arrive at a genuine intelligibility of the real.

REASON   Human reason is properly the intelligence considered in its discursive faculty, in contradistinction to the intellect, which is the intelligence as the power of intuition. The Thomistic notion of the human intelligence, as the intelligence of an essentially corporeal being, looks upon reason as applied to sensory data as the source of our natural knowledge. It allows of a certain obfuscation of this faculty as a consequence of original sin, not in itself, but because of the defective inclination of the will. It follows then that reason will meet with some difficulty in its functioning and doubly so when it is applied to the problems that concern our last *end* (q.v.). This has led the Church, particularly as a reaction against the excesses of modern *Rationalism*, to underline the weakness of the use of reason in the concrete condition of fallen man (*see* PHILOSOPHY, RATIONALISM, SIN). But, following St. Paul (cf. Rom. 1,18 ff.), the Church has no less strenuously maintained the capacity that human reason still has, in reflecting on the data of experience, to arrive at a belief in a creating God, as well as at a discernment of the basic moral obligations that are imposed on every man. (See in particular the statements of the First Vatican Council at the beginning of its chapter on revelation, Session III, Decree *De Fide Catholica*; D.B. 1785.) Again, the Church teaches that reason can demonstrate the fundamentals of faith and, enlightened by faith, it can arrive at some fruitful understanding of its mysteries, although they always exceed the created intelligence (*ibid.*, 1796–1800, as well as the canons that follow, 1806 ff.). These declarations and definitions of the First Vatican Council are in consistent line with tradition, which has always opposed any unwarranted depreciation of human reason, such as is found in Tertullian or at the time of the Reformation in Luther. To be otherwise would be to be unfaithful to Scripture itself, which, particularly in the Wisdom writings, has embodied within revelation the most sound products of human intelligence, rectifying them but also confirming them by this very fact. It would also be to run counter to the statement in the prologue of St. John that the Word of God made flesh is the *Logos* (q.v.) who enlightens every man (John 1,9). On all of this, see St. Thomas, *Sum. Theol.*, Ia, qq.1 and 12, as well as the whole beginning of the *Contra Gentiles*.

RECONCILIATION   *See* ABSOLUTION, PENANCE, and REDEMPTION

REDEMPTION   From the Latin *redimere*, this word signifies the buying back, or ransom, of a slave in order to assure his freedom. The biblical use of this expression to designate the saving action of God with regard to his People has made it the term par excellence for expressing the meaning of the cross of Christ.

God has appeared as the Redeemer of his People above all when he delivered them from bondage in Egypt, which is commemorated at Passover (*see* PASCH and SLAVERY). The use of this ransom image in regard to the cross will be made in reference with Jesus' own use, referring to himself, of the great text of Isa. 53, on the innocent servant suffering for the sinful people. The term *ransom* was not found in the text of the prophet (who speaks only of a sacrifice for sin, in Hebrew *asham*, in v.10). But the most expressive allusion by Christ to this text (cf. Matt. 20,28 and Mark 10,45) sums it up by expressly introducing the idea (in Greek, *lytron*). The result will be the union—a consistent one in Christian theology—of the two ideas of sacrifice and redemption, or ransom, to the extent that the tendency will be purely and simply to identify them.

However, it is noteworthy that the writers of the New Testament do not dwell on the idea of ransom in itself to explain the cross, but rather much more on the deliverance from bondage that is its result, with its concomitant reconciliation of the freed slaves with God, slaves who by this fact are adopted by him as his sons, in the Son who has ransomed them. The slavery from which we are ransomed by Christ is that of sin (cf. Rom. 6,18 and 8,2), death (Rom. 8,21; 2 Cor. 1,10), the power of darkness (Col. 1,23), the curse of the law (Gal. 3,13 and 4,5), and the wrath to come (1 Thess. 1,10). It will be noticed how St. Paul in these various texts uses both the technical term for redemption as well as the more general terms of purchase (*agorazein* or *exagorazein*), liberation (*eleutheroun*), deliverance (*ryesthai*), or just simply salvation (*sozein*). Behind all of this, the New Testament, like the Old Testament when it calls God redeemer, places more emphasis on a victorious struggle against the powers that have held us captive, than on the payment properly so-called of our ransom. (Cf. both a characteristic text of the Synoptics like the parable of the strong man and the stronger man who takes possession of his arms—cf. especially Luke 11,14–23—and the description of the cross as a triumph over the "powers" in Col. 1,13–14 and 2,15.) The consideration of ransom does not intervene directly, as we see quite well from the capital texts of the Synoptics that introduce it in order to expound on Isa. 53, except to underline the burdensome character of our salvation for the Saviour himself. New Testament emphasis, strictly speaking, is on the divine generosity that was manifested in the cross of Christ. This is what is said in a particularly revealing text of St. Paul that shows us the cross of Christ as the foremost manifestation of God's love, overturning all obstacles that have separated us from Him (Rom. 5,6–8). In the same sense, we must cite the other great text of John 3,16 on God's love for the world; it was so great that he gave his only Son to save those in the world who would believe in him. Let us note at this juncture that the notion of redemption as such is never directly formulated in the Johannine writings, but simply, in the Apocalypse, the idea that Jesus has purchased us by his blood (5,9 and 14,3 and 4).

The result is that we cannot understand redemption by the cross if we isolate it from its positive counterpart in the reconciliation with God. Again, if we wish to remain faithful to the teaching of the New Testament, we must in no way represent this reconciliation as simply posterior to the redemption properly so-called. In the view of St. Paul, it is quite the contrary, as he says emphatically in the Second Epistle to the Corinthians, because "God was in Christ, reconciling the world with Himself" (2 Cor. 5,19), by the blood of his cross, and he has delivered us from the slavery of sin and death. In other words, the love of God has not to be regained by man at the end of his deliverance: on the contrary, it is because this love has never been lacking to Him that God takes it upon Himself to deliver man, in His Son, in order to reconcile him with Himself, a reconciliation that furthermore cannot be separated from man's reconciliation with his fellows (cf. Col. 1,20 and 22, with Eph. 2,11–18).

Protestant historians, and Harnack in particular, have at times maintained that the Greek Fathers, following St. Irenaeus and St. Athanasius, tended to substitute for this biblical and especially Pauline doctrine of redemption through the cross the idea of a physical redemption, flowing solely from the Incarnation of the Word, on the basis of a Platonist notion on the unity of human nature, totally assumed and immortalized in Christ. This contradistinction is an idle dream, made up of a series of misconceptions.

In the first place, the solidarity between Christ and ourselves, through the common nature that we share, is very certainly, with these authors, a simple explicitation of what is assumed by the biblical writers: Christ saves *us* by what *he* did, only in virtue of the union between him and us resulting from the Incarnation (cf. Gal. 4,4). This solidarity was implied in the simple idea of the "Son of man who had come . . . to give his life as ransom," for it was already contained in the two biblical notions of the *"Son of man"* and of the *"Servant"* (qq.v.), which this idea combines. In the second place, the fact that Christ saves us from the moment that he assumes our nature did not mean, either for Irenaeus or for Athanasius or any other Father, that this would make his death useless, for they themselves emphasize that our nature is thereby saved, insofar as it has been assumed in Christ with everything this nature means for us, including death (or the *phthora*, i.e., the corruption that is death's principle, as they repeat, borrowing the expression from St. Paul: cf. Rom. 8,21; 1 Cor. 15,42; etc.). Finally, death in their eyes is by no means simply a physical reality: it sums up, according to biblical usage, this whole condition of sinful man that Christ took upon himself, even though He had no part in sin (cf. Rom. 8,3 and Heb. 4,15).

On the other hand, what will be something new in connection with the biblical doctrine of the Redemption, in the theology of the Fathers and the later theologians, are the various attempts to answer the question that the New Testament did not ask: to whom was the debt that was to be paid for our ransom, accomplished by the blood of the cross, actually paid? Tradition seems to be divided into two answers: some say (and they are the majority of the early Fathers) that it was paid to the devil who held us captive, while the others, beginning especially with St. Anselm (11th century), will say that it was paid to God.

It is quite obvious that both answers are only metaphors: the devil, properly speaking, could have no right to it; while with God, as the author of our redemption, the idea of a debt that He would pay to Himself appears still more incongruous. But these metaphorical expressions mask a profound reality, which can be all the better perceived when, instead of setting them in opposition, we see them as two complementary aspects of the same reality. In a general way, this debt to be paid expresses the fact that God's pardon could not simply wipe out man's sinful past like a *deus ex machina*. It is of the essence of sin to be a free act, and purely and simply to take it away would come down to destroying the freedom that, on the contrary, is to be restored. Under these circumstances, the debt paid to the devil would mean God's acceptance in man of the conditions in which he was placed by sin, in such a way that he would be removed from that state not by a sort of divine violence, but by a reparation that grace from heaven enables him to accomplish, through this new Head of his race who is Christ. Strictly speaking, the payment of the debt, then, is rather a dearly won victory that those Fathers who particularly develop the image of the debt to the devil express by saying that in jumping at what was offered to him, the devil was in fact deceived (which is merely a colorful way of expressing what St. Paul had already said in declaring that if the "powers" had known what they were about, in crucifying the Lord of glory, they would indeed have been much more careful, cf. 1 Cor. 2,8). This is the sense of the doctrine developed by a St. Gregory of Nyssa in the East and a St. Gregory the Great in the West.

Under the inspiration of the feudal idea of satisfaction for honor wronged, i.e., as a reparation for the insult inflicted upon a superior by his inferiors, St. Anselm proposes another way. He says that the infinite offense against God caused by man's sin could not be repaired except by an infinite satisfaction for which God himself became man, in order to restore man's honor by satisfying the honor of God whom he had wounded (this is the generative idea for his *Cur Deus Homo?*). Behind this new set of images, we again find the opposition set up by St. Paul (in Rom. 5) between Adam's act and its superabundant reparation by the act of the New Adam.

To be convinced that these two apparently contradictory developments are in reality complementary, it suffices to recall that redemption, according to St. Paul, ransoms us on the one hand from the bondage of sin, death, and the devil, and on the other from the curse of the divine law and wrath. The reconciliation of these two points of view depends on the very profoundly biblical notion of the divine Providence. According to this, the bondage of sin and death, indeed the domination of the devil over the world, when all is said and done, merely executes the divine judgments in such a way that it is from His own definitive judgment that God delivers us by rescuing us from these enemies.

We see then that these various speculations about the debt to be acquitted merely underline the human cooperation in a saving act that, before saving our freedom, could not, in order to save it, lessen its reality. Moreover, we may find, with St. Gregory Nazianzen (*Orat.* 45; P.G., 36, col. 653), that this image ultimately remains too inadequate for one to depend on it, however it is used, and therefore prefer to it the sacrificial notions. This is very precisely what St. Thomas Aquinas does in deepening the idea of the reparatory sacrifice implied in the redemption itself by a development of the idea of the reconciliatory sacrifice. He says then that the Passion of Christ has saved us by meriting our salvation in the new Head of mankind (just as Adam had merited our loss: here again we find, at the root of the whole synthesis, the fundamental opposition of Rom. 5), by making the reparatory satisfaction for our sin that we by ourselves were incapable of making, by accomplishing the reconciliatory sacrifice, and finally by redeeming us in this way from the slavery in which we have been placed by sin (see *Sum. Theol.*, IIIa, q.48, a.1 to 4). *See also* SACRIFICE, SIN, and SLAVERY.

REFORMED CHURCHES   A name assumed by Protestants who do not trace directly back to Luther and whom Catholic authors erroneously call Calvinists, even though the Calvinists were never more than a small minority among them. The Reformed Churches, which spread first in Switzerland and the Rhineland, owe much more to the traditions of a type of Reformation humanism, represented (more than created) by Zwingli, the Zurich Reformer (*see* ZWINGLIANISM). From Calvin, on the whole, they adopted only their presbyterian and synodal organization (*see* CALVINISM). Later, particularly in England, many of these Churches rejected this system and opted for congregationalism instead, where each local Church is independent (whence their name "Free Churches," which is still given to them) and all the members of the community (not only the "elders," who gave their name to the system called presbyterian) are expected to exercise directly their authority as a body. This congregationalism, upheld by Cromwell's Puritans and by certain Churches of Holland, was termed non-conformism by the Anglicans; it spread to America, in New England, where it was brought by the celebrated Mayflower expedition.

RELATION   As we have seen in the article PERSON, theology has come to define the divine persons as subsistent relations within the one divine essence. A distinction is made between the two active relations of fatherhood and the active procession of the Spirit, and the two corresponding passive relations of sonship and the passive procession of the Spirit. The Persons are distinct from the divine essence only by a distinction of reason, while the contradistinction of their relations establishes a real distinction among them. See St. Thomas, *Sum. Theol.*, Ia, qq.39 and 40.

RELIGION AND RELIGIOUS   Religion is generally explained etymologically as coming from the word *religare*, "to bind," and as that bond which unites man with God. St. Thomas sees it as part of the virtue of justice in that it causes us to render to God what is his due. But through the gift of *piety* (q.v.), it opens out into supernatural charity. See *Sum. Theol.*, IIa-IIae, qq.81 to 100.

In a more particular sense, the word *religion*, as well as the adjective *religious* taken substantively, refers to a life consecrated to God through the *vows* (q.v.) of poverty, chastity, and obedience. *See also* vows, and PERFECTION.

RELIGIOUS PROFESSION   A public pledge to enter the religious life in the technical sense of the word, i.e., a life dominated by the vows of religion. A distinction is made between temporary profession, generally made for a trial period of three years, and final profession. This in turn can either be simple, in which case the Church by her authority can always dispense from an obligation that was assumed simply before her, or solemn. In this latter case, the vow is considered as having the character of a consecration to God and the Church is only its witness, so that her authority could not dispense from the obligation contracted. At the very most, for a proportionately grave reason, she could commute its application. On these different points, see canons 571 ff., as well as the theological explanation of St. Thomas, *Sum. Theol.*, IIa-IIae, qq.88 and 189.

REMISSION   The word is used of the forgiveness of sins, considered (as in the original text of the Our Father) as the remitting of a debt. *See also* REDEMPTION.

RENUNCIATION   *See* ASCETICISM

REPENTANCE   The word designates precisely sorrow for sin in itself, in contradistinction to simple remorse that is only the fear of its consequences. *See also* PENANCE, and CONTRITION.

REPROBATION   The act whereby God rejects those who refuse His grace. *See also* HELL, and JUDGMENT.

RESPECT OF PERSONS   This expression refers to judgment of someone based on external appearances (i.e., on his *persona*, which first meant the mask or role of an actor), instead of considering him on his particular merits as an individual. In Deuteronomy we read: "You shall not show partiality" (16,19; cf. 1,17). St. Paul takes up the statement of 2 Par. 19,7: "There is no respect of persons with God" (Rom. 2,11), as does St. James (10,34).

RESURRECTION   The return of a dead man to life. The resurrection of Christ and of the blessed, of which the first constitutes the first fruits and the pledge, is quite different from a simple return to earthly life, even from the miraculous returns spoken of in Scripture, in that it is the result of a conclusive victory over death and is accompanied, as a consequence, by a spiritualization of the body that associates it perfectly to the life of the soul, itself fully united with God in the *beatific vision* (q.v.). As has already been explained in the articles BODY and SOUL (qq.v.), it has always been essential to biblical revelation to propose to man the hope not of a disembodied immortality, like that of the religious philosophy of Platonism, but rather of a return to life of his entire being, inseparably body and soul. This corresponds with the doctrine of creation in general, which looks upon God as the author of the body as well as of the soul, and more precisely with an anthropology that does not consider the union of the soul with the body as fortuitous, but rather as essential to the nature of the human soul itself.

It is in this light that we understand the primitive Christian faith, as explained so firmly by St. Paul in the 15th chapter of his First Epistle to the Corinthians, to be above all a faith in the Resurrection of Christ. By it, He manifests himself as the heavenly man whom we must come to resemble, just as in the beginning we were made simply in the likeness of Adam, i.e., as the name signifies, the man made from earth. On the contrary, the second, or rather last, Adam has become the lifegiving Spirit: his whole human nature is now vivified by the presence in him of the divine Spirit, radiating even in his body his power of immortalizing sanctification. The accounts of the appearances of the risen Christ in the four Gospels underline both the identity between the risen One and the One who died on the cross, as is stressed by the fact of the empty tomb, and the mysterious transformation that endows his body with extraordinary powers in such a way that the disciples at times found difficulty in recognizing him or even thought that they were having a vision. The earliest accounts in Acts, moreover, already emphasize that for the primitive Church this Resurrection is effectively the supreme testimony to Jesus' Messiahship, together with the assurance that *salvation* (q.v.) is in no other person.

The Resurrection of Christ or of those who belong to him remains a deep mystery, and theology must limit itself to maintaining both this continuity between our present being, in its profound unity, and this definitive transfiguration inseparable from the resurrection, which is already a fact in Christ and which we expect for ourselves. It appears furthermore as a datum of biblical revelation that the general resurrection will be inseparable from a transfiguration of the whole material universe. This universe will harmonize with the glory of the elect and will become a transparent manifestation, as it were, of the divine glory. Between the opposite extremes of the millenarist errors (*see* MILLENARIANISM), which unduly materialize this hope, and an exaggerated spiritualism, which simply destroys its reality, we must keep sight of these two statements of the Apostle: "Flesh and blood—i.e., the present condition of corporeal life—cannot inherit the Kingdom of God" (1 Cor. 15,50), and: "The Spirit . . . will give life to your mortal bodies" (Rom. 8,11). Anything else is only more or less hazardous speculation. Furthermore, let us note that Scripture, in its insistence upon the cosmic character that will accompany the resurrection of the righteous in the definitive victory of God over the forces of evil, seems indeed to admit a resurrection even of the damned, if only as a prelude to what seems to be a conclusive separation of the saved universe from the guilty and condemned "world." *See* PAROUSIA, and WORLD.

RETRIBUTION   *See* MERIT

RETURN OF CHRIST   *See* PAROUSIA

REVELATION   The divine action that uncovers for us the supernatural truths God has seen fit to have us know, and that sheds light upon a certain number of truths of the natural order which are more or less closely connected with the preceding. The word is also understood as the totality of truths that are the object of the act of revealing. Christian revelation is bound up with the more comprehensive fact of the divine *Word* (q.v.) and cannot be understood apart from this. This is why, on the one hand, we must not look upon revelation as the communication of a list of separate truths that are immediately expressed in definitive formulas, but rather as the essentially progressive communication of *one* truth with manifold aspects. Beginning with the first prophetic communications of the divine Word in the Old Covenant, revelation was objectively brought to its term at the death of the last *apostle* (q.v.). However, its explicitation in dogmatic formulas continues to be made in the Church in proportion to the needs to which the growth (*see* DEVELOPMENT) of the Church gives rise. On the other hand, revelation does not have an abstract truth as its object, but rather the truth about God and the relationship that he willed to establish with us in a totality of supernatural facts that make up sacred *history* (q.v.). Its high point is the redemptive Incarnation of his Son, and its term the eschatological end of the whole of human history (*see* ESCHATOLOGY). There exists, then, an essential correlation, of which we must never lose sight and which we have already mentioned in reference to the Word of God, between the prophetic illumination accorded to those whom God has willed to make the guides of his People (*see* PROPHECY), and these events that it accompanies.

Moreover, the Church has always admitted the possibility of authentic private revelations that God might make to privileged individuals if he saw fit. But she does not cease to put the faithful on their guard against the superstitious belief that such revelations can ever add anything essential to the revelation of himself that he willed to make to his entire People; its final word was given to us in the Gospel of his Son.

REVIVAL MOVEMENT   The term *réveil* (awakening) was used of a whole movement of religious revival that developed particularly in the French-speaking Protestant Churches in the 19th century. Under the more or less direct influence of *Wesleyanism* (q.v.) this movement developed in opposition to the deist rationalism of the 18th century and largely contributed toward a revival of an evangelical spirituality whose weakness was its inability to provide itself with a fairly consistent theology. Its most remarkable representatives were the pastor and preacher Adolphe Monod and the thinker Alexandre Vinet. In a popular form that concentrated on producing a conversion more or less marked with emotional elements, the movement branched out into more emotional movements, like the Welsh one that was studied particularly by the American philosopher William James. It is then at the root of the bursts of sectarianism thoughout the whole of contemporary Protestantism. "Pentecostalism" is the most bizarre, with its endeavor to resurrect a Church like that of Pentecost, i.e., with some sort of tangible manifestations of the communication of the Holy Spirit.

RIGHT   A distinction is to be made between the *objective right* that is due a person by virtue of the law, and the power an individual possesses (called a *subjective* right) of claiming these objective rights that are acknowledged by the law to be his. The early theologians looked upon the objective right as the foundation of the subjective right (cf. St. Thomas Aquinas, *Sum. Theol*, IIa-IIae, q.57, a.1). The objection raised by many persons in modern times, including Catholics, that such a position would make the subjective right of each person depend upon the subjective right of every lawmaker, does not hold, once it is admitted that the source of every right is ultimately only in the will of the supreme lawmaker, God.

RIGHTEOUSNESS   *See* JUSTICE.

RITE   A sacred action. The principal Christian rites are the sacramental rites, and above all the Eucharist. Unchangeable in their essential core, the rites can vary in the details of their celebration and in the accompanying formulas as well. It is the prerogative of the Church alone to specify the limits and modalities of these variations, with regard for the institution of the sacraments by her divine Head and their correlation with the communication of his Gospel to the world, which must be done in such a way that its intelligibility and its authenticity are always preserved as one. Granting the variations within mankind itself, this, moreover, can be done only by an effort of faithfulness and unceasing adaptation. At certain times, as in our own age, the Church is led to more or less radical reforms, but these always have as inseparable aims the return to the living sources of the highest tradition and the concern for present pastoral needs.

ROMAN CONGREGATIONS The name given to the agencies of the Roman Curia, consisting chiefly of cardinals to whom the Sovereign Pontiff delegates in varying degrees the exercise of his powers for the administration of the Church. This delegation, even in the case where the Pope himself does not preside as prefect of the particular congregation, is such that these agencies must be obeyed as expressing the authority of the Holy See itself. However, even the decisions of the Holy Office on faith and morals, when they are approved by the Pope *in forma communi,* do not directly involve his infallibility. This is why the objection often raised against pontifical infallibility on the grounds of Galileo's condemnation is irrelevant in this regard.

ROME In the Apocalypse, Rome, as the center of world government and of the pagan worship connected with it, appears as the seat of the Antichrist ("Babylon, the great," in 14,8, obviously refers to it). St. Peter was to establish himself there, both so that the center of the Church would correspond to the center of the ancient world, and that she would assert her authority in her struggle with the powers of this world (cf. the superscription of the First Epistle of Peter). It is therefore as the successor of St. Peter that the bishop of Rome is pope, i.e., the head of the episcopate. As a norm, the stability of local churches demands that this successor of the head of the apostles establish his see there in principle in a conclusive way. But just as St. Peter, after he had set himself up in Antioch, transferred not only his residence but his see to Rome, so it is that if serious circumstances should make it necessary it seems at least probable that a pope also could decide to transfer the Apostolic See again.

S

SABELLIANISM   A doctrine held by Sabellius in the 3rd century. It stated that the Father, Son, and Holy Spirit were not really distinct from one another. In a more subtle form called *Modalism* (q.v.), this heresy reappeared several times in the following centuries.

SACRAMENT   St. Augustine defines sacrament as a sacred sign; in profane language it seems that the word *sacramentum* was used particularly in reference to the whole gamut of consecratory ceremonies that accompanied the oath taken by Roman soldiers on the occasion of their enrollment. Early Latin Christian writing used the word not only in regard to all the liturgical signs, but also of all sacred facts. Hence its use in the early Latin versions of the Bible to translate the Greek *mysterion*. But we have gradually come to apply the word sacrament exclusively to the sacred signs instituted by Christ, and insofar as his sovereign will is expressed in them they are of themselves sources of grace (i.e., *ex opere operato*, as the theologians say, in contradistinction to those sacred actions initiated solely by the religious person himself, like prayer which is said to act *ex opere operantis*). In this light, it was defined that there are seven sacraments of the New Covenant. (The number 7 is already found in the confession of faith of Michael Palaeologus at the Council of Lyons in 1294, D.B. 465; again in the Decree for the Armenians of the Council of Florence in 1439, D.B. 695; and it was reasserted against the denials of the Protestants by the Council of Trent, Session VII, can. 1, D.B. 844). Eastern Christians, even those separated from Rome, although they continue to use the word *mysterion* in a broader sense, are in general agreement as to this number of the rites instituted by Christ, which because of this institution by Christ communicate of themselves his grace to us.

However, we ought not to look upon them as simply seven parallel channels of grace to man, an idea to which modern theology has unduly yielded. On the contrary, we should consider them as a framework of grace that is inseparable from the life of the Church to which it gives its structure, and which is profoundly one. This oneness is centered as it were in the Eucharist; St. Thomas says rightly that the Eucharist is the source of the whole sacramental order because it contains the Saviour himself (*Sum. Theol.*, IIIa, q.65, a.3). Through the Eucharist, the Church sustains and builds herself, in the eucharistic celebration of the sacrifice of the cross, the essential object of the evangelical proclamation, and more particularly by communion in this sacrifice with the One who is both its priest and its victim. On the other hand, the sacraments of initiation, baptism and confirmation, literally initiate us into the participation in the Eucharist by conforming us to Christ in his death and resurrection and by pouring out in us the gift of his Spirit. Penance merely restores to us this power that had been more or less seriously impaired in us by sin. Order prepares various baptized and confirmed members of the Church to perform the various public functions that the eucharistic celebration supposes, and particularly, in the case of the priesthood, it enables them to preside over the assembly in the name of its divine Head, and consequently to consecrate the Eucharist. Although the whole body offers it, the consecration itself remains their function alone. Lastly, marriage and anointing of the sick are singled out, from all the blessings arising from the eucharistic sacrifice, as corresponding to special promises of Christ in conjunction with the very special importance that the assimilation to the cross and Resurrection gives both to the natural fecundity of human life and its infirmity resulting from sin.

Furthermore, we shall single out as particularly necessary for the salvation of the individual, baptism, which engrafts him on Christ, and penance which restores this relationship to him if it was disturbed by subsequent sins. For the salvation of the Church, it is the sacrament of holy orders that is especially important, since it assures her perpetual bond with Christ through the apostolic succession (*see* APOSTLE).

The sacraments that imprint a permanent *character* (q.v.), because of this very fact, may not be repeated.

A further distinction is made between the *sacraments of the dead*, baptism and penance, which apply to those who are deprived of grace, and the *sacraments of the living* (all the others), which increase or sustain the grace already conferred by the preceding ones.

Lastly, in reference to the Eucharist, a distinction has been set up between two basic aspects of the sacraments: their form and matter. The matter is constituted by the materiality itself of the sign, and the form, by the words of the Saviour that specify its supernatural significance and guarantee its efficacy. In the case of marriage or penance, we need a certain deftness to use this distinction (the term quasi-matter is used, and it is constituted by the consent of the two parties, or the acts of the penitent in presenting himself for absolution). This distinction raises the debated problem of the efficacy of the sacraments. All Catholics, as opposed to most Protestants, hold that the sacraments are efficacious not merely because of the faith that they elicit in us and demand from us, but first because of the efficacious will to give us grace that Christ manifests in them (although this efficacy cannot be of benefit to us with-

out the faith that accepts it). But the precise way in which the sacraments are efficacious is freely discussed among theologians. Some hold to
an occasional efficacy, where the sign is only the occasion on which God
gives us his grace. Others admit a genuinely physical efficacy: the sign,
insofar as it is given by God in Christ, is efficacious of itself. Actually, as
is easily seen, these systems conflict because they do not understand the
sign in the same sense. The occasionalists look upon the materiality
alone as the sign, while the others, who are certainly more faithful to the
spirit of tradition wonderfully expressed by St. Thomas, consider the sign
to be both its materiality and what Christ willed and determined it to
signify, inseparably taken as a whole.

A final point that must be brought up in the Thomistic synthesis of
the sacraments is the distinction made between *sacramentum, sacramentum et res,* and *res tantum.* Actually this clarifies the whole sacramental
economy. First used in relation to the Eucharist, it singles out, under the
word *sacramentum,* the visible and tangible species of bread and wine.
These serve as a sign of a preliminary reality which is that of the body
and blood of the Saviour, separated by his saving death and reunited by
His resurrection. But, in turn, this reality itself has the part of a sign in
relation to an ultimate reality that is the end of the sacrament. Hence the
term *sacramentum et res* that it is given. The definitive reality, *res
tantum,* is then the achieved unity of the Mystical Body, which has
begun to be realized in the eucharistic communion. This same distinction is applied to the sacraments that entail the gift of a *character,* which
in this case fulfills the role of *sacramentum et res;* the grace proper to the
particular sacrament is the *res tantum.* In this way the proper function of
the sacraments is affirmed as an intermediary one between the reality of
the *mystery* (q.v.) of salvation, realized in the Saviour himself, and its
eschatological realization in the Church.

On all of this, see St. Thomas Aquinas, *Sum. Theol.,* IIIa, qq.60–90, as
well as qq.1–42 of the Supplement. See also the articles devoted to each
of the sacraments in particular.

SACRAMENTAL   From the time that the term sacrament was
reserved solely for the signs of grace instituted by Christ, the term
sacramental has been applied to the other religious signs instituted by
the Church. They are distinguished from the sacraments in that they do
not work *ex opere operato* (q.v.), but only *ex opere operantis Ecclesiae,*
i.e., simply in virtue of the subordinate sanctifying power that belongs to
the prayer of the Church. We must further distinguish among the
sacramentals those that consecrate persons, such as solemn religious
profession, the consecration of virgins or the blessing of abbots, as well as

the minor orders, from simple ceremonies added by the Church to the celebration of the sacraments, and finally from the simple *consecration* or *blessing* of objects (qq.v.).

SACRED Literally, the sacred is that which has been set off from the profane by its belonging in a special way to God. In the beginning, for primitive man everything in nature was sacred. As man became more and more conscious of his own autonomy (which, to make matters worse, became turned against God through sin), the sacred tended more and more to be confined until it appeared merely as a survival, indeed until man deluded himself, through his involvement with *magic* (q.v.), that if he could not actually produce the sacred, he could at least master it at will. The Jewish and Christian ideas of the sacred are distinguished by an awareness of the fact that God has reasserted his place in the world—a fact flowing from sacred history in which the divine action was sovereignly introduced so as to take upon itself the action proper to man.

SACRED HEART, HEART OF MARY The importance given in Scripture, particularly in the later prophets (Osee 11,15, but especially Jer. 31,31 ff.), to the heart (considered not merely as the seat of the emotions, but as the source of the deepest will, enlightened by an intelligence that is responsive to spiritual realities) was to bring the meditation of Christians to be centered about the heart of the Son of God made man. This was seen particularly in the Middle Ages in connection with reflections on the wound in the side of the Lord on the cross (John 19,34). Even before this the Fathers, undoubtedly in keeping with St. John's intention, had seen in the gushing out of water and blood of which he speaks, the symbol of the Church being born from the Saviour in his death, and more precisely, of the graces that his passion would communicate to the whole of mankind by baptism and the Eucharist (cf. St. Augustine, *Tractatus in Johannem, ad loc.*). It is in the Benedictine and Cistercian monasteries of the Rhine Valley that we see this devotion take form. St. Gertrude had a vision of Christ placing his own heart within her. However, it is the spiritual renewal of the 17th and 18th centuries that brought this veneration of the Sacred Heart to the point of development that we know today. St. John Eudes was the first to initiate it. He introduced the first attempt at a liturgical veneration of the hearts, or, as he said rather, of *the heart* of Jesus and Mary. This second manner of expressing his thought well demonstrates the symbolic character of the devotion such as he understood it. It is a more concrete equivalent of the devotion propagated by Jean-Jacques Olier to what he called the "inner life of Jesus and Mary." A more marked emphasis on the bodily heart of the Saviour characterized the new and important developments that the devotion was soon to experience. Although it was later to provoke a lively opposition from certain Jansenist or Protestant milieux, it is rather curious to ascertain that this emphasis first appeared in a beautifully expressed Protestant pamphlet by Cromwell's Puritan chaplain, Thomas Goodwin, as Bremond quite rightly points out.

But it was to the Visitandine nun of Paray-le-Monial, who was to become St. Margaret Mary Alacoque, as well as to Fr. de la Colombière, S.J., that we owe, along with the prodigious expansion of veneration to the Sacred Heart, the traits that were to characterize it: the bodily heart of the Saviour put to death for our sins is considered as especially wounded again by each infidelity of a Christian, and as never ceasing to radiate His redeeming love on sinners. This in return demands from us a penitent love, marked by a desire to make reparation, insofar as we are able, with the help of grace, for all the offenses undergone by this Heart so worthy of being adored, and especially for those that result from our negligence in welcoming it and in responding to it in the Eucharist. Thus, the modern devotion to the Sacred Heart, which is essentially eucharistic and reparative, is determined by practices such as the first Friday Communion. Despite the fact that it is sometimes inadequately presented because of sentimentality or bad art, this devotion was certainly one of the most powerful factors in the revival and deepening of spirituality in the course of the 18th and 19th centuries. It is an interior and apostolic devotion centered on Christ, on his redemptive passion, and on a better participation in this through Communion, and reverence for the Eucharist. One can find a spiritual progress report and a theological charter of the devotion to the Sacred Heart in the very fine Encyclical of Pius XII, *Haurietis aquas in gaudio.*

The veneration of the Immaculate Heart of Mary is naturally joined to the veneration of the Sacred Heart as an homage, full of inspiration for us, to the heart that has best responded to the love of the Redeemer's Heart.

A complaint is at times raised that veneration to the Sacred Heart seems no longer as relevant to the faithful of our day as it was to preceding generations. Actually, the most positive elements of this devotion have been incorporated into Christian piety to such an extent that it no longer represents a separate devotion as such. The whole renewal of the teaching on the Mystical Body and eucharistic practice has benefited greatly from this incorporation.

SACRIFICE   In modern times, both among theologians and laymen, discussions have multiplied as to a possible definition of sacrifice, and particularly as to the part played by the destructive immolation or the simple oblation of the victim. Actually, the history of religions seems to show decidedly that sacrifice is nothing else than a sacred meal, i.e., a meal where man believes that he is entering into communion with God. Either he looks upon the meal as an offering to God or else he supposes that God is there as his table-companion; inversely, it is God who is admitting him to His own table, even to the extent where He not only furnishes the food but is actually that food Himself. Yet, all these notions are not irreconcilable, and all of them can more or less clearly be seen in the sacrifices of primitive men. More generally, we may say that it is an essential point of sacrifice that it causes man to live in an interchange of life, indissolubly both physical and spiritual, between him and his gods. Hence, the importance of blood rites in most sacrifices, where blood represents life.

The sacrifices of the Hebrews, regulated by the Pentateuch and particularly in that part of Exodus that is called the Code of Holiness and in Leviticus, are in no way distinguished on any essential point in their materiality from the sacrifices offered by neighboring peoples, except for the fact that human sacrifices are strictly forbidden. But the notion becomes deeply modified as soon as it is expressly evident that their value stems only from their being the signs of the covenant and prescribed as such by God himself. All of them, in this way, are more or less part of the *memorial* (q.v.) that is particularly connected with the Passover sacrifice, the first and perhaps for some time the only sacrifice of the Hebrews. In other words, sacrifice in Israel becomes for the people a perpetually active and meaningful act that recalls the covenant that God had made with Israel on Sinai. By the same token, from the part of the people, through their constantly reasserted will to be faithful to the covenant, it is a reminder to God of his promises.

Under the influence of the prophets, sacrifice gradually became spiritualized in Israel, in the sense that both this express recalling of the *mirabilia Dei* (which are at the basis of Israel's faith) and the response to the divine initiatives through a faith that effectively hands itself over to God's action, become essential to it. Therefore, this helps in under-standing the tendency that appears in Jewish piety contemporary with the Gospel, and especially in the writings of Qumran and related texts: on the one hand, a sacrificial character is given to the whole life of the pious Israelite through the *berakoth*, i.e., the *blessings* (q.v.) that make him see in everything a sign and a seal of the Word of God, the Creator and Saviour, and at the same time, cause him to offer himself to God in obedient faith with every action; on the other hand, a better equivalent of the Temple sacrifices is sought in the community meals of the faithful united in the messianic hope. In these notions, we have an immediate preparation, as it were, for the Christian Eucharist. In taking over the two basic rites of these community meals (the breaking of bread with its short accompanying blessing at the beginning of the meal, and the serving of the last cup with its particularly elaborate solemn blessing at the end), Jesus transformed the meal itself into a new rite. Blessing the bread as the memorial of his body that is to be voluntarily handed over to death, and the chalice as the cup of the New Covenant that will be concluded in his blood, Jesus at the same time and inseparably gives his death a sacrificial significance and makes these community meals of his People, in the future, the memorial of this covenant until the end of time (see EUCHARIST).

In accordance with the basic nature of sacrifice as a sacred meal, it is evident that the factor which gives the cross itself a sacrificial character is that it was alluded to in this ritual meal of the messianic community as the element that would give substance to the sacrifice which was definitively to constitute and to sustain it. At the same time, we can see in this context the twofold misunderstanding that is at the root of the difficulties raised by the Protestants in the face of the traditional notion in the Catholic Church on the Eucharist. Far from saying that according to the New Testament only the cross can have a sacrificial character, and that the Eucharist is therefore merely a non-sacrificial memorial of it, we must say first that the biblical and Jewish notion of "memorial" is essentially sacrificial, to the point that it constitutes the essential element of the properly biblical sacrifice; it is this fact that justifies our consider- ing the Mass as the sacrifice of the Church. On the other hand, the cross derives its sacrificial significance from its relationship to the first Mass, and consequently to all others that follow. In instituting the Christian Eucharist at the Last Supper, Jesus made this ritual action of his the consecration of his offering that was immolated on the cross, thereby giving to the cross its substance as the new covenant sacrifice. At the same time, he made this unique offering the source for all time of all the eucharistic celebrations that would perpetuate this efficacious memorial. They would be guaranteed this character by the mysterious but su- premely real presence of the crucified body and the shed blood under the consecrated species, as a consequence of the Lord's words: "This is my body, this is my blood."

In a general way, in the New Testament, the concept of sacrifice, in accordance with the teaching of the prophets, is applied to the whole of Christian life, as a life lived from now on in the divine *agape*, as in this so characteristic text of St. Paul: "Present your bodies as a sacrifice, living, holy, pleasing to God—your spiritual service" (Rom. 12,1). To Christ himself and to his cross, the same apostle makes only one direct application of this sacrificial language, exactly in the same line of prophetic thought, when he says in the Epistle to the Ephesians: "Christ . . . delivered himself up for us an offering and a sacrifice to

God to ascend in fragrant odor" (Eph. 5,2). This is an evident allusion to Psalm 39(40), vv.6–8, where to the offering and the simply ritual sacrifice there is opposed the fulfillment by the chosen one of God of the divine will alone.

Another Pauline text, however, directly lays the groundwork for the application to Christ's death of the sacrificial expressions, and more especially of the images taken from the great yearly ritual of the *expiations* (q.v.). The whole Epistle to the Hebrews is constructed on this usage. It is the text of Rom. 3,24–25 which tells us that we "are justified freely by his grace through the redemption which is in Christ Jesus, whom God has set forth as a propitiation by his blood through faith." Again it must be noted that in this latter text it is rather the faith which takes on directly the value of a sacrifice, since Christ who is its object sheds his blood for us and takes his place, as it were, on the mercy seat of the Old Covenant. The Epistle to the Hebrews makes us look upon Christ's cross as the direct equivalent of the sacrifice of the day of expiation, although the focus is more on Christ's subsequent entry, as our forerunner, into the immediate presence of his Father than on the shed blood (which, in accordance with the Jewish understanding of this feast and of this sacrifice, is merely a means of purification preliminary to the resumption of normal relations with God).

In these different senses, the cross and the whole life of the Christian that it inspires appear as a spiritual sacrifice, in contradistinction to the ritual sacrifices. It is in this sense that the Fathers of the Church say many times to the pagans: "We have no sacrifices," understanding by this the sacrifices of immolated victims, like those of the pagans. But at the same time they say that the whole life of the Christian is a sacrifice that reproduces the spiritual offering of Christ on the cross. Insofar as the eucharistic celebration is the center of this spiritual sacrifice of the whole Church, in which this sacrifice draws its power from the unique oblation of Christ immolated on the cross, they also say that this is the only sacrifice of Christians and a sacrifice that is essentially unbloody (see, for example, St. Justin, *First Apology,* 13; P.G. 6, col. 345B, and *Dialogue with Trypho,* 117; *ibid.,* col. 746).

St. Augustine made the first synthesis of these different views in his distinction between the visible sacrifice and the invisible sacrifice of which, according to him, it is the sacrament, i.e., the sacred sign (*De Civitate Dei,* bk. 10, chap. 5). More generally in the following chapter he defines true sacrifice as *omne opus quod agitur ut sancta societate inhaereamus Deo:* "every work performed in order that we might adhere to God in a holy society" (*ibid.,* chap. 6). When St. Thomas wishes to explain in what sense the passion of Christ is sacrificial, it is these expressions themselves that he uses (*Sum. Theol.,* IIIa, q.48, a.3), although he specifies further on that the Eucharist is a sacrifice insofar as it "re-presents" the passion of Christ (*ibid.*, q.79, a.7).

Contrary to what modern theology, simply by confusing sacrifice and redemptive act (or, still more narrowly, sacrifice and *satisfaction*—q.v.) tends to think (Protestant theology more than Catholic, which, how-ever, it will influence dangerously on this point, if only because of the grounds of the polemic), it follows from the preceding that the essence of sacrifice is not in the simply negative aspect of a reparation for sin, but rather in the communion that has been established (or reestablished) with God. It is in this sense that sacrifice, as an act of man, accomplished by his handing himself over to God, and in Christianity, by God himself in man, expresses the whole positive fullness of the biblical notion of reconciliation with God (*see* REDEMPTION) in a way that the mere notion of satisfaction could not render as well. On the other hand, since this *communion* (q.v.) is possible today only on the basis of sin for which reparation has been made, we cannot distinguish separate Chris-tian sacrifices, namely, the sacrifice of the cross as the sole expiatory or satisfactory one, and on the other hand, the sacrifice of individual Christians or of the Church as merely a sacrifice of thanksgiving for the preceding one. This is the error held by Protestants that was condemned at the Council of Trent when it declared that the Mass is a genuine sacrifice and a propitiatory one, although it is nothing else than the sacrifice of the cross: "There is one and the same victim, the Same who offers himself today through the ministry of the priests, and who offered himself on the cross: it is only the manner of offering that is different" (Session XXII, *De Sanctissimo Missae Sacrificio*, chap. 2; D.B. 940).

SACRILEGE   The profanation of the sacred by man. See St. Thomas, *Sum. Theol.*, IIa-IIae, q.99. Disrespect for the divine name or receiving the sacraments without the requisite conditions of faith and the desire to submit oneself to the will of God are the most frequent forms of sacrilege.

SALVATION   Like the word Saviour, this expression, which is part of current usage in later Christianity, is relatively little used by the New Testament, undoubtedly because of the abundant use made of it in the religions of antiquity, particularly in the worship of sovereigns. In its proper Christian acceptation, salvation designates the effect, either individual or collective, of *redemption* (q.v.), and more particularly its ultimate effect in the Resurrection. As we have explained in the article ESCHATOLOGY, since the Christian vision of history is profoundly *one*—a unity stemming from the individual and collective unity of mankind in its spirituality and its corporality—the idea of a temporal salvation that could be attained separately from salvation in the fullest sense cannot be accepted literally.

SALVATION OF UNBELIEVERS   Since the Renaissance, a better evaluation of the vast extent of those populations still untouched by evangelization, and more recently, the massive dechristianization even of peoples that up to the present had been (or had seemed to be) Christian have led many Christian thinkers to look at the problem of the salvation of unbelievers in a more or less new light. While in traditional theology this salvation was looked upon as the aim and normal consequence of the evangelization received by souls of good will, many today have the tendency to ask themselves, not only as an additional question, but as a primary one, how unbelievers can be saved apart from evangelization. Several attempts at a solution have been and are still being made, and their conflicting answers seem to betray some uncertainty even as to the terms used. The Church has clearly condemned two types of extreme solutions: that of the ultra-Jansenists, like Quesnel, who sent off to inevitable perdition every pagan to whom the Gospel was not preached or who did not accept it; but also that of the laxist or naturalistic thinkers, who would admit that one could be saved from actual sin, or even from original sin, either by any act of nature left to its own devices, or by a supernatural act that would one way or another endanger the necessity of faith for salvation (see D.B. 1379 against Quesnel, and D.B. 1173 against the opposite extreme). Behind these condemnations there is 1) the certitude formulated by the Council of Trent: "Without [faith] justification has never come to anyone" (Sess. VI, Decree on Justification, D.B. 799), and: "We are said to be saved by faith, because faith is the beginning of man's salvation, the basis and the root of all justification, without which [i.e., faith] it is impossible to be pleasing to God and to enter into the family of his children" (*ibid.*, D.B. 801); 2) this other certitude generally expressed in the formula: "*facienti quod in se est Deus non denegat gratiam.*" This latter, however, is not without some ambiguity, for if "*quod in se est*" is understood "*naturaliter,*" it can be taken in a purely Pelagian sense; and if it is "*supernaturaliter,*" one runs the risk of stating nothing more than a tautology. Consequently, it would be better to simply resort to the formula of the First Epistle to Timothy: "[God] desires all men to be saved and to come to the knowledge of the truth" (2,4).

Among the solutions proposed to reconcile these two certitudes, there are some that are only apparent, not because they are false in themselves, but because they offer considerations that are related to quite a different question. Such is the solution based on the opinion of St. Thomas, according to which, once every man has arrived at adulthood, in the first free and responsible choice he makes he can only accept or reject the ultimate end which is to love God above everything. If he accepts it, by that very fact he is freed from original sin and placed in the state of grace (*Sum. Theol.*, Ia-IIae, q.89, a.6). Even if we follow this opinion, and it seems that we must unless we reject the very principles of all of Thomistic thought, it does not add anything to the present question (to which St. Thomas seems to have never intended to apply it) because we have no way of knowing if there are in fact many men who make this positive decision from the first, and because even if this were the case for all mankind, the totality of Thomist thought, echoing ancient Christian tradition and, it seems, Scripture itself, leaves but little or no hope for man's capacity for persevering in this state for any time without the help of the Church or at least of revelation explicitly known and accepted.

There remain then three systems or three types of systems: 1) that which is actually proposed by St. Thomas: in the case of someone who would follow faithfully the law of reason and who would have no material means of arriving at faith, God would certainly act in one way or another (a miracle or an inner illumination) in order to reveal to him the truths of salvation (cf. *In IV Sent.*, bk. III, dist. 25, q.2, a.1, sol.1 and ad 1um, and *De Veritate*, q.14, a.11, ad 1um); 2) that of Ludovico Cardinal Billot (1846–1931): the mass of humanity that seems to live apart from Christian salvation is in fact in a state far below what one may consider as a kind of morally adult state, so that, without being promised supernatural salvation, this mass of humanity could still not be damned but would be doomed to Limbo, where children who die without baptism are commonly relegated, and are deprived of the vision of God, but without any positive suffering (*see* LIMBO); and 3) finally, there are the various solutions that underline the different substitutes for the preaching of the Catholic Church. Through these substitutes non-Catholics may be given a certain more or less explicit knowledge of the salvation offered to man by a mediator sent by God, in such a way as to make the salutary act of faith possible for unbelievers in good faith. We must nevertheless mention in regard to the first solution (borrowed from St. Thomas) that it is hardly relevant to today's question as to the salvation of unbelievers, since it comes down to saying that even where it might seem that one could be saved without the explicit profession of Catholic faith, in fact this would not be the case at all. As regards the theory of Cardinal Billot, it does not have any weighty precedent in tradition (it is not enough to say in its defense that the problem itself is of recent origin), and in addition it offers no solution as regards salvation for unbelievers, but at the very most, merely concludes that in certain cases they are not damned. As for the systems of the third type, all they do is more or less to push back the frontiers where unbelief in the strict sense begins, while offering nothing in the cases where it is fully real.

Under these conditions, we may hold the opinion that, since the truths of faith have been given to us not that our taste for speculation might be satisfied, but in order that we might be led to salvation and lead others to salvation through our own profession of those truths, it is at least questionable that we can derive from such truths solutions to a problem that by definition is to be found outside of both cases. Perhaps the best we can do is to maintain intact our assurance that God is perfect justice and perfect mercy in all of his acts, without claiming either to pass judgment on hearts whose secret he alone knows, or even less, attempting to discern the ways that he may choose, in order to win them for himself, when he has not considered it good to enlighten us as to an action that in no way concerns us.

SATAN   See DEVIL

SATISFACTION   In the article REDEMPTION will be found what is relevant to the doctrine of satisfaction for our sins by the cross of Christ, as systematized by St. Anselm.

SAVIOUR   See SALVATION

SCHISM   From the Greek *schisma*, which signifies a split, the word was taken for a long time simply as a synonym for *heresy* (q.v.). Today it is distinguished from heresy in the sense that we call a schism any division of Catholic unity, even if it does not directly involve any doctrinal error that would make it properly heretical. The Churches of the East that are called Orthodox were cut off from the center of Catholic unity in the chair of St. Peter through various historical schisms, the most noteworthy being that of the Patriarch Michael Cerularius in the 11th century. However, not only may we not call them heretics, but, since this schism itself was never the object of a formal adhesion on the part of the whole episcopate of the East, and since reconciliations attempted since that time, such as at the Council of Florence in the 15th century, were not officially repudiated, they cannot strictly speaking even be called schismatics. The Apostolic See at various times has given instructions that this term not be used in their regard, and these certainly have not only a disciplinary but also a doctrinal import. The most flagrant case of schism, and without doubt the most scandalous in all of the history of Christianity, is the great schism of the West, where two and even three sections of Western Christianity were in opposition to one another, each rallying behind a pretender to the papacy (between 1328 and 1449).

SCHOLASTICISM The philosophy and theology of the Schools as developed from the 13th century on according to an essentially rational and deductive method. Excellent for the coherent statement of Christian truths, the scholastic method depends strictly on the quality of investigating the historical sources of revelation, and, as set down in principle by St. Thomas and recalled with a particular insistence by Cajetan (one of his greatest commentators), on a complete docility to the light of faith. Lacking these conditions, scholasticism risks degenerating into a mere rationalism that would distort the truths of faith instead of explaining them.

SCHOOL Because the Church received the commission from her divine Founder to teach the essential truths of salvation to all nations (Matt. 29,19), she not only has always been concerned with maintaining catechetical instruction for the schooling of her members in the Christian faith and life, but she has also always considered as an essential part of that commission to prevent her members from being side-tracked from their supernatural destiny by other forms of teaching that would not respect it. Christian education, in effect, is the formation of the whole man; and for a Christian, there can be no question of simply grafting it on to a general education that knows nothing of Christianity, even if it does not oppose it. As soon as the Church had emerged from persecution and was able to establish herself freely, she began to have schools. Actually, during the Middle Ages, all education, even in its most varied aspects, was in her hands. The forming of modern society and its gradual secularization put an end to this situation. But the Church may not cease to claim the right to have her own schools, or in the case of countries that are professedly Catholic, to demand the right to effectively supervise the teaching that, in principle, is in accord with the Catholic faith. Where the country is non-confessional, the Church may not permit Catholics to attend the state schools unless she has the positive guarantee not only that their faith will be respected, but also that they will be able, in accordance with the varying methods dictated by circumstances, to fill out their instruction with a religious training adequate to their particular situation. It is furthermore the right of the Church, and even her duty, to insist that the state never try to usurp as its own exclusive right the duty, resulting from the natural law and incumbent first of all on parents, of schooling their own children in all of their responsibilities as men and as Christian. These various principles that the Church authority has recently been induced to specify on numerous occasions, in a variety of local circumstances, govern the Church's attitude and must be understood and applied by all her members.

SCIENCE   In theology the Latin *scientia*, from which our English word comes, has had, successively, various acceptations that we must not confuse. The early Latin authors, like Cassian, and even some medieval authors like William of Saint-Thierry in the 12th century, used it as a translation of the Greek *gnosis*, with its religious sense studied in the article KNOWLEDGE. On the other hand, in contradistinction to Augustine's "wisdom," other medieval Latin authors look upon *scientia* in its religious sense as a simple discernment. In his analysis of the gifts of intelligence (*intellectus*) and knowledge (in this case, *scientia*), St. Thomas Aquinas understands the first of these gifts as a gift of supernatural understanding of the truths of faith, and the second as a gift of discernment with regard to what pertains or does not pertain to the faith (*Sum. Theol.*, IIa-IIae, q.9, a.1, ad 2um). In the same place, he distinguishes it from an extraordinary gift of convincing or refuting. In relation to this analysis and as an explanation of it, 13th-century theology adopted the Aristotelian notion of science, namely, a knowledge that was rationally constructed and worked out, in contradistinction to a simple opinion (*see* THEOLOGY).

In the modern sense of the term, science is the knowledge of the universe founded upon methodical experience and rationally analyzed. Starting with Descartes, the sciences of nature tended more and more toward a radical mathematicization of experience on the basis of determinist postulates (*see* DETERMINISM). Contemporary science, in this regard, is differentiated from Cartesian science by a new tendency to reject the idea that the ideal science is one that comes as close as possible to an entirely deductive rational mathematics starting from the simplest possible postulates. This is partially the result of what is called the determinism crisis in atomic physics. But scientists themselves are not in agreement as to whether this crisis is a merely passing one or actually irremediable. On the other hand, even if recent biological studies do not reject this trend toward the mathematicization of science, independently from the considerations of atomic physics, they are oriented toward new "comprehensive" mathematical systematizations, which absolutely reject the Cartesian tendency to explain integrally a whole by its parts. The sciences of man, on the other hand, particularly depth psychology and anthropology, seem more and more to rebel against the schema of rationalist materialism in which the 19th century had hoped to imprison them definitively. Every modern confrontation between science and theology obviously must be fully conscious of this situation, which no longer corresponds to what even recently could still have been thought to be classic.

In any case, we must acknowledge in principle that an experimental science of the physical universe could not conflict with a sound theology, since the same God is the author both of nature and grace; but in fact, since theology, like science, is the creation of men who are fallible for many reasons, conflicts can temporarily arise that must simply leave room on both sides for a more thoughtful analysis of the problems involved, and thereby sooner or later discover their solution. However, we shall expect this result from precise confrontations on carefully delineated borderline questions, rather than from overall general syntheses. In this latter case, it can be more difficult to conquer the temptation to a simple concordism that would artificially distort both the data of science and that of theology, ending up in a mere verbal agreement.

SCIENTIA MEDIA   According to Molina, this is the knowledge that God has of the free determinations of his creatures. It is depending upon this knowledge that he would give them efficacious grace or not. See PREDESTINATION.

SCOTISM   The philosophical and theological system of the Franciscan theologian John Duns Scotus, a contemporary of St. Thomas Aquinas. Its principal characteristics are voluntarism (particularly noticeable in his theory of the divine freedom to which he does not give even the rational limits assigned to it by St. Thomas), the rejection of the distinction between essence and existence in creatures, the refusal to put the principle of individuation in matter, and the assertion that the Incarnation would have taken place in any case, even if there had been no sin. In the article INCARNATION will be found the principles of a discussion of this last thesis.

SECULAR   This word is used of the clergy who remain in the world, not only because of their pastoral responsibilities, but also because they do not take religious vows. It also refers, in this latter sense, to the laity, and more particularly to the temporal authority that they can exercise. For a Christian, the word secular (any more than the word lay) cannot mean "profane" (*see* LAITY).

SEMI-PELAGIANISM   The error of those who, without following Pelagius completely, could not accept the formulas that St. Augustine used against him. *See* GRACE and PELAGIANISM.

SENSES   In accordance with the very positive biblical notion of the *body* (q.v.), orthodox Christian theology has always looked upon the corporeal senses as obviously limited means of knowledge, although they do have their own value within their context. What spiritual theology condemns is an importance given to a knowledge, and even more to a sensual enjoyment, that would overshadow the perception of the importance of spiritual realities, whether they are supernatural or even only rational. On the other hand, following Origen, theology has developed a doctrine of the spiritual senses, as the firstfruits of the transformation and spiritualization of the body itself that will be the result of the general resurrection.

SENSE OF SCRIPTURE   It is an established doctrine of the Church that the Scriptures have but one meaning, although this unity is mysterious and therefore lends itself to various aspects which are not contradictory but complementary. It is in this light that to the literal sense, which results from the immediate context, there has been added a spiritual sense, which flows from the text but in the light of the totality of the biblical perspectives. This sense itself can entail three aspects: the allegorical sense properly so-called, which relates to Christ; the tropological sense, which relates to the life of the individual Christian; and the anagogical sense, which relates to the eschatological fulfillment of the whole Mystical Body of Christ. As has already been said in the article ALLEGORY, we must carefully distinguish the principle of this distinction from the more or less fanciful allegories, which are called merely accommodative. These can be found in ancient and medieval tradition, but they are hardly more than figures of speech. Yet the traditional notion itself of these various senses, on their different levels, is far from being opposed to a truly scientific exegesis, and is completely justified by the way in which this exegesis has brought out how the progress of revelation is made throughout the Bible by a transposed reapplication of the same notions and the same images. It is in this way that notions as capital as those of the Redemption or the Messiah grew out of the deliverance of the Hebrews who were rescued from slavery in Egypt, or the notion of the king as the anointed one of the Lord.

SERVANT   This name is given by a whole series of texts in the second part of the book of Isaiah to a mysterious figure who appears to fulfill God's plans, but in a way other than man expected. They are essentially: Isa. 42,1–7; 49,3–6; 50,4–11; and especially 52,13–53,12. Other texts, either of Isaiah or of other books, like Isa. 61 or Ps. 21(22), seem to be connected with this same cycle. Three interpretations, which are not necessarily exclusive, seem to be shared by the exegetes with regard to this idea in Israel. According to one of them, this apparently rejected servant, suffering yet freeing the multitude by bearing their sins in his own body, is the people itself, or rather the "remnant" (*see* CHURCH) that has been purified by its trial. According to others, it is the prophet himself. Lastly, although with much hesitancy, it seems that certain people, particularly among the rabbis, saw it as a figure of the Messiah, although Jewish exegesis posterior to Christianity endeavored to combat or ignore this interpretation. There is no question that there is a collective aspect in the figure of the Servant, or that it was inspired by the sufferings of certain prophets, more particularly perhaps by those of Jeremiah. But certain details of the text can with difficulty be reconciled with an interpretation other than the one that looks upon the Servant as an individual called by God to bear not only the sins of the people but those of the whole world, and thus to offer a sacrifice of expiation with a universal import (cf. particularly Isa. 49,3–6).

It does not seem questionable that Christ made use of this figure to explain to his followers, in advance, what the meaning of his death would be. He did it particularly by combining a reference to Isa. 53 with the quite supernatural figure of the Son of man in Dan. 7, who comes on the clouds of heaven to establish the *Kingdom of God* (q.v.), as in these words spoken on the eve of His passion: "The Son of man has not come to be served but to serve, and to give his life as a ransom for many" (Matt. 20,28 and Mark 10,45). It is also this figure that will be fundamental in the interpretation that the apostles will give of the passion. (Cf. the *"pais theou"* of Acts 3,13 and 26,4,27 and 30, the literal Greek translation of the *ebed Adonai* of Isaias).

SEX   The whole Bible supposes that human sexuality and its fecundity are willed by God and are the pledge of his blessing (cf. Gen. 1,27–28 as well as Gen. 2,18–25). Nevertheless, once sin was committed by the human couple (occurring in the form of a mutual consent to a sensual suggestion—cf. Gen. 3), it follows that the divine curse will strike man and woman at the outset in their own relations, and it will carry on to their posterity, even though from the beginning they had the hope of a reparation. Not only, however, was the initial blessing granted to human fertility not taken away, but the prophets, following Osee and Ezechiel, do not hesitate to see in the human couple's intercourse an image of the relations between God and His people. They in turn pave the way for an exalted view of these relations in themselves. It is thus that the two great royal epithalamia of the Song of Solomon and of Psalm 44 (45) will be interpreted by the rabbis in the light of the restored union between God and his People in the future.

In the New Testament, Christ both recalls and renews the original blessing of marriage, and the requirements that this blessing implies, although he also clearly indicates that to sacrifice everything, including marriage, and follow him, can be still more noble (cf. Matt. 19 and par.). Similarly, St. Paul exalts Christian marriage to the point of making it a genuine participated image of this unique love that exists between Christ and his Church, while exalting virginity consecrated to Christ as a sacrifice of that image to the more perfect and more immediate realization of sanctity (cf. Eph. 5,21–33 and 1 Cor. 7). In the same way, far from setting them in opposition, Christian tradition constantly connects the consecration of virginity to Christ and marriage, as two ways of realizing the same charity, one being more expressive of the final flowering of the love of God in the love of men, and the other more radical in its realization of this end by its initial consent to this sacrifice.

We will note that the requirements with which Christianity surrounds the normal satisfaction of the sensual instinct in marriage are not based on a condemnation of it, but, on the contrary, on a very exalted view of its intrinsic value, as well as on a realistic view of the imbalance resulting from original sin to which man is subjected. This obliges him to an ascetical discipline, both in order to restore the purity of this instinct and to go beyond the instinct itself, if he is called to do so. Modern depth psychology, and particularly the most solid elements in the discoveries of Sigmund Freud, bring an unexpected confirmation to the importance of sexuality, and manifest more particularly how impossible, both psychologically and morally, it is for man to look upon it merely as some sort of sport in which he does not become completely involved.

SIMONY   From the name of Simon the Magician, and the episode narrated in Acts 8,9 ff., the word simony traditionally pertains to every buying or selling of spiritual realities, or temporal ones that are inseparable from these spiritual realities (like an ecclesiastic benefice). Considered as an especially grave sin and equivalent to heresy (see St. Thomas Aquinas, *Sum. Theol.*, IIa-IIae, q.100), simony has always been sanctioned in the Church with the most severe punishments, entailing the nullity of the conferral of whatever benefice or ecclesiastical function was involved. (See can. 727 ff.)

SIN   Properly speaking, sin is the resistance of the will of man to the will of God or his turning away from it. The notion of sin therefore is distinct from a simple moral fault by the introduction of an expressly religious consideration. Protestant theologians have underlined, and not without reason, that in the Bible sin as such is not contradistinguished so much from virtue as from faith. This is certainly evident in the picturesque description of the first sin that we find in the third chapter of Genesis: man sins by refusing to believe in the divine word and by preferring to it something more perceptible to his senses that arouses his own selfish sensuality. Yet this distinction ought not to be pushed too far since *faith* (q.v.), in the Bible, is never considered real unless it results in obedience. (Isaiah, who did more than any other Old Testament writer to shed light on what faith is, sets up an identification, as it were, between faith and obedience.) On the other hand, one of the most consistent traits of biblical religion is that it combines the primitive ritual notion of sin (i.e., as the profanation of what is sacred) with a moral notion. Even for Amos, sin was both an idolatry (worship due the Creator given instead to creatures) and an injustice toward one's neighbor (cf. Amos 4). The Decalogue, with its two tablets of the Law, is the clearest implicit expression of this identification that is so proper to the Bible.

In the New Testament, the notion of sin is deepened through the teaching of Jesus, especially in the Sermon on the Mount, and broadened so as to include internal acts as well as external actions, and faults of omission as well as positive faults. It is further developed theologically by St. Paul in chaps. 5 to 7 of the Epistle to the Romans. Sin is no longer looked upon as an isolated action, but rather as a state in which man finds himself immersed: a state that goes back to the very origins of mankind, and even more as a deeply mysterious power that kept us in a real bondage, as long as Christ had not come and the gift of his Spirit had not regenerated us. The original fault of the first man is now understood as having produced in his progeny—all mankind—a universal inclination; at the present mankind sins in all its members, and when man comes face to face with the Law, which reveals to him what his life ought to be, he merely becomes all the more painfully aware of his present powerlessness, despite his feeble desires that come to nothing. Only the cross of Christ has been able to break this curse and, in fact, only the gift of the Spirit, which is its fruit, equips us for a struggle against sin that is not vain.

To this must be added the close connection the Apostle makes between death and sin: "Therefore as through one man sin entered into the world and through sin death, and thus death passed unto all men because all have sinned" (Rom. 5,12). It may be said that around the exact interpretation of this text revolve all the later controversies over sin. But before we examine them, we must shed light on this connection between sin and death made by the Apostle. It supposes that death is not only a physical fact but the mark of the curse that sin carries within itself. Life, life in fullness, indissolubly physical and spiritual, was the goal of man's creation by God. But sin manifests its malice by bringing about death. On the other hand, death is not merely a punishment foreseen by God for sin, for in the cross of Christ it serves as the occasion of the reparation for sin. All of this is deeply rooted in the teaching of the prophets: on the one hand the affirmation that God was the spring of living water from which men have foolishly turned away in order to hew out broken cisterns that hold no water (Jer. 2,13), and, on the other hand, the vision of the tortured Servant whose wounds bring healing to the people (Isa. 53).

The error of Pelagius in the beginning of the 5th century led for the first time to posing the problem of the propagation of original sin. Pelagius actually taught that sin was passed on from the first man by imitation alone and not by generation, and that our nature remained, on the spiritual plane at least, endowed with the same possibilities for good that were man's in the beginning and that Adam's fault had nothing more than physical consequences in his descendents (namely, loss of the primitive immunities from death or sickness). In order to answer Pelagius and his disciples (in particular Julian of Eclanum who was to outdo his master in his optimism about the present state of human nature), St. Augustine set himself to defining how Adam's sin is propagated and comes down to us. He himself does not succeed in avoiding certain pessimistic exaggerations in the other direction (e.g., the idea that original sin is passed on by the fact of culpable concupiscence intrinsically connected with every conception). Above all, however, he unwittingly tended not only to distinguish but to separate this problem of the transmission of original sin from that of actual sin, to such an extent that it becomes difficult to accept the assertion that our guilt is derived from Adam's. This in turn, together with new reactions in the direction of an exaggerated optimism, led to a further definition of original sin that reduced it in us to an almost wholly juridical notion, which for that very reason was perhaps even more difficult to accept.

The Church, however, in the canons of the Councils of Carthage, and especially, in the following century, of Orange, did retain the following aspects of his teaching: 1) that original sin is truly transmitted to us (can. 2 of the Council of Carthage in 418; D.B. 102—an assertion that was to be resumed and specified by the Council of Trent, Sess. V., no. 3; D.B. 790); 2) that the sin of Adam not only brought harm to man's body (by death and the other infirmities that came to be its consequence, a thing which Pelagius himself, after having once denied it, ended up by acknowledging), but that man was entirely impaired by it (*in deterius commutatum*), his freedom in particular being injured (can. 1 of the Council of Orange; D.B. 174); 3) that it is not therefore only the punishment of sin but sin itself that has passed from Adam to all his race (*ibid.*, can. 2; D.B. 175).

St. Thomas Aquinas gives a balanced synthesis of the whole question, thanks to the use he makes of the metaphysical notion of *nature* (q.v.). He holds that, by original sin, all mankind was wounded in what was natural to it, in addition to being deprived from now on of all of its gratuitous gifts (together with *grace*, not only the *supernatural* gifts in the strict sense but also the so-called *preternatural* gifts—qq.v.). As for the particular wound in man's nature, he specifies that the constitutive principles of human nature remain unchanged, although man's inclination toward good is diminished and his original righteousness (i.e., reason's control over the concupiscence of the senses that he had received in the beginning in his primitive state of grace) is totally abolished. (*Sum. Theol.*, Ia-IIae, q.85, a.1.) As for the actual transmission of this fallen state, he explains it simply by saying that we receive it from Adam by receiving life from him through natural generation, since in this generation we are moved by him just as a limb is by the soul (*ibid.*, q.81, a.4). Finally, although original sin in us is not an act but an inborn state, it is nevertheless in us as a sin of nature, even prior to our sinning actually in the manner of an inborn *habit* (q.v.) (*ibid.*, q.92, a.1, the corpus of the article and *ad 2um*).

Again, St. Thomas defines original sin in our first parents as having been basically a sin of pride. However, because the pride of being equal to God destroyed original righteousness, this sin reached its climax in a fault of sensuality, since concupiscence was no longer governed by reason (*Sum. Theol.*, IIa-IIae, q.163, a.1 and 2; cf. in art. 1, ad 2um). Consequently, original sin subsists in us formally in our being deprived of original righteousness, and materially in the disordered concupiscence resulting from this (*Sum. Theol.*, Ia-IIae, q.82, a.3). Finally, St. Thomas gives what has become the classic explanation of the seven capital sins (vainglory, gluttony, lust, avarice, sloth, envy, and anger), and of the distinction between mortal and venial sin; mortal sin is directly opposed to the end of the spiritual life itself, namely, charity, while venial sin is only indirectly opposed to it (cf. *Sum Theol.*, Ia-IIae, q.84, a.4 and q.88).

With the Protestant Reformation there came an intensified return to what there was of exaggerated pessimism in Augustinianism as a reaction against the Neo-Pelagian (indeed, quite simply neo-pagan) optimism of the Renaissance. Consequently, the fifth session of the Council of Trent, in reasserting (indeed in making still more precise) the statements of the ancient councils on the reality of original sin and of its transmission (nos. 1–4; D.B. 787–791), rejected the Lutheran interpretation of the total corruption of human nature by this sin, at least in its consequence: namely, that baptism (or grace in general) could not really take away our sin, but only cause it no longer to be imputed to us. At this juncture, the Council specified that if concupiscence actually subsists after baptism, it is no longer a sin properly speaking for the baptized, since they now have the power of grace whereby they are able to overcome it (*ibid.*, no. 5; D.B. 792). In the same line, in the sixth session, the first chapter of the decree on justification made it clear that if free will was weakened by the fall, it was nevertheless not totally destroyed (D.B. 793). However, laxist tendencies were manifested in more than one of those who fought the Reformation, which at first was merely schismatic and only later heretical; these tendencies in turn provoked the Baianist and Jansenist reactions that, on this point in particular, practically reechoed the positions of original Protestantism.

In the Baianist or Jansenist propositions, and from the opposite camp in those of the various laxists, condemned in the 17th and 18th centuries, there is found an echo of this pendulum of Christian thought, in which the point of balance has perhaps not yet been fully reached. The growth of naturalistic rationalism in the 19th century was to lead the Church to emphasize, more than had been done in any document of the *magisterium* until then, the obfuscation of the human intellect that was the consequence of sin. (See D.B. 1616 and 1617, against Lamennais, 1634 ff., against Hermes, and especially a passage from the allocution *Singulari Quadam* of Piux IX, December 9, 1854; D.B. 1643.)

In conclusion, let us note some precisions of vocabulary. In original sin a distinction is made between *peccatum originans* (the act of our first parents) and *peccatum originatum* (the state resulting from it for all of human nature). In the *peccatum originatum*, on the other hand, there is the *reatus culpae* (the privation of the state of righteousness) that is distinct from the *reatus poenae* (the loss of the preternatural privileges, i.e., the exemption from suffering and death, for the present life, and the consequent incapacity of arriving at eternal life). Finally, we call "philosophical" sin a disobedience to the law of nature, which, when committed by men who do not know God or who pay no attention to him, could not have the malice of mortal sin nor, consequently, result in damnation for those committing it. That such a sin could exist was condemned by Alexander VII on August 24, 1690, as a scandalous and rash proposition (D.B. 1290).

SLAVERY   The condition of one who is looked upon as the property of another, and consequently cannot have any property himself. It is understood also of the institution itself. Slavery, in the ancient world, was always more or less tempered, if not by law, at least by custom, restricting to some extent the power of the master over the slave. It is in this light that the Justinian Code, reflecting an opinion not devoid of historical foundation, explains and justifies slavery by considering it as a mitigation of the primitive custom of putting prisoners of war to death: the word slave (*servus*) would come from *servare* ("to protect"), and not from *servire*. These considerations explain why Christianity from the outset did not condemn the institution as such, but simply, as we see in

St. Paul's Epistle to Philemon, reminded the master of his duty to treat the slave as a man and as a brother in Christ. Nevertheless, St. Paul also counsels the slaves who can obtain freedom to take advantage of it, for the Christian, properly speaking, cannot belong to anyone except Christ (1 Cor. 7,21–23). Feudal society made the *servus* (serf) into a man who remained attached to the seigniorial lands, but was bound to the seignior by a contract that carried with it reciprocal obligations for the seignior himself, in particular the defense of the serf and the guarantee of his well-being. The medieval slave (*sclavus*) was different from the serf in that he was always a prisoner of war who had come from peoples supposed to be hostile to Christianity (his name comes from *Slavus*). When the lands of America and Africa were discovered, the popes and theologians protested with increasing force against the claims of the Most Christian and Most Catholic kings to draw new slave resources from these territories, but it must be acknowledged that their protests had little effect for a long time. Certain Protestant theologians, on the other hand, were of the opinion that Negro slavery could be justified by the curse brought against their supposed ancestor, Ham (Gen. 9,25). At the end of the 18th century, these claims were forcefully refuted by the Anglican Englishman Wilberforce. He was the originator of the movement for the general suppression of slavery, which was encouraged by the Holy See since the Congress of Vienna in 1815.

The notion of slavery has played a great part in Christian theology and spirituality, on the basis of the texts of the second part of Isaiah, which describe Israel or the Messiah as the *ebed Adonai*, the "Servant" (or "slave") of the Lord. St. Paul presents fallen man as the slave of sin, death, and the devil (cf. Gal. 4 and Rom. 7). Christ has freed us from these tyrants (Rom. 6,18 and 8,2; cf. Gal. 5,1). But, St. Paul adds, "Having been set free from sin, you have become the slaves of justice . . . of God" (Rom. 6,18–22). He himself never ceases to proclaim himself "the slave of Christ" (Rom. 1,1; Gal. 2,10; Phil. 1,1). To his disciples, he even calls himself "your slave for Jesus' sake" (2 Cor. 4,5). And he invites them all to become "through love the servants of one another" (Gal. 5,13). For Christ himself, although he was the image of God, took on for us the image of a slave (Phil. 2,7). But it is through this action that he was led into the divine Seigniory in contrast to Adam, who, in his pride and his will for autonomy and domination, was made the slave of the evil powers (cf. the continuation of Phil. 2). Similarly, our being raised to the divine sonship, conferred upon us by the Spirit, supposes a voluntary subjection. Inversely, subjection to God will make us truly sons and truly free, in giving us over to the domination of the Spirit, a domination of charity. Whence the formula of Pauline asceticism: "I chastise my body and bring it into subjection, lest after preaching to others I myself should be rejected" (1 Cor. 9,27).

The spirituality of being a slave of Jesus (or of Mary, to whom Jesus himself had willed to be submitted), advocated by Bérulle or St. Louis-Marie Grignion de Monfort, must be interpreted in this sense and can be so justified.

SOBORNOST   See CATHOLICITY

SODOMY   From the sin of the inhabitants of Sodom (Gen. 19). It generally designates sexual relations against nature.

SON OF GOD   A title that has come to express in the formulas of faith the singular relationship which unites Christ to God the Father, as to his own Father, in an incommunicable sense. This expression in its primary sense among the Jews simply denoted a special adoption, which made of a privileged man, such as the king, the object of a special attention on God's part. It is in this way that the title was at first given to the Messiah as the ideal king. In the article JESUS CHRIST we have seen how Jesus revealed to his disciples the much deeper sense in which this appellation was to be applied to him. Thus for St. Paul, and even more for St. John, the doctrine of the divine sonship became the core of the Gospel.

SON OF MAN   So frequent in the Gospels, this title disappeared almost completely soon afterward, already in the other books of the New Testament. It can be understood only by alluding to the great vision of Dan. 7, in which a "son of man" appears in the clouds of heaven, i.e., a person who appears as a man but who is none the less quite supernatural in origin. This evangelical title, consequently, far from insisting upon the manhood of Christ, as might be believed, while it admits this as understood, does more than merely hint at a divine character. This is what St. Paul says in another manner when he calls Jesus the "heavenly man" (cf. 1 Cor. 15). The difficulty in understanding the meaning of such a paradoxical title outside of a Semitic context explains why it was so soon abandoned, despite the abundant use Jesus made of it in referring to himself. In fact, when it happened later that it was again revived, for example, among theologians who expounded the metaphysical theory of the Incarnation, they simply contrasted it with the expression "Son of God," since the two were supposed to designate the two natures in Christ. This contrast has remained familiar to preachers. But it must be noted that it does not correspond with the meaning of the words in the biblical sense taken literally (see JESUS CHRIST).

SONSHIP   The term denotes the relationship that exists between a son and his father; in the theological sense, especially between the Son and the Father in the heart of the Trinity. In regard to the faithful, the word *adoption* (q.v.) is preferably used. It must be emphasized that since sonship is a relationship between persons (and not, properly speaking, between natures), Christ, even considered in his manhood, is in no way the adopted son of the Father but only the Son in the sense primarily proper to his divinity (cf. St. Thomas Aquinas, *Sum Theol.*, IIIa, q.23, a.4). Sonship in the Trinity has been definied by the Council of Nicaea (325), against the Arians, as an eternal relationship which implies neither inferiority nor subordination.

SOTERIOLOGY   A name given to all of that part of theology which deals with *salvation* and *redemption* (qq.v.).

SOUL   In a very general way, the soul is understood to be the immaterial principle without which it seems impossible to explain the different movements and behavior of living beings in general, and the thought of human beings in particular. But this definition has to be made more precise, since the development of the notion of soul has had a rather complex evolution over the course of the history of philosophy and theology.

It can be said that the ancients' conception of the notion of soul took two different directions. One tended to emphasize the distance that separated soul from matter, and the other attempted to define as precisely as possible the soul's relationship to the matter it enlivened.

Certainly the most representative witness to the first tendency is Plato. Whatever the arguments he used as proof, he never ceased to insist upon the immortality of the soul and on its essential difference from the body. Immortality meant for him not only that the existence of the soul perdured after the death of the individual, but that this existence itself is in such a way prior to that of the individual the soul inhabits that the soul actually is the immortal person. From this comes the idea that the soul has to make the greatest effort to detach itself from the matter that dulls its perception, so that it may arrive at a better knowledge of itself and at a better existence. There is, however, no question here of a passage into eternity, for the immortality of the soul participates in the immortality of the world, and the better existence that it is bound to long for is still an existence in time.

From Plato on, a whole philosophical tradition developed that was both intellectual and mystical, and of a profoundly dualistic inspiration. It held that the soul could reach the fullness of its destiny only through emptying itself through contemplation and reflection of the matter that holds it a prisoner. Plotinus was the first representative of this tradition to have had any considerable influence on Christian spirituality. Among the moderns, Descartes (to whom we shall return) and especially Spinoza made use of the principle of Platonist dualism.

The second tendency appearing in antiquity is not so much concerned with the essence of the soul, but rather with the way it gives life to living beings. Aristotle defines it as "that by which we live, feel and especially, think" (*De Anima*, 414a,12). It is that whereby life, which was a potency in the body, becomes act, namely, the form of the body. That is, the soul could not be thought of without the body to which it gives life, and like the body it too is mortal. Everlasting life does not exist for the Aristotelian soul.

The Stoics are even stronger on this point. They hold that the soul of the world cannot be differentiated from the world itself, and that the individual soul is but a part of the world soul. But the teaching of the Stoics is above all the ethics of submission to the order of things, which is their definition of virtue. It follows that the soul's fate is bound up with the exercise of virtue. The wise man will see his soul survive at death and become identified with the soul of Zeus, although it will retain its personal awareness. The souls of the fool and the wicked man, however, will pass away at the hour of death, only to revive in an impersonal form in the flames of the cosmic hell. This manner of considering the nature and destiny of the soul from a moral point of view, which arises from a deep religious intuition, had a considerable influence on the development of Christianity.

Finally, for Epicurus, the soul is a "subtile body." Nothing that is thinkable can be anything other than material, and it is utterly fruitless to expect survival and approbation in an afterlife. Despite its elementary atomism, this theory will also influence the Christian thinkers of the first centuries, as well as, and this especially, a whole area of modern psychology.

From this quick survey of the historical horizon, two tendencies evidently come to light. The first is more metaphysical and insists on the immaterial and therefore immortal character of the soul, but at the same time runs the risk of cleaving the unity of human nature in two. The other, however, is more psychological and more interested in the way in which matter is made alive, although at the same time it risks ensnaring the notion of soul within the confines of its earthly existence. In any case, only a purely human notion of immortality can be derived from this. With the possible exception of Stoicism, there is no answer given as to how the soul can possess anything more than a hope of an immortality that is limited to the cyclic renewal of a world to which the soul never ceases to belong.

In the Bible, the problem is not at all posed in the same way. The far from speculative concern of the sacred writers was centered around a fact asserted by the divine word from the very beginning: living man is a being created by God. Two fundamental texts express the biblical view.

"Then the Lord God formed man of dust from the ground, and breathed into his nostrils the breath of life; and man became a living being" (Gen. 2,7).

"Then God said, 'Let us make man in our image, after our likeness; and let him have dominion over the fish of the sea, and over the birds of the air, and over the cattle, and over all the earth, and over every creeping thing that creeps upon the earth.'
So God created man in His own image, in the image of God He created him; male and female He created them" (Gen. 1,26–27).

From these two texts, three ideas at once come into relief. The first is that man has received directly from God something that is expressed here in a very concrete way and which makes him a being completely different from the animals. Although like him they are also formed from the earth, they do not receive this breath of life (Gen. 2,19). The second idea, formulated differently in the two accounts, is that man is master over the rest of the creation, as a being of another order. In the last and most important idea man exists after the image of God, an expression that for a long time to come was to stimulate theologians.

It is then a question here of a complete though quite rudimentary anthropology and not of philosophical reflections about the two components of human unity, spirit and matter.

Yet, the problem that most concerns the writers of the Old Testament in this anthropological view is the destiny of the whole man. They found themselves actually caught in a contradiction that the progress of revelation was to take a long time to solve. A complete solution was found only in the New Testament. On the one hand, the dignity that the Genesis text confers on man promises him at the same time a destiny bound up in one way or another with God. But in another respect, the brutal fact of death, as long as more precise reflections did not come to the fore to clear up the problem, seemed to be a separation not only from men, but also from God—a real disappearance. "When thou hidest thy face, they are dismayed; when thou takest away their breath, they die and return to their dust" (Ps. 104,29).

Perhaps the influence of Stoicism on the later books of the Old Testament introduced some more abstract notions into biblical thought (cf. Wis. 8,19–20, and Dan. 3,86), but that does not seem to modify to any great extent the essential difficulty of the problem for the ancient

Jews. Only progressively does the idea of resurrection come to the fore, as can be seen for example in all of the 37th chapter of Ezechiel, and especially in 2 Mach. 13,38–46. However, no unanimity was achieved among all the Jews as is demonstrated in the Pharisee-Sadducee disputes (Matt. 22,23–33; Acts 23,6–8).

Therefore, we must not look too hard in the Old Testament for something resembling a theory about the nature of the soul. The conviction about the superiority of man over the rest of the world and of his divine destiny, despite the anguishing problem of death, gives sufficient grounds to make the Chosen People think that there was something more in man than the slime of the earth from which he was formed. And that is enough.

The belief in the Resurrection constitutes without doubt the center of New Testament revelation. And it is precisely in the context of this belief that we look for the substructure of a teaching on the origin and the nature of the soul. Actually neither in Aramaic nor Hebrew is there a term that exactly translates the notion. The word *psyche*, at least in the Gospels, seems to correspond more to the Hebrew notion of breath of life than to what the Greek writers actually understood by it. There do exist, however, texts affirming very strongly the distinction between the spiritual and bodily principles of man. Thus Matt. 10,28, "And do not be afraid of those who kill the body but cannot kill the soul. But rather be afraid of him who is able to destroy both soul and body in hell."

In the same way the teaching of St. Paul depends in large measure on the traditional concepts of the Old Testament. So in 1 Cor. 15,45, he practically repeats the words of Genesis: "The first man, Adam, became a living soul [or rather, breath]." It is certain that he had no doubt about the distinction between the soul and the body. A text like 1 Thess. 5,23 is explicit. "May your spirit and soul and body be preserved sound, blameless . . ." But we cannot expect to find in St. Paul a precise psychological analysis, since this did not enter into his scope as a preacher of the Gospel.

Nevertheless it was St. Paul who introduced into theological language terms that up until then had been especially current in Greek philosophy. This allowed the introduction of certain interesting specifications. He actually did make use of words that may be translated "judgment, reason, intelligence" side by side with the words spirit and soul. So in 1 Cor. 14,15, "I will pray with the spirit, but I will pray with the understanding also," and Rom. 7,23, "I see another law in my members, warring against the law of my mind . . ." But, while in Greek philosophy the intellectual life was the highest activity of the soul, which found in it its most perfect expression, and on the other hand the breath of life was merely a component of much lesser dignity in the living being,

St. Paul overturned these notions and set them up in a new relationship. Prescinding from the various shades of meaning, it seems actually that intellectual activity for him is only an element of the total life of the soul, a life that comes from God and is destined to receive a spiritual completion which will give it its ultimate dignity. Let us examine 1 Cor. 15,45: "If there is a natural body, there is also a spiritual body. So also it is written, 'The first man, Adam, became a living soul'; the last Adam became a life-giving spirit." We can see then from this that the Pauline view remains uniquely dominated by the problem of the Resurrection, and that because of this fact, a distinction is established between the body on the one hand and the intellectual and spiritual character of the soul on the other. At least the soul's existence, if not the explanation of its nature and origin, is explicitly affirmed in this doctrine. This teaching, constructed as it is around the Resurrection, thoroughly modified the metaphysical and psychological views of Greek speculative thought; and it was to have the greatest consequences on later theological development, which was itself heir to both forms of thought.

In her infancy, the Church found herself faced on the one hand with a certitude of faith, the Resurrection, which implies the existence of the soul; and on the other hand with a conglomerate of heterogeneous philosophical teachings about the origin and nature of the soul. Neither the need for a psychological explanation nor the demands of preaching could really be content with this completely bare affirmation, nor with these disparate and contradictory analyses. It was necessary to unify these analyses around the first affirmation of faith and to shed light upon it through these analyses themselves. Over the long course of this theological research, the teaching authority of the Church did not intervene so much to solve the question metaphysically, but rather to condemn theories that seemed irreconcilable with the intangible data of faith. We shall consequently find these decisions cropping up along the whole course of theological research, compelling it each time to narrow down the problem a little more and to come closer and closer to a coherent doctrine.

One of the first attempts at reconciliation is found in St. Justin's *Dialogue with Trypho*. But even here there is only a juxtaposition of the belief in the immortality of the soul, as a gift of God, with the philosophical uncertainties about its precise nature and origin.

To Tertullian we owe the first tract *De anima*. He relies on the tradition of the Stoics and because of this had great difficulty in comprehending the immortality of the soul. This difficulty is all the greater since the completely concrete character of the biblical expressions seemed to him to confirm the confusion that the Stoics thought existed between the capacity of comprehending and the power of imagining. For him, the soul is "born of the breath of God, immortal, corporal and representable." We should be wrong to see here merely a follow-up to the materialism of the Epicureans. Tertullian's concern, on the contrary, was to emphasize profoundly the union of the soul and the body, to insist on the deep unity of human nature, and not to reduce the soul to a part of matter. From the same source also comes his way of conceiving the birth of the soul. In just the same way that the body is developed from the seed of its parents, so the soul is also a part of its parents' soul. This theory, commonly called traducianism, was definitely condemned in the canons of Benedict XII against the Armenian errors (D.B. 533). For a real understanding of Tertullian, however, it cannot be overlooked that behind this theory there was opposition to the Platonic ideas about the preexistence of the soul, ideas directly contrary to the text of Genesis that had been the starting point of this defender of the faith.

Origen, on the other hand, was a Greek and belonged to the current of Platonic thought; this strongly influenced his insistence on the spirituality of the soul. So strongly even, that he went so far as to think that souls were created before bodies. The fact that they were inserted into matter resulted from a forfeiture in them, but one that could be surmounted. It seems indeed that in this instance, although he actually did not go so far as to destroy the unity of the soul, Origen tended to see a distinction between the spirit and the soul. Since for him, this latter term meant the state of the spirit immersed in matter, the vocation of the soul was to become spiritualized so that it might find itself again in the image of God. Origen's doctrine of the preexistence of souls was condemned explicitly by Pope Vigilius (D.B. 203).

In fact, the uncertainties of Greek vocabulary did not make it easy to express the concept of the whole man as it is represented in the thought of the Bible. The reason is that the modes of expression of the two currents of thought bring totally different concepts to bear on the same problem. And this problem is soteriological. The Greeks naturally looked for salvation in the direction of what seemed to them to be the highest activity of the human personality, the intellectual life. St. Paul had, however, underlined the fact that for the Christian faith, it is the whole man who has the assurance of his salvation and of his resurrection. In addition, the use of the Greek vocabulary to express eschatological hopes could only fail as long as Christian thought did not occupy itself with formulating a psychology in which the various faculties of man would appear less like entities different from one another, and more like elements of one and the same existence. St. Augustine seems actually to have been the first to apply himself explicitly to this task, as well as the first to have arrived at a clear conception of the soul as a substance. The terms that may be translated as "vital principle, spirit, mind, reason, intelligence, intellect" are only various aspects of this unique substance. "The soul is a rational substance made to govern the body" (*De Quantitate Animae*, XIII, 22). But still it is difficult to give a definition of the whole man. The problem does not escape him, however, and for this reason he uses the formula "Man is a rational soul who uses a body" (*De Moribus Ecclesiae*, I, 27,52). He thus avoids the errors of both Origen and Tertullian. The birth of the soul is not prior to the body's, nor is the soul begotten as is the body, which developed from the seed of its parents. The parents beget a spiritual being, soul and body. This is the theory of generationism, and while it is not the most widespread theory, it has nevertheless never been the object of a condemnation by the magisterium of the Church.

The formulation that was to become standard was used for the first time in a canon of the Council of Vienne in opposition to the psychology of Peter Olivi, who broke the substantial unity of the soul apart by introducing the idea that it was actually threefold: vegetive, sensate, and intellectual. "The rational and intellectual soul is *per se* essentially the form of the body" (D.B. 481). It was taken up again practically word for word (*essentially* giving way to *immediately*) by Pius IX against Günther. (D.B. 1655.) In all of this the continuous trend of Christian thinking about the soul can be observed, but it was still necessary to justify it rationally in philosophy and psychology. This was the work of the great scholastics, and in particular of St. Thomas Aquinas.

We have already come across the concept of the soul as the form of the body. It is Aristotle's formula, which he used to explain the composition of a human being, and not to be the jumping-off point for a flight into the heaven of ideas. Aristotle bound the soul's destiny up with that of the body to which it gave its form, without however granting it any chance for an afterlife. This is why (at least insofar as it has come down to us) Aristotle's theory appeared to have no chance of serving as a basis for a Christian theology of the soul. The difficulties it had in adjusting to its new climate, once it reappeared in the West through the intermediary of the Arabs, demonstrate this quite well. At least in its beginnings Christian thought appeared to have been much more attracted by the quest of Platonic ideas or by the rigor of Stoic morality, which meant the acceptance and mastery of self, than by this realism that had no door opening out into eternity. However, when considering its aims, the Aristotelian view seemed actually to be more suitable than the other two schools of thought to describe philosophically this unity of man, a unity that God created in its totality with the promise of a future that did not imply its destruction. It was the genius of St. Thomas that perceived this. But how precisely was he able to do it?

Centuries before, St. Augustine's psychology had definitively estab-

lished the dignity of created man in the knowledge of his intellect. This
had been known of course since Plato, but still in Plato's time, as we have
seen, it would have had no application in the case of Adam. For the purpose of the intellectual life is not only to grasp intelligible things, but
especially to know the divine intelligible in the way that it understands
itself, since it recognizes the traces of this divine intelligible in itself. The
God of Augustine is more than pure Act, unaware of the contingent
realities that it drags along behind it. It is a living person who created man
in the beginning with his body and his soul so that he might know Him.
The formula "the soul is the form of the body" allows St. Thomas, then,
to escape the ever-immanent danger of dualism and to avoid falling into
a naturalism that would have no relation to the divine Person. The soul
is created unique and is the principle of existence for matter, which
without it would be precisely *nothing*. What makes it immortal, in
contradistinction to an animal soul, is precisely this character of intellectuality, which is made for the contemplation not only of sensible species
but also of the intelligible *in se*, the living God in whose image it was
made. It is important to emphasize here the way in which Aristotle and
St. Thomas arrived at their conclusion, since it was by virtue of this that
such a synthesis has become possible. The importance of this is not to be
underestimated in our examination of the problem as it is posed in the
modern period. Neither Aristotle nor St. Thomas began by making any a
priori distinction between the soul and bodies, in which the latter would
be denied any value from the very first, and no future reunification of the
concepts would ever be possible. Although they denied any form of
intelligibility *in se* to matter, they sought to define it in relation to the
function of the nature of the soul and thus arrived directly at the crux of
the problem. This is undoubtedly what was missing from the Platonism
of St. Augustine to perfect his theory. When we read his definition,
"man is a soul who makes use of a body," we are tempted to ask, for what
purpose? The answer here is very simple. Without a body, there would
be no soul either, since the definition of man is that he be first and
foremost a man, i.e., a living and intelligent being whose intelligence can
only be exercised through the intermediary of the senses. Only angels are
capable of directly apprehending the intelligible. We are not.

"The soul is a nature which has no relation to extension, nor to
dimensions, nor to the other properties of matter of which the body is
composed" (*Passions*, 1,30). Such is the definition Descartes gives. With
it we come back to Platonist dualism, but in a way that will end up in a
direction diametrically opposed to the Platonic conclusion. Actually,
while Plato saw in mathematics, as did Descartes, thought's most
intelligible expression, he used it to get back to his world of ideas. After
Descartes, mathematics was applied to the study of matter, of extension,

and thus gave rise to modern science. The concept that can be formed of the soul was thus completely modified, and the problem remained couched in such terms that the present age is only beginning to have an inkling about how it can be resolved.

Where thought was considered a substance completely independent from equally substantial matter, a whole philosophy developed in this pseudo-spiritualist direction, in which the problem of the soul is posed in uniquely intellectual terms. Spinoza, Malebranche, and Leibniz are the famous representatives of this tendency. Despite the enormous differences that divide them, their three schools of thought have at least this one thing in common, that each developed a notion of the soul that had no possible relationship to the material world. The limit of these speculations is marked by the theory of Leibniz's monads: the soul, a monad without door or window, is open only to the world of the divine. Only the fiction of the harmony pre-established by God allows the preservation of the concordance of sense knowledge.

The Kantian critique extends the consequences of the teaching still further. The faculty of understanding is not made for the pure intelligible. Only the *phaenomena* are within its grasp. God is unknowable. Nothing can be said about him. Nothing can be said about the essence of things, and in particular about the soul. "Metaphysical problems have to be exorcized," Taine said somewhat later. If there is a Cartesian spiritualism, it remains uniquely rationalistic and is resolved in a metaphysics that has no relationship to reality. The developments of modern science have enabled it to have a field day in opposing the objections of biology and psycho-physiology to this notion of a soul without earthly ties: there is no soul independent of the body, and since our study of bodies does not produce anything even resembling a soul, the soul is only an *epiphenomenon* of the movements of nature. Emptied of the Christian vestiges that it did not integrate into its synthesis, Cartesian parallelism is untenable. Actually, along with this spiritualistic rationalism, that ends up by losing itself in the maze of idealism, a scientific rationalism developed. Its central note was that it endeavored to rid this new synthesis of every metaphysical concept. The application of mathematics, not in exploring divinity but in the investigation of nature, resulted in the birth of modern science and its phenomenal success. From our point of view in this article, nothing can be said about this methodology to which all the material progress of our age owes its origin. But this methodology has also extended its scope to include the study of living matter. Modern biology a priori sees in a living thing nothing more than a network of causal relations, and although these relations may be more complex than they are in brute matter, they are nevertheless of the same nature. It is not our concern here to give any criticism of this a priori method, nor to show how it is not at all certain that the biological discoveries actually do give a complete explanation of all the phenomena of life. It remains merely to say that, thanks to this method, biology has known unquestionable and most beneficial progress.

But the method came to have an even wider application and took up a field of study that had seemed, up until then at least, to have escaped the investigation of direct observation, i.e., the life of the mind and the intellect itself. This was the uproar that resulted from the appearance of Binet's test at the beginning of the century: the intelligible also is measurable. Since this discovery, purely mechanistic psychologies have been multiplying in the style of the theses of Epicurus. But they have been even more radical. The soul is not even a subtile body. It is a useless hypothesis, for example, in the Behaviorism of America and in the Pavlovism in Russia (not to mention an obsolete associationism), where the highest mental activities are reduced to the reflex arc or to a chain of conditioned reflexes. Only one problem exists, and that concerns the entirely determined relations among the motivations of environment, the situation itself, and the responses of the subject who is immersed in them. But just as biology seems unable to completely explain the finality inherent in certain adaptative responses of the differentiated minus of living things, so even less does exclusively scientific psychology seem to be able to explain even the most elementary human behavior. The examination of certain aspects of behavior like love-making, for example, as it was analyzed in so-called depth psychology, seems to be bound to show that the human problem, far from being uniquely a problem of adaptation to given situations, is more deeply a problem of relation. "All personality illnesses are illnesses of intercommunication." In this way, by a sort of regressive procedure of scientific criticism, it appears that everything that is in the realm of matter or materiality (i.e., measurable), in both the human sciences and the others, is a medium of relation, of communication. Cartesian thought is language, and language still belongs to extension. It is easy to see to what solution this road will lead. If all observable reality is a medium of relation, then there is something that enters into the relation and that escapes direct observation. That something is the soul.

Thus it seems that the means of investigation worked out by the progress of the sciences, which is unquestionably the result of the Cartesian method, ends up by creating a complete reversal of the original conclusions of this method. The soul is a nature that in all respects is related to extension. We have proceeded here according to the Aristotelian and Thomistic method, which consists in defining the relation of matter to the soul, instead of starting off from an a priori definition of the soul, differentiating it completely from the world of bodies. From all of this, the soul appears still more clearly to be what the man from Stagira and St. Thomas called it, the form of the body.

M. B.

SPECIES　In theology this word (in the Latin sense of appearances) designates the *accidents* (q.v.) of the elements consecrated in the Eucharist, which subsist absolutely unchanged for the senses after the consecration, and the *transubstantiation* (q.v.) that results from it. These species do not correspond to a proper substance, but since they are no longer anything but the sign of the presence of the body and blood, the reverence given to them is given directly to Christ himself. Since the sacramental presence is bound up with them, it ceases with their adulteration. On the other hand, since the eucharistic species are not the accidents proper to the substance of the body and the blood of the Saviour, nothing that affects them affects Him. See St. Thomas Aquinas, *Sum. Theol.*, IIIa, q.75–77.

SPIRITUAL WARFARE　Stemming from this verse in the Epistle to the Ephesians: "For we are not contending against flesh and blood, but against the Principalities and the Powers, against the world-rulers of this darkness, against the spiritual forces of wickedness on high," (6,13), the spiritual combat remained a familiar theme of spirituality up until modern times, as the title of a celebrated work of Lorenzo Scupoli proves. But the place occupied by this notion in biblical revelation and patristic theology still remains too little known.

The fundamental event in the religious consciousness of Israel (the Passover in which God bound his People to Himself by delivering them from bondage in Egypt) made the saving God definitively the *gibor*, i.e., the powerful warrior, and his redemptive work especially became a victory (cf. the Canticle of Moses in Ex. 15). The appearance and the progressive growth of the concept of the *Messiah* (q.v.) in the expectation of Israel unfolds this theme. The Messiah is to restore the Kingdom of the Lord by a decisive victory over his enemies, and because of this he is precisely the Anointed One of the Lord. This is the reason for the important place given in the Psalms to the idea of the conflict in which God comes to help his People because the battle they are to wage is his battle. Jewish apocalyptic literature, beginning with the Book of Daniel, expands this vision to cosmic proportions. All of history becomes like the lists for a combat in which God and his faithful angels fight against mysterious rebel "powers." The earthly kingdoms of these powers, following one upon the other, are only their instruments and, as it were, their tangible manifestation. Onto this battlefield the heavenly figure of the "Son of Man," appearing on the clouds of heaven, makes his first entrance and prepares to replace the still earthly figure of a merely human Messiah anointed from on high, with the figure still of a "man," but a man who comes himself from on high to win the decisive victory. It is he who will replace the kingdom usurped by the rebel "powers" with the fully real, and therefore only definitive kingdom, the Kingdom of God.

From the very first, Jesus made use of this figure to explain his work. The parable of the "stronger man" who comes to drive away the "strong man" (which obviously is the Devil) in order to wrest his weapons from him, and also the very world itself which had practically become his lair, shows how essential this aspect of struggle and reconquest is to the idea He wishes to impart of His mission (Matt. 12,22–30 and parallels). But at the same time he systematically combines the very glorious and heavenly vision of the *Son of Man* (q.v.) in Dan. 7 with the idea of the *Servant* (q.v.) in Isa. 53, who suffers and is humiliated for the redemption of his people. Thus his cross is shown to be this heavenly victory in which the hostile "powers" that had enslaved the world are conquered forever. There are few texts more expressive of this notion than Col. 2,15, where St. Paul shows us that these powers are chained to the triumphal chariot that his cross has become for the Crucified (cf. the allusion of 1 Cor. 2,8). But this must be seen in the light of Phil. 2,5–11, in order to understand how this victory won in the humiliation of apparent defeat is nothing more than the victory of the *agape*, of the love of God, triumphant in and for man himself, the victory over sin. St. John draws this idea to its natural conclusion and along with St. Paul sees above all in the cross the revelation of the *agape* in a sinful world (cf. Rom. 5,8 and John 15,13), and systematically identifies the idea of Christ's being raised up on the cross with another "raising up," that of his exaltation in the spiritual triumph of the Ascension in which he involves all mankind (cf. John 3,14; 8,28; 12,32).

In relation to this victory of Christ, which is God's victory in and for man, the New Testament describes the enemies that He conquered by his cross. They are first of all, sin and death, which in the 5th chapter of the Epistle to the Romans appear clearly as being only two aspects of one and the same reality, i.e., the voluntary separation from God (vv.12 ff.). Sin and death are therefore merely the two complementary faces of the prince of this world, or of this age (i.e., the one who reigns in the present dispensation that is only passing—cf. John 12,31 and 1 Cor. 2,6, where it is a question not of one but of several evil-working "princes" who become only one in Eph. 2,2). This mysterious person, who is obviously Satan, St. Paul goes so far as to call the "god of this world" (2 Cor. 4,4), implying by this formula both the one who is the ultimate object of all idolatries, and the one who has temporarily usurped God's dominion over His work. Satan, however, acts as it were through his ministers, through the "flesh" and the "world." As will be seen from the explanation of these two terms, neither one nor the other (the first in St. Paul, the second in St. John) refers to physical creation in itself (considered as within us in the first case and around us in the second). They are only the perversion of creation wrought by the power hostile to God through sin. It was sin that put creation in the hands of this power and brought death to it. But it must still be emphasized that these enemies of man, although they are first and foremost enemies of God, whatever they may attempt, end up only in accomplishing the judgment of the divine wrath or the divine law against all iniquity (cf. Rom. 1,18 and 4,15; also Eph. 2,3 and 1 Thess. 1,10). And this has the paradoxical consequence of making Jesus' victory to be a victory of the *agape* both over the divine wrath and even over the divine law (cf. Col. 2,14, where the document annulled by Christ's victory is most certainly the law). But as the fourth Gospel shows so clearly, the wrath of God is only the judgment of his love when it is not accepted.

This vision of struggle and triumph, which fills the Johannine Apocalypse, marks the whole theology and spirituality of the patristic age. It is what is so beautifully expressed in the Easter liturgy and in the fundamental concept of monastic *asceticism* (q.v.). That the Middle Ages began to minimize the role of these notions in the living faith of Christians is assuredly one of the most serious gaps of that period, and unless we recover the spirit of these notions, we shall never be free from juridicalism and depressing psychologism.

STATE   In its proper sense this word designates the body politic in its entirety; improperly, it is applied at times solely to the government of that body. The clear distinction between the State, as an organization of human society geared to its temporal ends, namely, its present life on earth, and the Church is implied in the saying of Christ, "Render, therefore, to Caesar the things that are Caesar's, and to God the things that are God's," explained by its whole context (Matt. 22,15–22 and parallels). This distinction supposes the proper composition of the temporal order and consequently a necessary distinction between the authority of the State and that of the Church. But it also supposes the acknowledged subordination of the temporal ends of man to his spiritual and eternal ends, or at least its *de facto* acceptance. This does not mean that the Church can recognize only the authority of an explicitly Christian State as legitimate. Where all of the people, or at least the majority, are not Christian, it would be artificial to have a Christian State. But in all cases, the State may never set itself up as the supreme end of man nor claim to appoint a supreme end for him, other than that of revelation. A non-Christian State is legitimate, then, only insofar as it respects, at least in fact, and if possible explicitly, these conditions. It is to be noted in this regard that the totalitarian tendencies of the modern State, already noticeable at the end of the Middle Ages, arose from the fact that some States, as they ceased effectively to be Christian, still wanted to preserve the concessions that the Church had granted them in certain mixed spheres (like education), or even directly spiritual ones (like the nomination of Church offices), at a time when they were still actually Christian, although they now wanted to replace the Christian notion of *authority* (q.v.) as a service with the pagan idea of authority as a *dominium*. It is the duty of the Church to protest against these confusions, which are so baneful for the proper ends of the State, as well as for the higher ends for which she is responsible. See St. Thomas Aquinas, *De Regimine Principum*, along with the encyclicals of Leo XIII: *Immortale Dei* (1885), *Rerum Novarum* (1891); of Pius XI: *Quadragesimo Anno* (1931), *Divini Redemptoris* (1937); and of Pius XII: *Summi Pontificatus* (1939).

SUBCONSCIOUS   In modern psychology this term designates all of those memories, impressions, or tendencies that we carry within ourselves and that more or less escape our conscious awareness. Philosophers have acknowledged the existence of the subconscious for a very long time. Plato in particular brought it out through the analysis of memory. But it is in modern (depth) psychology that we find the first attempt to explore all of its richness in detail and to determine its importance in the life of the mind. Certain psychologists, particularly among the followers of Freud, have found themselves so tempted by the importance of these discoveries as to minimize the reality of the conscious awareness itself (and the conscience) and to deny its freedom. But these exaggerations should in no way cause us to reject summarily the very great enrichments that may accrue to our knowledge about man through the study of the rootedness of his conscious awareness in a subconscious that is the result of his bodily condition, and of the whole very strict connection between us and the universe that it implies. If such an exploration of the depths of the soul contradicts the illusions of a Cartesian ultra-spiritualism (*see* CARTESIANISM), it is in full accord with biblical anthropology and that systematization given to it by St. Thomas when he explains the human soul as the substantial form of the body.

SUBJECT   In logic, the subject is that about which one affirms or denies something; in psychology, it is the knower, as opposed to the object known; in metaphysics, it is everything that is capable of receiving a *form* (q.v.).

SUBORDINATIONISM   This word is used of erroneous or formally heretical theologies that lose sight of the equal divinity of the three divine persons, and particularly of the Son in relationship to the Father, as was the case of different ancient errors, of which the best known is *Arianism* (q.v.). They were influenced by the Hellenic notion of *Logos* (q.v.), which is only God's instrument of creation. These errors have been revived in more recent times in various forms of rationalist or liberal Protestantism, which refuse to acknowledge the full divinity of the Saviour.

SUBSISTENCE   A technical theological term used particularly with regard to the Incarnation. It designates the mode of substantial existence (*see* SUBSTANCE) that belongs properly and incommunicably to an individual being. We speak of the subsistence of the humanity of Christ in his divine Person.

SUBSTANCE   A substance is that which exists in itself and not in another, as opposed to an *accident* (q.v.). We distinguish the primary substance, which is the concrete individual subject, from the secondary substance, which is its abstract essence (e.g., a certain man and his humanity).

SUFFERING   Suffering is the consciousness that a living being has of something that is harmful to life in him. It is therefore not so much an evil as a primary reaction to the threat against life. That being the case, if looking for suffering is in itself a certainly morbid act, to accept it in the spirit of reparation for sin, as Christ did and his saints after him, can become an act of virtue. Christianity does not encourage any unhealthy algolagnia; on the contrary, it offers us the possibility of making suffering, like death itself, fruitful.

SUNDAY   The day of the Lord, i.e., the day on which the Lord rose from the dead, the first day of the week, which for that reason replaced the Sabbath of the Old Testament as a day of rest devoted to prayer and public worship. The expression *dominica* (*dies*) is found only in the Apocalypse (1,10), but even in St. Paul we see that this day was publicly sanctified by Christians (1 Cor. 16,2; cf. Acts 2,7). It seems that at first there was a time when Christians observed the Sabbath as well as Sunday, but the celebration of Sunday must have generally been substituted for the other at least by the 2nd century, and it became the object of exclusive precepts at the Council of Laodicea (5th century). The obligation of observing Sunday, such as it has gradually come to be defined, includes two elements. The first and most important is the obligation of taking part in the eucharistic celebration through which the Church herself takes form in the union of her members in the sacrifice of her Head. This is why, although the concern for providing a permanent means of instruction for the faithful, as well as nourishment for their personal prayer is certainly envisioned in this precept, in the spirit of the Church the best private meditation cannot be substituted for assistance at Mass. The second of these elements is the abstaining from work required for everyday living, or from that which is not merely a leisure occupation. Thus Sunday, the weekly feast of the Resurrection, comes to be understood as the Church's anticipation in time of everlasting life, since it is devoted to God's celebration, i.e., to the worship of God who is known and loved by the whole Church gathered together. Secondarily, it also looks forward to the full flowering of all men in peace and joy.

SUPEREGO   By this word modern psychologists understand that part of the psychological subconscious that is constituted by moral obligations and inhibitions. In it, therefore, we distinguish two aspects: one, fully normal, which corresponds to the imperatives actually founded in human nature; and the other, pathological, which is behind all the false idealisms of morbid self-punishment. Odier has proposed that they be set apart by calling the first *Über-ich* and the second *Über-es*. The second is obviously only a caricatural deformation of the first.

SUPERNATURAL   An adjective that designates what is superior in us to the forces not only of our nature but of all nature whether created or creatable. On the other hand, the term *preternatural* is reserved for that which is beyond our nature, but which would not necessarily be so for a creature superior to man. Again, we must distinguish the supernatural *quoad essentiam*, which is the supernatural in the strict sense, i.e., everything that is directly connected with the life of divine grace in us, from the supernatural *quoad modum*, which is in fact the product of a supernatural action, but which could also have been produced, under other conditions, by simply natural or preternatural forces. This is the case with the visions of the saints or miracles like supernatural healings.

The genuine supernatural, being a direct intervention of the life of God in that of his creatures, must not be understood merely as a superior nature. In this regard, the substantive use of the word *supernatural* (recent in theological usage), and even more the use of a term such as *supernature* (which should be abolished) are capable of completely misleading us. Grace is not a superior nature affixed to our own, but an infusion into our nature of a vitality that belongs properly and can belong properly only to the divine nature alone. This is what Thomistic theology means by teaching that grace is, as it were, a supernatural accident created in our nature in order to adapt it to the divine life.

Hence both the radical gratuitousness of everything that is supernatural in the proper sense (no created nature, of itself, could postulate it) and its harmony with human nature, or more generally, spiritual created nature. Every spiritual being, by the fact of its creation in the image of God, has a capacity for the supernatural, and we can even say that it bears within itself a certain obscure desire for it to the extent that it would be incapable, in the deepest part of its will, of not aspiring to come as close as possible to the divine life. Nevertheless, this desire is essentially conditional, and it is not capable of clearly defining its object for itself, since this object can be proposed to it only by a free divine initiative. Outside of this initiative the life of God in itself remains a mystery, impenetrable for the most elevated creatures. But this natural preadaptation of every spiritual creature to the supernatural life explains why, since this life was once offered as an actual possibility to human nature, man was not able to refuse it without irremediably unbalancing his own nature, in contradiction with his deepest will. The result is the wound of nature that is the inevitable and, of itself, irreparable consequence of the loss of the supernatural gifts.

This whole notion, so essential and yet so delicately balanced, is threatened either by errors like that of Baius, who supposes that nature is so weak of itself that it could not subsist without being elevated to the supernatural state, or those like that of Pelagius, who believed he could attribute to the created nature alone inamissible gifts that in fact could not be present in it without grace. *See* GRACE, NATURE, SIN, and PELAGIANISM.

SUPERNATURAL ADOPTION   This term refers to the fact that God looks upon us as his children. As St. John underlines in his first Epistle (3,1), we are not only called the children of God, but actually *are* his children. In other words, supernatural adoption is not merely a juridical fiction but an ontological reality. The Old Testament already expresses the idea that Israel is the "Son of God" (Osee 1,1) and even God's "first-born" (Ex. 4,22–3), i.e., the one to whom the divine inheritance preeminently belongs. Ezechiel describes in particularly expressive terms the reality and generosity of this adoption (16). The teaching of Christ in the Synoptic Gospels, particularly in the Sermon on the Mount, shows the reality of our adoption to be the uppermost Gospel teaching. We are all called to be "sons" of the heavenly Father, in that we are called to a life that shares the likeness of his own: "Do you, therefore, be perfect as your heavenly Father is perfect" (Matt. 5,48). St. Paul in his development of this notion is the first to show a formal relationship between our adoption and the unique sonship of Jesus. This he does in two particularly remarkable passages (Rom. 8,14–7 and Gal. 4,4–7). He shows that adoption has been conferred upon us by the redemptive Incarnation of the Son of God in our flesh, and that the seal of its reality is found in the gift of the Spirit of the Son, which we have received accordingly. Further in the Epistle to the Galatians, the Apostle shows that we receive this adoption by faith in our baptism in which we put on Christ (3,26–28; cf. Rom. 6,5, which states that in baptism we have become as one identity with Christ). Everything that is proper to Christ is appropriated to us by grace. This is the significance of the expression that St. Paul uses in the two great texts of Romans and Galatians when he says that we are co-heirs with Christ. He repeats the same idea in another way when he says that Christ is the "first-born among many brethren" (Rom. 8,29). St. John expresses himself somewhat differently to emphasize the different sense in which Christ is "the Son," the "Only-Begotten Son" (1,18), and he reserves this appellation of "Son" for Christ alone, calling us merely the "children" of God. He nevertheless underlines, as we have already seen in the beginning of the article, the reality that is contained in this appellation (John 1,12; 1 John 3,1–2,10; cf. 5,2). St. Thomas Aquinas sums up the whole of the biblical teaching in this regard by saying that our adoption belongs to the Father as its author, to the Son as its exemplar, and to the Holy Spirit as the one who stamps on our souls the likeness of this exemplar (*Sum. Theol.*, IIIa, q.33, a.2 ad 3um).

There has been much discussion among modern theologians about the formal cause of this adoption. The Council of Trent in fact teaches that the unique formal cause of our justification is God's justice, i.e., not that by which he himself is just, but rather that by which he makes us just. (Sess. VI, chap. 7; D.B. 795). Since the Council tended to identify justification with adoption (Sess. VI, chap. 7; D.B. 799) it has been generally thought that sanctifying grace is the formal principle of adoption itself. Lessius, Petau, and Scheeben, all of whom insisted upon the presence of the Spirit in us (primarily from the Scriptures, but also following the Greek Fathers) as being essential to the reality of our adoption, were opposed on the grounds that they were supposedly teaching a position that somehow detracted from this doctrine. Actually, sanctifying grace itself cannot be separated from the gift of the Spirit since it is not a substance (i.e., a "super-nature") but rather a supernatural accident infused into our nature to prepare it for a share in the life of God, i.e., the very life of the Trinity where the Spirit is the substantial gift of the Father in the Son.

SUPERSTITION   For the ancient Romans, *superstitio* was any form of exaggerated or extravagant religion. For Christian theology, it is to attach a religious import to something that has none, or in any case not the significance attributed to it. Superstition can involve the prayers of the Church or the sacraments themselves, once we are concerned merely with their materiality and not with the attitude of faith that they require. Condemned by Christ in many of the practices of the Pharisees (cf. Matt. 23), superstition is a danger against which Christians ought also to be put on their guard, for it ends up in a genuine degeneration of the most exteriorly correct piety. See St. Thomas Aquinas, *Sum. Theol.*, IIa-IIae q.92–96.

SUPPOSITUM   This Latin word designates the subsistent, substantial individual (*see* SUBSISTENCE). Note that the word subject is sometimes taken in the precise sense of *suppositum*.

SYMBOL   From a Greek word meaning to "bring together," this term is used to designate the synthesized statements of the Christian faith, like the Symbol of the Apostles (or Apostles' Creed), used in the Roman baptismal liturgy, or the Symbol of Nicaea–Constantinople, the work of the first two ecumenical councils, and used in the greater part of the eucharistic liturgies of both East and West.

Besides this special usage, we call symbols the sacred signs that are at the basis of all rituals and all expressions of religious reality. According to Thomistic theology, there is a symbolic element at the root of all of our expressions of the spiritual, since our intelligence is directly applied to the knowledge of the sensible and raises itself to the level of spiritual reality only by starting from sensory data. Hence the doctrine of *analogy* (q.v.). In this regard, we must mention that the symbols which are capable of lending themselves to an effective religious knowledge are the natural symbols to which revelation will bring a higher significance, which is furthermore not an arbitrary one: e.g., the symbolism of the waters of baptism, or food in the Eucharist, or again the symbols borrowed from human relations like fatherhood. Quite another thing, however, are the artificial symbols that man can create from abstract ideas. They are merely calculated signs that are more or less arbitrary.

SYNAGOGUE   From a Greek word meaning "assembly" (*ekklesia* is practically synonymous with it), this word was first used for the assemblies of sacred reading and prayer in Judaism, and was then applied to the building in which they were held, and finally to the ideal assembly of the Jewish people, considered in its essential religious beliefs and practices. The synagogue, as such, is as it were the immediate predecessor of the Church. In detaching herself from it, the Church condemned only its refusal to go beyond itself, a thing that was basic to the tradition of the Synagogue itself. The condemnation brought by Christ against the synagogal traditions must be understood then only with regard to those traditions that become static and deformed by refusing to listen to the promptings of the Spirit. *See* TRADITION.

SYNCRETISM   From the Greek *synkratein*, "to pour together." It is a name given to the system, or rather the Hellenistic trend of thought, that tended to mingle and confuse the most different cults. This name at times has also been given in modern times to endeavors to reunite divided Christians, which were content more or less with proposing a fusion of rituals and doctrines (it is in this sense that we speak of the syncretism of Leibniz).

T

TABERNACLE   This word, which means "tent," was used of the tent described in Ex. 25–26 as a portable sanctuary in which God willed to make himself the companion of the Israelites in their peregrination by indicating his presence with them in a special way. At the time of the erection of the tabernacle (Ex. 40), this presence manifested itself in the luminous cloud (*see* CLOUD, and GLORY). Exodus also states (same chapter, last verses) that the Israelites struck camp when the cloud left the tabernacle. The prophets took this as an image of the free condescension that brings the Lord to dwell among his People but that could not chain him to them. Quite the contrary, the presence in the tent (which the rabbis will call the *Shekinah*—from the verb *shakan*, "to sojourn under a tent") was the proof of the faithfulness of their sovereign Guide.

In the New Testament, it becomes evident that the definitive tabernacle is the humanity of the Saviour (cf. John 1,14) in which, St. John tells us, the Word has willed "to dwell [in a tent] among us" (in Greek, *skenoun*, equivalent to *shakan*). Similarly, the Apocalypse (21,3) states that the heavenly Jerusalem is the *skene*, i.e., the tabernacle, in which God will dwell with men. Lastly, St. Paul, who calls our bodies the temple of the Lord (1 Cor. 3,16–17 and 6,19), gives the name *skenos* to our mortal body in contradistinction to the resurrected body (2 Cor. 5,1.4).

The Feast of Tabernacles (cf. Deut. 16,1–17), primitively the feast of the harvest, with the tabernacles, or more exactly the huts of branches that were built as a reminder of the journey through the desert with the presence of the Lord, seems to have been the memorial of his life-giving presence with his own People and a renewal of the expectation of his manifest Kingdom (cf. Lev. 23,42 ff., and Jer. 2,2). We can see in this feast a perpetual renewal, as it were, of the people's betrothal to their God.

TEMPLE   At first, God refused David's idea of building a temple; the prophets saw in this wish to have the Lord dwell in a stone temple something of the magic illusion of the Chanaanites in which they imagined that they could keep their gods under their control (cf. Jer. 7 and the whole development of the same ideas in the discourse of Stephen, Acts 7,46 ff.). It was subsequently built by Solomon (cf. 2 Kings 7 and 3 Kings 6–8), desecrated and then destroyed at the time of the exile (2 Kings 25), and rebuilt for the first time under Ezra (Esther 6). It was again desecrated, although not destroyed, under Antiochus IV Epiphanes (1 Mach. 1), and Judah Machabee purified it (1 Mach. 4,41 ff.). At the time of Our Lord, the Temple was in the process of being rebuilt through the initiative of Herod (cf. John 2,20). The purification wrought by Jesus in casting out the money-changers (cf. John 2,13 ff., and its par. in the Synoptics), together with his mysterious words about its destruction and reconstruction, which Christians applied to the Resurrection of the Lord (cf. John 2,21), but which was one of the chief points of accusation against him (cf. Matt. 26,61), expresses the sense of the renewal of the covenant: the Temple of God, from now on, is the Body of Christ himself, and St. Paul states that it is also the body of Christians in whom His Spirit lives (cf. 1 Cor. 3,16–17 and 6,19, with 2 Cor. 6,16 and Eph. 1,21).

TEMPTATION   The New Testament word *peirasmos*, translated by temptation, has actually the broader sense of a trial (hence the formula of the Lord's Prayer: *ne nos inducas in tentationem*, which ought rather to be translated by "lead us not into that which would be an occasion of temptation"). For as the Epistle of James says: "God himself tempts no one; but each person is tempted when he is lured and enticed by his own desire" (i.e., the disordered concupiscence resulting from original sin— 1,13–14). Actually, in the full sense of the word, temptation exists only where there is a certain connivance with evil and its feasibility is proposed. This is the reason why theologians say that if Christ was tempted in all things as we are, yet was without sin, according to the Epistle to the Hebrews (4,15), this total absence of sin in him prevented him from ever having experienced such a connivance. On this point, see St. Thomas Aquinas, *Sum. Theol.*, IIIa, q.41.

TESTAMENT   The Greek *diatheke* used to translate the Hebrew *b'rith*, which means covenant, can also have the sense of last will and testament. The author of the Epistle to the Hebrews deliberately plays on this possible dual sense in order to emphasize the very close connection between the New Covenant and the death of Christ (indicated in the words of consecration of the chalice at the Last Supper). Hence the expression "New Testament" that in all languages is looked upon as a synonym for the New Covenant.

THEANDRIC   An adjective made up of two Greek words meaning God-man. Used in a hardly orthodox way by the Monophysites, the term was nevertheless retained, thanks especially to the writings of the Pseudo-Dionysius who made great use of it, to designate those works of the Lord in which his divinity became evident through the instrumentality of his humanity, i.e., everything which is connected with our redemption and our sanctification through the power of the cross.

THEOCENTRIC   A term used at times to underline how the orientation of the life of charity in us, and particularly the life of prayer, is directed basically toward God himself as our ultimate end. Our own real happiness is also involved, but as inseparable from his holy will.

THEOLOGICAL CONCLUSIONS   Today this term refers to the truths theology deduces by reason from the data of revelation. From this viewpoint a distinction is made between two kinds of theological conclusions, according to whether the minor and major are both derived from revelation or whether only one of the premises arises from it, while the other is a truth of the natural order that is held to be certain. But two things must be observed here. The first is that the primary object of theology, according to St. Thomas, is, insofar as possible, not to multiply new conclusions but to explain the directly revealed truths themselves by inter-relating them as conclusions are related to principles. Besides the fact that new conclusions are therefore only the margin of theology, far from being its most important work, it must be added that the whole task of theology can only be accomplished by means of the analogy of faith. Conclusions can therefore be proposed that have the appearance of compelling logic but which are only illusory because the middle term is not considered, according to Cajetan's expression, "in the divine light," i.e., in the light of faith. In this way the Arians deduced that the Son was inferior to the Father, according to the sole process of logic applied to the notion of sonship as it is ordinarily understood, without taking into account the correctives brought to the notion by revelation's applying it to Christ.

The result is that all theological conclusions are not definable as truths of faith on the mere grounds that they seem irrefutable to good minds, while it is quite possible that one day truths could be defined as of faith that logic alone would not have been adequate to extract from revelation. On the use of theological conclusions to explain revelation as from inside, see St. Thomas Aquinas, *In Boet. de Trinitate*, q.3, a.1, ad 4um; on theological conclusions not formulated by revelation itself, see John of St. Thomas, *Curs. theol.*, Iam, q.1, disp. 2, a.6 and 7.

THEOLOGICAL PLACES or SOURCES   This expression was used to designate theological propositions by different authors, particularly during the Renaissance and the Reformation period. But since the publication of the celebrated posthumous work of the theologian Melchior Cano, O.P., with this title (Salamanca, 1563), the term has thereafter come to be reserved to what he himself calls the "seats," or what are also called the "domiciles" of the arguments that may be put forth in theology. He singles out ten, and attempts in each case to define the authority attached to it and the manner in which it may be used. He has been generally followed, although a classification, resulting chiefly from his own observations regarding these seats of theological argument, has been introduced into the schema he pointed out. First, there are the two places that are called *proper* or *constitutive:* 1) Holy Scripture; 2) the apostolic traditions, i.e., those that can be traced back to the apostles themselves for their source. Next come the *declarative* places: 3) the Church taken as a body, in all of the most diverse expressions she gives to her faith, among which liturgy and canon law are of particular importance (although their testimony must be taken in its entirety in those things on which there is consistent agreement, and not as a simple mass of isolatable arguments); 4) the decisions, and especially the definitions of the councils; 5) the teaching and the definitions of the popes. These last three places are related to the first two, since they specify the sense in which the Church understands them. To these are added the following (also declarative), even though their value does not exceed simple probability unless they are in agreement: 6) the Fathers of the Church, i.e., the most ancient theologians who had given precision to her faith through their explanations of it, and whose authority has been acknowledged by the whole Church and especially by the papal and episcopal *magisterium,* and therefore to a lesser extent and in proportion to the authority that is generally conceded them under the same conditions; 7) the theologians and canonists (although in these latter, undoubtedly wrongly, Cano did not wish to acknowledge any authority greater than one derived from that of the theologians). Finally, as *supplementary* places, he adds 8) natural reason; 9) philosophers and jurists; 10) the data of history and human tradition.

This schematization has often been criticized and different systems have been proposed to improve or to supplant it. But as a whole it remains the most practical and the most ordered that we possess.

THEOLOGICAL SCHOOLS This expression applies to the different forms of theological tradition that the Church intends to respect and has respected without exclusively opting for one of them, but rather in giving them all common approbation. This approval in no way prejudges the validity of all of their principles, nor even less of all their conclusions, but rather maintains the freedom necessary for the exploration of the many questions for which, for the moment, there does not seem to be enough evidence to require a particular solution. It is in this way that we speak of the Thomist, Scotist, Suarezian, etc., schools. The more balanced quality as well as the particular soundness of the teaching of St. Thomas Aquinas explain why the Church insists upon using the teaching of this doctor as a basis, in particular, for the formation of her clergy. But it does not signify any absolute canonization of all of the theses of the Thomistic school in general, nor even of St. Thomas in particular, as is sufficiently proved by the fact that the Church, in the case of the Immaculate Conception, for example, defined a doctrine that St. Thomas did not favor; and there are other points where the Church, without yet having pronounced herself, has allowed a teaching opposed to what he held, as in the distinction between the episcopacy and the priesthood of second rank, to be worked out and to prevail.

On the other hand, by the expression "school of theologians," we understand the common teaching of theologians at a particular period. This agreement obviously constitutes a strong presumption in favor of the theses thus currently taught in the Church, but it does not necessarily involve the *magisterium* that may allow a doctrine to spread for a while without thereby taking a definitive position on its validity.

THEOLOGICAL SYSTEMS   It is one of the essential tasks of theology to organize the revealed truths in a coherent manner by virtue of the *analogy* of faith, itself based on the analogy of being, without which the divine mysteries would in no way be communicable to us (*see* ANALOGY). Yet since the truths of revelation remain essentially mysterious in their revelation itself, and the human mind can never claim to understand them completely, the best theologies, particularly in their systematic organization, cannot claim to exhaust the whole content of revelation. Therefore, while the Church especially recommends certain systems for the training of her clergy (notably the Thomistic synthesis), she does not thereby limit herself to all their details. Nor does she condemn other systems, such as those of St. Bonaventure, Duns Scotus, or Suarez, which though less definitive, can as well demonstrate certain aspects of revealed truth.

THEOLOGY   The science of divine things. In antiquity, theology was at first a hymn in which God was glorified rather than explained by the human mind. This understanding remained very much alive among the Fathers of the Church, and even with men like Origen, who made the greatest instrumental use of notions borrowed from Greek philosophy, or others, like the great theologians whom we call the Cappadocians (St. Basil of Caesarea, St. Gregory Nazianzen and St. Gregory of Nyssa), who used these same notions especially to refute the errors resulting from a rationalizing illusion about our ability to clarify the divine mysteries. For the Pseudo-Dionysius, mystical theology was the only theology really worthy of the name since it surpasses inadequate analogies by an experience that declares itself to be ultimately inexpressible. In a general way, until quite late in the Latin Middle Ages, theology was conceived, particularly in the monasteries, less as a proper science of the divine things than as a meditation of the mysteries. It made no call upon reason except in order to avoid false interpretations of these mysteries that would destroy them, and to prepare for contemplation in which theology itself would be surpassed. This is still true of a writer like St. Anselm, who yet was one of the first to make more stringent use of dialectic thought in theology. However, in the 12th century, Abelard's tendency to rationalize theology completely (which produced an impassioned rejection in St. Bernard, for example) caused other thinkers, even among those who were closest to St. Bernard, like William of Saint-Thierry, to endeavor to make a more systematic use of a rational criticism of the concepts and to set up a rational framework of the truths of faith in an ordered system. This was to end up in the 13th century, with St. Albert the Great and especially St. Thomas Aquinas, in the notion of theology as a sacred science. Beginning with a clearer recognition of supernatural truths, those received from revelation alone, theology ordered the totality of the truths of faith into a rational synthesis when it added those truths about God attainable by reason alone. This plainly happened only when men developed a clear metaphysical conception of things and beings which allowed them to make a radical distinction between these and supernatural realities as such (*see* NATURE, and SUPERNATURAL). This is precisely what is perhaps the most salient point of Thomistic theological thought.

Yet St. Thomas still maintained that theology as a science remains the science of faith, and as such can be pursued only in the light of faith. This was disregarded, either merely in fact or even in principle, by many of those who came after him; hence the decadence of scholastic theology at the end of the Middle Ages, a decadence from which it was not able to recover except under the inspiration of forceful minds who would rediscover the full sense of the principles of Thomistic thought, like Cajetan in the 16th century.

As St. Thomas conceived it, theology demands that the rational strength of dialectic thought be constantly associated with not only an extensive but a penetrating exploration of the whole of the data of revelation and tradition, within the safeguard of the living *magisterium* of the Church and in a spirit of living faith. In this case it really will be a sacred science in the sense that it will not foster the rash and futile claim to substitute itself for the Word of God, confided to the Church, particularly in Holy Scripture, but only the hope of respectfully exploring its depths, not by destroying its mystery, but by enabling us to put it in better perspective with regard to our merely natural knowledge. Systematic theology must then be constantly nurtured by positive theology that is confined to making an inventory and an exegesis of the Word of God in its authentic documents. In addition it must always remain in close contact with the developments in merely human thought, although remaining within the living school of the Church and in a profound communion of faith with her.

THEOSOPHY   Literally, divine wisdom. The word seems to have been used for the first time in modern times by the Neo-Platonists of the Renaissance, but it was especially popularized by the writings of Jakob Boehme in the 17th century to designate a mystically oriented speculation, rather than a speculative mysticism. In the nineteenth century, the Catholic thinker Franz von Baader, like the philosopher Schelling and the whole school of Russian thinkers that stems from Vladimir Solovyëv, took over the word to designate their own speculations on the divine Wisdom. The same word was taken over again at the end of that century by a popular and rather crass form of *occultism* (q.v.) that claimed to unveil the esoteric quintessence of the religions of the Far East.

THOMISM   It is difficult to give the essential points of a theologico-philosophical system like Thomism, i.e., the form of religious thought that can be legitimately said to have originated with St. Thomas Aquinas, since its value and its strength lie more in a certain spirit than in defined or definable theses. Yet we may point out certain sign posts: 1) a moderate *realism* (q.v.) in philosophy, in the service of 2) an intellectualism of being which supposes that the intellect is a faculty of knowing being through the concepts that it makes of it, and 3) that the will itself is dependent upon this being to the extent that it is immediately apprehended by the intellect. In theology, there follows 4) the possibility of a distinction between created natures and the supernatural intervention of God in order to associate spiritual created beings with His own life, but without any extrinsicism that would make them incommunicable. Out of this comes 5) the fact that all theology is based on the principle of the *analogy of being* that permits God to reveal his own life to us in a positive way, and enables us thereby to reflect upon this revelation so as to assimilate it without destroying its mystery. Let us add to these points both a respect for, and a positive openness, to the whole of tradition. All of this results in particularly balanced theses on problems as delicate as that of grace and human freedom or on the question of the motive of the Incarnation, and intuitions as felicitous as that of the instrumentality, joined to the divinity, of the Saviour's humanity, which synthesizes in a very illuminating way the doctrine of the Redemption of Christ and of its application in the Church through the sacraments. These are, at the very least, the chief reasons that explain why the Church insists on recommending such a system of thought to all of her clergy charged with teaching in her name.

TIME   Contrary to the Greek notion, in which the divine eternity had no relation to time, the Jewish notion sees the time of creation as immersed in the divine eternity. Through sacred history, and more particularly through the Incarnation, God breaks into the time of men. In this way he brings history to its conclusion, where the "world to come," i.e., the new economy where God reigns, is substituted for the present "world," subjected to the domination of the "powers" who revolted against the Creator (*see* KINGDOM OF GOD). At the final resurrection, the righteous will pass from time into the eternity of God. *See* ETERNITY.

TOLERANCE   At the very least, the passive acceptance of principles or patterns of behavior that one does not approve. In the article FREEDOM we point out how respect for the freedom of the human person (without which the freedom essential for faith would not even be possible) imposes a certain tolerance as a Christian duty.

TRADITION   In a general way, this word is used of any passing on, as from hand to hand, of knowledge, or practices, or both (in Greek *paradosis*; that which is handed on by tradition being termed *paratheke*, or "deposit"). The rabbis already had the very clear idea that the Word of God (q.v.) was handed down in and by the People of God in this way. If Christ keenly criticized certain traditions of the "scribes and Phari-sees" (cf. Matt. 23) as being opposed to the authentic tradition of the Word, in the same text (v.2) he did authenticate the principle of tradition most conclusively. The New Testament in turn presents the doctrine of the Gospel as the *paratheke* (1 Tim. 6,20 and 2 Tim. 1,14), communicated by the *paradosis* of the apostles (1 Cor. 11,2 and 2 Thess. 2,15; cf. 3,6). It can be said that until the 3rd century the Church writers all propose Christian doctrine to men in this way. When the canon of Scripture (*see* CANON) was definitively established, these Scriptures, inspired by God, drew more and more attention to themselves as constituting the care or rather the heart of Christian tradition, but without any suggestion of ever being separated from the totality of this tradition (or a fortiori of being opposed to it). In the struggle against the Gnostics, the Fathers underlined many times (St. Irenaeus in particular, but the Alexandrians as well) that it is vain to claim to quote the Bible in favor of interpretations that would not be in agreement with those current in the Church.

In this tradition, however, as Cardinal Newman luminously pointed out in his *Via Media* (London, 1880), we always distinguish a twofold aspect: 1) what he calls *prophetic tradition*, handed down by the whole body of the Church and in which any individual, whether cleric or layman, can take the part of a witness to the Spirit working through the whole Church, to keep living and pure within her that truth which was once entrusted to the apostles; and 2) what he calls *episcopal tradition*, which is not another tradition, but rather an officially authenticated expression of tradition in general by those who, as successors to the apostles, have the special responsibility of preserving the divine deposit of the Word from ever being contaminated by merely human traditions that have gone astray. This is what modern theologians understand by the *magisterium* (q.v.). It was only at the time of the Protestant Reformation that a formal opposition came to be made between the Word of God as directly formulated by the Holy Scriptures insofar as they are inspired (*see* INSPIRATION), and the tradition of the Church.

Hence the Council of Trent's statement that it receives "*pari pietatis affectu et reverentia* all the books both from the Old and New Testaments . . . as well as the traditions themselves, dealing either with faith or morals, which were as it were dictated by the mouth of Christ or the Spirit and preserved in the Catholic Church by a continual succession," as containing the same truth and discipline promised by the prophets, promulgated by Christ, and preached by the apostles (Sess. IV, *Decretum de Canonicis Scripturis*, D.B. 783). It is very remarkable that the Council put aside a first redaction that twice used the word *partim* (partly) before the mention of Scripture and before that of traditions. The Fathers of the Council obviously wished to keep to the ancient position, which held that Scripture makes up one whole together with the totality of tradition, and could not be set in opposition to it. However, the controversy itself led modern Catholic theologians to speak like Protestants about Scripture *and* Tradition, as if they were speaking of two forms of handing on the Word of God that were relatively autonomous, even though complementary. This policy is regrettable for it unwittingly yields much more than necessary to the error that they wish to refute and makes it rebound. Let us rather say that the Word of God, given once and for all to the Church by the apostles as coming from Christ himself in the Spirit, is kept alive in her within the totality of tradition such as we have described it, and of which tradition the inspired Scriptures forever remain the heart.

TRADITIONALISM A doctrine held by Louis de Bonald and Joseph de Maistre and embraced enthusiastically by Lamennais, with the purpose of refuting the individualistic rationalism of the 18th century. Traditionalism claimed to see in the original tradition of mankind, conveyed by all the common beliefs that can be found beneath the totality of myths and politico-religious institutions, the sole source of truth. It was rejected by the Church to the extent that it unduly underestimated the powers of reason and tended to confuse supernatural *tradition* (q.v.) with an original tradition that was most vague.

TRANSCENDENCE We have explained in the article IMMANENCE how the sense of these two words was defined and evolved together. The divine transcendence prevents us either from confusing the being of God with that of the world as *pantheism* (q.v.) does in its various forms, or, by way of consequence, from ever placing the divine action on the same plane with the action of creatures. But in the traditional Judeo-Christian notion, it does not exclude the reality of an immanence, i.e., of a presence and an action of God in his works, and in particular in spiritual creatures. Quite the contrary, it can be said that the true notion of divine transcendence is what makes this immanence possible, without its in any way slipping into a confusion between God and the world or the created spirit. St. Thomas, in his notion of the *analogy* (q.v.) of being, furnished the most balanced principles for an understanding of this necessary connection.

TRANSFIGURATION The transfiguration of Christ, as reported in the three Synoptic Gospels (Matt. 17,1–13; Mark 9,2–13; Luke 9,28–36) and commented upon by the Second Epistle of Peter (1,16–19), in allowing the glory of his divinity to shine through his humanity, was an omen, as it were, of his Resurrection and of the definitive transformation that it would produce in him—a pledge of that which all of his followers expect at the end of time. Oriental mysticism, particularly, looks upon it as the principle of the mystical doctrine of assimilation to Christ through the contemplation in the faith of his glorified humanity, in accordance with St. Paul's words: "And we all, with unveiled face, beholding the glory of the Lord are being changed into his likeness from one degree of glory to another; for this comes from the Lord who is the Spirit" (2 Cor. 3,18), or with those of St. John: "We know that when he appears we shall be like him, for we shall see him as he is" (1 John 3,2). We will note besides that the presence of Moses and Elijah on the mountain of the Transfiguration does not merely signify, as is usually said, the testimony given to Jesus by the Law and the prophets, but that they are present with Him as the two most important personages of the Old

Testament who had been allowed to see the glory of God, which now shines forth from the face of Jesus (cf. Ex. 33 and 3 Kings 19). Lastly, certain exegetes think that St. Peter's allusion to the possibility of erecting tents is connected with the liturgy of the *tabernacles* (q.v.), where the presence of the Lord with his People was celebrated in the expectation of the definitive coming of his Kingdom.

TRANSUBSTANTIATION   A name given in the Church (as the Council of Trent recalls, but without imposing any particular definition) to the mysterious transformation of the elements of the Eucharist that makes them, by the power of the Word of Christ, his own body and blood (Sess. XIII, *Decretum de S. Eucharistia*; D.B. 877). Although Tertullian had already used the word, Christian antiquity preferred the Greek expression *metabole*, translated into Latin by *conversio* (a term repeated by the Council). The word transubstantiation came to be used by preference during the Middle Ages, both as a reaction against certain theologians like Ratramnus who tended to see in the Eucharist only a virtual and not a real presence of the body and blood of the Lord, and against others like Paschasius Radbertus, who expressed this presence as if it were a question of a material and sensible one. To speak of transubstantiation comes down then to stating that it is indeed the very reality of the body of Christ that we have on the altar after the consecration, yet in a way inaccessible to the senses and in such a manner that it is neither multiplied by the multiplicity of the species, nor divided in any way by their division, nor passible in any way whatsoever. The theologians explain this by saying that the *substance* (q.v.) alone of the bread and wine is mysteriously transformed into the substance of the body and blood, while the *accidents* (q.v.) remain absolutely unchanged, even though they no longer have any proper substance of their own and serve simply as sensible signs of this presence. See St. Thomas Aquinas, *Sum. Theol.*, IIIa, qq.75–77. The more or less far-fetched theories that were developed in order to make an analysis of this mystery that would go further than the holy doctor had gone are too unsatisfactory to be worth mentioning here.

TRINITY   A Church doctrine stating that in God there are three persons who are really distinct within the unity of one sole nature, or essence. The New Testament does not in any way speculate on the Trinity (the use of the term is introduced later), but reveals to us the Father through the Son in the Holy Spirit. The triadic formulas, however striking they may be (like the conclusion of the First Epistle to the Corinthians), are less striking in this regard by themselves than the total view of this communicated divine life that emerges from all the texts taken together, allowing us to catch a faint glimpse, as it were, of something of its mystery in its communication. The articles INCARNATION and JESUS CHRIST show how the belief in the divinity of Christ and in his *consubstantiality* (q.v.) with the Father was set down and defined, and the article HOLY SPIRIT how there followed the fully explicit recognition and definition of the equal divinity and consubstantiality of the Spirit. The articles NATURE, ESSENCE, and PERSON will furnish the necessary particulars concerning the words used in these definitions. We shall limit ourselves here to underlining how liturgical usage, especially in the Roman liturgy, has kept for us the essentially spiritual and dynamic vision of the discovery of the Trinitarian life of God in our participation in it through grace. Early Greek theology, for its part, always begins with a consideration of the persons in order to end up by showing, by an analysis of their *processions* through their *missions* (qq.v.), how a unique essence is shared among them. In this it remains closer to the perspective of the Word of God than medieval Latin theology which starts with the divine essence in order to deduce the persons from that notion. Although aided by analogies, like those proposed by St. Augustine (*see* PROCESSIONS), from human psychology, Latin theology runs the risk of giving the impression that this is a question merely of artificially substantiated abstractions. In reality, the Trinity is the Christian mystery seen under its most divine aspect, and we cannot claim, therefore, to plumb completely this divine aspect, which illumines the most vital mystery there is: our *adoption* (q.v.) by the Father, in his Son, by the gift of the Spirit of holiness.

TRUTH   *See* FAITHFULNESS, and INTELLIGENCE

TYPES   From a Greek word meaning "model." We see this expression already being used by the New Testament in regard to the realities of the Old Testament that are images and omens of these New Testament realities: St. Paul uses the name Adam in relation to Christ (Rom. 5,14) and speaks of the People of God of the Old Testament in relation to the Church (1 Cor. 10,6). Although the school of Antioch, in its opposition to Alexandria, refused to admit an allegorical sense in the biblical texts themselves, it did declare that there are certain realities spoken of by the sacred writers that are revealed afterward to be "types" of the realities to come, even though the writers themselves did not formally intend it. In fact, the Antiochians, starting from this principle, were at times still more fanciful than the Alexandrians in their typical interpretation of scriptural (or liturgical) realities. The word "type," particularly but not exclusively in this school was also used in regard to the sacramental signs. Certain Protestants wished to look upon this as a pre-Calvinist notion of the sacraments. Yet they are most assuredly wrong, for the same writers, like Theodore of Mopsuestia, who give this name in their catecheses to the elements of the Eucharist, for example, indicate unequivocally in other places that they have no doubt about the real and objective presence of the reality beneath the "type."

U

ULTRAMONTANISM   This name was given by the Gallicans (*see* GALLICANISM) to the opposite doctrine that was current "beyond the mountains" (whence the name), i.e., the supremacy of the papal power over the episcopal power and its total independence with regard to the secular powers. It is this latter aspect of Ultramontanism that gained for it, from the beginning of the 19th century, a very general return to favor among both French and German Catholics who looked upon it as the sole means of assuring the Church's independence from the more and more secularized political powers. Moreover, at the same time that Ultramontanism became the doctrine admitted by some liberal Catholics, it found a certain justification in the so-called traditionalist school (*see* TRADITIONALISM) of Louis de Bonald and Joseph de Maistre, which held, quite to the contrary, to an absolutist theory of authority. De Maistre went so far as to explicitly identify the infallibility of the pope with the doctrine of the secular jurists who held that "the king cannot be wrong." However, this was understood no longer in a juridical, but in a quasi-mystical, sense. The confusion reached its high point in the Lamennais affair. After having been a particularly extreme partisan of the theses of Bonald and De Maistre, Lamennais became in the second phase of his Church career the defender of a no less extreme political liberalism, combined at first with the same Ultramontanism that he had held from the beginning, but ultimately rejected. This is the reason for the strange incoherence of the debates that preceded the definition of pontifical infallibility given by the First Vatican Council. Some of its most outspoken defenders combined it inextricably with the most absolutist theses in politics, while others (or the same ones) connected it with the idea of the Pope-King, which in turn was defended as if it were a dogma. The conciliar definition managed to disentangle these doctrines in a satisfactory way by specifying that the infallibility of the pope is not that of any ordinary absolute monarch, but that of the whole Church, and by introducing nothing in this definition that would connect it in any way either to any particular political theory or to the question of the pope's sovereignty over his own States. In fact, following new circumstances that the Church was to accept in the Lateran concordat, the papal sovereignty was maintained by the contemporary papacy only in principle, as a juridical protection for the independence of the ecclesiastical power in its Head, who could not be subservient to any earthly power without endangering this independence.

UNION AND UNITY These terms are frequently used in Scripture and theology in a sense that is not always easy to define. The Trinitarian controversies brought out clearly that the unity of God the Trinity is that of one sole nature (or essence or substance) in three persons who proceed from a unique source or principle: the Father. The unity of Christ, for its part, appears as the result of the union of the two natures, divine and human, in the unity of one sole person (*see* INCARNATION, and TRINITY). The problem of the unity of human nature among the individuals of which it is composed is evidently more delicate. The Fathers, and particularly the Greeks, seem often to see in this unity more than the unity of an abstract essence. They are unquestionably helped in this by the elements of Platonist *realism* (q.v.) in their thought. But whatever may have been said about this, it is more than questionable that this is actually the source of their thought on the matter. We must seek that source in the conviction of a unity in the destiny of all mankind on a supernatural basis, a conviction based on revelation. This unity stems from the kinship among its members resulting from the union in which God wills to establish them as one sole People. The unicity of the original human pair, to the Fathers at least, seems to be the expression of this fact of faith (*see* MONOGENISM). And the assumption by the divine Word of an individual human nature constitutes for them the principle of a reunion in him of a mankind dismembered by sin, which therefore immediately involves all men. But if the possibility of the redemptive Incarnation certainly results in their eyes from a certain unity that is at least already latent in mankind, that unity, according to them, achieves its manifestation and realization only through the Incarnation itself. For St. Athanasius and still more precisely for St. Cyril of Alexandria, the Logos is the model of creation, and especially of the creation of man; by becoming flesh, he became a universal man in a mysterious sense. The least that can be said about it is that it is still more true to say this of him than it is of Adam.

Yet this capacity that he has of including us with himself in some way becomes effective only through the Resurrection and the Ascension. Having thus become, according to the Pauline expression, the "life-giving Spirit" (cf. 1 Cor. 15,45), Christ, by communicating his "spiritualized" body to us in the Eucharist and thereby pouring out his Spirit, as the divine Spirit, in us all, reunites us all in himself. This unity upon which St. Cyril comments in his writings both on First Corinthians and on the discourse after the Last Supper in the fourth Gospel, he does not hesitate to call a *henosis physike*. Surely this expression must not be understood in the technical sense in which Aristotelian philosophy takes it, viz., as designating the fusion of two substances into a third, but rather in the sense of a real participation by man in the divine unity of Christ in his humanity. The Encyclical *Mystici Corporis* of Pope Pius XII has clearly declared that both the union of Christ with his own in the Church and the union of the Mystical Body which is the Church and results from it, must be considered as *sui generis:* i.e., as surpassing the merely moral union of wills in a mysterious but real communication, only imperfectly expressed by the natural analogies of the body and its members, or the vine and its branches, used by Christ and the apostles. This union and this unity are both interior and exterior: they are expressed and produced in the sacramental life of the Church, in the unity of her apostolic hierarchy which is its primary means, but are realized in each of us by grace and the communication of the Spirit who pours himself out in supernatural charity, a participation itself in God's own life.

A point resulting from all of this is that the unity of the true Church is a supernatural gift that she could not lose, but which must find its more and more positive manifestation in the bringing of all mankind together in the one body of Christ. The result is that divisions among Christians, if they do not weaken the potential unity of the Church, which rests on her institution by Christ on the basis of the apostolate and on the continued presence of Christ among his own through the sacraments, are harmful to the positive shining forth of this presence and its full flowering in charity.

UNITARIANISM   A form of modern Protestantism characterized by the rejection of belief in the dogma of the Trinity. Having first appeared in the 16th century with Socinus, Unitarianism experienced a sudden growth among the Presbyterians and Congregationalists of Great Britain and especially the United States in the 19th century, particularly under the influence of William E. Channing. It is much in decline today, and most of its members have passed purely and simply into agnosticism or else returned to more traditional Churches.

UNIVERSE   *See* WORLD

UNIVERSALISM   This name is given especially to the progressive vision of the Jewish prophets with regard to God's plan for the whole universe, beyond the limits of a particular people. But we must be careful not to confuse this properly biblical universalism which presupposes that the definitive historical roots of the Church were first in Israel and a reintegration of all mankind in this one Christ, with a simple abstract universality that practically denies the absolute and definitive value of salvation history.

UNIVOCITY OF BEING   A notion according to which the being of God is understood in the same sense as that of a creature. Its practically inevitable consequence is *pantheism* (q.v.).

V

VALIDITY   The exercise of authority in the Church, particularly in the performance of the sacramental functions, is said to be valid when the objective conditions that follow from Christ's institution are respected. Validity can coexist with unlawfulness, when these functions are performed in subjective conditions disapproved by the Church because they do not correspond to the finality of authority or of the sacraments, as when a priest who is unworthy celebrates them or when they are administered to faithful who do not receive them worthily.

VIRGIN BIRTH   The Gospel of the infancy, both in St. Matthew and St. Luke, states that Jesus was born of Mary and that she remained a virgin. It seems that St. John, for his part, alludes to this fact in verse 13 of his prologue, if we adopt the text that is generally accepted as more certain by the critics, giving the singular form ("*he* who was born, not of blood, nor of the will of the flesh, nor of the will of man, but of God"). The supposition by some contemporaries that this belief came from a literal understanding of Isaiah 7,14 (cited by Matt. 1,23) is groundless. No rabbi who lived at the time of Christianity's beginnings understood it in this way, and it is clear on the contrary that the certainty of the fact itself brought Christian writers to this interpretation of the text. As for the notion that the idea of the virgin birth was borrowed from the mythological notion of the demigods, i.e., persons born from the union of a god and a mortal, it is impossible to suppose that Christians who came from Judaism could ever have allowed themselves to be contaminated by such fantastic ideas, while nothing was less virginal than what was evoked by them. Christian tradition appears from the beginning to have looked upon this birth, which was an exception from the ordinary laws of generation, as the sign of the divine preexistence of the Saviour: the Son of God in being born as a man does not come into existence the way other men do, but simply assumes a human existence. Nor is he simply one man among others, but the New Man, the last Adam, in whom all other men are to live again, just as they had come into natural existence through their descendence from Adam. Cf. St. Irenaeus, *Adversus Haereses*, III, xx, 2 and 3 and xxiii, as well as V, i, 3 (Harvey edition, vol. 2, pp. 104–105,110 and 216). The idea that the purpose behind such a manner of being born would have been to have him escape original sin came later (its first appearance was in Origen, and it was scarcely developed except in St. Augustine). The Fathers who admit it often bring it up merely as an appendage to the primary motive (as in the case of St. Cyril of Alexandria and St. Leo). See St. Thomas Aquinas, *Sum. Theol.*, IIIa, q.28.

VIRGINITY   Virginity consecrated to Christ in the expectation of the divine kingdom, blessed and exalted by him even above marriage (whose holiness and dignity he rewards—cf. Matt. 3,12), is similarly recommended by the apostles as a most excellent way of being faithful to Christ for those who are called to it (cf. 1 Cor. 7,25 ff.). The Church herself is described as a virgin who has prepared and adorned herself for her Bridegroom, Christ (cf. 2 Cor. 11,2 and Apoc. 21,9 ff.). This, together with the fruitful virginity of Mary as described in the infancy Gospel in St. Luke, let us see in holy virginity, along with bloody martyrdom, a preeminent form of Christian holiness (cf. Apoc. 14,4). But it is essential that Christian virginity be viewed not as a negative condemnation or depreciation of marriage, but as a means of hastening, through the generosity of a voluntary sacrifice, the full realization of this union between Christ and the Church of which marriage itself is an efficacious sign.

VIRTUE   From the Latin *virtus*, used to translate the Greek *arete*. The word virtue designates first of all the energy proper to the well-born or well-formed soul. In the Aristotelian-Thomistic systematization, virtue is a good habit (*see* HABITUS), as against vice which is a defective habit. To the acquired natural virtues, theology adds the supernatural virtues infused by divine grace. These latter are differentiated into the theological virtues that have no natural equivalent (i.e., faith, hope, and charity—charity being considered as giving full flower to faith and hope in that they disappear within it when it finds its own perfection in eternal life) and into the moral infused virtues. These correspond to the natural virtues in that they are, like them, simply a development of nature according to a law immanent within it. But since they are coordinated to the ultimate triumph of charity, they receive from it as it were a new coloration. Among the moral virtues, a further distinction is made between the cardinal virtues of prudence, justice, fortitude (or courage), and temperance, and the related virtues that are, as it were, potential parts of them. Finally, in the Thomistic synthesis, the *gifts of the Holy Spirit* (q.v.) are joined to the virtues to complete them in supernatural charity by creating in us a particular docility to the ways of the Spirit. See St. Thomas Aquinas, *Sum. Theol.*, IIa-IIae, qq.1–170.

VISION   In the New Testament the vision (or sight) of God and Christ are opposed to faith, but as a fulfillment of that toward which faith tends and into which it disappears. It is in this sense that the Epistle to the Hebrews defines faith as "the assurance of things hoped for, the conviction of things not seen" (Heb. 11,1). The vision of God is promised in the beatitude of Matthew (5,8) to the pure of heart. When St. Paul says: "I shall know even as I have been known" (1 Cor. 13, 12), specifying that we shall then see face to face, he certainly has the same thing in mind. But it is St. John who has best developed this hope, as when he says: "Now we are God's children, and it has not yet appeared what we shall be. We know that, when He appears, we shall be like to him, for we shall see him just as he is" (1 John 3,2). In this last phrase, it is probable that "He" refers to God himself as manifested in the glorious Christ.

It is actually a familiar thought for St. John that to see Christ and to see God is one and the same thing (cf. John 14,9). More exactly, it seems that there is for him a dialectic between the vision of Christ, the Word of God made flesh, which leads to belief in his divinity, and the faith that leads us even now to "know" him effectively in love (*see* KNOWLEDGE). This is a knowledge that in turn will reach its full flower in the heavenly vision (cf. John 6,40 and 11,40). People have at times wanted to see in these texts an influence of the religious ideas of Hellenism, and in particular of a transforming contemplation that would be attributed to the tradition of Platonism. But as we have shown in the article CONTEMPLATION, if Platonism indeed has an idea of an assimilation to God that permits man to contemplate him, we must on the contrary see a quite biblical origin in the idea of a purely gratuitous revelation of God, which will assimilate us to him in causing us to know him better and better. This is what is shown so well by the Pauline text of 2 Cor. 3,18 that could be taken for a condensation of the whole Johannine mystical doctrine of the vision of God in Christ, even though all of its references are explicitly from the Old Testament.

The vision promised to the righteous is a vision of the *glory* of God in Christ (cf. John 17,24), and an eschatological vision, i.e., one that corresponds to the final consummation of all things. But two questions are posed of Christian tradition. The first is to what extent this vision can be anticipated even in this present life, and the second, whether the beatific vision itself will cause us to see the essence of God.

On the first point, it is evident from the whole of patristic tradition that the ecstasy of St. Paul (mentioned in 2 Cor. 12,1–4) must have been an anticipation of the beatific vision, and many think that the vision of Moses in Ex. 33,12 ff., and even that of Elijah in 3 Kings 19 must be put in the same category (which coincides with rabbinical traditions that are probably considerably prior to Christianity). At the same time, speculative mysticism, as it was developed especially in monasticism following

St. Gregory of Nyssa, Evagrius Ponticus, and the Pseudo-Dionysius, encourages us to think that such experiences, however rare they may be, are not impossible for especially fervent Christians, since God for them remains always the sole master of his gifts, and especially of such an eminent gift. But it is emphasized that such an experience, if it does take place on earth, can be only evanescent, indeed that it could not be completely disengaged from the shadows of faith, except as a first dawning of that vision properly so-called. This is particularly the case with St. Augustine, who, after having been relatively optimistic about the actual possibilities of experiences of this kind, under the influence furthermore of his Neo-Platonist formation, later becomes much more reserved. St. Thomas, for his part, without excluding the possibility of a transient vision of the *lumen gloriae*, particularly in the cases of St. Paul, Moses, and perhaps Adam, seems to consider it as completely exceptional. (Cf. *Sum. Theol.*, IIa-IIae, q.180, a.4 and 5; see also q.175, on ecstasy; and *Contra Gentiles*, bk. III, chap. 47.)

As for the second question, the Fathers in general, particularly the Cappadocians, as a reaction against the claims of the second generation Arians to know the divine essence in an exhaustive way, seem very reserved. The vision of the divine glory such as it is accessible to man, either in eternal life or a fortiori in this life, and even such as the highest creatures like the angels can attain it through grace, appears to them still to be a vision of God like that of Moses, a "vision from behind" as St. Gregory Nazianzen and St. Gregory of Nyssa say. Nevertheless they insist upon the fact that it is an authentic vision of God, without intermediary. As we have mentioned in the articles MYSTICISM, and CONTEMPLATION, the result is a twofold tradition. Byzantine mysticism speaks of the vision of an uncreated light, and therefore a divine light, but one that nevertheless does not allow us to perceive the essence of God as it is in itself, but only the "divine energies" that are really distinct from this essence, and by which he is communicated to his creatures. This is the solution that is systematized by the theologian Gregory Palamas, Bishop of Thessalonica, after having been a monk of Athos in the 14th century. The view of what could be called Western mysticism, on the contrary, finds its formulation in the thought of St. Thomas, according to whom the *lumen gloriae*, like the grace that prepares us for it, is a created light, but one that adapts us to the vision of the uncreated essence, although this vision can never be exhaustive for us. It is obvious that the real distinction made in God between the divine essence itself and energies that would also be uncreated is most unsatisfactory from the metaphysical point of view. But it must be admitted that the notion of created grace or of a created light adapting us to see the uncreated essence also poses insoluble problems.

VOCATION   A calling by God to accept his graces. In the article ELECTION we have examined what concerns the Christian vocation in general. A particular problem has been raised since the last century about the vocation to the priesthood. As a reaction against the age of the Counter-Reformation, where there had been an insistence on the personal sense of vocation in order to put an end to ordinations conferred upon men who had no genuine spiritual concern, certain authors rightly devoted themselves to underlining that since the priesthood is a public function in the Church, it is for the Church authority definitively to judge who is fit or not. From this, some people, like the Abbé Lahitton in France, even came to consider that a vocation consisted in the exterior call made by the bishop, regardless of any subjective consideration. A lively controversy resulted that is still going on. The least one can say is that the supreme authority has not shown itself well disposed to the extreme theses, neither in one direction nor in the other. It seems then that we are arriving at a notion of vocation where subjective factors, like the spontaneously experienced attraction, have an acknowledged place, along with objective qualities, namely the authority's judgment on the whole question guided by a consideration of supernatural prudence. The same thing could be said about the vocation to the religious life, except that the importance of the subjective factors in this case is merely more weighty, since this involves a vocation ordained for the spiritual welfare of the subject himself and not for the welfare of Christian society.

VOLUNTARISM   This name is given to all the philosophies or theologies that, either in God alone or in man himself, tend to render the will completely autonomous in relation to the intellect, making this latter in turn depend on the will. Thomism is opposed in this regard to the voluntarism of Scotus and the Nominalists, in that it holds that even in God it is the being as apprehended by the intellect that governs the will.

VOW   An engagement made before God, which entails a consideration that St. Thomas calls quasi-sacramental as soon as it involves the solemn public vows of religion: poverty, chastity, and obedience (see *Sum. Theol.*, IIa-IIae, q.88; cf. also qq.186 ff.). It is for this reason that the Church does not acknowledge that she is capable of dissolving the obligations of a solemn public vow, but only of commuting its application within a certain degree. On the other hand, since simple vows, even when they are public, are taken only before the Church, her authority can completely dispense from them if she judges it good. See can. 1307 ff.

W

WATER   In the liturgy and in Holy Scripture, water plays a symbolic role based on a twofold natural symbolism. Water appears in all primitive civilizations both as a symbol of life and as a symbol of death. This latter aspect is suggested particularly by the waters of a raging ocean or of rivers in spate, whose destructive power is concretized in mythical monsters like the Leviathan. The beneficent aspect of the waters as an instrument of fecundity comes from the waters of a spring or the showers of springtime.

Similarly, in the Bible, on the one hand, we have the waters of the primordial chaos (Gen. 1,2,6 ff.), those of the Flood (Gen. 7), the waters of the Nile that buried Pharaoh's armies (Ex. 14; cf. 15,4–5), etc. On the other hand, there are the waters of Siloam, which represent God's presence among his People as the spring of life (Isa. 8,6; cf. 12,3), or the supernatural spring that Ezechiel made gush forth from the Temple in the rebuilt city in order to fertilize the whole promised land (Ezech. 47), etc. The same is true of the New Testament, with the destructive waters that washed away the house built on sand (Matt. 6,25–27), the mention of the fact that the sea will no longer exist in eternity (Apoc. 21,1) contrasting with the abundant references to living water in the Johannine texts (John 4, 10–15; 7,38, etc.; Apoc. 7,17; 21,6, etc.).

The symbolism of baptism connects these two ideas in the notion formulated by St. Paul that the waters of baptism bury us with Christ in his death in order to associate us with his Resurrection (Rom. 6,1–11). This has given rise to meaningful comparisons, either with the waters of the Nile that buried the Egyptians and freed the Israelites at the time of the Exodus (cf. 1 Cor. 10,2), or with those of the Flood, which annihilated the unbelieving while saving the believers along with Noah (1 Pet. 3,20–21).

The different baptismal liturgies have made abundant use of these biblical symbols, as can be illustrated, for example, in the prayer of the blessing of fonts during the Easter Vigil. The theme of a purifying ablution, as found in the prophets (cf. Isa. 1,16; Ezech. 36,28), if it has any place in this context, nevertheless remains secondary in relation to the fundamental theme of a death in which the divine judgment against sin is accomplished, and of the resurrection that associates us with the divine life in giving us a heavenly rebirth (cf. the whole conversation with Nicodemus in St. John 3,1–8).

WESLEYANISM   Still called Methodism (from an early nickname given to the piety of its inspirer, John Wesley), Wesleyanism sprang from Pietism and transformed it. An Anglican clergyman of the 18th century who had been formed at first in a rather "High Church" climate (i.e., in the most traditional aspects of Anglicanism), John Wesley developed a whole movement of popular evangelization in an England that was in the throes of industrialization. His preaching was dominated by a call to conversion, identified with a more or less sudden experience of salvation through a living faith in the power of the blood of Jesus Christ to wash us of all our faults, and it was responsibile for mass meetings that were to be extended into a general and organized effort to achieve a positive sanctification of existence. Toward the end of his life, having been misunderstood and rejected by the Anglican authorities, who confused him with sectarians of preceding generations, Wesley reluctantly prepared for the transformation of his movement into an autonomous Church. With a rather unsystematic mind, much drawn to many aspects of the spiritual tradition of Catholicism, although filled with the prejudices of his environment with regard to the Catholic Church, Wesley, despite an at times uncritical acceptance of the sentimentalism and moralism of his age, contributed more than anyone else to restoring to Protestant spirituality many of the essential traits of Catholic spirituality, and above all toward strengthening the necessary connection between justification by faith and the sanctification of all existence. His influence lives on in all the Protestant "Revival" movements.

WHITSUNDAY   *See* PENTECOST

WILL   The will is the faculty of loving, i.e., the faculty that the mind, endowed with knowledge, has of inclining toward a good that attracts it. A distinction in this regard is made between the profound or primary will, which could only be inclined toward the good, and the secondary will, which is determined by a specific good. Since for us this is always some particular good, and since evil is never anything but an imperfection of good, the free creature can will evil in the sense that he can will a concrete particular good that is in fact in conflict with the supreme good (e.g., an immediate pleasure, leaving aside the deeper considerations that under the circumstances make what he wants unlawful). Contrary to the Scotist or Nominalist theory, which makes the divine will, leaving aside any other consideration, the sole arbiter of the good, Thomistic theology, while maintaining both that the will of God is free and that it could not be evil, maintains also that for this will good follows from being, as known by the intellect. See *Sum. Theol.*, Ia, qq.5,6, and 9.

WINE   Since the vine was taken by the prophets as the symbol of Israel, and by Christ himself as the image of the life of his faithful living in him (cf. Isa. 5,1–7 and John 15), the cup of wine, which furnished its theme to the greatest blessing of the Jewish community meals, became in the Christian Eucharist the cup of the New Covenant in His blood (cf. 1 Cor. 10,16 and 11,25).

WISDOM   Throughout the ancient Eastern Mediterranean world, wisdom was looked upon as the art of carrying on and organizing human life, based on the cumulative experience of tradition and clarified by a reflection itself nurtured by that tradition. Therefore, wisdom was essentially the art of kings or their collaborators. In Israel, its introduction at first came up against the same objection that was made by the prophets about having a king (cf. 1 Kings 8). Is the Lord not the King of Israel? Must his Word not take the place of wisdom for Israel? However, just as kingship was finally allowed, although only if exercised in the name of the Lord and by his own power, wisdom was also assimilated, with the proviso that its principle become the fear of the Lord and the observance of his commandments (cf. Prov. 1,7). Thus Solomon is looked upon as the preeminent man of wisdom because he made wisdom the object of his prayer from the moment of his accession (cf. 3 Kings 3,4 ff.). Yet with the collapse of the Jewish kingship, the idea took shape that God is the only wise man, just as he is the only King, and that there is no other wisdom than the plan that is concealed in him and that dominates the whole course of history, despite men's fancy. This plan then can be known only through his Word, which he reveals to those whom he wills (cf. Dan. 2). Hence the identification of Wisdom with the divine Word that is so characteristic of the later Wisdom books (cf. Ecclus. 24,23–24), and the passing over from Wisdom to "apocalypse," i.e., God's revelation of his supernatural direction of history, which we can observe in the book of Daniel. At the same time, like the divine Word, yet even more clearly, we see Wisdom becoming personified as another self that God sends into the world to conform it to the image of his living thought.

All of this is brought together and expanded in the New Testament, particularly in the first chapters of the First Epistle to the Corinthians, where St. Paul sets up an opposition between worldly wisdom that ultimately is mere foolishness, and the mysterious Wisdom of God that is folly in the world's eyes and that was revealed in Christ, particularly in the mystery of his cross (*see* MYSTERY). Finally, the Epistle to the Hebrews in its prologue applies to Christ what was said of wisdom in the *Wisdom of Solomon* (cf. Heb. 1,3 and Wis. 7,25), while in St. John's prologue, in calling Christ the *Logos* (q.v.), the evangelist brings together in Christ what was said both of the Word and of Wisdom in the Old Testament.

The Wisdom of God, as God's plan for the world, moreover, finds its final realization in the Church as the Bride of Christ (cf. Eph. 3,10). Tradition distinguishes then between the divine Wisdom as directly manifested in Christ and its created realization in the Church and in the world. The Virgin Mary very soon appears as its most perfect created manifestation, both because she is the particularly faithful "handmaid" of the Lord and because in her, as Mother of Christ, the divine plan has found all its fulfillment. With the heretical Gnostics these speculations on the created wisdom as the reflection of the uncreated tended to degenerate into mythological forms. The same trend is reflected in many modern speculations on Wisdom, particularly with the Lutheran mystic Jakob Boehme in the 17th century, and the whole German idealist philosophical tradition in the line of Schelling, that was inspired by Boehme, as well as with Catholic thinkers like Franz von Baader, or especially Russian Orthodox ones like Vladimir Solovyëv, Fr. Paul Florensky, or Fr. Sergius Bulgakoff. Yet, intermingled with speculations that are at least risky, we do find in more than one of these thinkers, and especially in the last named, a fruitful use of certain themes of the most authentic Christian tradition on the close connection that God willed to establish between himself and his work.

In another line of thought that is spiritual and psychological rather than metaphysical, St. Augustine develops a whole notion of wisdom as the knowledge of God inseparable from charity (*see* KNOWLEDGE), which the Latin Middle Ages picked up from him and which found its final development in the Thomistic theology of the gift of wisdom (see *Sum. Theol.*, IIa-IIae, q.45).

WOMAN   In the Genesis accounts, woman appears as man's equal, although at the same time subordinate to him as his complement (Gen. 1–3). She appears as the one through whom sin comes into the world, even though it is man who is definitively responsible for it. On the other hand, her role as a mother makes hope for redemption possible (3,15). In Israel, the woman had no priestly function, nor was she allowed any official participation in worship. But this does not impede her from being recognized as a prophetess on occasion (cf. Miriam, the sister of Moses, or Deborah; Ex. 5,20 f. and Judges 4), nor of course does it prevent her from exerting her influence in religious matters as in other areas of life.

The New Testament maintains her exclusion from worship functions such as preaching (1 Cor. 14,34–37). But in the *deaconesses* (q.v.), the primitive Church did recognize a ministry proper to woman, and from the outset placed her on a footing of absolute equality with man in the area of lay participation in the liturgical and sacramental life. The virginity of the woman who consecrated herself to God in Christ, moreover, at an early date is evidently a privileged sign of the union of Christ and the Church. The supernaturally fruitful virginity of the Virgin Mary throws increasing light on this primitive theme of Christian spirituality. Alongside the public and visible role of the apostolate that is reserved to men, it seems therefore that women in the Church from the beginning were to have the no less important role of witnessing to the irreplaceable values of intercession and contemplation, as well as the exercise of active charity in its most unobtrusive but also most humane forms. For this reason, if man plays the role of the representative of the Head of the Church in the Church's daily life as he does in Christian marriage, then it is the woman alone who furnishes the Church with an adequate image of herself (cf. Eph. 5, and Apoc. 12).

WORD OF GOD   The word is the act whereby one human mind communicates with another. Modern psychologists and philosophers have underlined the importance—even in the merely human word—of the act: the word is not merely the communication of thought, but the personal intervention of the one speaking in the life of the one addressed. This aspect becomes still more important when we speak of the word of God in its biblical sense. Indeed, since the God who speaks to man is all-powerful, with Him, unlike with man, there will be no disagreement or gap between the word and the effective action. Not only is the Word of God true, in the sense that God could neither deceive himself nor deceive us, but it is true in a superior sense in that it is enough that his will be expressed for it to be realized.

From these elementary considerations it follows immediately that we cannot reduce the notion of the Word of God to *revelation* (q.v.). To be most specific, revelation in the Word of God is inseparable from a personal communication that is in the highest degree creative. Finally, the Word of God is recognized as another self, a divine Person who became incarnate in mankind to whom he addressed himself, a Person who brings about a new creation in mankind.

In Israel, it is in the phenomenon of *prophecy* (q.v.) that we find the Word of God expressed. The prophet is the man to whom the Word of God makes itself heard, although in the most varied forms. It may be the object of a vision or a dream (cf. Num. 12,6 and 3 Kings 22,13–17), of a completely interior inspiration (Jer. 1,4), or of an intuition brought about through the simple consideration of an object that is evidently fortuitous (Amos 8,1–3 or Jer. 1,11–12) or finally, with those who are called writer prophets and with the wisdom writers, of an inspiration that simply impregnates the most normal processes of reflection (cf. Prov. 8,4–21). But in all cases, there is the same conviction that not only do they not utter disconnected oracles, but that there is but one word animating them. This is not only because in each of them it proceeds from the same God, but because it is the same object that this word tends to express and realize through them. This consistent object of the Word appears under a twofold aspect, but the unity of these two inseparable aspects is constantly reasserted. It is, first of all, the revelation of the divine *Name* (q.v.) that Moses received in the burning bush on Mount Horeb (Ex. 3). In other words, it is the communicated *knowledge* (q.v.) of God himself, a knowledge where through his revelation of himself he hands himself over, and in some way binds himself, to those whom he thereby leads into his intimacy. Out of this came the second aspect: the *covenant* (q.v.) that was defined by the *law* (q.v.) given somewhat later on the same mountain (Ex. 20 ff.). But the law itself merely impresses the mark of the divine Name on those whom he has made his own by revealing himself to them as he did. (Hence the refrain in Leviticus: "Be holy as I am holy," which is reechoed in the Sermon on the Mount: "Be perfect as your heavenly Father is perfect.") More generally, the Word of God, by introducing itself into history and reshaping it, tends entirely toward the realization of a plan, which is the effective adoption of the *People of God* (q.v.), i.e., the creation of a new people that is truly a people according to the heart of God (cf. in Jer. 31 the description of the expected new covenant). Whether we think of the details of the providential or miraculous events that are announced (cf. Ezech. 4 and 5, where the prophet acts out in advance the events he is proclaiming in a symbolic action; there is no doubt that by this he is asserting the fact that the Word not only announces these events but will actually produce them), or whether, a fortiori, we allude to their final outcome (cf. Isa. 56), the Word has within itself the power of fulfillment. For the wisdom writers (*see* WISDOM), it is evident that God is the one who holds the key to the world's history in his hand, and that he alone knows and can reveal its vicissitudes, because it is he who controls them (cf. Dan. 2). At the end of the Old Testament revelation, the Word appears as having been from the beginning the principle of all things coming into being (cf. Gen. 1); it was sent by God into the world that it might infallibly make His plans a reality. (Cf. Isa. 55,10–11: "For as the rain and the snow come down from heaven, and return not thither but water the earth . . . so shall my word be that goes forth from my mouth: it shall not return to me empty, but it shall accomplish that which I purpose, and prosper in the thing for which I sent it.")

This text, like others, particularly in the Psalms (cf. 147,18), already expresses a personification of the Word. It does not seem that we can reduce this personification to a simple figure of speech. In the later biblical writings and even more in the Judaism contemporary with the beginnings of Christinity, we observe the same tendency making itself more and more felt, either with regard to the Word itself or to other realities closely bound up with it, like *Wisdom* and the *Shekinah* (i.e., the special presence of God among his People) manifested in the radiance of *Glory* (qq.v.). It is remarkable that the prologue of St. John, which decidedly asserts the personal character of the Word in identifying it with Jesus, identifies it at the same time with these other notions. The *Memra* (an Aramaic term for "word") of the *targumim* is certainly something quite other than a metaphor in its description that is given to us, where we see it not only descending upon Israel as the preeminent divine blessing, remaining with it, fighting against its enemies for it, but also interceding with God on its behalf.

However, with the New Testament, the assertion that the Word was made flesh in Jesus Christ has its immediate preparation in the conviction first of all that the "good news," the gospel of salvation that he brought to the world, is the definitive Word of God; and then that this Word, which announces our adoption to us, finds its content in the eternal Son who has come to us. In this coming, it is through him that God has "spoken" to us definitively (cf. Mark 4,33; Acts 13,26; Heb.1).

The Greek Fathers naturally connected this Word of God made flesh with the Stoic or Neo-Platonist *Logos* (Greek expression for "word"), a demiurgic power that imparts existence to everything that exists, or an eternal model of the world in the thought of God. It is not impossible that the author of the fourth Gospel wished to make reference to this idea that was widespread among his hearers of Hellenic origin, but the content of his own notion of the Word remains basically biblical. Instead of an ideal reality or an intermediary between God and the world, his Logos is in the strictest sense divine, although he does become incarnate in order to save the world. If the more or less strict apologetic identification that the Fathers worked out between the Greek Logos and the Johannine one made the Christian faith easier to grasp for minds trained in the school of Greece, it nevertheless had two serious drawbacks. The first was that it made heresies like *Arianism* (q.v.) possible, heresies that saw the Son-Logos merely as the first among creatures, the instrument that God used in creating the world. And even when this exaggerated assimilation of the Word made flesh to the Logos of Hellenism was rejected, along with all the deviations it implied, the tendency remained to understand the Word in an exaggeratedly intellectualistic sense that, even today, has kept Christian theology from using to its fullest so fertile a biblical and evangelical notion, a notion that so well lends itself to unifying the whole Christian perspective around the work and person of Christ. Protestants, particularly Karl Barth in our own day, have developed a theology of the Word in which many elements are of real value. But they have done this onesidedly, remaining prisoners of this intellectualism without realizing it, particularly in the way in which they oppose Word to sacrament, or else, on the contrary, reduce the sacraments to a visible word without objective reality. The personalist realism of the biblical notion of Word ought to help us make them understand that Catholic sacramental realism is quite far from making the sacraments alien to the perspectives of God's authentic Word. On the contrary, since the Word made flesh instituted the sacraments, their reality is the simple result of the fact that, by them and in them, through his divine power, the Word brings what He intended them to signify to fruition. *See* LOGOS, and SACRAMENT.

WORK   Work, or labor, i.e., the endeavor to harness nature in accordance with man's needs, was ordained for man in Paradise (Gen. 2,15). After the Fall, it assumed an arduous and expressly penitential aspect: "by the sweat of your brow" (Gen. 3,17–19). The Decalogue, in prescribing the Sabbath rest, implies expressly that the other days will be consecrated to work (Ex. 20,9). The New Testament states: "If anyone will not work, let him not eat" (2 Thess. 3,10). Primitive monasticism was categorical on the fact that the primary and basic asceticism of the monk must be to earn his food and even, since food was reduced to the barest minimum, to contribute by his work toward the feeding of the poor who have not voluntarily chosen a life of poverty. It is undeniable that a certain influence of the contempt of ancient philosophy for manual labor, which it considered to be inferior, combined with the growth of monastic properties, contributed toward obscuring this view of things for the Middle Ages. The first Cistercians forcefully restored it to its proper status. Although we have rich elements for a theology of work in Christian tradition, we must acknowledge that its development remains quite sketchy.

WORKS   In theology we understand by this term good actions in their relationship to salvation. This is at the root of the debates over justification by works or justification by faith, which are already found in the New Testament (cf. Rom. 4 and James 2,14 to the end, which at first sight seem to be contradictory) and which were resumed at the time of the Protestant Reformation. *See* JUSTIFICATION.

WORLD   All of creation, considered as a unified whole. It is noteworthy in this regard that throughout the whole of Scripture there is a duality in the notion proposed to us of the world. Nothing expresses this better than the apparent paradox found in bringing together these two verses of St. John: the first is in his Gospel: "For God so loved the world that he gave his only Son, that whoever believes in him should not perish but have eternal life" (3,16), and the second in the first Epistle: "Do not love the world or the things in the world," together with this explanation: "the whole world is in the power of the evil one" (2,15 and 5,19). In the first case, the world is viewed within the perspective of its being created by God and of the divine plan that it is ultimately to realize; while in the second, it is viewed in its present organization that sin has given over to the power of evil. Against the background of these texts two essential truths stand out. One is that the unity of the world is, as it were, a reflection of a spiritual solidarity among all created freedoms, angelic or human. It follows that the physical world itself is only the fringe and manifestation of a spiritual universe, dominated at present by a conflict beween the evil "powers" and the Spirit of God in Christ struggling to free the world from these powers (cf. Rom. 8,19–23). The other is that the world must not be considered as a static reality, but as the field of successive economies that at present is in a period of agonizing transition. The present "aeon," or, as it is generally translated, the present world, is dominated by a sovereignty usurped by created powers in revolt against their Creator. The "aeon," or the world to come, will again be completely in the hands of the Creator. But, through Christ, the world to come has already arrived in the world that it is to supplant. And now, through the Spirit, in the Body of Christ that is the Church (i.e., as St. Paul again says, in all of those who are "in Christ"), it is already present, suffering violence in its members as it had first suffered in Him (cf. Matt. 13,39; Mark 10,30; Luke 18,30; Rom. 12,2; Gal. 1,4, etc.). But "if we endure [i.e., suffer], we shall also reign with Him" (2 Tim. 2,12; cf. 1 Cor. 4,8 and Rom. 8,17). In Christian asceticism the result is the inevitable tension between the love of the world that will save the world, and the liberation from the world whereby we shall be saved from it. But the two are only apparently contradictory; it is only in ceasing "within the world" to be "of the world" because we shall have freed ourselves from it, and in freeing ourselves, that we shall be able to contribute to our own deliverance (cf. John 17,15–16). Thus, the flight of the monks from the world is never anything but a primary phase in the spiritual combat; after that, freed by their own self-effacement, they return to the world as liberators (cf. St. Athanasius's plan of the *Life of St. Antony*, the monk who fled into the desert to fight, like Christ, with the spirit of evil, and, once he is possessed and dominated by the Spirit of God, comes back among men to play the role of a spiritual father among them).

WORSHIP In the strict sense of the word, it is the honor given to God, especially in the public celebration of the prayer of the liturgy. As a translation of the Latin word *cultus*, it has a broader meaning and may be understood as the honor the Church gives to the saints in commemorating their example and invoking their intercession in her public worship. The more usual English term in this sense would be *veneration*. On the distinction between the worship of *latria* and of simple *dulia, see* ADORATION.

Z

ZWINGLIANISM   The doctrine of the Zurich Reformer Ulrich Zwingli. It is essentially a strongly rationalizing humanism that claims to bring the Church back to the Gospel, which it understands in a singularly more optimistic, if much more superficial, way than Luther. What has been retained of Zwingli's thought is especially his opposition to any idea of a presence of Christ in the elements of the Eucharist (which caused the great controversy between him and Luther at the Colloquy of Marburg). Yet we must be grateful to him, on the other hand, for having insisted upon the communal character of the Eucharist as a festive banquet of the Christian fellowship—a notion that had been lost sight of by the other Protestant Reformers even more than had already been the case in the individualistic piety of the Middle Ages. Despite the endeavor and the relative influence of Calvin, the ideas that Zwingli had expressed, rather than initiated, have remained characteristic of a stronger current of inspiration among the Reformed Churches of Switzerland and France. We can see in it at least the germ of the rationalism or the *liberalism* (q.v.) of later Protestantism.

TOPICAL READING OF

THE DICTIONARY

The following table will permit the chief articles of this volume to be read in a logical sequence, arranged and based on the Creed. In this way the **Dictionary of Theology** may be used as an introduction to the study of theology. The center column gives the essential articles, and the column to the right indicates the more secondary ones which can be considered as appendices to the principal articles. (Words mentioned for the second time appear in parentheses.)

I

Believe

Philosophy 347
{
Realism 381
Nominalism 323
Materialism 301
Aristotelianism 38
Marxism 295
Existentialism 150
Immanence 225
Transcendence 446
Modernism 309
Gnosticism 180
Humanism 213
}

Reason 382
Atheism 45
Agnosticism 14
Absolute 3

Apologetics 31
{
Certitude 78
Credibility 107
Rationalism 379   Fideism 166
}

Revelation 390   Dogma 126   Articles of Faith 39

Word of God 465
Gospel 191
Holy Scripture 207
}
{
Inspiration 240   Canon of Scripture 69
Inerrancy of Holy Scripture 235
Prophet and Prophecy 369
Senses of Scripture 408   Exegesis 149
Allegory 18
}

Tradition 444
{
Deposit of Faith 117
Development 119
Fathers of the Church 164
}

Magisterium 288
{
Assistance of the Holy Spirit 44
Infallibility 236
Interpretation 243
}

Faith 155
{
Catechesis 73
Catechism 73
Catechumenate 74
}

Theology 441
{
Theological places 439
Theological Systems 441 {
Augustinianism 48
Thomism 443
}
Analogy 21
Theological Conclusion 439
}

Mystery 313
{
Knowledge 261
Contemplation 101
Mysticism 316 {
Light 273
Face 155
Cloud 90
Darkness 111
Night 322
}
}

In God

The Father

Almighty

Creator

of Heaven

and Earth

and in Jesus Christ
His Only Son
Our Lord

Who Was Conceived
by the
Holy Spirit

Born of the
Virgin Mary

World 468   Time 444

Matter 302

Adam 11   Monogenism 310

Man 290
{
Body 64   Soul 417
Image of God 220
Intelligence 242
(Freedom) 168
History 204
}

Fall 160   Conscience 98

Evil 147   Devil 120

Sin 410
{
(World) 468
Flesh 167
Death 113
}

Jesus Christ 245
{
Salvation 401
Messiah 305
Son of Man 416   Son of God 416
Servant 408
Lord 278
Logos 278   Word of God 465
Imitation 222
Impeccability 229
}

Incarnation 230
{
Arianism 38
Adoptionism 13
Nestorianism 322
Monophysitism 311   Monothelitism 311
}

Virgin Birth 455

Mary 299
Perpetual Virginity 345
Immaculate Conception 223
Assumption 44
}
{
Presentation in the Temple 365
Purification 377
Motherhood of Mary 312
Mediation of Mary 304
Mariology 291
}

Suffered under
Pontius Pilate

Was Crucified
Died
and Was Buried

He Descended
into Hell

the Third Day
He Rose from
the Dead

Ascended into
Heaven

Sits At the
Right Hand of the
Father Almighty

Passion 336

Transfiguration 446
Pasch 335   Lamb of God 228

Kenosis 259

Impassibility 228

Last Agony 266

Redemption 383

Expiation 152

Sacrifice 397

Immolation 227

Descent into Hell 118

Resurrection 388

(Pasch) 335

Ascension of Christ 40

Parousia 334

Whence He Shall
Come to Judge the
Living and the
Dead

and in the
Holy Spirit

The Holy
Catholic
Church

Judgment 252   Day 111

Holy Spirit 208   Pentecost 343

                                ⎧ Nature 320
Grace 193   ⎨ Supernatural 432   Preternatural 365
                                ⎩ Pelagianism 339

Virtue 456   Habitus 199

Gifts of the Holy Spirit 176

Indwelling of the Divine   (Appropriation) 37
    Persons 235

                                Synagogue 435
Church 81   Tabernacle 437
                                Temple 437

                                ⎧ Schism 404   Heresy 202
                                │ Indefectibility 233
                                │ East and West 129
                                │ Ecumenism 134
                                │ Protestants 370
Union and Unity 452 ⎫   ⎨ Liberalism 271
Catholicity 75   ⎭   │ Barthism 54
                                │ Lutheranism 284
                                │ Calvinism 67
                                │ Zwinglianism 471
                                │ Anglicanism 27
                                ⎩ Wesleyanism 462

                                Authority 49
Apostle 33   Law 267
                                Abrogation of Laws 2

The Communion
of Saints

The Forgiveness
of Sins

Pope 352
Council 102
Bishop 60
Clergy 89
Priesthood 365
Deacons 112
Lay, Laity, Layman 268

Hierarchy 203
Vocation 459
Character 79

Sacrament 393 Sacramental 395

Mass 300
Communion 91
Eucharist 144

Liturgy 277
Altar 20
Offertory 328
Preface 362
Canon 68
Epiklesis 141 Consecration 100
Concelebration 95
Transubstantiation 447
(Presence) 363

Baptism 51
Confirmation 96

Water 461 Chrism 80 Holy Oils 206
Supernatural Adoption 433
Justice 253
Justification 254
Salvation of Unbelievers 402

Prayer 357
(Faith) 155
Hope 211
Love 279

(Holiness) 206
Beatification 55
Canonization 72
Martyrdom 294
Icon 217

Concupiscence 96
Penance 340
Absolution 8
Ascetic, Asceticism 42
Spiritual Warfare 427

Attrition 47
Indulgences 234
Punishment 376

Perfection 344

Vow 459
Poverty 356
Virginity 456
Obedience 327

Marriage 292 Sex 409

Anointing of the Sick 29

Healing 199
(Holy Oils) 206

The Resurrection of the Body

and Life Everlasting

Eschatology 141

Fire 166
(Darkness) 111

(Resurrection) 388
(Flesh) 167
(Body) 64
(Heaven) 200

Paradise 333

Election 137   Number of the Elect 324

Hell 201
Purgatory 376

Limbo 276

Beatitude 55
Life 272
Glory 177

Millenarianism 307
(Eternity) 143
Vision 456